Multistate Performance Test Workbook

Table of Contents

Professor Peter Jan Honigsberg

To be used in conjunction with the Summer 2009 and Winter 2010 BAR/BRI Bar Review Courses

MULTISTATE PERFORMANCE TEST WORKBOOK

TABLE OF CONTENTS

I. INTRODUCTION

These materials are designed to assist you in preparing for the Multistate Performance Test ("MPT"). They will acquaint you with that portion of the exam, suggest strategies and approaches in taking it, and help you build your confidence.

The MPT tests lawyering skills rather than legal knowledge. It is developed by the National Conference of Bar Examiners and has been adopted by more than 30 jurisdictions as a part of their bar examination. Presently, a majority of those jurisdictions require bar applicants to take two MPTs. However, some jurisdictions will administer only one of these exams. Check with your local bar examiners. All MPTs are administered on Tuesday or Thursday of the bar exam, and each is 90 minutes long.

Each jurisdiction determines the weight of the MPT in relation to the rest of its exam, and also establishes its own grading guidelines and policies including the length of the answer. Because of the resulting variations in grading guidelines and standards, the National Conference of Bar Examiners does not release a model answer to the exam, although it does provide "Drafters' Point Sheets" for each exam. Jurisdictions on their own may release sample answers. BAR/BRI provides sample answers that would be passing in any jurisdiction.

As stated above, the MPT measures fundamental lawyering skills, namely: legal analysis and reasoning, fact analysis, fact gathering, problem solving, and recognizing and resolving ethical dilemmas. It also tests your ability to communicate and to organize and manage a legal task. The exam will provide a library of legal authorities (*i.e.*, the law you need to complete the task) and a client's file (*i.e.*, the information you need to know about the client and your case). The client's file includes a task memo from the supervising attorney instructing you on what you need to do.

Because the MPT is not testing your specific knowledge of law outside the library, some people have described this exam as an "open book" exam. However, just because it is open book does not mean it is easy. Nor does it mean that people who have had experience working in a law office need not prepare. The bar examiners are requiring you to demonstrate your skills ***under exam conditions***. Preparing and writing these documents over days or weeks is very different from creating them in 90 minutes. No matter how well you can write and analyze, you need to remind yourself that you are primarily taking an exam, not writing a genuine legal document.

II. PARTS OF THE MULTISTATE PERFORMANCE TEST

A. LIBRARY

Nearly every exam will contain a library. The library contains the legal authorities you need to complete the task assigned and sometimes authorities that are not relevant. The library may consist of cases, statutes, regulations, rules of professional conduct, and secondary materials (such as a Restatement or a portion of a treatise). The cases may be actual cases, actual cases that have been modified by the examiners, or cases entirely written for the examination. Other materials in the library may also have been modified. Consequently, even if you are familiar with the subject matter or the case names, ***you will still need to read all the material in the library***. Do not assume that the material is precisely what you have read in law school or in practice. It is

also possible that the bar examiners may include some major statutes such as the U.C.C. or the Federal Rules of Evidence ***without changes***. If so, they may tell you that. Read the instructions carefully.

1. **No Library**
   The bar examiners may give a performance test without a library. If so, any necessary law will be provided in the file. For example, if you are required to write a closing argument, the file could include jury instructions setting out the relevant law.

2. **Jurisdiction**
   The MPT is set in a fictitious state, in the fictitious Fifteenth Circuit of the United States. In this state, the trial court of general jurisdiction is the District Court, the intermediate appellate court is the Court of Appeal, and the highest court is the Supreme Court. The cases and other authorities in the library may all be from the same jurisdiction or from several jurisdictions.

B. FILE

The file contains information about your case. For example, the file could include: a transcript of an interview with a client; depositions or interviews of witnesses and/or parties; interrogatories answered by the other party; a complaint and answer; a memorandum written by an associate of the firm; a partial transcript of the trial; a contract, will, deed, trust, probation report, lease, police report, or newspaper articles; and any other relevant documents. Just as in a real life situation, the facts in the file may not be accurate. You may need to work with and identify facts that appear to be ambiguous, conflicting, inconsistent, unreliable, or even missing.

C. TASK MEMORANDUM

The most important document in the materials is the task memorandum. It is part of the file. In the memorandum, the supervising attorney or partner assigns the task for you to perform. Take the time to read this memo carefully. Make sure you ***answer the questions*** and perform the assigned tasks as precisely as possible.

III. SKILLS TESTED ON MULTISTATE PERFORMANCE TEST

A. IDENTIFIED SKILLS

Although the National Conference of Bar Examiners has identified the following discrete skills as those being tested by the MPT, you may have to use more than one of these skills when drafting certain documents.

1. **Legal Analysis and Reasoning**
   In a legal analysis document, you will need to demonstrate the ability to ***identify and formulate legal issues***, ***analyze the relevant legal rules and principles***, and ***apply*** the rules and principles ***to the relevant facts***. Examples of legal analysis documents include a memorandum to a supervising attorney, a persuasive memorandum or brief, a letter to a client, a letter to an opposing attorney, and a letter or memo to a legislator or administrative agency.

2. **Fact Gathering**
   In a fact gathering problem, you will be required to ***investigate and gather*** all the favorable and unfavorable evidence relevant to your case. Examples of fact gathering documents you

may be required to draft include an investigation plan, a discovery plan, and a set of interrogatories.

3. **Fact Analysis**
In a fact analysis problem you will need to ***analyze and use facts***, separating the relevant from the irrelevant. Unlike in a legal analysis exam, your focus is entirely on the facts. The law is given or agreed upon, and is used only to help you organize your material. Examples of fact analysis documents include a closing argument, an opening statement, jury instructions, and an affidavit or declaration.

4. **Problem Solving/Tactics**
In a problem solving task, you will need to demonstrate your ability to ***develop and evaluate strategies and tactics*** for solving a problem and accomplishing the client's goals. The problem solving process requires you to ***identify the problem, generate alternative solutions and analyze the consequences*** of each alternative, and ***develop and implement a plan of action***. Examples of problem solving exams would include drafting or redrafting a will, contract, or other document; developing a client-counseling plan evaluating courses of action; and creating a settlement proposal.

5. **Recognizing and Resolving Ethical Dilemmas**
The bar examiners expect applicants to demonstrate the ability to represent a client within the bounds of applicable ethical standards. Thus, you will be required to ***identify and resolve ethical dilemmas*** as well as know the nature and sources of ethical standards and the means by which the standards are enforced. An ethical problem may require you to apply rules of professional conduct to the relevant facts in the file. Or the examiners could raise an ethical problem without providing any such rules in the library, in which case, you will be expected to use your general knowledge of appropriate ethical behavior in resolving the problem.

B. OTHER REQUIRED SKILLS

1. **Communication**
For any task, you must ***organize and express your ideas*** with "precision, clarity, logic and economy." You will also need to write to your intended ***audience***, such as a client, lawyer, or judge.

2. **Organization and Management of a Legal Task**
As an attorney, you will have to manage your time, effort, and resources efficiently, and perform your tasks within certain time constraints. These same abilities are expected on the MPT. Organization is always the key!

C. ADDITIONAL POINTS

1. **Thinking**
Good writing reflects good thinking; fuzzy writing reflects fuzzy thinking. Be sure you think the problem through ***before*** you begin writing. And as you write, show the reader how you are solving the problem step by step.

2. **Common Sense**
Lawyers use common sense whenever they are solving problems. They rely on their experience of the world and their understanding of human nature, and you should too. The bar examiners are looking for lawyers. Trust your instincts.

3. Answering the Question Asked
The bar examiners need standards in grading the exams. One of the most likely standards your jurisdiction will use is whether you have ***actually answered the question asked***. A competent attorney answers the question. Make it easy for the grader—stay focused on the task memorandum.

4. Using Given Format
If the bar examiners want you to use a particular format in creating your document, they will provide you with an instruction sheet that sets out the format to be used. If the exam does not suggest a format to follow, you are not obligated to use any particular format in your answer. Nevertheless, we will provide examples of typical formats to help prepare you for the MPT.

a. Unfamiliar Document
If you encounter a document that is new to you, do not panic. You do not have to be familiar with the document tested by the examiners. Remember, the important factor is the underlying skills being tested. You are not being tested on documents; you are being tested on those skills.

5. Using the Proper Tone
Your document can be effective only if it speaks in the appropriate tone. Are you writing to a client? An opposing attorney? A judge? A legislator? An investigator? You write differently to a layperson than you would to a lawyer. Know your audience, and know whether the document should be objective or persuasive.

6. Knowledge of the Law
The MPT tests your ability to work with a given set of legal materials to perform certain tasks using certain skills. You are ***not being tested on your specific knowledge of the law outside the materials***—that knowledge will be tested on the essay and Multistate Bar Exam sections of your exam. In fact, the substantive area of law on the MPT can be outside the specific areas of law tested in your jurisdiction. For example, the library could include international law, bankruptcy law, or maritime law. Nevertheless, the examiners do expect you to have a "general knowledge" of the law based on the fact that you have gone to law school. That general knowledge of the law will assist you in assessing the relative values of the various authorities and facts and in selecting and applying the most appropriate principles of law raised by the library.

IV. APPROACH TO THE MULTISTATE PERFORMANCE TEST

A. INTRODUCTION

On the MPT, you will have 90 minutes to:

- Read and organize the file;
- Read and organize the cases and other authorities in the library; and
- Write one or more documents or parts of documents.

To work efficiently and to successfully complete the tasks, you need to develop your strategy ***before you walk into the exam***. Become comfortable with your approach and stick with it. Do not let a problem on the exam unnerve you, causing you to substitute a new and unpracticed strategy.

B. SUGGESTED STRATEGY

We suggest the following approach when taking the MPT:

1. Read the General Directions

Even though you may be familiar with the general directions since they appear on the back cover of all the exams, you cannot be certain that the bar examiners will not change them on your exam. Do not take chances. Also, if there is more than one task on the exam, the general instructions may identify the percentage weight of each task. If so, gauge your time accordingly.

2. Read the Letter/Memorandum (the Task Memo) from the Supervising Attorney

This is the ***most important document*** in the materials. It sets out the call of the question, the thing(s) you must do. Read the task memo very carefully. Make sure you answer the questions asked and draft the appropriate tasks.

3. Outline the Call of the Question (the Task Memo)

By briefly outlining the task memo and identifying the specific tasks, you keep yourself focused on the questions asked. Stick to the language of the question as you outline it. Many, but not all, jurisdictions provide scratch paper. If your jurisdiction does not, a good place to outline the task memo is on the inside front cover of the exam booklet.

4. Outline the Document Instruction Sheet

If the exam includes an instruction sheet on how to set out the document, outline the key points of the instructions on the same sheet as your outline of the task memo.

5. Read and Organize the File and Library

a. In General

At this point, consider whether to read the library or the file first. Many people read the library before they read the file. They believe that since the task memo sets out the broad sweep of the problem, they can go directly to the library and identify the relevant issues and elements. Then, when they read the file, they can efficiently select the relevant facts that apply to the identified issues and elements. Other people begin with the file, wanting to know the full factual situation before researching the law in the library. ***We suggest that you practice on several exams, and see which approach works better for you***. Whichever approach you take, remember you do not have the time to move back and forth between the library and file. To be efficient, you need to collect and organize all the relevant information ***with one reading*** of each part.

b. Reading and Organizing the File

We suggest you use the ***table of contents*** to organize the materials in the file. (If you are provided scratch paper, you can itemize the table of contents on your scratch paper and work off it.) In the space beneath the listing of each document, jot down the ***key words*** that highlight the relevant facts of each document. Along with the key facts, add

page number references, in case you have to return to the file to check on some point. In this way, the table of contents also becomes an index to the file.

c. **Reading the Library**

1) **Read Carefully**
Even if you happen to be familiar with the subject of the problem or with the name of the particular cases, do not assume you can whiz through the material. The cases and other authorities in the library may have been rewritten in whole or in part by the bar examiners. Remember, you are not being tested on how much you know about the subject independently, but on your analysis of the material presented.

2) **What If You Do Not Understand a Case?**
If you have a problem interpreting a case, move on and see whether later cases help explain the point that is confusing you. If not, make the best of it. In all likelihood, many of the other examinees are also finding the case difficult. You are not alone!

3) **Statutes and Regulations**
If there are only a few statutes or regulations, read them carefully. If the library contains many statutes or regulations, such as A.B.A. rules or U.C.C. sections, use your judgment in deciding which are the most relevant provisions. You probably will be using only a few of them. The cases and task memo can guide you in focusing on the key provisions.

4) **Read the Footnotes**
The bar examiners use the footnotes to drop in valuable information. Do not overlook them.

d. **Organizing the Library**
There are two ways to organize the library:

1) **Table of Contents**
Just as with the file, you can use the library's ***table of contents*** as your outline for the library. As you read each case, jot down ***key words*** of the case, with page number references. With statutes and regulations, select the relevant ones (based on the cases and the task memo) and note them. Keep all your notes about the library materials on this one sheet of paper. The page number references allow you to return to the materials efficiently, if you need to do so.

2) **Honigsberg Grid**
If the task memo requires you to draft a legal analysis document, analyzing the cases and the law, you might want to use the Honigsberg Grid instead of the table of contents to organize your library—especially if there are several cases in the library and you like charts. The Honigsberg Grid helps you immediately see how one case compares to another in reference to a particular issue. In fact, you can often draft legal analysis documents by using your grid as an outline. An illustration of the Honigsberg Grid follows.

SAMPLE GRID:

FACTS & ISSUES

AUTHORITIES	**Facts** (of each case)	***Issue #1** (*e.g.*, defamation)	***Issue #2** (*e.g.*, right of privacy)	***Issue #3** (if necessary)	***Issue #4** (if necessary)
Name of First Case					
Name of Second Case					
Name of Third Case (if necessary)					
Name of Fourth Case (if necessary)					
Name of Fifth Case (if necessary)					

*Identify ***by name*** at the top of your grid each issue you intend to include. The legal issues usually come from the cases.

The columns at the top of the Honigsberg Grid should be for the facts of the cases in the library and for the major legal issues in the exam. There should be no more than three or four major issues. Subissues should be keyed into the appropriate issue boxes under the main issues. The cases will identify the major issues, and so you should develop your grid as you go along. Along the left side of the Grid, list the cases in the library. In the boxes created by the intersecting lines, indicate how the case treats the particular issue you noted on top. Think in terms of ***key words***, and use abbreviations. You are not trying to squeeze an entire case brief into a box. ***Stick to essentials***. Along with the key words, add ***page numbers***, and make the grid an index to the library. In the first column, be sure to include the key facts of the case you are gridding. This allows you to later compare and contrast the cases in the library with your own situation.

a) Statutes
Note that you can also grid statutes since they too speak to issues. But limit your gridding of statutes to one or two major provisions. If you need to take notes on other provisions, put them in the margin, or in your outline.

6. Time Factor
Reading and organizing the library and file is very important to analyzing your task and writing your document(s). Thus, you need to spend a fair amount of time on this part of the exam. However, in order to have sufficient time to write your document(s), you should complete your reading and organization of the library and file in about ***40 minutes*** or possibly less, depending on the length of the materials.

7. **Return to the Task Memo and Your Outline of the Task Memo**
After you have read and organized the library and the file, take five minutes to review the task memo and your outline of the task memo. ***Make sure you are clear about the questions asked*** and how you intend to answer them. Think of the "big picture" as you decide what organization you will use to answer the question, and what issues, elements, and facts you will be focusing on.

8. **Write Your Document(s)**
When you begin writing, you should have two outline sheets in front of you: (i) your brief outline of the task memo (written on the inside front cover of the exam booklet or on scratch paper), including an outline of the document instruction sheet (if one is included); and (ii) your outline of the file and library (which should be on the table of contents or on scratch paper). (*See* below.) Be sure you have allowed yourself sufficient time to write—we suggest ***45 minutes***—and be sure to budget your time among your tasks and issues. If the instructions assign percentage weights to differing tasks, use these values as guidelines for the amount of time to spend on each section.

THE TWO SHEETS OF PAPER YOU SHOULD HAVE BEFORE YOU WHEN YOU WRITE YOUR ANSWER

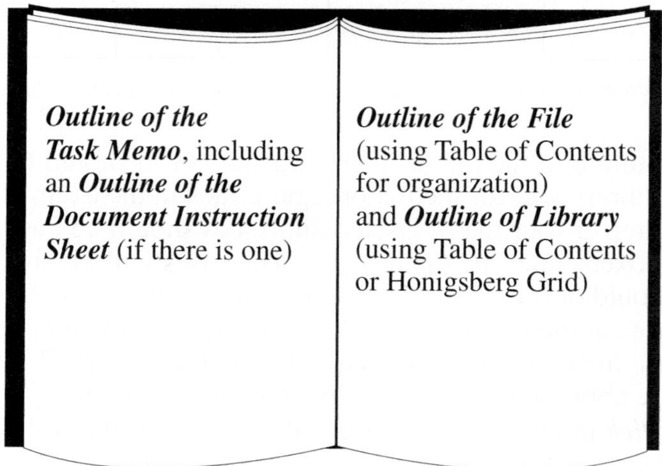

Outline of the Task Memo, including an ***Outline of the Document Instruction Sheet*** (if there is one)
Outline of the File (using Table of Contents for organization) and ***Outline of Library*** (using Table of Contents or Honigsberg Grid)

V. LEGAL ANALYSIS AND REASONING

A. THE SKILL

Legal analysis and reasoning is frequently tested on the MPT. With this type of test, you will need to identify and formulate legal issues, analyze relevant legal rules and principles, and apply the rules and principles to the relevant facts. The examiners may test this skill by using a familiar document, such as a memorandum of law, or an unfamiliar document, such as a theory of the case memorandum. But as stated earlier, the name of the document is not the issue; the important factor is the underlying skill.

B. TYPES OF DOCUMENTS TESTED ON A LEGAL ANALYSIS EXAM

The following is a list of the kinds of documents that the examiners could require you to draft in testing legal analysis skills. This list is certainly not exhaustive. The bar examiners could easily require you to draft a legal analysis document not mentioned in this list.

1. **Memorandum of Law**
This is an ***objective*** memo to a supervising or associate attorney.

2. **Persuasive Brief; Brief in Support of a Motion; Memorandum of Points and Authorities**
All three of these documents are the same. They all represent a ***persuasive*** document that accompanies a motion to the court. (An example of an instruction sheet for drafting persuasive memoranda is included in Appendix I.)

3. **Memorandum to a Judge**
If you are assigned this document, be clear on whether you are representing a client and thus need to ***persuade*** the judge to act—in which case this is a persuasive document—or whether you are clerking for the judge and asked to give an ***objective*** assessment—in which case you are drafting an objective document.

4. **Trial Brief**
A trial brief is designed to ***persuade*** the trial judge what law to apply at trial.

5. **Appellate Brief**
An appellate brief is a ***persuasive*** brief. It may be submitted at any stage of the appellate level.

6. **Theory of the Case Memorandum**
This document is relatively unfamiliar. A theory of the case memorandum is a working hypothesis of how the law and facts will fit together to support the result sought by the client. Note that a portion of this type of memo is ***persuasive*** in tone, while the remainder is ***objective***. (*See* an instruction sheet describing this document in Appendix I.)

7. **Client Letter**
This is a letter to a client advising the client on the law and the status of her case. It is ***always objective***. If the client is a layperson, write in the appropriate tone, *i.e.*, in a significantly less legal tone than you would use in a memo to a lawyer. You may cite authorities, but keep your analysis of the law to a level that the layperson would understand.

8. **Letter to an Opposing Attorney**
A demand letter, a negotiation letter, or any other letter written to an opposing attorney is ***always persuasive***. However, because you are writing to another attorney, your tone should be less formal than if you were writing to a judge.

9. **Position Paper**
A letter or a memo to a legislator or administrative agency is called a position paper. To the extent that you are trying to persuade the official to act, the letter is ***persuasive***.

10. **Case Planning Memorandum**
This is an internal document used to prepare for court. It identifies and evaluates the client's claims, counterclaims, defenses, and remedies. (*See* an instruction sheet and example in Appendix I.)

C. CONSIDERATIONS IN DRAFTING LEGAL ANALYSIS DOCUMENTS

1. **Is the Document Objective or Persuasive?**
Be sure you are clear on whether the document you are to draft is objective or persuasive.

   a. **Objective**
   In objective writing, you should be more balanced in your assessment of the situation. You should look at the strengths and weaknesses of both sides—although you always need to keep your client's interests in the forefront. The favored approach is to present the law in the best light you can, with judicious references to pitfalls and other concerns.

   b. **Persuasive**
   If you are drafting a persuasive document, you must "***believe in your client***." Thus, you must be reasonable in the presentation of your analysis, but your client's situation should always be presented in the best light possible. In your analysis, convince the reader that your position should prevail. Emphasize your strong points. Also, begin with your best argument and authorities, and convince the court of the correctness of your position early on. Do not dispose of your opponent's arguments until you have established your position. And always use the facts to make your client look good.

2. **Citations**
Citations are not necessary. Neither do you need to cite to the full name of the case; a reference to the plaintiff's or defendant's name will do.

3. **Note Importance of Each Authority**
The library may contain several different authorities. Be sure you understand the precedential and persuasive value of each. Generally, you should focus on primary authorities first (*i.e.*, the statutes, cases, and regulations), and use secondary authorities (Restatements, treatises, law reviews, etc.) as supporting authorities. Remember, the MPT can include authorities that are not relevant.

4. **Using a Format**
Since lawyers in different states and even in different firms use various formats, the bar examiners cannot expect a uniform formatted answer—unless they provide the format. Thus, on many of the legal analysis exams, the examiners may include an instruction sheet setting out a format. (*See* examples in Appendix I.) If no instruction sheet accompanies the exam, you do not need to worry about particular formatted sections.

D. APPROACH TO LEGAL ANALYSIS AND REASONING

When writing a legal analysis document, whether objective or persuasive, remember the following:

1. **Instruction Sheet**
If there is an instruction sheet setting out a format, follow that format.

2. **Clearly Set Out the Issue and the Rule**
Make sure that you clearly set out each issue and the applicable principle of law drawn from the library. When you are using a case, mention a few facts of that case so that you can compare and contrast that case with your client's situation. In most situations, you will also want to identify the reasoning behind the rule so that you can later analyze whether that reasoning would also apply to your client's situation.

3. **Be Sure to Apply the Rule to the Facts**
As a lawyer, you need to solve a client's problem. The more you identify the relevant facts

and work with those facts, the more you demonstrate your lawyering skills. As you analyze the problem, focus on how the rule applies to the facts of your case.

4. **Distinguish Opposing Authorities**
Distinguish authorities that oppose your position. Do not ignore them. The bar examiners need to see how you handle any opposing authority—they need to see how you think! You can distinguish cases on their facts, their reasoning, public policy grounds, and fairness. Although you can also distinguish cases on their jurisdiction and their age, distinguishing cases on these two factors is less important because it does not demonstrate insightful analytical thinking.

5. **Draw a Conclusion**
Lawyers make decisions. Be a lawyer. Make a decision after analyzing the issues and applying the rules of law to the facts.

E. SOME ADDITIONAL THOUGHTS ON LEGAL ANALYSIS AND REASONING

1. **Organization**
If the task memo does not provide you with an organizational approach, organize your legal analysis document issue by issue if it is objective, or argument by argument if it is persuasive.

2. **Statement of Facts**
If the examiners want you to add a statement of facts to your document, they will tell you. If so, be sure to focus on the ***legally significant facts***—*i.e.*, the facts on which the issues turn. But do not ignore background facts and emotional facts (*i.e.*, facts with a human interest that make your client look good). Make sure that you place your client in a sympathetic light. Play up the favorable facts, but do not ignore damaging facts that are legally significant. You must include them, but surround them with positive facts. (*See* the sample instruction sheet for persuasive documents in Appendix I.)

3. **Questions Presented/Statement of Issues**
You generally do not need to draft a "questions presented" or statement of issues section in your answer. If, however, you are asked to do so, write your issues or questions presented in terms of the facts. There should be a separate statement or question for each major issue. If you are drafting a persuasive document, be sure to phrase your issues/questions in a way that engenders sympathy towards your client and guides the reader to the results you want.

4. **Summary of Argument**
A summary of the argument encapsulates the points and arguments you will make in your answer. The summary is written before you write your analysis of each issue so you must have outlined or worked through your answer before you begin writing. You do not need to draft a summary of the argument unless you are told to do so. If so, write a brief paragraph (two or three sentences) for each major issue. Be sure the summary is written in terms of the facts.

5. **Point, Argument, or Subject Headings**
Different jurisdictions and lawyers use these terms interchangeably. Thus, for purposes of the exam, a point heading, an argument heading, and a subject heading are all the same.

They all appear in persuasive documents and summarize, in a sentence, the point of law you want the court to adopt. They are written ***in terms of the facts*** and should include a reason. Since you should precede each argument with a heading, these headings can help you organize your document. (*See* the sample instruction sheet for persuasive documents in Appendix I.)

VI. FACT GATHERING

A. THE SKILL

Perhaps more than anything else, lawyers gather facts. Fact gathering is essential for any case. Lawyers gather facts by hiring an investigator and preparing an investigation plan, or by using various means or tools of discovery and preparing a discovery plan. But whatever the document is called, and however the lawyer gathers facts, the process is the same.

B. APPROACH TO FACT GATHERING

The lawyer needs to do the following:

1. Identify the Theory or Ultimate Fact You Want To Prove

Consider what it is that you ultimately want to prove at trial. For example, in a criminal case, is the person guilty or not? Or, in an action on a disputed contract, has a contract been formed?

2. Identify the Elements or Factors Underlying the Theory or Ultimate Fact

Next, think about the elements or factors you need to show for that theory or ultimate fact. For example, in the contract situation, you may need to show whether there was an offer, acceptance, and consideration, or a defense to formation such as duress in the inducement of the contract. These are the elements or factors important to your contract formation (or nonformation) theory. Since this is a closed universe exam, the exam materials (usually the library) will provide you with the appropriate elements or factors.

3. Gather Facts for Each Element or Factor

Figure out what facts you need in order to show that there was, for example, an offer (or no offer). You have some facts in the file, but you need to look as well for facts ***outside*** the file. What evidence is missing from the file? Be objective in your fact gathering. Do not limit yourself to facts that support your position. ***Gather all facts—favorable and unfavorable***— and explore all possibilities. As you gather facts, look for facts on the ***background*** of the situation as well as for facts concerning the ***incident*** itself.

4. Identify the Sources for Each Fact

Next, ask who has access to these facts? What documents will assist your investigation? What physical evidence will help? Think ***"DPT"***—*i.e.*, ***documentary, physical, and testimonial evidence***. (We include demonstrative evidence, *e.g.*, a map, within the "physical" evidence category.)

5. Identify the Tools or Means Used to Gather the Facts, If Requested by the Task Memo

If the task memo requires you to identify the tools or the means for gathering facts, you will want to consider using: interrogatories, depositions, requests for admission, requests for production of documents, requests for physical or mental examinations or blood tests, requests for inspection of real property, and a *subpoena duces tecum*. (*See* D., *infra*.)

6. **Explain the Reasons Why You Are Gathering the Facts Where the Explanation Is Not Obvious**
Because you are writing under time pressure, you do not have the time to explain why you are gathering every fact. So, unless the task memo tells you otherwise, limit your explanations of why you are seeking the particular facts to those facts that are not obvious.

C. SOME ADDITIONAL THOUGHTS ON FACT GATHERING

1. **Look for the Obvious**
The materials in the library and file will give you ideas about the kinds of facts to gather. You will want to collect every document mentioned in the file. Also, you should check with every person mentioned in the file. Each person is likely to provide some evidence, whether documentary, physical, or testimonial.

2. **Make No Assumptions**
Do not censor yourself. Gather whatever fact you think might be helpful. You never know what could turn up. Also, check all pieces of information from a client. Clients do lie at times, so don't take chances. Verify everything.

3. **Organize Your Fact Gathering Answer**
Unless directed otherwise by the task memo, you should organize your answer ***element by element*** (or ***factor by factor***). That is, under each element or factor underlying the theory or ultimate fact, identify the facts you have as well as the facts you will need and the sources for those facts (including the tools used to get them, if requested by the task memo). Also, unless the examiners suggest an outline format for your answer, we recommend that you write a full prose, paragraph-by-paragraph answer, not merely a laundry list.

4. **Don't Worry About Admissibility**
The basic criterion for discovery is that the information requested be ***relevant to the subject matter***. Relevance to the subject matter means that the information requested be reasonably calculated to lead to discovery of admissible evidence. The immediate information sought need ***not be admissible in itself***—as long as it is reasonably calculated to lead to the discovery of other evidence that is admissible. Thus, for purposes of this exam, unless instructed otherwise, do not concern yourself with admissibility. Just gather as many facts as you think may be helpful.

D. TYPES OF TOOLS USED IN DISCOVERY

If the bar examiners want you to use tools or means of discovery, they will probably include definitions on the exam. Nevertheless, the basic discovery devices are briefly described below so that you can become familiar with them before you take the exam.

1. **Interrogatories**
Interrogatories are ***written questions*** propounded to a ***party***. They may not be sent to a nonparty witness. The party receiving the interrogatories must respond under oath and in writing, and may be required to do some investigation in order to answer the questions. Interrogatories are designed to gather basic and specific background information about the

opposing party and about the incident. The questions can also cover damages, injuries, the existence of documents, and the names of witnesses. Generally, if the information to be gathered is particularly critical to the case, the attorney is more likely to raise the question at a deposition than through interrogatories.

a. **Drafting Interrogatories**
The examiners may require you to draft a set of interrogatories. If so, they will provide an instruction sheet with examples. Interrogatories should be clear and sharply focused, and may be framed as questions or declarative statements. You will probably also be asked to explain why you are proposing each interrogatory—*i.e.,* how it will help you prove the elements of the case and determine your theory or ultimate fact. (A primer on interrogatories taken from an actual exam appears in Appendix I.)

2. **Depositions**
Depositions are usually ***oral examinations*** of witnesses made under oath. A reporter is present. Occasionally, the questions are presented in writing. The person deposed need not be a party, but may be anyone who might have relevant information. The opposing attorney may cross-examine the witness. The transcript of the deposition may be admitted into evidence at trial in certain instances, such as where the deponent is unable to appear. Also, a witness may be impeached at trial by conflicting deposition testimony. Depositions are helpful not only in gathering facts but also in helping attorneys evaluate the strength of the opponent's case and the credibility and demeanor of the witness.

3. **Requests for Admissions**
Requests for admissions are requests made to a ***party*** to admit the truth of a basic fact or the genuineness of a document. For example, you might ask the opposing party to admit that she went to medical school.

4. **Requests for Production of Documents and Things for Inspection**
These requests are directed to the ***opposing party*** to allow the requesting party an opportunity to examine relevant documents or other items, such as a piece of property.

5. **Requests for Physical or Mental Examinations or Blood Tests**
These types of examinations may be requested, although the moving party must usually obtain a ***court order*** before compelling the opposing party to submit to an examination.

6. ***Subpoena Duces Tecum***
This is a subpoena for the purpose of obtaining documents or other tangible evidence. It is usually served with a notice of deposition, directing the deponent to bring certain named documents to the deposition. As with depositions, it may be directed to ***nonparties*** who have control over relevant documents.

VII. FACT ANALYSIS

A. THE SKILL

Fact analysis is different from legal analysis in that it centers almost exclusively on the facts. The law is given or agreed upon, but is used only to help focus and organize the document. The facts are analyzed or argued within the structure of the law. A closing argument is the most common type of fact analysis exam tested by the bar examiners. But fact analysis can be tested in other ways, such as in drafting an opening statement, jury instructions, affidavit, declaration, or witness cross-examination plan.

B. TYPES OF FACT ANALYSIS DOCUMENTS

1. Closing Argument

A closing argument is a ***persuasive*** piece presented at the end of trial to the trier of fact, usually a jury. It is designed to sum up your case and to present your contentions as to what the evidence has shown. Essentially, you are convincing the jury to accept your interpretation of the evidence. A closing argument is almost entirely fact-based. The facts come from the trial transcript; you do not gather new facts. The only references to the law are in the theory you are trying to prove and in the accompanying elements or factors.

a. Organization

Just as you do with fact gathering exams, you should structure your closing argument in a "theory-elements" approach. That is, you should try to convince the jury that a ***theory*** (or ultimate fact) has or has not been met, and that the appropriate ***elements or factors*** have or have not been met. Thus, as with fact gathering, the organization is element by element. Don't forget to introduce yourself (applicant) and your client and to identify the theory and the elements before you begin your argument.

1) Elements or Factors

The elements may come from several different sources. The exam could provide jury instructions setting out the elements. Or the library could include cases, statutes, or regulations that identify the elements.

2) Approach

Under each element, (i) begin by showing how the facts from the trial transcript support your position, stressing those facts that are particularly favorable; and then (ii) rebut any evidence that favors the opposing party. You can rebut facts by:

- showing evidentiary gaps in your opponent's case (*e.g.*, if the plaintiff did burn his scalp as he says he did, why did he not wear a bandage on his head?);

- questioning the credibility of the witness (*e.g.*, the witness was biased, he had prior relevant convictions, his testimony was laden with contradictions or was inconsistent with that of other witnesses); and

- showing that what appears to be evidence damaging to your case can be otherwise interpreted (*e.g.*, the plaintiff was not waving good-by—she was brushing her hair from her face).

After you rebut the most prominent unfavorable facts, draw your conclusion and move on to your next element. Do not bother the jury with lots of unconnected details. Stick to a tight theory-elements organization. If the opposing argument is included in the file, you may point out its weaknesses and downplay its logic, but do not spend much time challenging the opposing party's closing. Remember, the main thrust of your closing should be on presenting and interpreting the evidence to support your position.

b. Tone
If your closing argument is to a jury, be sure to use the appropriate tone for your audience. Keep in mind that you are talking to laypeople.

c. Persuasive
A closing argument is persuasive. To write a good persuasive argument, you must ***believe in your client***. Thus, be careful about conceding certain positions. You are the advocate, not the jury. Do the best you can for your client with the facts you have, and let the jury decide.

d. Burden
If you are the party required to meet the burden of proof, be sure to stress how you have met it. If the other party has the burden, show how that party has failed to meet the burden.

e. Instruction Sheet
An example of an instruction sheet for a closing argument is included in Appendix I.

2. Opening Statements
Opening statements begin the trial. A party's opening statement is essentially a promise of what the evidence will show. It is not argumentative; rather, in opening statements the attorney ***tells a story***. Therefore, you should avoid trying your case in the opening statement.

a. Organization and Approach
Your opening statement is designed to provide the context for the upcoming trial. Tell the jury the story of your case, not pieces of unconnected testimony. Focus on an overall theme or theory, with elements woven into your narrative.

1) Presentation
In telling your story, make your client appealing to the jury. Use specific facts and personalize the names. Think about telling your story in the third person and using the present tense. If you do, a jury is more likely to listen. Do not become over-absorbed in the details—save most of those for trial—and avoid a witness-by-witness account of what evidence will be presented. And although you might want to mention a few weak spots, to keep your credibility and to blunt the opposing party's raising them, be careful about undermining your own position.

2) Tone
Distinguish an opening statement from a closing argument. An opening statement is not argumentative. Rather, it is a narrative designed to set the stage in a light favorable to your client. And remember, you are talking to laypeople. Know your audience.

b. Instruction Sheet
An example of an instruction sheet for an opening statement is included in Appendix I.

3. Jury Instructions
Both parties suggest jury instructions. The judge then reviews the proposed instructions and decides whether to adopt all or part of either party's instructions. Thus, if you must draft

instructions, keep in mind that they are not argumentative and cannot misstate the law. Your instructions should, however, emphasize factors that are favorable to your client's position.

a. **Presentation**
As in a closing argument, you will also need to focus on the ***theory*** and ***elements*** of your case. Jury instructions should set out the theory of your case and identify the elements that need to be proven. Naturally, you will want to present the elements and discuss whether they can be proven in a manner that is advantageous to your client. Also, if you need to set out the theory of the case in legal terms (*e.g.,* whether the testator was under undue influence when she made the will), be sure to define the legal term ("undue influence") as well as provide the appropriate elements. Also, draft the instructions to be ***fact specific***—*i.e.*, refer to the ***specific*** people, companies, and events involved in the lawsuit.

b. **Tone**
Again, remember to write for your audience—*i.e.*, laypeople.

c. **Instruction Sheet and Example**
An example of an instruction sheet for drafting jury instructions is in Appendix I. An example of jury instructions is in Appendix II.

4. **Declaration or Affidavit**
A declaration or affidavit is a sworn statement by a party or witness, testifying to certain facts in support of a legal position in a motion or in another legal document. States differ in how and when they require affidavits and declarations to accompany motions and legal documents. For purposes of this exam, these documents are very similar in style.

a. **Form**
Your affidavit or declaration should be presented in numbered paragraphs, with each paragraph containing ***only one factual statement***. Begin your affidavit or declaration by identifying the declarant or affiant (paragraph 1) and follow with the declarant's or affiant's basis for knowledge (paragraph 2). Then proceed by stating the facts as the declarant or affiant knows them to be. The facts come from the file, and should support your client's position as asserted in the accompanying document. The affidavit or declaration should include only those facts that are truthful, relevant, material, and ***personally known*** by the declarant or affiant.

b. **Inferred Facts**
The bar examiners may ask you to include inferred facts in your affidavit or declaration. Inferred facts are those that can be deduced from the statements of the declarant or affiant that are contained in the file.

c. **Instruction Sheet and Example**
An example of an instruction sheet for drafting affidavits and declarations is in Appendix I. An example of an affidavit/declaration is in Appendix II.

5. **Witness Cross-Examination Plan**
A witness cross-examination plan is just that—it is your plan of how to cross-examine an opposing party or witness. The bases for challenging the witness's credibility will be obvious from the materials in the file and the library. An example of an instruction sheet for a witness cross-examination plan is included in Appendix I.

6. Complaints and Pleading Causes of Action

In drafting a complaint and pleading a cause of action, you must state the minimum allegations necessary to plead the legal elements of your claim. Thus, if you were drafting a complaint for negligence, you would allege the facts that show the elements of negligence: duty, breach of duty, causation, and damages. The allegations are set out in separately numbered paragraphs. An example in included in Appendix I.

7. Will, Contract, and Other Documents

The bar examiners may ask you to draft or redraft a document such as a will, contract, or trust, or they may ask you to draft or redraft a statute. The exam should provide you with guidelines. Generally, no matter what document you are asked to draft, you are essentially performing the same task: ***regulating*** one or more persons' ***behavior*** in order to meet certain ***goals***. Thus, in drafting or redrafting a document, always think of the following before you begin writing:

- What are the client's goals?
- How do you intend to meet these goals?
- Whose behavior is being regulated?
- What behavior is being regulated?
- What assumptions, if any, have you made?
- How do you intend to resolve problems and conflicts that may arise and still meet the client's goals? (This question ties into tactics and problem solving issues—*see* VIII., *infra.*)

a. Organization

Unless the bar exam instructions direct otherwise, your document should follow these guidelines:

1) ***Begin with a title*** (such as "Will of Lefcadio Hearn").

2) ***In an introductory clause identify the parties*** whose behavior is being regulated. Do not use "party of the first part." Use actual names or identifying labels (*e.g.*, "Edith Ho, tenant").

3) ***If the purpose or situation is not clear*** from the title of the document, you can include a ***statement of purpose*** or description of the situation, but keep it short.

4) ***Identify the terms*** of the document. The terms should reflect the ***client's goals*** and the concerns of the parties involved. The terms should be ***fact specific***, and each term should be in a separately numbered paragraph.

5) ***If your document has more than one section***, consider using headings for each section. Sections should have a logical progression.

6) ***Define terms*** in the text the first time you introduce them, or you may include a separate definitional section in your document.

7) ***Standard ("boilerplate") clauses*** usually are not required, but if they are, instructions or examples will be provided.

b. **Tone**
If the document is for a layperson, make sure a layperson will understand it. Define technical terms. Draft provisions precisely. Your document should reflect your client's goals, but do not be unreasonable.

c. **Instruction Sheet and Examples**
An instruction sheet for drafting a will appears in Appendix I. Examples of a will, a contract (a prenuptial agreement), and a trust appear in Appendix II.

d. **Memo or Letter**
You will probably be asked to include a letter or memo explaining to the client why you drafted the document the way that you did.

VIII. PROBLEM SOLVING AND TACTICAL CONSIDERATIONS

A. THE SKILL
Problem solving tests your ability to develop and evaluate tactics and strategies for solving an assigned problem and meeting a client's goal.

B. APPROACH

1. **Identify the Problem**
Begin by identifying the problem in terms of the client's goals.

2. **Consider Various Options**
Next, generate options or plans of action that can meet the client's goals. Be sure to consider both ***legal and nonlegal*** options and plans of action, and evaluate each option or plan of action by analyzing the ***legal and nonlegal consequences*** of each. It is important not to overlook the social and economic consequences as you consider the legal consequences. The examiners also may ask you to identify and evaluate the opposing party's options or plans of action.

3. **Select an Option**
After you have identified and evaluated various options and analyzed the consequences, you may be asked to select and implement one solution, recommendation, or plan of action.

4. **Organization**
Unless otherwise instructed, organize your problem solving exam option by option. Analyze the relevant consequences under each option.

C. INSTRUCTION SHEET
An example of an instruction sheet for a problem solving exam is in Appendix I (*see* Sample Instruction Sheet for Pre-Counseling Letters).

IX. RECOGNIZING AND RESOLVING ETHICAL DILEMMAS

A. THE SKILL
The bar examiners expect you to demonstrate the ability to represent a client within the bounds

of applicable ethical standards. To do this you must know the relevant ethical standards and their means of enforcement, and use that knowledge in recognizing and resolving ethical dilemmas.

B. TYPES OF ETHICAL DILEMMA TESTS

Essentially, the examiners can test ethical dilemmas in two ways:

1. Legal Analysis

The examiners may include professional responsibility rules in the library and expect you to apply them to the behavior of one or more attorneys mentioned in the file. This type of exam is simply a legal analysis exam, requiring you to apply the law in the library to the facts in the file.

2. Problem Solving

The examiners may create an ethical dilemma in the file, but include no rules or law in the library for you to draw upon. If this happens, you still are expected to identify and resolve the problem. The best approach in this situation is to:

a. ***Identify the ethical dilemma*** (*e.g.*, you may see a conflict of interest);

b. ***Suggest alternative ways of resolving the issue*** (*e.g.*, in a conflict of interest situation, you may suggest that the attorney (i) withdraw; (ii) disclose the conflict to the client and obtain the client's consent; or (iii) suggest that the client obtain a second opinion; and

c. ***Select one of your options*** as your recommendation for resolving the dilemma. Be sure that you are consistent with ethical standards.

X. CONCLUSION

A few reminders for the Multistate Performance Test.

- Remember, you are ***primarily taking an exam***, not drafting a real document.
- ***Become comfortable with the skills tested*** on the MPT—legal analysis, fact gathering, fact analysis, problem solving, and solving ethical dilemmas—as well as the skills of communicating with your audience and organizing and managing a legal task.
- Make sure you ***answer the question asked***.
- Think about the ***proper tone***: Is the document objective or persuasive? And be sure to write to your audience.
- ***Practice*** taking MPTs ***under exam (timed) conditions***, and become comfortable with the process and format. This is critical!
- Always ***use your common sense***.

GOOD LUCK!

APPENDIX I

SAMPLE INSTRUCTION SHEETS

For 25 years, the California Bar Exam has required students to take Performance Tests. Many of these tests contained instruction sheets for drafting the various documents assigned by the task memo. Since the Multistate Performance Test was created a decade after the introduction of the California exam, fewer instruction sheets have appeared on the MPT. Thus, we have included in this appendix copies of California's instruction sheets as well as those from the MPT to serve as ***guidelines*** for formats of documents and for drafting particular portions of documents.

The following pages are samples of the different types of instruction sheets the MPT and the California bar examiners have issued through the July 2008 exams. The first eight instruction sheets (one of which is the primer on interrogatories) are taken from MPT exams. Although instruction sheets are becoming more standardized, the National Conference of Bar Examiners may change or modify these sheets on your MPT exam. So if your exam includes an instruction sheet similar to one that is included in this appendix, ***do not assume it is identical***. Rather, ***read the instruction sheet on your exam*** carefully and completely.

SAMPLE INSTRUCTION SHEET FOR PERSUASIVE BRIEFS

Calomen & Sanchez
2714 Meadowood Drive - Suite 100
Weston Hills, Franklin 33332

MEMORANDUM September 8, 1995

To: All Lawyers

From: Director of Litigation

Re: Persuasive Briefs

All persuasive briefs, including Briefs in Support of Motions (also called Memoranda of Points and Authorities), shall conform to the following guidelines.

All briefs shall include a Statement of Facts. The aim of the Statement of Facts is to persuade the tribunal that the facts support our client's position. The facts must be stated accurately, although emphasis is not improper. Select carefully the facts that are pertinent to the legal arguments. In the case of a motion for summary judgment, our arguments must be based on undisputed facts.

The firm follows the practice of breaking the argument into its major components and writing carefully crafted subject headings that illustrate the arguments they cover. Avoid writing briefs that contain only a single broad argument heading. The argument heading should succinctly summarize the reasons the tribunal should take the position you are advocating. A heading should be a specific application of a rule of law to the facts of the case and not a bare legal or factual conclusion or a statement of an abstract principle. For example, *improper:* THE UNDERLYING FACTS ESTABLISH PLAINTIFF'S CLAIM OF RIGHT. *Proper:* BY PLACING A CHAIN ACROSS THE DRIVEWAY, BY REFUSING ACCESS TO OTHERS, AND BY POSTING A "NO TRESPASSING" SIGN, PLAINTIFF HAS ESTABLISHED A CLAIM OF RIGHT.

The body of each argument should analyze applicable legal authority and persuasively argue how the facts and law support our client's position. Authority supportive of our client's position should be emphasized, but contrary authority also should generally be cited, addressed in the argument, and explained or distinguished. Do not reserve arguments for reply or supplemental briefs.

The lawyer need not prepare a table of contents, a table of cases, a summary of argument, or the index. These will be prepared, where required, after the draft is approved.

SAMPLE INSTRUCTION SHEET FOR OPINION LETTERS

Elmore, Anderson & Reed
Attorneys at Law
3722 Page Park Road
Bradley Center, Franklin 33092
(489) 555-7108

MEMORANDUM September 8, 1995

To: Associates

Re: Opinion Letters

The firm follows these guidelines in preparing opinion letters to clients:

- State each client question independently.
- Following each question, provide a concise one-sentence statement giving a "short answer" to the question.
- Following the short answer, write an explanation of the issues raised by the question, including how the relevant authorities combined with the facts lead to your conclusions and recommendations.
- Bear in mind that, in most cases, the client is not a lawyer, so use language appropriate to the client's level of sophistication. Remember also to write in a way that allows the client to follow your reasoning and the logic of your conclusions.

SAMPLE INSTRUCTION SHEET FOR BRIEFS ON EVIDENTIARY PROFFERS

Office of the District Attorney
Victoria County
145 East Harold Street
Beckley, Franklin 33331
(901) 555-1111

MEMORANDUM September 8, 1995

To: Attorneys

From: Andrea Preston, District Attorney

Re: Trial Briefs on Evidentiary Proffers

This memo is for the purpose of clarifying the expectations of the District Attorney's Office and to provide guidance to Assistant District Attorneys. All trial briefs on evidentiary offers shall conform to the following guidelines.

We follow the practice of writing carefully crafted subject headings that illustrate the arguments they cover. The argument heading should succinctly summarize the reasons the tribunal should take the position you are advocating. A heading should be a specific application of a rule of law to the facts of the case and not a bare legal or factual conclusion or a statement of an abstract principle. For example, *improper:* THE WITNESS IS COMPETENT TO TESTIFY. *Proper:* A FIVE-YEAR-OLD WHO ADMITTED HER MOTHER WOULD NOT PUNISH HER FOR LYING, BUT STILL TESTIFIED SHE KNEW THAT LYING WAS WRONG, IS COMPETENT TO TESTIFY.

The body of each argument should incorporate the relevant facts, analyze applicable legal authority, and persuasively argue how the facts and law support our position. Authority supportive of our position should be emphasized, but contrary authority should generally be cited, addressed, and explained or distinguished. Do not reserve arguments for reply or supplemental briefs.

Unless specifically assigned, Assistant District Attorneys should not prepare separate statements of facts. Tables of contents, tables of cases, summaries of arguments, and indices for a trial brief on evidentiary proffers will be prepared, where required, after the draft is approved.

SAMPLE INSTRUCTION SHEET FOR CLOSING ARGUMENTS

COLUMBIA PRISON ASSISTANCE PROGRAM
An Equal Justice Project of the Columbia Bar Association

MEMORANDUM April 10, 1991

To: All Lawyers

From: Director of Litigation

Re: Closing Arguments/Jury Trials

You should begin with an understanding of the legal principles that will be applied to the facts in the case. In some cases, you will be provided with jury instructions. In other cases, the instructions will not yet be drafted and you will have to rely upon an analysis of legal authority. The instructions or legal authority will give you the framework for your closing argument. However, the closing argument should not discuss, or make reference to, these authorities; a closing argument is not a legal brief or an essay. The argument must show how the evidence presented meets the legal standards which are, or will be, set forth in the jury instructions. The argument is based on the evidence presented, not histrionics or personal opinion. Write out your argument exactly as you plan to give it.

It's important that the argument be in your own words, but remember that you're communicating with a group of laypeople. Your job is to help them understand how the law relates to the facts presented, and to persuade them that they have no choice but to find for your client. In doing that, you should consider the following:

- State explicitly the ultimate facts that the jurors must find in order for your client to prevail.
- Organize the evidence in support of the ultimate facts.
- Incorporate relevant legal principles or jury instructions into your argument.
- Discuss the sufficiency of the evidence and the credibility of witnesses.
- Draw reasonable inferences from the evidence to support positions you have taken.
- Anticipate opposing counsel's arguments, and point out weaknesses in his case.
- Refer to equities or policy considerations that merit a finding for our client.

The most important factors are organization and persuasiveness; if you immerse the jury in a sea of unconnected details, they won't have a coherent point of view to discuss in the jury room. Never hold back any argument assuming that you will have a second opportunity to make it on rebuttal.

PRIMER ON INTERROGATORIES TAKEN FROM ACTUAL EXAM

WALKER ON DISCOVERY

A Primer On Discovery Techniques

In civil litigation, depositions, interrogatories, requests for production of documents, and requests for admissions are primary discovery tools used by parties to lawsuits. The purpose of this text is to inform attorneys whose experience is limited or those who need a refresher on discovery techniques. Careful attention to the techniques will facilitate the process of gathering information at a relatively low cost.

* * *

Written Interrogatories: Written interrogatories are, plainly and simply, a series of written requests for information submitted by one party to another. The recipient is required to respond in writing and under oath and to disclose all pertinent information known to it, reasonably available to it, and within its possession and control. Interrogatories may not be sent to nonparties, although they may request information known to the recipient ***about*** nonparties.

An interrogatory may be phrased as a question (*e.g.,* "What goods does ABC, Inc. manufacture?") or as a declarative statement (*e.g.,* "Describe the goods that ABC, Inc. manufactures."). In order to be effective and to avoid objections that they are vague or overbroad, interrogatories must be sharply focused and unambiguously worded.

For example, in an employment discrimination case, the plaintiff might want to obtain information on other employees who have charged the employer with discrimination and what documentary evidence there is of the charges. The following interrogatory would probably be subject to an objection for vagueness and overbreadth:

> INTERROGATORY NO. 1: Please describe each document that contains information regarding the names and addresses of the employees of ABC, Inc. who have filed charges of employment discrimination with the EEOC.

A more focused inquiry will avoid the objection and be more likely to produce the information sought. For example:

> INTERROGATORY NO. 2: What is the name and address of each employee who, within the past two years, has filed with the EEOC a charge of employment discrimination against ABC, Inc.?

Interrogatories may be sequential and may have subparts that seek information related to the main thrust of the interrogatory. For example:

> INTERROGATORY NO. 3: Within the past two years, have any employees of ABC, Inc. filed against ABC, Inc. charges of employment discrimination with the EEOC?
>
> INTERROGATORY NO. 4: If the answer to the preceding interrogatory is in the affirmative, please state the following with regard to each such employee of ABC, Inc.:
>
> a. The name, address, and telephone number of the employee;
>
> b. The name of the custodian of ABC, Inc.'s records regarding ABC, Inc.'s investigation of and response to each such charge filed with the EEOC.

Care must be taken, however, in using interrogatories with subparts. Because there is the potential that counsel might abuse the process by serving burdensome interrogatories, many courts, by local rule, limit the number of interrogatories a party may serve. Typically, the local rules treat each subpart of an interrogatory as a separate interrogatory for purposes of measuring the number of interrogatories served; *e.g.,* Interrogatory No. 4, above, would be counted as two interrogatories.

Although interrogatories cannot be used to require the recipient to ***produce*** documents (*i.e.,* make documents available), they can be used effectively to seek ***identification*** of relevant documents. For example:

> INTERROGATORY NO. 5: Describe the computerized and/or manually prepared records that are used in your company to keep track of the racial, ethnic, and gender make-up of your workforce.

Such interrogatories can be followed up later with written requests for production of documents.

The key to the productive use of interrogatories is for the proponent to think carefully about the specific underlying facts he or she wishes to elicit in order to support the legal elements of the claim and to draft straightforward, plainly worded inquiries. It is best to request the information in small doses. One can always send follow-up interrogatories if further explication is necessary. Convoluted or complex inquiries that encompass too many topics or too much subject matter are ordinarily a waste of time and will not draw useful answers. *See, e.g.,* Interrogatory No. 1, above.

* * *

SAMPLE INSTRUCTION SHEET FOR DRAFTING CAUSES OF ACTION

Miller & Killebrew LLP

OFFICE MEMORANDUM

To: Attorneys

From: Tania Miller

Re: Drafting Causes of Action

Date: September 5, 2004

In pleading a cause of action, firm practice requires attorneys to draft the minimum allegations necessary to plead the required legal elements of the claim, presented in separately numbered paragraphs. The practice of pleading the required legal elements minimizes the risk of the court dismissing an action for failure to state a claim.

For example, a complaint for negligence must usually allege four elements: that the defendant had a duty, that the defendant breached that duty, that the defendant's breach was the proximate cause of injury to the plaintiff, and that this injury caused the plaintiff to suffer compensable damages. The following complaint for negligence provides an example of a negligence pleading consistent with the firm's pleadings practice:

1. When driving his car on the streets of Franklin City, Joe McMann owed other persons using the streets the duty to drive his car as a reasonable and prudent person would.

2. On December 5, 2002, Joe McMann breached his duty by driving his car at a speed in excess of the posted speed limit and through a red light at the corner of First Avenue and K Street in Franklin City.

3. When Joe McMann breached his duty, his car struck Sally Young, who was a pedestrian lawfully walking in a crosswalk at the intersection of First Avenue and K Street.

4. As a result of Joe McMann's breaching his duty, Sally Young suffered serious bodily injury and other damages.

SAMPLE INSTRUCTION SHEET FOR DRAFTING A WILL

Reilly, Ingersol & Powell, P.C.

MEMORANDUM September 8, 1995

To: All Attorneys

From: Robert Reilly

Re: Will Drafting Guidelines

Over the years, this firm has used a variety of formats in drafting wills. Effective immediately, all wills drafted for this firm should follow this format:

Introduction:

A. Set forth the introductory clause with the name and domicile of the testator.

B. Include an appropriate clause regarding the revocation of prior testamentary instruments.

C. Include a clause describing the testator's immediate family (parents, sibling(s), spouse, children, and grandchildren).

Part ONE: Dispositive Clauses (to be set forth in separate subdivisions or subparagraphs by type of bequest or topic). Bequests should be set forth in the following order, as appropriate:

A. Specific bequests

1. Real property
2. Tangible personal property
3. Other specific bequests
4. Any other clauses stating conditions that might affect the disposition of the real and tangible personal property

B. General bequests

C. Demonstrative bequests

D. Residuary clauses

Part TWO: Definitional Clauses. Clauses relating to how words and phrases used in the will should be interpreted.

Part THREE: Boilerplate Clauses. These are clauses relating to the naming of fiduciaries and their administrative and management authority, tax clauses, attestation clauses, and self-proving will affidavits.

SAMPLE INSTRUCTION SHEET
FOR CASE PLANNING MEMORANDUM

The Legal Aid Society ***March 4, 2003***

Case Planning Memorandum Guidelines

Our office follows the practice of using a case planning memorandum (CPM) to prepare for court. A CPM is an internal document that identifies and evaluates, as applicable, the client's claims, counterclaims, defenses, and/or remedies. For each of these, cite the **Legal Authority,** including statutory and case law as applicable; the **Elements** that must be proven in order to establish the client's right to prevail; and the **Supporting Evidence** available to establish each element, including testimonial evidence, documentary evidence, and physical evidence.

A CPM should not include a separate statement of facts, as it is intended as a reference tool for attorneys already familiar with the case. Attached as an example is an excerpt from a CPM drafted for *Jimenez v. Brown Apartments,* a case we litigated in January 2002 (*see* next page).

Excerpt from *Jimenez* Case Planning Memorandum

Claim: Breach of Franklin Fair Housing Law/Unlawful Housing Discrimination

Legal Authority: § 530 of the Franklin Fair Housing Law prohibits a landlord from rejecting a prospective tenant's rental application solely because the application does not meet a particular income-to-rent ratio. A landlord's rejection of an application, notwithstanding the tenant's proof of actual ability to pay, is prima facie evidence of a violation of this section. *(Mooney v. Lutz Management Co.)*

Element #1: The landlord refused to lease residential premises to a prospective tenant because the tenant did not meet the minimum income-to-rent ratio.

Evidence available to show Brown Apartments refused to rent to David Jimenez based on his income level:

- Testimony of Jimenez that he completed Brown's standard rental application form, including providing information about his income.
- Copy of the application Jimenez submitted to Brown.
- Copy of Brown's standard rental application form, stating (in very fine print) that all tenants must have monthly income equal to four times monthly rent.
- Letter from Brown rejecting Jimenez's rental application.

Element #2: The prospective tenant established actual ability to pay rental amount.

Evidence available to show Jimenez's actual ability to pay rent charged by Brown:

- Jimenez's bank statement showing $5,000 in savings account.
- Written financial reference from previous landlord.

Remedy: Punitive Damages

Legal Authority: A court will award punitive damages to a tenant for a violation of § 530 when such conduct is a pervasive practice by a landlord. *(Chong v. Riverside Apartments, LLC*—punitive damages upheld where landlord exhibited repeated disregard for the rights accorded tenants under § 530)

Element: The landlord's pervasive practice is to reject applicants based on income level without considering actual ability to pay rent.

Evidence available to prove Brown's pervasive practice violates § 530:

- Copy of Brown's standard rental application form.
- Testimony of Brown's rental agent that the standard rental application form is used for *all* prospective tenants in Brown's five high-rise complexes in Avon.
- Copy of Brown's rental agent manual, which states that "rental agents must screen each prospective tenant for compliance with minimum income requirements using payroll statements only. . . ."

SAMPLE INSTRUCTION SHEET FOR OPENING STATEMENTS

MEMORANDUM July 30, 1994

To: All Lawyers

From: Executive Committee

Subject: Opening Statements

The purpose of an opening statement is to explain to the fact finder, in plain language, the evidence that you have a good faith basis to believe will be introduced and how that evidence fits into the theory of your case.

All opening statements, whether to be given in a jury trial, bench trial or administrative hearing, shall conform to the following organizational structure:

- Introduce the participants.
- State the theory of your case in a way that will command the fact finder's attention.
- Develop a logical organization of the substantive part of the statement. The substantive portion of the statement should be organized by presenting a narrative statement in the nature of a story, with reference to specific witnesses and documents within the narrative. This type of narrative is often chronological (*e.g.*, a chronology of a car accident) or a series of related topics (*e.g.*, in a custody case: mother, father, home, school, etc.).
- Anticipate defenses and reveal and appropriately deal with weaknesses in our case. Personalize institutions and unsavory clients and witnesses.
- Do not argue the law, but limited references may be helpful (*e.g.*, plaintiff will not be able to meet its burden of . . .).
- Tell the fact finder what you want it to do (*e.g.*, return a specific verdict).

Remember this is an opening statement, not a closing argument. Arguments are inferences you ask the fact finder to draw and are improper in opening statements. On the other hand, do not be timid about emphasizing the evidence that is important to our case, *e.g.*,

Improper: It isn't sex discrimination just because a less experienced male employee got the promotion instead of the plaintiff.

Proper: A better qualified male employee was promoted. He was less experienced, but had a higher performance rating.

SAMPLE INSTRUCTION SHEET FOR JURY INSTRUCTIONS

Finley, Frost and Van Cleave
Attorneys at Law
7814 Harrowgate
Clinton, Columbia

MEMORANDUM January 22, 1994

To: Attorneys

From: Lynda Frost

Re: Jury Instructions

This firm follows the policy of insuring that jury instructions are viewed as an integral part of our persuasive presentation. As such, the instructions must be carefully crafted to present the law to the jury in a clear and understandable manner consistent with the theory of our case. To accomplish this, jury instructions must conform to the following standards:

The instructions must be understandable by the average layperson. Remember the instructions will be read by the judge to the jury. You, for example, may have had months to learn torts; the jury may have minutes.

The instructions must be clear.

The instructions must be particularized to the specific case being litigated. The jury will have sat through the entire trial having heard about specific people, corporations, transactions, and occurrences. The instructions, therefore, will be more easily understood and will provide much more guidance if they refer to the specific people, corporations, transactions, or occurrences involved in the lawsuit.

Since the instructions must be adopted and delivered by the judge as a neutral third party, they cannot be argumentative, or misstate or distort the controlling legal authority. The objective is to fairly state the law while emphasizing factors that support a favorable result for our client.

The jury instructions must fairly state the law, yet be consistent with the legal and factual theory of your case. For example, the fact that we may represent a defendant in a personal injury action does not mean that we do not submit a jury instruction that addresses the plaintiff's obligation to establish a prima facie case. We will draft our version and then argue to the court why it is more appropriate than plaintiff's version.

While form instructions are often helpful, they can do no more than provide a general guide. Form instructions, given their generality, will never have sufficient particularity to the facts of our specific case.

The following instructions are examples that meet the above standards. They are taken from several of our cases involving negligent infliction of emotional distress.

- The plaintiff, Nancy Crater, is entitled to recover damages for serious emotional distress if a cause of such serious emotional distress was the negligent conduct of the defendant, Stanley Manufacturing, Inc. Serious emotional distress is an emotional reaction which is not an abnormal response to the circumstances. It is found where a reasonable person would be unable to cope with the mental distress caused by the circumstances. The elements of a cause of action for negligent infliction of serious emotional distress are:

1. The defendant engaged in negligent conduct;

2. The plaintiff suffered serious emotional distress;

3. Such negligent conduct of the defendant was a cause of the serious emotional distress.

- If you find that Harry Jones, as an adjacent landowner to the Chesterfield airport, suffered emotional distress as a result of the noise from aircraft landing, taking off, and in-flight, you may award damages to the plaintiff.

- If you find that the employee of the defendant, Speedy Process Service, made an invalid service of the writ on Mary Williams and thereafter knowingly filed a false affidavit of valid service, you may award damages to the plaintiff for negligent infliction of emotional distress.

SAMPLE INSTRUCTION SHEET FOR CROSS-EXAMINATION PLANS

Freeman, Duke and Woolridge
3000 Paragon Place
Frederick, Columbia

MEMORANDUM August 1, 1992

To: All Associates

From: Executive Committee

Re: Witness Cross-Examination Plan

When preparing a witness cross-examination plan, you should (1) state the topic of each series of questions; (2) under each topic, list the precise questions you propose be asked of the witness; (3) identify any objections you anticipate will be lodged by opposing counsel; (4) state the best response(s) to the objection; and (5) state the likely ruling. For example, the following was taken from the cross-examination plan in *Smith v. Jones*:

Topic: Witness's prior inconsistent statement concerning who had right of way.

Questions: Q. On direct, you testified that the light was green for Defendant, is that correct?

A. Yes.

Q. Immediately after the accident, you spoke to a police officer, is that correct?

A. Yes.

Q. You told the police officer that the light was green for Plaintiff, didn't you?

A. Yes.

Objections Anticipated: Hearsay.

Response: Prior inconsistent statement offered to show two stories, not for truth of either version.

Likely ruling: Admitted with limiting instruction.

SAMPLE INSTRUCTION SHEET FOR AFFIDAVITS

CENTRAL COLUMBIA
LEGAL SERVICES

MEMORANDUM

To: All Attorneys & Paralegals

From: Executive Committee

Re: Affidavits in Support of Motions or Other Requests for Judicial or Administrative Action

Affidavits should meet the following requirements:

1. Affidavits are to be limited to statements of fact. Those facts should be those necessary to support the legal position asserted in the motion or other request.

2. The facts should be presented in numbered paragraphs and each numbered paragraph, to the extent possible, should contain only one factual statement.

3. Only those facts which are personally known to the affiant and which are truthful, logically relevant, and material shall be included.

Assume that the person signing the affidavit will be subject to cross-examination concerning the contents of the affidavit. Particular care must be taken to insure that person's credibility will not be impeached.

The materials you rely upon may not always contain precisely the facts you need. There often are, however, other facts that can be inferred from existing statements of the person who will sign the affidavit. If you have a good faith basis to believe that he or she has personal knowledge of those inferred facts, include them. We will then check with the person to confirm he or she actually does have personal knowledge of the inferred fact.

Captions, signature lines, and sworn acknowledgement will be added by support staff.

SAMPLE INSTRUCTION SHEET FOR PRE-COUNSELING LETTERS

Rubineau and Boyle
Attorneys at Law
1200 Second Street
Fort Gaines, Columbia 89334

MEMORANDUM February 24, 1994

To: All Lawyers

From: Executive Committee

Re: Pre-Counseling Letter Guidelines

Often members of the firm will be required to conduct a counseling session with a client who is confronted with several significant and difficult choices. In such a situation, the lawyer is advised to prepare and deliver to the client a Pre-Counseling Letter. In addition to helping prepare the client for the counseling session, the letter will serve as an organizing aid for the lawyer conducting the session.

All pre-counseling letters will use the following format:

- State your understanding of the client's goals.
- Identify all courses of action the client can take or that may be taken against the client.
- For each course of action, identify the possible consequences or results, whether legal, economic, or personal.
- Be sure to explain the possible consequences or results, why they are possible, and how likely they are to occur. This will require a discussion of the interrelationship of the law and facts. Remember that most pre-counseling letters are written to lay clients. Although discussion of underlying law is necessary, you must structure this discussion having in mind the client's level of sophistication.
- Where a possible course of action, consequence, or result is unclear, identify what additional information we need, why we need it, and how it can be obtained.

SAMPLE INSTRUCTION SHEET FOR PRE-LITIGATION COUNSELING LETTERS

Atwood, Hoffmann & Paff
One Carlyle Plaza, Suite 1400
Middletown, Columbia

MEMORANDUM

To: All Lawyers

From: Litigation Committee

Re: Pre-Litigation Counseling Letter Guidelines

Often members of the litigation section will be required to conduct a counseling session with a client before actually filing suit. In such a situation, the lawyer is advised to prepare and deliver to the client a Pre-Litigation Counseling Letter. In addition to helping prepare the client for the counseling session, the letter will serve as an organizing aid for the lawyer conducting the session.

All pre-litigation counseling letters will use the following format:

- Identify your understanding of the specific results our client wants to achieve and against whom he wants to achieve them. Be as specific as possible. IMPROPER: Force the school to educate Mary properly. PROPER: Require the school to provide a sign language interpreter for Mary during the entire school day.

- For each specific result, identify each potential legal theory that could be asserted. Be sure to explain the likelihood of success on each theory. This will require a discussion of the interrelationship of the law and facts. Remember that most pre-litigation counseling letters are written to lay clients. Although discussion of underlying law is necessary, you must structure this discussion having in mind the client's level of sophistication.

- Remember, the client is looking for information upon which to make a decision.

The client wants our judgment as to the likelihood of success. Where there is a clear answer, indicate so and explain why. Where the answer is not clear, indicate what you believe the likely result will be and indicate why you reached that judgment.

SAMPLE INSTRUCTION SHEET FOR THEORY OF CASE MEMORANDUM

CENTRAL COLUMBIA
LEGAL SERVICES

To: All Staff Attorneys

Re: Theory of the Case Memorandum

A theory of the case is a working hypothesis of how the law and facts will fit together to support the result sought by our client. The statement of facts should include, in addition to a statement of those facts presently known, a statement of those facts that need to be developed. The statement of law is a summary explanation of why specific legal authorities compel a decision in our client's favor on the basis of those facts. Although it is to be stated in detailed and definite terms, the theory of the case is necessarily provisional, and may be revised and refined as fact development proceeds.

In writing the theory of the case memo, the staff attorney must begin with one or more overarching statements of what we will ask the court to hold. For example, in an age discrimination in employment case, an overarching statement of the plaintiff's case theory might be:

> The defendant employer is liable under the Federal Age Discrimination in Employment Act for damages, injunctive relief, and attorney's fees for having terminated our client because of his age. Our client will make out a prima facie case based on the facts that he was in a protected age category at the time of his termination, was qualified to perform the job, was replaced by a younger person, and was terminated in a workforce reduction which disproportionately impacted persons over 40 years old. Defendant's effort to establish that our client was unqualified to perform the assigned work will fail to rebut the prima facie case.

Next, each element of the case theory must be identified. Any legal principles that affect an element of the case theory must be briefly analyzed. Known facts that support an element of the case theory must be stated and facts that need to be developed must be identified.

In the preceding age discrimination example, this analysis would be as follows:

- *Element:* A showing of disparate impact alone establishes a prima facie case of age discrimination.
- *Analysis:* In *Greggs v. Maryland Power,* the United States Supreme Court held that disparate impact alone establishes a prima facie case of race discrimination, because it raises a permissive inference with regard to a protected class. The same analysis should apply in age discrimination cases, because of congressional intent to create a protected class.
- *Known facts:* 12 of 20 persons terminated in plaintiff's department were over 40 years old.
- *Facts to be developed:* Age distribution of defendant's overall work force reduction and remaining work force.

APPENDIX II

EXAMPLES OF COMMON DOCUMENTS

SAMPLE AFFIDAVIT/DECLARATION

DECLARATION OF GLORIA GREEN

Gloria Green, under penalty of perjury, declares that the following is true and correct:

1. I am an aunt of plaintiffs Elizabeth and Debbie Powell; I am the sister of their late mother, Martha; and I am the guardian of plaintiff Elizabeth Powell.
2. Although I did not live with Martha and Ronald Powell, I visited them frequently during their marriage and had many opportunities to observe their family.
3. From the time of Ronald Powell's marriage to Martha, he held out Elizabeth as his daughter. Until his death, she lived in his home.
4. From the time of the marriage, Elizabeth began to use the name of Elizabeth Powell. I heard Ronald introduce her many times as "my daughter, Elizabeth."
5. Ronald treated Elizabeth as though she was his child, even though, as far as I know, he never formally adopted her. He took her to school and shopping, taught her to ride a bike and swim, and helped her with her homework. For all the world, he was her father. Elizabeth believed Ronald was her father; he was the only father she ever knew.
6. After Debbie was born, Ronald treated Elizabeth in the same manner as Debbie. It was impossible for anyone to know that only Debbie was his natural daughter, and only a few close friends and members of the family, like myself, knew that Elizabeth was not Ronald's natural daughter.
7. Ronald always provided for both Debbie and Elizabeth, and continued to take care of and support Elizabeth, without any support from her natural father, even after Martha's death. He paid to have both girls attend a private school. A small insurance policy he had from work (for $500) listed both Debbie and Elizabeth as co-equal beneficiaries.
8. As far as I know, neither Ronald nor Martha ever requested that Elizabeth's natural father provide for her financial support. Elizabeth's natural father's whereabouts are unknown to me.
9. I know that Ronald would have wanted to see that both Debbie and Elizabeth were treated alike. As much as I love Debbie, it would not be Ronald's wish that only Debbie be included among his heirs.
10. Ronald had a preoccupation with fires. The Powell house had fire extinguishers and smoke detectors in every bedroom and the kitchen. He insisted that ***all*** of Elizabeth's and Debbie's clothing be fireproof. Ronald told me many times that he would never stay in "cheap" motels because they were "fire traps."

Gloria Green

Gloria Green

SAMPLE JURY INSTRUCTIONS

Introductory instructions will be given on the duty of the jury, including its duty to follow the judge's instructions on the law, drawing inferences from circumstantial evidence, weighing conflicting testimony, and judging the credibility of witnesses. Other approved instructions follow:

(1) The contestants (Mrs. Crenshaw's children) have the burden of establishing by a preponderance of the evidence all of the facts necessary to prove the grounds of contest.

By a preponderance of the evidence is meant such evidence as, when weighed with that opposed to it, has more convincing force and the greater possibility of truth. In the event that the evidence from each side is equally balanced so that you are unable to say that the evidence on either side of a ground of contest preponderates, then your finding upon that ground of contest must be against the contestant.

(2) Every person of sound mind, over the age of 18 years, and not acting under undue influence, has the right to make a will directing the disposition of her property upon her death in any way she sees fit. Mrs. Crenshaw, the decedent, was under no obligation to make such disposition as will meet with the approval of a judge or jury.

The right to dispose of property by will is a fundamental right assured by law and does not depend upon a wise use of the right.

A will cannot be set aside simply because dispositions in the will may appear to you to be unreasonable or unjust.

(3) A will that is made by a person who is not of sound mind is not valid. However, in this case the court has decided Mrs. Crenshaw was of sound mind and therefore had the capacity to dispose of her property by will. That matter has been decided for you by the court and is no longer in issue.

(4) A will that is obtained by undue influence is not valid and may not be admitted to probate. Your sole responsibility in this case is to determine whether Mrs. Crenshaw's will was obtained by undue influence.

Undue influence consists of acts or conduct by which the mind of the decedent is overcome by the will of another person.

Mere general influence is not undue influence. In order to constitute undue influence, it must be used directly to obtain the will. It must amount to coercion destroying Mrs. Crenshaw's free will, substituting for her own another person's will, and compelling Mrs. Crenshaw to make a disposition she would not otherwise have made.

(5) In determining the issue of undue influence, you may consider, among other things, these questions:

1. Do the provisions of the will prefer strangers in blood to the persons who would naturally be considered by Mrs. Crenshaw, the decedent?

2. Does the will unduly benefit Richard and Alice Waterman, the chief beneficiaries thereof?

3. Is there a variance between the terms of the will and Mrs. Crenshaw's expressed intentions?

4. Was there an opportunity afforded by the Watermans' relationship to Mrs. Crenshaw to influence Mrs. Crenshaw?

5. Was Mrs. Crenshaw's mental and physical condition such as to permit her free will to be overcome?

6. Were the Watermans active in procuring execution of the will?

(6) If you find that a confidential relationship existed between Mrs. Crenshaw and Richard or Alice Waterman, that the Watermans or either of them were active in obtaining the will and that either of them unduly profited from it, you shall presume that the will was obtained by undue influence of either or both of the Watermans. That presumption may be overcome by the Watermans if they establish by a preponderance of the evidence that the will was not the result of undue influence.

A confidential relationship exists whenever trust and confidence is reposed by one person in the integrity and fidelity of another.

SAMPLE WILL

LAST WILL AND TESTAMENT

I, ROGER WINTHROP STERN, a resident of Golden City, Columbia, declare that this is my last will and testament.

FIRST: I revoke all Wills and Codicils that I have previously made.

SECOND: I am a widower and have only one child, my son, GORDON ALLEN STERN, who was born on May 29, 1946. I have no deceased children.

THIRD: I give all of my estate to my son Gordon, if he survives me.

FOURTH: If my son Gordon is not living at the time of my death, I give all of my estate to my alma mater, THE UNIVERSITY OF COLUMBIA, Golden City, Columbia.

FIFTH: I nominate COLUMBIA BANK AND TRUST of Golden City, Columbia, as Executor of this Will. The term "my Executor," as used in this Will, shall include any personal representative of my estate.

I authorize my Executor to sell, with or without notice, at either public or private sale, and to lease any property belonging to my estate, subject only to such confirmation of court as may be required by law.

Because of their familiarity with my business and personal affairs, it is my desire that my Executor employ the law firm of COLLIER & FRAZEE, of Golden City, Columbia, to assist in the administration of my estate.

I subscribe my name to this Will this 23rd day of June, 1977, at Golden City, Columbia.

Roger Winthrop Stern
ROGER WINTHROP STERN

(The will was properly executed and witnessed under Columbia law.)

SAMPLE CONTRACT

PREMARITAL PROPERTY AGREEMENT

This agreement is entered into this 25th day of September, 1996, in Golden City, Columbia, between ROGER WINTHROP STERN and ANNETTE ELY LOCKWOOD. The parties contemplate marriage on or about October 5, 1996, and by this agreement seek to define their respective rights in the property each now holds and in property that may be acquired after their marriage. In furtherance of this purpose, the parties mutually agree as follows:

I. At the present time each of the parties has separate property consisting of real property, investments in stocks and bonds, bank accounts, and a lifetime's accumulation of personal items. Roger's holdings are substantial and include a controlling interest in a business now managed by others; Annette's are less substantial, but have provided a comfortable income during her widowhood. Each wishes to retain the power to manage and control this separate property and to dispose of the same by will, while at the same time recognizing the rights and obligations that flow from marriage.

II. It is the intent of the parties that Annette's rights under the community property laws of this state be fully protected, and that in the event Roger predeceases her, she will have sufficient property as the result of their marriage to enable her to maintain the lifestyle to which she has become accustomed. To this end Roger specifically agrees that, within 30 days of the parties' marriage, he will do the following:

A. Transfer to Annette an undivided interest in his home at 77 Firwood Drive, Golden City, valued at approximately $400,000, so that he and Annette hold this residence as joint tenants with right of survivorship. He will also pay off the balance of the mortgage on this property.

B. Procure and thereafter pay all premiums on a life insurance policy in the amount of $200,000, which policy will name Annette as sole beneficiary.

C. Open a joint savings account between himself and Annette and thereafter maintain a balance of at least $30,000, that being the amount agreed on by the parties as necessary to provide a smooth transition in the event of Roger's death.

D. Open a joint checking account between himself and Annette and thereafter deposit all sums necessary to enable the parties to meet monthly expenses and enjoy a comfortable and gracious lifestyle during their marriage.

III. It is agreed by the parties that the value of the property transferred to Annette under Paragraph II, if she should survive Roger, equals or exceeds the value of any community property that might be acquired after marriage, and Annette specifically accepts these transfers, once they become final, as full satisfaction of her community property rights.

IV. It is also agreed by the parties that during the marriage Annette's separate property shall remain her separate property, and that she alone will be entitled to all rents and profits therefrom, whether or not some part of this income might be characterized as community property.

V. Finally, it is further agreed by the parties that beyond the specific transfers above mentioned, neither shall have any interest in the separate property of the other, and in particular, each party specifically waives the right to inherit from the estate of the other. Each of the parties has a child

or children from a previous marriage, and it is understood that each has willed or intends to will most if not all of his or her separate estate to these children.

In witness whereof, the parties have signed this agreement this 25th day of September, 1996.

Roger Winthrop Stern
ROGER WINTHROP STERN

Annette Ely Lockwood
ANNETTE ELY LOCKWOOD

(The agreement was properly executed under Columbia law.)

SAMPLE TRUST

Andrew Cook of DeVane, Columbia, as Trustor, and Jean Hemphill of DeVane, Columbia, as Trustee, agree as follows:

1. The Trustor hereby transfers and delivers to the Trustee the property listed in Schedule "A," which is attached to this document [not included in this example], together with all his interest in the property described in Schedule "A." The Trustee shall hold the property, together with any additions to the property, as provided in this trust agreement as a Trust Estate. The Trustee shall invest and reinvest the property and shall distribute the net income ("income") and principal for the benefit of the Trustor's children, Michael and Elizabeth.

2. Until Michael and Elizabeth both reach their 30th birthdays, the Trustee shall expend both income and principal to such extent and in such manner as she in her sole discretion deems advisable for the beneficiaries' welfare, comfortable support, maintenance, and education. The Trustee shall also add any excess income to principal and invest it as such.

3. When both beneficiaries have reached their 30th birthdays, the Trust shall terminate and the principal and any accrued or undistributed income shall be transferred and delivered to the beneficiaries, in equal amounts, free of trust.

4. If a beneficiary should die prior to the time he or she is entitled to receive distribution of the Trust Estate, one-half of the principal and one-half of any accrued or undistributed income shall be distributed to the beneficiary's then living children, in equal shares. If there is no living child of the beneficiary, then the beneficiary's share shall be distributed to the Homeless Foundation in Columbia.

5. Neither the principal nor income of the Trust Estate held by the Trustee shall be subject to assignment or other anticipation by any beneficiary of this trust. Nor shall any beneficiary's interest be subject to any attachment by garnishment or by any other legal proceeding or action for any debt or other obligation of a beneficiary to this Trust.

6. This Trust shall not be revoked or terminated by Trustor or any other person, nor shall it be amended or altered by Trustor or any other person.

SAMPLE TRUST

PRACTICE TESTS AND ANSWERS

NOTE REGARDING ANSWERS

The model answers provided discuss the major arguments that could be made. They are not intended to be definitive answers. Your answers could be *considerably shorter* than the answers provided, and you could still receive a passing grade, even an excellent grade, without covering all of the items discussed in the model answers.

Multistate Performance Test

In re Kiddie-Gym Systems, Inc.

National Conference of Bar Examiners

Preface

This Multistate Performance Test is a reprint of one of the second two MPTs, which were administered in July 1997 in eight states: Colorado, District of Columbia, Georgia, Hawaii, Iowa, Missouri, Nevada, and New Mexico.

The instructions for the test appear on the next page. On the actual MPT, they will appear on the back cover of the test.

INSTRUCTIONS

1. You will have 90 minutes to complete this session of the examination. This performance test is designed to evaluate your ability to handle a select number of legal authorities in the context of a factual problem involving a client.

2. The problem is set in the fictitious state of Franklin, in the fictitious Fifteenth Circuit of the United States. Columbia and Olympia are also fictitious states in the Fifteenth Circuit. In Franklin, the trial court of general jurisdiction is the District Court, the intermediate appellate court is the Court of Appeal, and the highest court is the Supreme Court.

3. You will have two kinds of materials with which to work: a File and a Library. The first document in the File is a memorandum containing the instructions for the task you are to complete. The other documents in the File contain factual information about your case and may include some facts that are not relevant.

4. The Library contains the legal authorities needed to complete the task and may also include some authorities that are not relevant. Any cases may be real, modified, or written solely for the purpose of this examination. If the cases appear familiar to you, do not assume that they are precisely the same as you have read before. Read them thoroughly, as if they all were new to you. You should assume that cases were decided in the jurisdictions and on the dates shown. In citing cases from the Library, you may use abbreviations and omit page references.

5. Your response must be written in the answer book provided. If you are taking this examination on a laptop computer, your jurisdiction will provide you with specific instructions. In answering this performance test, you should concentrate on the materials provided in the File and Library. What you have learned in law school and elsewhere provides the general background for analyzing the problem; the File and Library provide the specific materials with which you must work.

6. Although there are no restrictions on how you apportion your time, you should be sure to allocate ample time (about 45 minutes) to reading and digesting the materials and to organizing your answer before you begin writing it. You may make notes anywhere in the test materials; blank pages are provided at the end of the booklet. You may not tear pages from the question booklet.

7. This performance test will be graded on your responsiveness to the instructions regarding the task you are to complete, which are given to you in the first memorandum in the File, and on the content, thoroughness, and organization of your response.

In re Kiddie-Gym Systems, Inc.

FILE

LIBRARY

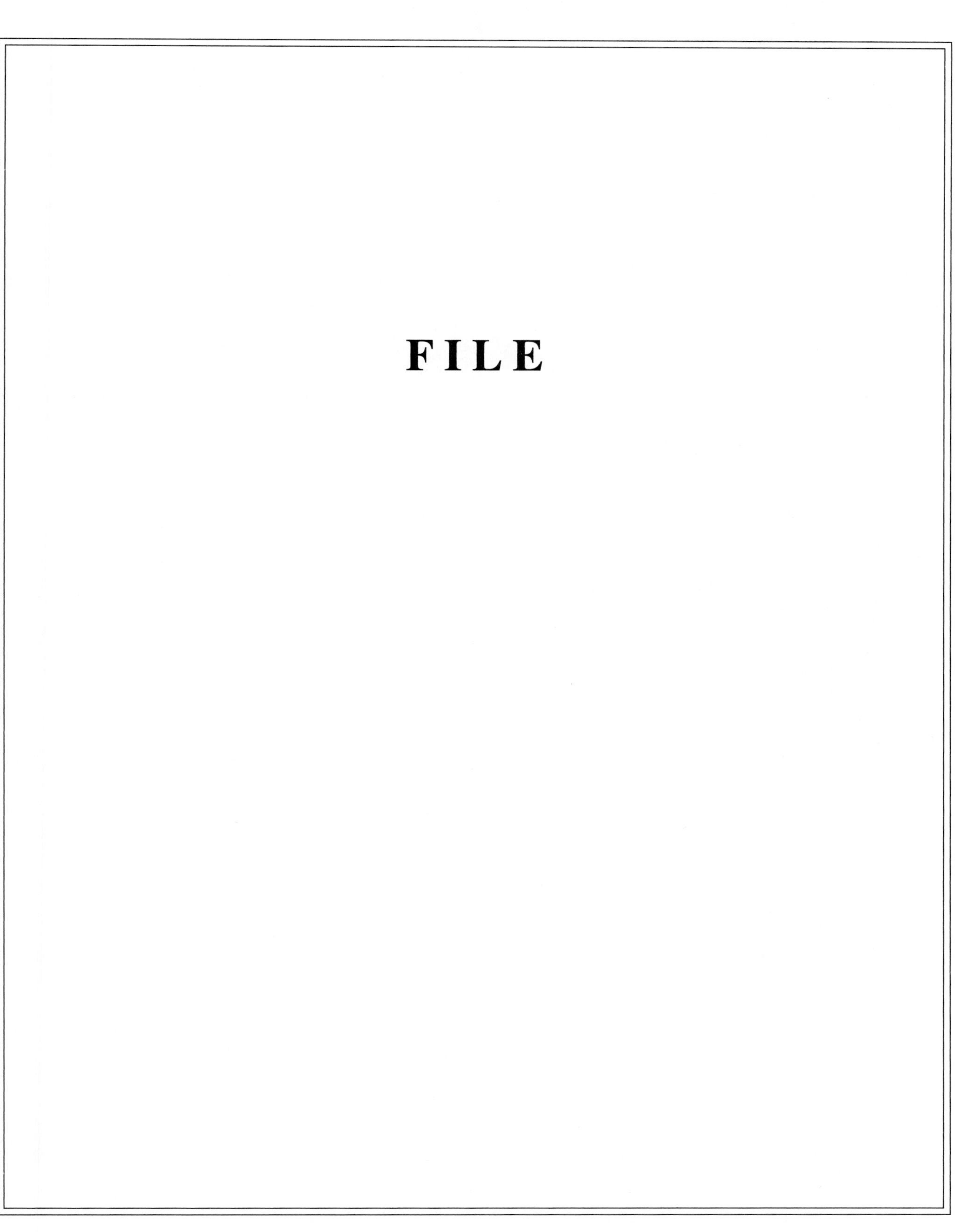

FILE

Elmore, Anderson & Reed
Attorneys at Law
3722 Page Park Road
Bradley Center, Franklin 33092
(489) 555-7108

MEMORANDUM

To: Applicant

From: Marla Reed

Date: July 29, 1997

Subject: Kiddie-Gym Systems, Inc.

Our client, Kiddie-Gym Systems, Inc. (KGS), has been in business for almost a year. It furnishes and installs prefabricated indoor playground equipment for developers and operators of shopping malls, day-care centers, fast-food outlets, and other entities that want to provide such facilities for children of their customers. Earlier today, Jerry Martin, the president of KGS, came in to get our advice on a business problem involving playground equipment KGS bought from Poly-Cast, Inc. and installed at Bradley Center Mall, one of Cornet Development Corporation's shopping malls. The playground equipment was destroyed by a fire at the mall. I told him we would give him a written opinion within a few days.

I've transcribed my notes of the discussion I had with Mr. Martin, and they are included in the file along with some documents Mr. Martin left with me. I've also included parts of the Franklin Commercial Code (which is identical in substance to the Uniform Commercial Code) and some cases that may or may not be relevant. Here's what I would like you to do for me:

Draft for my signature an opinion letter to Mr. Martin addressing the following questions:

(1) As between KGS and Cornet, which bears the risk of loss for playground equipment destroyed in the fire at Cornet's Bradley Center shopping mall?

(2) Is KGS obligated to pay the shipping and handling charges billed by Poly-Cast?

Attached for your guidance is a memorandum regarding our firm's practice in writing opinion letters.

Elmore, Anderson & Reed
Attorneys at Law
3722 Page Park Road
Bradley Center, Franklin 33092
(489) 555-7108

MEMORANDUM

September 8, 1995

To: Associates

Re: Opinion Letters

The firm follows these guidelines in preparing opinion letters to clients:

- State each client question independently.
- Following each question, provide a concise one-sentence statement giving a "short answer" to the question.
- Following the short answer, write an explanation of the issues raised by the question, including how the relevant authorities combined with the facts lead to your conclusions and recommendations.
- Bear in mind that, in most cases, the client is not a lawyer, so use language appropriate to the client's level of sophistication. Remember also to write in a way that allows the client to follow your reasoning and the logic of your conclusions.

NOTES OF DISCUSSION WITH JERRY MARTIN, PRESIDENT OF KGS
JULY 29, 1997

KGS installs indoor molded plastic playground equipment in places like fast-food restaurants, shopping malls, day-care centers, etc.

- A little over 2 months ago, KGS landed its largest contract so far—with Cornet Developers—3 major shopping centers in Franklin—1st one, in Bradley Center, just completed and opened to the public on July 23, 1997—2 other malls under construction. Contract drafted by Cornet's attorneys.
- Martin shopped Cornet's specifications around and found a new supplier, Poly-Cast, Inc., located in Copley, about 100 miles from here—Poly-Cast's playground equipment meets Cornet's specs—got what he thought was very favorable pricing from Melissa Parker, Poly-Cast's sales manager.
- Poly-Cast shipped 1st playground system to Bradley Center job site on time and in good condition—it arrived at the site in heavy protective wooden crates—unnecessary as far as Martin is concerned—it just costs Poly-Cast money to do the crating and costs KGS time and labor to uncrate and dispose of the wood.
- Re Bradley Center Mall, KGS crew began assembly on July 21, 1997 and finished physical installation of playground equipment and general site clean-up on July 22—removed construction barriers at end of the day and told Charlie Short, Cornet's job superintendent, Martin would be back the next day to do final site check and crew would return within 2 weeks to do final "tune-up."
- Martin went to job site the next day, July 23, about 11:00 a.m. and found 20 - 30 kids already playing on the equipment; checked with Charlie Short and learned that he had given the mall manager the green light to let the kids begin using the playground—Martin did a visual check, found things in order, and left, intending to send crew back in two weeks to do final tune-up per contract.
- Fire broke out at Bradley Center Mall on July 24—damaged part of the mall and destroyed the playground equipment—best guess is that the fire started from a cigarette someone threw into a trash bin.
- Charlie Short has told Martin that KGS won't get paid for Bradley Center job until it installs replacement equipment—Charlie also said no pay because title to the playground system hadn't yet passed to Cornet.

- Martin says Short had already given his OK for kids to begin using the equipment—can't understand why KGS should bear the loss—the fire wasn't KGS's fault—KGS hasn't been able to afford insurance for this kind of loss; is pretty sure Cornet is insured. KGS might be willing to make some accommodation on labor costs during installation of replacement system at Bradley Center Mall, at least to the extent of Cornet's insurance deductible, if any.
- Obviously, KGS can't perform final tune-up on the system that was destroyed—Martin says final tune-up is no big deal—the Poly-Cast systems shouldn't need much if any final adjustments and, at most, it would've been an hour's work by 2 workers.
- To make matters worse, Martin just received Poly-Cast's invoice for the first system, and Poly-Cast has included a $2,500 charge for shipping and handling (amount not surprising, judging from the fancy wooden crate job)—Martin got a range of quotes that would meet specs from Melissa Parker, Poly-Cast's sales manager; the one for Model PC 443-7 was $25,000 per playground system—no mention of additional charges—that's why KGS's purchase order states "price all inclusive."
- Martin didn't look too closely at Poly-Cast's acknowledgement form when he received it on or about June 16, 1997, other than to notice that it agreed with the price on KGS's purchase order—just yesterday, noticed the fine print re shipping and handling.
- Even if KGS doesn't have to pay the cost to replace the Bradley Center unit, if KGS has to pay the $2,500 in freight charges, KGS will barely break even (maybe even take a slight loss) on the Cornet contract after labor and overhead. If he'd known, he could have had his own driver pick up the shipment at Poly-Cast plant—no trouble for him to do that.
- KGS is between a rock and a hard place with respect to both Cornet and Poly-Cast—can't afford to eat the loss on the Bradley Center Mall or agree to pay the Poly-Cast freight, but needs to preserve relations with both because of the other 2 malls.

CONSTRUCTION AND SERVICE CONTRACT

This contract for construction and services is made and entered into by and between Cornet Development Corporation ("Cornet") and Kiddie-Gym Systems, Inc. ("KGS") this 23rd day of May, 1997.

1. Work: KGS shall furnish all labor, equipment and materials necessary for the installation of molded plastic indoor playground equipment ("playground systems") at each of the three (3) Cornet shopping malls listed below. The playground systems shall be installed at locations designated by Cornet within each mall and shall conform to the specifications prepared by Cornet and delivered previously to KGS. Not later than 30 days after completion of installation of each playground system, KGS shall perform a follow-up inspection and make such final adjustments ("tune-up") of the system as shall be required, if any, as the result of initial use by patrons of the mall.

2. Mall Sites and Projected Opening Dates: KGS shall perform its work at the following mall sites and shall complete installation no later than one day before the projected opening date of each mall: Bradley Center, due to open July 23,1997; Sedona Hills, due to open September 29, 1997; and Mayfair, due to open January 26, 1998.

3. Price and Payment Terms: The total price to be paid by Cornet to KGS is $120,000, each playground system to be paid for at $40,000 ("site price") upon completion of the work at each mall site.

4. Passage of Title: Title to each playground system shall pass to Cornet upon completion by KGS of the final tune-up of the system.

5. Penalty for Delay: KGS shall forfeit $500 for each day of delay in the completion of the installation of the playground system at each site.

6. Entire Agreement: This writing sets forth the entire agreement of the parties, and any prior or contemporaneous promises or representations made and not set forth in this writing shall be of no effect. No modification of this agreement may be made except in a writing executed by both parties.

Cornet Development Corporation

By Thomas G. Bodette

Thomas G. Bodette
Vice President for
Development

Kiddie-Gym Systems, Inc.

By Jerome A. Martin

Jerome A. Martin
President

PURCHASE ORDER

Date: May 29, 1997

No. 447A

Kiddie-Gym Systems, Inc.
4722 Industrial Way
Bradley Center, FN 33087
(489) 554-6249

Seller: Poly-Cast, Inc.
790 Polypropylene Way
Copley, FN 33124

Ship To: Per Instructions

This constitutes order by Kiddie-Gym Systems, Inc. of three (3) Poly-Cast molded playground systems, Model No. PC443-7. Systems per sample shown and to conform to Cornet Development specifications furnished to Poly-Cast.

Systems to be delivered by Poly-Cast to Cornet Development job sites per instructions to be given by Kiddie-Gym Systems. First system to be delivered to Bradley Center Mall job site not later than July 21, 1997. Delivery to other job sites (Sedona Hills and Mayfair) per later instructions.

Price: $25,000 per unit, all-inclusive, per quote from Melissa Parker. Payable net 60 days after delivery.

General Conditions

Seller warrants all goods are of merchantable quality and fit for the intended purpose. Seller warrants that all goods are free and clear of all liens and claims by third parties and that Seller possesses all rights to sell said goods free and clear.

Date: May 30, 1997

Authorized Signature: Jerome A. Martin
Jerome A. Martin

ACKNOWLEDGEMENT OF ORDER

POLY-CAST, INC.
Premier Molded and Extruded Plastic Products
790 Polypropylene Way
Copley, FN 33124
(489) 550-0900

No. 277695

Date: June 9, 1997

Buyer: Kiddie-Gym
4722 Industrial Way
Bradley Center, FN 33087
(489) 554-6249

Ship To: Per Instructions

Contact: Jerry Martin

Poly-Cast hereby acknowledges your Order per your PO #447A dated May 29, 1997:

- Three (3) Model PC443-7 playground systems Unit price $25,000
- Systems to conform to Cornet Development specs
- Will ship first system to Cornet site at Bradley Center Mall by July 21, 1997 per instructions
- Will wait for shipping and delivery instructions on Sedona Hills and Mayfair sites
- Payable net 30 days from date of invoice

Arthur Haskins

Arthur Haskins
Vice President/Sales

Conditions Applicable To All Sales: All goods subject to limited warranties of merchantability and fitness. All shipments subject to charges for shipping and handling to be paid net 30 days from date of invoice. Goods are guaranteed against defects discovered and reported within ten (10) days of delivery. Late charges at 10% per month for past due payments; minimum late charge $10.00. Shipments travel at the risk and cost of Buyer. Risk of loss passes to Buyer at time of identification of goods to the contract at Seller's loading dock.

POLY-CAST, INC.
Premier Molded and Extruded Plastic Products
790 Polypropylene Way
Copley, FN 33124
(489) 550-0900

INVOICE

Date: July 25, 1997 No. 114076-96

Customer: Kiddie-Gym
4722 Industrial Way
Bradley Center, FN 33087

Attention: Jerry Martin

Your PO# 447A

Quantity	Description	Price
1	Poly-Cast playground system - Model PC443-7 delivered July 21, 1997 per customer's instructions	$25,000.00
	Shipping & handling	$ 2,500.00
	Total Due (net 30 days)	$27,500.00

Make checks payable to Poly-Cast, Inc.

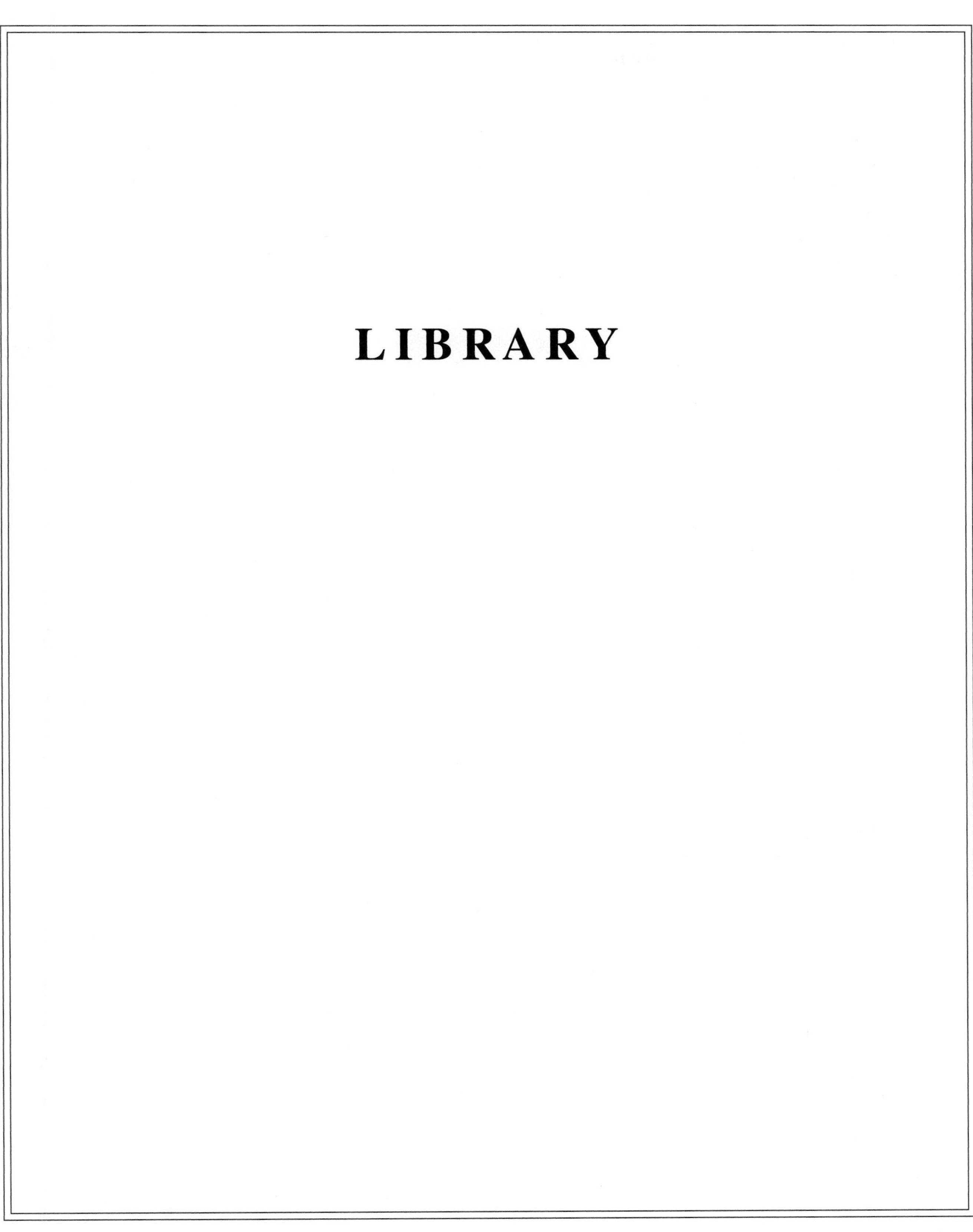

LIBRARY

Franklin Commercial Code

* * * *

§ 2102. Scope: Unless the context otherwise requires, this division of the Commercial Code applies only to transactions in goods; it does not apply to any transaction which is solely for the sale of services.

* * * *

§ 2104. Definitions: "Merchant"; "Between Merchants":

(1) "Merchant" means a person who deals in goods of the kind . . . involved in the transaction . . . .

(2) "Between merchants" means any transaction with respect to which both parties are chargeable with the knowledge or skill of merchants.

§ 2105. Definitions: "Goods": "Goods" means all things (including specially manufactured goods) which are movable at the time of identification to the contract for sale other than the money in which the price is to be paid.

* * * *

§ 2207. Additional Terms in Acceptance or Confirmation:

(1) A definite and seasonable expression of acceptance or written confirmation which is sent within a reasonable time operates as an acceptance even though it states terms additional to or different from those offered or agreed upon, unless acceptance is expressly made conditional on assent to the additional or different terms.

(2) The additional terms are to be construed as proposals for addition to the contract. Between merchants such terms become part of the contract unless:

(a) The offer expressly limits acceptance to the terms of the offer;

(b) They materially alter it; or

(c) Notification of objection to them has already been given or is given within a reasonable time after notice of them is received.

(3) Conduct by both parties which recognizes the existence of a contract is sufficient to establish a contract for sale although the writings of the parties do not otherwise establish a contract. In such a case the terms of the particular contract consist of those terms on which the writings of the parties agree, together with any supplementary terms incorporated under any other provisions of this code.

* * * *

§ 2319. F.O.B.:

(1) Unless otherwise agreed the term F.O.B. (which means "free on board") at a named place, even though used only in connection with the stated price, is a delivery term under which:

(a) When the term is F.O.B. the place of shipment, the seller must at that place ship the goods and bear the expense and risk of putting them into the possession of the carrier; or

(b) When the term is F.O.B. the place of destination, the seller must at his own expense and risk transport the goods to that place and there tender delivery of them.

* * * *

§ 2401. Passing of Title: Each provision of this division of this code with regard to the rights, obligations and remedies of the seller, the buyer, purchasers or other third parties applies irrespective of title to the goods except where the provision of this code refers to title. Insofar as situations are not covered by the other provisions of this division of this code and matters concerning title become material the following rules apply:

(1) Title to goods cannot pass under a contract for sale prior to their identification to the contract. Subject to these provisions, title to goods passes from the seller to the buyer in any manner and on conditions explicitly agreed on by the parties.

(2) Unless otherwise explicitly agreed title passes to the buyer at the time and place at which the seller completes his performance with reference to the physical delivery of the goods.

* * * *

§ 2503. Manner of Seller's Tender of Delivery: Tender of delivery requires that the seller put and hold conforming goods at the buyer's disposition and give the buyer any notification reasonably necessary to enable him to take delivery.

* * * *

§ 2509. Risk of Loss in the Absence of Breach: The risk of loss passes to the buyer on his receipt of the goods if the seller is a merchant; otherwise the risk passes to the buyer on tender of delivery. The provisions of this section are subject to contrary agreement of the parties.

Coakley, Inc. v. Washington Plate Glass Co.
Franklin Court of Appeal (1991)

PER CURIAM: Washington Plate Glass Co. had a contract "to furnish and install aluminum and glass curtain wall and storefront work" on a building owned by Coakley, Inc. To accomplish its contractual undertaking, Washington purchased the glass required from Shatterproof Glass Corp. Other materials were acquired elsewhere.

The contract price under the Coakley/Washington contract was $262,500. The glass purchased from Shatterproof cost $87,715. The other materials necessary for the performance of the contract, aluminum, anchor clips, fittings, field fasteners, etc., cost approximately $80,000.

Within a year, the glass began to discolor. When Coakley complained to Washington and Shatterproof, they declined to replace the glass, so Coakley filed suit against them in the Franklin District Court. Coakley alleged breach of implied warranties of merchantability and fitness for a particular purpose created by Franklin Commercial Code §§2314 and 2315.

Shatterproof moved for dismissal on the sole ground that the FCC was inapplicable. The District Court granted the motion and Coakley appeals.

Whether the FCC applies turns on whether the contract between Coakley and Washington involved principally a sale of goods or a provision of services. Unless there has been a buyer of goods, the implied FCC warranties of merchantability and fitness do not apply. Thus, the question as to the availability of warranties comes down to whether the transaction between Coakley and Washington was a sale of goods or the provision of services. Any requirement for privity between Coakley and Shatterproof is abolished if the FCC applies. See FCC §2314(1)(b): "Any previous requirement of privity is abolished as between the buyer and the seller in any action brought by the buyer."

The cases dealing with this issue turn upon whether the thrust of the contract is to supply goods or to furnish services. The mixed character of the contract does not remove it from the ambit of the sales division of the FCC. The words of §2102 of the FCC support this conclusion: The sales division of the FCC "does not apply to any transaction which is solely for the sale of services."

Therefore, we apply the test articulated in *Wilson v. Sharpe* (Franklin Supreme Court, 1974): in situations where the contract is a mixed contract involving both the sale of goods and the rendition of services, it will be deemed that the contract comes within the sales division of the Franklin Commercial Code if the value of the goods being furnished under the contract exceeds one-half of the total contract price. By that measure, at least, it can be clearly said that the predominant factor in the contract is the sale of goods and that the sale of goods is more than merely incidental to the contract.

Applying that principle to the case at hand, we note that more than one-half of the price in the Coakley/Washington contract is attributable to the value of the goods to be furnished thereunder. The contract therefore falls within the Franklin Commercial Code. Accordingly, we reverse.

Hughes v. Al Green, Inc.
Franklin Court of Appeal (1993)

Laura Hughes purchased a new 1989 Lincoln Continental from Al Green Dodge-Lincoln. She tendered a cash down payment and arranged to finance the balance through a local bank. In the meantime, she completed the necessary application for a certificate of title. The parties agreed that Hughes would take immediate possession of the automobile but that she would return it to the dealership on the following Monday for certain new car preparations and installation of the CD player. En route from the dealership to her home, Hughes was involved in a collision and the automobile was substantially damaged. The title documents, showing Hughes as the legal owner, were subsequently delivered to her.

Hughes refused to pay the balance and sued Al Green, Inc. for breach of contract alleging that the vehicle had been transferred to her in a damaged condition. Her claim is based on the notion that, when the certificate of title was issued to her, thereby legally transferring title to her, she no longer possessed that for which she had bargained, i.e., an undamaged 1989 Lincoln Continental.

A jury found for Green. The case is now before us on appeal.

We must determine whether the buyer or the seller bore the risk of loss or damage to the automobile at the time of the collision. To say that the buyer had the risk of loss at the time the goods were destroyed is to say that the buyer is liable for the price. To say that the seller had the risk of loss at the time the goods were destroyed is to say that the seller is liable in damages to the buyer for nondelivery unless he tenders a performance in replacement for the destroyed goods.

Franklin Commercial Code §2509 provides that "the risk of loss passes to the buyer on his receipt of the goods if the seller is a merchant; otherwise the risk passes to the buyer on tender of delivery." This provision represents a significant shift away from the prior importance of the concept of title in determining the point at which risk of loss passes from seller to buyer. Under the common law, title to the contract goods determined the locus of risk of loss. Under the Commercial Code, however, each provision relating to the rights, obligations and remedies of sellers and buyers applies irrespective of title except where the provision of the code itself refers to such title. (FCC §2401.)

FCC §2509 sets forth a contractual approach, as distinguished from the property concept of title, to solving issues arising when goods are damaged or destroyed. The section focuses on specific acts, such as tender of delivery by the seller or receipt of the goods by the buyer. Title is relevant under this section only if the parties provide that risk of loss shall depend upon the locus of title. Unless the contract specifically provides that risk of loss depends upon the locus of title, it is irrelevant where title resides.

In this case, the buyer had received possession of the automobile as partial execution of a merchant-seller's obligations under a purchase contract. There is no question but that the buyer, having physical possession and use of the vehicle, had "receipt" within the meaning of the FCC. Nothing in the contract purported to shift the risk of loss dependent upon the locus of title. Thus, Hughes, as a buyer in receipt of goods identified to the contract, must bear the risk of loss of the car's value resulting from the collision.

Affirmed.

Album Graphics, Inc. v. Craig Adhesive Company
Franklin Court of Appeal (1995)

Plaintiff Album Graphics, Inc. brought a complaint against Craig Adhesive Company alleging a breach of express and implied warranties. The trial court dismissed.

Album manufactures containers for cosmetics. Craig manufactures and sells adhesives (glue). A salesperson employed by Craig visited Album's plant and, after discussions with Album's manufacturing superintendent, offered to manufacture a special glue that would meet Album's needs for the assembly of newly designed cosmetics packages. During a later visit, the salesperson demonstrated the glue and instructed plaintiff's personnel on its use. As a result of the two meetings, Album ordered a quantity of the glue and used it on the new packages. Album sold a number of the new cosmetics packages to a customer. The packages fell apart, and Album had to recall and replace them using a different glue.

The parties in the present case do not dispute that a contract for sale was entered into, or that express or implied warranties may have been created on the basis of the facts pleaded in Album's complaint. Craig alleges that such warranties were effectively disclaimed. Craig asserts its disclaimer theory on two grounds. First, each container of glue delivered to Album had a label on which there was conspicuously printed language to the effect that the only warranty made was that all goods were manufactured of standard materials and, if any material proved to be defective, Craig would either replace the goods or refund the price. Second, Craig's invoices also contained explicit disclaimers of warranties.

Though it may be questionable that the labels and invoices are "confirmatory memoranda" of the agreement reached by the parties, we will, for the purpose of analysis, accept the defendant's contention and assume that they are. Hence, they would be "written confirmation" of the prior agreement entered into by the parties as that term is used in Franklin Commercial Code §2207.

The general purpose of §2207 is to allow the parties to enforce their agreement, whatever it may be, despite discrepancies between an oral agreement and a written confirmation, and despite discrepancies between a written offer and a written acceptance. Also, it allows for additional terms stated in an acceptance or written confirmation to become terms of the agreement in certain cases. Hence, the section allows a written confirmation to "operate" as acceptance for the above purposes.

Here, the question is only whether the additional terms in the written confirmations became part of the agreement. For this, we must look at §2207(2), which states in part: "Between merchants such terms become part of the contract unless: *** (b) They materially alter it. . . ."

Official Comment 4 to the FCC gives as examples of typical clauses that would materially alter the contract and so result in surprise or hardship if incorporated without the express awareness by the other party: "a clause negating such standard warranties as that of merchantability or fitness in circumstances in which either warranty normally applies. . . ." We believe that Craig's unilateral disclaimer of warranties and limitation of damages clauses are such as to result in "surprise or hardship" and therefore could not become part of the contract under §2207(2) because they "materially alter it." On that basis alone, Craig's disclaimers were ineffective.

There is, however, an additional basis for reaching the same result. Here, the parties effectively performed their contract without taking cognizance of the conflicting terms that later resulted in this dispute. That is to say, Album ordered the goods, Craig shipped them, and Album used them. In such circumstances, §2207(3) comes into operation. Under that section, if the conduct of the parties recognizes the existence of a contract, then a contract for sale is formed even though the writings of the parties do not establish a contract. In such a case, the contract contains "those terms on which the writings of the parties agree," and all other terms either "drop out" or are supplied by the "gap-filling" provisions of the Commercial Code.

In the present case, since Craig's labels and the invoices do not contain a term which also appears as part of the writing sent by Album, the label and invoice terms cannot become part of the contract. The terms relating to the warranty issue are then supplied by §§2314 and 2315, which are sections of the Code that statutorily create the implied warranties of merchantability and fitness for a particular purpose. The warranties created by those sections are imported as "gap fillers" into the contract by operation of §2207(3). The contract is then deemed to contain the implied warranties. Accordingly, we reverse.

In re Kiddie-Gym Systems, Inc.

Sample Answer

Dear Mr. Martin:

This letter is in response to your inquiries concerning your company, Kiddie-Gym Systems ("KGS") and its installation of playground equipment bought from Poly-Cast and installed at Bradley Center Mall, one of Cornet Development Corporation's shopping malls. As you know, the playground equipment was destroyed by a fire at the mall.

1. Does KGS or Cornet bear the risk of loss for the playground equipment destroyed in the fire at Cornet's shopping mall?

The risk of loss should fall on Cornet since the fire occurred after Cornet received the playground equipment.

The first issue is to determine the applicable law. The Franklin Commercial Code ("FCC") applies to all transactions in goods, but does not apply to transactions that are solely for the sale of services. (Section 2102) Our situation involves both the sale of goods (the playground equipment would be "goods" under section 2105) and the sale of services (construction and installation services) and therefore is a mixed goods services contract.

In a Franklin appellate court case, *Coakley v. Washington Plate Glass*, the court was confronted with a similar situation wherein a business sold and installed materials, just as KGS did. The court held that where a contract involves both a sale of goods and the furnishing of services, the court must look to see "whether the thrust of the contract is to supply goods or to furnish services." The court stated that the FCC controlled where the value of the goods being furnished under the contract exceeded one-half of the contract price. Here, the goods were purchased for $25,000, and the total contract price was $40,000. (Since the contract calls for separate "site prices," payment, delivery dates and sites, the contract is divisible, and performance at each site can be treated separately.) Therefore, the value of the goods exceeded one-half of the contract price, and thus the FCC applies.

The next issue is who bears the loss for the goods under the FCC. Under FCC section 2509, where neither party is in breach and where the seller of goods is a merchant, the risk of loss passes to the

buyer upon receipt. Here, there is no evidence of a breach and KGS is a merchant because KGS regularly deals in goods of the kind, i.e., playground equipment. (Section 2104) Therefore, the risk of loss passed to Cornet when Cornet received the goods from KGS.

The next issue is when did Cornet receive the goods? In the *Hughes* case, the court found that a buyer had received the goods and therefore bore the loss when the buyer had physical possession and use of the goods, even though title had not yet passed. In our situation, Cornet received the goods before the mall opened, as required under the contract. KGS had completed the installation, removed all the barriers, and turned the equipment over to the mall manager. The mall manager, having physical possession and use of the goods, put the equipment into use. Only the final tune-up for minor adjustments, if any, required as the result of the initial use by mall patrons, remained to be done. Thus, Cornet had receipt of the equipment at the time of the fire, and the risk of loss passed to Cornet.

Cornet may argue that it is not required to pay because title to the equipment had not passed under the contract. However, absent a contrary agreement on risk of loss (and there was none here), risk of loss has nothing to do with the passage of title.

2. <u>Is KGS obligated to pay the $2500 shipping and handling charges billed by Poly-Cast?</u>

KGS should not be required to pay these charges because they either (a) materially alter the agreement or (b) the conduct of the parties is inconsistent with the charges.

The threshold issue of whether a contract was formed is met. Although the terms of KGS's order form are different from Poly-Cast's acknowledgement form, a contract was still formed. Under section 2207(1), a written confirmation operates an acceptance even though it contains additional or different terms unless acceptance is expressly made conditional on assent to the additional or different terms. Here Poly-Cast's acknowledgement was not made expressly conditional on assent by KGS to the additional or different terms. Thus, a contract was formed. The only question is what are the terms of the contract.

Because the shipping and handling charges were included on Poly-Cast's acknowledgement form but not on KGS's purchase order to buy the playground equipment from Poly-Cast, we must first determine whether they are part of the contract between KGS and Poly-Cast, which would require KGS to pay the stated charges. Under FCC section 2207, a merchant dealing with another merchant is bound by additional terms unless the additional terms materially alter the agreement.

In the *Album Graphics* case, the court dealt with a similar situation. It noted that clauses added to a contract without the express awareness of the other party materially alter the contract if the additional terms result in surprise or hardship. Such would be the case here. If KGS had to pay the shipping and handling charges, its profit would essentially be eliminated, which certainly is a hardship. Also, the purchase order stated that the price was "all-inclusive"; thus, KGS was surprised to learn that shipping and handling charges would be added. In fact, had KGS known about the charges, KGS would have sent its own driver to pick up the shipment and save the expenses. Therefore, the additional terms requiring payment of shipping and handling charges materially alter the agreement and thus are not binding on KGS.

In addition, an argument could be made that there is no contract based on the exchange of the documents because the terms are inconsistent: KGS's purchase order states "price all-inclusive," while Poly-Cast's acknowledgment form adds $2500 for shipping and handling. In such a situation, a contract would be formed based on the conduct of the parties. (FCC section 2207(3)) Here, KGS ordered the equipment, Poly-Cast shipped it, and KGS used it. This conduct would create the contract. Under section 2207(3), the contract would contain the terms on which the writings of the parties agree. All other terms would be left out. Therefore, the shipping and handling charges would not be part of the contract, and KGS would not be liable for them.

Sincerely,

Multistate Performance Test

In re Gardenton Board of Education

National Conference of Bar Examiners

Preface

This Multistate Performance Test is a reprint of one of the two MPTs which were administered in February 1998.

The instructions for the test appear on the next page. On the actual MPT, they will appear on the back cover of the test.

INSTRUCTIONS

1. You will have 90 minutes to complete this session of the examination. This performance test is designed to evaluate your ability to handle a select number of legal authorities in the context of a factual problem involving a client.

2. The problem is set in the fictitious state of Franklin, in the fictitious Fifteenth Circuit of the United States. Columbia and Olympia are also fictitious states in the Fifteenth Circuit. In Franklin, the trial court of general jurisdiction is the District Court, the intermediate appellate court is the Court of Appeal, and the highest court is the Supreme Court.

3. You will have two kinds of materials with which to work: a File and a Library. The first document in the File is a memorandum containing the instructions for the task you are to complete. The other documents in the File contain factual information about your case and may include some facts that are not relevant.

4. The Library contains the legal authorities needed to complete the task and may also include some authorities that are not relevant. Any cases may be real, modified, or written solely for the purpose of this examination. If the cases appear familiar to you, do not assume that they are precisely the same as you have read before. Read them thoroughly, as if they all were new to you. You should assume that cases were decided in the jurisdictions and on the dates shown. In citing cases from the Library, you may use abbreviations and omit page references.

5. Your response must be written in the answer book provided. If you are taking this examination on a laptop computer, your jurisdiction will provide you with specific instructions. In answering this performance test, you should concentrate on the materials provided in the File and Library. What you have learned in law school and elsewhere provides the general background for analyzing the problem; the File and Library provide the specific materials with which you must work.

6. Although there are no restrictions on how you apportion your time, you should be sure to allocate ample time (about 45 minutes) to reading and digesting the materials and to organizing your answer before you begin writing it. You may make notes anywhere in the test materials; blank pages are provided at the end of the booklet. You may not tear pages from the question booklet.

7. This performance test will be graded on your responsiveness to the instructions regarding the task you are to complete, which are given to you in the first memorandum in the File, and on the content, thoroughness, and organization of your response.

In re Gardenton Board of Education

FILE

LIBRARY

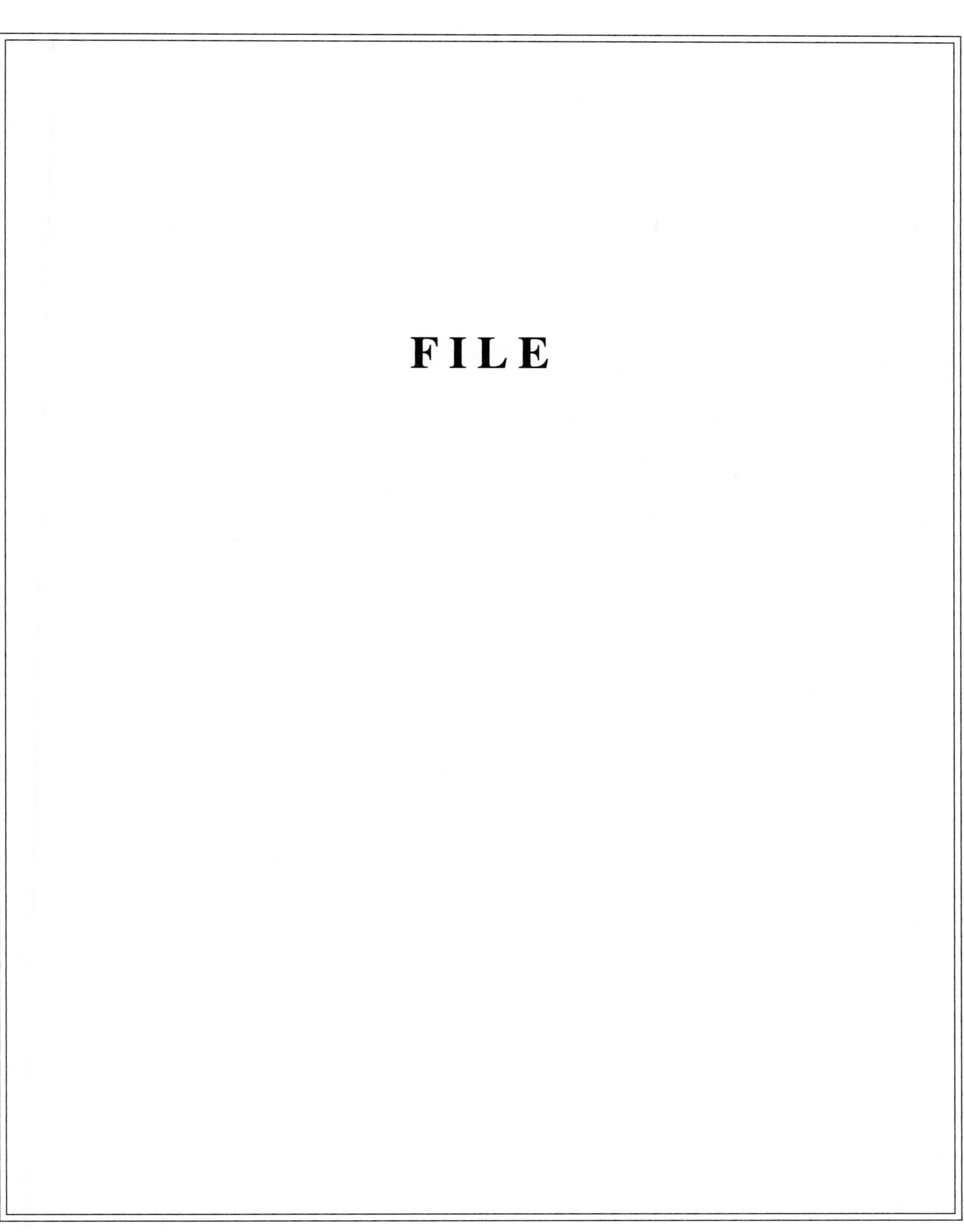
FILE

ALLEN, EISNER & THOMAS
Attorneys at Law
1427 Marsden Place
Gardenton, Franklin 33301
(434) 277-8901

M E M O R A N D U M

TO: Applicant

FROM: Frank Eisner

DATE: February 24, 1998

SUBJECT: Gardenton Board of Education—Proposed Communications Code for Gardenton High School

---

Dr. Edwina Kantor, the President of the Gardenton Board of Education, came to see me a few days ago about a new code to regulate the content of student communications at our public high school, Gardenton High. At its next meeting, the Board wants to present for public comment the most restrictive communications code permissible, one that gives the school the greatest flexibility to prevent the publication of offensive material. Dr. Kantor wants me to meet with and advise the Board in advance of that meeting and to be prepared to respond to comments from members of the public who have signed up to speak pro and con about the code.

Over the last few months, parents and civic groups have objected to what they consider to be intemperate, irresponsible reporting, profanity, and sexually charged material of questionable taste appearing in the various student media.

I've included in the file a transcript of my conversation with Dr. Kantor so you can get a better idea of what the issues are and how she'd like to have this matter resolved.

Please prepare a memorandum in which you evaluate the preamble and each of the guideline provisions in the draft of the communications code that Dr. Kantor left with me. Identify the legal issues that can give rise to constitutional challenges to each of the provisions and analyze whether each such provision is likely to be found legally permissible. Make suggestions for deleting, modifying, or adding any items in order to help the Board achieve its goal. Be sure to state your reasons for concluding that each guideline provision is legally permissible or impermissible, as well as the reasons for any suggestions you make. Support your reasons with appropriate discussion of the facts and law.

TRANSCRIPT OF DISCUSSION WITH DR. EDWINA KANTOR

Lawyer: Thanks for allowing me to record this discussion, Dr. Kantor. It'll make it easier to reconstruct it later on.

Kantor: That's fine. This problem is becoming a real headache.

Lawyer: Tell me what the situation is.

Kantor: With increasing frequency, we've been getting complaints from local residents, some city leaders, parents, and various church and civic groups about the degenerating quality of the subject matter being reported in *The Weekly Cougar* and the language being used by students in their student theatrical and video productions. In fact, we've come pretty close to being sued for defamation by a number of really irate citizens who've read or seen things published about themselves or their families.

Lawyer: *The Weekly Cougar*—that's the student newspaper, right?

Kantor: That's right. It's published by the students in the senior journalism class. Students in drama and theatrical arts classes also publish plays. The performances are produced a couple of times a year. Sometimes there are live performances and sometimes the plays are filmed or videotaped by the students in the cinematography department and then shown in the auditorium or in classrooms in lieu of live plays.

Lawyer: Is the *Cougar* circulated beyond the student body? Who is invited to attend the student theatrical productions?

Kantor: Well, we don't consciously circulate the *Cougar* off campus. It's intended to be an educational vehicle for training students, but there's nothing to prevent anyone who's interested from getting copies. In order to finance the costs, the students solicit advertisements from local merchants and business operators. But it's not a newspaper of general circulation.

As far as the theatrical productions are concerned, the regular annual live performances are advertised around town and admission is charged. The targeted audiences are made up mostly of students and their friends and relatives. Some of the smaller productions—I mean videos and films—are just for student consumption. We've never tried to open either the live plays or the smaller productions to the public at large.

Lawyer: What's the problem?

Kantor: Well, the student reporters for the *Cougar* have reported stories about individuals, relying on rumor and innuendo, without verifying the facts, without exercising mature judgment, and generally exceeding the boundaries of responsible journalism. They have used some profanity in their stories. They just don't have the experience to know better. As a result, there have been some pretty defamatory and tasteless things published.

The plays and theatrical productions have sometimes bordered on being obscene. They frequently deal with sexually charged and morally questionable subject matter that parents, community leaders, and civic groups have found offensive. And, I've got to tell you that I agree with them.

Lawyer: Haven't the school administrators and classroom teachers been able to control the contents sufficiently to avoid these problems?

Kantor: Not really. It's not that they don't want to. It's just that they haven't had any guidelines, and they've been unsure how far they can go to squelch what some people say is free speech. The Board has worked up some guidelines as part of a communications code that we'd like to implement. I'll just leave this copy with you.

Lawyer: All right. Where would you like to end up with this thing?

Kantor: Well, in the best of worlds, we'd like to be able to implement each and every one of the controls we've listed in the draft. It was supposed to be a working draft and was supposed to be kept secret until we were ready to go public with it. Somehow it got out, and the next thing we know the opposition groups are coming out of the woodwork, and we're being threatened with litigation from both sides. The Union for Freedom of Speech is threatening to sue us if we promulgate any code at all, and the Gardenton Civic League is threatening to sue us if we don't.

We really want to go as far as the law will allow us in controlling what the kids can publish and in giving the school district and the high school administration something they can enforce without being tied up in litigation. We have to satisfy the parents and the community that we're doing something to curb the problem and, at the same time, convince the students and free speech activists that what we're doing is within the law.

Lawyer: What, specifically, can I do to help?

Kantor: The next public meeting of the Board is scheduled for a week from Friday. The public session begins at 8:00 p.m. We already know from the sign-up list that there are going to be a lot of speakers on both sides of the issue. We are particularly concerned about the Union for Freedom of Speech, which we believe is champing at the bit to sue us. They've told us they'll sue to enjoin us. I think they believe that publication of <u>any</u> code would be a violation of the students' constitutional right of free speech.

We'd like you to meet with us before the meeting to advise us on whether or not the draft of the guidelines is something we can lawfully implement. If not, tell us why not, and tell us what we can do. We're not wedded to all the items in the draft. The main thing is that we be able to censor unacceptable language and morally questionable subject matter that runs counter to our educational goals, especially things that open us up to suits for libel and slander and invasion of privacy.

Lawyer: What about procedures for implementing the guidelines?

Kantor: One step at a time. First, let's get agreement on these substantive guidelines at the Board meeting. Then we can turn our attention to the procedures for applying them. Later on, we'll draft some procedures and ask you to look at them.

Lawyer: OK, Dr. Kantor. Let me get to work. I'll see you at the Board meeting at 6:00 p.m.

DRAFT

STUDENT COMMUNICATIONS CODE FOR GARDENTON HIGH SCHOOL

Preamble: This Communications Code shall apply to all student publications and media representations produced either as a result of course work or intramural extracurricular activities that are published, distributed, or otherwise disseminated on or off campus. This code shall apply to school newspapers, yearbooks, plays and other literary publications, films, movies, videos, signs, posters, and other photographic productions and graphic displays.

Guidelines for Student Publications and Productions:

1. All student publications and productions shall maintain professional standards of English language and journalistic style.

2. All student publications and productions shall avoid language and depictions that are not in good taste, having regard for the age, experience, and maturity of the general student population.

3. No stories or reports of events shall be published unless the accuracy of the facts and any quotations from individuals have first been verified to the satisfaction of the teacher supervising the publication.

4. No person shall be quoted or photographically depicted in any student publication or production without that person's prior permission and, in the case of a minor, the permission of the minor's parent or guardian, except that persons posing for group photographs shall be deemed to have given their implied consent.

5. No publication, literary piece, play, film, video, or other student production shall include material that:

   a. is libelous or slanderous or violates any person's right of privacy;

   b. contains profanity, which means language that would not customarily be used in local newspapers, to wit: *The Gardenton Times* or *The Morning Herald*;

   c. criticizes or demeans any public official, including officials, administrators, and teachers of the school; or

   d. is deemed by the principal not to be in the school's best interest.

6. Material must receive the prior approval of the principal before it is published, distributed or otherwise disseminated.

Procedures for Implementation: [to come later.]

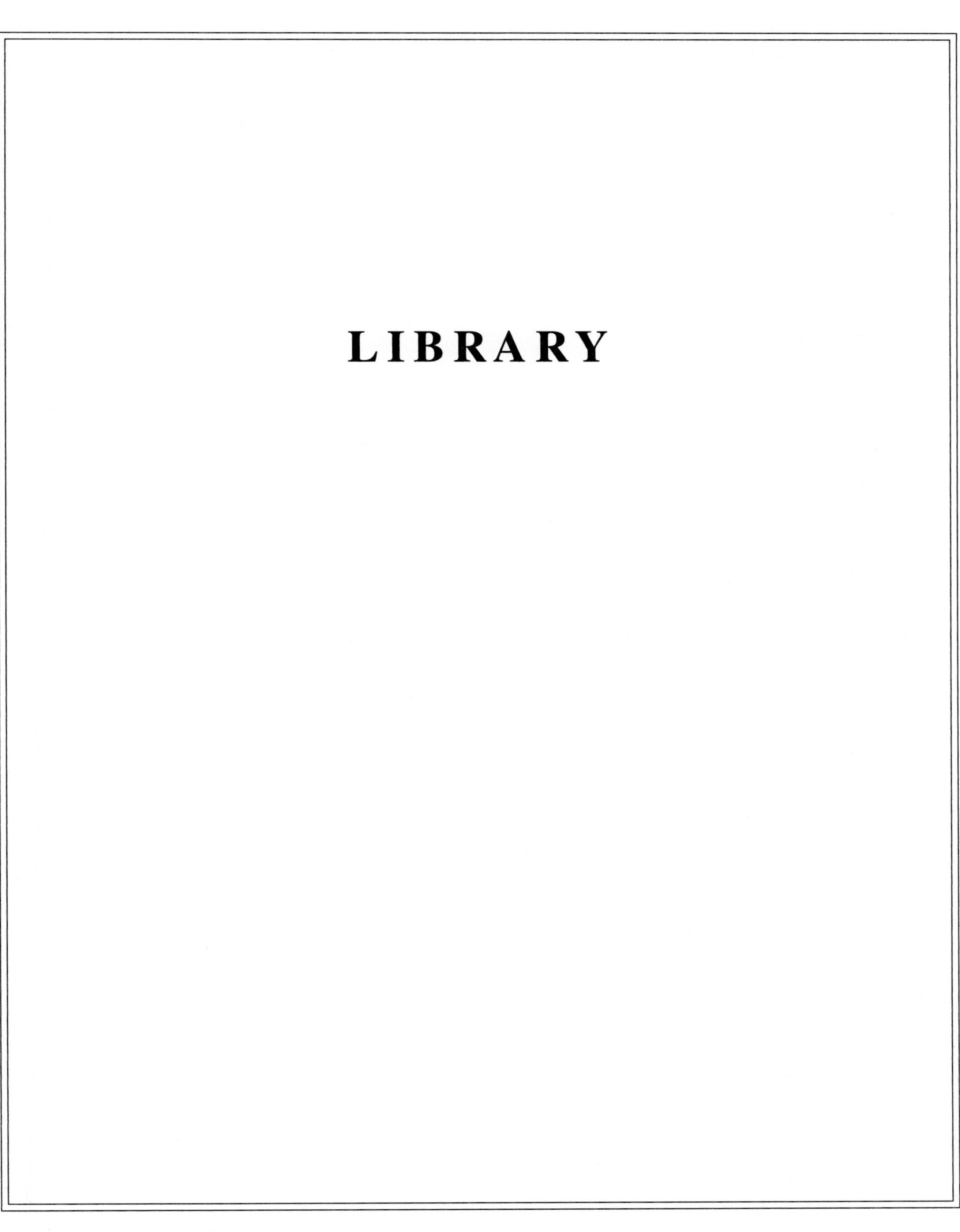

LIBRARY

The Constitution of the United States

Amendment I

Congress shall make no law respecting an establishment of religion, or prohibiting the free exercise thereof; or abridging the freedom of speech, or of the press; or the right of the people peaceably to assemble, and to petition the Government for a redress of grievances.

Constitution of the State of Franklin

Article I

Section 2. Every person may freely speak, write, or publish his or her sentiments on all subjects, being responsible for the abuse of this right. A law may not restrain or abridge liberty of speech or press.

Franklin Education Act

Section 48. Student Exercise of Freedom of Speech or Press

Students of public schools shall have the right to exercise freedom of speech and of the press including, but not limited to, the use of bulletin boards, the distribution of printed materials or petitions, the wearing of buttons, badges, and other insignia, and the right of expression in official publications, whether or not such publications or other means of expression are supported financially by the school or by use of school facilities, except that expression is prohibited which is obscene, libelous, or slanderous. Also prohibited shall be material which so incites students as to create a clear and present danger of the commission of unlawful acts on school premises or the violation of lawful school regulations, or the substantial disruption of the orderly operation of the school.

Student editors of official school publications shall be responsible for assigning and editing the news, editorial, and feature content of their publications subject to the limitations of this section. However, it shall be the responsibility of journalism advisers or advisers of student publications within each school to supervise the production of the student staff, to maintain professional standards of English and journalism, and to maintain the provisions of this section.

"Official school publications" refers to material produced by students in the journalism, newspaper, yearbook, or writing classes and distributed to the student body either free or for a fee.

Hazelwood School District v. Kuhlmeier

United States Supreme Court (1988)

Respondents contend that school district officials violated their First Amendment rights by deleting two pages of articles from the May 13, 1983 issue of *Spectrum,* the Hazelwood High School student newspaper. Written and edited by the Journalism II class at Hazelwood High, the newspaper was distributed to students, school personnel, and members of the community.

The practice at Hazelwood was for the journalism teacher, Robert Mackinac, to submit each *Spectrum* issue to Eugene Reynolds, the school principal, for his review prior to publication. On May 10, Reynolds objected to two of the articles scheduled to appear in the May 13 edition. One of the stories described three Hazelwood students' experiences with pregnancy; the other discussed the impact of divorce on students at the school, quoting a student's remarks about the cause of her parents' divorce. Reynolds directed Mackinac to withhold the two stories from publication.

The district court found that Principal Reynolds' concern that the pregnant students' anonymity would be lost and their privacy invaded was "legitimate and reasonable," given "the small number of pregnant students at Hazelwood and several identifying characteristics that were disclosed in the article." The deletion of the article on divorce was seen by the court as a reasonable response to the invasion of privacy concerns raised by the named student's remarks. Because the student's parents had not been offered an opportunity to respond, there was cause for "serious doubt that the article complied with the rules of fairness which are standard in the field of journalism and were covered in the textbook used in the Journalism II class."

The Court of Appeals for the Eighth Circuit reversed. We granted certiorari, and we now reverse the decision of the Eighth Circuit and affirm the district court.

The First Amendment rights of students in the public schools are not automatically coextensive with the rights of adults in other settings and must be applied in the special circumstances of the school environment. A school need not tolerate student speech that is inconsistent with its basic educational mission, even though the government could not censor similar speech outside the school. Accordingly, we have held that a school could discipline a student for having delivered a speech that was "sexually explicit" but not legally obscene at an official school assembly, because the school was entitled to disassociate itself from the speech in a manner that would demonstrate to others that such vulgarity is wholly inconsistent with the fundamental values of public school education. The determination of what manner of speech in the classroom or in school assembly is inappropriate properly rests with the school board, rather than with the federal courts. It is in this context that respondents' First Amendment claims must be considered.

We deal first with the question of whether *Spectrum* may appropriately be characterized as a forum for public expression. The public schools do not possess all the attributes of streets, parks, and other traditional forums that have been used for purposes of assembly and discussion of public questions. Hence, school facilities may be deemed to be public forums only if school authorities have by policy or practice opened those facilities for indiscriminate use by the general public or by some segment of the public, such as student organizations. The government does not create a public forum by inaction or by permitting limited discourse, but only by intentionally opening a nontraditional forum for public discourse.

Educators have authority over school-sponsored publications, theatrical productions, and other expressive activities that students, parents, and members of the public might reasonably perceive to bear the imprimatur of the school. These activities may fairly be characterized as part of the school curriculum so long as they are supervised by faculty members and designed to impart particular knowledge or skills to student participants and audiences.

Educators are entitled to exercise greater control over this form of student expression to assure that participants learn whatever lessons the activity is designed to teach, that readers or listeners are not exposed to material that may be inappropriate for their level of maturity, and that the views of the individual speaker are not erroneously attributed to the school. Hence, a school may in its capacity as publisher of a school newspaper or producer of a school play disassociate itself not only from speech that would substantially interfere with its work or impinge upon the rights of other students, but also from speech that is, for example, ungrammatical, poorly written, inadequately researched, biased or prejudiced, vulgar or profane, or unsuitable for immature audiences. A school must be able to set standards that may be higher than those demanded in the "real" world.

In addition, on potentially sensitive topics, a school must be able to take into account the emotional maturity of the intended audience. Sensitive topics might range from the existence of Santa Claus in an elementary school setting to the particulars of teenage sexual activity in a high school setting. A school must also retain the authority to refuse to associate the school with any position other than neutrality on matters of political controversy. It is only when the decision to censor a school-sponsored publication, theatrical production, or other vehicle of student expression has no valid educational purpose that the First Amendment is so directly and sharply implicated as to require judicial intervention to protect students' constitutional rights.

We cannot reject as unreasonable Principal Reynolds' conclusion that the students who wrote these articles had not sufficiently mastered those portions of the Journalism II curriculum that pertained to the treatment of controversial issues and personal attacks, the need to protect the privacy of individuals whose most intimate concerns are to be revealed in the newspaper, and the legal, moral, and ethical restrictions imposed upon journalists within a school community that includes adolescent subjects and readers. Accordingly, no violation of the First Amendment occurred.

Lopez v. Union High School District

Franklin Supreme Court (1994)

The issue presented is whether a school district is precluded by Section 48 of the Education Act and Article I, Section 2, of the Franklin Constitution from requiring, on the ground of educational suitability, that a film arts class instructor have his students delete the profanity in a student-produced film. We hold that school authorities may restrain such expression because it violates the "professional standards of English and journalism" provision of Section 48.

Plaintiffs, students at Union High School, wrote and produced a film entitled *Melancholianne* in a film arts class. The film addresses the problems faced by teenaged parents. The film dialogue contains profanity and references to sexual activity that the students believed made the film characters more realistic and "real world." The school principal, upon review of the draft of the script, found the language highly offensive and educationally unsuitable. After public hearings, the school board held that "sound educational policy" as well as a district administrative regulation required that the profanity be deleted.[1] Plaintiffs sued for declaratory and injunctive relief challenging the censorship of the videotape script.[2]

We need not decide whether the legislature intended to include the profanity at issue within the term "obscene expression." Legislative history demonstrates the legislature intended to preclude the students' use of "four-letter words" under the auspices of the "professional standards of English and journalism" provision of Section 48. The words of the statute permit prior restraint of material prepared for official school publications when the material "violates" the statute. Further, the legislative history of Section 48 indicates the legislature did not intend to protect student expression that constitutes profanity, especially when the expression is aimed at minors rather than adults. The school authorities have a substantial interest in protecting the student audience from expression that could be embarrassing or detrimental to their stage of development. Censorship of "four-letter words" does not unduly hinder the students' ability to express their ideas or opinions on any subject. It enjoins only the indecent manner in which an idea is expressed.

Having concluded that Section 48 permits prior restraint of profane student expression in official

---

[1]The administrative regulation in question is a "Student Publications Code" that, among other things, confers upon school authorities the power to require that school-sponsored publications maintain "professional standards of English grammar and journalistic writing style" and to prohibit the publication of "obscene" or "profane" material, defining those terms to mean language that would not ordinarily be used in certain specified local newspapers of general circulation.

[2]The parties have not raised or briefed the issue of whether the video is an "official school publication" within the meaning of Section 48. Nevertheless, we see no policy reason for distinguishing between student expression in school-sponsored activities solely on the basis of the medium by which the expression is conveyed.

student publications, we must consider whether such restraint is constitutional under the federal or state constitutions. The question is easily answered under the First Amendment. Teaching students to avoid vulgar and profane language is obviously a legitimate pedagogical concern and proper under the First Amendment. *Hazelwood School District v. Kuhlmeier* (U.S. Supreme Court, 1988).

The answer is the same under the Franklin Constitution. This court has adopted a forum analysis to determine when the government's interest in limiting the use of its property to its intended purpose outweighs the interest of those wishing to use the property for other purposes. We have divided public property into three categories: public, nonpublic, and limited.

A public forum is the traditional soapbox in a town square; no one can be denied access, and prior restraints are rarely permissible. A nonpublic forum is public property that is not a public forum by tradition or design, such as a military base or a jail or a "house organ" school bulletin for dissemination of educational or administrative information to students or faculty, over which school officials retain full power to regulate access and content.

The so-called limited forum is property the state has opened for expressive activity by part or all of the public. "Official school publications" in Franklin fall into the limited forum category. *Melancholianne* is conceptually no different from a school yearbook or newspaper produced in a journalism class. While the primary purpose for producing the videotape is to teach the students writing and film-making skills, the film also serves as an avenue of student expression. Thus, *Melancholianne* is a limited public forum.

When a school publication is deemed to be a limited public forum, school officials must demonstrate that the particular regulation of student expression advances a compelling state interest. Here, the compelling state interests advanced by the board are to maintain an environment where the educational process may occur without disruption, to teach students the boundaries of socially appropriate behavior, to promote "moral improvement," and to teach students to refrain from the use of profane and vulgar language.

School officials must also show that the speech regulations are narrowly drawn to achieve the compelling interest and sufficiently precise to avoid a challenge on grounds that they are void for vagueness. The board has done so here. The board has not censored the students' expression of ideas; rather, the board has prohibited their expression of those ideas by the use of profane language. The board's directive cannot be construed as the type of censorship we have deemed unconstitutional—censorship based on a disagreement with the views presented or censorship designed to avoid discussion of controversial issues. Rather, the board's directive was content neutral and served a valid pedagogical purpose.

Accordingly, the judgment is affirmed.

Leeb v. DeLong

Franklin Court of Appeal (1995)

David Leeb was the student editor of the Rancho High School newspaper. On March 29, 1994, Leeb submitted for the school principal's approval, as required by the school district's communication code, the April Fool's edition. An article appeared under the headline "Nude Photos: Girls of Rancho." According to the article, the July issue of Playboy magazine would carry nude photographs of Rancho students, and those interested in posing should sign up at the school darkroom. The article was accompanied by a photograph of five fully clothed female students standing in line with their school books, purportedly with applications in hand. Principal DeLong recognized each of them.

Mr. DeLong formed the opinion that "the article and photograph taken together are damaging to the reputation of each of the girls in the photograph." He was also of the view that the reputation of the school and the school district would be injured by the publication of the material. On March 30, he prohibited distribution of the newspaper. Leeb sued for declaratory and injunctive relief, and the court below granted summary judgment in favor of the school district.

Section 48 of the Education Act and Franklin decisional authority clearly confer editorial control of official student publications on the student editors alone, with very limited exceptions. The broad power to censor in school-sponsored publications for pedagogical purposes recognized by the U.S. Supreme Court in *Hazelwood School District v. Kuhlmeier* (1988) is not available to this state's educators. Student free speech rights under Section 48 are broader than rights arising under the First Amendment.

Under Education Act Section 48, a school district may constitutionally censor expression from official school publications which it reasonably believes to contain an actionable defamation. A school district may not, however, censor defamatory material that is not actionable because it is privileged or deals with a public figure without malice. *New York Times v. Sullivan* (U.S. Supreme Court, 1964). For example, an article suggesting that a public official is wrong, illogical, or was a poor choice for office could never lead to a recovery in tort, and could for that reason not be suppressed. But the girls in the photograph in this case are not public figures, and the principal's concerns were justifiable. The censorship in this case was not, therefore, precluded either by the federal or state constitutions or by Section 48.

To the extent that the school district's communication code suggests that an article such as one mentioned above about a public official could be censored, the code should be amended. The code should also be amended to require that any decision to delete an item thought to be defamatory should, insofar as it is possible, be limited to the offending material itself.

Judgment affirmed.

In re Gardenton Board of Education

Sample Answer

MEMORANDUM

To: Frank Eisner
From: Applicant
Re: Gardenton Board of Education—Proposed Communications Code

This case demonstrates a tension between the free speech rights contained in the United States and the Franklin Constitutions and section 48 of the Franklin Education Act. Students do not have the same freedom of speech rights under the United States Constitution as adults. In *Hazelwood School District v. Kuhlmeier*, the United States Supreme Court held that schools may censor student expression to protect immature students from inappropriate materials and to ensure that the materials are not attributed to the school. As long as the censorship has a valid educational purpose, it does not violate the First Amendment. [Hazelwood]

While Article I of the Franklin Constitution does not appear to give students any broader rights than the United States Constitution, section 48 of the Franklin Education Act clearly does. In *Leeb v. DeLong*, the Franklin Court of Appeal stated that "[t]he broad power to censor in school-sponsored publications . . . recognized by the U.S. Supreme Court in *Hazelwood* . . . is not available to [Franklin] educators." Section 48 gives the students editorial control, but it also allows the school to place some restraints on speech to prohibit obscene, libelous, and slanderous speech and to maintain professional standards of English and journalism.

Although section 48 gives students broad rights, it also requires school faculty advisers to supervise the students to maintain professional standards. The Communications Code may be justified as fulfilling part of the school's responsibility.

In analyzing the proposed guidelines, note that the level of scrutiny a court would use depends on whether the speech in question is in a public, nonpublic, or limited forum. [Lopez v. Union High School District—Franklin Supreme Court discussed standards relative to student-produced film] For example, in a limited forum, such as a school newspaper, the school must demonstrate that it has a compelling interest and that the censorship is narrowly drawn and precise. [Lopez] Every provision in the proposed code would be subject to this standard. The only items in the proposed code that could arguably be subject to a different standard concern the school plays. It may be argued that the plays are a public forum because they are advertised around town and admission is charged, but only students and faculty participate in the plays and the audiences are mostly students and their friends and relatives. Thus, this point is debatable.

Under the compelling interest/narrowly drawn standards, the proposed code is permissible with a few modifications.

Preamble

First, although section 48 of the Franklin Education Act refers specifically to written publications, the fact that this preamble includes other types of student works such as films and videos should not be a problem. The Franklin Supreme Court has indicated that there is no reason to distinguish between student expression in school-sponsored activities based on medium [Lopez, footnote 2] and has held that a student film was "no different from a school yearbook or newspaper. . . ." [Lopez] Therefore, to the extent that this code is legally permissible for written publications, it is also permissible for other types of student works.

On the other hand, the portion of the preamble that refers to off-campus materials is probably not permissible and should be removed. It is simply too broad. Any justification the school may have to review and possibly censor student expression is weakened considerably when the expression occurs off campus. Therefore, this section should be amended to delete "or off" campus.

Guideline 1

This section is legally permissible. The language is similar to that in Franklin Education Act section 48, which states that the advisers may supervise the students "to maintain professional standards of English and journalism."

Guideline 2

Parts of this guideline are probably too vague to be permissible. Forbidding language and depictions "not in good taste" is too subjective a standard and may well violate students' free speech rights under section 48. This provision could be rewritten to forbid "obscene" materials, which would be in line with section 48, with the restrictions being measured against those used by other newspapers. [*See* Lopez, footnote 1] On the other hand, the portion about "age, experience, and maturity" was upheld in *Hazelwood* and is similar to a concern in *Lopez* for protecting students from "expression that could be . . . detrimental to their stage of development." Thus, this portion is probably permissible.

Guideline 3

This guideline is probably permissible. While on the one hand this may improperly limit the editorial discretion guaranteed the students in section 48, on the other hand it is the responsibility of the school to "maintain professional standards of English and journalism." [Section 48] Clearly, verification of facts and quotes is a standard part of professional journalism.

Guideline 4

This guideline would also be permissible as an example of maintaining the professional standards of journalism. [Section 48]

Guideline 5

This guideline needs significant revision. Section a. could use a little clarification. The school may censor material that is ***actionably*** libelous or slanderous or violates any person's right of privacy, but it may not censor defamatory material that is privileged or deals with a public figure without malice. [Leeb]

Section b. is permissible. The school may place prior restraints on profanity. [Lopez; Section 48—use of profanity violates the "professional standards of English and journalism"] While the Union for Freedom of Speech may argue that this standard is too vague, the Franklin Supreme Court has already upheld a similar provision in another case. [Lopez]

Section c. is not permissible. As mentioned in regards to section a. of this guideline, schools may not censor materials that deal with a public figure without malice. [Leeb—citing New York Times v. Sullivan] Therefore, this section will need to be removed or amended to bring it in line with the malice standard.

Section d. is also impermissible. It gives the principal too much discretion in determining what would not "be in the school's best interest." The school is limited by the Franklin Education Act which allows censorship only of obscene, libelous, and slanderous language as discussed above, language that incites the students and creates a clear or present danger of unlawful acts or violation of lawful school regulations, or language that would substantially disrupt the operation of the school. This provision should be stricken or strictly revised to reflect these grounds.

Guideline 6

This section is permissible. As discussed above, there are some grounds on which the principal may censor. Therefore, it would be proper for the principal to examine the material first to see if it contains any of these items.

Multistate Performance Test

State v. Robert Baker

National Conference of Bar Examiners

Preface

This Multistate Performance Test is a reprint of one of the two MPTs which were administered in July 1998.

The instructions for the test appear on the next page. On the actual MPT, they will appear on the back cover of the test.

INSTRUCTIONS

1. You will have 90 minutes to complete this session of the examination. This performance test is designed to evaluate your ability to handle a select number of legal authorities in the context of a factual problem involving a client.

2. The problem is set in the fictitious state of Franklin, in the fictitious Fifteenth Circuit of the United States. Columbia and Olympia are also fictitious states in the Fifteenth Circuit. In Franklin, the trial court of general jurisdiction is the District Court, the intermediate appellate court is the Court of Appeal, and the highest court is the Supreme Court.

3. You will have two kinds of materials with which to work: a File and a Library. The first document in the File is a memorandum containing the instructions for the task you are to complete. The other documents in the File contain factual information about your case and may include some facts that are not relevant.

4. The Library contains the legal authorities needed to complete the task and may also include some authorities that are not relevant. Any cases may be real, modified, or written solely for the purpose of this examination. If the cases appear familiar to you, do not assume that they are precisely the same as you have read before. Read them thoroughly, as if they all were new to you. You should assume that cases were decided in the jurisdictions and on the dates shown. In citing cases from the Library, you may use abbreviations and omit page references.

5. Your response must be written in the answer book provided. If you are taking this examination on a laptop computer, your jurisdiction will provide you with specific instructions. In answering this performance test, you should concentrate on the materials provided in the File and Library. What you have learned in law school and elsewhere provides the general background for analyzing the problem; the File and Library provide the specific materials with which you must work.

6. Although there are no restrictions on how you apportion your time, you should be sure to allocate ample time (about 45 minutes) to reading and digesting the materials and to organizing your answer before you begin writing it. You may make notes anywhere in the test materials; blank pages are provided at the end of the booklet. You may not tear pages from the question booklet.

7. This performance test will be graded on your responsiveness to the instructions regarding the task you are to complete, which are given to you in the first memorandum in the File, and on the content, thoroughness, and organization of your response.

State v. Robert Baker

FILE

LIBRARY

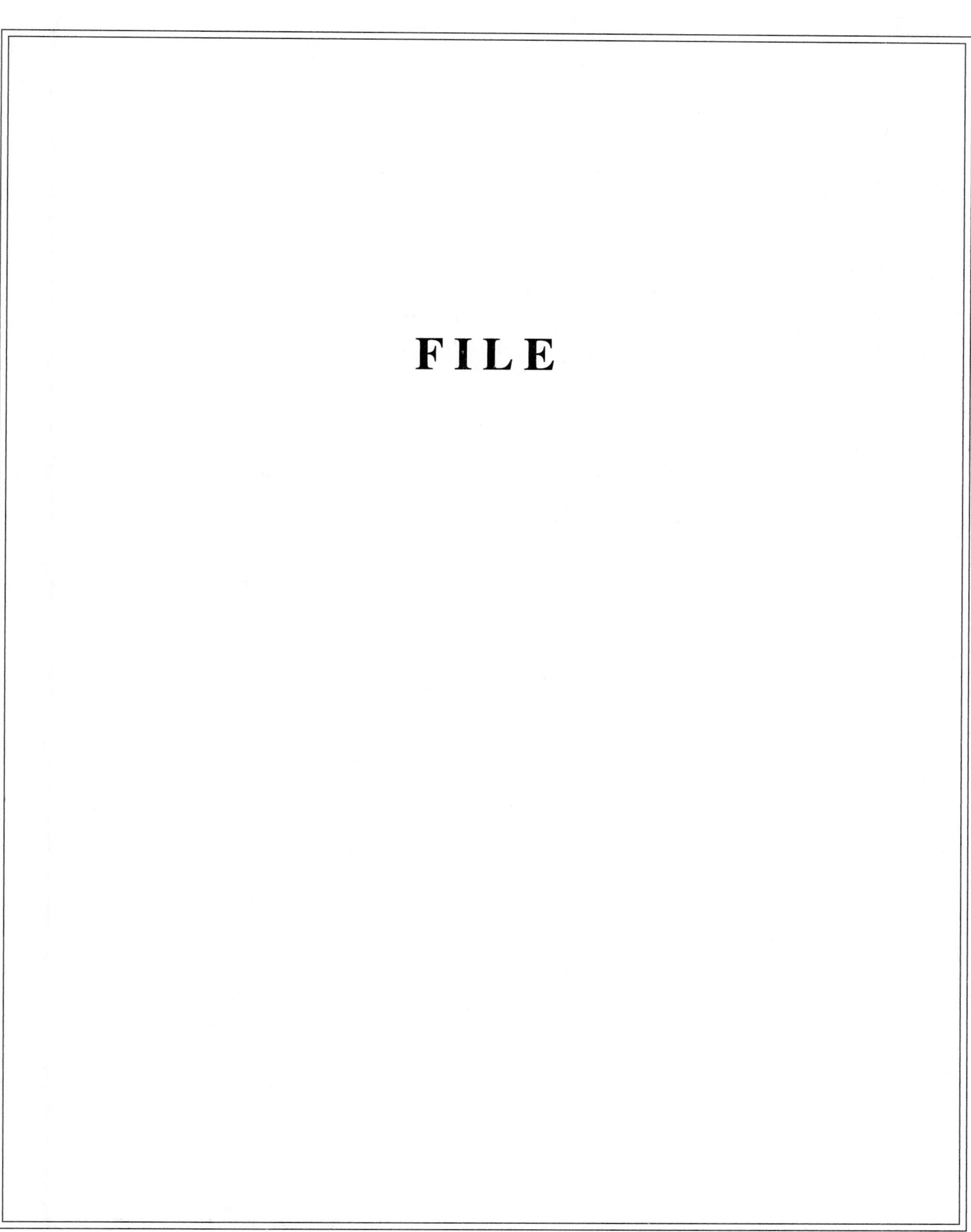
FILE

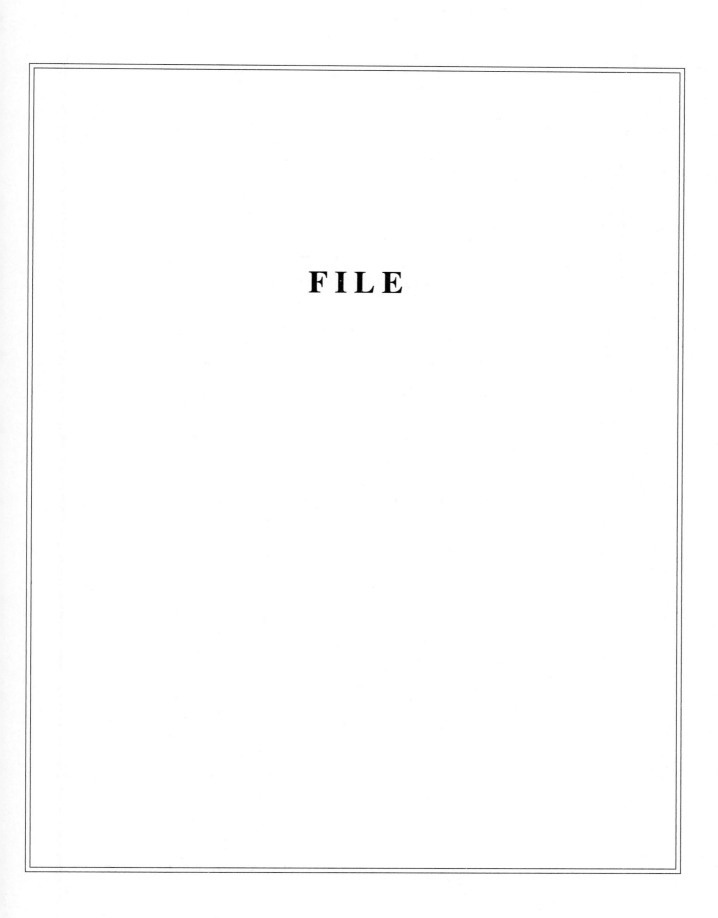

Office of the District Attorney
2371 Michigan Street
Island City, Franklin 00101

July 28, 1998

TO: Applicant

FROM: Harvey Feldman, Assistant District Attorney

RE: State v. Robert Baker

I need your help on the Baker prosecution. The defendant was indicted two weeks ago by the grand jury for the crime of larceny by false pretense, and it is now time to begin preparing the case for trial. We decided not to indict him on conspiracy. I've attached a copy of the indictment and the transcript of the grand jury testimony. I haven't taken the time to sort through the transcript, which seems to include a lot of irrelevant testimony. We need to organize the facts and make sure we can prove our case.

Here is what I would like you to do. Write a memorandum to me in which you do the following:

1. Identify from the statutes and the case law the elements of the crime for which Baker was indicted and, using each element as a heading, discuss under each heading the specific facts in the transcript that support each element.

2. Tell me whether you believe there is any flaw in the indictment as it is now worded that would prevent us from obtaining a conviction. If not, tell me why not. If so, tell me what choices are available to us as to how and at what stage in the proceedings we can cure any defect in the indictment, and tell me which choice is most appropriate.

We do not know at this time if any witnesses other than those who testified before the grand jury will be available for trial. Therefore, assume we must proceed with only the three we have.

FRANKLIN }
} In the Superior Court of the City of Island City
City of Island City }

July 14, 1998

BILL OF INDICTMENT

The grand jury charges that:

On or about February 16, 1998, in the City of Island City, Robert Lee Baker did commit larceny by false pretense, namely by taking one 1998 Jeep having a value of $200 or more belonging to Jasper Motor Company operating as Jeep Sales & Service Co., with intent to permanently deprive the owner of the value thereof,

against the peace and dignity of the State of Franklin.
Franklin Code Section 98

A True Bill

Paul Smith
Foreperson

Diane Thompson
Clerk

TRANSCRIPT OF GRAND JURY PROCEEDINGS

EXAMINATION: Gerald Story by Ms. Cushman

Q: Mr. Story, where are you employed?
A: Thompson Toyota.
Q: Were you so employed on February 16, 1998?
A: Yes, ma'am.
Q: Were you working on that date?
A: Yes, I was.
Q: And where was that?
A: We had a tent sale at Parker Field, you know, the ball field.
Q: On that date, did anything of an unusual nature happen?
A: Yes. We had a gentleman come in and inquire about a red 1983 Toyota pickup that had just been traded in.
Q: What did you do?
A: I let the man drive the Toyota pickup around on the Parker Field lot. I was with another customer. He was supposed to be just driving around the lot.
Q: Then what happened?
A: Approximately 30 minutes later when I had finished with my previous customer, I started looking for the truck and the man. They were gone. We walked the whole lot. We could not find the truck or the man anywhere.
Q: Did you see the truck that day again?
A: No, ma'am.
Q: What make was the truck?
A: A Toyota pickup.
Q: Do you remember the color?
A: Red.
Q: Did you ever see that truck again?
A: Not until we went over to pick it up at Jasper Jeep.
Q: Who is "we"?
A: My supervisor Mack Griswald and me.

Q: Is that where you saw it?
A: Yes, ma'am, and it was kinda' funny.
Q: What do you mean?
A: Mack and I both thought the guy who took the truck sure had nerve, no doubt about it. It was funny standing there on the Jasper lot and seeing Mack in awe of the thief's audacity.
Q: Okay, when was that, sir, approximately?
A: Approximately two days later.
Q: Was anyone else with the person that took the truck at Parker Field?
A: No one that I saw.
Q: Had you ever seen that person before?
A: No.
Q: Do you know who the person who took the truck is?
A: I didn't at the time, but I've since learned that his name is Shumaker.
Q: Do you know what city or county Parker Field is located in?
A: Island City.
MS. CUSHMAN: That's all I have. Thank you very much. You're excused, sir.

EXAMINATION: Richard Carter by Ms. Cushman

Q: Where are you employed, Mr. Carter?

A: Jasper Jeep.

Q: And where is that located?

A: 7300 Brook Road.

Q: Is that in Island City?

A: Yes, it is.

Q: How long have you been employed there?

A: Since 1986.

Q: And you're the General Manager?

A: Yes, I am.

Q: You were so employed on February 16, 1998?

A: Yes, I was.

Q: Were you working on that day?

A: Yes, I was.

Q: And on that date, did anything happen of an unusual nature that you recall?

A: Yes. A vehicle was taken from our lot and was not returned.

Q: Do you remember how that happened?

A: We were extremely busy that day. We were short two salespeople. Customers were all over the lot. To give you some background, our new car and used car operations are separate, our used cars being across the street from us. And quite frequently when a customer is looking at both new and used cars, we'll go back and forth. When we're short of salespeople, we'll try to get to everyone as quickly as we can. And on occasion we'll let someone try out a vehicle without a salesman with him.

Q: Is that policy?

A: No, it is not.

Q: What happened on this occasion?

A: On this occasion I saw the gentleman come onto the lot.

Q: What was he driving?

A: He was driving a red pickup truck, a Toyota truck. I was inside the showroom and saw him go by the window, the plate glass window. He came into the showroom and waited around for a

bit, while we were helping other customers. I went back across the street over to the used car lot. As I was returning to the new car side, he was standing by a Jeep, a 1998 silver Cherokee.
Q: Then what happened?
A: I talked with him a bit. I told him that he could take the Jeep for a ride around the block, that I was busy with some other customers, and that as soon as they returned from their demonstration ride I would go with him and fully demonstrate the vehicle to him. We had to move a motorcycle, in order to get the Jeep out. It was in his way. He took the Jeep and never returned with it.
Q: Now, had he not driven a vehicle onto the lot, would he have been allowed to take a drive in that Jeep?
A: No, he would not have.
Q: Did he have permission to keep that Jeep?
A: No, he did not.
Q: Had you ever seen this person before?
A: No.
Q: Did you ever see him after that day?
A: The police asked me to come to the jail and I identified him in a lineup.
Q: Did he have permission to have your Jeep?
A: No, he did not.
Q: Did anyone?
A: No.
Q: Was any money paid for the Jeep?
A: No.
Q: Did you ever sign title to the Jeep over to this man?
A: No.
Q: Could you tell the members of the jury what the retail value or the list price of that Jeep was?
A: It was a new vehicle. It had not been put in demonstration yet, because it wasn't ready.
Q: All right. Could you tell what it was worth at that time?
A: The retail value, approximately $29,000.
Q: Did you come to see that Jeep again?
A: Yes, I did.

Q: Can you say approximately how much later that was?
A: Five or six weeks later.
Q: And where did you see it?
A: It was towed back to our lot from Sand, Franklin.
Q: Could it have been driven back from Sand to Island City?
A: Well, we weren't sure. We just didn't know. The distance from Sand to Island City one way is maybe 50 miles and we didn't know what condition the Jeep was in.
Q: Now, on that February 16th date, that you testified to, about the person who drove the Jeep off your lot, anything else you remember about that day? Any other people or encounters?
A: It was a busy day, and the only other noticeable type of encounter that stuck with me was four other people that were on the lot.
Q: All right. What kind of people—what gender—were these?
A: Two males and two females.
Q: How long did you talk with them?
A: Just briefly. A few minutes.
Q: And did you see how they left?
A: Yes, I did.
Q: How did they leave?
A: They left in a Ford station wagon, a white Ford station wagon.
MS. CUSHMAN: That's all I have. You're excused, sir.

EXAMINATION: Donald Shumaker by Ms. Cushman

Q: Mr. Shumaker, how old are you?

A: Twenty-two.

Q: And do you know Robert Baker?

A: Yeah, I do.

Q: How do you know Mr. Baker?

A: I met him through some other friends of mine.

Q: Who were those friends?

A: Bill Sales and Susan Kennedy.

Q: How do you know Bill Sales and Susan Kennedy?

A: I used to work for them.

Q: When did you first meet Mr. Baker?

A: Late 1993. We were at a party.

Q: I direct your attention back to February of this year. Where were you living at that time?

A: With Bill and Susan.

Q: Did you ever have a meeting with Mr. Baker concerning a Jeep?

A: Yes.

Q: When was the first time you had contact with Mr. Baker about a Jeep?

A: The 15th of February.

Q: How did that meeting come about?

A: It started with a telephone conversation.

Q: And who spoke on the phone from your end?

A: Bill Sales.

Q: Did you speak on the phone?

A: I did afterwards.

Q: Did you recognize the voice on the phone?

A: Yes.

Q: How did you recognize the voice?

A: I had talked to the person many times in the past.

Q: Who was on the other end?

A: Robert Baker.

Q: And what was said?
A: Just that he had a man that needed a Jeep, that I could pick up $1,000.
Q: All right. Is that all he said to you on the phone?
A: Over the phone, yes, ma'am.
Q: What happened then?
A: I went out and looked at some Jeeps.
Q: Did you see Mr. Baker that day?
A: No. He came up the next morning.
Q: Where did he go?
A: To the apartment.
Q: Was he with his wife?
A: Yes, ma'am. Her name is Carla.
Q: Who else was at the apartment?
A: Bill and Susan.
Q: And yourself?
A: Umm huh.
Q: What did you-all do at the apartment?
A: We sat around the apartment for a while just trying to figure out where we were going to get the Jeep from.
Q: Who was talking about that?
A: All of us.
Q: All five of you?
A: Yes.
Q: How long were you at the apartment?
A: A couple of hours. Well, we were there all that morning.
Q: What did you do after you left the apartment?
A: Well, I went out first, then I went to look at a couple of Jeeps, and then realized that you had to drive a car onto the lot to drive another one off.
Q: What did you do then?
A: Then I went back to the apartment, told them this. We sat around for a while, looked in the paper. We had the radio on, and there was an advertisement for this car sale at Parker Field, so

we decided to go up to Parker Field and get a car, take it to another place, or get a Jeep if we could find one there. If not, we'd get a car from there and then drive to another car lot.
Q: All right. So, what did you do?
A: We went up to Parker Field.
Q: Now, who's "we"?
A: The five of us. Me, Robert, Carla, . . .
Q: All right. And how did you get there?
A: We went in Robert's car.
Q: And what kind of car is that?
A: About a '70 station wagon, Ford.
Q: Do you know what color it is?
A: White.
Q: And where did you go?
A: To Parker Field.
Q: What was at Parker Field?
A: They had a car sale. A couple of dealers were there.
Q: And what did you do once you got there?
A: We pulled up, stopped and got something to eat, and while we were in there, I went over to test drive a truck, went over to this salesman to get the keys and tags to a truck. I got in the truck, drove it out off the lot, going to Jasper Jeep.
Q: While you were test driving the truck, where were the others?
A: About 50 yards from me.
Q: What did you do once you were in the truck?
A: I drove the truck on towards the end of the field you had to go around to get back to the road, and after I got in the truck and started driving around, they all walked back to Robert's car. I passed them as I came out, and then I just went on down, up the Boulevard.
Q: And where did you go?
A: I went about a mile or so past Parker Field, pulled over, waited a second, saw them come out of Parker Field, then I went on.
Q: What happened then?

A: I drove to Jasper Jeep, parked, got out, and walked around. The others pulled into the parking lot across the street, which is another Jasper parking lot, got out, looked around. We started walking around looking at some Jeeps.
Q: Were you with them?
A: No, I was by myself then.
Q: Why was that?
A: So nobody wouldn't see us all together.
Q: What, if anything, did you see the others doing on the lot while you were there, when you first got there?
A: When I was on one end of the lot, they were on the other end of the lot. We were just looking at some Jeeps.
Q: Then what happened?
A: Robert hit the hood of one Jeep.
Q: And which way was he facing at that time?
A: We were facing each other.
Q: All right. What happened then?
A: I went inside the building, told the salesman I wanted to test drive the Jeep Robert had hit. The salesman came outside, got the serial number, went back in, got the keys and tags. I drove the Jeep on off the lot.
Q: Which Jeep did you test drive?
A: The one Robert hit with his hand.
Q: And where did you go?
A: I went about, I guess, two miles down the highway. I pulled off the side of the highway, waited a few minutes, saw them coming, pulled back out on the road in front of them. I got off the highway onto the ramp and stopped again.
Q: What did you do when you stopped on the ramp?
A: They pulled in behind me. I got out of the Jeep and walked back to their car.
Q: Then what happened?
A: Robert gave me 10 one-hundred-dollar bills and I got back into the Jeep.
Q: Did you know where to go at that point?
A: Yes, ma'am.

Q: Okay. And where did you go?
A: To the apartment.
Q: Did you make a stop before you got to the apartment?
A: We got off at the Maury Street exit. I drove the Jeep from Jasper Jeep to Maury Street, behind a factory, and we stopped at a red light. Bill got out of Robert's car and into the Jeep.
Q: Which side of the Jeep?
A: On the driver's side.
Q: And what did you do?
A: I got over in the passenger side.
Q: What happened then?
A: We drove to the apartment.
Q: At the apartment, what happened?
A: We all went inside. Robert got out the DMV title registration form . . .
Q: Do you mean by "DMV," the Department of Motor Vehicles?
A: Yeah. Well, Robert had these title forms that you pick up at the DMV and he filled one out and forged a name and listed Jasper Jeep as the dealer. You know, to give to the guy they got the Jeep for. Then, they got in the Jeep and left. A couple of minutes later, Robert's wife got in the station wagon and left.
Q: Did you see Mr. Baker after that?
A: Not until we were arrested.
MS. CUSHMAN: That's all I have. Please go with the deputy here.

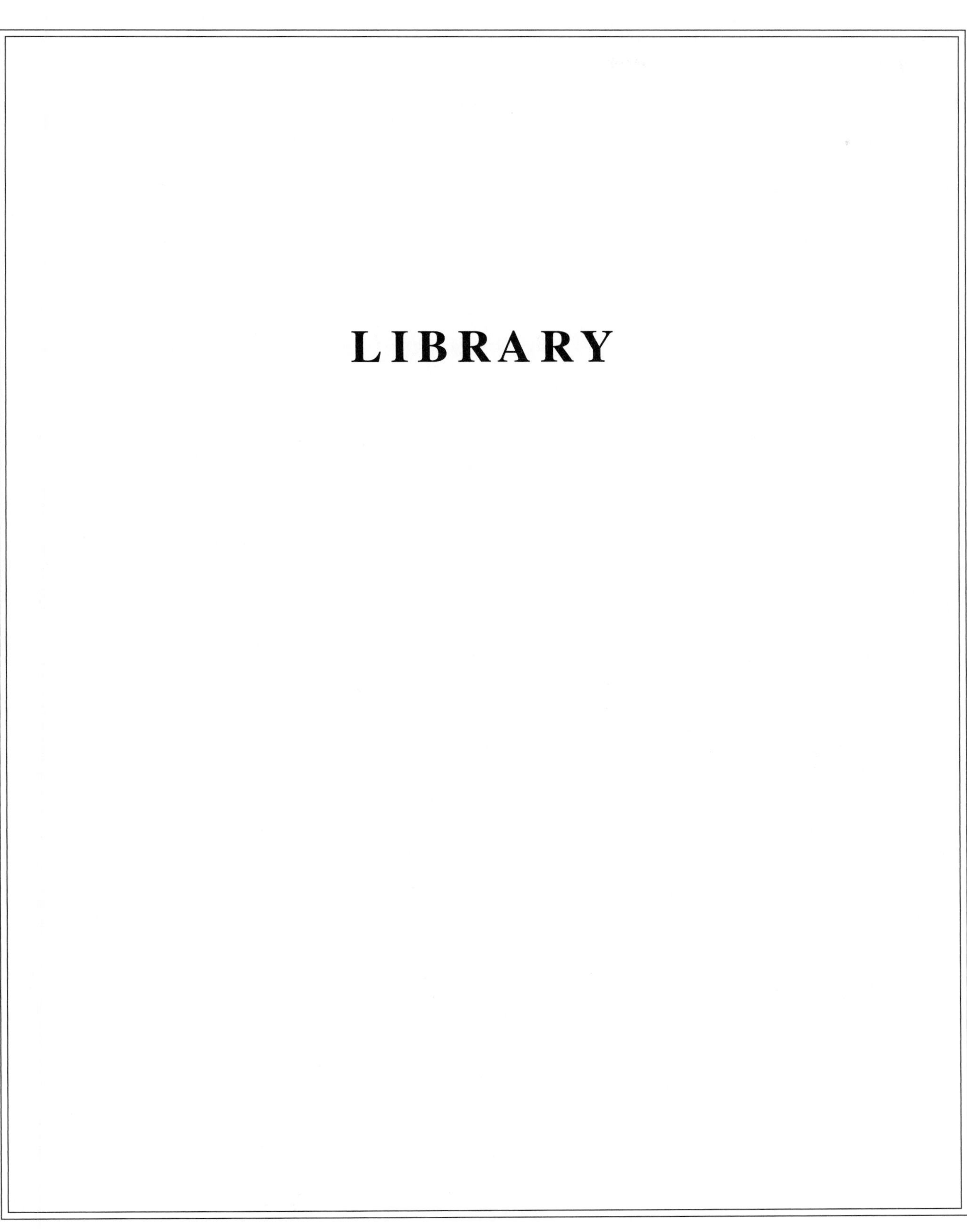

LIBRARY

Franklin Criminal Code

§11. Liability for conduct of another; complicity:

(1) A person is guilty of an offense if it is committed by his own conduct or by the conduct of another person for which he is legally accountable, or both.

(2) A person is legally accountable for the conduct of another person when he is an accomplice of such other person in the commission of the offense.

(3) A person is an accomplice of another person in the commission of an offense if, for the purpose of promoting or facilitating the commission of the offense, he

(a) solicits such other person to commit it; or

(b) aids or agrees or attempts to aid such other person in planning or committing it.

(4) An accomplice may be convicted on proof of the commission of the offense and of his complicity therein, though the person claimed to have committed the offense has not been prosecuted or convicted or has been convicted of a different offense or degree of offense or has an immunity to prosecution or conviction or has been acquitted.

* * * *

§94. Larceny; defined: If any person obtains unauthorized control over the property of another with the intent permanently to deprive the owner of that property, he shall be guilty of larceny.

§95. Grand larceny; how punished: Any person who (1) commits larceny from the person of another of money or any other thing of value of $5 or more, (2) commits simple larceny not from the person of another of goods and chattels of the value of $200 or more, or (3) commits simple larceny not from the person of another of any handgun, rifle or shotgun, regardless of the handgun's, rifle's or shotgun's value, shall be guilty of grand larceny, punishable by imprisonment in a state correctional facility for not less than one nor more than twenty years or, in the discretion of the jury or court trying the case without a jury, by confinement in jail for a period not exceeding twelve months or by a fine of not more than $2,500, either or both.

* * * *

§98. Grand larceny; obtaining money, property or signature, etc., by false pretense: If any person obtains, by any false pretense or token, from any person, with intent to defraud, money or

other property which may be the subject of larceny, he shall be deemed guilty of larceny by false pretense thereof; or if he obtains, by any false pretense or token, with such intent, the signature of any person to a writing, the false making whereof would be forgery, he shall be guilty of larceny by false pretense. In both instances the person shall be punishable by imprisonment in a state correctional facility for not less than five nor more than thirty years or, in the discretion of the jury or court trying the case without a jury, be confined in jail for a period not exceeding two years or fined not more than $5,000, either or both.

* * * *

§231. Amendment of indictment, presentment or information: If there be any defect in form in any indictment, presentment or information, or if there shall appear to be any variance between the allegations therein and the evidence offered in proof thereof, the court may permit amendment of such indictment, presentment or information, at any time before the jury returns a verdict or the court finds the accused guilty or not guilty, provided the amendment does not change the nature or character of the offense charged. After any such amendment, the accused shall be arraigned on the indictment, presentment or information as amended, and shall be allowed to plead anew thereto, if he so desires, and the trial shall proceed as if no amendment had been made; but if the court finds that such amendment operates as a surprise to the accused, he shall be entitled, upon request, to a continuance of the case for a reasonable time.

* * * *

§247. When judgment not to be arrested or reversed: Judgment in any criminal case shall not be arrested or reversed upon any exception or objection made after a verdict to the indictment or other accusation, unless it be so defective as to be in violation of the Constitution.

Franklin Code of Professional Responsibility

DR 7-103 Performing the duty of public prosecutor or other government lawyer.

(A) A public prosecutor or other government lawyer shall not institute or cause to be instituted criminal charges when he knows or it is obvious that the charges are not supported by probable cause.

(B) A public prosecutor or other government lawyer in criminal litigation shall make timely disclosure to counsel for the defendant, or to the defendant if he has no counsel, of the existence of evidence, known to the prosecutor or other government lawyer, that tends to negate the guilt of the accused, mitigate the degree of the offense, or reduce the punishment.

Davies v. State of Franklin

Franklin Supreme Court (1992)

In a jury trial, Ralph Donald Davies (Davies) was convicted of two counts of grand larceny by false pretense. On appeal, he contends that the trial court erred in refusing to instruct the jury that it must find that Davies obtained title to the property.

On August 21, 1990, Davies filed a credit application in the name of Brian Stark at a Circuit City store. He produced an identification card in the name of Brian Stark. Upon approval of his credit application, Davies purchased on credit a camcorder, a tripod, and a car stereo. The value of this property totaled $1,306.16. Davies signed the sales slip acknowledging his receipt of the property and took it from the store premises.

On the credit application, Davies claimed to be Brian Stark, an attorney employed by the firm of Tate and Bywater. However, neither "Brian Stark" nor Davies had ever been employed by that firm. On September 5, 1990, Davies admitted that Brian Stark was not his real name and he was not so employed.

At trial, Davies offered instruction "F," which would have required the jury, in order to find Davies guilty of grand larceny by false pretense, to find that the owner of the property parted with both "possession of and title to" the property. Over the objection of defense counsel, the trial court deleted the words "and title to" and granted the instruction as amended.

Proof that the accused obtained money by false pretense will sustain an indictment for larceny under Franklin Criminal Code §94. In order to convict one of larceny by false pretense under §98, however, the State must also prove four elements of the offense charged: (1) an intent to defraud; (2) an actual fraud; (3) use of false pretense for the purpose of perpetrating the fraud; and (4) accomplishment of the fraud by means of the false pretense used for the purpose; that is, the false pretense to some degree must have induced the owner to part with his property. Moreover, the false pretense must be a representation as to an existing fact or a past event. The gravamen of the offense, as pertinent to these facts, is the obtainment of ownership of property by false representations or pretense.

It is elementary that a jury must be informed as to the essential elements of the offense; a correct statement of the law is one of the essentials of a fair trial. An essential element of larceny by false pretense is that both title to and possession of property must pass from the victim to the defendant. The requirement that the defendant obtain ownership of the property, rather than mere possession, distinguishes the offense of larceny by false pretense from the offense of larceny.

Therefore, the trial court's refusal to instruct the jury regarding the essential elements of the offense was error.

However, we find that the error in failing to instruct the jury regarding the passage of title was harmless. The crux of the harmless error analysis is whether the defendant received a fair trial on the merits and substantial justice has been achieved.

The evidence produced at trial showed that Davies obtained possession of the electronic equipment from Circuit City on the basis of the fraudulent information provided in the credit application. The property was delivered to Davies, who took possession of the property and left the store with the property. This is unlike a situation involving a motor vehicle, which requires a document to transfer title. Here the evidence produced at trial showed that Davies obtained ownership, or "title," of the property by false pretense upon the seller's delivery and Davies's simultaneous receipt of the goods. Consequently, because the undisputed evidence established as a matter of law that ownership (albeit voidable because of his fraud) of the goods passed to Davies, the erroneous instruction did not affect the verdict. We hold, therefore, that the trial court's refusal to instruct the jury that "title" to the property must pass was harmless error. Affirmed.

However, we find that the error in failing to [illegible] the jury regarding the passage of title was harmless. The crux of the harmless error analysis [illegible] the defendant received a fair trial [illegible] and substantial justice has been done.

The evidence produced at trial showed that Davis obtained possession of the electronic equipment from Circuit City on the basis of the fraudulent information provided in the credit application. The property was delivered to Davis, who took possession of the property and left the store with the property. This is unlike a situation involving a motor vehicle, which requires a document to transfer title. From the evidence produced at trial, however, it is clear that ownership or title of the property was transferred upon the seller's delivery and Davis's simultaneous receipt of the goods. Consequently, because the undisputed evidence established as a matter of law that ownership or title would be considered to have passed when the goods passed to Davis, the erroneous instruction did not affect the verdict. We hold, therefore, that the trial court's refusal to instruct the jury that title to the property must pass was harmless error.

Affirmed.

State v. Robert Baker

Sample Answer

MEMORANDUM

To: Harvey Feldman, Assistant District Attorney
From: Applicant
Re: State v. Robert Baker

I. ELEMENTS OF LARCENY BY FALSE PRETENSE

A. Liability

As Donald Shumaker was the one who actually drove the Jeep away from the Jasper Jeep lot, we first need to establish that the defendant, Robert Baker, is also liable for this crime. Baker can be held legally responsible for his own actions and Shumaker's actions as an accomplice. Accomplice liability is defined in Franklin Criminal Code section 11. A person is legally accountable for the conduct of another when he solicits the other person to commit a crime or aids the other person in planning or committing a crime. There are sufficient facts in this case to prove that Baker both solicited Shumaker to commit the crime in question and aided him in the planning and commission of the crime. Shumaker testified that Baker called him and offered him money for getting a Jeep. Baker and Shumaker then worked out the details of the plan. Baker drove Shumaker to Parker's Field where he stole a truck that he used to gain access to the Jeep. Once at Jasper Jeep, Baker directed Shumaker toward the Jeep that he wanted him to steal by hitting the Jeep's hood. After Shumaker drove off the lot with the Jeep, Baker paid Shumaker money for taking the Jeep. Finally, Baker forged some DMV forms so that he could transfer the Jeep to someone else. The facts clearly establish that Baker is legally accountable for this crime.

B. Larceny

1. <u>Taking the property of another/subject of larceny</u>

The first element that we must prove is that the item taken, the Jeep, is of the type of property that may be the subject of larceny. Larceny is defined in Franklin Criminal Code section 94 as the taking of another's property. Jasper Jeep's employee, Richard Carter, testified that the Jeep belonged to Jasper Jeep and that he did not give Shumaker permission to keep the Jeep. Shumaker admits that he took the Jeep from Jasper Jeep. Thus, we can easily establish that the Jeep was property belonging to another.

2. <u>With the intent to permanently deprive the owner</u>

The next element that we must prove is that Baker intended to permanently deprive Jasper Jeep of the property. Shumaker's testimony proves this element. He testified that they intended to steal the Jeep and transfer it to someone else. Baker's intent to deprive Jasper Jeep of the property is also evidenced by the fact that he forged some DMV title documents so he could transfer the Jeep to someone else. Finally, the circumstances of the Jeep's return also suggest that Baker had the intention of permanently depriving Jasper Jeep of the property. The Jeep was found weeks later, miles away from Jasper Jeep, and had to be towed back to its owner.

C. Larceny by false pretense

The elements that are necessary to prove that larceny was accomplished by false pretense are laid out in *Davies v. State of Franklin.*

1. **Intent to defraud**

The first element of the offense of larceny by false pretense is that there was an intent to defraud. There is ample evidence of that intent in this case. Shumaker testified that he knew that he would have to drive another vehicle to Jasper Jeep to gain access to a new Jeep. Therefore, according to Shumaker, Baker and he formulated a plan to steal another vehicle, drive it onto the Jasper Jeep lot, then use that vehicle to convince the Jasper Jeep employees to allow him to take the Jeep on a test drive so that he could steal it.

2. **Actual fraud**

Next, we must establish that there was an actual fraud committed. This element is also easy to prove. Gerald Story testified that Shumaker stole a truck from Parker's Field. Shumaker admits that he drove the stolen vehicle onto Jasper Jeep's lot. He used that truck as a way to get approval for a test drive of the new Jeep. According to Carter, Shumaker would not have been allowed to drive the Jeep if he had not driven his own vehicle onto the lot. Thus an actual fraud was committed.

3. **Use of false pretense**

The next element that we must establish is that there was a use of false pretense for the purpose of perpetrating the fraud. A false pretense is defined as a representation as to an existing fact or a past event. Here, Shumaker, by his actions, represented to Jasper Jeep that he was in lawful possession of the truck. He knew that he would not be permitted to test drive the Jeep without creating that impression. Furthermore, while at Jasper Jeep, Shumaker stayed away from the rest of the group so no one would realize they were together. Baker selected the Jeep he wanted Shumaker to steal by hitting the Jeep on the hood. Shumaker then said that he wanted to test drive that Jeep when he was really planning to steal it. Shumaker clearly used a false pretense to gain access to the Jeep.

4. **Accomplishment of fraud: passage of title**

The final element of larceny by false pretense is the accomplishment of the fraud. The defendant must obtain ownership of the property, not just mere possession. In the case of a motor vehicle, this requires a documentary transfer of title. We cannot establish this element. Jasper Jeep did not sign title to the Jeep over to Shumaker or Baker. The fact that Baker forged some DMV papers is irrelevant. Baker did not obtain the signature ***of another*** by false pretense; instead he signed the papers himself. This was not a valid transfer of title. Thus he never obtained title to the Jeep.

II. THE INDICTMENT

The indictment in this case is faulty because one of the elements of larceny by false pretenses cannot be proved: Neither Shumaker nor Baker ever obtained title to the Jeep. Thus we will not be able to convict Baker of larceny by false pretense. On the other hand, given the facts discussed above and that the value of the stolen Jeep was $29,000, we may be able to convict Baker of the lesser crime of grand larceny. Baker through Shumaker obtained unauthorized control of the Jeep owned by Jasper Jeep with the intent permanently to deprive Jasper Jeep of that property which was worth more than $200.

Franklin Criminal Code section 231 allows the court to amend an indictment when there is a variance between the allegations and the evidence. In this case we could seek to amend the indictment from larceny by false pretense to grand larceny any time before the jury returns a verdict. However, this may only be done if the amendment would not change the nature or the character of the original offense charged. Here, Baker is likely to argue that amending the indictment to grand larceny would change the nature of the offense charged and would submit him to undue surprise. However, we could argue that any error in the wording of the indictment is harmless as long as Baker receives a fair trial and the proof we offer at trial is sufficient. [*See* Davies v. State of Franklin—harmless error in failing to instruct jury that title to property must pass for charge of larceny by false pretense when evidence established that the defendant took possession of the property and thus took title of the property as a matter of law]

More problematic is our ethical problem. The Franklin Code of Professional Responsibility forbids a prosecutor from instituting criminal charges that he knows are not supported by probable cause. [DR 7-103(A)] Furthermore, a prosecutor must make timely disclosure to the defense of any information that could mitigate the degree of an offense or reduce the punishment. [DR 7-103(B)] Here it is obvious that there is no probable cause to establish larceny by false pretense. In light of our ethical obligations as prosecutors, the best course of action would be to drop the current indictment and re-indict Baker for the lesser crime of grand larceny.

Multistate Performance Test

Meley v. Boundless Vacations, Inc.

National Conference of Bar Examiners

Preface

This Multistate Performance Test is a reprint of one of the three MPTs which were administered in February 1999.

The instructions for the test appear on the next page. On the actual MPT, they will appear on the back cover of the test.

INSTRUCTIONS

1. You will have 90 minutes to complete this session of the examination. This performance test is designed to evaluate your ability to handle a select number of legal authorities in the context of a factual problem involving a client.

2. The problem is set in the fictitious state of Franklin, in the fictitious Fifteenth Circuit of the United States. Columbia and Olympia are also fictitious states in the Fifteenth Circuit. In Franklin, the trial court of general jurisdiction is the District Court, the intermediate appellate court is the Court of Appeal, and the highest court is the Supreme Court.

3. You will have two kinds of materials with which to work: a File and a Library. The first document in the File is a memorandum containing the instructions for the task you are to complete. The other documents in the File contain factual information about your case and may include some facts that are not relevant.

4. The Library contains the legal authorities needed to complete the task and may also include some authorities that are not relevant. Any cases may be real, modified, or written solely for the purpose of this examination. If the cases appear familiar to you, do not assume that they are precisely the same as you have read before. Read them thoroughly, as if they all were new to you. You should assume that cases were decided in the jurisdictions and on the dates shown. In citing cases from the Library, you may use abbreviations and omit page references.

5. Your response must be written in the answer book provided. If you are taking this examination on a laptop computer, your jurisdiction will provide you with specific instructions. In answering this performance test, you should concentrate on the materials provided in the File and Library. What you have learned in law school and elsewhere provides the general background for analyzing the problem; the File and Library provide the specific materials with which you must work.

6. Although there are no restrictions on how you apportion your time, you should be sure to allocate ample time (about 45 minutes) to reading and digesting the materials and to organizing your answer before you begin writing it. You may make notes anywhere in the test materials; blank pages are provided at the end of the booklet. You may not tear pages from the question booklet.

7. This performance test will be graded on your responsiveness to the instructions regarding the task you are to complete, which are given to you in the first memorandum in the File, and on the content, thoroughness, and organization of your response.

Meley v. Boundless Vacations, Inc.

FILE

LIBRARY

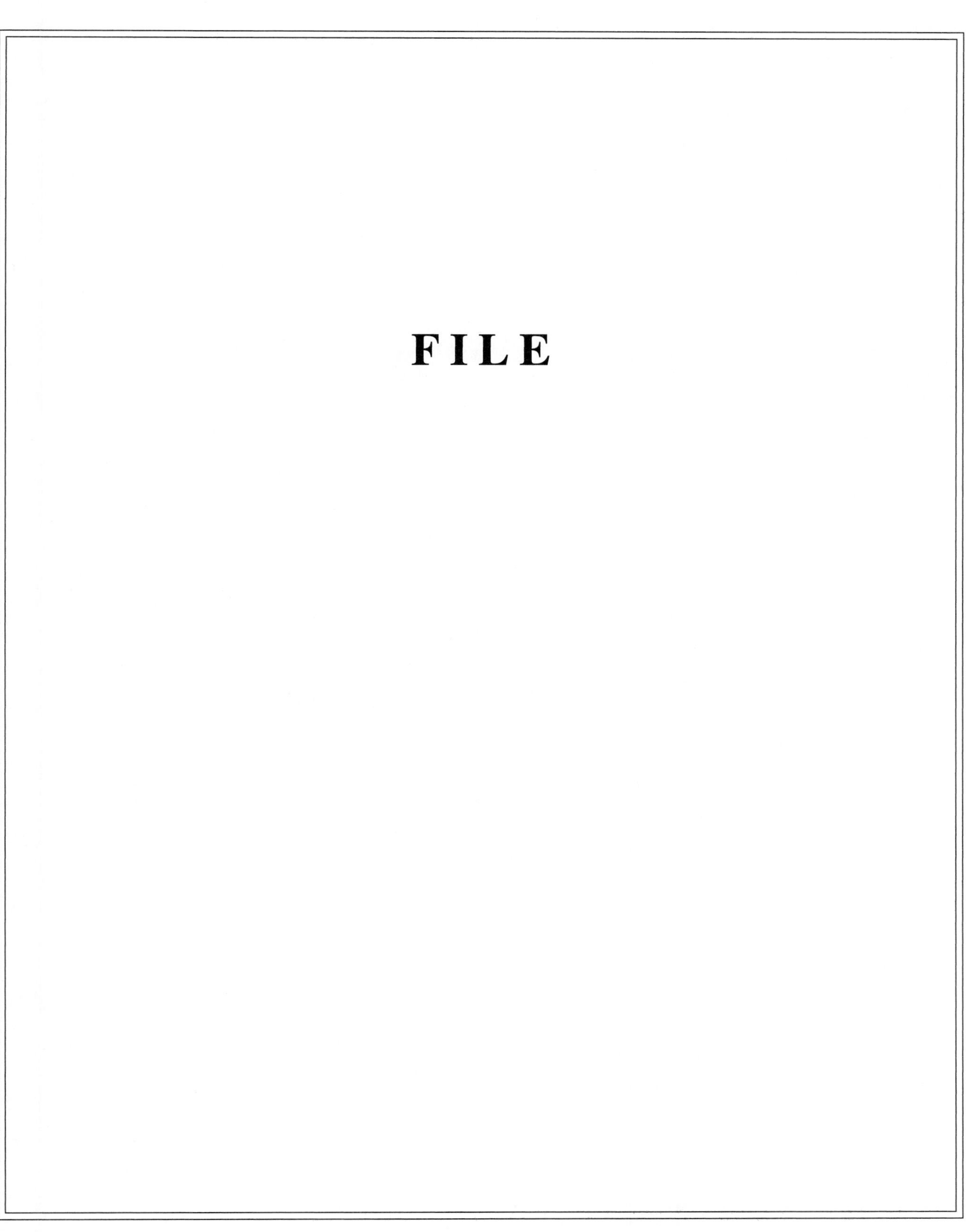
FILE

Chen, Massive & Schwartz
10070 Arvida Parkway, Suite 300
Plantation, Franklin 00135
(555) 349-0980 chenmasch@ultra.com

TO: Applicant

FROM: Dillon Massive

RE: *Meley v. Boundless Vacations, Inc.*

DATE: February 23, 1999

One of our newest clients is Boundless Vacations, Inc. (BVI), a full-service travel agency with a dozen locations throughout the metropolitan area. A former BVI customer, Philip Meley, is threatening BVI with a negligence suit. Meley was assaulted and robbed while on a business trip booked by BVI. The essence of Meley's claim is that BVI, as his agent, negligently booked him into a motel located in a dangerous section of a city he was visiting in another state.

BVI notified its insurance company of Meley's claim. Since the potential liability involved is less than the deductible under BVI's policy, BVI is permitted to choose its own counsel and has asked us to handle the matter.

Although this is a small claim, it's a great opportunity for us. As part of the firm's client development strategy, I have developed expertise in travel law, an emerging specialty that tracks the remarkable growth in the travel, tourism, and hospitality industry. The airlines, cruise lines, car rental agencies, tour operators, travel agents, hotels, destinations, and timeshares that make up this industry face a wide range of similar legal problems. I am making a considerable effort to attract local travel businesses such as BVI as new clients.

Before I contact Kevin Byrne, counsel for Meley, I want you to prepare a memorandum evaluating the merits of Meley's claim in which you do the following:

(1) Analyze the legal and factual bases of BVI's potential liability.

(2) Incorporated into your analysis, be sure to discuss how the facts we already know support or undercut BVI's position.

(3) Identify additional facts that might strengthen BVI's position, state why they are helpful, and indicate from what sources we might be able to obtain them.

INTERVIEW WITH DONNA GORE

President, Boundless Vacations, Inc.

Attorney: I'm delighted, Donna, that you've entrusted the firm with Boundless Vacations' legal work.

Gore: Well, Dillon, my colleagues and I were very impressed with the presentation you made to us. As a travel professional, I'm very aware of the rapid growth in the industry.

Attorney: I'm glad we decided to develop a specialty in the field.

Gore: Me, too. We're excited to have a real expert in our corner.

Attorney: I hope we'll live up to your expectations. Now, tell me about this controversy.

Gore: It's really a frivolous claim, Dillon. Just look at this letter from Kevin Byrne.

Attorney: Thanks. I'll look at it later. Meantime, tell me what you know about the problem.

Gore: We had a business client, Phil Meley, a former Franklin state policeman. We've booked sales trips for him for about nine months or a year now. Phil invented some kind of lightweight bulletproof vest and he's been trying to market it to police departments all over the country. BVI handled all of his flights out of Franklin International Airport and reserved his rental cars wherever he traveled. Up until that trip to the state of Olympia last month, everything was fine.

Attorney: What happened on that trip?

Gore: Meley got beat up and robbed in the parking lot of the motel where he was staying, and now he's trying to blame BVI because the motel is in a high-crime area.

Attorney: Did you handle Meley's motel reservation?

Gore: Well, I didn't personally do the booking. Meley always dealt directly with Linda Gates, the manager of our office at the Weston Mall, to handle all of his travel, including the motels.

Attorney: Did she know the area around the motel had a high incidence of crime?

Gore: I'm sure she didn't know anything about that particular location, other than it was a Highland Inn. After all, it happened in a state halfway across the country.

Attorney: Was there a way she could have learned that the motel was in a dangerous location?

Gore: Well, we checked the most recent issue of the USTA bulletin and didn't see anything that suggested that to be the case.

Attorney: What's a USTA bulletin?

Gore: The United States Travel Association. It puts out bulletins from time to time identifying travel suppliers who pose risks to travelers, anything from circumstances that might cause injury to the client to a supplier in a shaky financial condition that might cause it to fold. I'll have to check the back issues.

Attorney: I'll make an appointment to meet with Linda to get the details of BVI's relationship with Meley. If you learn anything from your review of the USTA bulletins, call me immediately. What commission does Highland Inn pay BVI for bookings?

Gore: Zero. As a mid-level motel chain with locations across the country, Highland relies on heavy advertising to get travelers themselves to make reservations through its 1-800 system. They pay nothing to travel agents.

Attorney: If you don't get paid, why do you do it?

Gore: To make sure we get the traveler's airline and car rental business as well as future family vacations that include major hotels and resorts where we make excellent commissions. We call it an accommodation booking. What kind of reaction do you think we'd get if we told the client, "Well, we got our commission by booking your flights and your rental car. Here's the 800 numbers of a couple of motels; you're on your own"?

Attorney: I get your point. Do you have any idea why Meley is coming after BVI? Why isn't he focusing on the motel?

Gore: I don't know; it's not right. I did hear that the franchise owner of the Nova City Highland Inn went bankrupt because crime in the area drove away so much business. I guess we are a convenient target.

Attorney: With your permission I'm going to see if I can get a private investigator to do a preliminary analysis of the situation.

Gore: That's fine. What do you think our chances are?

Attorney: Well, Donna, there is legal authority for the proposition that a travel agent may be liable for certain injuries or losses suffered by a traveler.

Gore: Do you mean to tell me BVI is responsible for what criminals in the state of Olympia did to Meley?

Attorney: No, I'm not saying that. What I am saying is that it's not as clear cut as you may think. Let me do some factual and legal research before providing you with an analysis of BVI's position. I'll get back to you before responding to Byrne.

* * * *

Byrne, Hall and Steinberg

Attorneys at Law
Bonaventure Plaza, Suite 1200
Marlin, Franklin 00121
555-310-2700

January 18, 1999

Donna Gore, President
Boundless Vacations, Inc.
Century Village Station
Adventura, Franklin 00155

Dear Ms. Gore:

Byrne, Hall and Steinberg represents Philip Meley, a client of Boundless Vacations, Inc. Mr. Meley was seriously injured when he was assaulted and robbed in the parking lot of the Highland Inn, Nova City, Olympia, on December 16, 1998. Boundless Vacations was acting as his agent when it booked Mr. Meley at the Nova City Highland Inn as part of an extended business trip to Olympia. When Boundless Vacations failed to inform or warn Mr. Meley that the Inn is located in the highest crime area of Nova City and that many other guests of the Inn had been victims of similar violent crimes against the person, Boundless Vacations negligently breached the duty of care it owed to Mr. Meley. That is particularly true because Mr. Meley notified your agent he was concerned about crime, especially theft.

Mr. Meley has suffered significant damages to date. Medical costs, including a two-day hospital stay and continuing counseling expenses, amount to $2,947. During the period he has been unable to work on his new enterprise, Mr. Meley has lost more than $10,000 in net business income. In addition, Mr. Meley continues to suffer significant lingering pain directly related to his injuries.

I hope we can reach agreement on an appropriate compensation package for Mr. Meley. Such an understanding will avoid a costly and embarrassing lawsuit against Boundless Vacations. I encourage you to forward this information to your insurance carrier.

Sincerely,

Kevin T. Byrne, Esquire
For the Firm

Meley/Boundless Vacations.ltr

INTERVIEW WITH LINDA GATES
Manager, Boundless Vacations, Inc.
Westin Mall Office

Attorney: Thanks for meeting with me, Ms. Gates.

Gates: You're quite welcome, sir. Please call me Linda.

Attorney: Certainly, Linda. Tell me a little bit about Philip Meley.

Gates: Oh, he's a very nice person, and he's brought us steady business over the past year. That is, until he got injured on his trip to Nova City last month.

Attorney: How did he become BVI's steady customer?

Gates: Well, after he retired.... You know he's a former Franklin state policeman?

Attorney: Uh huh.

Gates: Well, anyway, after he left the state police, Mr. Meley took over as head of security at Dingle's Department Store here in the mall. He'd stop in for help with trips for him and his wife. Last year he came in and said he had resigned his job at Dingle's, that he had patented a super-light bulletproof vest, and that he planned to personally sell it to police departments across the country. As a former cop, he thought he could land some big contracts and then turn the sales operation over to others. He asked me to handle his business travel.

Attorney: How many trips did BVI book for him prior to the Nova City one?

Gates: I'll have to look it up to be exact but....

Attorney: A close approximation will do for now.

Gates: OK, I think we booked about a dozen trips for him. Mostly large cities in several states. We'd fly him into one city, get him a car, and book his motel. Then he'd drive to a couple of other cities in the state and then we'd fly him out of the last one back here to Franklin. I remember a big trip he took to Florida. He flew into Miami, then we booked Highland Inns for him in Fort Lauderdale, Fort Myers, Tampa, Orlando, Tallahassee, and finally Jacksonville, from which he flew back to Franklin.

Attorney: Was last month's trip to Nova City different from the others?

Gates: Nope. We did just what he always asked for. We booked Delta flights so Mr. Meley got his Skymiles; a Hertz car so he got extra mileage credit; and Highland Inns so he received RepeatGuest points. The car was a full-size. As a former cop, he wanted a big car because he thought he'd be more protected in case of a crash. And the Highland Inns were all close to downtown and within one mile of an interstate highway.

Attorney: Did he always stay at Highland Inns?

Gates: Always. With RepeatGuest points he earned with every stay, Mr. Meley was able to stay free about every tenth night. That adds up when you're starting a new business.

Attorney: What's this about downtown locations near the interstate?

Gates: Mr. Meley insisted that we book only Highland Inns near the center of the city and not more than a mile from the interstate highway. That way, he said, he'd be close to the police departments and city halls he had to visit, and he could easily find the motel in a strange city if it was close to the highway.

Attorney: How'd you pick that particular Highland Inn in Nova City?

Gates: Just like anyone would. I did what I did all the other times I booked Mr. Meley's lodging. I used the American Travel Association TourGuide that covers Nova City and found the only Highland Inn location that met Mr. Meley's requirements. The ATA Guide is one of the top two travel directories in the country. I pulled it off my shelf so I could show you. You can see here that the Highland Inn we booked him into is three-quarters of a mile from I-17 and close to downtown.

Attorney: What does "Silver Lodging" mean?

Gates: ATA rates accommodations as Bronze, Silver, Gold, and Platinum. That's similar to AAA's Diamond ratings. A Silver Lodging means the motel is clean, private, and comfortable, with nice but not upscale décor. ATA Silver Lodges generally appeal to the budget-oriented traveler.

Attorney: Does ATA evaluate safety issues of motels it lists in its TourGuides?

Gates: The only safety things they look at are in the guest rooms. They check for the presence of dead bolts, locks on the windows, view ports in the doors, stuff like that.

Attorney: Did Meley ever say anything about checking into criminal activity near the motels?

Gates: No, not that I recall. Oh, I remember once, right at the beginning, Mr. Meley said something about industrial espionage and people trying to steal one of his vests so they could copy it and cheat him out of what he was due. It was kind of a general comment about how tough his new work was going to be.

Attorney: Did you have any information about criminal activity or the safety of the area around this particular Highland Inn?

Gates: Nothing. How could I? Nova City is hundreds of miles away. All I could do was to grab the TourGuide and find a Highland Inn that met Mr. Meley's needs.

Attorney: What about the USTA bulletin? Did you check that? Or what would have happened if you had called the folks at the American Travel Association; would they have been able to give you a status report on that Highland Inn?

Gates: I don't know much about USTA. Donna gets the bulletin and deals with them exclusively. As to the ATA, I guess it's possible they have some kind of information hot line for travel agents or members to update their TourGuides. I'll have to call and find out. But I don't think they keep any information on criminal activity stuff.

Attorney: OK, let me know what you find out and thanks for all of your help. Can I get a copy of that Highland Inn listing?

Gates: Sure. I hope I did the right thing. I don't want BVI to get sued or anything.

Attorney: Don't you worry, Linda. It's my responsibility to deal with Meley.

American Travel Association
Olympia TourGuide (1998)

Highland Inn, Nova City 1P $39 2P/1B $45 2P/2B $58 (222) 615-7755 ***Silver Lodging*** **Location:** I-17, exit 29, east 3/4 mile to 2801 Adams St.; near downtown, driving distance (3.5 m) to State Capitol/City Hall complex. **Terms:** Sr. discount, credit card guarantee, no pets, RepeatGuest points. **Facility:** 79 rooms, interior corridors, pool, 2 meeting rooms. **Services:** Coin-operated laundry, vending machines, drive (1.75 m) to nearest rated restaurant. **Rooms:** Cable TV, coffee makers. **Credit Cards:** AE, DS, MC, VI

Ripka Investigation Services

1216 Meade Street
Reading, Franklin 00122
555-777-6309

John Paul Ripka
Licensed Civil/Criminal Investigator

TO:	Dillon Massive, Chen, Massive & Schwartz	February 10, 1999
FROM:	J.P. Ripka	
RE:	Meley v. BVI: Preliminary Report	

At your request, I made a detour from the Park City investigation to conduct a preliminary review of the circumstances surrounding the assault on Philip Meley at the Highland Inn, Nova City, Olympia, on 16 December 1998.

Police Investigation: I reviewed the Nova City Police Department offense report and spoke to Det. Adsani, the investigating officer. Following is from the offense report:

> At 0125, responded to report of robbery, Highland Inn parking lot, 2801 Adams St. Found WM, later identified as Philip Meley, age 63, Weston, Franklin, in dazed condition with severe head lacerations. Meley, former Franklin SPD officer, was struck with blunt object as he exited his vehicle in the Highland Inn parking lot. Two WMs, early 20s (#1- 5'10" 160-175 lbs, light hair; #2- 6'+ 180-200 lbs, dark hair/complexion) took victim's wallet containing $225 and credit cards. Descriptions/MO same as those reported by 5 other robbery victims accosted at same location in last 3 weeks.

Det. Adsani confirmed that the Highland Inn is located in the Soma Section, the area of Nova City with the highest crime index. Significant criminal activity has been reported in immediate vicinity of the Highland Inn in the last 6 months, including burglary of rooms (7); auto break-in (13); robbery (8); rape (1); homicide (1). Arrests have occurred in 3 burglaries, 5 auto break-ins, the rape and homicide. No suspects apprehended in robberies.

The Hotel: Older property with obvious deferred maintenance. To reach motel from I-17 must drive through light industrial area with warehouses and trucking facilities. No retail business between I-17 and motel. Street and parking lot lighting clearly inadequate for safety.

Meley registered at Inn for 3 nights, scheduled to leave 16 December. Each evening asked for restaurant recommendation: no restaurants nearby, so he was referred to dining at some distance from motel. Returned by car after midnight each evening. Joe Lawlor, owner of Highland Inn, filed for bankruptcy protection two weeks ago. Claims rising criminal activity in last 6 months has driven away customers. Vacancy rate has jumped from 15% to more than 35%. Couldn't afford to employ private security or improve lighting in parking lot.

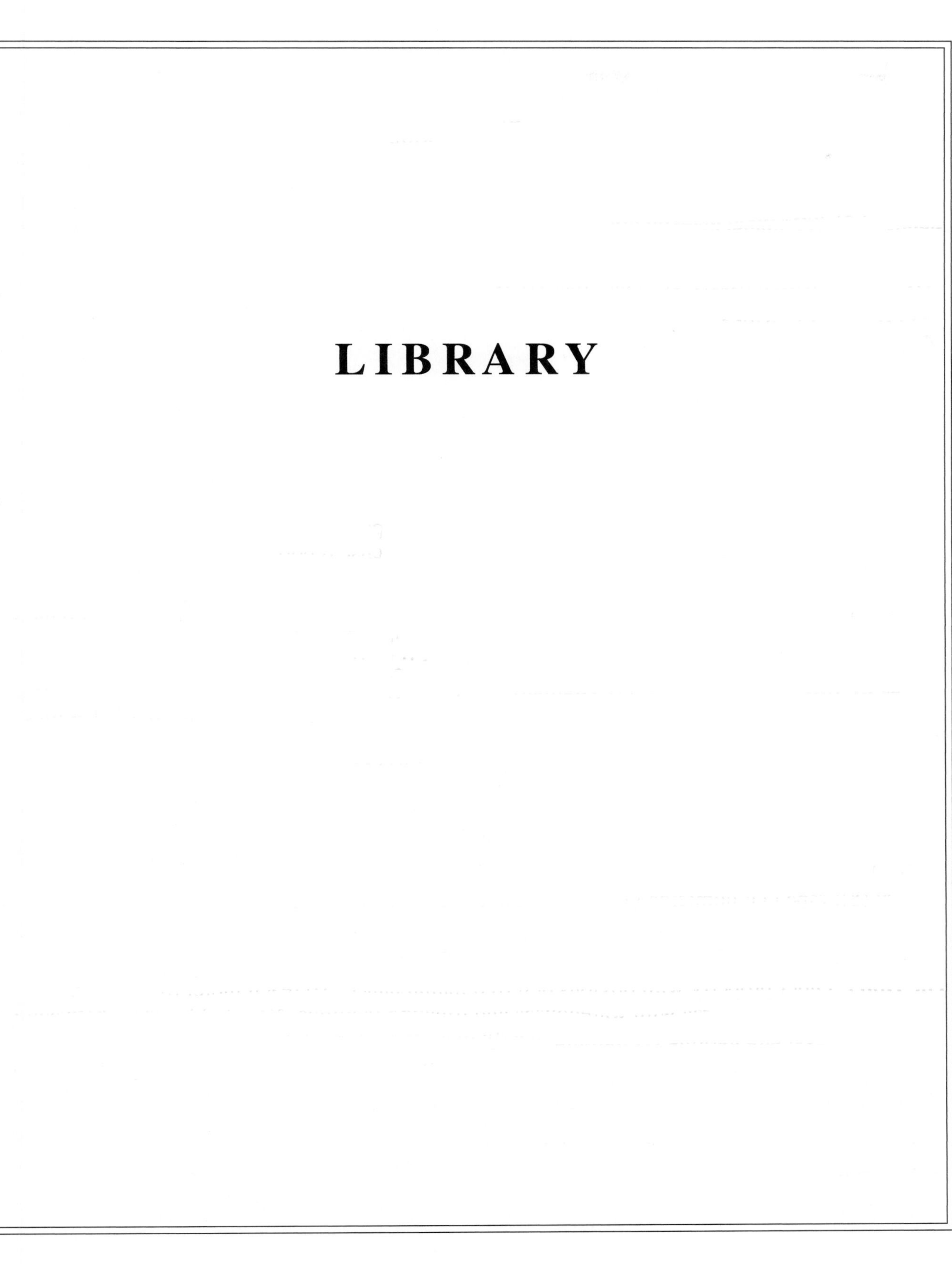

LIBRARY

Restatement (Second) of Agency

§1. Agency; Principal; Agent

(1) Agency is the fiduciary relation which results from the manifestation of consent by one person to another that the other shall act on his behalf and subject to his control, and consent by the other so to act.

(2) The one for whom action is to be taken is the principal.

(3) The one who is to act is the agent.

Comment:

Agency is a legal concept which depends upon the existence of required factual elements: the manifestation by the principal that the agent shall act for him; the agent's acceptance of the undertaking; and the understanding of the parties that the principal is to be in control of the undertaking. The relation which the law calls agency does not depend upon the intent of the parties to create it, nor their belief that they have done so. To constitute the relation, there must be an agreement, but not necessarily a contract, between the parties; if the agreement results in the factual relation between them to which are attached the legal consequences of agency, an agency exists although the parties did not call it agency and did not intend the legal consequences of the relation to follow.

A gratuitous agent, one who is to receive no compensation for his services, is subject to the same duty to give loyal service and to account as is a paid agent. His duty of obedience is the same except that he need not obey orders to continue to act as agent. He is subject to a duty of care, but the fact that his services are gratuitous is considered in determining the extent of his undertaking and the amount of care he should exercise.

* * * *

§379. Duty of Care and Skill

(1) Unless otherwise agreed, a paid agent is subject to a duty to the principal to act with standard care and with the skill which is standard in the locality for the kind of work which he is employed to perform and, in addition, to exercise any special skill that he has.

(2) Unless otherwise agreed, a gratuitous agent is under a duty to the principal to act with the care and skill which is required of persons not agents performing similar gratuitous undertakings for others.

Comment:

The mutual duties of the principal and agent are, in the absence of statute, controlled by the agreement which the parties make.

If the agent receives compensation, he is subject to liability in an action of contract or of tort. The gratuitous agent is subject to liability in an action of tort. In such actions, the burden of proving negligence and damage therefrom is upon the principal.

The paid agent is subject to a duty to exercise at least the skill which he represents himself as having. Unless the circumstances indicate otherwise, a paid agent represents that he has at least the skill and undertakes to exercise the care which is standard for that kind of employment in the community. An agent who is given discretion as to the manner in which he performs his duty is under a duty to act competently and carefully. A mistake in judgment resulting from a failure to have the standard knowledge or to use the standard care subjects the agent to liability to the principal. The liability of gratuitous agents to their principals for failure to exercise care is determined by the same principles which apply to the liability of persons who are not agents and who gratuitously act for the benefit of others, such as gratuitous bailees and hosts rendering services to guests.

* * * *

§381. Duty to Give Information

Unless otherwise agreed, an agent is subject to a duty to use reasonable efforts to give his principal information which is relevant to affairs entrusted to him and which, as the agent has notice, the principal would desire to have and which can be communicated without violating a superior duty to a third person.

Comment:

An agent may have an implied duty to act upon, or to communicate to his principal or to another agent, information which he has received, although not specifically instructed to do so. The duty exists if he has notice of facts which, in view of his relations with the principal, he should know may affect the desires of his principal as to his own conduct or the conduct of the principal or of another agent. The duty of the agent is inferred from his position, just as an authority is inferred. The extent of the duty depends upon the kind of work entrusted to him, his previous relations with the principal, and all the facts of the situation.

Loretti v. Air Land Travel Bureau

Franklin Court of Appeal (1993)

Karen Loretti, wishing to take a vacation, contacted Joan Lyons, a travel agent for Air Land Travel Bureau, in June of 1991. Lyons informed her that a tour booked by the Police Benevolent Association was scheduled to leave in September for Freeport in the Bahamas. Those on the tour were scheduled to stay at the Bahamas Princess Hotel.

Although Loretti had never been to the Bahamas, she had gone on other trips arranged through defendant Air Land. What little Loretti knew about the Caribbean islands had made her concerned about personal safety. Loretti expressed these concerns to Lyons, who assured her that they would be staying at the Bahamas Princess Hotel, a well-known resort, and that they would be traveling with a police group.

Lyons drove the plaintiff to the airport and at this time told her that because the Bahamas Princess Hotel had been overbooked she would be staying at the Holiday Inn. Lyons assured her that the Holiday Inn was just as nice as the Bahamas Princess and had the advantage of being situated on the beach.

Upon her arrival at the Holiday Inn, Loretti was assured by a Holiday Inn security guard that it was safe to walk on the beach. The plaintiff later attended a meeting conducted by a man employed by the defendant who described activities available to tourists and stated that it was safe in the pool or on the beach at any time of day or night. That evening Loretti and another guest staying at the Holiday Inn took a walk on the beach and were accosted by two men who raped and assaulted the plaintiff at gunpoint.

Air Land presented evidence that it believed the Holiday Inn was a safe place for guests, having sent several clients to that location in the months preceding Loretti's trip. Air Land's manager stated in his affidavit that he had not received complaints from any of more than a half dozen clients who had stayed at the Inn and that the agency relied on the positive general reputation of Holiday Inns. On the other hand, the plaintiff offered evidence that in the months before her visit the Holiday Inn was the locale for several crimes, including two robberies of guests on the beach at knifepoint.

In this negligence action, the trial court granted Air Land's motion for summary judgment on the ground that even when the facts were construed in the light most favorable to Loretti, there was no evidence that Air Land breached any duty owed to the plaintiff.

In reviewing the lower court's judgment, we must define the duty, if any, of defendant Air Land to warn Loretti of the danger of crimes against the person on the beaches in the Bahamas. No Franklin court has addressed the issue of a travel agent's duty to warn clients of criminal activity.

In *Wilson v. Trans Air, Inc.* (Indiana 1989), a traveler suffered injuries as a result of a criminal assault at the hotel where she was staying in the Cayman Islands. The court held that a travel agent ordinarily had no duty to investigate the safety and security of the accommodations or conditions it arranged, absent a specific request from the traveler. The travel agency, which regularly planned and operated tours to the Cayman Islands, gave the plaintiff the option of staying at the hotel where the assault occurred or at other venues. The traveler alleged that there was substantial criminal activity involving guests at the hotel in the months preceding the attack, but there was no evidence the hotel was in a high-crime area or that it had experienced more safety problems than other hotels on the island. The agency denied any knowledge of significant criminal activity at the hotel and relied on the general reputation of the hotel, the fact that the hotel employed security guards, and the lack of complaints from other clients.

In *Cretean v. Liberty Travel, Inc.* (New York 1991), on the other hand, plaintiffs sued defendant travel agency in negligence when they were robbed (and one was raped, at gunpoint) at a hotel while vacationing in Jamaica. The court said the defendant would be liable if the agency, an experienced provider of travel services in the Caribbean, knew or could easily have learned about a rising crime rate in Jamaica and other relevant safety factors about which it failed to warn plaintiffs.

This court concludes that a travel agency is more than a mere ticket agent. An agency deals with carriers; plans an itinerary; arranges for hotel accommodations, guides, and tours of each city; and sets up the traveler's schedule. A travel agent cannot reasonably be expected to guarantee that a traveler will have a good time or will return home without having experienced an adverse adventure or harm. Nor can it reasonably be expected to divine or forewarn a traveler of the innumerable litany of tragedies and dangers inherent in foreign and domestic travel. This cannot mean, however, that a travel agent owes no duty to its client. Rather, we hold, a travel agent who has relevant information that his client would want to have has an obligation to provide that information to his client. This duty applies unless that information available to the client is so obvious that, as a matter of law, the travel agent would not be negligent for failing to disclose it.

Assuming that Loretti expressed a concern for her personal safety to Air Land's agent, Air Land would have had a duty to disclose reasonably obtainable information about the safety of the area which the plaintiff would be visiting. The defendant claims that it fulfilled this duty, and its manager stated in her affidavit that she found the Holiday Inn to be safe and would not hesitate to recommend it.[1] The plaintiff reports,

[1] In support of this proposition, defendant refers to *Klinghoffer v. S.N.C. Achille Lauro* (S.D.N.Y. 1993), a case involving the tragic hijacking of a cruise ship and the subsequent death and injury of passengers at the hands of

however, that an examination of the Holiday Inn's records showed there had been twenty incidents of crime within three months of the plaintiff's visit and that two of the crimes involved knifepoint robberies of Holiday Inn guests on the Inn's beach.

The court believes that there are at least two issues of material fact. The first issue is whether the beach near the Holiday Inn was safe. If a jury were to conclude that the beach was safe, then defendant Air Land would have satisfied its duty to the plaintiff by accurately reporting that there was no safety problem on the trip. If a jury were to conclude that the beach was unsafe, then it would have to reach the second issue of whether information that the beach was unsafe was reasonably obtainable by defendant Air Land. Even if the plaintiff is successful in showing that the defendant breached its duty to disclose reasonably obtainable information, if actual observations or the information available to her would have led a reasonable person to conclude the beach area was dangerous at night, Loretti cannot cast blame upon the defendant.

The court reverses the grant of Air Land's motion for summary judgment.

---

criminals. There the court exonerated a defendant tour operator who established that before the 1985 hijacking Lauro was well respected within the travel industry, and it had received no complaints about security procedures aboard any Lauro ships.

Yanase v. Automobile Club of Southern California

California Court of Appeal (1989)

George Yanase was injured by an unknown assailant at night in a parking lot of a motel in which he was staying. The theory of Yanase's complaint against Auto Club is negligent misrepresentation, i.e., Auto Club negligently failed to determine and publish information on the safety of the area and the existence and effectiveness of security measures.

The trial court found the complaint failed to state facts sufficient to constitute a cause of action against Auto Club. We affirm.

Yanase was a member of Auto Club. American Automobile Association (AAA), a codefendant, and Auto Club are in the business of endorsing travel accommodations and services through their Tourbooks. Their Tourbooks contain listings of various hotels and motels in designated geographical areas and a rating system with reference to those accommodations. The California/Nevada edition of the Tourbook states:

> This Tourbook has only one purpose: to make your trip as enjoyable as possible by providing accurate, detailed information about attractions and accommodations in the area through which you are traveling. AAA field representatives cover the length and breadth of the North American Continent. These efficient, highly trained individuals are constantly on the move, systematically searching the highways for accommodations and restaurants that meet AAA's requirements for recommendation to our more than 22 million members. For every establishment selected to be listed in the Tourbooks, many others were inspected and found to be lacking in some important consideration. We believe, in the best interests of our members, that our standards are important. We will not lower them simply to achieve a greater volume of listings.

The complaint alleges that because of the relationship between Yanase and Auto Club, and AAA and Auto Club's business practice of endorsing travel accommodations and services, the defendants had a duty through their field representatives to determine the relative safety of the area where the recommended hotels and motels were located, to determine the existence and effectiveness of the security measures offered to the patrons, and to publish the information in the Tourbook. Further, Yanase alleges that had Auto Club exercised reasonable care it would have known that the motel "was located in a high-crime area wherein robberies and muggings were commonplace in the immediate radius of the motel and that the motel offered inadequate security for its patrons." Yanase claims to have read the Tourbook and relied on it in selecting the motel. Moreover, he would not have selected the motel if Auto Club had determined it was in a high-crime area and offered inadequate security.

Negligent misrepresentation consists of making a false statement honestly believing it is true but without reasonable ground for such belief. The tort is a form of deceit without, however, the element of scienter. Since the tort requires a "positive assertion," the doctrine does not apply to implied representations.

There is nothing in Auto Club's Tourbook listing or rating that consists of a positive assertion concerning neighborhood safety or the security measures taken in connection with the motel. In fact, as we discuss in more detail below, those matters are not even implied in the Tourbook listing or rating. Accordingly, the complaint does not state facts sufficient to constitute a cause of action in negligent misrepresentation.

We next consider the question of whether there exists a duty of care, a question of law to be determined on a case-by-case basis. The fact that Auto Club's Tourbook gives "information about attractions and accommodations" adds nothing to the analysis. So far as we are concerned, the Tourbook speaks only of accommodations, i.e., "something that is supplied for convenience or to satisfy a need . . . lodging, food, and services (as at a hotel)." Webster's Third New International Dictionary (1968 ed.). Making trips enjoyable through providing information about accommodations is the stated purpose of the listing and rating in the Tourbook. Nothing is said about inspecting for dangerous neighborhoods or determining the presence or absence of personal security measures taken by the owners of the accommodations on behalf of their patrons.

The puffing statements concerning the efforts of AAA's representatives in searching for accommodations and inspecting them do not suggest neighborhood safety or security measures are aspects of the listing and rating. In fact, the rating description speaks only of "physical and operational categories," "comfortable and attractive accommodations," and listing "on the basis of merit alone." Again, the quality of "accommodations" is the focus of the Tourbook listing and rating.

From what we have said, it follows that the "special relationship" described by Yanase as one "defined by a dependency and reliance" on Auto Club "in all matters of vehicular travel and services connected therewith," if it exists at all, is limited to the listing and rating of accommodations and does not include within its scope matters of neighborhood safety or security measures.

The present case is to be contrasted with cases such as *McCollum v. Friendly Hills Travel Center* (California 1985), where we held that a travel agent who arranges vacation plans is a special agent for the purpose of the transaction between the parties and thus owes a duty to disclose reasonably obtainable material information to the traveler unless the information was so clearly obvious and apparent to the traveler that, as a matter of law, the travel agent would not be negligent in failing to disclose it. Here, of course, Auto Club had no such special agency relationship with Yanase. Accordingly, we affirm.

Meley v. Boundless Vacations, Inc.

Sample Answer

TO: Dillon Massive
FROM: Applicant
RE: Meley v. Boundless Vacations, Inc.

Our client, Boundless Vacations, Inc. ("BVI") was clearly acting as Meley's agent when it booked accommodations for him at the Nova City Highland Inn. It is likely that it was a paid, rather than gratuitous, agent and thus was subject to the standard of care that generally is exercised by other travel agents in the locality. We need more facts before reaching a definitive conclusion as to whether BVI breached its duty of care to Meley, but even if it did, it is possible that Meley cannot recover because the safety/security problems at the motel were readily observable by him. The additional facts that may help our case are incorporated into the analysis below.

I. AGENCY RELATIONSHIP

The fiduciary relationship of agency arises when (i) there is a manifestation by one person (the principal) that another person (the agent) shall act for him; (ii) the agent accepts the undertaking; and (iii) the parties understand that the principal is in control of the undertaking. [Restatement (Second) of Agency ("Rest. 2d") §1]

That BVI was acting as Meley's agent is clear from the interviews with BVI's president, Donna Gore, and Linda Gates, the BVI manager who has handled Meley's travel arrangements for the past year. Gates had booked approximately 12 trips for Meley. Meley was obviously in control of the bookings as evidenced by his insistence that BVI book only with specific companies. As regards his motel, Meley dictated the use of only Highland Inns (so he could receive RepeatGuest points entitling him to a free night every 10th time he booked with the chain). In addition, Meley insisted that his motel be near the city center and not over one mile from the interstate. Clearly there was an agency relationship between the parties.

There is a question whether BVI was a paid or gratuitous agent. This categorization would have an effect on the standard of care required of our client. Although we need to ascertain from Gore whether Meley paid any fees to BVI, it does not appear that he did. BVI did not receive any compensation from Highland Inn for booking Meley with the motel chain. Therefore, an argument can be made that BVI was a gratuitous agent as to the Highland Inn bookings. However, Gore stated that BVI did receive commissions from booking Meley with Hertz and Delta Airlines. Since BVI did receive compensation for arranging Meley's trip, it is probable that the undertaking would be viewed as a whole and our client would be considered to be a paid agent.

II. STANDARD OF CARE

Assuming that BVI is a paid agent, the Restatement Second establishes a duty to act with the care and skill that is standard in the locality for the type of work the agent is hired to do. [Rest. 2d §379] Here that standard would be the ***care and skill exercised by travel agents in the locality***. When the agent has discretion in the manner of performing the undertaking, she must act carefully and competently, and a mistake in judgment resulting from failure to exercise the required standard of care subjects the agent to liability to the principal. [Rest. 2d §379, comment]

The facts we have indicate that BVI acted carefully and competently in booking Meley's room at the Highland Inn. Gates booked at least 12 other trips for Meley at Highland Inns and heard no complaints from him. Her booking for this trip too met his requirements. She acted competently in booking motels for him.

As for careful action, according to Gore, she checked the most recent issue of a periodic bulletin issued by the United States Travel Association ("USTA"), a publication that identifies risks to travelers. There was no mention of Highland Inn in the bulletin. However, we do not yet know whether Gore routinely checked the bulletins or whether there was a warning regarding this specific motel in past issues. We need to determine those facts from Gore. If there were warnings in past issues, this could hurt our position, but we should find out if other local travel agents use USTA for this purpose and whether agents generally check more than just the current issue.

Gates stated that she used one of the two top industry directories, the American Travel Association TourGuide ("ATA Guide") to locate the motel in Nova City. Again, we need to determine if this guide is used by most travel agents in booking accommodations. If so, that is helpful to our case. According to Gates, the ATA Guide's evaluation of safety is limited to room safety and does not consider the general location of the motel. Gates opined that perhaps the ATA Guide may have some sort of "hot line" from which one could obtain current information regarding a location. However, since the ATA Guide lists information such as location, specifics of accommodations, services provided, rating, etc., it is doubtful that safety and security concerns would be on a hot line. This needs to be investigated and whether the hot line (if it exists) is something generally used by other travel agents in the area when making arrangements for their clients. Thus, although we are not yet completely clear on the standard practices of other travel agents in the locality, it seems likely that BVI acted carefully and competently in booking Meley. Once we get the information about other agents' practices we can make a better determination of this issue.

We could also argue that BVI had no actual discretion in selecting the motel. Meley insisted on Highland Inns and only those within a specific proximity of the interstate and the center of the city. BVI agents had no discretion here to choose a Highland Inn because there was only one that met Meley's specifications. Thus, BVI competently did what it was engaged to do—reserve Meley a room at his chosen motel.

(Note that if BVI were found to be an unpaid agent, its standard of care would be minimal—merely that of a nonagent acting gratuitously. [Rest. 2d §379])

III. BVI'S DUTY TO WARN MELEY REGARDING SAFETY AND SECURITY IN MOTEL AREA

A. INFORMATION KNOWN TO BVI

An agent must use reasonable efforts to transmit to the principal information known to the agent that is relevant to the undertaking and that the agent should know the principal would be interested in knowing. [Rest. 2d §381] Under this rule, the agent must disclose only information ***actually known*** to the agent which she knows may affect the desires of the principal. [Rest. 2d §381, comment]

It is clear that BVI had no knowledge of the unsafe conditions at the Highland Inn. According to Gates, Meley had stayed at Highland Inns approximately 12 times in the past year with no complaints. This particular Highland Inn is located far from where BVI is located and there is no indication that the agents know anything about the area of Nova City in which the motel is located. Also, the ATA Guide and the current USTA bulletin consulted by BVI contained no information that would alert our client to any danger. Therefore, BVI had no knowledge of a dangerous condition to transmit to Meley.

BVI also did not have any indication that Meley was concerned about safety. He set the requirements for the motel—both the chain and location. He had stayed in Highland Inns 12 times before and never complained or even inquired about their safety. The only thing he ever said about safety was a casual comment that he was concerned about industrial espionage. That statement was made early in the relationship, never brought up again, and clearly is not related to concerns for his personal safety.

Furthermore, as discussed above, BVI agents had no discretion in booking Meley. He ***insisted*** on staying in only Highland Inns that were close to the city center and no more than a mile from the interstate. The motel booked by BVI was the only motel in Nova City that met Meley's requirements. BVI, in its previous bookings for Meley, had neither given, nor been asked to give, information regarding personal safety issues at Meley's distant destinations. There were no indications from the parties' past dealings that any such information was expected.

Therefore, assuming that past USTA bulletins contained no relevant warnings, or that Gore was not aware of those warnings, BVI had no notice of unsafe conditions in the area of the motel. Thus, under the Restatement view, BVI had no duty to warn Meley of unknown safety hazards at the motel.

B. INFORMATION REASONABLY OBTAINABLE BY BVI

In *Loretti v. Air Land Travel Bureau* (1993), a case of first impression in Franklin, the court of appeals determined that a travel agent has a duty to communicate known relevant information to the client. (This is basically the standard of the Restatement Second, *see* above.) However, the court stated a different standard ***when a client expressed concern for safety***. In that case the agent would have a duty to disclose "***reasonably obtainable***" information about the safety of the area. [Loretti] However, an agent would not, as a matter of law, be negligent for failure to disclose that information ***if the lack of a safe environs is obvious*** to the client. [Loretti]

Clearly, BVI had no actual knowledge of unsafe conditions at the motel (*see* discussion above). And *Loretti* (*citing Wilson v. Trans Air, Inc.*) states that a travel agent ordinarily does not have a duty to investigate safety and security arrangements unless a client makes a ***specific*** request concerning personal safety. Meley's attorney contends that Meley told Gates that he was concerned about "crime, especially theft." However, as mentioned, Meley made a casual statement at the beginning of the relationship that he feared that people were trying to steal one of his vests to make copies. According to Gates, this was merely a general comment on the difficulty of his new work and did not amount to an expression of concern for his personal safety that would trigger BVI's duty to investigate. Thus, under the Restatement and *Loretti*, BVI met its duty to Meley.

(Regarding Meley's concern about the safety of his vests, Gates did check the Nova City Highland Inn in the ATA Guide, which evaluates safety measures in the motel room, such as door and window locks, etc. Thus, BVI did investigate the general concern casually mentioned by Meley, *i.e.*, theft of a vest.)

Even if Meley's statement were interpreted as an expression of concern for his personal safety, we may be able to show that BVI met its duty regarding "reasonably obtainable" information. Of course, as mentioned before, this may depend on what, if anything, is contained in back issues of the USTA bulletins regarding the particular motel. If there are risks mentioned, this will be harmful, as Gore's knowledge of the information source would be imputed to Gates under the law of agency, and BVI would have failed to give Meley "reasonably obtainable" information. If no risks were mentioned in back issues, this would indicate a lack of "reasonably obtainable" facts.

We also need to discover whether the ATA Guide has relevant updates or a hot line. If not, the Guide appears only to offer information relating to ratings, services, and amenities of accommodations.

It was determined in *Yanase v. Automobile Club of Southern California* (Cal. Ct. App. 1989) that a similar listing in a tour guide does not encompass "matters of neighborhood safety or security measures," and BVI had no duty to investigate the safety of the area surrounding Meley's motel.

Therefore, unless our investigation of other travel agents in the locality reveals some other commonly used source of information, there probably was no "reasonably obtainable" information about the Highland Inn for BVI to give to Meley.

C. OBVIOUS INFORMATION DEFENSE

The duty to communicate known or "reasonably obtainable" relevant information to a client applies unless the information is so obvious that, as a matter of law, a travel agent would not be negligent for failure to disclose the information. [Loretti] Even if safety and security risks are noted in a past USTA bulletin, principles of contributory negligence will be a complete defense to our client. If actual observations or available information would have led a reasonable person in Meley's situation to conclude that an area is dangerous, the blame cannot be attributed to the agent. [Loretti]

As a retired police officer, Meley should have recognized that the neighborhood was unsafe. Our investigator, Ripka, found that the motel is located in a light industrial area containing warehouses and trucking facilities, with no retail businesses. According to Ripka, the street and parking lot lighting is "clearly inadequate for safety." The motel is in a somewhat neglected condition. Meley's specialized knowledge gained from his police work should have alerted him to the unsafe conditions. He should have known that the centers of large cities are often a high crime area, and that an industrial area where there are no retail businesses is somewhat isolated and therefore ripe for criminal activity. Also, he should have noticed the motel's condition and the lighting in the area and parking lot.

Although Meley might not have known initially that the motel was in a high crime area of Nova City, it is highly likely that during Meley's meetings with the local police department, he would have learned that fact. Surely after seeing the motel's location and lack of concern for safety, he should have asked the police about it. Clearly the police were aware of the crimes that have occurred at the Inn.

Meley also may have seen something about the area in the local newspapers. Most motels have newspapers available and business travelers often read the paper while eating or to learn about the businesses in the area, to check the weather, etc. We could check to see whether the motel chain offered a free paper as some chains do and whether there was anything in the papers on those days about the crime in the area.

Meley had reservations for three nights, but after seeing the place, he did not make a change of motel or complain to BVI. Instead he decided to remain there despite the conditions and the fact that he had to travel some distance each night for dinner and return quite late. (He was assaulted and robbed on the last night of his stay.) Given his past profession, his current dealings with Nova City police officers, and the readily apparent character of the motel neighborhood, the safety risks must have been obvious to him. However, his desire for RepeatGuest points apparently took precedence over any concern he may have had for his safety. Since Meley did not act as a reasonable person would in his situation, no negligence can attach to BVI.

Multistate Performance Test

In re Steven Wallace

National Conference of Bar Examiners

Preface

This Multistate Performance Test is a reprint of one of the three MPTs which were administered in July 1999.

The instructions for the test appear on the next page. On the actual MPT, they will appear on the back cover of the test.

INSTRUCTIONS

1. You will have 90 minutes to complete this session of the examination. This performance test is designed to evaluate your ability to handle a select number of legal authorities in the context of a factual problem involving a client.

2. The problem is set in the fictitious state of Franklin, in the fictitious Fifteenth Circuit of the United States. Columbia and Olympia are also fictitious states in the Fifteenth Circuit. In Franklin, the trial court of general jurisdiction is the District Court, the intermediate appellate court is the Court of Appeal, and the highest court is the Supreme Court.

3. You will have two kinds of materials with which to work: a File and a Library. The first document in the File is a memorandum containing the instructions for the task you are to complete. The other documents in the File contain factual information about your case and may include some facts that are not relevant.

4. The Library contains the legal authorities needed to complete the task and may also include some authorities that are not relevant. Any cases may be real, modified, or written solely for the purpose of this examination. If the cases appear familiar to you, do not assume that they are precisely the same as you have read before. Read them thoroughly, as if they all were new to you. You should assume that cases were decided in the jurisdictions and on the dates shown. In citing cases from the Library, you may use abbreviations and omit page references.

5. Your response must be written in the answer book provided. If you are taking this examination on a laptop computer, your jurisdiction will provide you with specific instructions. In answering this performance test, you should concentrate on the materials provided in the File and Library. What you have learned in law school and elsewhere provides the general background for analyzing the problem; the File and Library provide the specific materials with which you must work.

6. Although there are no restrictions on how you apportion your time, you should be sure to allocate ample time (about 45 minutes) to reading and digesting the materials and to organizing your answer before you begin writing it. You may make notes anywhere in the test materials; blank pages are provided at the end of the booklet. You may not tear pages from the question booklet.

7. This performance test will be graded on your responsiveness to the instructions regarding the task you are to complete, which are given to you in the first memorandum in the File, and on the content, thoroughness, and organization of your response.

INSTRUCTIONS

1. You will have 90 minutes to complete this session of the examination. This performance test is designed to evaluate your ability to handle a select number of legal authorities in the context of a factual problem involving a client.

2. The problem is set in the fictitious state of Franklin, in the fictitious Fifteenth Circuit of the United States. Columbia and Olympia are also fictitious states in the Fifteenth Circuit. In Franklin, the trial court of general jurisdiction is the District Court, the intermediate appellate court is the Court of Appeal, and the highest court is the Supreme Court.

3. You will have two kinds of materials with which to work: a File and a Library. The first document in the File is a memorandum containing the instructions for the task you are to complete. The other documents in the File contain factual information about your case and may include some facts that are not relevant.

4. The Library contains the legal authorities needed to complete the task and may also include some authorities that are not relevant. Any cases may be real, modified, or written solely for the purpose of this examination. If the cases appear familiar to you, do not assume that they are precisely the same as you have read before. Read them thoroughly, as if they all were new to you. You should assume that the cases were decided in the jurisdictions and on the dates shown. In citing cases from the Library, you may use abbreviations and omit page references.

5. Your response must be written in the answer book provided. If you are taking the examination on a laptop computer, your jurisdiction will provide you with specific instructions. In answering this performance test, you should concentrate on the materials in the File and Library. What you have learned in law school and elsewhere provides the general background for analyzing the problem; the File and Library provide the specific materials with which you must work.

6. Although there are no restrictions on how you apportion your time, you should be sure to allocate ample time (about 45 minutes) to reading and digesting the materials and to organizing your answer before you begin writing it. You may make notes anywhere in the test materials; blank pages are provided at the end of the booklet. You may not tear pages from the question booklet.

7. This performance test will be graded on your responsiveness to the instructions regarding the task you are to complete, which are given to you in the first memorandum in the File, and on the content, thoroughness, and organization of your response.

In re Steven Wallace

FILE

LIBRARY

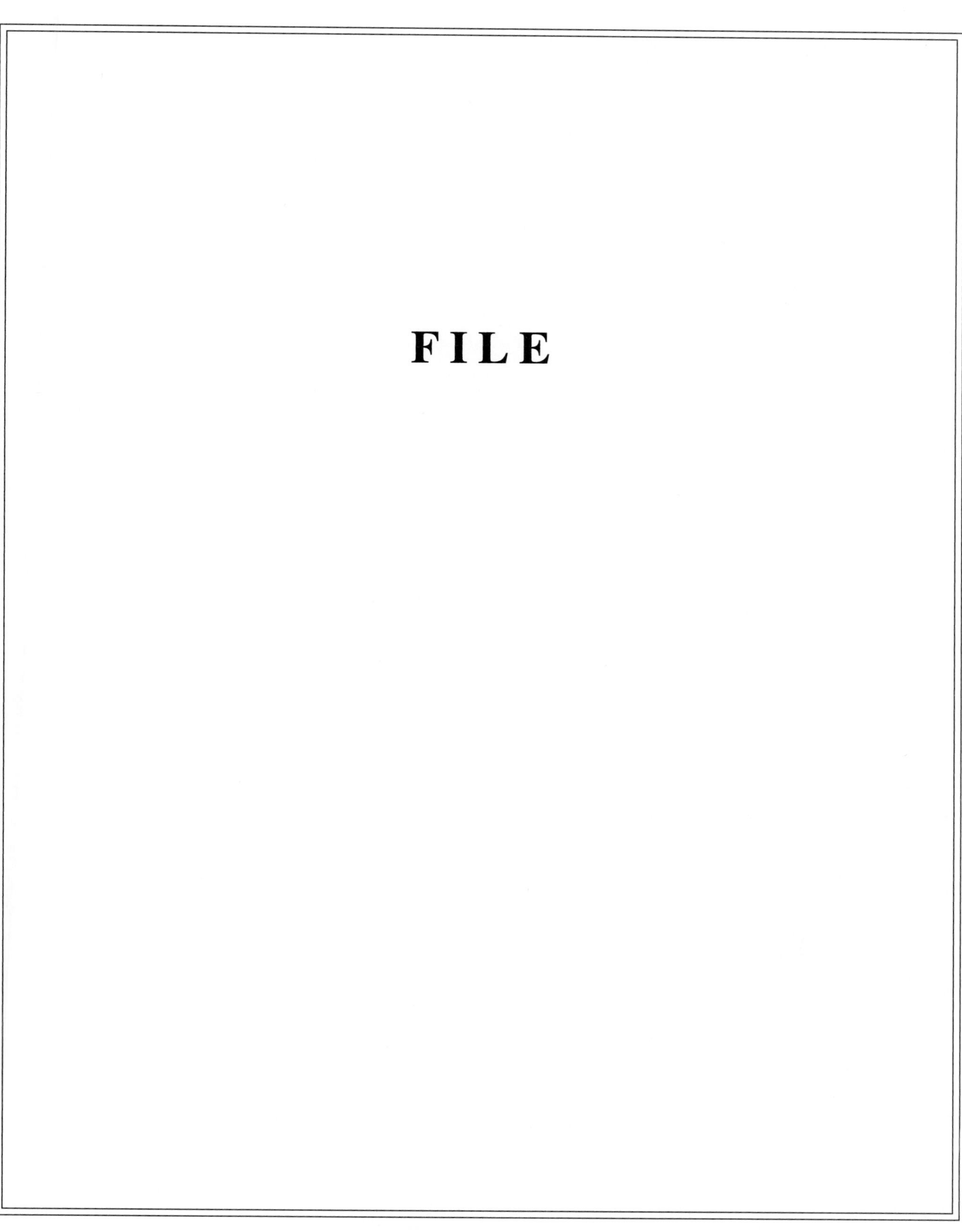
FILE

Piper, Morales & Singh
Attorneys at Law
One Dalton Place
West Keystone, Franklin 33322

M E M O R A N D U M

To: Applicant

From: Eva Morales

Date: July 27, 1999

Subject: Steven Wallace - Painting Titled "Hare Castle"

Steven Wallace, a long-time friend of mine, recently retired as Chair of the English Department at the University of Franklin to pursue full time what has until now been his avocation as an artist. He came in yesterday to get my advice and brought the documents I've included in the file. On reviewing the file, I can see that there are other facts we need in order to advise him properly.

About a year ago, Steven left one of his paintings, a canvas he had titled "Hare Castle," with Lottie Zelinka, an art dealer friend of his, with the understanding that she would try to sell it for him. Ms. Zelinka is the owner of Artists' Exchange, an art gallery here in West Keystone. Ten days or so ago, Ms. Zelinka returned the painting to Steven. A few days ago, he received a letter from Martin Feldner, a bankruptcy practitioner here in town. Mr. Feldner represents Charles Sims, the court-appointed Trustee in Bankruptcy. The letter advises Steven that Ms. Zelinka has filed for bankruptcy and demands that Steven turn "Hare Castle" over to the Trustee in Bankruptcy. Naturally, Steven is upset by this turn of events and wants to know how to respond.

Please draft for me a two-part memorandum:

> First, analyze the legal and factual bases of the trustee's claim that the painting is an asset of the bankruptcy estate under the Bankruptcy Act and the Franklin Commercial Code (FCC).
>
> Second, for each of the four defenses under FCC §2-326(3), discuss how the facts we already know support the defense, identify additional facts that might be helpful to us, state why they would be helpful, and indicate from what sources we might be able to obtain them.

Notes of July 26, 1999 Meeting with Steven Wallace

- Steven can't believe this letter he got (copy attached) two days ago—a bankruptcy attorney is demanding that Steven turn over one of his best paintings ("Hare Castle") to a Trustee.
  - A friend of his, Lottie Zelinka, has an art gallery in West Keystone—the gallery is called Artists' Exchange. She operates it as a sole proprietorship.
  - Lottie has a sizeable inventory of paintings and sculptures—Steven thinks (but isn't sure) that most of the art in the gallery is on consignment from artists and that Lottie doesn't really own it. That's how Steven and every other artist he knows deal with the galleries in town—*i.e.*, by consignment. He's pretty sure that's how galleries work everywhere. Maybe Lottie owns some of the art, but, mainly, she shows the art, sells it for the artists, and makes her money on the sales commissions.
  - Steven thinks (but is not sure) Lottie had placed a sign in the window at the front of the gallery that said something like, "All offers will be considered and forwarded to the artists."
  - About a year ago, Lottie was at Steven's house for dinner with Steven and Ella, his wife. Lottie saw "Hare Castle" (oil on canvas - about 2' × 3') hanging on the dining room wall. She admired it and said she thought she could sell it for "a lot of money," maybe as much as $25,000 (some of Steven's recent paintings have been fetching pretty good prices, but he'd never thought about trying to sell "Hare Castle"—it was one of his favorite paintings and had been hanging in his dining room since he finished it a couple of years ago). Lottie told Steven, if he's interested, to bring it to her gallery and she'd put it up for sale.
  - Steven and Ella talked it over and, although they had recently purchased a new rug for their dining room that coordinated with the colors in the painting, $25,000 sounded like a lot of money, so they decided to see if Lottie was right. Steven took "Hare Castle" to Lottie's gallery, they did some paperwork (copies attached), and Steven left the painting with Lottie. He had put a label (about 2" × 3") on the back of the painting that said: "Hare Castle—Property of Steven Wallace (+ his address and phone number)."
  - From time to time, Lottie called Steven to tell him about offers for the canvas—three offers all told—the highest one for $6,000. Steven rejected them—not enough money.

could not sell

- Maybe 10 days ago, Lottie called Steven at about 10 p.m.—told him she was going to come right over and leave "Hare Castle" at his house—she didn't think she could sell it and she needed the space in the gallery. He thought it was strange, but he didn't ask any questions and Lottie didn't let on that anything was unusual. Now he realizes she tried to do him a favor by returning the painting—apparently, she filed for bankruptcy.

- Steven is now into painting full time—retired from Univ. of Franklin at the end of the last school year. His paintings seem to have caught on, and he's been selling more and more of them (in fact, he has offered to buy back for $750 paintings he originally sold for $500—says he can probably sell them now for $2,500).

- He now has a studio in a loft on Parker St.—up until now, he's been working out of a spare room at home.

- Steven can't believe he jeopardizes his paintings every time he puts them up for sale in a gallery!

ARTISTS' EXCHANGE
West Keystone's Premier Gallery
9 Wharf Alley
West Keystone, Franklin 33322
(555) 942-5060

Inventory Receipt

Date: August 15, 1998

Artist: Steven Wallace

Agent: none

Address: 749 Galewood Circle
West Keystone, Franklin 33322

Phone: (555) 942-3342

40%

Medium	Inventory Number	Size	Title	Artist's Net
Oil/Canvas	C 6076	2' × 3'	Hare Castle	Sale price minus 40% commission to Gallery

General Conditions:

Definition

The item(s) of artwork listed above is (are) being placed by the Artist or his/her agent, as consignor, on consignment with Artists' Exchange (Gallery), as consignee, to be sold by Gallery for the account of Artist. Artist retains title to the artwork until sold by Gallery. Gallery makes no representations regarding its ability to sell any or all of said artwork or the sales price thereof. Gallery may return artwork to Artist at any time if not sold. All offers shall be communicated to Artist by Gallery, and Artist shall have the right to accept or reject any offers. Artist shall have the right to determine price of sale, except that if an offer exceeds the appraised value of the artwork plus the amount of Gallery's commission, Artist shall be required to accept the offer. Risk of loss over and above amount of Gallery's liability and hazard insurance shall be borne by Artist. Artist's Net shall be paid to Artist upon payment in full of sale price by buyer.

Lottie Zelinka
Artists' Exchange
By: Lottie Zelinka

Steven Wallace
Artist or Agent

APPRAISAL OF ARTWORK

Date: August 15, 1998

Title: "Hare Castle"

Artist: Steven Wallace

Medium: Original Oil on Canvas

Value: $25,000.00

Owner: Steven Wallace

THE ABOVE INFORMATION IS TRUE AND CORRECT TO THE BEST OF OUR KNOWLEDGE.

Signed: Lottie Zelinka
Lottie Zelinka

Title: Owner
ARTISTS' EXCHANGE

Martin R. Feldner
Attorney at Law
2298 West Arden Boulevard
West Keystone, Franklin 33322
(555) 942-4324

July 23, 1999

Mr. Steven Wallace
749 Galewood Circle
West Keystone, Franklin 33322

Re: In the Matter of Lottie Zelinka dba
Artists' Exchange
Bkpcy No. 980-7 (99)

Dear Mr. Wallace:

I represent Charles A. Sims, Trustee in Bankruptcy in the Chapter 7 bankruptcy case of Lottie Zelinka dba Artists' Exchange ("Debtor"). The Debtor filed a petition for bankruptcy under Chapter 11 of the Bankruptcy Act on May 25, 1999. She converted the case to a liquidation under Chapter 7 on July 19, 1999, on which date Mr. Sims was appointed trustee.

The Debtor has recently provided us with an accounting and business records detailing certain actions taken by her after the filing of the petition. According to Ms. Zelinka, she transferred a piece of artwork titled "Hare Castle" to you on July 20, 1999. The transfer was improper under Franklin Commercial Code §2-326 and §544 of the Bankruptcy Act.

The Trustee has elected to exercise his power under §549 of the Bankruptcy Act to avoid improper transfers made during the pendency of a bankruptcy case. Accordingly, demand is hereby made that you forthwith return to the Trustee the artwork titled "Hare Castle" or all proceeds from the sale thereof. If you fail to do so within 15 days of the date of this letter, the Trustee will commence legal action to recover the artwork or the proceeds.

Very truly yours,

Martin R. Feldner

Martin R. Feldner

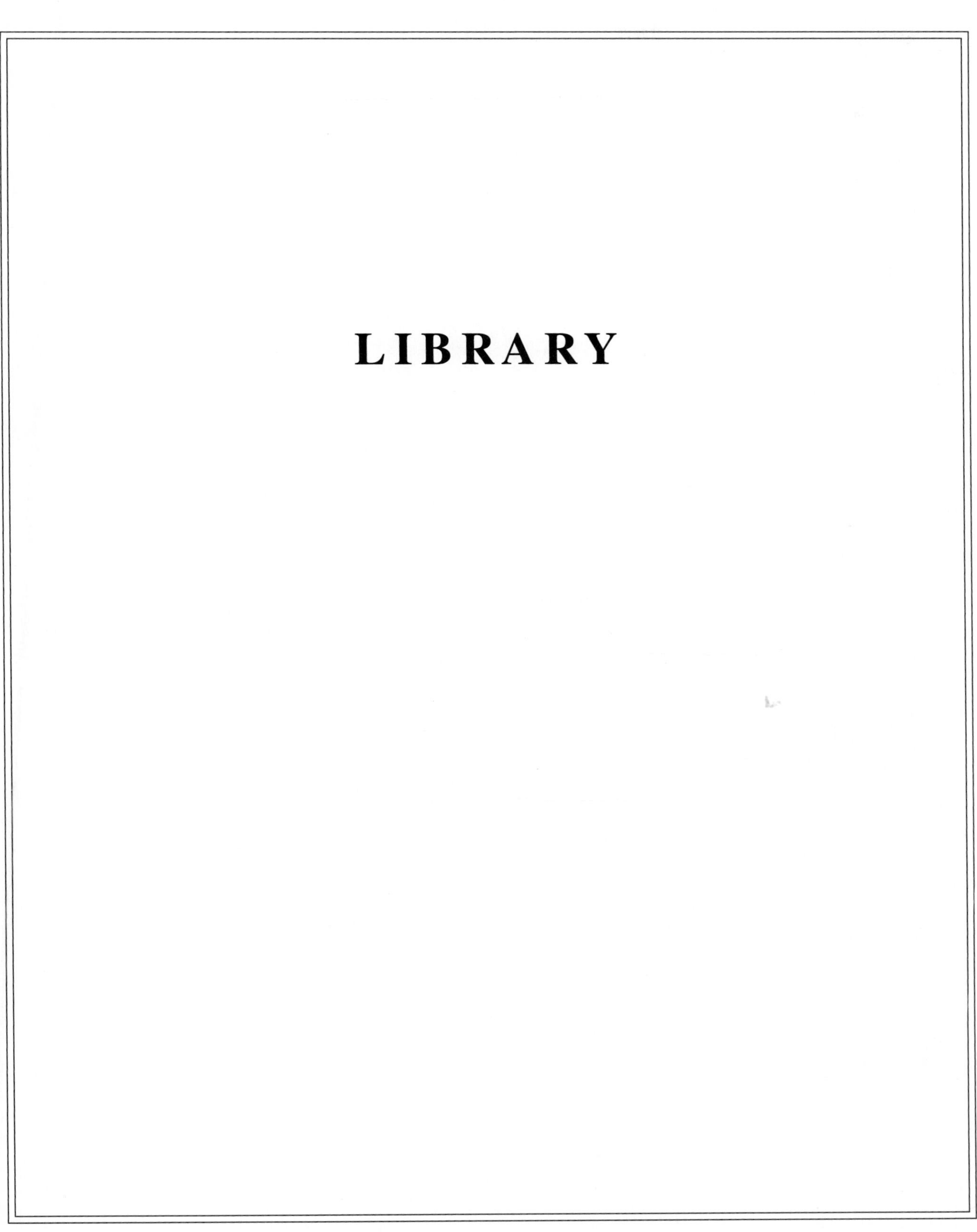

LIBRARY

Walker On Bankruptcy (3d Ed. 1995)
A Short Course for the Non-Bankruptcy Lawyer

§4 - Definitions:

* * *

§4.07 - Chapter 11: A petition for a Chapter 11 "reorganization" commences a proceeding in which the insolvent debtor continues to operate as an ongoing business with certain restrictions. The business operates by the direction of the Bankruptcy Court under the management either of a court-appointed trustee or the debtor (debtor-in-possession). The Bankruptcy Act provides for an automatic stay of legal and self-help proceedings against the debtor pending the preparation and execution of a "plan of arrangement" pursuant to which the debtor "works out" its obligations to its creditors over an extended period of time.

§4.08 - Chapter 7: Often, Chapter 11 proceedings that fail are converted to Chapter 7 cases. A petition for bankruptcy under Chapter 7 commences a proceeding for liquidation of the debtor's assets for the benefit of its creditors. A court-appointed trustee takes possession of the business, including all items in inventory, which thereafter come under the exclusive control of the trustee. The trustee is vested with all the rights possessed by the creditors of the bankrupt debtor prior to the filing of the petition. The trustee's principal function is to marshall and, subject to the rights of secured creditors, sell the assets and distribute the proceeds proportionately to the creditors in accordance with their interests. Under §549 of the Bankruptcy Act, "the trustee may avoid a transfer of property of the estate . . . that occurs after commencement of the case . . . ."

* * *

§4.27 - Schedules of Assets, Debts, and Creditors: It is incumbent on the debtor in any bankruptcy proceeding to file with the court schedules of its assets, debts and creditors. All property, including goods delivered on consignment and accounts receivable, in which the debtor has any interest must be described and its location shown on the schedule of assets. Likewise, the amount of each debt and the name and address of the creditor to whom each debt is owed are required to be listed on the schedules of debts and creditors, with designations in each case as to whether the particular creditor is secured or unsecured. The schedules of secured creditors must describe with particularity the property of the debtor in which the creditor has a security interest.

Franklin Commercial Code

* * *

§2-326. Sale on Approval and Sale or Return; Consignment Sales and Rights of Creditors.

(1) Unless otherwise agreed, if delivered goods may be returned by the buyer even though they conform to the contract, the transaction is

(a) a "sale on approval" if the goods are delivered primarily for use, and

(b) a "sale or return" if the goods are delivered primarily for resale.

(2) Except as provided in subsection (3), goods held on approval are not subject to claims of the buyer's creditors until acceptance; goods held on sale or return are subject to such claims while in the buyer's possession.

(3) Where goods are delivered to a person for sale and such person maintains a place of business at which he deals in goods of the kind involved, under a name other than the name of the person making the delivery, then, with respect to claims of creditors of the person conducting the business, the goods are deemed to be on sale or return. The provisions of this subsection are applicable even though an agreement purports to reserve title to the person making delivery until payment or resale or uses such words as "on consignment" or "on memorandum." However, this subsection is not applicable if the person making the delivery

(a) complies with an applicable law providing for a consignor's interest or the like to be evidenced by a sign, or

(b) establishes that the person conducting the business is generally known by his creditors to be substantially engaged in selling goods of others, or

(c) complies with the filing of provisions of the Article on Secured Transactions (Article 9), or

(d) delivers goods which the person making delivery used or bought for personal, family, or household purposes.

* * *

Franklin Civil Code

§3533 - Sign Law.

If a person transacts business and identifies his place of business by a sign and fails by another sign or signs in letters easy to read and posted conspicuously in his place of business to state that he is dealing in property in which others have an interest and identifying such property, then all the property, stock of goods, money, and choses in action used or acquired in such business shall, as to the creditors of such person, be liable for his debts and be in all respects treated in favor of his creditors as his property unless the provisions of Franklin Commercial Code §2-326(3)(b) through (d) are applicable.

First National Bank v. Marigold Farms, Inc.

Franklin Court of Appeal (1997)

In this case, we determine the priority of the claims of First National Bank (the Bank) and Marigold Farms, Inc. (Marigold) to $139,000 in a bank account (the Fund) of Pacific Wholesalers (Pacific). The trial court held that the Bank was entitled to the Fund. Marigold appeals.

The Bank had loaned $600,000 to Pacific and Pacific, in turn, had executed a security agreement granting the Bank a security interest in certain assets of Pacific. The Bank had perfected its security interest by filing a financing statement with the Secretary of State. Pacific defaulted on the loan and the Bank sued. Pacific and the Bank negotiated a settlement pursuant to which cash received by Pacific in the conduct of its business would be delivered to the Bank and applied to the balance of the loan. Marigold asserted claims to the same cash and also asserted that its claims had priority over any claim of the Bank. The court approved the settlement subject to resolution of the competing claims of Marigold and the Bank and ordered $139,000 of Pacific's cash receipts held in a "blocked" account (*i.e.*, the Fund).

The facts of the relationship between Marigold and Pacific are undisputed. Marigold was a grower of flowers. Pacific was a flower wholesaler. They had a longstanding relationship under which Marigold would deliver flowers to Pacific and obtain a delivery receipt. Pacific would mark the flowers with Marigold's name, package them, and attempt to sell them to retail florists at prices determined by Pacific. If the flowers were sold and Pacific received payment, Pacific would remit to Marigold 75% of the sale price, retaining 25% as its commission. If the flowers were not sold, Pacific would with Marigold's approval discard them, and Marigold would receive nothing for those flowers. It is also undisputed that the Bank had no actual knowledge of the nature of the commercial arrangement between Marigold and Pacific.

The Bank's financing statement and the security agreement between Pacific and the Bank describe the collateral as: "All inventory used in Pacific's business now owned or hereafter acquired; and all accounts and rights to payment of every kind now or hereafter arising in favor of Pacific out of Pacific's business, including all proceeds from the sale of inventory."

Under the Franklin Commercial Code, it is clear that, upon delivery of Marigold's flowers to Pacific, the flowers became part of Pacific's "inventory" because they were held by Pacific for sale. The Fund consists of "proceeds" of this inventory.

Marigold contends that its sale of flowers to Pacific was a "consignment sale," that Pacific never had title to the flowers and that, therefore, Pacific never owned the collateral (inventory) to which the Bank's security interest could attach. Marigold also asserts that Franklin Commercial Code §2-326(3) is inapplicable in this case.

A consignment sale is one in which the merchant takes possession of goods and holds them for sale with the obligation to pay the owner of the goods from the proceeds of the sale. If the merchant does not sell the goods, the merchant may return them to the owner (or, as in this case of perishable flowers, discard them) without obligation. In a consignment sale transaction, title to the goods generally remains with the original owner. The arrangement between Marigold and Pacific was a consignment sale arrangement; Marigold was the consignor and Pacific was the consignee. Under FCC §2-326(3), which clearly governs this transaction, the retention of title by Marigold is irrelevant to the ability of the Bank to obtain a security interest in the collateral.

Marigold does not contend that it complied with the filing requirement under the secured transactions division of the FCC as provided for in §2-326(3)(c). Nor does Marigold claim that it complied with an applicable "sign law" under §2-326(3)(a) or that it had delivered goods it had "used or bought for personal, family, or household purposes" as provided for in §2-326(3)(d).[1] Rather, Marigold claims that, as provided for in §2-326(3)(b), Pacific was generally known by its creditors "to be substantially engaged in selling goods of others."

At the evidentiary hearing, Bank officials testified unequivocally that the Bank was unaware that Pacific was selling the goods of others. Three flower growers who also consigned flowers to Pacific testified that Pacific was "well-known as a commission selling agent" and that other flower growers knew it as well.

---

[1] The obvious reason for the exception for goods "used or bought for personal, family, or household purposes" is to avoid the situation where one who is not a merchant, and who should not therefore be deemed to know of the intricacies by which merchants protect their interests under the commercial code, unwittingly loses his right to property. If a householder occasionally delivers an item of property to a dealer to see if the dealer can sell it for him, the FCC protects that item from claims of the dealer's creditors. On the other hand, if the deliverer is one who deals in goods of the kind sold by the person to whom he delivers the goods, he should be held to the rules in the FCC that bind merchants. There are hybrid situations such as, for example, where one collects gemstones for his personal use and enjoyment but also regularly places the gems on consignment with jewelers to test the market and sell if the price is right. At some point the casual collector crosses over the line from being the householder, whom the personal goods exception is designed to protect, to being a merchant or dealer, who is bound by the filing or other protective provisions of §2-326. In this case, Marigold is clearly at the extreme end of the merchant spectrum.

Although it is true that consignors, all of whom are necessarily also creditors, might know that Pacific deals in the goods of others, such knowledge cannot be extrapolated into a fact "generally known by its creditors." The purpose of §2-326(3) is to protect general creditors of the consignee from claims of consignors who have undisclosed arrangements with the consignee. To impute as a matter of law the self-interested knowledge of the consignors/creditors to the general creditors does not give general creditors the opportunity to protect themselves from the undisclosed interests of the consignors.[2]

A consignor asserting that the consignee is "generally known by his creditors to be substantially engaged in selling the goods of others" must establish such general knowledge by proof other than that a few other consignors know that fact. He must establish that nonconsignor creditors possess the requisite knowledge. Marigold failed to meet that burden of proof.

Accordingly, we affirm.

---

[2] The result might be different if all or most of Pacific's creditors were flower consignors but that fact does not appear from the evidence in this case. If all or most of the creditors *were* consignors, then one might be able to conclude that the creditors did have such "general knowledge."

In re Levy

Bankruptcy No. 29054

United States District Court, E.D. Pennsylvania (1993)

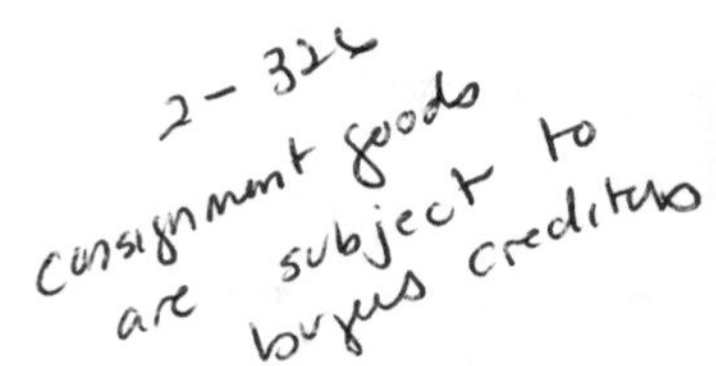

In December 1992, Bernard Levy, owner of a retail shoe store in Reading, Pennsylvania, filed a voluntary petition in bankruptcy. One of his suppliers, Acme Shoe Co. (Acme), had delivered a stock of shoes to Levy for resale in his store under the terms, of a written agreement in which Levy, the bankrupt, acknowledged that the shoes were "on consignment" and could be returned to the consignor at any time.

Acme has filed a reclamation petition to recover the shoes it delivered to the bankrupt. The trustee resists the petition on the ground that the transaction was one of "sale or return," and, since there had been no compliance with §2-326(3) of the Pennsylvania Uniform Commercial Code, the stock of shoes while in Levy's possession was subject to the claims of Levy's creditors.

Acme concedes that it had not filed any financing statements in the public records offices. Acme did, however, produce evidence that small cards had been placed upon certain sections of shelving in Levy's store where Acme's shoes were stored and displayed, identifying the shoes placed on those sections of the shelving as shoes manufactured by Acme.

Under §2-326 of the UCC, if goods are delivered to a consignee primarily for resale with the understanding that they may be returned by the consignee, the transaction is one of "sale or return" and such goods are subject to the claims of the buyer's creditors while in the buyer's possession even though the consignor has retained title. The consignor may avoid the consequences of having the goods subjected to the claims of the consignee's creditors by doing one or more of three things: (a) complying with "an applicable law" evidencing a consignor's interest or the like by a sign to that effect, or (b) establishing that the consignee is generally known by his creditors to be substantially engaged in selling the goods of others, or (c) complying with the provisions for filing financing statements and other notice documents under UCC Article 9 having to do with secured transactions.

There was no filing under Article 9. There was an effort by Acme to protect its goods by posting signs on the sections of shelving where its shoes were kept, but Acme has failed to show that there is in Pennsylvania "an applicable [sign] law" as that term is used in §2-326(3)(a). The phrase "an applicable law" means a statute, and there is no such statute in Pennsylvania. Absent such a statute or an Article 9 filing, Acme is left with the burden of proving that Levy was generally known by his creditors to be substantially engaged in selling the goods of others.

Acme argues that, although the absence of a sign law might mean that the cards Acme caused to be placed on the shelves did not invoke the "sign law" subsection of §2-326, the cards nonetheless served to impart knowledge that Levy was selling the goods of others. That argument might have had some merit if Acme could have shown that the cards did in fact impart such knowledge to Levy's creditors to such an extent that it was "generally known" by the creditors and that the cards also suggested that Levy was "substantially engaged" in selling goods not owned by him. On the record before the court, however, the most that can be said is that the cards were designed to impart to Levy's *customers*, not his creditors, the knowledge that the shoes were Acme's. Thus, Acme's proof fell short.

Under §544 of the Bankruptcy Act, the trustee is vested with the rights that the creditors had prior to the filing of the petition in bankruptcy. Section 2-326(2) of the UCC expressly makes goods held on sale or return subject to the claims of the debtor's creditors. That is the situation in this case.

Acme's petition for reclamation is denied.

In re Steven Wallace

Sample Answer

MEMORANDUM

TO: Eva Morales
FROM: Applicant
RE: Steven Wallace—"Hare Castle" Painting

INTRODUCTION

In this case we must show that our client, Steven Wallace, is entitled to retain possession of his painting, "Hare Castle," and that he is not obligated to turn the painting over to the Trustee in Bankruptcy. We must prove that either (i) the painting is not an asset or part of the inventory of Artists' Exchange, or (ii) if the painting is an asset, it is still exempt from the interests and claims of Artists' Exchange's creditors because the consignment is subject to at least one of the four defenses provided in section 2-326(3) of the Franklin Commercial Code ("FCC"). Part I of this memorandum will examine the first issue and analyze the legal and factual bases of the trustee's claim that the painting is an asset of the bankruptcy estate of Artists' Exchange. Part II will discuss the four defenses under the FCC in relation to the facts of our client's case.

I. IS "HARE CASTLE" AN ASSET OR PART OF THE INVENTORY OF ARTISTS' EXCHANGE?

Under FCC section 2-326(3), where goods are delivered to a person for sale, and such person maintains a place of business dealing in goods of the kind involved under a name other than the name of the person making the delivery, the goods are deemed to be on "sale or return." This is so ***even though*** the agreement purports to reserve title to the person making delivery until payment or resale, or uses a word such as "consignment." This rule was applied in *First National Bank v. Marigold Farms, Inc.,* where Marigold regularly delivered flowers to Pacific Wholesalers for resale. If Pacific sold the flowers, Marigold was given 75% of the proceeds. If Pacific did not sell the flowers, the flowers (because they were perishable) were discarded with Marigold's permission, and Marigold did not receive any money. The court concluded that the flowers became part of Pacific's inventory upon delivery by Marigold because they were held by Pacific for sale, and that retention of title by Marigold was irrelevant to the ability of another creditor (the bank) to obtain a security interest in the goods.

It is clear that our client delivered "Hare Castle" to Artists' Exchange on consignment. Mr. Wallace expressed his belief that most of the art in Artists' Exchange was on consignment from artists. Furthermore, he took steps to assure that he would retain title to the painting by labeling the back of the painting and by signing the inventory receipt that contained the explicit language that he would retain title and the right to accept or reject offers. Therefore, this was a sale on consignment.

However, a court applying FCC section 2-326(3) would find the arrangement to be a sale or return, and under the *Marigold Farms* case would conclude that once Mr. Wallace delivered "Hare Castle" to Artists' Exchange, the painting became part of the shop's inventory. This conclusion would also be supported by the fact that the receipt signed by our client included the words "Inventory Receipt" in large print near the top. Our client's steps to retain title would probably be viewed as irrelevant with respect to a creditor's claim.

Thus, "Hare Castle" is an asset of Artists' Exchange, is subject to the requirements of the Bankruptcy Act, and is under the exclusive control of the Trustee in Bankruptcy.

There is an issue we need to examine. Section 549 of the Bankruptcy Act states that the trustee may avoid a transfer of property that ***occurs after commencement*** of the case. Our file notes are unclear as to the exact date that the painting was returned to Mr. Wallace, but it appears that it was about July 16 or 17, 1999. The Chapter 7 case commenced on July 19, 1999. Therefore, it is arguable that the transfer of the painting occurred before commencement of the case. However, the Chapter 11 case commenced on May 25, 1999, well before the transfer. We need to research to see which date is relevant for purposes of section 549—the date of the Chapter 7 case or the date of the original Chapter 11 case.

II. DOES STEVEN WALLACE HAVE A DEFENSE UNDER FCC §2-326(3)?

This section will examine the defenses separately and the relevant helpful facts.

A. Sign Law

To take advantage of the defense contained in section 2-326(3)(a), there must be an applicable sign law. Franklin has such a law. [Franklin Civil Code §3533] For the sign law to apply to our client's case, we must prove that Lottie Zelinka, the owner of Artists' Exchange, posted an easy to read, conspicuously placed sign in the shop that (i) states that Artists' Exchange deals in property in which others have an interest and (ii) identifies such property. Mr. Wallace believes that there is a sign at the front of the store stating that all offers would be forwarded to the artists; however, he is not ***positive*** that such a sign exists. Nor do we know whether that language is adequate to notify parties that others have an interest in the artwork in the shop and whether it identifies the particular property. There is also a question of whether Ms. Zelinka owns some of the items. At this point, we need to determine whether there actually is a sign in the shop and exactly what it says. We can determine this by asking Ms. Zelinka, although we may have to go through her attorney as well as the trustee. One of our law clerks could also pay a visit to the shop to see if there is a sign and where it is located, although we may have to proceed through the same channels for permission to enter the shop. Hopefully, we can get pictures of the sign. We also need to find out from Ms. Zelinka or the trustee if all items for sale in the shop are owned by the artists and are there on consignment. Furthermore, we need to review other sign cases regarding visibility and notice issues.

B. Establishing that Artists' Exchange Is Generally Known by its Creditors to be Substantially Engaged in Selling Goods of Others

To be entitled to this defense [FCC §2-326(3)(b)], a consignor must establish that a consignee is "generally known by his creditors to be substantially engaged in selling the goods of others." We must determine who Ms. Zelinka's creditors are. If they are mainly consignors, then clearly they would know that she sells goods of others. We could ask Ms. Zelinka, her attorney, or the trustee about her creditors, and probably we could find out information from the bankruptcy petition and court records.

If the majority of her creditors are not consignors, based on *Marigold Farms*, we would have to show that these nonconsignor creditors knew that she substantially sold the goods of others. We need to determine whether it is a well-known fact (or common knowledge) that ***many or most*** art galleries sell the goods of others. The knowledge that most galleries operate on consignment arguably could be imputed to creditors of Artists' Exchange, regardless of whether they are artists. We should be able to determine this rather easily by calling the various galleries in the area and by contacting an expert in the field of art dealing. We should also contact other artists and ask them and perhaps peruse their contracts. We should also talk to other creditors and review the Artists' Exchange's advertising to see whether it indicates a consignment arrangement.

Also lending support to our position is the sign that our client believes is posted in the shop and possibly the labels on the backs of the paintings, although the court in *In re Levy* held that cards placed on certain sections of shelving where a consignor's shoes were displayed were not adequate. Again, we need to check all the details of the sign and see whether labels exist on all the consigned paintings. We should also check on how long Ms. Zelinka has been operating the gallery to see how well-known it is and, consequently, how well-known its practices are.

C. Compliance with FCC Article 9

Nothing in our facts indicates that our client filed any financing statements or other documents pursuant to FCC Article 9. [FCC §2-326(c)] Thus, this defense is inapplicable to our client's case. However, we should ask Mr. Wallace to be sure that he did not file.

D. Goods Used for Personal, Family, or Household Purposes

Section 2-326(3)(d) provides a defense for persons who do not normally deal in consignments, but may occasionally deliver an item to a consignee for resale. It does not apply to a merchant, who we can define as one who normally deals in the goods delivered to the consignee. Facts that would support our use of this defense include the fact that "Hare Castle" was a painting that Mr. Wallace created for his own pleasure and not for sale, it originally hung in his dining room and was hanging there for two years, and he never thought about trying to sell it before Ms. Zelinka approached him with the idea. The fact that Mr. Wallace and his wife selected and bought a carpet to coordinate with the colors in the painting strengthens our argument that "Hare Castle" was intended for personal use (enjoyment) by the Wallace family.

Also, we should argue that while Mr. Wallace had previously sold a few of his works, he did not deal in the sale of his artwork on a regular basis, certainly not regular enough to be considered a merchant. We can use his statement that he could not believe that his paintings were jeopardized every time he put them up for sale in a gallery to support that he was unaware of the FCC rules affecting merchants and therefore had no idea of the possible consequences of entering into a "sale or return" situation. We should also confirm Mr. Wallace's beliefs by talking to his wife and other family members and friends who are aware of the situation. Although Mr. Wallace is now creating artwork full time, this is irrelevant to his position at the time of the transaction at hand.

Thus, depending on what our investigation shows about the sign and the creditors' knowledge, we may have those defenses available to us. At this point, however, our best defense appears to be the personal use defense.

Multistate Performance Test

Kantor v. Bellows

National Conference of Bar Examiners

Preface

This Multistate Performance Test is a reprint of one of the three MPTs which were administered in July 1999.

The instructions for the test appear on the next page. On the actual MPT, they will appear on the back cover of the test.

INSTRUCTIONS

1. You will have 90 minutes to complete this session of the examination. This performance test is designed to evaluate your ability to handle a select number of legal authorities in the context of a factual problem involving a client.

2. The problem is set in the fictitious state of Franklin, in the fictitious Fifteenth Circuit of the United States. Columbia and Olympia are also fictitious states in the Fifteenth Circuit. In Franklin, the trial court of general jurisdiction is the District Court, the intermediate appellate court is the Court of Appeal, and the highest court is the Supreme Court.

3. You will have two kinds of materials with which to work: a File and a Library. The first document in the File is a memorandum containing the instructions for the task you are to complete. The other documents in the File contain factual information about your case and may include some facts that are not relevant.

4. The Library contains the legal authorities needed to complete the task and may also include some authorities that are not relevant. Any cases may be real, modified, or written solely for the purpose of this examination. If the cases appear familiar to you, do not assume that they are precisely the same as you have read before. Read them thoroughly, as if they all were new to you. You should assume that cases were decided in the jurisdictions and on the dates shown. In citing cases from the Library, you may use abbreviations and omit page references.

5. Your response must be written in the answer book provided. If you are taking this examination on a laptop computer, your jurisdiction will provide you with specific instructions. In answering this performance test, you should concentrate on the materials provided in the File and Library. What you have learned in law school and elsewhere provides the general background for analyzing the problem; the File and Library provide the specific materials with which you must work.

6. Although there are no restrictions on how you apportion your time, you should be sure to allocate ample time (about 45 minutes) to reading and digesting the materials and to organizing your answer before you begin writing it. You may make notes anywhere in the test materials; blank pages are provided at the end of the booklet. You may not tear pages from the question booklet.

7. This performance test will be graded on your responsiveness to the instructions regarding the task you are to complete, which are given to you in the first memorandum in the File, and on the content, thoroughness, and organization of your response.

Kantor v. Bellows

FILE

LIBRARY

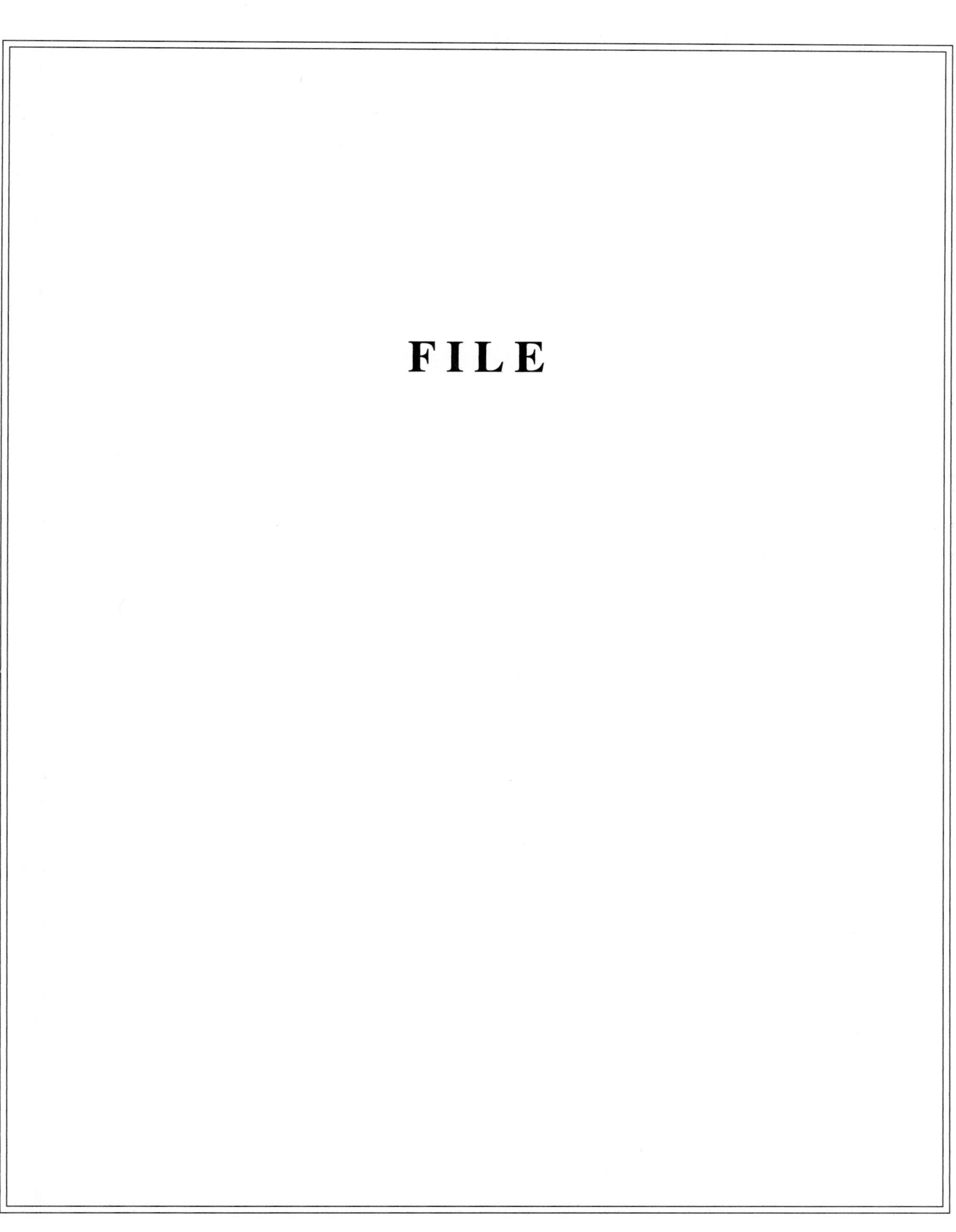

FILE

Crystal, Hughes & Bernstein
Attorneys at Law
47 Bridge Street
Oakton, Franklin 33311

Memorandum

July 27, 1999

To: Applicant
From: Pat Moore
Re: Linda Kantor

Linda Kantor has asked us to represent her in her divorce from her husband, Bill Bellows. The only contested issue is whether the enhanced earning capacity created by Bill's law degree will be treated as property, subject to division between the parties. Franklin has an equitable distribution statute as part of its divorce law, but two divisions of our Court of Appeal are in conflict on the issue of how to treat spousal contributions to professional degrees. The Franklin Supreme Court has not ruled on this issue.

I want to persuade Bill's lawyer, Shawn Martin, that we have a good chance of convincing a court that the enhanced earning capacity created by Bill's law degree and license to practice law is property subject to equitable distribution. As the law now stands in Franklin, there are two conflicting policy views. It won't do us any good to simply distinguish the two cases. Our job is to convince the other side that the Supreme Court will most likely end up adopting the view that favors us.

As the first step in the negotiation process, I want to send a letter to Shawn Martin that:

- argues that Linda is entitled to a share of Bill's enhanced earning capacity;
- addresses counter-arguments that would deny or diminish her share; and
- includes a specific dollar demand that is justified in light of these arguments.

Please draft such a letter for my signature. Be sure to discuss both the legal principles and the facts of our case in making the arguments. Shawn is a thoroughly competent family law practitioner and a straight-shooter. I have no hesitancy in honestly laying out my entire case.

Crystal, Hughes & Bernstein
Attorneys at Law
47 Bridge Street
Oakton, Franklin 33311

Memorandum June 1, 1999

To: File
From: Pat Moore
Re: Linda Kantor - Interview Notes

Linda Kantor, who is 29, has been married to William Bellows, also 29, for seven years. They have one child, Jason, who is three. They have agreed that they want to be divorced, and Linda believes that they are in agreement as to most issues. The only issue about which there seems to be dispute is how William's law degree will be treated in the divorce.

The parties married soon after they both graduated from the University of Franklin in June 1992. Linda began work as a programmer for Computech, a computer consulting firm specializing in the development of software, and Bill as a legislative aide in the office of Andy Pepper, a state assemblyman from Oakton. Three years later, Bill entered law school at the University of Franklin Law Center, which is in Oakton. Linda was also interested in attending law school, but the parties decided that Bill would attend first, with Linda attending after Bill graduated. They both wanted to have children soon and thought it would be easier to stagger their law school careers. Jason was born just as Bill began law school in the fall of 1995. Linda got a three-month, paid parental leave from Computech, after which she returned to work full time. Linda arranged to share with another couple who have a child Jason's age the cost of hiring a child care worker to care for the two children from 8:30 a.m. to 5:30 p.m. While Bill was in law school, Linda did most of the housework and child care. (She estimates that she did more than 75% of each.) She usually did Jason's morning routine with him, picked him up from the child care worker at 5:30 p.m., gave him dinner and a bath, and played with him in the evening. Bill participated in these activities, but usually in a secondary kind of role. Because of flexible policies at Computech, Linda was able to take time off work when Jason was sick.

Linda has continued at Computech to the present, where she has advanced steadily, gaining an increasingly important role in the development of specialized software programs for small- to medium-sized institutions. The company is committed to personnel development, devoting significant resources to those employees it sees as promising. Although Linda has been identified as one of the "stars," she has not been able to take full advantage of all the educational opportunities they offer because of her many responsibilities at home. She has been able to attend only one extended, out-of-town workshop in software design each year, but could have gone to as many as three each year at the company's expense if her circumstances had permitted it. In addition, the company pays for employees to take up to four graduate-level courses in computer science each year at the university, but Linda has been able to take advantage of this opportunity only one semester in which she took one course. Linda has contributed all of her earnings to the family. When she first started at Computech, her salary was $16,000. She has received steady raises as her responsibilities have increased, and she currently earns $35,000 per year.

Bill was successful in law school, graduating in June of 1998 *magna cum laude*, with a special award for the high quality of his performance in the clinical program. During the three years Bill was attending law school, Linda contributed her entire pay of $85,000 to support the family. Bill's tuition averaged approximately $12,000 per year; he obtained loans amounting to $25,000, and his parents gave him another $10,000. For two of the six semesters, he worked 10 hours per week, earning a total of $3,000 from this employment. Last summer, he took and passed the Franklin bar exam. He obtained a position in the prestigious Honors Program at the Franklin State Attorney General's Office, which he began in September 1998. In that program, he rotates for a year through the different divisions in the A.G.'s office and at the end of the year can choose a permanent position among any of the positions available, if he wishes. His salary for the first year of the program is $35,000, but it will go up to $40,000 the following year if he decides to work there on a permanent basis. Because of his excellent law school record and the prestige of the Honors Program, he would have no trouble getting a job with a major law firm in Oakton, or anywhere else in the state, where a beginning salary could be as high as $61,000.

Linda and Bill have accumulated almost no assets during their marriage. Before Bill entered law school, they purchased two cars, one in the first year of their marriage and the other in the third year, both of which they continue to drive. They rent the modest two-bedroom house they live in. They

accumulated savings of approximately $3,000 when they were both working, but that money was spent after Jason was born and Bill began law school. All of their money has gone into paying living expenses, raising a child, and putting Bill through school.

Linda feels very strongly that, as part of the divorce, she should be able to share in the benefits from Bill's law degree. They decided together that he would go to law school first, and she worked very hard for three years to make that possible. Now it's supposed to be her turn. She also is anxious to get on with her own education, although she has decided that she would like to pursue full-time graduate studies in computer science rather than go to law school. Although Computech has been a good place for her, she has become interested in the more theoretical aspects of computer science. After all her sacrifices, Linda feels that she should be able to share in the benefits of Bill's law degree.

Although Linda and Bill have been able on their own to agree that they will share joint legal and physical custody of Jason and that Bill will pay child support, they have not been able to agree on how to treat Bill's law degree. I discussed with Linda litigation of this issue, including the uncertain state of the law. She is not averse to trial on the issue, if necessary, but she would prefer to resolve the matter through negotiation because she would like to avoid the expense of a trial and maintain a cordial relationship with Bill.

Franklin State University

Bentonville, Franklin 33312

Millicent Elstein, Ph.D.
Professor of Economics

July 20, 1999

Patricia Moore
Crystal, Hughes & Bernstein
Attorneys at Law
47 Bridge Street
Oakton, Franklin 33311

Dear Ms. Moore:

Please excuse the delay in responding to your inquiry. As requested, I provide the following summary of my analysis of the value of the law degree held by Bill Bellows.

In arriving at the present value, I began by comparing the projected life earnings of an average college graduate to the projected earnings of two types of lawyers: a lawyer engaged in private practice in a large law firm and a lawyer employed in government service. I used the time between Mr. Bellows' admission to practice and his 65th birthday in making these projections. I then considered the impact of taxes, inflation, and interest rates. From all this, I calculated the present value of these projected earnings.

Based on these calculations, it is my opinion that the present value of Mr. Bellows' law degree is $520,000 should he choose to remain in government service and $820,000 should he enter the private practice of law.

A complete report will follow under separate cover. If I can be of any additional assistance, please let me know.

Sincerely,

Millicent Elstein

Millicent Elstein, Ph.D.

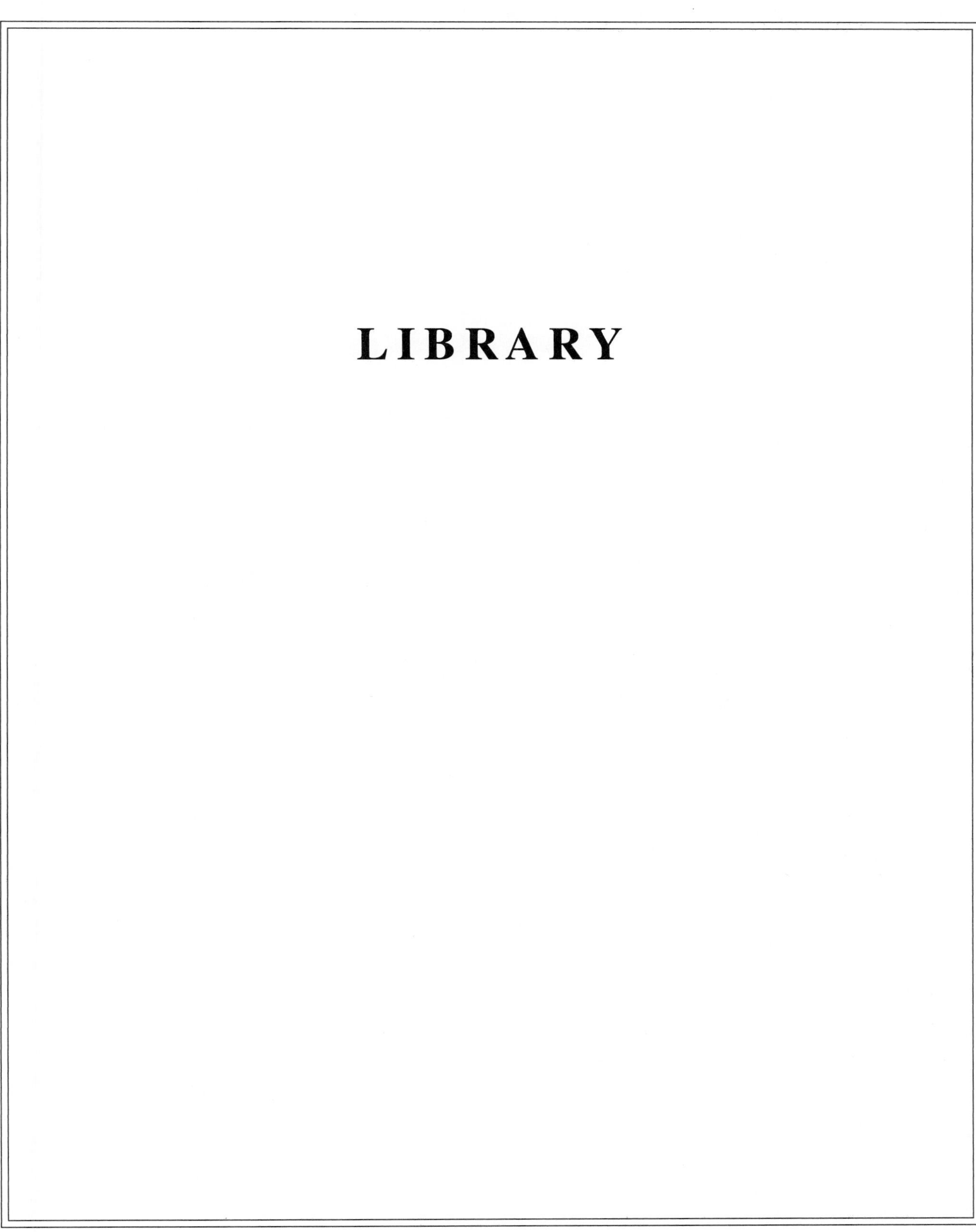

LIBRARY

Franklin Domestic Relations Law

Section 3 - The term "marital property" shall mean all property acquired by either or both spouses during the marriage. Marital property shall not include separate property as hereinafter defined.

Section 4 - The term "separate property" shall mean

A. property acquired before marriage or property acquired by bequest, devise, or descent, or gift from a party other than the spouse;

B. compensation for personal injuries;

C. property acquired in exchange for or the increase in value of separate property as defined in subpart (A) of this section, except when the increase is attributable to the direct or indirect contribution by the party not having title;

D. property described as separate property by valid written agreement of the parties.

Section 5 - Disposition of property in divorce actions.

A. The court, in an action for divorce, shall determine the respective rights of the parties in their separate or marital property.

B. Separate property shall remain such.

C. Marital property shall be distributed equitably between the parties, considering the circumstances of the case and the respective parties.

D. In determining an equitable disposition of property under paragraph C, the court shall consider

(1) the income and property of each party at the time of marriage and at the time of the commencement of the action;

(2) the duration of the marriage and the age and health of both parties;

(3) any equitable claim to, interest in, or direct or indirect contribution made to the acquisition of such marital property by the party not having title, including joint efforts or expenditures and contributions and services as a spouse, parent, wage earner and homemaker, and to the career or career potential of the other party;

(4) the liquid or non-liquid character of all marital property;

(5) the probable future financial circumstances of each party;

(6) the impossibility or difficulty of evaluating any component asset or any interest in a business, corporation, or profession, and the economic desirability of retaining such asset or interest intact and free from any claim or interference by the other party.

E. In any action in which the court determines that an equitable distribution is appropriate but would be impractical or burdensome or where the distribution of an interest in a business, corporation, or profession would be contrary to law, the court, in lieu of equitable distribution, shall make a distributive award in order to achieve equity between the parties.

Section 6 - Maintenance.

A. Except where the parties have entered into an agreement, in any divorce action the court may order temporary maintenance or maintenance in such amount as justice requires, having regard for the standard of living of the parties established during the marriage, whether the party in whose favor maintenance is granted lacks sufficient property and income to provide for his or her reasonable needs, whether the other party has sufficient property or income to provide for the reasonable needs of the other, and the circumstances of the case and the respective parties. In determining the amount and duration of maintenance, the court shall consider

(1) the income and property of the respective parties, including marital property distributed pursuant to Section 5;

(2) the duration of the marriage and the age and health of both parties;

(3) the present and future earning capacity of both parties;

(4) the ability of the party seeking maintenance to become self-supporting and, if applicable, the period of time and training necessary therefor;

(5) reduced or lost lifetime earning capacity of the party seeking maintenance as a result of having foregone or delayed education, training, employment, or career opportunities during the marriage;

(6) the presence of children of the marriage in the respective homes of the parties;

(7) contributions and services of the party seeking maintenance as a spouse, parent, wage earner, and homemaker, and to the career or career potential of the other party.

B. The court may award permanent maintenance, but an award of maintenance shall terminate upon the death of either party or upon the recipient's valid or invalid marriage.

Reginald Morgan v. Victoria Morgan

Franklin Court of Appeal, Second Appellate Division (1998)

The question in this case is whether the defendant, Victoria Morgan, has the right to share the value of a professional business (MBA) degree earned by her former husband, Reginald Morgan, during their marriage. The court must decide whether the plaintiff's degree is "property" for purposes of Franklin Domestic Relations Law Section 3. If the MBA degree is not property, we must still decide whether Victoria can nonetheless recover the money she contributed to her husband's support while he pursued his professional education. We hold that Reginald's professional degree is not property and therefore not subject to equitable distribution but that Victoria may be reimbursed for her financial contributions to Reginald's professional training.

When the parties married in 1984, Reginald had an engineering degree and Victoria had a bachelor of science degree. From that time until the parties separated in October 1991, they generally shared all household expenses. The sole exception was the period between September 1988 and January 1990, when the plaintiff attended the Wharton School of the University of Pennsylvania and received an MBA degree.

During the 16-month period in which Reginald attended school, Victoria contributed $26,000 to cover household expenses plus another $10,000 for Reginald's tuition. Reginald made no financial contribution while he was a student. After receiving his degree, Reginald went to work as a commercial lending officer for Franklin National Bank. Meanwhile, in 1989 Victoria began a part-time graduate program at Franklin State University, paid for by her employer, that led to a master's degree in microbiology one year after the parties had separated. Victoria worked full time throughout the course of her graduate schooling.

The trial court granted a divorce. At the time of trial, Reginald's annual income was $48,200 and Victoria's income was $40,000. No claim for maintenance was made. The parties owned no real property and they divided the small amount of their personal property by agreement. The only issue at trial was Victoria's claim for an equitable share of the present value of the enhanced future earning capacity of plaintiff attributable to the MBA degree.

The trial court did not attempt to determine the value of Reginald's MBA degree. Instead, the court held that the education and degree obtained by Reginald constituted a property right and reimbursed Victoria for the contribution she made to acquiring the degree. The court awarded her the $10,000 she contributed to Reginald's tuition and 50% of her $26,000 contribution to household expenses during the educational period.

This court must decide whether the legislature intended an MBA degree to be "property" so

that, if acquired by either spouse during a marriage, its value must be equitably distributed upon divorce. Since there is no legislative history on the meaning of the word "property" and the statute itself offers no guidance, statutory construction in this case means little more than an inquiry into the extent to which professional degrees and licenses share the qualities of other things that the legislature and courts have treated as property.

Franklin courts have subjected a broad range of assets and interests to equitable distribution, including vested but unmatured private pensions, military retirement pay and disability benefits, and personal injury claims. This court, however, has never subjected to equitable distribution an asset whose future monetary value is as uncertain and unquantifiable as a professional degree or license. A professional license or degree cannot be sold and its value cannot readily be determined. It represents the opportunity to obtain an amount of money only upon the occurrence of highly uncertain future events. The value of a professional degree is nothing more than the possibility of enhanced earnings that the particular academic credential will provide, income that the degree holder might never acquire. Moreover, any assets resulting from future income for professional services would be property acquired after the marriage; the statute restricts equitable distribution to property acquired during the marriage.

Valuing a professional degree in the hands of any particular individual at the start of his or her career would involve a gamut of calculations that reduces to little more than guesswork. Even if such estimates could be made, however, there would remain a world of unforeseen events that could affect the earning potential—not to mention the actual earnings—of any particular degree holder. A person qualified by education for a given profession may choose not to practice it, may fail at it, or may practice in a specialty, location, or manner which generates less than the average income enjoyed by fellow professionals. The potential for inequity to the failed professional or one who changes careers is at once apparent; his or her spouse will have been awarded a share of something which never existed in any real sense.

Valuing educational assets, even if they were marital property, in terms of the cost to the supporting spouse of obtaining the degree would be an erroneous application of equitable distribution law. The cost of a professional degree has little to do with any real value of the degree and fails to consider at all the nonfinancial efforts made by the degree holder in completing his course of study. The cost of a spouse's financial contributions has no logical connection to the value of that degree. The cost approach is not conceptually predicated on a property theory at all but rather represents a general notion of how to do equity. Equitable distribution in these cases derives from the proposition that the supporting spouse should be reimbursed for contribution to the marital unit that, because of the divorce, did not bear its expected fruit for the supporting spouse.

Although the trial court found that the degree was distributable property, it actually reimbursed the defendant without attempting to give her part of the value of the degree. This court does not support reimbursement between former spouses in maintenance proceedings as a general principle. Marriage is not a business arrangement in which the parties keep track of debits and credits, their accounts to be settled upon divorce. Rather, marriage is a shared enterprise, a joint undertaking in many ways akin to a partnership. It is improper for a court to treat a marriage as an arm's-length transaction by allowing a spouse to come into court after the fact and make legal arguments regarding unjust enrichment. Courts should assume, in the absence of contrary proof, that the decision to obtain a professional degree was mutual and took into account what sacrifices the husband and wife needed to make in furtherance of that decision. But every joint undertaking has its bounds of fairness. Where a partner to marriage takes the benefits of his or her spouse's support in obtaining a professional degree or license with the understanding that future benefits will accrue and inure to both of them, and the marriage is then terminated without the supported spouse giving anything in return, an unfairness has occurred that calls for a remedy.

In this case, the supporting spouse made financial contributions towards her husband's professional education with the expectation that both parties would enjoy material benefits flowing from the professional license or degree. It is therefore patently unfair that the supporting spouse be denied the mutually anticipated benefit while the supported spouse keeps not only the degree, but also all of the financial and material rewards flowing from it. Furthermore, in this case a supporting spouse has contributed more than mere earnings to her husband with the mutual expectation that both of them will realize and enjoy material improvements. Also, the wife has presumably made personal financial sacrifices, resulting in a reduced or lowered standard of living. She has postponed present consumption and a higher standard of living for the future prospect of greater support and material benefits. If the parties had remained married long enough after the husband had completed his postgraduate education so that they could have accumulated substantial property, the court would have determined how much of the marital property to allocate to the wife, taking into account her contributions to her husband's earning capacity. In this sense, an award that is referable to the spouse's monetary contributions to her partner's education significantly implicates basic considerations of marital support and standard of living.

Although not explicitly provided for in Section 6 of our Domestic Relations Law, to provide a fair and effective means of compensating a supporting spouse, we now introduce the concept of *reimbursement maintenance* into divorce proceedings. Regardless of the appropriateness of permanent maintenance or the presence or absence of marital property to be equitably distributed, there will be circumstances where a supporting spouse should be reimbursed for the financial contributions he or she made to the spouse's successful professional training. Such reimbursement maintenance should cover all

financial contributions towards the former spouse's education, including household expenses, educational costs, school travel expenses and any other contributions used by the supported spouse in obtaining his or her degree or license. Although courts may not make any permanent distribution of the value of professional degrees and licenses, whether based upon estimated worth or cost, where a spouse has received financial contributions used in obtaining a professional degree or license with the expectation of deriving material benefits for both, that spouse may be called upon to reimburse the supporting spouse for the amount of contributions received.

We do not hold that every spouse who contributes toward his or her partner's education or professional training is entitled to reimbursement maintenance. Only monetary contributions made with the mutual and shared expectation that both parties to the marriage will derive increased income and material benefits should be a basis for such an award. For example, it is unlikely that a spouse who has been married to a financially successful executive and returns to school after many years of homemaking would upon divorce be required to reimburse her husband for his contributions toward her degree.

We remand the case so the trial court can determine whether reimbursement maintenance should be awarded and, if so, what amount is appropriate.

Michael Sooke v. Loretta Sooke

Franklin Court of Appeal, Fourth Appellate Division (1999)

In this divorce action, the parties' only asset of any consequence is the husband's medical degree. The principal issue is whether that degree, acquired during their marriage, is marital property. The trial court held that it was and made a distributive award in the wife's favor. It also granted her expert witness fees.

Michael and Loretta Sooke married in 1982. Both were employed as teachers. Loretta had a bachelor's degree and a temporary teaching certificate but required 18 months of post-graduate classes at an approximate cost of $3,000, excluding living expenses, to obtain permanent certification in Franklin. She relinquished the opportunity to obtain permanent certification while Michael pursued his education. In 1984 the parties moved to Guadalajara, Mexico, where Michael became a full-time medical student. Loretta taught and contributed her earnings to their joint expenses. The parties returned to Franklin in 1987 so that Michael could complete the last two semesters of medical school and internship training here. Loretta resumed her former teaching position, where she remained at the time this action was commenced. Michael was licensed to practice medicine in 1991 and filed for divorce two months later. At the time of trial, he was a resident in general surgery. During the marriage, both parties contributed to paying the living and educational expenses. In addition to performing household work and managing the family finances, Loretta contributed 76% of the parties' income exclusive of a $10,000 student loan obtained by Michael.

Loretta presented expert testimony that the present value of Michael's medical degree was $950,000. Her expert testified that he arrived at this figure by comparing the average income of a college graduate and that of a general surgeon between 1996, when Michael's residency would end, and 2023, when he would reach age 65. Taking into account taxes, inflation, and interest rates, he gave his opinion that the present value of Loretta's contribution to Michael's medical education was $210,000. Michael offered no expert testimony on the subject.

The court made a distributive award to Loretta of $380,000, representing 40% of the value of the degree, and ordered it paid in 11 annual installments. The court also ordered Michael to pay Loretta's counsel fees of $20,000 and her expert witness fee of $5,000. We affirm.

Our statutes contemplate only two classes of property: marital and separate. The former, which is subject to equitable distribution, is defined broadly as "all property acquired by either or both spouses during the marriage." Michael does not contend that his license is separate property, but rather, relying on *Morgan v. Morgan* (Franklin Court of Appeal, 1998), he claims that it is not property at all.

We disagree with the decision of the Second Appellate Division in that case.

The Franklin Domestic Relations Law recognizes that spouses have an equitable claim to things of value arising out of the marital relationship and classifies them as subject to distribution by focusing on the marital status of the parties at the time of acquisition. Those things acquired during marriage and subject to distribution have been classified as marital property, although they hardly fall within traditional property concepts because there is no common-law property interest remotely resembling marital property. Having classified the property subject to distribution, the legislature did not define it but left it to the courts to determine what interests come within its terms.

Section 5 provides that in making an equitable distribution of marital property, the court shall consider "any equitable claim to, interest in, or direct or indirect contribution made to the acquisition of such marital property by the party not having title, including joint efforts or expenditures and contributions and services as a spouse, parent, wage earner and homemaker, and to the career or career potential of the other party [and] . . . the impossibility or difficulty of evaluating any component asset or any interest in a business, corporation or profession . . . ." Where such difficulty exists, the court shall make a distributive award in lieu of an actual distribution of property. The words mean exactly what they say: an interest in a profession or professional career potential is marital property which may be represented by direct or indirect contributions of the non-titleholding spouse, including financial contributions and nonfinancial contributions made by caring for the home and family.

Few undertakings better qualify as the type of joint effort that the statute's implicit economic partnership theory is intended to address than contributions toward one spouse's acquisition of a professional degree. The legislature has decided, by its explicit reference in the statute to the contributions of one spouse to the other's profession or career, that these contributions represent investments in the economic partnership of the marriage and that the product of the parties' joint efforts should be considered marital property. It does not matter whether the spouse has established a practice or whether he or she has yet to do so. An established practice merely represents the exercise of the privileges conferred upon the professional spouse by the degree, and the income flowing from that practice represents the receipt of the enhanced earning capacity that a professional degree allows.

Michael contends that alternative remedies should be employed, such as reimbursement for direct financial contributions. Limiting a working spouse to a maintenance award not only is contrary to the economic partnership concept underlying the statute but also retains the uncertain and inequitable economic ties of dependence that the legislature sought to extinguish by equitable distribution. Maintenance is subject to termination upon the recipient's remarriage, and a working spouse may never receive adequate consideration for his or her contribution and may even be penalized for the decision to remarry. When a marriage ends, each of the spouses, based on the totality of the contributions made to it, has a stake in and right to a share of the marital assets accumulated while it endured, not because that share is needed, but because those assets represent the capital product of what was essentially a partnership entity.

Turning to the question of valuation, it has been suggested that even if a professional degree is considered marital property, the working spouse is entitled only to reimbursement of his or her direct financial contributions. Such a result is completely at odds with the statute's requirement that the court give full consideration to both direct and indirect contributions. If the degree is marital property, then the working spouse is entitled to an equitable portion of it, not merely a return of funds advanced. Its value is the enhanced earning capacity it affords the holder and, although fixing the present value of that enhanced earning capacity may present problems, the problems are not insurmountable. Certainly they are no more difficult than computing tort damages for wrongful death or diminished earning capacity resulting from injury, and they differ only in degree from valuing a professional practice, which courts routinely do. The trial court retains the flexibility and discretion to structure the distributive award equitably, taking into consideration factors such as the working spouse's need for immediate payment and the current ability of the spouse with the degree to pay. Once it has received evidence of the present value of the degree and the working spouse's contributions toward its acquisition, it may then make an appropriate distribution of the marital property, including a distributive award for the professional degree. For these reasons, we affirm.

DISSENT by Meyer, J.
Michael Sooke's principal argument is that a professional degree is not marital property because it does not fit within the traditional view of property as something which has an exchange value on the open market and is capable of sale, assignment or transfer. I agree.

An educational degree is simply not encompassed even by the broad views of the concept of "property." It does not have an exchange value or any objective transferable value on an open market. It is personal to the holder. It terminates on death of the holder and is not inheritable. It cannot be assigned, sold, transferred, conveyed or pledged. An advanced degree is a cumulative product of many years of previous education, combined with diligence and hard work. It may not be acquired by the mere expenditure of money. It is simply an intellectual achievement that may potentially assist in the future acquisition of property. In my view, it has none of the attributes of property in the usual sense of that term. My interpretation is in accord with the Second Appellate Division of this court. I would reverse.

Kantor v. Bellows

Sample Answer

Dear Mr. Martin:

I am writing to summarize our position that my client, Linda Kantor, is entitled to a share of the enhanced earning capacity that your client, Bill Bellows, enjoys partly as a result of his wife's work and sacrifice. I am confident that I will convince the court that (i) the equities favor compensating Linda for her contribution and (ii) Bill's enhanced earning capacity created by his law degree and license is property subject to equitable distribution. Furthermore, I believe that the court will agree that Linda is entitled to a distributive award of $335,000.

(I. Linda must be compensated for her contribution.)

As I'm sure you are aware, Linda made significant contributions and sacrifices to allow Bill to receive his law degree and the accompanying enhanced earning capacity. This state has a policy of compensating upon divorce a spouse who has made such sacrifices for the education and training of the other spouse. For example, Franklin Domestic Relations Law section 5D(3) states that the court should consider any equitable claim based on services as a spouse, parent, wage earner, and homemaker, and contributions to the career potential of the other party in making an equitable distribution of property. In addition, section 6A(5) allows an award of maintenance based on forgone or delayed education or career opportunities. Clearly, the legislature intends for spouses to be compensated in such cases.

There can be no doubt that Linda made a valuable contribution to Bill's future earning capacity. Linda worked full-time while Bill went to law school and contributed her entire salary of $85,000 over those years to the family. In addition she did more than 75% of all the housework and child care. Meanwhile, Bill worked only 10 hours per week for two of the six semesters he attended law school, contributing only $3,000 to the family over a three-year period of time. Also, he played only a secondary role in child rearing. Clearly, it was Linda who was supporting the family.

In addition to her contributions of time and money, Linda also made great professional sacrifices for the sake of Bill's degree. Based on her agreement with Bill, she put her own plans for graduate school on hold so that they could "stagger" their education. While he was earning his degree, she had to turn down many educational opportunities offered by her employer, thus hampering her career as a "star" employee.

It is of little importance that Linda did not pay the actual tuition for Bill's law degree. She provided him with food, clothing, shelter, housekeeping services, and child care services while he pursued his degree. She also supported their child, which is an obligation of both parents. Likewise, it is not a convincing argument that Bill's degree is due to his previous education, effort, and diligence. While we do not want to minimize Bill's achievement, we will point out that Bill did not do this alone. Thanks to Linda's support, Bill was able to devote his energies to school, rather than a job. Without all of this aid, Bill would not have been able to earn his degree, let alone devote the time necessary to his education to graduate *magna cum laude*, with a special award for his performance in the school's clinical program.

Although Bill may feel that Linda's actions were just part of the normal obligations of marriage, and thus not entitled to compensation, clearly this is not the case. In fact, this is one point on which both the second and fourth appellate divisions agree. Although the *Morgan* court held that a professional degree is not property and thus not subject to equitable distribution, it stated: "Where a partner to marriage takes the benefits of his . . . spouse's support in obtaining a professional degree . . . with the

understanding that future benefits will accrue and inure to both of them, and the marriage is then terminated without the supported spouse giving anything in return, an unfairness has occurred that calls for a remedy." The *Morgan* court thus reimbursed the wife for her financial contributions to her husband's training. Similar sentiments were expressed by the fourth appellate division in *Sooke v. Sooke.* Now that Bill has obtained his degree, it would be inequitable for him alone to reap the benefits of Linda's contributions.

Furthermore, there can be no argument that Linda's contributions were meant as a gift to Bill. The couple explicitly agreed before Bill went to law school that Bill would attend school first, with Linda attending after Bill graduated, so that they could have children sooner. The fact that she has now decided to go to graduate school for computers, rather than law school, makes no difference; the type of contributions required would be the same. Bill knew that Linda was sacrificing now, in exchange for a later reward.

(II. Bill's degree should be treated as marital property subject to equitable distribution.)

Since there is no doubt that Linda is entitled to compensation for her contributions to Bill's degree and enhanced earning capacity, the next issue that arises is what form this compensation should take. I am confident that the state supreme court will align with the fourth appellate division in *Sooke v. Sooke* and find that enhanced earning capacity based on a professional degree is marital property subject to equitable distribution.

Franklin Domestic Relations Law section 3 defines marital property as "all property acquired by either or both spouses during the marriage." Bill's professional degree was acquired during the marriage. Section 3 also specifically excludes separate property, which is defined in section 4. A professional degree does not fall under that definition: it is not property acquired before marriage or by bequest, devise, or descent or by gift, nor is it acquired in exchange for or is it the increase in value of those things; it is not compensation for personal injuries; and here at least it is not property described as separate by valid written agreement. Thus, it is marital property.

Although a professional degree is unlike some other forms of property because it is not exchangeable on the market, terminates on death, and is not inheritable, it is similar to other types of property mentioned in the statute, such as an interest in a business. [*See* §5(E)] Like a business, a degree and its accompanying future earnings are created by a combination of monetary contributions, hard work, and ability. Similarly, good will in a business may be personal to the owner, terminate on his death, and not be inheritable by his heirs. This is particularly true in a field like law, where a client may take his business elsewhere if he cannot have the personal services of a particular lawyer. In fact, if our clients' divorce were taking place a few years in the future, after Bill had built a practice, there is no doubt that Linda would be entitled to her share of that practice as marital property. The same result should be reached now.

Although the amount of Linda's award will be addressed below, it should at this point be noted that the court should have no trouble dividing the property despite its unique nature. First, Bill's future earnings are not too speculative for distribution. In many other areas, the law gives present values based on uncertain future events, *e.g.,* in personal injury awards. Expert testimony is available to determine a fair estimate of the future earnings that will be earned thanks to the law degree. (*See* below.) Furthermore, the legislature has already empowered the court to make a distributive award in lieu of equitable distribution when equitable distribution is appropriate but would be impractical. [§5(E)]

Although Bill may argue that "reimbursement maintenance" would be appropriate compensation, it is not. The second appellate division in *Morgan* erred when it created the concept. Reimbursement maintenance is not consistent with the policies of this state and is simply unfair. Under that concept, a spouse would be "reimbursed" for her contributions in the form of maintenance payments. This theory has two major flaws: (i) mere reimbursement for the spouse's economic contributions is inadequate to do justice in these types of cases, and (ii) maintenance payments are a grossly unjust method of compensation.

As noted by the fourth appellate division, merely reimbursing a spouse for her economic contributions is not an adequate solution because an education is an investment that the parties believe will create much larger returns than their initial contributions. Thus, reimbursement is unjust.

In addition, the whole concept of reimbursement maintenance violates the public policy of this state. Maintenance was designed to aid dependent spouses upon divorce, as evidenced by its concern for factors such as the future earning capacity of the parties, the age and health of the parties, and the presence of children in the home. [§6] In this case, Linda is not dependent on her husband for support, nor does she wish to be classified as such in the future. Instead, she is asking for her fair share of property that she and Bill have jointly earned, *i.e.*, the degree and accompanying enhanced earnings. She should not be tied to Bill, waiting for his payments to supply her with what is rightly hers.

Finally, perhaps the most troubling aspect of an award of reimbursement maintenance is its intrusion on Linda's ability to exercise her fundamental right of marriage. In this state, maintenance terminates on the death of either party or ***upon the recipient's marriage***. Again, Linda has earned the money in question; she is not asking for Bill to "take care of her" until she remarries. If Bill were to remarry anytime after their divorce, no one would even suggest that his portion of their investment should be terminated; Linda should be entitled to the same treatment. Likewise, it would be inequitable to deprive Linda's estate of her share of the property if she were to die before collecting it.

(III. Linda should receive a distributive award of $335,000.)

Our expert, Dr. Millicent Elstein, has determined that the present value of Bill's degree is $520,000 if he remains in government service and $820,000 if he enters private practice. Although Bill is currently in government service, he is young and may switch to private practice later on. Therefore, a fair estimate of his degree is probably somewhere between these two figures. The average of these two amounts is $670,000, and I will base my request on that amount.

In determining an equitable disposition of property the court will consider factors such as the incomes of the parties at the time of the marriage and in the future, the duration of the marriage, and the parties' contributions to the acquisition of the property. [§5] Although the court in *Sooke v. Sooke* awarded the wife only 40% of the value of the husband's degree, the facts of our case call for a higher distribution: Linda should be awarded one-half of the value of Bill's enhanced earning capacity, or $335,000. The reason for granting her one-half the value is that the parties agreed to an equal division. They entered the marriage on an equal footing (as unemployed college graduates) and agreed that each in turn would be given the opportunity to attend law school. In that sense, they agreed to equal career goals and equal support during the pursuit of their educations. Now that the parties are divorcing, Linda will not get her turn to attend school while Bill supports the family. This half of the deal will not be completed. Thus, she should be awarded one-half of his degree's value.

In addition, during the years Bill was in law school, Linda was the family's primary breadwinner and did more than 75% of the housework. In *Sooke,* the wife provided 76% of the parties' income and apparently did most of the housework and finance management. Because Bill earned only $3,000 during his law school years, Linda provided significantly more than 76% of the family income (Bill's loan proceeds all went towards tuition). Also, unlike the Sookes, Linda and Bill have a child. Linda apparently paid for all of the outside child care, and she provided over 75% of the care in the home—handling the morning and evening routines, giving the child dinner, staying home with him when he was sick, etc. Therefore, there were more demands made on Linda than on the wife in *Sooke*.

In conclusion, for the reasons stated above, Bill's law degree is property subject to equitable distribution. Linda is entitled to a share of Bill's enhanced earning capacity based on that degree in the amount of $335,000.

Sincerely,

Pat Moore

Multistate Performance Test

In re Emily Dunn

National Conference of Bar Examiners

Preface

This Multistate Performance Test is a reprint of one of the three MPTs which were administered in July 1999.

The instructions for the test appear on the next page. On the actual MPT, they will appear on the back cover of the test.

INSTRUCTIONS

1. You will have 90 minutes to complete this session of the examination. This performance test is designed to evaluate your ability to handle a select number of legal authorities in the context of a factual problem involving a client.

2. The problem is set in the fictitious state of Franklin, in the fictitious Fifteenth Circuit of the United States. Columbia and Olympia are also fictitious states in the Fifteenth Circuit. In Franklin, the trial court of general jurisdiction is the District Court, the intermediate appellate court is the Court of Appeal, and the highest court is the Supreme Court.

3. You will have two kinds of materials with which to work: a File and a Library. The first document in the File is a memorandum containing the instructions for the task you are to complete. The other documents in the File contain factual information about your case and may include some facts that are not relevant.

4. The Library contains the legal authorities needed to complete the task and may also include some authorities that are not relevant. Any cases may be real, modified, or written solely for the purpose of this examination. If the cases appear familiar to you, do not assume that they are precisely the same as you have read before. Read them thoroughly, as if they all were new to you. You should assume that cases were decided in the jurisdictions and on the dates shown. In citing cases from the Library, you may use abbreviations and omit page references.

5. Your response must be written in the answer book provided. If you are taking this examination on a laptop computer, your jurisdiction will provide you with specific instructions. In answering this performance test, you should concentrate on the materials provided in the File and Library. What you have learned in law school and elsewhere provides the general background for analyzing the problem; the File and Library provide the specific materials with which you must work.

6. Although there are no restrictions on how you apportion your time, you should be sure to allocate ample time (about 45 minutes) to reading and digesting the materials and to organizing your answer before you begin writing it. You may make notes anywhere in the test materials; blank pages are provided at the end of the booklet. You may not tear pages from the question booklet.

7. This performance test will be graded on your responsiveness to the instructions regarding the task you are to complete, which are given to you in the first memorandum in the File, and on the content, thoroughness, and organization of your response.

In re Emily Dunn

FILE

LIBRARY

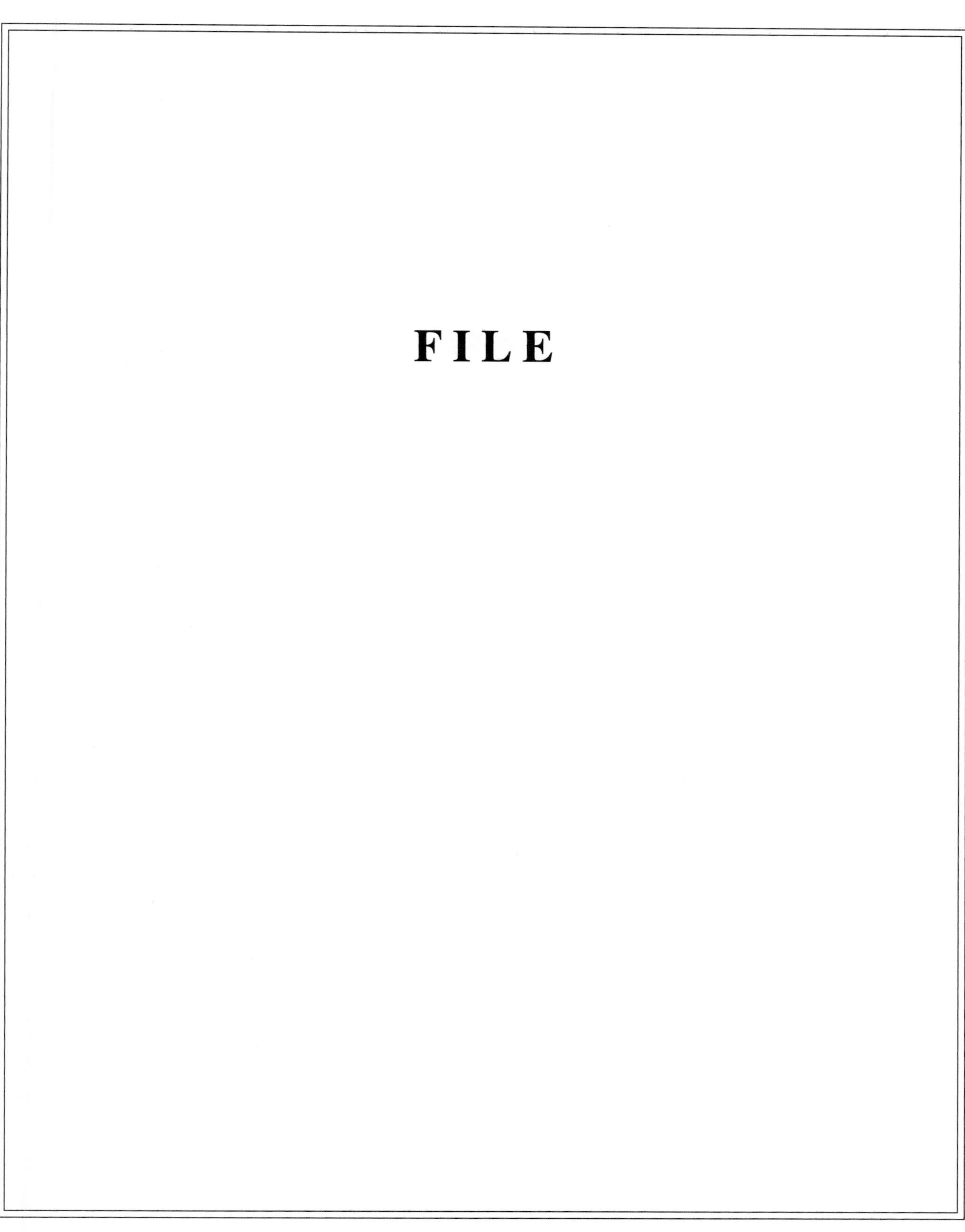

FILE

Reilly, Ingersol & Powell, PC

Attorneys-at-Law
300 Willis Road
Jackson City, Franklin 33399

(555) 999-4567
(555) 999-4555 (Fax)
e-mail: rip@aol.com

MEMORANDUM

July 29, 1999

To: Applicant

From: Robert Reilly

Re: Emily Dunn

Yesterday I met with Emily Dunn, who was recently widowed. She has asked me to prepare a new will for her.

The transcript of the interview should give you a good overall sense of what Mrs. Dunn is trying to accomplish. Looking back over it, however, I see some potential holes in my understanding of her precise intentions. In particular, I'm concerned about how she wants to deal with the disposition of potential insurance proceeds, her gifts of stock, the equalization of gifts to her grandchildren, and the distribution of the residuary estate. These ambiguities are not surprising. There are always some unresolved details that we must review with a client at a subsequent meeting. At such meetings, however, I find it useful to have a draft of the will to help clients refine their choices. I'd like you to do the following:

1. Draft the introductory and all dispositive clauses for Mrs. Dunn's proposed new will. Please set them forth in separately numbered paragraphs and in an order consistent with our firm's Will Drafting Guidelines. Don't concern yourself with the definitional and boilerplate clauses.

2. In drafting the dispositive clauses regarding the four areas I've said I'm concerned about, you will have to fill in the gaps left in the interview by making some assumptions about exactly what Mrs. Dunn wants. Therefore, in drafting a dispositive clause that requires an assumption about the insurance, the stock, the grandchildren, or the residuary estate, following that clause write a short explanatory paragraph that does two things:

    A. Tells me what assumptions you've made about the facts and Mrs. Dunn's intentions;

    B. Tells me why, based on those assumptions, you drafted the particular clause the way you did.

Reilly, Ingersol & Powell, PC

MEMORANDUM September 8, 1995

To: All Attorneys

From: Robert Reilly

Re: Will Drafting Guidelines

Over the years, this firm has used a variety of formats in drafting wills. Effective immediately, all wills drafted for this firm should follow this format:

Introduction:

A. Set forth the introductory clause with the name and domicile of the testator.

B. Include an appropriate clause regarding the revocation of prior testamentary instruments.

C. Include a clause describing the testator's immediate family (parents, sibling, spouse, children, and grandchildren).

Part ONE: Dispositive Clauses (to be set forth in separate subdivisions or subparagraphs by type of bequest or topic). Bequests should be set forth in the following order, as appropriate:

A. Specific bequests
   1. Real property
   2. Tangible personal property
   3. Other specific bequests
   4. Any other clauses stating conditions that might affect the disposition of the real and tangible personal property

B. General bequests

C. Demonstrative bequests

D. Residuary clauses

Part TWO: Definitional Clauses. Clauses relating to how words and phrases used in the will should be interpreted.

Part THREE: Boilerplate Clauses. These are clauses relating to the naming of fiduciaries and their administrative and management authority, tax clauses, attestation clauses, and self-proving will affidavits.

Reilly, Ingersol & Powell, PC

Attorneys-at-Law
300 Willis Road
Jackson City, Franklin 33399

(555) 999-4567
(555) 999-4555 (Fax)
e-mail: rip@aol.com

May 27, 1999

Mrs. Emily Dunn
23 Ipswich Lane
Jackson City, Franklin 33399

Dear Emily:

It was quite a shock to learn of Chuck's sudden heart attack given how fit he had been all of his life. He was a wonderful friend, and he will be sorely missed.

I am enclosing the completed documents finalizing your gift to the Franklin Museum of Art of the Claude Monet painting that you inherited from your grandfather.

When we last talked, you asked me to review your files and see if other things require your attention. In light of Chuck's death, it is appropriate that you review your 1965 will to see what changes you might like to make. A copy of that will is enclosed.

Please call me for an appointment to talk about possible revisions to your will. When we meet, we can talk about your family and other people to whom you might want to leave your property.

I look forward to seeing you soon.

Sincerely,

Bob

Robert Reilly

\vins
Enclosure

LAST WILL AND TESTAMENT

I am Emily Dunn, a resident of Jackson City, Franklin. This is my Last Will, and I revoke all previous wills and codicils.

ONE: A. I give all of my tangible personal property to my husband, Charles Dunn, if we are married to each other at the time of my death.

B. I give my family home located at 23 Ipswich Lane, Jackson City, Franklin to my husband, Charles Dunn, if we are married to each other at the time of my death.

C. At the present time my husband is Charles Dunn, and we have two children, Andrea and Jonathan.

D. I give 500 shares of Wilson Corporation stock to my cousin, Alice Dunn.

E. If Alice Dunn does not survive me, I give those 500 shares to her son, Drew Dunn.

F. I give the Claude Monet painting I inherited from my grandfather to the Franklin Museum of Art.

TWO: The remainder of my estate shall be disposed of in the following manner:

A. I give the sum of $25,000 to Bea Willis who for many years was my governess and who now lives in Sarasota, Florida.

B. I give the sum of $50,000 to Thomas Hardman who for 25 years served my parents faithfully as a gardener, provided he is married at the time of my death.

C. The balance of my residuary estate I give to my husband, Charles Dunn, or if he does not survive me or if we are not married at the time of my death, I give the balance of my residuary estate equally to our two children if they survive me, or all thereof to the survivor, or if none of my children survives me, I give the balance of my residuary estate to the Franklin Museum of Art.

THREE: A. I nominate First Federal Bank as Executor of my estate. I empower my Executor to exercise all administrative and management powers conferred on it as Executor by the laws of the State of Franklin. I direct that my Executor not be required to post a bond.

IN WITNESS WHEREOF, I, Emily Dunn, have signed this, my Last Will, on the 18th day of January, 1965.

Emily Dunn

Witnesses

Margaret Carnegie

Judy Carter

EXCERPTS OF TRANSCRIPT OF INTERVIEW WITH EMILY DUNN

July 28, 1999

****

Attorney: By the way, are you going to be OK financially?

Dunn: I'll be fine. Chuck insured everything we own and I should be able to get by on what he left me.

Attorney: Good. I know we could go on talking about Chuck for hours and that it's hard to go from talking about Chuck to talking about your own will, but we need to go over a number of facts so that I can revise the will you signed in 1965.

Dunn: I realize my will is really out of date. Both Bea Willis and Thomas Hardman are dead.

Attorney: Let me go over some basics. When and where were you born?

Dunn: 1928 in Jackson City, Franklin.

Attorney: When did you and Chuck marry?

Dunn: On June 15, 1947. He died on April 30, 1999.

Attorney: What are the names and ages of your children and their spouses?

Dunn: I have three children: Andrea Dunn Little, age 45; Jonathan Dunn, age 42; and Bertha Dunn, age 30. My daughter Andrea is married to Elliott Little. Jonathan and Bertha are single.

Attorney: What are the names and ages of your grandchildren?

Dunn: I have four grandchildren. Andrea's kids are Nelson Little, age 12; Becky Little, age 9; and Steven Little, age 5. Also, there is my grandson, Sidney Dunn, age 8, who is my daughter Bertha's only child.

Attorney: Let's talk about how you'd like to divide your property. Is there anyone to whom you would like to give cash?

Dunn: Yes, $20,000 to Helen Rossini, a good friend of mine whose husband, Harry, recently died. He left her his car. Apparently, it has been stolen and now there is some question about whether the insurance proceeds are payable to her or to her husband's children from his first marriage. She is very upset, as she should be. What a terrible thing. Wouldn't you think that she would get the insurance if she also got the car under his will?

Attorney: That must have been very hard for Helen, but that's a lesson to us about how careful we have to be when we're setting up our wills. How old is Helen?

Dunn: Oh, she's a little older than I am, about 75.

Attorney: What would you like to have happen with the $20,000 if Helen doesn't survive you?

Dunn: If Helen dies before me, I suppose I don't really care, although I'd like the money to stay in my family.

Attorney: What else do you have that you'd like to give away?

Dunn: Well, I have 10,000 shares of Wilson Corporation stock, and I want to give my grandchildren, Nelson, Becky, Steven, and Sidney, 500 shares each. Of course, if I have more grandchildren before I die, as I hope, I'd like each of them to receive 500 shares, too. Oh, and I'd like to give some stock to the children of my cousin, Alice Dunn. She's dead now, but she had three children, Drew, Bobby, and Marilyn, who is the child of her husband from his first marriage whom she adopted. While I haven't had much contact with any of them, I'd still like to leave her kids 600 shares of Wilson. After all, it is the family-owned company founded by our great-grandfather. The 600 shares should be divided equally among any of Alice's three children if they are still alive when I die.

Attorney: So you want to treat your grandchildren equally with respect to the gift of stock.

Dunn: Yes, I've always tried to treat them equally. After all, I love them all the same.

Attorney: Now, if your grandchildren die before you, you can make the gift to another person, including any of their children. What would you like to have happen with the stock if one of the grandchildren does not outlive you?

Dunn: If any of them dies before me, I suppose the stock should go to their kids. I mean, I would want any children of a grandchild who might die before me to get what his or her parent would have gotten.

Attorney: What about other personal property?

Dunn: I want Andrea and Bertha to have my jewelry. They should split it up between them as they see fit.

Attorney: What if Andrea and Bertha can't agree on how to divide it?

Dunn: Then my executor will have to divide it up as equally as possible.

Attorney: What if one of them dies before you?

Dunn: In that case, let my executor divide it up and then sell the share of the one who died before me.

Attorney: Other than the jewelry, how would you like the rest of your property divided?

Dunn: Jonathan should get the things located in my home, as well as the house itself.

Attorney: What if Jonathan dies before you?

Dunn: If he dies before me, the house and the things in the house should be sold and the money from the sale should be distributed along with everything else I have left.

Attorney: OK. Then let's talk about how you would like the balance of your estate to be disposed of.

Dunn: Now that Chuck's gone, I want what's left of my estate to go equally to my kids, or their families, of course.

Attorney: When you say "family," do you mean to include spouses of your children?

Dunn: No. Just my kids.

Attorney: What if all your children and grandchildren outlive you?

Dunn: Then I would just want things divided up equally among the kids, not the grandchildren.

Attorney: What if one or two of your children die before you, leaving grandchildren? Would you still want the balance of your estate divided into three equal parts?

Dunn: Yes. But would that mean my grandchildren wouldn't be treated equally?

Attorney: It might, depending on whether any of your children dies before you.

Dunn: It's hard for me to think about that now. Let me tell you this. I want my estate divided equally among my three children whether or not they are alive when I die. Then, I want all the children of my deceased children to be treated equally.

Attorney: We may not be able to do that without setting up a trust because we don't know at this time whether any of your kids will die before you.

Dunn: No, I don't want a trust. I want my heirs to have the total freedom to do what they want with my property when I die.

Attorney: OK, I think I have a fairly clear picture of how you would like your estate handled. I'll have a revised will prepared for you within the next few weeks. I'll call you to set up an appointment so that we can go over it together and make sure it's what you want.

Dunn: Well, you won't be able to reach me for a few weeks. I always wanted to see the Great Wall of China, and Helen and I are leaving tomorrow for Beijing and beyond. I'll call you when I return.

Attorney: Have a wonderful trip, Emily. We'll get together when you get back.

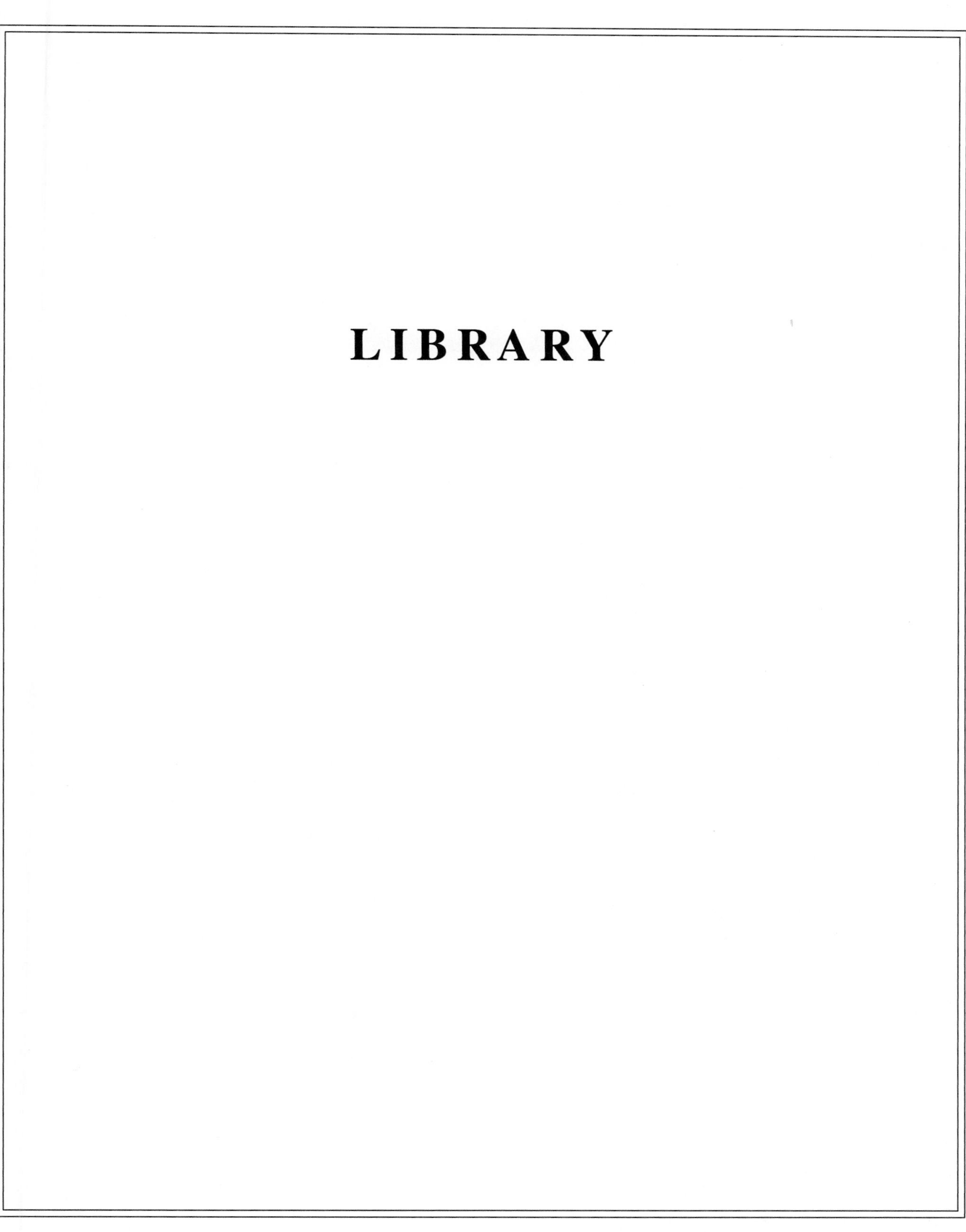

LIBRARY

In re Estate of Rich

Franklin Supreme Court (1996)

Harry Dawson, a legatee under the will of Michael Rich, and the Estate of Tom Rich appeal the judgment of the Franklin Probate Court approving the final accounting of the executor of the Estate of Michael Rich.

Decedent, Michael Rich, died on April 15, 1994, a domiciliary of Parklane, Franklin, leaving a Last Will dated February 4, 1991. Under the terms of this will, decedent bequeathed:

1. All of my household goods to my daughter, Sylvia Rich Yankow;

2. My summer home on Lake Forest, State of Franklin to my best friend, Harry Dawson;

3. 100 shares of New Pioneer, Inc. common stock to my aunt, Nancy Rich, if she survives me;

4. $50,000 to my friend, Ellen Gray, if she survives me; and

5. The residue of my estate to my daughter, Sylvia Rich Yankow, and my son, Tom Rich, in equal shares.

Other than his son, Tom Rich, who died during the Gulf War, all of decedent's named beneficiaries survived him.

Decedent died leaving an estate of over $1,000,000, including his summer home on Lake Forest. Two months following decedent's death, the summer home was totally destroyed by fire. Home Casualty Insurance Company, which had issued the fire insurance policy on this home, immediately paid $150,000, the value of the home, to the executor.

In the final accounting for the estate, the executor determined that the insurance proceeds and all of the other residuary assets of the estate should be paid to Sylvia Rich as the sole surviving residuary legatee under the will. Both Harry Dawson, the legatee of the summer home, and the Estate of Tom Rich appeal.

Harry Dawson claims that, as the specific legatee of the summer home, all insurance proceeds payable thereon as a result of its destruction following the decedent's death are payable to him rather than to the residuary legatee under the decedent's will. The Estate of Tom Rich claims that one-half of the residuary estate should have been distributed to it under the terms of the residuary clause in the will.

Walker on Wills, one of the country's leading treatises on wills, notes that all bequests under wills are classified as either (1) general, (2) specific, (3) demonstrative, or (4) residuary.

A *general* legacy (typically a gift of money) is defined as a "bequest payable out of general estate assets or to be purchased for a beneficiary out of general estate assets." Walker on Wills, §501.

A *specific* legacy is defined as a "bequest of a specific asset." Id. at §502(a).

A *demonstrative* legacy is a bequest of a "specific sum of money payable from a designated account. Such legacy is specific as to the funds available in the account to pay the bequested amount and general as to the balance." Id. at §502(b).

Lastly, Walker states that a *residuary* bequest is a "bequest that is neither general, specific or demonstrative and includes bequests that purport to dispose of the whole estate." Id. at §503.

The bequest to Harry Dawson is of specific property, the summer home of the testator. If the identical thing bequeathed is not in a decedent's probate estate, the legacy is "adeemed" and the legatee's rights are gone. Walker on Wills, §600. In this case, the summer home was in existence at the time of the decedent's death, so the bequest to Harry Dawson did not adeem. On the other hand, it was totally destroyed by fire following the decedent's death. The question raised is whether the specific legatee is entitled to receive the casualty insurance proceeds payable as a result of the fire. In resolving this question, the court, as it does in construing wills generally, must consider the testator's intent. Here, testator's will is completely silent regarding who should receive the insurance proceeds under the facts as they occurred. Thus, we are unable to ascertain the testator's intent. As such, the insurance policy must be treated like any other estate asset that is not the subject of a specific bequest. While there are cases in other jurisdictions to the contrary, we believe that the insurance policy insuring the summer home is merely another asset of the decedent's estate and forms part of the residuary estate because it was not specifically bequeathed to any other legatee. Accordingly, the Franklin Probate Court correctly upheld the decision of the executor to distribute such proceeds as part of the residuary estate.

Having determined that the insurance proceeds were part of the residuary estate, we turn to the claim of the Estate of Tom Rich.

Section 331 of the Franklin Probate Code ("Lapse Statute") provides that: "If a legatee or devisee predeceases the testator, the bequest or devise that would have passed to the deceased legatee or devisee passes to his issue that survive the testator, unless the will otherwise provides." Cases in this jurisdiction have repeatedly held that unless a decedent's will *expressly* conditions a residuary or other bequest on survivorship, the bequest passes to the estate of a deceased legatee unless the legatee dies leaving issue who survive the testator.

Unlike the specific bequest of the stock and the general bequest of cash, decedent's will does not expressly condition the residuary bequests to Sylvia Rich Yankow and Tom Rich on survivorship, and Tom Rich predeceased the testator leaving no surviving issue. In light of the statute and relevant cases, the probate court erred in holding that the Estate of Tom Rich was not entitled to one-half of the decedent's residuary estate.

Order of the Franklin Probate Court affirmed in part and reversed in part.

In re Estate of Young

Franklin Supreme Court (1978)

Decedent, Harry Young, died on March 12, 1974, a resident of Jackson City, Franklin. Mr. Young was a successful businessman in Jackson City and by the time of his death had accumulated a substantial fortune.

Two provisions of Mr. Young's will were called into question by the residuary legatees under his will. The first reads: "I give 100 shares of Gemet Corporation stock to my nephew, Ron Winky." Gemet Corporation stock is publicly traded on the New York Stock Exchange. Mr. Young did not own any Gemet Corporation stock at the time of his death and there is no evidence whether he ever owned any such stock. Mr. Winky argues that the bequest of stock was a general bequest to be purchased for his benefit with assets of Mr. Young's estate. The residuary legatees argue it is a specific bequest that adeemed because no such stock was in the decedent's probate estate at the time of his death.

Generally, whether a gift of specific shares of stock is a specific or general bequest depends on the intent of the testator. Gifts of specific stock are presumptively specific. If the stock was not owned at the time the will was signed, the bequest is more likely general. See generally, Walker on Wills, §10320. If the stock was owned by testator at the time the will was executed or was stock in a closely held corporation—or if there is language in the will evidencing such ownership at the time the will was signed, such as "my stock"—the bequest is specific and, if such stock is not in the estate when testator dies, the bequest adeems. In the absence of evidence to the contrary and given the presumption of classification as specific, we affirm the Probate Court's finding that the gift to Ron Winky adeemed.

The second contested provision of the will reads: "I give $100,000 to my friend, Phil Darby, or if Phil predeceases me, to his children." Phil Darby predeceased decedent. While none of Darby's children survived the decedent, he had two grandchildren who did. One of these grandchildren had been adopted by Mr. Darby's deceased child. The grandchildren claim to be entitled to the $100,000 as alternate beneficiaries under the will. The residuary legatees claim the bequest lapsed under §331 of the Franklin Probate Code.

The question on appeal is what the decedent meant or intended when he used the word "children." Mr. Darby's grandchildren argue that, when Mr. Young signed his will, Mr. Darby's children had already been dead for five years and that his grandchildren who lived with him were known to the decedent. Thus, they argue, it is reasonable to believe that, when decedent referred to "Mr. Darby's children," he was thinking of these grandchildren. We find this argument persuasive and hold that, for *purposes of this case,* the word "children" means *issue*.

We hold that the $100,000 passes to the grandchildren of Mr. Darby and affirm the judgment of the Probate Court.

Walker on Wills

§11200: In construing wills, all courts adhere to the principle that testator's intent controls in the interpretation of the language in the will. For this reason, there is a very high premium on drafting wills in which the language is clear and unambiguous. Attorneys who draft wills also must be aware of governing rules of law that can affect how wills might be construed if the language is not clear.

For example, suppose a testator bequeaths "my 100 shares of X Corporation stock to B" but at the time of the testator's death, she owns 200 shares of X Corporation stock. Is B entitled to only 100 shares of the X Corporation stock or to the 200 shares of that stock that testator owns at death? The answer to this question often depends on how testator acquired the additional 100 shares of stock.

If the additional shares were acquired either as a stock split or stock (as distinguished from cash) dividend, most courts hold that they pass to the specific legatee because they represent the stated gift in its current form. However, since this matter is not always free of doubt, if a testator intends that result, a will construction proceeding to resolve the question could be avoided if, for example, the will had read: "I give my 100 shares of X Corporation stock to B, including any additional shares I receive between the date of the execution of this will and the date of my death as either a stock split or as a dividend paid to me by X Corporation in its own shares."

* * * *

§14920: There had been much confusion surrounding how property should be distributed among class members where the class gift is limited to persons potentially of different generational levels to the named ancestor, such as a gift to "issue." Fortunately, the matter has been universally resolved in all states by their adoption of the Uniform Act on Per Capita and Per Stirpes Distributions. This act provides that:

1. If property is distributed "per capita" to the "issue" or "descendants" of a named ancestor, each person who is an issue or descendant of the named ancestor takes an equal share.

2. If property is distributed "per stirpes" to the "issue" or "descendants" of a testator, the property is distributed among the issue or descendants most closely related to the testator. However, if there would have been other issue or descendants at the same generational level who, had they survived, would have participated in the gift, then their issue or descendants, if any, take the share these deceased persons would have taken. The following example illustrates distribution "per stirpes":

(1) Testator (T) had three children, A, B, and C.

- A dies before T and had 7 children.
- B dies before T and had 1 child.
- C survives T and has 1 child.

(2) A's children each take 1/7 of the 1/3 share A would have received had he lived.

(3) B's child gets the entire 1/3 share B would have received had he lived.

(4) C takes a 1/3 share and C's child takes nothing.

As can be seen, in a "per stirpes" distribution, grandchildren with dead parents get a proportionate share of what their parents would have gotten.

3. If property is distributed "per stirpes but per capita at each generation" to the "issue" or "descendants" of a testator, the outcome is quite different. The following example, using the same facts that were used to illustrate "per stirpes" distribution, illustrates distribution "per stirpes but per capita at each generation":

(1) Testator (T) had three children, A, B, and C.

- A dies before T and had 7 children.
- B dies before T and had 1 child.
- C survives T and has 1 child.

(2) A and B's children each take 1/8 of the 2/3 share A and B would have received had they lived.

(3) C takes a 1/3 share and C's child takes nothing.

As opposed to a pure "per stirpes" distribution, in this case the grandchildren with dead parents each get an equal share of what all the dead parents would have gotten. In this example, B's child gets much less. Instead of a 1/3 share, B's child shares equally with all the grandchildren whose parents have died.

In re Emily Dunn

Sample Answer

LAST WILL AND TESTAMENT

(PARTIAL FIRST DRAFT)

I am Emily Dunn, a resident of Jackson City, Franklin. This is my Last Will, and I revoke all previous wills and codicils. At the present time, I have three children, Andrea Dunn Little, Jonathan Dunn, and Bertha Dunn, and I have four grandchildren, Nelson Little, Becky Little, Steven Little, and Sidney Dunn.

ONE: A. 1. I give my family home, located at 23 Ipswich Lane, Jackson City, Franklin, and its contents except as provided below, to my son, Jonathan Dunn, if he survives me. If he does not survive me, the house and its contents shall be sold and the proceeds distributed with my residuary estate. In the event the home is destroyed before or after my death, Jonathan is to receive the casualty insurance proceeds payable as a result of its destruction.

In drafting paragraph 1., I assumed that Ms. Dunn would want her son, Jonathan, to receive the potential insurance proceeds resulting from the destruction of the family home whether the home was destroyed before or after her death. Because the gift of the home is a specific bequest, if it were destroyed before Ms. Dunn's death, it would not be in the estate at her death and would be adeemed, which would mean that Jonathan would not be entitled to the home. The insurance proceeds would be added to the residuary estate and Jonathan would only receive a portion of the proceeds, at most one-third. In Ms. Dunn's meeting with us, in discussing her friend Helen Rossini, Ms. Dunn indicated that she thought that a devisee under a will should be entitled to insurance proceeds; thus, I assumed that she would want that result in this case.

I further assumed that if the house were destroyed after Ms. Dunn's death, but before the estate is distributed, Ms. Dunn would still want Jonathan to receive the insurance proceeds. It is prudent to specifically state that Jonathan is entitled to the insurance proceeds even if the house is destroyed after Ms. Dunn's death given the court's holding in *In re Estate of Rich* (1996), which held under similar facts, that where the will is silent on the matter, the specific devisee is not entitled to the insurance proceeds.

2. I give my jewelry to my daughters, Andrea Dunn Little and Bertha Dunn, if they survive me, to be divided between them as they see fit. In the event Andrea and Bertha cannot agree on a division of the jewelry, my Executor shall divide the jewelry between them in approximately equal shares. If one of my daughters does not survive me, I direct my Executor to divide the jewelry in substantially equal shares, give one share to the surviving daughter, and sell the other share and distribute the proceeds with my residuary estate.

In drafting paragraph 2., I assumed from the interview transcript that Ms. Dunn would want the proceeds of a sale of a deceased daughter's share of the jewelry to be distributed with the residue of her estate. Ms. Dunn indicated that she wanted the share of a deceased daughter to be sold but she did not indicate what to do with the proceeds.

> 3. I give to each of my grandchildren 500 shares of my Wilson Corporation stock. If any grandchild predeceases me, his or her shares shall pass to the that grandchild's surviving issue. If no issue survives, then those shares shall pass with my residuary estate.

In drafting paragraph 3., I assumed from the transcript of the interview with Ms. Dunn that Ms. Dunn meant to make a specific bequest of the stock to the grandchildren; that is, I assumed that she wanted the grandchildren to have the stock itself and not, should the shares not be in her estate at her death, the value of the shares. Thus, I have written "500 shares of ***my*** Wilson Corporation stock." I assumed this because the shares represent part of the family-owned business founded by her great-grandfather, and because she has held the shares for a long time (at least since before her previous will). However, we should explain to Ms. Dunn that if the shares are not in her estate at her death, her grandchildren will get nothing (the gift adeems), and if this is not Ms. Dunn's intent, the word "my" should be deleted and the language changed to "500 shares of Wilson Corporation stock," which would make this a general bequest not subject to ademption.

Since Ms. Dunn was clear in expressing her intention to have each of her grandchildren receive 500 shares of Wilson stock at her death, I did not include any language that would allow them to receive additional shares of Wilson stock resulting from stock dividends or stock splits.

I did not name the grandchildren individually because Ms. Dunn indicated that she wanted the class to remain open to include any grandchildren born after her will was executed.

Also, Ms. Dunn indicated that if any of her grandchildren predeceases her, she would want the stock to go to that grandchild's children. This would be the apparent result under the lapse statute [Franklin Probate Code §331] and so it might seem that we could stop with the first sentence of paragraph 3. However, *In re Estate of Rich* states that if no issue survives a predeceasing legatee, the gift passes to the predeceasing legatee's estate. This is probably not what Ms. Dunn would want—shares passing to a grandchild's estate could go to the grandchild's spouse or other beneficiaries, and since Ms. Dunn did not want her children's spouses to take, she probably would not want her grandchildren's spouses to take either. Also, as indicated above, this is a family-owned business and so Ms. Dunn probably wants to keep the stock in the family. Therefore, I drafted paragraph 3. so that it was clear that only issue of grandchildren take the stock or if none, the stock would pass with her residuary estate.

> 4. I give 600 shares of my Wilson Corporation stock to the children of my cousin, Alice Dunn, namely Drew, Bobby, and Marilyn, in equal shares. If one of them does not survive me, the shares shall be divided between the surviving two, and if two of them do not survive me, all shares shall go to the survivor.

In drafting paragraph 4., I assumed that Ms. Dunn would want to give her cousin's children only the Wilson stock, and not its value if the stock were not in her estate at her death. Therefore, as in paragraph 3., I used the phrase "my Wilson Corporation stock." Also, I assumed that Ms. Dunn would not want the issue of Alice Dunn's children to share in the gift of the Wilson stock in the event the children predecease Ms. Dunn. Therefore, I conditioned the gift on survival. Also, I named the children specifically because Marilyn is an adopted child of Alice Dunn. Generally adopted children are included in a gift to "children," but it is best to avoid any question of Ms. Dunn's intention.

B. I give $20,000 to my friend, Helen Rossini, if she survives me.

C. The balance of my residuary estate I give to my descendants per stirpes but per capita at each generation. If none of my descendants survive me, I give the balance of my residuary estate to the Franklin Museum of Art.

Ms. Dunn indicated that she did not want the spouses of her children to share in the residue of her estate, but she does want to include children of any child who predeceases her; thus, I used the word "descendants." She further stated that if any of her grandchildren are to receive shares, she wants them to be treated equally. I drafted paragraph C. so that all of Ms. Dunn's children will share equally in the residue of her estate if they all survive, and if grandchildren take, they too will receive equal shares. In a straight per stirpes distribution, grandchildren with dead parents would not receive equal shares; instead, they would receive a proportion of their dead parent's share and the distribution among grandchildren may be unequal. However, under the above distribution, if more than one of Ms. Dunn's children predeceases, the grandchildren with dead parents each get an equal share of what all the dead parents would have gotten.

I assumed, based on Ms. Dunn's former will, in the unlikely event that no descendants survive, Ms. Dunn would still want the balance of her estate to go to the Franklin Museum of Art.

TWO: To be completed later.

THREE: To be completed later.

IN WITNESS WHEREOF, I, Emily Dunn, have signed this, my Last Will, on the __th day of July, 1999.

____

Witnesses:

____

____

Multistate Performance Test

Pauling v. Del-Rey Wood Products Co.

National Conference of Bar Examiners

Preface

This Multistate Performance Test is a reprint of one of the three MPTs which were administered in July 2000.

The instructions for the test appear on the next page. On the actual MPT, they will appear on the back cover of the test.

INSTRUCTIONS

1. You will have 90 minutes to complete this session of the examination. This performance test is designed to evaluate your ability to handle a select number of legal authorities in the context of a factual problem involving a client.

2. The problem is set in the fictitious state of Franklin, in the fictitious Fifteenth Circuit of the United States. Columbia and Olympia are also fictitious states in the Fifteenth Circuit. In Franklin, the trial court of general jurisdiction is the District Court, the intermediate appellate court is the Court of Appeal, and the highest court is the Supreme Court.

3. You will have two kinds of materials with which to work: a File and a Library. The first document in the File is a memorandum containing the instructions for the task you are to complete. The other documents in the File contain factual information about your case and may include some facts that are not relevant.

4. The Library contains the legal authorities needed to complete the task and may also include some authorities that are not relevant. Any cases may be real, modified, or written solely for the purpose of this examination. If the cases appear familiar to you, do not assume that they are precisely the same as you have read before. Read them thoroughly, as if they all were new to you. You should assume that cases were decided in the jurisdictions and on the dates shown. In citing cases from the Library, you may use abbreviations and omit page references.

5. Your response must be written in the answer book provided. If you are taking this examination on a laptop computer, your jurisdiction will provide you with specific instructions. In answering this performance test, you should concentrate on the materials provided in the File and Library. What you have learned in law school and elsewhere provides the general background for analyzing the problem; the File and Library provide the specific materials with which you must work.

6. Although there are no restrictions on how you apportion your time, you should be sure to allocate ample time (about 45 minutes) to reading and digesting the materials and to organizing your answer before you begin writing it. You may make notes anywhere in the test materials; blank pages are provided at the end of the booklet. You may not tear pages from the question booklet.

7. This performance test will be graded on your responsiveness to the instructions regarding the task you are to complete, which are given to you in the first memorandum in the File, and on the content, thoroughness, and organization of your response.

Pauling v. Del-Rey Wood Products Co.

FILE

LIBRARY

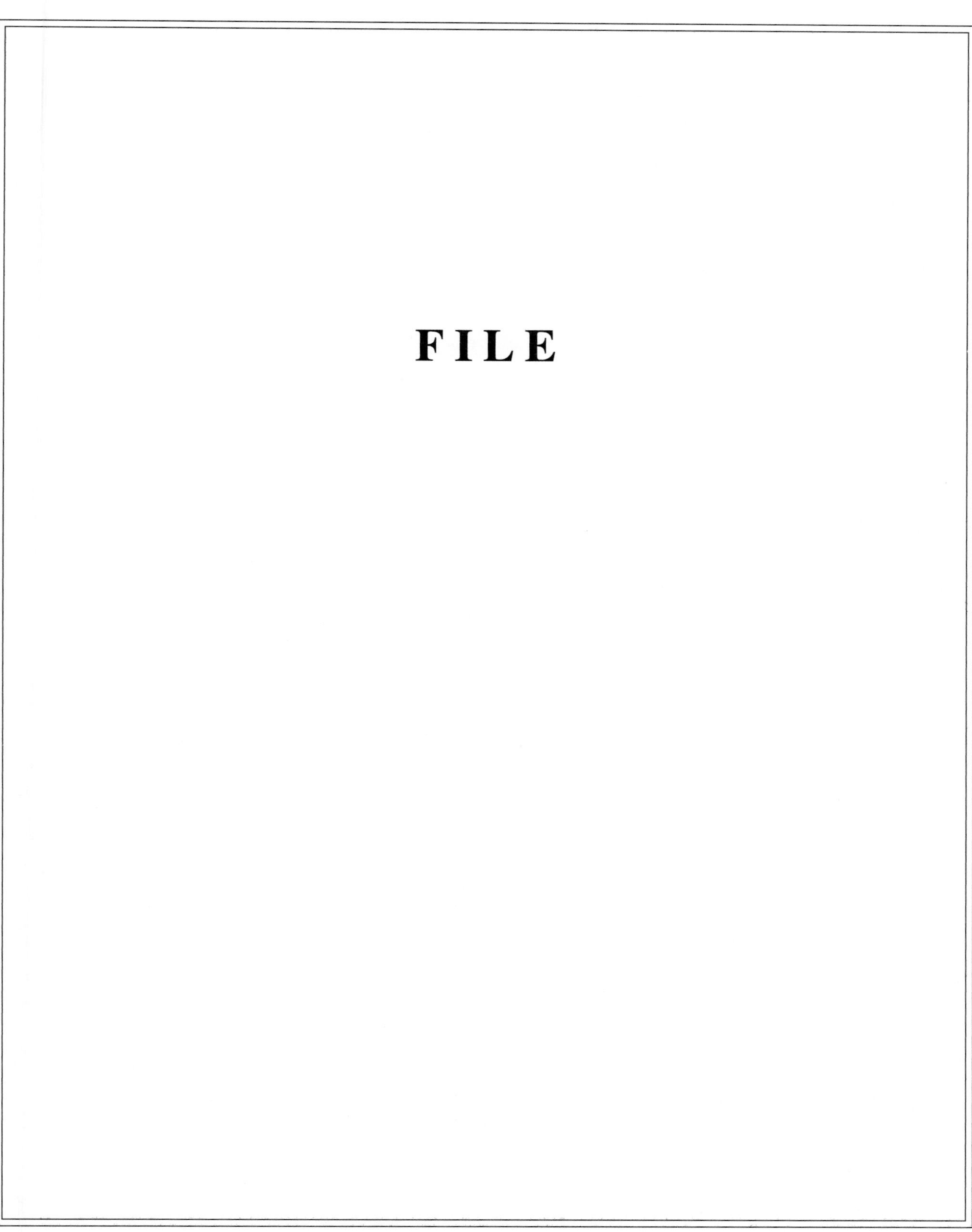

FILE

Law Offices of Andrew J. Reed
509 Dawkins Avenue
Marina, Franklin 33405
(555) 521-7108

MEMORANDUM

To: Applicant

From: Andrew Reed

Date: July 25, 2000

Subject: Letitia Pauling v. Del-Rey Wood Products Co.

Our client Letitia Pauling worked for a small, local company called Del-Rey Wood Products for three years. She was recently fired. She came to see me complaining that she and her co-workers had regularly worked between 50 and 60 hours per week and that the company had never paid any of the workers time and a half for overtime.

I filed suit against Del-Rey alleging that Del-Rey violated the Fair Labor Standards Act (the "Act") by failing to pay time and a half after 40 hours a week. In its answer to the complaint, Del-Rey denies that it or its employees are covered by the Act. If there is no coverage, Del-Rey has no obligation to pay overtime, and Ms. Pauling has no claim.

Some of Ms. Pauling's co-workers who are still employed by Del-Rey have expressed interest in joining the lawsuit. There is certainly a basis in what Ms. Pauling told me to assume that the Act applies to Del-Rey's employees, but, since Del-Rey has denied it, we need to pin it down. Before I take this matter any further and possibly jeopardize the co-workers' relationships with Del-Rey, I want to send a set of interrogatories to find out whether the Act applies. There are two bases for establishing the application of the Act to employees: "enterprise coverage" and "individual coverage."

Here's what I'd like you to do:

1. Please draft for my review a set of six clear and sharply focused interrogatories designed to obtain information on whether there is any basis for asserting "individual coverage" of

the Del-Rey employees under the Fair Labor Standards Act. I'm working on the interrogatories for "enterprise coverage," and I've attached the three I've finished as examples. Your task is to focus on "individual coverage" and nothing else.

2. To help me understand why you are proposing each interrogatory, follow each one with a short statement of why you are proposing it and how, based on the law and the facts, it will help us determine whether "individual coverage" exists under the Act. I've included such statements with the three interrogatories I drafted to give you an idea of what I'm looking for.

Our word processing program will supply the correct format, introductory remarks, definitions and the like, so you need not concern yourself with such matters.

Notes of Interview with Letitia Pauling

June 20, 2000

Letitia Pauling was referred to me by her cousin, Alfred Markum, whom I once represented successfully in a backwage suit against his employer.

- Pauling started working for Del-Rey Wood Products Co. here in Marina a little over 2 years ago—she can't remember actual date of employment.
- She worked as Del-Rey's shipping and receiving clerk—her job was to receive, store and maintain records on incoming materials and to ship finished goods per instructions from front office.
- She thinks the company is run by Delbert and Reynaldo Dragowitz—not sure if it's a corporation or what—front office people and bosses are all members of the Dragowitz family.
- She started at $6.50 per hour—got 2 raises while she was there—her last wage was $7.25 per hour. She was paid every week with a paycheck bearing a printed logo that said "D & R Enterprises—Recognized Around the World for Fine Furniture."
- Del-Rey's business is making parts for wood furniture, *e.g.,* decorative legs for tables and chairs, fronts for desk drawers and things like that. The parts are mostly manufactured to drawings and specifications Del-Rey gets from D & R Furniture Manufacturing Co., which has a plant in the industrial park across town on the south side of Marina.
- Most of the goods that Pauling remembers taking in as receiving clerk were raw lumber that she stacked with a fork-lift—specialty woods such as cherry, walnut, maple, used for making parts—as far as she remembers, most of the wood came from a local lumber yard—she doesn't know where the timber came from or where the logs were cut into lumber.
- Once in a while, she'd receive other materials such as woodworking tools, saws, lathe parts, miscellaneous supplies and the like. She has no recollection where the materials came from, although she thinks she remembers about once a month receiving shipments of saw blades from an out-of-state supplier.
- The stockroom clerk would fill the orders for finished parts and box them up for shipment—Pauling's job was to handle the paperwork and put the boxes on the trucks at the loading dock—mostly on Del-Rey's own flatbed truck for delivery across town to D & R Furniture's

warehouse. That's where Del-Rey ships almost all of its production. Once in a while an outside trucking company picked up a few orders for delivery to a customer in another part of the state—she remembers only one order shipped to an out-of-state customer, although she never paid close attention to the addresses, so there may have been more.

- Pauling isn't sure what the connection is, but she thinks the Dragowitz brothers also run D & R Furniture Mfg. Co. She thinks D & R Furniture makes high quality wood furniture and has about 300 employees. She knows that Delbert and Reynaldo spend a lot of their time over at the D & R Furniture plant. She has no idea where D & R Furniture gets its materials other than what Del-Rey ships to them or who D & R Furniture sells to or whether D & R Furniture ships any furniture out of state. All she knows about "D & R Enterprises" is that the logo appears on her paycheck. Maybe if we can lay hands on the financial statements for all three companies, they will tell us something about the intercompany relationships.
- Del-Rey only has about 20 workers in the shop—a couple of working foremen, a quality control inspector, a local pick-up and delivery truck driver (*i.e.,* the one who drives Del-Rey's flatbed and delivers to D & R Furniture), a stockroom clerk, a shipping and receiving clerk, a janitor, a mechanic who keeps the machines working; the rest of the Del-Rey employees operate various woodworking machines making wood parts. Pauling doesn't know what the hourly wages are for the other employees but she believes she and the janitor were the lowest paid in the shop.
- Regular shop hours at Del-Rey were 7 a.m. to 3:30 p.m., with 1/2 hour for lunch, Monday through Friday, but it wasn't unusual for Pauling to work through her lunch period and grab a sandwich on the run; she'd usually work until 4:30 - 5 p.m. loading trucks every day; she also had to work 4 to 5 hours almost every Saturday and about one Sunday a month.
- She got paid straight time for all her hours, but the company never did pay time and a half for overtime—whenever she asked about overtime pay, one of the bosses would say something like, "It's not company policy to pay time and a half."
- Pauling says all the other shop workers are fed up with the long hours. Most of them would like to sue for back pay, but they're afraid to say anything or to report it to the government. She says that 7 or 8 of them want to come see me about suing for them. I told her to hold off on that until I've had a chance to look into it further.

Law Offices of Andrew J. Reed
509 Dawkins Avenue
Marina, Franklin 33405
(555) 521-7108

MEMORANDUM

To: Applicant

From: Andrew Reed

Date: July 25, 2000

Subject: Enterprise Coverage Interrogatories

Here are the first three interrogatories I've drafted regarding "enterprise coverage." I'll write other ones later, but this ought to give you an idea of how I want you to go about drafting the interrogatories for the "individual coverage" issue.

INTERROGATORY NO. 1: State in dollars the gross annual volume of sales of or business done by Del-Rey Wood Products Co. for each of the past three years.

Reason for proposing: One of the components of enterprise coverage is showing annual dollar volume of $500,000. If that dollar volume can be established vis-à-vis Del-Rey alone, we will have established the threshold statutory requirement under §203(s)(1)(A)(ii).

INTERROGATORY NO. 2: State the names of all persons, corporations, partnerships, or other entities having an ownership interest in, or who is an officer, director, or shareholder of, Del-Rey Wood Products Co., D & R Furniture Manufacturing Co., and D & R Enterprises.

Reason for proposing: We need to know the relationships among the three companies to establish that the three entities are related through unified operations or common control, as suggested by the facts and required by §203(r)(1).

INTERROGATORY NO. 3: In each of the past three years, what has been the combined gross annual dollar volume of sales of or business done by Del-Rey Wood Products Co., D & R Furniture Manufacturing Co., and D & R Enterprises?

Reason for proposing: If these companies together do in fact constitute an "enterprise," their combined dollar volume is relevant to the $500,000 threshold.

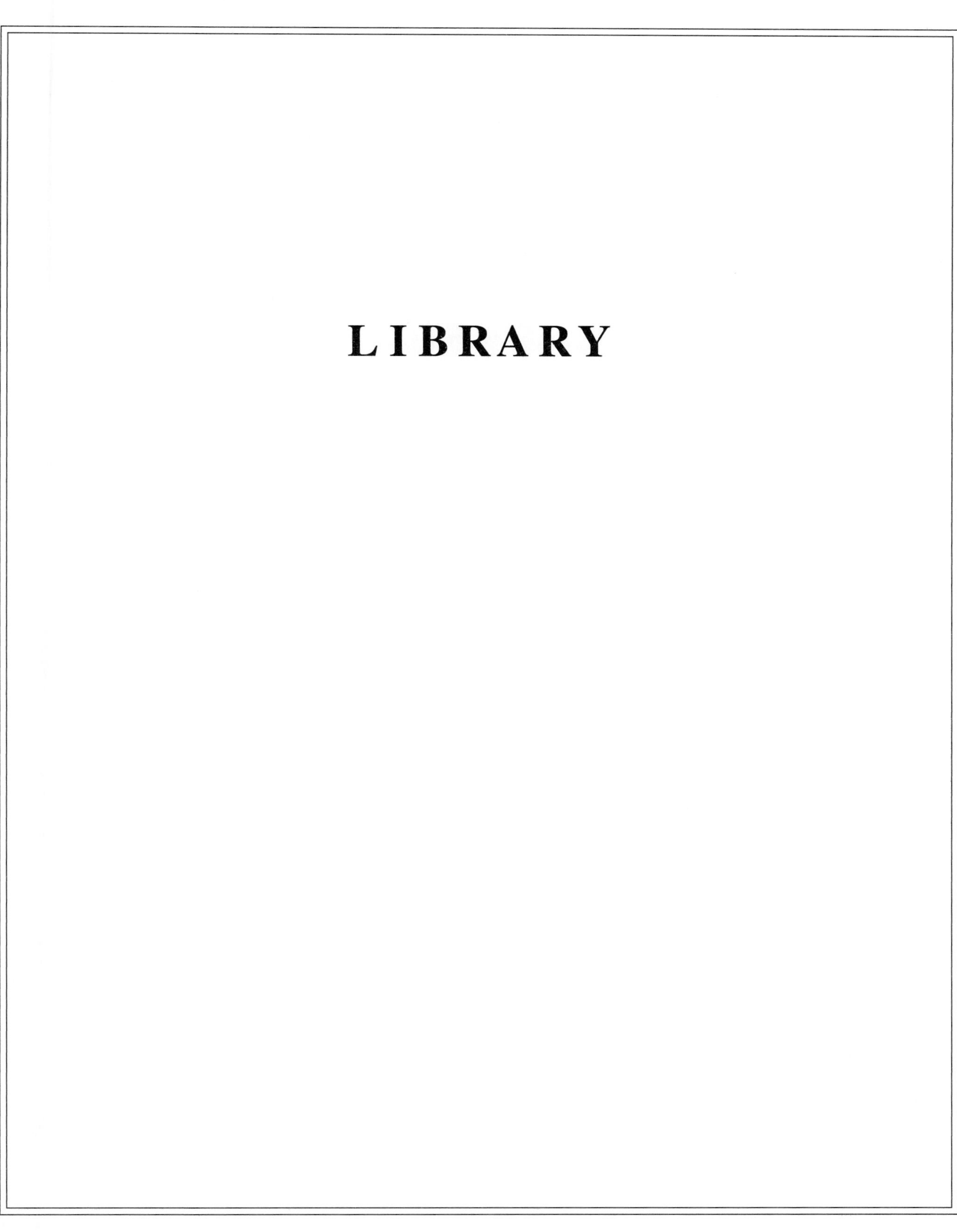
LIBRARY

WALKER ON DISCOVERY

A Primer On Discovery Techniques

In civil litigation, depositions, interrogatories, requests for production of documents, and requests for admissions are primary discovery tools used by parties to lawsuits. The purpose of this text is to inform attorneys whose experience is limited or those who need a refresher on discovery techniques. Careful attention to the techniques will facilitate the process of gathering information at a relatively low cost.

* * *

Written Interrogatories: Written interrogatories are, plainly and simply, a series of written requests for information submitted by one party to another. The recipient is required to respond in writing and under oath and to disclose all pertinent information known to it, reasonably available to it, and within its possession and control. Interrogatories may not be sent to nonparties, although they may request information known to the recipient about nonparties.

An interrogatory may be phrased as a question (*e.g.,* "What goods does ABC, Inc. manufacture?") or as a declarative statement (*e.g.,* "Describe the goods that ABC, Inc. manufactures."). In order to be effective and to avoid objections that they are vague or overbroad, interrogatories must be sharply focused and unambiguously worded.

For example, in an employment discrimination case, the plaintiff might want to obtain information on other employees who have charged the employer with discrimination and what documentary evidence there is of the charges. The following interrogatory would probably be subject to an objection for vagueness and overbreadth:

> INTERROGATORY NO. 1: Please describe each document that contains information regarding the names and addresses of the employees of ABC, Inc. who have filed charges of employment discrimination with the EEOC.

A more focused inquiry will avoid the objection and be more likely to produce the information sought. For example:

> INTERROGATORY NO. 2: What is the name and address of each employee who, within the past two years, has filed with the EEOC a charge of employment discrimination against ABC, Inc.?

Interrogatories may be sequential and may have subparts that seek information related to the main thrust of the interrogatory. For example:

> INTERROGATORY NO. 3: Within the past two years, have any employees of ABC, Inc. filed against ABC, Inc. charges of employment discrimination with the EEOC?
>
> INTERROGATORY NO. 4: If the answer to the preceding interrogatory is in the affirmative, please state the following with regard to each such employee of ABC, Inc.:
>
> a. The name, address, and telephone number of the employee;
>
> b. The name of the custodian of ABC, Inc.'s records regarding ABC, Inc.'s investigation of and response to each such charge filed with the EEOC.

Care must be taken, however, in using interrogatories with subparts. Because there is the potential that counsel might abuse the process by serving burdensome interrogatories, many courts, by local rule, limit the number of interrogatories a party may serve. Typically, the local rules treat each subpart of an interrogatory as a separate interrogatory for purposes of measuring the number of interrogatories served; *e.g.,* Interrogatory No. 4, above, would be counted as two interrogatories.

Although interrogatories cannot be used to require the recipient to ***produce*** documents (*i.e.,* make documents available), they can be used effectively to seek ***identification*** of relevant documents. For example:

> INTERROGATORY NO. 5: Describe the computerized and/or manually prepared records that are used in your company to keep track of the racial, ethnic, and gender make-up of your work force.

Such interrogatories can be followed up later with written requests for production of documents.

The key to the productive use of interrogatories is for the proponent to think carefully about the specific underlying facts he or she wishes to elicit in order to support the legal elements of the claim and to draft straightforward, plainly worded inquiries. It is best to request the information in small doses. One can always send follow-up interrogatories if further explication is necessary. Convoluted or complex inquiries that encompass too many topics or too much subject matter are ordinarily a waste of time and will not draw useful answers. *See, e.g.,* Interrogatory No. 1, above.

* * *

Local Rules of the District Court for Oceola County

<u>Local Rule 33-1</u>: Written Interrogatories

Without leave of court or written stipulation, a party may serve upon any other party written interrogatories, not exceeding 20 in number including all discrete subparts to be answered by the party served or, if the party served is a public or private corporation or a partnership or association or governmental agency, by any officer or agent, who shall furnish such information as is available to the party. Leave to serve additional interrogatories shall be granted liberally, but shall require a showing of cause. Any memorandum in support of a motion for leave to propound additional interrogatories shall set forth the additional proposed interrogatories and the reasons for their use.

Zorich v. Long Beach Fire Department

Franklin Court of Appeal (1997)

Jerome Zorich brought suit against his employer, Long Beach Fire Department (LBFD), seeking regular and overtime wages under the Fair Labor Standards Act (FLSA or Act), 29 U.S.C. §201, et seq. That Act requires employers to pay covered employees at least the established minimum wage and time and one-half their regular rates of pay for all hours worked in excess of 40 in a week.

The district court granted summary judgment in favor of LBFD, concluding that LBFD did not qualify as an "enterprise" covered by the FLSA. Under 29 U.S.C. §203(s), an "enterprise" is covered by the Act if (1) it has covered employees in its workforce and (2) it has an annual gross volume of sales made or business done of not less than $500,000. LBFD does not satisfy the $500,000 test. Thus, the district court found that LBFD is not a covered enterprise and its employees are therefore not entitled to the benefits of the Act.

"Enterprise" coverage, however, is not the only basis upon which employees may be covered by the FLSA. Individual employees who are engaged in commerce or in the production of goods for commerce may be individually covered by the Act even if their employer is not a covered enterprise. The district court erred when it failed to consider whether Zorich was individually covered by the Act.

Zorich is currently employed as a paramedic by LBFD. The paramedics work four consecutive 24-hour shifts weekly. In each 24-hour period, a paramedic spends four hours on site at the station and 20 hours on call. Zorich filed a complaint alleging that his on-call time is compensable pursuant to the FLSA and that LBFD owes him additional regular and overtime pay for the time spent on call.

LBFD argues that in order for employees to fall within the protection of the FLSA, their employer must be a covered enterprise. Zorich, on the other hand, asserts that the FLSA covers employees by two independent means: 1) individually, if they are "engaged in commerce or in the production of goods for commerce," or 2) through their employer, if they are "employed in an enterprise engaged in commerce or in the production of goods for commerce." Zorich is correct.

The regulations governing the FLSA support Zorich's argument that individual employee coverage survived the amendment by which the concept of enterprise coverage was added to the Act:

> Before the amendments of 1961 and 1966 to the Fair Labor Standards Act, general coverage of the Act depended on the traditional basis of engagement by individual

> employees "in commerce or in the production of goods for commerce." The amendments broadened coverage by extending it to other employees on an "enterprise" basis when "employed in an enterprise engaged in commerce or in the production of goods for commerce" as defined in subsections 203(r) and (s) of the Act. Employees covered on an individual basis remain so covered under the amended Act; the effect of the amendments was to extend coverage to those employees of covered enterprises who might not have been theretofore individually covered. (29 C.F.R. §776.0 (1996).)

The FLSA provides two independent types of coverage. An employee who engages in interstate commerce is individually covered regardless of whether his employer qualifies as a covered enterprise.

We reverse and remand to the district court for its consideration of whether plaintiff is engaged in commerce or in the production of goods for commerce and, if so, whether he is due additional compensation under the Act.

Excerpts from Fair Labor Standards Act
29 U.S.C. §203, et seq.

§203: Definitions

* * *

(b) **"Commerce"** means trade, commerce, transportation, or communication among the several States or between any State or any place outside thereof.

* * *

(i) **"Goods"** means goods, wares, products, commodities, merchandise, or articles or subjects of commerce of any character, or any part thereof, but does not include goods after their delivery into the actual physical possession of the ultimate consumer thereof other than a producer, manufacturer, or processor thereof.

(j) **"Produced"** means produced, manufactured, mined, handled or in any other manner worked on in any State; and for purposes of this statute an employee shall be deemed to have been engaged in the production of goods if such employee was engaged in producing, manufacturing, mining, handling, transporting, or in any other manner working on such goods, or in any closely related process or occupation directly essential to the production thereof, in any State.

* * *

(r)(1) **"Enterprise"** means the related activities performed (either through unified operation or common control) by any person or persons for a common business purpose, and includes all such activities whether performed in one or more establishments or by one or more corporate or other organizational units.

(s)(1) **"Enterprise engaged in commerce or in the production of goods for commerce"** means an enterprise that—

(A)(i) has employees engaged in commerce or in the production of goods for commerce, or that has employees handling, selling, or otherwise working on goods or materials that have been moved in or produced for commerce by any person; and

(A)(ii) is an enterprise whose annual gross volume of sales made or business done is not less than $500,000; . . .

* * *

§207: Maximum Hours

(a)(1) Except as otherwise provided in this section, no employer shall employ any employee who in any workweek is engaged in commerce or in the production of goods for commerce, or is employed in an enterprise engaged in commerce or in the production of goods for commerce, for a workweek longer than 40 hours unless such employee receives compensation for his employment in excess of the hours above specified at a rate not less than one and one-half times the regular rate at which he is employed.

Excerpts from
Regulations on the General Coverage of the Wage and Hours Provisions of the Fair Labor Standards Act
29 C.F.R. Part 776

§776.2 Employee basis of coverage.

If employees are found to be engaged in covered work, their employer cannot avoid his obligations to them under the Act on the ground that the employer is not "engaged in commerce or in the production of goods for commerce."

§776.3 Persons engaged in both covered and noncovered activities.

The Act makes no distinction as to the percentage, volume, or amount of activities of either employee or employer which constitute engaging in commerce or in the production of goods for commerce . . . . Employees doing work in connection with mere isolated, sporadic, or occasional shipments in commerce of insubstantial amounts of goods will not be considered covered by virtue of that fact alone. However, every employee whose engagement in covered activities is regular and recurring, even though small in amount, is covered by the Act.

* * *

§776.10 Employees participating in the actual movement of commerce.

Employees doing work involving or relating to the movement of persons or things (whether tangibles or intangibles and including information and intelligence) in commerce are covered by the Act. Under this principle, the Act applies to employees such as those in telephone, telegraph, television, radio, transportation, and shipping industries, since these industries serve as the actual instrumentalities and channels of interstate and foreign commerce. Similarly, employees of such industries as banking, insurance, newspaper publishing, and others which regularly utilize the channels of interstate commerce (such as telephones, the mails, wire and wireless communications and the like) in the course of their operations are generally covered by the Act. Likewise, employees whose work is an essential part of the stream of commerce, in whatever type of business they are employed, are covered by the Act. For example, employees of a warehouse whose activities are connected with the receipt or distribution of goods across state lines are covered. This does not mean that any use by an employee of the mails and other channels of communication is sufficient to establish coverage. But if the employee, as a regular and recurrent part of his duties, uses such instrumentalities in obtaining or communicating information or in sending or receiving written reports or messages, or orders for goods or services, he comes within the coverage of the Act.

* * *

§776.16 Employment in "producing, * * * or in any other manner working on" goods.

Employees employed in producing, manufacturing, handling or in any other manner working on goods (including parts or ingredients thereof) for interstate commerce are covered by the Act. This is true of employees doing such work as handling ingredients (scrap iron) of steel used in building ships which will move in commerce; transporting within a single state lumber to a mill where the products of the mill will be shipped out of state; transporting parts or ingredients of other types of goods or the finished goods themselves between processors, manufacturers, and storage places located in a single state, where the goods will leave the state in the same form or will be altered or incorporated into other goods and leave the state in some other form. Employees of independent employers who provide other employers with materials or articles which become parts or ingredients of goods produced by such other employers for commerce are covered. Thus, for example, employees of an independent employer that gathers and processes pine cones and sells them to an unrelated manufacturer of Christmas wreaths that incorporates the pine cones as components of the wreaths and ships the wreaths across state lines are covered.

§776.17 Employment in a "closely related process or occupation directly essential to" production of goods.

Employees whose work is closely related and directly essential to the production of goods for commerce are also covered by the Act. The terms "closely related" and "directly essential" are not susceptible of precise definition, but they describe a situation where, under the particular circumstances, the process or occupation in which the employee is engaged bears a relationship to the production of goods for interstate commerce (1) which can reasonably be considered close, as distinguished from remote or tenuous, and (2) in which the work of the employee directly aids production in a practical sense. Examples of such processes or occupations are bookkeepers, clerks, accountants, auditors, payroll clerks, draftsmen, inspectors, industrial safety personnel, labor relations, advertising, promotion and public relations activities, servicing, repairing and maintaining buildings, equipment and machinery.

Pauling v. Del-Rey Wood Products Co.

Sample Answer

PROPOSED INTERROGATORIES ON INDIVIDUAL COVERAGE

INTERROGATORY NO. 1: State the names and addresses of all suppliers of all raw materials, including lumber, used in the production of Del-Rey products in the past three years, and the source of such materials.

Reason for proposing: An individual is covered by the Act if she is engaged in commerce or in the production of goods for commerce. [Zorich v. Long Beach Fire Department] Commerce in this context means interstate commerce. [29 U.S.C. §203(b) — "trade, commerce, transportation, or communication among the several States or between any State or any place outside thereof"] An employee employed in the producing, manufacturing, handling, etc. of goods (or parts thereof) for interstate commerce is covered by the Act. [29 U.S.C. §203(j); 29 C.F.R. §776.16] Also, an employee whose activities are connected to the receipt of goods across state lines would be covered. [29 C.F.R. §776.10] As part of her job duties, Pauling received and stacked lumber used for the making of the furniture parts. She does not know where the timber originally came from or where the logs were cut into lumber, but it is possible that the materials were from out of state and thus part of interstate commerce, bringing her, as well as workers finishing the lumber, under the Act.

INTERROGATORY NO. 2: State the names and addresses of all suppliers of equipment, including woodworking tools, saws, lathe parts, and saw blades, used at Del-Rey Wood Products Co. during the past three years.

Reason for proposing: Similarly, we need to know whether equipment used by Del-Rey Wood Products came from an out-of-state supplier. Part of Pauling's job was to receive equipment and supplies, and Pauling believes that at least some of the equipment used in making Del-Rey's products (the saw blades) were from an out-of-state supplier. If so, her work and that of other employees would be covered under the Act. [29 C.F.R. §§776.10, 776.16]

INTERROGATORY NO. 3: State the names and addresses of all purchasers of Del-Rey Wood Products finished parts within the last three years.

Reason for proposing: We need to know if Del-Rey shipped any of its own products out of state. As stated above, an employee is deemed to have been engaged in the production of goods if she was engaged in the handling, transporting, etc. of goods for commerce. Part of Pauling's and other employees' jobs was to handle the paperwork for the finished parts and to load boxes of them onto trucks. If these items were then sent to out-of-state customers, Pauling and these other employees would be covered by the Act. [29 C.F.R. §§776.10, 776.16]

INTERROGATORY NO. 4: State the names and job duties of all Del-Rey employees who work or have within the past three years worked on orders (including communicating about, processing, shipping, and receiving such orders) of all raw materials covered in Interrogatory No. 1, equipment covered in Interrogatory No. 2, and/or finished parts covered in Interrogatory No. 3.

Reason for proposing: Employees who obtain or communicate, such as by telephone or fax, information or send or receive orders for goods or services are covered by the Act if such activity is a regular and recurrent part of their job. [29 C.F.R. §776.10] This information will help us to determine which Del-Rey employees are involved in ordering, receiving, or handling raw materials, equipment, and finished parts and if it is a regular part of their job.

INTERROGATORY NO. 5: State the names and addresses of all purchasers within the last three years of D & R Manufacturing Co. products and D & R Enterprises products that use or incorporate Del-Rey parts.

Reason for proposing: We know that many of Del-Rey's parts are shipped to D & R Furniture Manufacturing Company, located nearby, but we need to know if D & R Furniture Manufacturing then ships its goods out of state. Also, Pauling's paychecks bore a logo that said "D & R Enterprises—Recognized Around the World for Fine Furniture." Thus, it would seem likely that D & R Enterprises, if not D & R Furniture Manufacturing, ships finished goods out of state, and some of those goods may well include Del-Rey parts. This interrogatory might also provide us with other purchasers who use Del-Rey parts for their goods, which are then shipped in interstate commerce. This information would be useful because if Del-Rey employees provide other, independent employers with materials or articles that become parts or ingredients of goods produced by those other employers for commerce, Del-Rey employees would be covered by the Act. [29 C.F.R. §776.16]

INTERROGATORY NO. 6: Please state the names and job titles of all current and former Del-Rey Wood Products employees, including employees who do not work directly with Del-Rey parts, such as front office or other support staff, within the last three years and give a detailed job description for each and the frequency with which each duty is/was performed.

Reason for proposing: We need to know the duties of each potential plaintiff. If an employee is engaged in both covered and noncovered activities, the employee is still covered by the Act if the covered activities are regular and recurring, even if small in amount. [29 C.F.R. §776.3] Also, employees whose work is "closely related and directly essential" to the production of goods for commerce are covered. [29 C.F.R. §776.17] This would allow coverage of some Del-Rey employees who do not work directly with goods or shipments but whose work is still essential to Del-Rey's business, such as front office employees. (*Note:* This interrogatory, which asks for the names of all current and former employees in a three-year period, would be too broad if the company were quite large. However, since Del-Rey has approximately 20 current employees, and three years is not a very long period, this request is not that broad or burdensome.)

[***EDITOR'S NOTE:*** The exam required only six interrogatories, and there are many others you could have asked. In fact, passing answers from various jurisdictions were organized differently. For example, some passing answers broke down Interrogatory No. 4 into separate interrogatories instead of asking all about the various employees in one interrogatory. The key to a passing answer was to ask interrogatories that would elicit information about Del-Rey's connection to interstate commerce through its goods or activities, and about its employees' duties that directly or indirectly relate to commerce. Also, questions pertaining to enterprise coverage (rather than individual coverage) should have been avoided.]

Multistate Performance Test

March v. Betts

National Conference of Bar Examiners

Preface

This Multistate Performance Test is a reprint of one of the three MPTs which were administered in July 2000.

The instructions for the test appear on the next page. On the actual MPT, they will appear on the back cover of the test.

INSTRUCTIONS

1. You will have 90 minutes to complete this session of the examination. This performance test is designed to evaluate your ability to handle a select number of legal authorities in the context of a factual problem involving a client.

2. The problem is set in the fictitious state of Franklin, in the fictitious Fifteenth Circuit of the United States. Columbia and Olympia are also fictitious states in the Fifteenth Circuit. In Franklin, the trial court of general jurisdiction is the District Court, the intermediate appellate court is the Court of Appeal, and the highest court is the Supreme Court.

3. You will have two kinds of materials with which to work: a File and a Library. The first document in the File is a memorandum containing the instructions for the task you are to complete. The other documents in the File contain factual information about your case and may include some facts that are not relevant.

4. The Library contains the legal authorities needed to complete the task and may also include some authorities that are not relevant. Any cases may be real, modified, or written solely for the purpose of this examination. If the cases appear familiar to you, do not assume that they are precisely the same as you have read before. Read them thoroughly, as if they all were new to you. You should assume that cases were decided in the jurisdictions and on the dates shown. In citing cases from the Library, you may use abbreviations and omit page references.

5. Your response must be written in the answer book provided. If you are taking this examination on a laptop computer, your jurisdiction will provide you with specific instructions. In answering this performance test, you should concentrate on the materials provided in the File and Library. What you have learned in law school and elsewhere provides the general background for analyzing the problem; the File and Library provide the specific materials with which you must work.

6. Although there are no restrictions on how you apportion your time, you should be sure to allocate ample time (about 45 minutes) to reading and digesting the materials and to organizing your answer before you begin writing it. You may make notes anywhere in the test materials; blank pages are provided at the end of the booklet. You may not tear pages from the question booklet.

7. This performance test will be graded on your responsiveness to the instructions regarding the task you are to complete, which are given to you in the first memorandum in the File, and on the content, thoroughness, and organization of your response.

March v. Betts

FILE

LIBRARY

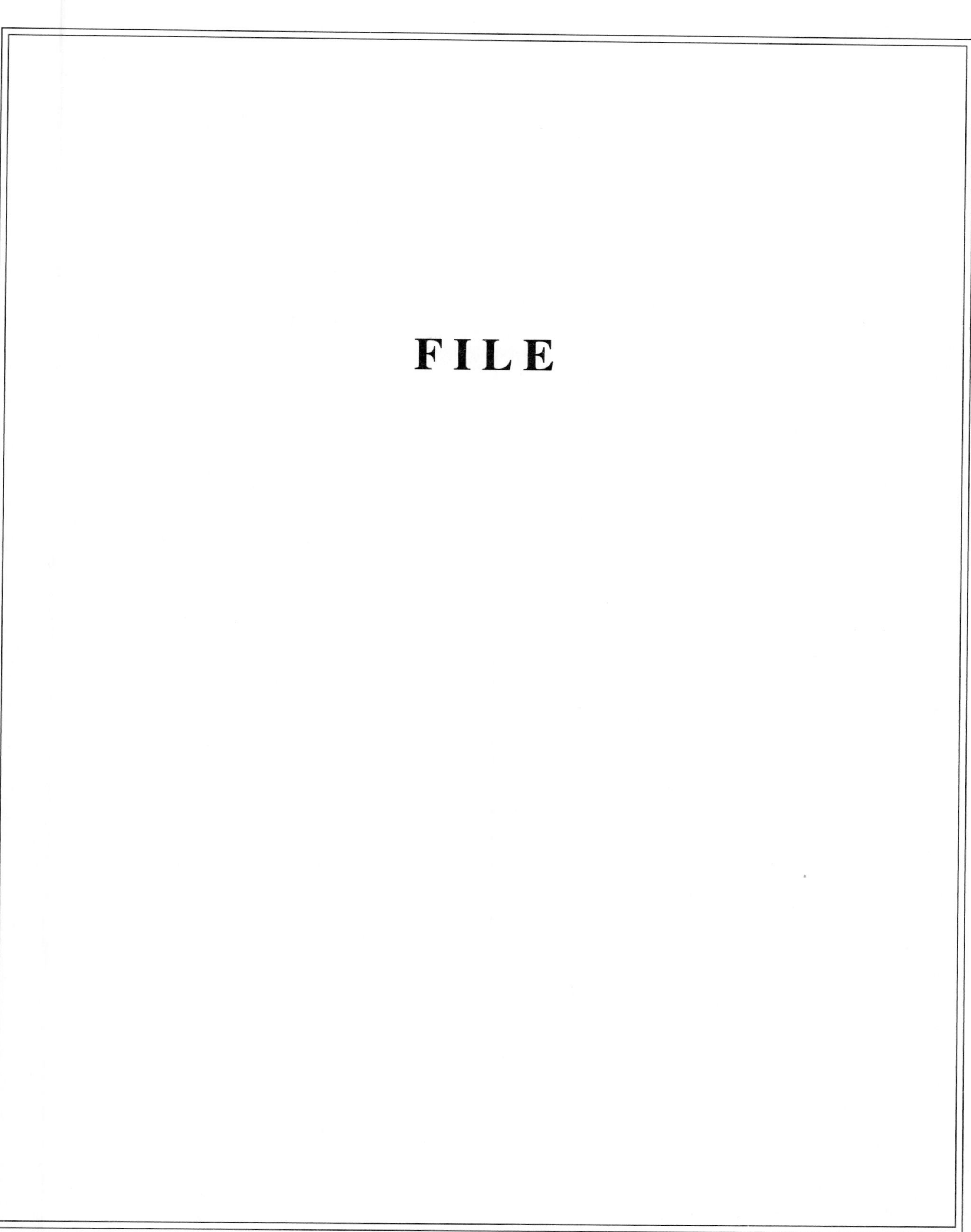

FILE

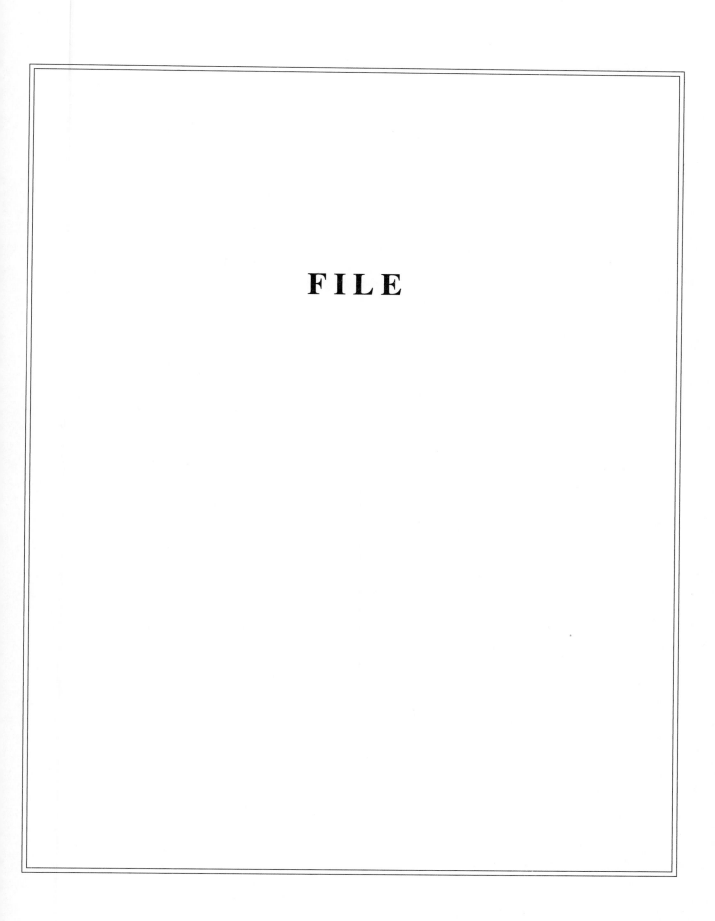

Mitchell, Fitch & Dawson
2205 Crescent Lane
Porter City, Franklin 33214

To: Applicant

July 25, 2000

From: Craig Dawson

Re: Arlene March - Mediation Statement

Last week, while staffing the Bar Association Pro Bono Clinic, I agreed to represent Arlene March. Last month, Ms. March rode home in a Sun Cab taxi with her wheelchair folded up in the trunk. An expensive custom-built back brace, which needed to be detached when the wheelchair was folded up, was left in the trunk when the taxi drove away. Efforts to retrieve the back brace have failed, and Sun Cab has denied all responsibility. In response to Ms. March's complaint to the Porter City Taxi Commission and her election to pursue mediation, the Commission has ordered mandatory mediation of the matter.

We need to file a persuasive written mediation statement with the Taxicab Commission's mediator. I intend to rely on three legal theories: that the cab driver breached a contract of bailment; that the cab driver was negligent; and that, in both cases, Sun Cab Association and the owner of the cab are vicariously liable.

Please draft a mediation statement for my signature in accordance with Sections 3a. and 3b. of the Taxicab Commission's mediation procedures. After you have completed this assignment, I will meet with Ms. March to discuss what relief she really wants, so don't draft Section 3c. of the letter.

Mitchell, Fitch & Dawson
2205 Crescent Lane
Porter City, Franklin 33214

July 18, 2000

To: File

From: Craig Dawson

Re: Notes of Interview with Arlene March

Arlene March sustained a serious spinal cord injury in a hit and run accident five years ago that left her largely paralyzed from the neck down. Because her spine was not completely severed, she still has some movement in and control over parts of her body. She is unable to work, and her only source of income is Supplemental Security Income (SSI). She requires 24-hour care. She is assisted by a nurse from Homecare, Inc. four hours a day, the maximum that medical assistance will pay for. The rest of the time, she is helped by her cousin, Maxine Taylor, who lives in Arlene's apartment rent-free in return for providing care and performing housekeeping duties.

Ms. March has two wheelchairs, one electric (which she can maneuver on her own, but which is not very portable and therefore difficult to take to places without wheelchair access) and one manual (in which she needs to be pushed). The electric wheelchair has built-in back support that enables Ms. March to sit up straight and alleviates some pain produced by sitting. The manual wheelchair, which folds up easily, has a custom-made, form-fitting back brace that must be inserted in place of the normal sling on the back of a folding wheelchair to provide the necessary support for Ms. March when she is using that wheelchair.

Last month, Ms. March and Ms. Taylor took a cab with the insignia of the Sun Cab Association home from Porter City Park, where they go on an average of two times a month to listen to concerts, watch the tennis players, or play chess at the outdoor chess tables. Because of the need for cab transportation between their home and the park, they took the manual wheelchair. The driver placed the wheelchair and the back brace in the trunk of the cab. When they reached Ms. March's home, Ms. March and the cabdriver got into a dispute about the fare, and her back brace was left in the trunk when the driver, Gary Betts, drove off. The dispute is described in the complaint Ms. March filed with the Taxicab Commission, a copy of which she brought with her (attached).

Since losing her back brace, Ms. March has been trying to get a replacement. The Porter City Rehabilitation Institute, where she received treatment as an inpatient after her accident and where she has continued ever since, got her both wheelchairs and the back brace in the first place. Although her doctor, Dr. Maureen Korn, wrote her a new prescription for a replacement brace, Jeremy Steel, her social worker, said that Medicaid would not pay for it unless she were an inpatient. The cost of a new brace is over $1,600, which she cannot afford out of her monthly SSI grant of $328.

Ms. March wants to recover, at a minimum, two components of damages: the money to replace the lost brace and compensation for the limitations on her activity caused by not having the use of the back brace. I spoke to her at length about the choice between filing a lawsuit or seeking mediation under the new Porter City Taxicab Commission Mediation Program. She liked the fact that mediation could result in a much faster resolution of the problem and decided to pursue the mediation choice.

The Commission's files show that Cynthia Maxon is the owner of the cab and that she pays dues to and is a member of the Sun Cab Association. That gives her the right to buy insurance coverage through the Association, use the Association's logo and color scheme, and use the Association's dispatch services. There is no record in the Commission's files of Gary Betts as a registered driver for either Sun Cab or Cynthia Maxon.

Porter City Taxicab Commission

Disputes Between Passengers and Taxicab Drivers, Owners, and Associations

Procedures for Mediation

If the parties are unable to resolve their dispute among themselves, the passenger may ask that the complaint be referred to the Commission's Mediation Program. The following procedures shall be followed:

1. The Secretary of the Commission shall appoint a mediator from the existing panel of mediators who shall be members in good standing of the Porter City Bar Association.
2. Within 30 days from the referral, a mediation session will be scheduled and the parties notified by mail of the session.
3. No later than 10 days prior to the date set for the mediation session, the passenger shall file with the Commission a written mediation statement, which shall be in letter format and which shall:
    a. describe the dispute;
    b. explain the legal and factual reasons why the taxicab driver, owner and/or Association is/are responsible and should be held to account;
    c. state the relief sought.
4. No later than 5 days prior to the date set for the mediation session, the taxicab driver, owner, or Association shall file with the Commission a written reply to the mediation statement, which shall be in letter format and which shall:
    a. describe its version of the dispute;
    b. explain the legal and factual reasons why it is not responsible and should not be held to account;
    c. state what resolution, if any, it proposes.

Porter City Taxicab Commission
Complaint - Form 220

Complainant: Arlene March **Complaint No.** 7639

Address: 2705 Hawthorne St., Porter City

On Sunday, June 11, 2000, at 7:00 p.m., myself and my cousin, Maxine Taylor, were picked up at Porter City Park and taken to 2705 Hawthorne Street by Sun Cab #206. I require help when traveling. When I arrived at my destination, the driver tried to charge me $10. I knew that the amount that he told me was too much so I gave him $8 instead. The driver insisted that the fare was $10 and he started to argue with me and tried to show me how many zones he went through to get to my destination. While in the cab I looked at his license and got his name, Mr. Gary Betts. Maxine got out of the cab to get the wheelchair out of the trunk. While she was helping me into the chair, the cabdriver got upset, slammed the trunk, and drove off before we could get my back support out of the trunk.

On Monday, I called Sun Cab and spoke to Mr. Abner, the dispatcher. I explained my situation to him and Mr. Abner told me to call back the next day and he could give me some more information on Mr. Betts. I called the next day, which was Tuesday. Mr. Abner informed me that he and the driver had looked in the cab and couldn't find anything in the trunk. I told Mr. Abner that I needed my back support and he told me to call the place where I got my back support and to get an estimate. I called Porter City Rehabilitation Institute to get the price and it is valued at $1644. When I called back and gave Mr. Abner the price, he told me the driver was let go, but they are not responsible. So I informed Mr. Abner that I would contact the Taxi Commission. I called the Commission and they told me to try and work it out with Sun Cab. I called back and spoke to Mr. Abner and he tried to estimate the cost of my back support himself and wanted to give me $100 for it and $8 back for the fare. On Wednesday, I called the Commission again and spoke to Mr. Smith and he sent Inspector Hall over to my house so I could make this formal complaint.

Date: June 20, 2000 **Signature** Arlene March

Porter City Taxicab Commission
2041 Winter Avenue
Porter City, Franklin 33214

July 5, 2000

Ms. Cynthia Lea Maxon
1201 S. Courthouse Road
Porter City, Franklin 33214

Mr. Marvin Shaw, Operations Manager
Sun Cab Association, Inc.
2100 Vidal Avenue
Porter City, Franklin 33214

Dear Ms. Maxon and Mr. Shaw:

You are hereby notified that Arlene March has filed with Porter City Taxicab Commission a complaint regarding Sun Cab Association vehicle #206, which our records show is owned by Cynthia Maxon and operates under the trade name and colors of Sun Cab Association. Under the regulations of the PCTC, you must attempt informal resolution of this matter. If that is not successful, the passenger may choose to pursue mediation under the PCTC Mediation Program.

Failure to obey these procedures is a violation of Taxicab Commission regulations and may result in a hearing before the Commission's Panel on Adjudication. If found guilty, you may receive a **suspension** or **revocation** of your privilege to own or operate public vehicles in Porter City and/or the imposition of a fine up to $500.

Sincerely,

Sharon T. White

Sharon T. White
Taxicab Dispute Resolution Specialist

Enclosure

SUN CAB ASSOCIATION

2100 Vidal Avenue
Porter City, Franklin

July 11, 2000

Sharon T. White
Taxicab Dispute Resolution Specialist
Porter City Taxicab Commission
2041 Winter Avenue
Porter City, Franklin 33214

RE: Sun Cab #206

Dear Ms. White:

In response to your letter of July 5, I submit to you the following:

We tried our best to recover the back support from the alleged driver, who was driving the Taxicab illegally and without our permission or knowledge, without much success. However, we did confiscate the Tags of the Taxicab and handed them over to Inspector Hall.

At this time, due to extreme financial hardship, we can only offer a sum of $200 as a donation towards the purchase of a back support. As you are aware, we try our best to run our business according to the rules and regulations set forth by the Taxicab Commission, but there are times when some incidents take place over which we do not have any controls. This, unfortunately, is one such mishap.

Yours sincerely,

Marvin Shaw

Marvin Shaw
Operations Manager

FMIC

FIRST MADISON INSURANCE COMPANY
3341 Denning Road
Porter City, Franklin 33214

July 11, 2000

VIA CERTIFIED MAIL
Marvin Shaw
Sun Cab Association
2100 Vidal Avenue
Porter City, Franklin 33214

RE: Complaint of Arlene March to Porter City Taxicab Commission

Dear Mr. Shaw:

Thank you for forwarding the complaint filed by Ms. March with the Porter City Taxicab Commission.

Our records reflect that the driver of the accident vehicle, Gary Betts, was not a covered driver under a policy of insurance you have with this company covering vehicle #206 owned by Cynthia Maxon. We cannot, therefore, provide coverage to you for this accident.

We suggest that you retain counsel to defend you in this case. We are sorry that we could not assist you in this matter.

Respectfully,

Michael W. Wood

MICHAEL W. WOOD
Claims Manager

cc: Porter City Taxicab Commission

NO. B 149254

Porter City Department of Consumer and Regulatory Affairs

CERTIFICATE OF OCCUPANCY

April 14, 1993
(date)

Permission is hereby granted to Sun Cab Association, Inc. to use the 1st floor(s) of the building located at the premises known as 2100 Vidal Avenue for the following purpose(s) Taxicab Office, Rent, Buy, Repair & Sell Cabs & Cars, Related Auto Repairs & Auto Body Repairs.

EXPIRATION DATE: December 31, 2000 FEE $134.08

Donald G. Murray, Acting Director

By Donald G. Murray

PORTER CITY TAXICAB COMMISSION PCTC
TAXICAB LICENSE
NUMBER 27991
VALID 01/01/00 to 12/31/00

MAXON, CYNTHIA LEA
1201 S. COURTHOUSE ROAD
PORTER CITY, FRANKLIN 33214

OWNER ID 486685385
ASSN/COMPANY NO:
SUN CAB ASSN 206
INSURANCE COMPANY
FIRST MADISON INS
VEHICLE IDENTIFICATION NO.
1G1BN69HOFY150134

YEAR	MAKE	MODEL	TAG NUMBER	COLOR
96	CHEV	4D	HPC 472	Silver

STATE OF FRANKLIN
AUTOMOBILE REGISTRATION CERTIFICATE

Tag No.	Sticker No.
HPC 472	180056

Title No.	Make	Year	Body	Wgt	Cl
J95431V	CHEV	96	TX	40	A

Vehicle ID No.	Fee
1G1BN69HOFY150134	98.00

MAXON, CYNTHIA LEA
1201 South Courthouse Road
Porter City, Franklin 33214
Expires March 31, 2001
VALIDATED: BMVS
Department of Public Works

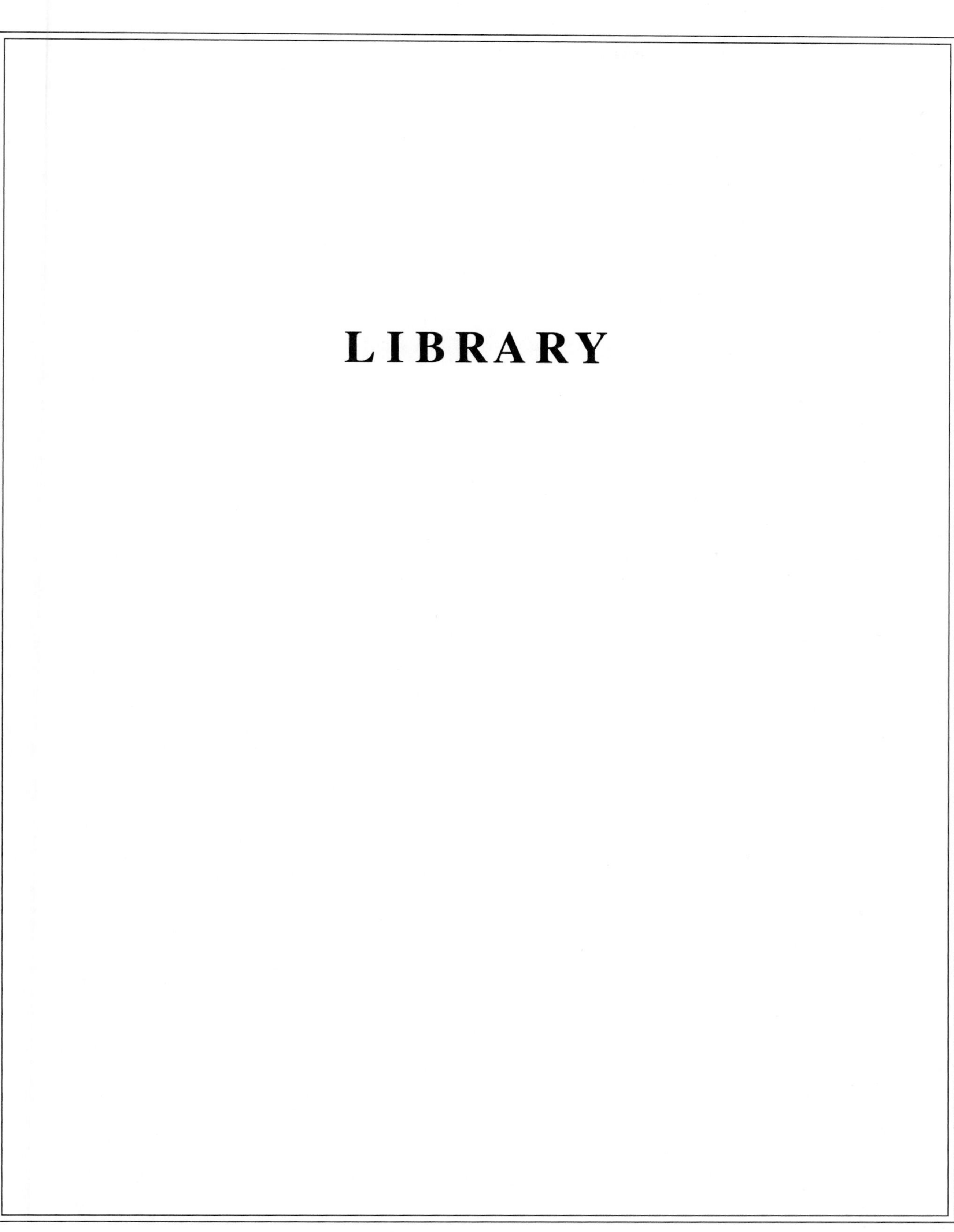
LIBRARY

Franklin Code

Title 400—Motor Vehicles and Traffic

Section 408: Operator deemed to be agent of owner

Whenever any motor vehicle shall be operated upon the public highways of Franklin by any person other than the owner, with the consent of the owner, express or implied, the operator thereof shall be deemed to be the agent of the owner of the vehicle. Proof of the ownership of the motor vehicle shall be prima facie evidence that such person operated said motor vehicle with the consent of the owner.

Marchetti v. Olyowski

Franklin Supreme Court (1980)

Annie Olyowski was injured on February 16, 1978, when the cab in which she was a passenger collided with another vehicle. She sued the driver, the former owner of the vehicle, and the taxicab association for personal injury.

She had met the driver, Anthony Nolan, a few days earlier when he was driving a Diamond Cab. On the day of the accident, Nolan had picked Ms. Olyowski up by pre-arrangement to drive her to Charlotte, Franklin for $150. On that day, he was driving a vehicle showing the color scheme and trade name of American Cab Association. The cab was registered with the Public Utilities Commission in the name of Philip Marchetti. It showed him as the owner and insured under a general liability policy carried by the American Cab Association, of which Marchetti was a member.

A few days before the accident, Nolan had purchased the vehicle from Marchetti, but no one had notified American of the sale of the vehicle. Nolan registered it in his name but not as a taxicab.

American Cab Association does not own or operate taxicabs, operate a garage, advertise, or furnish telephone call service. The extent of its activity is to permit its members to use its trade name and color scheme and to obtain public liability insurance, coverage under which is indicated by a windshield sticker.

Nolan's negligence is not at issue in this appeal. Drivers of taxicabs have the duty to transport passengers and their property safely. *Johnson v. Sales* (Franklin Supreme Court, 1979). Nolan breached his duty of care when he ran a red light and collided with another car.

At the trial, the judge instructed the jury that, if it found against Nolan, it must also find against Marchetti and American. Marchetti and American appeal based on that instruction.

We first consider the propriety of the instruction with respect to American. We held in *Callas v. Independent Taxi Owners' Association* (Franklin Supreme Court, 1965) that a taxicab bearing the peculiar colors and trade name of a cab association is rebuttably presumed, when involved in an accident or other loss, to have been in the custody of, and engaged in the business of, that association. If the presumption is overcome by uncontradicted proof, the association cannot be found liable.

Here the uncontradicted evidence showed that Nolan was a total stranger to American, with no authority, express or implied, to operate the cab in the name or under the colors of the Association and whose use of the cab was without its knowledge or consent. Nor was there any evidence of reliance by the injured passenger upon the name or colors of the defendant Association. Accordingly, the trial court's instruction was erroneous.

We are not dissuaded by *Rhone v. Try Me Cab Co.* (Franklin Supreme Court, 1970), where this court held the cab association was estopped to deny liability for damages negligently inflicted by the driver of a cab carrying its colors. The driver in that case was the agent of the owner, who was a member of the defendant cab association; and the plaintiff called the association for service, which responded by sending a cab bearing its insignia. The plaintiff relied, and had a right to rely, upon the Try Me Cab Company. Here Olyowski made her contract with Nolan when he was using a Diamond Cab and did not know he would appear later in a cab marked American Cab Association.

However, the court's instruction vis-à-vis Marchetti was correct. Without notifying American, he turned over to Nolan the taxicab bearing the colors of the Association of which Nolan was not a member and bearing also the insurance sticker issued in Marchetti's name. He made it possible for Nolan to operate the taxicab in an unauthorized manner. Under *Rhone,* he is estopped to deny liability.

Affirmed in part and reversed in part.

Dovell v. Arundel Supply Corporation

Franklin Court of Appeal (1986)

Ann Dovell sued John Skouzes and Arundel Supply Corporation for damages arising from an injury suffered when she was struck by a truck while crossing a street. Skouzes was the driver-owner of the truck. Arundel was alleged to be vicariously liable for the actions of Skouzes. The trial court granted Arundel's motion for summary judgment on the basis that Skouzes, as a matter of law, was an independent contractor and dismissed the complaint against Arundel. This appeal followed.

John Skouzes owned two dump trucks. He drove one and hired a driver for the other. Skouzes kept the trucks at a garage he rented and was responsible for their maintenance. From 1980 until this accident in November 1982, he worked for Arundel, who had a daily right of first refusal of Skouzes' services. He could seek other work only if Arundel did not need him. The contract of employment was oral and could be terminated by either party. Arundel would load the truck with gravel and measure the load. A representative of Arundel would designate its recipient, leaving the choice of route up to the driver. Arundel required a certain number of deliveries to a particular location in a day. To prove delivery, a receipt would be obtained at the destination. Arundel paid Skouzes weekly on a ton-mile basis without any deductions. On a delivery, the accident occurred.

Franklin courts leave to the jury on these facts the question whether Skouzes was an independent contractor or an employee. We look to five factors at least in the determination of the relationship of master and servant: (1) the selection and engagement of the servant, (2) the payment of wages, (3) the power to discharge, (4) the power to control the servant's conduct, and (5) whether the work is a part of the regular business of the employer. Standing alone, none of these indicia, excepting (4), seems controlling. The decisive test is whether the employer has the right to control and direct the servant in the performance of his work and in the manner in which the work is to be done. It is not essential that the alleged master actually exercise the authority to control and direct the action of the servant; it is his *right* to do so that is important. *Silver Auto Co. v. Magruder* (Franklin Court of Appeal, 1975).

In *Keitz v. National Paving and Contracting Co.* (Franklin Court of Appeal, 1965), where a truck was an integral and necessary part of the alleged master's business and subject to the same direction and control as his own trucks, the court held "there was sufficient evidence to require the submission to the jury." In *Grace v. Miller* (Franklin Court of Appeal, 1968), where the question was whether "coal hustlers" who stored coal at the place of a coal customer after its delivery by the company were independent contractors or employees, the court noted that the storage of coal was an essential part of appellant's business and subject to the control of the company. "Nothing could be more destructive of the goodwill of a business than improper service at the point of contact between the company and the customer."

The trial court erred in granting a motion for summary judgment. A jury determination is required. Material facts are in dispute. For example, while Skouzes independently owned the two trucks, he was not brought in to perform a function unrelated to Arundel's supply business as would be a plumber to repair a leaking faucet in Arundel's office. His function was directly related to and essential to the supplying of gravel by Arundel to Arundel's customers.

In the final analysis, however, it may not matter whether Skouzes is found to be an employee or an independent contractor. In this case, we find that he is an agent of Arundel, and Arundel may be vicariously liable on agency principles. See *Miller v. Pickering* (Franklin Supreme Court, 1961) (principal is liable for torts committed by his agent in the course and scope of the agency).

Reversed and remanded for further proceedings.

Morris Properties v. Noble

Franklin Supreme Court (1995)

Morris Properties appeals the judgment in favor of tenant Noble for $269.95 for the cost of a stereo tuner delivered to the landlord's apartment building but never delivered to Noble. In reviewing the findings by a trial court, we may reverse only if the findings are clearly erroneous and without evidentiary support, or if there was an error of law. The trial court found that, in February 1994, Noble ordered a stereo tuner from a store in Maine. It was shipped to his apartment in appellant's building and delivered on February 20, 1994. Paulette McLean, the receptionist, signed the receipt for and received the tuner and placed it on a shelf in a small room next to her desk where packages for tenants were kept. McLean routinely accepted packages on behalf of tenants. Access to the room was limited; McLean and the night receptionist had keys to the door and there were bars on the windows.

When McLean was replaced by the night receptionist, the package was on the shelf. Noble later informed McLean that he had never received his tuner. McLean had assumed that he had received it since the tuner was not on the shelf when she returned to work the next morning. Thereafter, McLean gave Noble the empty box in which the tuner had been packaged. The box had been found outside the building.

A bailment requires a delivery by the bailor and the acceptance by the bailee of the subject matter of the bailment. The bailee does not acquire title to the property but merely holds it according to the terms of the bailment. A bailment is a form of contract and, thus, requires the mutual consent of the parties. If there is no express agreement, an implied in fact bailment can be found if it appears that such was the intent of the parties.

A plaintiff may establish a prima facie case for breach of the contract of bailment by showing the bailment and the loss of his/her property. Where a breach of the contract of bailment has occurred, the plaintiff may recover contract damages.

A prima facie case for breach of the contract of bailment also raises a presumption of negligence on the part of the bailee. When there is no evidence in rebuttal, the plaintiff may recover tort damages, such as compensatory damages.

A landlord may occupy the dual position of landlord and bailee, and the nature of the bailment will determine the proper standard of care. If the bailment is gratuitous, liability is limited to acts of gross negligence, willful acts, or fraud. When a bailment is for hire, the standard of care imposed on the bailee is that of ordinary care.

In this case, the landlord provided the locked room for packages received for tenants. A

bailment for hire was created when McLean placed Noble's package on the shelf. The landlord was required to exercise ordinary care, and proof by Noble of delivery and failure to produce the tuner established a prima facie case of negligence by the landlord.

Finally, the trial judge did not err in finding that the night receptionist was negligent and imputing the negligence to the landlord. It was a question of fact as to whether the landlord's evidence of due care rebutted the inference of negligence arising from the prima facie case. The circumstantial evidence of negligence is supported in the record. See *Smith's Transfer & Storage Co.* (Franklin Supreme Court, 1987) (circumstantial evidence of negligence where uncontradicted testimony established that missing items were previously delivered).

Affirmed.

March v. Betts

Sample Answer

Porter City Taxicab Commission
2041 Winter Avenue
Porter City, Franklin 33214

RE: Complaint #7639

Dear Commissioners:

The complainant, Arlene March, is paralyzed from the neck down and therefore uses a wheelchair with a custom back brace. On June 11, 2000, Ms. March and her cousin, Maxine Taylor, took a cab home from the city park. The cab, which bore the insignia of the Sun Cab Association, was driven by Gary Betts. Mr. Betts put Ms. March's folding wheelchair and the back brace into the trunk of the cab. At the destination, Ms. March and Mr. Betts got into a dispute over the fare, which was normally $8 for that route, but Mr. Betts charged her $10, a 25% increase. Mr. Betts angrily drove off with Ms. March's back brace still in the trunk of the cab.

The next morning, Ms. March telephoned Sun Cab and explained the situation to the dispatcher, Mr. Abner. Mr. Abner told Ms. March that he and Mr. Betts looked in the cab but could not find the brace. Mr. Abner told Ms. March to get an estimate of the cost to replace the brace. The estimate is $1,644 for a replacement brace. When Ms. March called Mr. Abner back, he told her that the cab company let Mr. Betts go, but it would not pay for the replacement back brace. Instead, he offered Ms. March only $100 and a refund of the cab fare. Thus, Ms. March filed a formal complaint with the Commission.

The cab involved is owned by Cynthia Maxon. Ms. Maxon is a member of the Sun Cab Association. As a member, she uses the Association's logo and color scheme on her cab and the Association's dispatch services. She also can buy insurance coverage through the Association. The Association refuses to pay Ms. March's claim because Mr. Betts is not registered as a driver for either Sun Cab or Ms. Maxon, and its insurance company has refused to cover the incident.

Betts's Breach of Bailment Contract: The driver of the cab, Gary Betts, is clearly liable to Ms. March for breach of the contract of bailment. In *Morris Properties v. Noble,* the Franklin Supreme Court states that a bailment is created by delivery of an item by the bailor and acceptance by the bailee. Because a bailment is a form of contract, there must be mutual consent of the parties, but an express agreement to create a bailment is not necessary. A bailment can be implied in fact if it appears that was the intent of the parties. The court also held that the establishment of a bailment and a loss of the property in question establishes a prima facie case for breach of the contract of bailment. Here, a bailment was created when Ms. March gave Mr. Betts her back brace and he accepted it by placing it in the trunk of his cab. It was clearly the parties' intent that the brace be transported along with Ms. March and delivered to her at her destination. Now the object of that bailment, the back brace, is lost. Thus, Mr. Betts is liable to Ms. March based on his breach of the contract of bailment.

Betts's Negligence: Mr. Betts is also liable to Ms. March based on his negligence in losing the back brace. A prima facie case for breach of the contract of bailment raises a presumption of negligence on the part of the bailee. [Morris Properties] Since Mr. Betts breached the contract of bailment when he lost the back brace, the presumption of negligence applies. Furthermore, negligence by Mr. Betts is easily established in this case. The bailment between Ms. March and Mr. Betts was a bailment for hire, since she was paying for his taxi services. When a bailment is for hire, the bailee is held to an ordinary care standard of care. [Morris Properties] An item simply would not be lost from a closed trunk by one exercising ordinary care. Since the back brace is now missing, Mr. Betts breached that duty, causing Ms. March to suffer damages. Mr. Betts is liable for his negligence.

Vicarious Liability of Maxon: Ms. Maxon, as the cab's owner, is vicariously liable for the actions of her driver, Mr. Betts. By statute, a driver of a motor vehicle who acts with the express or implied consent of the owner of the vehicle is presumed to be the agent of the owner. [Franklin Code Title 400, §408] Proof of ownership of the vehicle is prima facie evidence that the person operated the motor vehicle with the consent of the owner. [Franklin Code Title 400, §408] Ms. Maxon was the owner of the cab driven by Mr. Betts as evidenced by the automobile's registration certificate and the taxicab license. She either expressly or impliedly consented to Mr. Betts's operation of the car. Although he was not a registered operator, there is no evidence that she did not know that he was driving her cab or that she tried to stop him from doing so prior to the incident (*e.g.*, she never reported the cab stolen or had him charged with illegally operating her cab). Therefore, Mr. Betts was the agent of Ms. Maxon when he committed the tort against Ms. March. A principal is liable for torts committed by her agent in the course and scope of the agency. [Dovell v. Arundel Supply Corporation, *citing* Miller v. Pickering] Since Ms. Maxon is Mr. Betts's principal, she is liable for the torts he committed while acting as a cab driver in her car and thus is liable for his breach of contract of bailment and negligence.

Vicarious Liability of Association: Likewise, the Sun Cab Association is also liable for Mr. Betts's actions. The Franklin Supreme Court has held that a taxicab bearing the colors and trade name of a cab association is rebuttably presumed to have been engaged in the business of that association. [Marchetti v. Olyowski, *citing* Callas v. Independent Taxi Owners' Association] Unlike the situation in *Marchetti,* where the driver had no express or implied authority to operate the cab under the taxicab association's name or colors, Mr. Betts had at least implied authority to drive the cab bearing the insignia of the Sun Cab Association. Thus, he is rebuttably presumed to have been engaged in business of the Association. Although the Association may attempt to rebut that presumption by claiming that there was no relationship between it and Mr. Betts—that in fact Mr. Betts was operating the cab illegally—the facts are to the contrary. Mr. Abner, the dispatcher for Sun Cab, stated that after the incident Mr. Betts was "let go," thus implying that there was indeed some form of prior employment relationship with the Association. Furthermore, the court in *Dovell* sets out five factors to determine whether a person is an employee or independent contractor. Of those factors the most relevant here are the right to control the worker's conduct and whether the work is part of the regular business of the employer. Here, regarding control, the facts show that upon learning of the incident, Mr. Abner was able to summon Mr. Betts back to the Association's base so that he and Mr. Betts could look for the back brace. This implies that there was at least some minimal control over Mr. Betts. More importantly, driving a cab is clearly a part of the regular business of the Association. Thus, Mr. Betts is arguably an employee of the Association, but even if it were determined that he is an independent contractor, there is clearly some agency relationship between him and the Association. Also, at the time Ms. March reported her loss, Mr. Abner did not appear alarmed that Mr. Betts had been driving "illegally"; he did not call the police or take any similar action. Thus, even if Mr. Betts was not an officially registered driver, the Association is liable for his actions.

Finally, as established above, Mr. Betts was the agent of Ms. Maxon, a member of the Association, at the time of the incident. In a similar case, *Rhone v. Try Me Cab Co.*, a cab association was estopped from denying liability for the negligence of a cab driver who was the agent of the cab's owner, a member of the association. In that case the plaintiff called the association for service, which responded by sending a cab bearing its insignia and driven by an agent of one of its members. While here Ms. March simply hailed the Sun Cab, rather than called ahead for it, a similar result should be found because as discussed above, the facts indicate that the association had a relationship with the driver and Ms. March had a right to rely on that relationship.

Multistate Performance Test

Steinberg & Son, Inc. v. Wye

National Conference of Bar Examiners

Preface

This Multistate Performance Test is a reprint of one of the three MPTs which were administered in February 2001.

The instructions for the test appear on the next page. On the actual MPT, they will appear on the back cover of the test.

INSTRUCTIONS

1. You will have 90 minutes to complete this session of the examination. This performance test is designed to evaluate your ability to handle a select number of legal authorities in the context of a factual problem involving a client.

2. The problem is set in the fictitious state of Franklin, in the fictitious Fifteenth Circuit of the United States. Columbia and Olympia are also fictitious states in the Fifteenth Circuit. In Franklin, the trial court of general jurisdiction is the District Court, the intermediate appellate court is the Court of Appeal, and the highest court is the Supreme Court.

3. You will have two kinds of materials with which to work: a File and a Library. The first document in the File is a memorandum containing the instructions for the task you are to complete. The other documents in the File contain factual information about your case and may include some facts that are not relevant.

4. The Library contains the legal authorities needed to complete the task and may also include some authorities that are not relevant. Any cases may be real, modified, or written solely for the purpose of this examination. If the cases appear familiar to you, do not assume that they are precisely the same as you have read before. Read them thoroughly, as if they all were new to you. You should assume that cases were decided in the jurisdictions and on the dates shown. In citing cases from the Library, you may use abbreviations and omit page references.

5. Your response must be written in the answer book provided. If you are taking this examination on a laptop computer, your jurisdiction will provide you with specific instructions. In answering this performance test, you should concentrate on the materials provided in the File and Library. What you have learned in law school and elsewhere provides the general background for analyzing the problem; the File and Library provide the specific materials with which you must work.

6. Although there are no restrictions on how you apportion your time, you should be sure to allocate ample time (about 45 minutes) to reading and digesting the materials and to organizing your answer before you begin writing it. You may make notes anywhere in the test materials; blank pages are provided at the end of the booklet. You may not tear pages from the question booklet.

7. This performance test will be graded on your responsiveness to the instructions regarding the task you are to complete, which are given to you in the first memorandum in the File, and on the content, thoroughness, and organization of your response.

Steinberg & Son, Inc. v. Wye

FILE

LIBRARY

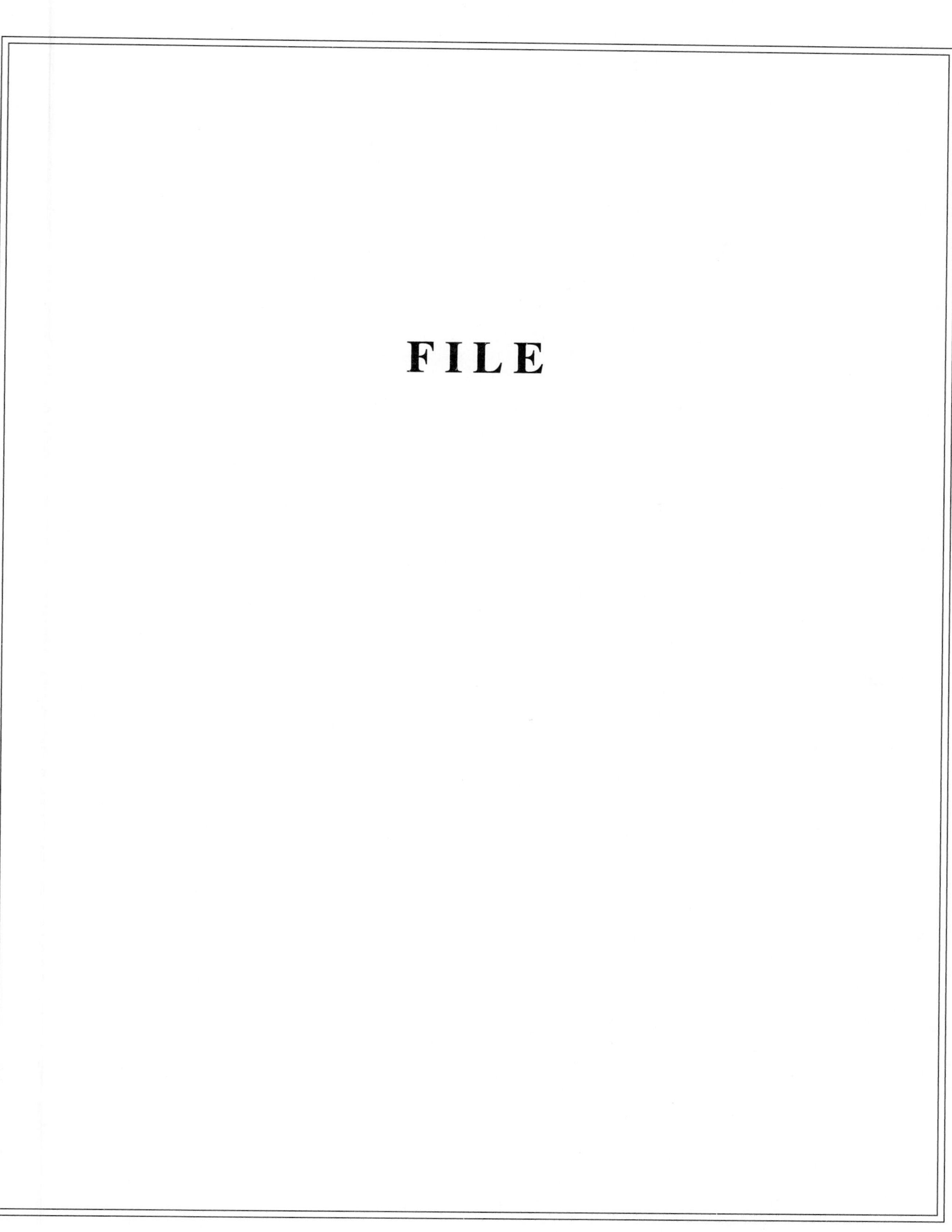
FILE

Shelley, Polikoff and Wolfe
Attorneys at Law
3200 Brooklawn Boulevard
Rosslyn, Franklin 33135
(555) 213-1000

TO: Applicant
FROM: Steven Shelley
DATE: February 27, 2001
RE: *Jack Steinberg & Son, Inc. v. Wye*

Our client, a closely held corporation, Jack Steinberg & Son, Inc., is the plaintiff in a complex lawsuit concerning a contract between the corporation and Murray Wye, an engineering consultant retained to design and supervise the construction of a new plant for the corporation. The litigation has been acrimonious throughout the four years it has been going on. Wye misrepresented his qualifications as an engineer, and the project ended up with huge cost overruns.

The action was begun for our client by Purta & Paul (P & P), a law firm that had represented the corporation and its president, Jack Steinberg, from the time the business was started in 1988 until August, 1999. P & P's only office is here in Rosslyn, and the firm has about 20 lawyers. Mr. Steinberg discharged P & P because he believed they committed malpractice on another matter. We were immediately retained and have represented Mr. Steinberg and his company ever since. The defendant in this case, Murray Wye, has been represented by the law firm of Doyle & Davis (D & D) since the inception of this action four years ago.

I learned about a month ago that Philip Fine, an associate at P & P during the entire time that firm represented our client, has left P & P and joined D & D as a partner. Mr. Steinberg remembers dealing with Fine in corporate business matters only. He doesn't remember ever talking to him about this litigation. Nevertheless, Mr. Steinberg is particularly aggrieved by the fact that a lawyer from P & P is now working for the law firm that is representing his adversary.

Our correspondence file contains the facts we know. I have attached some excerpts from the Franklin Rules of Professional Conduct, which are identical to the ABA's Model Rules, and the only Franklin case I could find decided under our Rules.

To assist me in determining whether to file a motion to disqualify D & D as counsel in this case, please draft a memorandum for me that analyzes the likelihood that such a motion would be successful. Be sure to give me the reasons for your conclusion. If you believe additional facts would assist us in our analysis, identify those facts and tell me why we need them.

Shelley, Polikoff and Wolfe
Attorneys at Law
3200 Brooklawn Boulevard
Rosslyn, Franklin 33135
(555) 213-1000

February 13, 2001

Ms. Dede Allen, Esq.
Doyle & Davis
Attorneys at Law
7603 Maple Avenue
Rosslyn, Franklin 33135

Dear Dede:

It has come to my attention that Philip Fine, formerly an associate at Purta & Paul, has, within the past several weeks, joined your firm as a partner. I think you already know that Purta & Paul served for a number of years as attorney for our clients, Jack Steinberg & Son, Inc. and its founder, Jack Steinberg. Among other matters that Purta & Paul handled for my client prior to being discharged was the original action that we have scheduled for trial against your client on June 4, 2001. This means, of course, that your continuing to represent Murray Wye, the defendant in *Jack Steinberg & Son, Inc. v. Wye* (Franklin District Court C.A. 97-1255), constitutes a conflict of interest.

Mr. Fine and Purta & Paul represented Jack Steinberg throughout the period during which Mr. Steinberg was organizing his business. Mr. Fine personally counseled Mr. Steinberg as to the form of the business and drafted and filed the articles of incorporation for Jack Steinberg and Son, Inc. Other lawyers in Purta & Paul represented the corporation in several real estate transactions, in all labor and employment matters, and in all litigation from 1988 until August, 1999. As a consequence, Mr. Steinberg shared with Purta & Paul his confidences and secrets and those of the company. Although I realize that Mr. Fine specialized in transactional and corporate work, he is presumed to have acquired confidential information that he is required to protect.

My clients will not waive the conflict of interest. Moreover, they continue to assert all privileges regarding any communications with Purta & Paul and any information in the possession of Mr. Fine. We expect that you will immediately withdraw from your representation of Mr. Wye in this matter and that you will so advise the court. Furthermore, we ask that you assure us that you have no other clients whose interests are adverse to those of Mr. Steinberg or the corporation.

In the event that you choose not to comply with this demand, we intend to file a motion for disqualification with the court.

Very truly yours,

Steven Shelley

Steven Shelley
Attorney at Law

Doyle & Davis

Attorneys and Counselors at Law

7603 Maple Avenue
Rosslyn, Franklin 33135
(555) 213-2300

1010 Pennsylvania Avenue, N.W.
Washington, D.C. 20002
(202) 555-1010

555 Park Avenue
New York, N.Y. 10020
(212) 666-4000

23 Embarcadero
San Francisco, CA 90001
(415) 200-7700

Dede Allen, Esq.
Managing Partner
Rosslyn Office

February 19, 2001

Steven Shelley, Esq.
Shelley, Polikoff and Wolfe
Attorneys at Law
3200 Brooklawn Boulevard
Rosslyn, Franklin 33135

Dear Steven:

This is in response to your letter of February 13, 2001, regarding the litigation between your clients, Jack Steinberg & Son, Inc. and Mr. Steinberg, and ours, Murray Wye. We were well aware of the fact that our newest partner, Philip Fine, worked for the firm that originally represented the Steinberg interests in this litigation. Consistent with the practice of this firm whenever new attorneys join us, we make careful inquiry regarding all conflicts of interest that may result from the affiliation.

Our routine practice, whenever we discover that an imputed conflict of interest has the potential to raise problems in any of the ongoing work of the firm, is to build an ethical wall between the new attorney and the rest of the firm. Even though Mr. Fine was not involved in the current litigation in any way during his previous employment, I want to assure you that we have protected the interests of your clients by isolating Mr. Fine from any involvement in the representation of Murray Wye. He did not bring any files relating to the Steinbergs or to the Steinberg Corporation with him nor has he shared with any member of this firm any confidential information he may have acquired during that representation.

For your information, I have attached the memorandum that I, as managing attorney of this office, sent to all personnel of this firm before Mr. Fine actually joined the firm. I trust this will reassure you as well as your client that nothing improper will occur.

It would constitute an undue hardship for my client to find new counsel at this late stage of litigation that has been going on for more than four years. It would also, no doubt, inflict costs on your client and delay the resolution of the pending cases were new counsel to be brought in now. We will resist any attempt you might make to disqualify us.

Very truly yours,

Dede Allen

Dede Allen
Attorney at Law

DA/lt
Enclosure

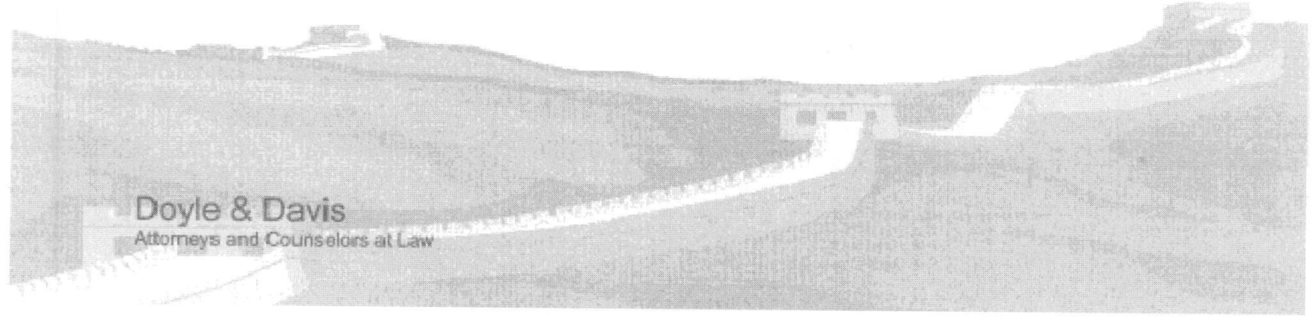

MEMORANDUM

TO: All Attorneys and Staff
FROM: Dede Allen, Managing Partner
RE: Ethical Wall - *Jack Steinberg & Son, Inc. v. Wye*
DATE: January 2, 2001

This office represents Murray Wye, who is presently a defendant in litigation brought by Jack Steinberg & Son, Inc. and Jack Steinberg. The Steinberg interests were previously represented by Purta & Paul. Philip Fine, formerly an associate with Purta & Paul, will become a partner of this firm on January 29, 2001.

It is our intention to build an "ethical wall" between Mr. Fine and all matters with which he might have a conflict of interest. Therefore, with respect to this litigation or any other matter regarding the Steinberg interests and Mr. Wye, the following rules will apply:

1. Do not discuss this litigation or any matters that might relate in any way to Mr. Steinberg, to the Jack Steinberg and Son, Inc. entity, or to Mr. Wye with Mr. Fine or any member of the support staff assigned to work with him.

2. Do not request any information or documents from Mr. Fine regarding this matter.

3. All files regarding this litigation will remain in the locked file room to which Mr. Fine will have no access.

4. Philip Fine and all new employees will be advised of these procedures as well.

c: Philip Fine

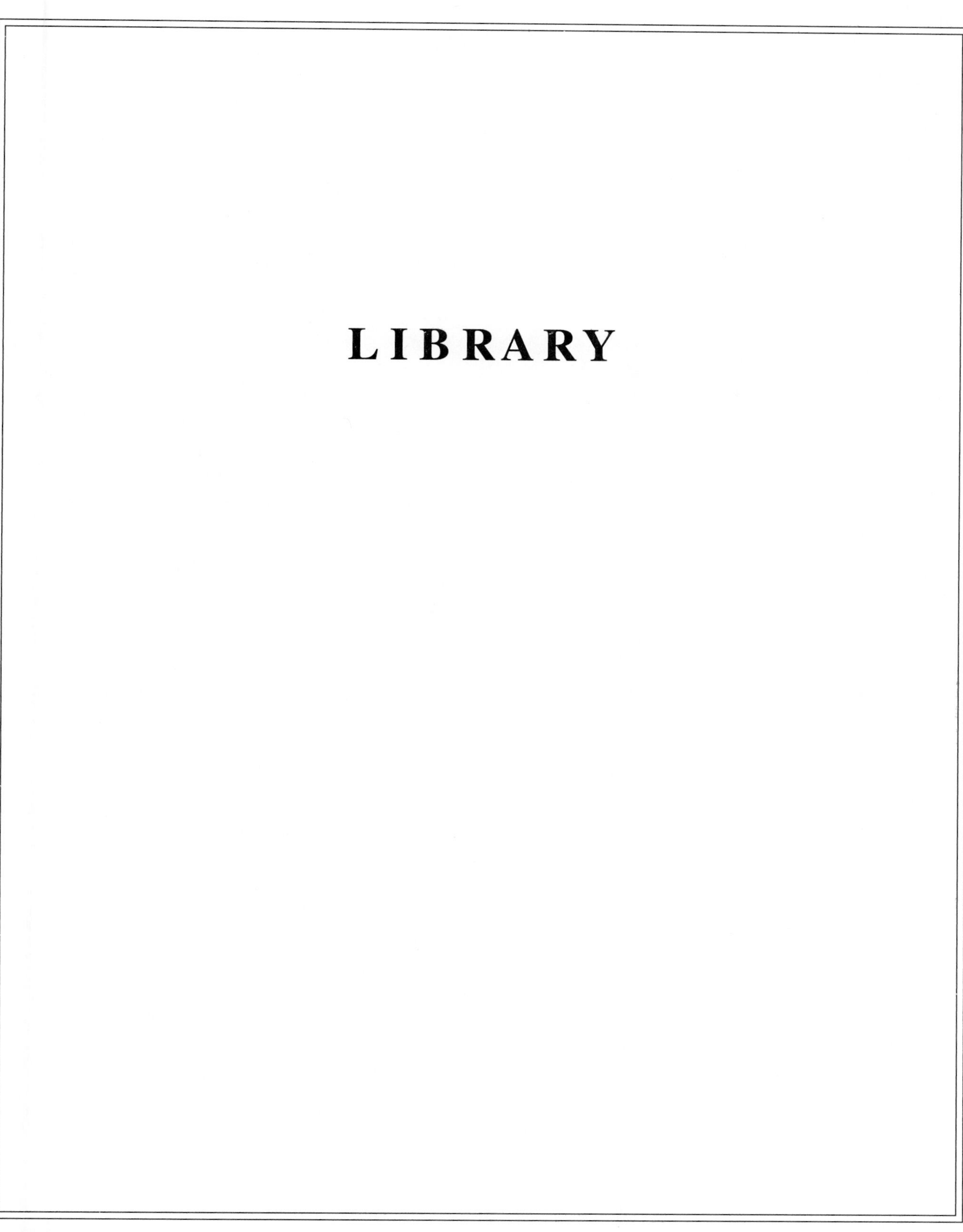

LIBRARY

Franklin Rules of Professional Conduct

RULE 1.6 Confidentiality of Information

(a) A lawyer shall not reveal information relating to representation of a client unless the client consents after consultation, except for disclosures that are impliedly authorized in order to carry out the representation . . . .

* * * *

RULE 1.7 Conflict of Interest: General Rule

(a) A lawyer shall not represent a client if the representation of that client will be directly adverse to another client, unless:

(1) the lawyer reasonably believes the representation will not adversely affect the relationship with the other client; and

(2) each client consents after consultation.

* * * *

COMMENT:

* * * *

Conflict Charged by an Opposing Party

[15] Resolving questions of conflict of interest is primarily the responsibility of the lawyer undertaking the representation. In litigation, a court may raise the question when there is reason to infer that the lawyer has neglected the responsibility . . . . Where the conflict is such as clearly to call in question the fair or efficient administration of justice, opposing counsel may properly raise the question. Such an objection should be viewed with caution, however, for it can be misused as a technique of harassment.

* * * *

RULE 1.9 Conflict of Interest: Former Client

(a) A lawyer who has formerly represented a client in a matter shall not thereafter represent another person in the same or a substantially related matter in which that person's interests are materially adverse to the interests of the former client unless the former client consents after consultation.

(b) A lawyer shall not knowingly represent a person in the same or a substantially related matter in which a firm with which the lawyer formerly was associated had previously represented a client:

(1) whose interests are materially adverse to that person; and

(2) about whom the lawyer had acquired information protected by Rules 1.6 and 1.9(c) that is material to the matter; unless the former client consents after consultation.

(c) A lawyer who has formerly represented a client in a matter or whose present or former firm has formerly represented a client in a matter shall not thereafter:

(1) use information relating to the representation to the disadvantage of the former client except as Rule 1.6 . . . would permit or require with respect to a client, or when the information has become generally known; or

(2) reveal information relating to the representation except as Rule 1.6 . . . would permit or require with respect to a client.

COMMENT:

* * * *

[2] The scope of a "matter" for purposes of this Rule may depend on the facts of a particular situation or transaction. The lawyer's involvement in a matter can also be a question of degree. When a lawyer has been directly involved in a specific transaction, subsequent representation of other clients with materially adverse interests clearly is prohibited. On the other hand, a lawyer who recurrently handled a type of problem for a former client is not precluded from later representing another client in a wholly distinct problem of that type even though the subsequent representation involved a position adverse to the prior client. The underlying question is whether the lawyer was so involved in the matter that the subsequent representation can be justly regarded as a changing of sides in the matter in question.

Lawyers Moving Between Firms

[3] When lawyers have been associated within a firm but then end their association, the question of whether a lawyer should undertake representation is more complicated. There are several competing considerations. First, the client previously represented by the former firm must be reasonably assured that the principle of loyalty to the client is not compromised. Second, the rule should not be so broadly cast as to preclude other persons from having reasonable choice of legal counsel. Third, the rule should not unreasonably hamper lawyers from forming new associations and taking on new clients after having left a previous association. In this connection, it should be recognized that today

many lawyers practice in firms, that many lawyers to some degree limit their practice to one field or another, and that many move from one association to another several times in their careers. If the concept of imputation were applied with unqualified rigor, the result would be radical curtailment of the opportunity of lawyers to move from one practice setting to another and of the opportunity of clients to change counsel.

[4] . . . One approach to the reconciliation of these competing principles has been to seek per se rules of disqualification. For example, it has been held that a partner in a law firm is conclusively presumed to have access to all confidences concerning all clients of the firm. Under this analysis, if a lawyer has been a partner in one law firm and then becomes a partner in another law firm, there may be a presumption that all confidences known by the partner in the first firm are known to all partners in the second firm. This presumption might properly be applied in some circumstances, especially where the client has been extensively represented, but may be unrealistic where the client was represented only for limited purposes. Furthermore, such a rigid rule exaggerates the difference between a partner and an associate in modern law firms.

* * * *

[6] A rule based on a functional analysis is more appropriate for determining the question of disqualification. Two functions are involved: preserving confidentiality and avoiding positions adverse to a client.

Confidentiality

[7] Preserving confidentiality is a question of access to information. Access to information, in turn, is essentially a question of fact in particular circumstances, aided by inferences, deductions or working presumptions that reasonably may be made about the way in which lawyers work together. A lawyer may have general access to files of all clients of a law firm and may regularly participate in discussions of their affairs; it should be inferred that such a lawyer in fact is privy to all information about all the firm's clients. In contrast, another lawyer may have access to the files of only a limited number of clients and participate in discussions of the affairs of no other clients; in the absence of information to the contrary, it should be inferred that such a lawyer in fact is privy to information about the clients actually served but not those of other clients.

[8] Application of paragraph (b) depends on a situation's particular facts. In such an inquiry, the burden of proof should rest upon the firm whose disqualification is sought.

[9] Paragraph (b) operates to disqualify the lawyer only when the lawyer involved has actual knowledge of information protected by Rules 1.6 and 1.9(b). Thus, if a lawyer while with one firm

acquired no knowledge or information relating to a particular client of the firm, and that lawyer later joined another firm, neither the lawyer individually nor the second firm is disqualified from representing another client in the same or a related matter even though the interests of the two clients conflict . . .

[10] Independent of the question of disqualification of a firm, a lawyer changing professional association has a continuing duty to preserve confidentiality of information about a client formerly represented. See Rules 1.6 and 1.9.

Adverse Positions

[11] The second aspect of loyalty to a client is the lawyer's obligation to decline subsequent representations involving positions adverse to a former client arising in substantially related matters. This obligation requires abstention from adverse representation by the individual lawyer involved, but does not properly entail abstention of other lawyers through imputed disqualification. Hence, this aspect of the problem is governed by Rule 1.9(a). Thus, if a lawyer left one firm for another, the new affiliation would not preclude the firms involved from continuing to represent clients with adverse interests in the same or related matters, so long as the conditions of paragraphs (b) and (c) concerning confidentiality have been met.

* * * *

RULE 1.10 Imputed Disqualification: General Rule

(a) While lawyers are associated in a firm, none of them shall knowingly represent a client when any one of them practicing alone would be prohibited from doing so by Rules 1.7, . . . , 1.9 or . . .

* * * *

COMMENT:

* * * *

Principles of Imputed Disqualification

[6] The rule of imputed disqualification stated in paragraph (a) gives effect to the principle of loyalty to the client as it applies to lawyers who practice in a law firm. Such situations can be considered from the premise that a firm of lawyers is essentially one lawyer for purposes of the rules governing loyalty to the client, or from the premise that each lawyer is vicariously bound by the obligation of loyalty owed by each lawyer with whom the lawyer is associated. Paragraph (a) operates only among the lawyers currently associated in a firm . . . .

* * * *

Reyes and RI Partners v. Grobard Builders, Inc.

Franklin Court of Appeal (1993)

This matter comes to us as a permissible interlocutory appeal from the district court. Defendants, Grobard Builders, Inc. ("GBI"), appeal the decision of the district court disqualifying the law firm that had been representing them, Quinto & Grady.

In 1985, plaintiff Thomas J. Reyes became a limited partner in a partnership (the "Partnership") for the purpose of developing a hotel. The Partnership in turn contracted with Grobard Builders, Inc. to construct the hotel. The Partnership never built the project, however, and the parties have ever since been involved in a legal dispute regarding performance of the Partnership Agreement.

From April 1985 through September 1985, Reyes was, in some capacity, represented by Attorney Mary Stark of the law firm of Nance and Bernard. Stark left the Nance firm in 1986 and joined the law firm of Shust and Stevens, where she practiced for six years. Then Stark joined the law firm of Quinto & Grady ("Quinto").

Quinto had represented GBI since 1988. Reyes and other partners (the "Plaintiff Partners"), represented by the law firm of Freed, Jonathan & Michaels, commenced a lawsuit in 1989 alleging that GBI breached the Partnership Agreement. Quinto, and specifically Attorney Wallace, a member of the Quinto firm, had represented defendants since the inception of the lawsuit.

Reyes became aware that Stark had joined Quinto on March 12, 1992. Quinto did not obtain Reyes' consent to its representation against him, and Reyes demanded that Quinto withdraw from further representation on the basis of Stark's past representation of him.

Before Stark joined Quinto, the firm performed a conflicts review. At that time, Stark did not disclose her past representation of Reyes. On March 13, 1992, Attorney Gary David of Freed, Jonathan & Michaels, representing Plaintiff Partners, telephoned Stark concerning the matter. Stark told David that she could not recall anything about her past representation of Reyes. In response to David's concerns, Quinto took measures to insulate Stark from all contact with this case. As part of Quinto's screening arrangement, all files containing GBI material were separated and kept locked, with access limited to Wallace and a paralegal. In addition, Stark was barred from participating in any discussions related to the merits of this case. Lastly, access codes to any information related

to this case stored on electronic software were kept secret.

There are currently 185 lawyers in Quinto's Franklin City office. Stark and Wallace work on different floors in different departments.

Reyes moved for disqualification of Quinto & Grady on the basis of Attorney Stark's past representation of him. The district court found in favor of Reyes, holding that Stark had a conflict of interest and that the conflict should be imputed to Quinto. GBI appeals.

We recognize, of course, that one party's interest in preserving confidential communications conflicts with the opposing party's interest in being represented by the counsel of its choice. Motions to disqualify counsel, moreover, should be resolved with extreme caution because they may be used abusively as a litigation tactic, when, for example, a movant is facing a formidable opponent. A successful movant may thus create both psychological hardship, by requiring an opponent to obtain and trust different counsel, and financial hardship, by requiring an opponent to incur additional fees while new counsel becomes familiar with the litigation.

The scope of Stark's representation, which was the basis for Reyes' motion, is disputed. Reyes alleges that Stark represented him personally with regard to the Partnership Agreement that he signed on May 31, 1985, the hotel project, and the Partnership's affairs. The Nance firm's file cataloguing the Reyes representation firm contains over thirty (30) separate items of written correspondence related to the hotel project. Except one, all are addressed to or from Stark.

Defendants argue that almost all of Stark's work involved a consulting agreement between Reyes and the Partnership. None of those matters is at issue in this case. No correspondence to or from Stark, they claim, makes any reference to the Partnership Agreement at issue in this case.

The district court found that Stark entered an attorney-client relationship with Reyes in his personal capacity. Among other things, Reyes retained Stark to draft the Consulting Agreement executed by Reyes and the Partnership, review the Commitment and Development Agreements entered into by the franchisor, and review the one-page agreement signed by GBI, Nelson, and Reyes on January 24, 1985. This work is consistent with Reyes' obligations under the Partnership Agreement. Reyes and Stark, therefore, entered an attorney-client relationship. Pursuant to this relationship, Reyes submitted confidential information to Stark with a reasonable belief that she was representing him in his capacity as a limited partner.

Our finding that Stark entered an attorney-client relationship with one or more of the parties involved in the above-captioned matter is enough to satisfy the threshold inquiry. Stark, therefore, was subject to the ethical obligation of preserving confidential communications. Accordingly, Stark could not later use the confidential information she obtained from Reyes, and possibly the other partners, against them on behalf of another client.

The next question is whether Stark's prior representation is substantially related to Quinto's present representation of defendants. Under Franklin Rules of Professional Conduct Rule 1.9, the trial court must apply the substantial relationship test, which requires a three-part inquiry. First, the court must factually reconstruct the scope of the prior legal representation. Second, it must determine whether it is reasonable to infer that the confidential information could have been given to a lawyer representing a client in the prior matters. It is not necessary to prove that the lawyer actually received useful confidential information, only that the lawyer could have. Third, the court must decide whether that information is relevant to the issues raised in the litigation pending against the former client.

The district court found that Quinto's present representation of defendants was substantially related to Stark's prior representation of Reyes and/or the Partnership. We agree. First, Reyes retained Stark to help him fulfill his obligations under the Partnership Agreement. In drafting the agreements between Reyes and the Partnership, Stark must have been aware of the goals and intentions of the partners in setting up the Partnership. Although Stark may not have been involved in negotiating and drafting the Partnership Agreement—the subject of this litigation—she was clearly privy to information concerning the partners' intentions and goals in entering the Partnership, as well as their performance under the Partnership Agreement.

As to the second prong, it is reasonable to infer that confidential information about the Partnership Agreement could have been given to Stark during her representation of Reyes. In fact, the record indicates that Stark extensively advised Reyes as to his performance under the Partnership Agreement. On this evidence, it is reasonable to infer that confidential information could have been given to a lawyer in Stark's former position as Reyes' attorney.

Third, the information obtained by Stark is relevant to the issues raised in the pending litigation. A simple reading of the complaint makes this clear. We therefore affirm the district court's finding that Quinto's present representation and Stark's former representation satisfy the three prongs of the substantial relationship test.

Because the two representations are substantially related, a presumption arises that the lawyer received confidential information during his or her prior representation. When a lawyer switches sides in a matter, the presumption of shared confidences is irrebuttable and thus disqualification is proper. See Franklin Rules of Prof. Conduct 1.9(a). However, where a lawyer moves from one firm to another, that lawyer or his or her new firm may represent an adversary of the client of his or her former firm in certain circumstances. In such a case, even if the two matters are substantially related, the lawyer and his or her new firm may rebut the presumption of shared confidences and avoid disqualification.

The presumption is rebutted if, for example, the lawyer whose change of employment created the disqualification issue was not actually privy to any of the confidential information that his or her prior law firm received from the party now seeking disqualification of his or her present firm. Defendants did not rebut the presumption that Stark was privy to confidential information during her prior representation. They offered no affidavit from Stark, the court notes, stating that she did not receive confidential information. Stark did not sustain her burden of proving that she did not receive confidential information.

The lower court therefore properly disqualified Stark based on defendants' failure to rebut the presumption of shared confidences during her former representation. We also affirm the district court's ruling imputing Stark's conflict of interest to Quinto.

To avoid the firm's disqualification, Quinto must rebut the presumption of intra-firm sharing of confidences as to Stark's former representation. A targeted law firm can rebut the latter presumption by demonstrating that specific institutional mechanisms (*e.g.*, ethical walls) had been employed to prevent the participation of the "tainted" lawyer in the matter in dispute and to screen the flow of any confidential information from the "tainted" lawyer to any other members of his or her present firm.

In this, we hold defendants have also failed. Quinto did make arrangements, the court notes, to screen Stark from the present litigation on March 13, 1992, by denying her access to all files containing GBI materials, restricting her access to any information kept on an electronic database, and banning all discussion of the case with her. The lower court also inferred some insulation of Stark from the firm's size—185 lawyers in Franklin City. There, Wallace, the lawyer representing defendants, and Stark work on different floors and in different departments.

We find that, although Quinto set up an ethical wall, it was untimely. Screens must be in place when the potentially disqualifying event occurs.

We find that Quinto should have been aware of a potential conflict of interest in its representation of defendants and set up an ethical wall on or before March 12, 1992, which is the date Stark joined the firm. The court finds, therefore, that defendants have not rebutted the presumption of intra-firm sharing because Quinto failed to screen Stark when they should have been aware of her conflict.

Defendants have not provided the type of clear and effective proof required to rebut the presumptions of shared confidences. Since any doubt as to the existence of an alleged conflict of interest must be resolved in favor of disqualification, Reyes must prevail.

Judgment affirmed.

Steinberg & Son, Inc. v. Wye

Sample Answer

TO: Steven Shelley
FROM: Applicant
RE: Jack Steinberg & Son, Inc. v. Wye

Our client, Jack Steinberg & Son, Inc. ("JSI"), seeks to have the law firm of Doyle and Doyle ("D & D") disqualified from representing the defendant, Murray Wye, because of a conflict of interest that was created when D & D recently hired Philip Fine as a partner. Mr. Fine had previously worked for the law firm of Purta and Paul ("P & P"), which represented JSI in the current litigation against Mr. Wye prior to our taking over representation two years ago. You have asked me to examine whether a motion to disqualify D & D is likely to succeed.

It is important to note in analyzing whether we should move to disqualify D & D that both the Comments to the Franklin Rules of Professional Conduct ("RPC") and case law provide that motions to disqualify opposing counsel should be viewed with extreme caution. [RPC 1.7, Comment 15; Reyes and RI Partners v. Grobard Builders, Inc.] Because such motions can be used as a litigation tactic to harass opposing counsel and can inflict psychological and financial hardship on the opposing party by requiring him to obtain new counsel, the court will likely be hesitant to grant our motion.

Before we can move to disqualify D & D, we must establish a conflict of interest under the RPC. The RPC provide that a lawyer must not represent a person in the same or a substantially related matter in which the lawyer or a firm with which the lawyer formerly was associated had previously represented a client whose interests are materially adverse to that person and about whom the lawyer had acquired confidential information that is material to the matter. [RPC 1.9(a), (b)] Whether the lawyer acquired confidential information in the previous representation is crucial in the disqualification of the lawyer because the RPC prohibit a lawyer who has previously represented a client, or whose former firm previously represented a client, from disclosing confidential information related to the representation. [RPC 1.9(c)]

Therefore, our first analysis in determining whether D & D should be disqualified under RPC 1.9 is to decide if the matter in which D & D is representing Mr. Wye and the matter in which P & P represented JSI are the same or substantially related. In *Reyes and RI Partners v. Grobard Builders, Inc.*, the court proposed a three-part test to determine whether a matter is substantially related. However, we do not need that test because the matter is the same. Specifically, Mr. Wye hired D & D to represent him in the lawsuit filed against him four years ago by JSI. JSI alleged that Mr. Wye misrepresented his qualifications as an engineer and the misrepresentations supposedly resulted in damages to JSI in the building of a plant. D & D has been representing Mr. Wye since the inception of the lawsuit. Mr. Fine was an associate at P & P the entire time that P & P represented JSI. While Mr. Fine did not personally represent JSI in the litigation against Mr. Wye, other members of P & P did; thus, D & D's representation of Mr. Wye involves the same matter as that in which P & P represented JSI while Mr. Fine was an associate. Also, the interests of Mr. Wye and JSI are materially adverse because they are opposing parties in litigation.

Having established that the same matter is involved, we must now determine if Mr. Fine acquired confidential information that is material to the matter. In the *Reyes* case, the court stated that a presumption arises that a lawyer received confidential information during his prior representation. Also, when two matters are the same or substantially related and a lawyer switches sides in the matter, the presumption of shared confidences is irrebuttable. [Reyes and RI Partners v. Grobard Builders, Inc.] However, when a lawyer moves from one firm to another, the presumption may be rebutted if the

lawyer can establish that he did not in fact obtain confidential information that is material to the matter. [Reyes and RI Partners v. Grobard Builders, Inc.] The rebuttal of the presumption is necessary because otherwise the rules of imputation would apply and the lawyer's new firm would be severely limited in its representation of clients due to its hiring of the new lawyer. The Comments to the RPC recognize that lawyers practice in firms and change firms numerous times in their careers; if the concept of imputation of conflicts were applied too rigorously, it would impede the opportunity of lawyers to change firms. [RPC 1.9, Comment 3]

As stated, the matter in which P & P represented JSI is the same as the matter in which D & D is representing Mr. Wye. Also, Mr. Fine has switched sides in the matter, and therefore the presumption that Mr. Fine acquired confidential information regarding the JSI lawsuit would arise. However, because Mr. Fine moved from one law firm to another, the presumption can arguably be rebutted by evidence establishing that Mr. Fine did not receive confidential information regarding the matter. While Mr. Fine was an associate at P & P, he did not personally represent JSI in the litigation against Mr. Wye, although he did represent JSI and its president, Jack Steinberg, in corporate business matters. Mr. Fine counseled Mr. Steinberg regarding the form of entity he should create before Mr. Steinberg decided to incorporate JSI, and Mr. Fine also filed JSI's articles of incorporation. Thus, Mr. Fine did receive some confidential information regarding Mr. Steinberg and JSI. The RPC prohibit Mr. Fine from disclosing this information.

It can be argued that this information is not material to the current litigation because Mr. Fine's representation of JSI related to corporate matters and the current matter involves litigation and construction of a plant (a real estate matter); thus, Mr. Fine would not be disqualified from representing Mr. Wye in the current litigation and neither would D & D because there would be no conflict of interest to impute to D & D. However, the facts and law do not necessarily support this argument. Even if Mr. Fine did not represent JSI in the current litigation against Mr. Wye while he was employed at P & P, other lawyers in the firm did. These lawyers clearly obtained confidential information regarding the matter while representing JSI in the litigation. Therefore, Mr. Fine may have received confidential information regarding the matter. The law firm of P & P was relatively small—about 20 attorneys—and Mr. Fine may have discussed the litigation with the attorneys at P & P who worked on the litigation or he may have had access to files regarding the litigation.

Moreover, a partner in a law firm is conclusively presumed to have access to all confidences concerning the firm's clients, and when the partner changes firms, there may be a presumption that all confidences known by the partner in the first firm are known to all partners in the second. [RPC 1.9, Comment 4] This presumption is necessary to preserve confidentiality of a client's confidential information. Although Mr. Fine was not a partner at P & P, the RPC basically extend this presumption to other attorneys in a firm by creating an inference that when a lawyer has general access to files of all clients and may regularly participate in discussion of their affairs, the lawyer is privy to information about all the firm's clients. [RPC 1.9, Comment 7] Mr. Fine was an associate at P & P the entire time P & P represented JSI. Also, he personally represented JSI on some corporate matters and did have access to some confidential information of JSI. However, we do not have enough facts to know if Mr. Fine had general access to all client files. It would help our case if we could find that P & P attorneys handling different areas of law work in close proximity, share support staff, etc. Also, we should try to determine from bills and other records if Mr. Steinberg and Mr. Fine ever met regarding the litigation. Even without that information, however, the inference under the RPC that Mr. Fine was privy to all confidential information regarding all clients, including information regarding the JSI litigation, will probably apply.

Because P & P clearly acquired confidential information regarding the JSI litigation against Mr. Wye, and Mr. Fine may have confidential information concerning the litigation, Mr. Fine should be disqualified from representing Mr. Wye under RPC 1.9(b). However, the issue here is not whether Mr. Fine should be disqualified, but whether Mr. Fine's conflict should be imputed to D & D to disqualify it from representing Mr. Wye. There is a presumption that all confidences known by a partner in a firm are known to all partners in the firm. [RPC 1.9, Comment 4] Mr. Fine is a partner at D & D; therefore, the presumption is that any confidential information he acquired from P & P, particularly regarding the JSI litigation, would be known by D & D partners. However, D & D may rebut the presumption that Mr. Fine has shared confidences regarding the JSI case. A firm can do so by demonstrating that it employed a mechanism (ethical wall) to prevent the participation of the tainted lawyer in the matter and to screen the flow of any confidential information from the lawyer to any members of the present firm. The screening mechanism must be in place before the tainted lawyer joins the new firm. [Reyes and RI Partners v. Grobard Builders, Inc.]

Based on the information provided by Dede Allen, the managing partner of D & D, it appears that D & D employed a screening mechanism to prevent any disclosure by Mr. Fine of confidential information regarding the JSI lawsuit to any members of D & D and that this mechanism was instituted prior to Mr. Fine's joining the firm. Ms. Allen sent a memorandum to all attorneys and staff alerting them to the fact that Mr. Fine was joining the firm and that his former firm represented the plaintiff in the suit against Mr. Wye. Ms. Allen also instructed the staff not to communicate with Mr. Fine regarding the litigation or request any documents or information regarding the matter. She also noted that all files regarding the litigation would be contained in a locked file room to which Mr. Fine would have no access.

Consequently, it would appear that D & D built the appropriate ethical wall to prevent the disclosure of any confidential information from Mr. Fine regarding JSI to the members of D & D and therefore D & D should not be disqualified from representing Mr. Wye. We should, however, explore whether the wall is solid; that is, does it really block the D & D litigation attorneys from Mr. Fine? For example, we need to discover how close Mr. Fine is to those attorneys both physically (office location) and socially. Also, are the files really secure—does, for example, Mr. Fine as a partner have access to attorneys' computer files, and do the attorneys carefully follow procedures for locking paper files up each night?

Even if the wall does not hold, we would still have a difficult time winning our motion because Mr. Fine's knowledge of confidential information regarding the JSI suit against Mr. Wye is probably minimal considering he did not actually work on the litigation. Also, the court would likely find that disqualification of D & D would impose a substantial hardship on Mr. Wye considering the fact that D & D has represented Mr. Wye since the lawsuit was commenced four years ago and the matter is to go to trial soon. The disqualification would cause delay and inflict unnecessary cost on Mr. Wye if he has to obtain new counsel because new counsel would have to be brought up to speed on the matter. Thus, if we file a motion to disqualify D & D, it is unlikely we would prevail.

Multistate Performance Test

True Values Television Network, Inc.

National Conference of Bar Examiners

Preface

This Multistate Performance Test is a reprint of one of the three MPTs which were administered in July 2001.

The instructions for the test appear on the next page. On the actual MPT, they will appear on the back cover of the test.

INSTRUCTIONS

1. You will have 90 minutes to complete this session of the examination. This performance test is designed to evaluate your ability to handle a select number of legal authorities in the context of a factual problem involving a client.

2. The problem is set in the fictitious state of Franklin, in the fictitious Fifteenth Circuit of the United States. Columbia and Olympia are also fictitious states in the Fifteenth Circuit. In Franklin, the trial court of general jurisdiction is the District Court, the intermediate appellate court is the Court of Appeal, and the highest court is the Supreme Court.

3. You will have two kinds of materials with which to work: a File and a Library. The first document in the File is a memorandum containing the instructions for the task you are to complete. The other documents in the File contain factual information about your case and may include some facts that are not relevant.

4. The Library contains the legal authorities needed to complete the task and may also include some authorities that are not relevant. Any cases may be real, modified, or written solely for the purpose of this examination. If the cases appear familiar to you, do not assume that they are precisely the same as you have read before. Read them thoroughly, as if they all were new to you. You should assume that cases were decided in the jurisdictions and on the dates shown. In citing cases from the Library, you may use abbreviations and omit page references.

5. Your response must be written in the answer book provided. If you are taking this examination on a laptop computer, your jurisdiction will provide you with specific instructions. In answering this performance test, you should concentrate on the materials provided in the File and Library. What you have learned in law school and elsewhere provides the general background for analyzing the problem; the File and Library provide the specific materials with which you must work.

6. Although there are no restrictions on how you apportion your time, you should be sure to allocate ample time (about 45 minutes) to reading and digesting the materials and to organizing your answer before you begin writing it. You may make notes anywhere in the test materials; blank pages are provided at the end of the booklet. You may not tear pages from the question booklet.

7. This performance test will be graded on your responsiveness to the instructions regarding the task you are to complete, which are given to you in the first memorandum in the File, and on the content, thoroughness, and organization of your response.

True Values Television Network, Inc.

FILE

LIBRARY

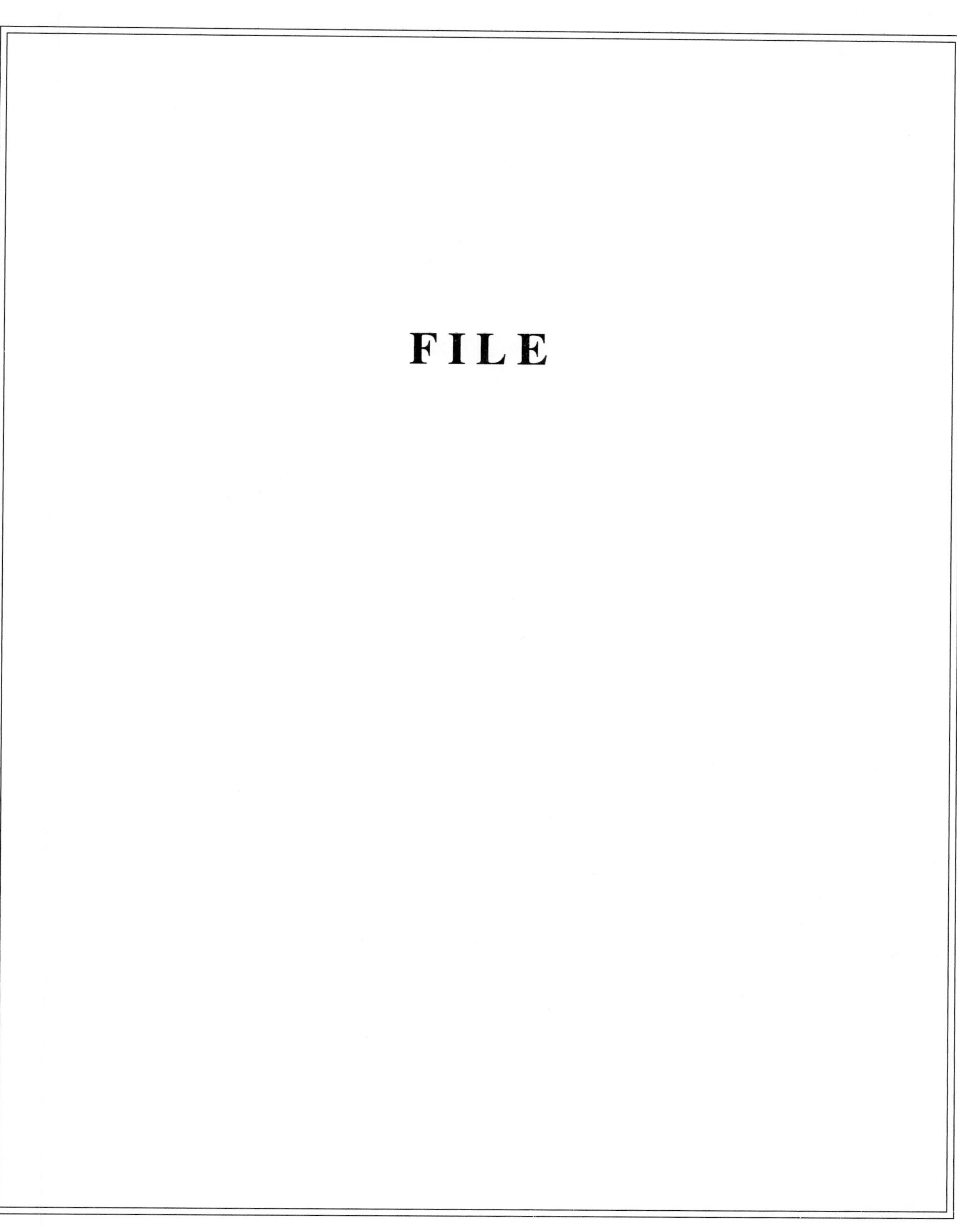
FILE

Grohman, Marty-Nelson, Kalevitch & Gilmore, P.A.
Attorneys and Counselors at Law
The Meadows Corporate Center
Suite 200-300
Easton, Franklin 33333

MEMORANDUM

TO: Applicant
FROM: Joe Grohman
RE: TVTV Hostile Takeover
DATE: July 24, 2001

We serve as outside corporate counsel for True Values Television Network, Inc. (TVTV), a Franklin entity that owns and operates television stations in major and minor media markets throughout the U.S.

A short time ago, TVTV received a hostile offer from Metro Communications Corporation (Metro) to buy all of TVTV's assets. Rudy Braccia, founder, chairman of the board and primary shareholder of TVTV, is adamantly opposed to this takeover. In his attempt to thwart Metro's planned takeover, Braccia has stepped up merger discussions with the Family Friendly Publishing Company (Friendly).

As you can see from the materials in the File, there are various shareholder groups with differing interests, some of whom favor the deal with Metro and some of whom might be better off with the Friendly deal.

For example, Corporate Resources Investment Fund (CRIF), a major institutional investor in TVTV, is demanding, on behalf of itself and other shareholders, that TVTV abandon its attempt to reach an agreement with Friendly and instead cooperate with Metro's acquisition efforts.

On the other hand, the TVTV Board is not at all sure that it is in the best interest of the corporation or other shareholder groups to accept either offer. If there is going to be a transaction, however, the Board favors a deal with Friendly.

Section 103(c) of the Franklin Corporations Code refers to various other groups, in addition to the corporation and its shareholders, whose interests the Board is entitled to consider when making a decision regarding the best interests of the corporation and its shareholders.

To help me in counseling the Board about its options, please draft a memo that:

1) **Describes what are the conflicting interests of the corporation, each shareholder group, and each of the other groups identified in Section 103(c); and**

2) **Analyzes whether and how, consistent with its fiduciary duty, the Board can justify a decision to negotiate exclusively with Friendly in spite of the various conflicting interests.**

In structuring part one of your memo, please identify and discuss the interests of the corporation and each of the shareholder groups and other groups *separately*. Write part two of your memo in straight narrative form.

Zanetti Kaufman Ono & Krause
One Lauderdale Plaza - Suite 400
Davie, Franklin 33212
555/777-5555

July 10, 2001

Rudolph Braccia, Chairman of the Board
True Values Television Network, Inc.
100 TVTV Drive
Dania, Franklin 33113

Dear Mr. Braccia:

Corporate Resources Investment Fund (CRIF) is an institutional investor with significant holdings of True Values Television Network, Inc. (TVTV) stock. CRIF's Board of Directors has directed me to inform you of its strong objections to the TVTV Board's de facto rejection of the recent offer by Metro Communications Corporation (Metro) to buy all of TVTV's assets. The CRIF Board is similarly concerned with the TVTV Board's reported intention to pursue a possible merger with the Family Friendly Publishing Company (Friendly).

CRIF understands that Metro has offered to purchase all of TVTV's assets at a price that is the equivalent of $47 per share. CRIF also understands that the Friendly merger offer that is being favorably viewed by the TVTV Board can be fairly valued at only $38 per share, almost 20% below the Metro proposal.

The reason the TVTV Board is continuing the discussion with Friendly is the belief that Friendly is committed to the "family friendly" programming philosophy that marks the operation of TVTV. In contrast, the Board has rejected the Metro offer apparently because it is unlikely Metro will continue to follow the current TVTV programming format.

The CRIF Board wants to maximize immediate financial return to investors. The CRIF Board, therefore, holds strongly to the position that, if the TVTV Board were to act in the fashion and for the reasons described above, it would amount to a breach of the duty owed to the stockholders, including CRIF and the three other institutional investors. *See* Cole Corporation v. Nord, Inc., Franklin Supreme Court (1992).

If the TVTV Board fails to carry out its legal obligations, CRIF will sue to block the TVTV Board from pursuing a business relationship with Friendly and to obtain other appropriate relief.

Sincerely,

Reu C. Shotland, Esq.
For the Firm

cc: Members of the TVTV Board of Directors
Richard Schwartz, Chairman of the CRIF Board of Directors

Metro Communications Corporation
World Headquarters

MC Boulevard
Metro, Columbia 11115

July 9, 2001

Rudolph Braccia, Chairman of the Board
True Values Television Network, Inc.
100 TVTV Drive
Dania, Franklin 33113

Dear Mr. Braccia:

On behalf of Metro Communications Corporation (Metro), I extend to True Values Television Network, Inc. (TVTV) and its shareholders Metro's offer to purchase all of TVTV's assets for $282 million, which is equivalent to $47 per share. TVTV shares closed yesterday at $34 per share.

Metro offers this premium price because of the value of these assets and the positive fit between Metro and TVTV. Metro and TVTV have crossover operations in 49 markets that could be owned by a single company under FCC regulations. Because 42 of our crossover stations are located in the 50 largest markets in the nation, TVTV's broadcast license assets are valuable to Metro.

Metro's expertise in operating television stations across the country allows it to determine which minor market outlets should be sold and which stations will be operated by Metro's personnel rather than by TVTV's personnel. Metro will close any TVTV stations that cannot be profitably operated or sold.

Metro's formal proposal is being sent under separate cover. Failure to respond positively to our offer within 45 days will cause irreparable injury to Metro and force us to take remedial legal action against the TVTV Board.

Sincerely,

Marilyn B. Cane

Marilyn B. Cane, President

Excerpts from Confidential Report to TVTV from

Goldman, Morgan, Smith & Barney

Investment Bankers
New York, New York

True Values Television Network, Inc. (TVTV)
May 29, 2001

TVTV owns 80 television stations (42 located in the 50 largest U.S. markets), down from 90 a year ago. TVTV broadcasts a variety of family-oriented programs, including syndicated reruns of popular network shows (*e.g.,* Touched by an Angel; Highway to Heaven), as well as a few original programs produced exclusively for TVTV (*e.g.*, Happy Island; Adventures of Louis the Saint) and made-for-TV movies (G or PG rated). In the past year, the Company sold its 10 best stations in the minor media market to raise much-needed capital.

The outstanding shares of TVTV stock total 6 million:

- Rudy Braccia, founder and Board chairman, and the Board members who do not represent institutional shareholders—2.5 million shares (about 42%)
- Institutional investors, led by CRIF—1.5 million shares (25%)
- Individual investors—the remaining 2 million shares (33%) (See below for breakdown as between *Good Times* subscribers and others.)

Trading in TVTV shares is light, an average of 70,000 shares a day, slightly more than 1% of the stock. In the last year, the price of TVTV stock has ranged from a low of $25 a share to a high of $39 a share.

A stock ownership anomaly is the large number of shares owned by TVTV's dedicated viewers. At the time of the launch of the TVTV network, management promoted the sale of shares through places of worship within its broadcast areas. Those who purchased five shares of TVTV stock were entitled to receive the Company's monthly program guide, *Good Times,* at a deeply discounted rate.

Almost 250,000 individuals bought at least five shares. While some of those who originally bought Company stock in response to this promotion (primarily those who live in the markets where TVTV sold its stations) have sold their shares, a remarkable percentage of the Company's stock is held by those who, according to a year-2000 marketing survey, appear to be committed to TVTV's broadcasting philosophy. Today, more than 200,000 individuals, who own at least 1 million shares of TVTV stock (about 17%), subscribe to *Good Times* at the special stock ownership rate.

* * * *

It is difficult to place a value on TVTV. The Company has not met its goals. It has performed poorly and continues to decline. It has lost an increasing amount of money each year since its creation three years ago, and last year it lost $69 million. The Company's declining viewership translates into weak advertising sales, effectively capping income while production and other expenses continue to rise.

On the other hand, TVTV controls valuable assets. Despite its modest viewership, the Company's assets have risen in value as a result of the Federal Communications Commission's ruling that allows one company to own two stations in a single market. Inevitably, TVTV will be the target of takeover attempts by other broadcast companies or those who wish to enter the field.

Taking all of these factors into consideration, it is the judgment of the firm that the present value of TVTV is $309 million (or $50 per outstanding share).

Grohman, Marty-Nelson, Kalevitch & Gilmore, P.A.
Attorneys and Counselors at Law
The Meadows Corporate Center
Suite 200-300
Easton, Franklin 33333

INTEROFFICE MEMORANDUM

TO: TVTV File
FROM: Joe Grohman
RE: NOTES OF INTERVIEW WITH RUDY BRACCIA
DATE: July 20, 2001

Braccia reviewed status of offers from Metro and Friendly.

- Metro's offer is to pay TVTV $282 million for all of the Company's assets (broadcast licenses, station equipment, etc.), the equivalent of $47 per share. If TVTV accepted this offer, it would become a mere shell company with cash to distribute to shareholders.

- Friendly has upped offer to equivalent of $40 per share. TVTV shareholders would not get cash but would receive 2 shares of Friendly stock for each TVTV share held (Friendly presently trading at $20/share). Braccia believes Friendly will increase offer to $45 (2.25 shares of Friendly for each share of TVTV) if it appears Metro is likely to be successful. When pressed, Braccia admitted Metro may up its merger offer to the equivalent of $50, the "fair value" projected by Goldman, Morgan, but doubts Friendly will go over $45 per share.

- Friendly will absorb TVTV's broadcast operations and has committed to follow the "family friendly" broadcast philosophy of TVTV and has agreed to make that commitment an element of the merger agreement. Friendly's president also gave assurance that stations in smaller markets would be retained; most of those are in the heartland of America where Friendly's present products sell well.

- Braccia questioned Friendly president, Mark Dobson, about Friendly's ability to carry out its commitment because Friendly has no experience in broadcasting. Dobson said Friendly will depend heavily on TVTV's experienced personnel to manage and to implement Friendly's

broadcast plan. Emphasized that Friendly's successful implementation of the same philosophy in other media can be carried over to broadcasting. Dobson will continue TVTV's efforts to support the production of "family friendly" programming.

- Braccia firmly believes Friendly has the resources and the business strategy to make "family friendly" broadcasting financially successful. Friendly shares have quadrupled in value over the last three years (from $5 to $20 per share). By merging with Friendly, TVTV shareholders are likely to benefit from what Braccia believes will be Friendly's growth as it branches into broadcasting. Of course, Braccia acknowledges there is a real risk that Friendly will be unsuccessful in implementing the "family friendly" television philosophy.

- Braccia is worried about what's going to happen to the 400 TVTV employees who work in 30+ small market stations. He is also concerned that the people in these small communities will be denied access to "family friendly" programming and that the producers of such programs will lose their outlet.

Media Daily **News from the Communications Industry** July 12, 2001

INDUSTRY ANALYSIS by **SIMON SCOTT**

Will TVTV's Braccia Dance with the Media Devils?

Rudy Braccia, the "angel" behind TVTV, had hoped that "feel good" programming would be the answer to the network's financial prayers. It doesn't appear, however, that those prayers have been answered. TVTV continues to wallow in low viewer numbers despite the wide geographic reach of its 80 stations (42 of the top 50 markets).

But Braccia may be "saved" by a miracle, so to speak. An FCC rule change allowing broadcasters to own two outlets in a single market has made smaller networks, like TVTV, attractive takeover targets.

The word on the street is that media giant Metro has made a bid to capture TVTV. How will Braccia and a board dominated by fans of "family friendly" programming react to the broadcast "heathens"? If Metro gets its hands on TVTV's juicy stations, you can be sure "Touched by an Angel" will be replaced by Metro's brand of "sex, crime and rock 'n roll." The FCC has handed Rudy Braccia a gift, a chance to share ownership in his struggling operation or even sell all of his company to a competitor, like Metro. What will Braccia decide? And will it be just a matter of money?

Braccia, who recently referred to the network he created as "the most eligible bachelor at the media dance," is said to have initiated discussions with an unlikely partner, the Family Friendly Publishing Company. Friendly is not involved in television in any way. Its business is limited to book publishing, greeting cards, and Internet communications. Successful, cash-rich, and family-friendly, Friendly is an ideological match for Braccia and TVTV, but one wonders if it can compete in the dog-eat-dog world of broadcasting.

It won't be long before we learn whether Braccia will "dance with the media devils." As usual, stay tuned!

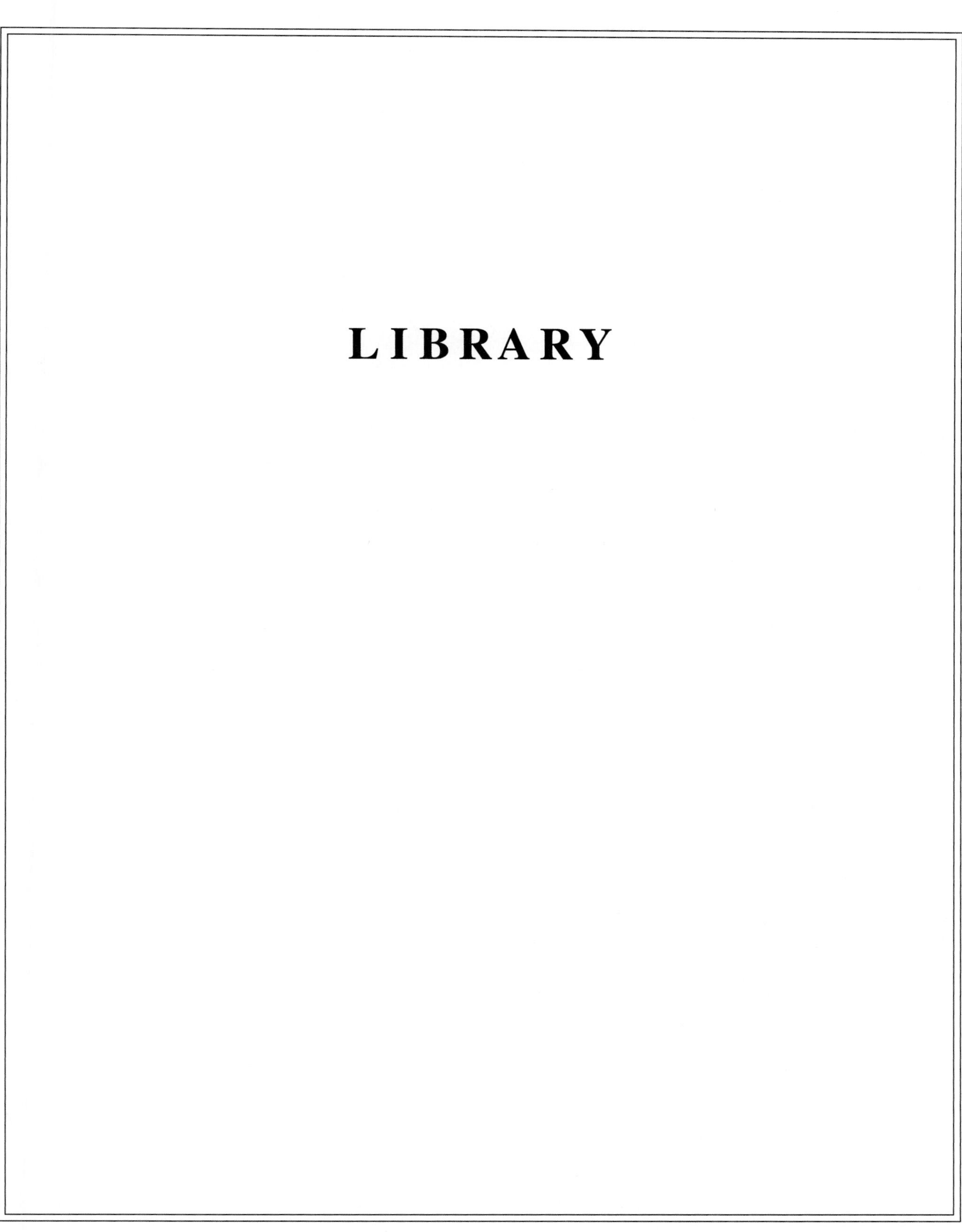

LIBRARY

Franklin Corporations Code

§103. Board of directors

(a) The business and affairs of every corporation organized under this chapter shall be managed by or under the direction of a board of directors, whose duty is to promote the best interests of a corporation and its stockholders.

(b) A member of the board of directors shall, in the performance of such member's fiduciary duties, be fully protected in relying in good faith upon the corporate records and upon such information, opinions, reports or statements presented to the corporation by any of the corporation's officers or employees or by any other person as to matters the member reasonably believes are within such other person's professional or expert competence and who has been selected with reasonable care by or on behalf of the corporation.

(c) A director may, in considering the best interests of a corporation and its stockholders, consider the effects of any action on employees, suppliers, and customers of the corporation, and communities in which offices or other facilities of the corporation are located, and any other factors the director considers pertinent.

(d) A director shall not be personally liable to the corporation or its stockholders for monetary damages for breach of fiduciary duty as a director, provided that this provision shall not eliminate or limit the liability of a director: (1) for any breach of the director's duty of loyalty to the corporation or its stockholders, and (2) for acts or omissions not in good faith.

* * * *

§251. Merger; Sale of Corporate Assets

(a) The board of directors of each corporation that desires to merge shall adopt a resolution approving an agreement of merger and declaring its advisability. The agreement shall state the terms and conditions of the merger. This agreement shall be submitted to the stockholders of each constituent corporation at an annual or special meeting for the purpose of acting on the agreement. Approval requires a majority vote by the holders of a majority of the outstanding stock of the corporation entitled to vote thereon at a meeting duly called.

(b) Every corporation may at any meeting of its board of directors sell all or substantially all of its property and assets upon such terms and conditions and for such consideration as its board of directors deems expedient and for the best interests of the corporation, when and as authorized by a resolution adopted by the holders of a majority of the outstanding stock of the corporation entitled to vote thereon at a meeting duly called.

Cole Corporation v. Nord, Inc.

Franklin Supreme Court (1992)

This case involves the attempted hostile corporate takeover of Nord, Inc. (Nord) by Cole Corporation (Cole) and the intervention of a "white knight," Wright Co. (Wright), favored by Nord's board of directors. In an action filed by Cole, the District Court concluded that Nord's directors had breached their fiduciary duty by making certain concessions to facilitate Wright's takeover and granted a preliminary injunction.

In this permissive interlocutory appeal we consider two issues: (1) the validity of the defensive measures taken by the Nord board in the face of an active bidding contest for corporate control; and (2) the power of the directors to take into consideration the impact of the takeover on a constituency other than the shareholders.

The Takeover Battle and the Defensive Measures Undertaken by the Nord Board: The controversy began when Cole made an unsolicited tender offer of $45 per share for the outstanding shares of Nord. At the time, Nord's shares were trading on the New York Stock Exchange for $38 per share. Upon analysis of the offer, Nord's investment bankers advised the board that $45 was a grossly inadequate price; that Nord had a value of $55 per share; and that the likelihood was that, upon acquisition, Cole intended to sell off all of Nord's assets rather than operate the company intact. The board expressed its opposition to any such sell-off and rejected Cole's offer.

The board implemented two defensive measures: (1) it began repurchasing its shares to bolster the share price; and (2) it issued debt in the form of bonds, which contained covenants limiting the sale of any of Nord's assets while the debt was outstanding, provided, however, that the board could waive the covenants. Soon thereafter, Wright appeared on the scene, and the board agreed to negotiate exclusively with Wright.

A bidding war ensued. Nord's board rejected a new offer of $48 per share from Cole, asserting as its principal ground for rejection the fact that Cole intended to sell off all of Nord's assets. Reconciling itself to an eventual sale of the company, the board accepted an offer of $55 from Wright. Under this proposal, Wright would assume liability for the bonds that had been issued to fend off Cole's takeover attempt, and Nord would waive the covenants against the sale of any of Nord's assets. In Wright's offer, it promised that it would sell off only two of Nord's divisions to generate cash to pay for the acquisition.

When the waiver of the debt covenants became known, the market value of the bonds fell by 15%. The bondholders immediately threatened to sue Nord and the directors individually.

Cole then offered $56 per share, subject to the waiver of the debt covenants. Wright made a new offer in which it agreed to pay $57 per share and to guarantee the value of the debt. The board unanimously accepted Wright's offer on the grounds that it was for a higher price than Cole's and it protected the bondholders.

Cole raised its bid to $58 per share, again conditioned on waiver of the debt covenants. Nord rejected the offer, and Cole sued to enjoin the sale to Wright. The District Court granted the injunction on the ground that the Nord directors had breached their fiduciary duty by making concessions to Wright out of concern for their personal liability to the bondholder constituency rather than maximizing the price to be paid to their principal constituency, the shareholders.

Discussion: To obtain a preliminary injunction, the plaintiff must demonstrate both a likelihood of success on the merits and irreparable harm if the injunction is not issued.

First, we conclude that Cole has a likelihood of success on the merits. The directors are responsible for managing the affairs of the corporation, Franklin Corp. Code §103(a), and, under the business judgment rule, they are ordinarily given wide latitude. However, the business judgment rule does not absolve directors of their fiduciary duty. In making business decisions to implement anti-takeover measures, the board is especially vulnerable to the charge that the measures will serve the board's financial interests rather than those of the shareholders. Accordingly, the directors bear the burden of proving that the defensive measures taken were in the best interests of the shareholders, that they had reasonable grounds for believing there was a danger to the corporate policy and effectiveness, and that the measures are reasonable in relation to the threat posed.

Repurchase of Nord Shares: The board acted in the best interests of the shareholders by preventing a takeover at a price below the stock's intrinsic value. The effect of the repurchase program was to increase the market price of the shares and was a factor that caused Cole and Wright to raise their bids substantially. It was therefore a reasonable measure in relation to the threat that the early offers were too low.

Issuance of the Bonds: Initially, the board acted in good faith and on an informed basis with reasonable grounds to believe that Cole's intention to break up the corporation and sell off the assets was a threat to the corporate

enterprise. The issuance of the bonds with the restrictive sale-of-assets covenants was a proper exercise of the directors' legal powers, duties, and responsibilities to ward off what they saw as a threat to the continued existence of the corporation.

However, by the time Cole offered $56 per share, the board had already accepted an offer from Wright, it was clear that the company was for sale, and it was inevitable that there would be a breakup of Nord. The board's duty then changed from preserving Nord as a corporate entity to obtaining the best price for the shareholders.

The threat of litigation that arose when the board waived the sale-of-assets covenants in response to Wright's first offer then became a major factor influencing the board's actions. It was no longer justifiable for the directors to deal selectively and to favor Wright's offer on the ground that it would guarantee the debt. In doing so, they improperly preferred the bondholder interests, whose rights were fixed by contract, and their own interests to avoid personal liability. Their sole focus should have been on obtaining the highest possible price for the shareholders.

The directors correctly point out that Franklin law permits them to consider the interests of constituencies other than the shareholders, Franklin Corp. Code §103(c), and they argue that their decision to protect the bondholder interests was a reasonable exercise of this power. In the abstract, that is a correct assertion, but not on the facts of this case. A significant by-product of Wright's offer to guarantee the value of the debt was to absolve the directors of personal liability to the bondholders. By ending the bidding once they were assured of protection against personal liability for consequences flowing from the adoption of previous defensive measures, they breached the fiduciary duty they owed to the shareholders.

<u>Exclusive Negotiation with Wright</u>: It is not inherently unlawful for the Nord board to have favored a white knight to the total exclusion of a hostile bidder. It is, however, impermissible when a board's primary duty is to auction the company to the highest bidder. When, as here, the competing bidders make relatively similar offers and the dissolution or breakup of the company becomes inevitable, market forces must be allowed to operate freely to bring the best price available for the shareholders' equity. The board's decision to negotiate exclusively with Wright prevented that from happening.

Accordingly, we conclude that Cole is likely to prevail on the merits of its suit.

<u>Irreparable Harm</u>: The District Court correctly ruled that Cole's opportunity to bid for Nord

would be lost unless the preliminary injunction issued. Given the conclusion that the board's obligation was to obtain the highest price for the shareholders, issuance of the injunction outweighs any harm to the defendants.

Conclusion: Initially, the directors' defensive measures were justified because they prevented a hostile takeover at an inadequate price. But, once the sale and break-up became inevitable and the prices offered became realistic, their duty shifted. They were no longer justified in seeking to protect the interests of the bondholder constituency. Moreover, in limiting the scope of negotiations and waiving the asset sale restrictions only after assurances that they would be protected from personal liability, the directors allowed their own financial welfare to override their consideration of shareholder profit. Because the business judgment rule offers no safe harbor under these circumstances, we affirm.

True Values Television Network, Inc.

Sample Answer

MEMORANDUM

TO: Joe Grohman
FROM: Applicant
RE: TVTV Hostile Takeover
DATE: July 24, 2001

You asked me to describe the conflicting interests of the corporation, the shareholder groups, and the other groups identified in Franklin Corporations Code ("FCC") section 103(c) relating to the TVTV hostile takeover bid by Metro Communications Corporation ("Metro"). You also asked me to analyze how the board can justify negotiating exclusively with Family Friendly Publishing Company. My responses are as follows:

1) CONFLICTING INTERESTS

The conflicting interests of the parties are as follows:

The Corporation: While a corporation is an entity under Franklin law, it is unclear whether the corporation can have any interest apart from its shareholders. If the corporation has any interest at all, it would probably be to continue to survive to carry out the purposes stated in its charter. The file does not include an express statement of the corporation's purpose, but it seems that the purpose is to provide "family friendly programming." To continue such programming, the corporation would prefer to accept an offer from Friendly because Friendly has vowed to keep TVTV generally intact, and Metro has indicated that it would change TVTV's programming. On the other hand, it can be argued that the corporation would also have an interest in obtaining the best price for its shares, and that would probably mean accepting an offer from Metro.

Rudy Braccia and Board Members Not Representing Institutional Investors: Mr. Braccia is the founder and CEO of TVTV. He and his supporters on the board of directors comprise the largest shareholder voting block—controlling about 42% of the outstanding shares of TVTV stock. The file does not explicitly say where Mr. Braccia's interests lie, but because he is the founder of TVTV, presumably the company's current policies reflect his interests, and he would like to continue running a company that offers family friendly programming in as many markets as possible. This goal could be met by maintaining current ownership or by agreeing to a share exchange with Friendly. It is unclear whether Mr. Braccia and his supporters have a great interest in making a profit from their investment in the company. This is something we need to look into.

Institutional Investors: There appear to be four institutional investors who hold only about 25% of TVTV's outstanding stock. Their interest, as summed up by the board of directors of one of them—Corporate Resources Investment Fund ("CRIF"), is to maximize immediate financial return to investors. In other words, they would like the greatest return on their investment in the shortest time. At this point, that would mean selling TVTV's assets to Metro.

Individual Investors: Individual investors own about 33% of TVTV's outstanding stock, but this group really should be split into two subgroups: *Good Times* (TVTV's programming guide) subscribers and non-*Good Times* subscribers.

> ***Good Times* Subscribers:** About 17% of TVTV's outstanding stock is owned by *Good Times* subscribers. Generally, each subscriber purchased and owns only five shares of TVTV stock. Presumably, their interest is not in turning a big profit on their small investments, but rather they

are more interested in having a television station in their area that offers family friendly programming. This is evidenced by the fact that most of the individuals in this group who originally purchased shares still own them, the main exception being purchasers who live in markets where TVTV was forced to sell its stations. The interests of these shareholders can best be served by maintaining the current ownership structure of TVTV or selling out to Friendly. Thus, the interests of these shareholders seem to be aligned with the interests of Mr. Braccia and his supporters on the board. It should be noted that together, these groups make up a majority of the outstanding TVTV stock (about 59%).

Non-*Good Times* Subscribers: Individual investors who do not subscribe to *Good Times* own about 16% of TVTV's outstanding stock. The file does not contain any specific information about these individuals. Presumably these are regular investors who are looking for a good return on their investment, and they have no interest in whether family friendly programming continues in any particular market. This is something that we need to verify. It is hard to say what course of action would best serve the interests of these investors. Some might agree with the institutional investors that they are interested in getting the greatest return on investment in the shortest time and would want TVTV's board to sell its assets to Metro to make a quick profit. On the other hand, others might favor a stock exchange with Friendly, given that Friendly shares have quadrupled in value over the past three years. The one course of action that most of the investors in this group would probably reject is to continue operating TVTV as it has been operated, since TVTV has consistently lost money and has been forced to sell off assets to keep operating.

Employees: Section 103(c) allows the board to consider the effect that corporate action will have on employees in addition to the effects the action will have on shareholders. A sale of assets to Metro will cost many TVTV employees their jobs, as Metro has indicated that it will close stations in unprofitable markets and use its own personnel to run other stations. A merger with Friendly, on the other hand, would not be as devastating. Friendly has indicated that since it has no expertise in television, it will retain most of TVTV's current staff and will sell off only a few stations in order to raise money to help with costs associated with the merger. This course of action might be more beneficial to employees than continuing down TVTV's current path, given TVTV's current losses.

Customers: Section 103(c) also allows the board to consider the effect that corporate action will have on customers. This is difficult to assess because it is unclear whether a television station's customers are its advertisers or its viewers. Advertisers probably want to reach the most people they can with their television ads. Because Metro's programming seems to have broader appeal than TVTV's programming, selling out to Metro might better serve the interests of advertisers. On the other hand, certain advertisers might be interested in targeting their ads to people who watch family friendly television and would prefer to have a station specializing in such programming. Their interests would be aligned with TVTV's viewers, the other possible "customers," who clearly want to watch family friendly programming. This interest would best be served by maintaining TVTV's current structure or by a share exchange with Friendly.

Communities: Section 103(c) allows the board to consider the interests of the communities in which the corporation's facilities are located. A sale of TVTV assets to Metro would deprive viewers of family friendly programming, as Metro has indicated that it will not continue such programming. Additionally, the sale would take away jobs in communities with smaller unprofitable stations, as Metro has said it will close such stations. The closures will also deprive minor market communities of local television stations. Maintaining the current TVTV structure or implementing a share exchange with Friendly would best serve the interests of most communities by protecting both viewing options and jobs.

Suppliers: Finally, the producers of family friendly programming, such as "Adventures of Louis the Saint" and "Touched by an Angel," would prefer that TVTV deal exclusively with Friendly so that there will continue to be a market for their products.

2) DEALING EXCLUSIVELY WITH FRIENDLY

Conclusion: The board probably can justify dealing exclusively with Friendly.

Issue: At issue is whether TVTV's board of directors can fulfill their fiduciary duty to act in the corporation's and shareholders' best interests by negotiating exclusively with Friendly despite the various conflicting interests.

Discussion: Franklin Corporations Code section 103(a) places a duty on directors to act in the best interests of the corporation and its shareholders, and under the business judgment rule, directors are ordinarily given wide latitude, but they are not absolved of the fiduciary duty. [Cole Corporation v. Nord, Inc.] Corporations Code section 103(c) states that in performing their duty, directors may consider the effects that a corporate action will have not only on the corporation and its shareholders, but also on employees, suppliers, customers, and the communities in which corporate facilities are located. Despite the conflicting interests of the various parties, it would seem that the TVTV board would be justified in deciding to deal exclusively with Friendly because, as discussed above, that would serve the interests of most of TVTV's shareholders, employees, customers, and suppliers, and would be best for most of the communities in which TVTV facilities are located. There is only one problem with this course of action: The effect of section 103(c) may be limited by *Cole Corporation v. Nord, Inc.,* a 1992 Franklin Supreme Court decision.

Cole involved a takeover target that rejected offers from one corporation and dealt exclusively with another. In *Cole*, the supreme court held that while section 103(c) permitted directors to consider the interests of constituencies other than the shareholders and favor a white knight (*i.e.*, friendly takeover bidder) when making corporate decisions, once a corporation made a decision to be sold, the board's primary duty was to obtain the best price possible for the shareholders; the board may not deal exclusively with any bidder. However, the court also held that before a sale and break up of the company becomes inevitable, the board is free to take defensive measures to prevent a hostile takeover of the corporation at an inadequate price (*e.g.*, below estimated market value).

Cole currently does not seem to be an obstacle to dealing solely with Friendly because TVTV's board has not yet determined whether to sell the corporation. Moreover, Metro's current offer, which is equivalent to $47 per share, is below the $50 estimated market value of TVTV shares, as determined by Goldman, Morgan, Smith & Barney. Under Corporations Code section 103(b), the board may reasonably rely on the Goldman report in determining what action to take. Thus, despite *Cole*, the TVTV board can take defensive measures to prevent Metro's hostile takeover, including dealing exclusively with Friendly, in order to protect the corporation and all interested parties from Metro's inadequate offer.

If the TVTV board eventually decides to sell the corporation, *Cole* appears to prohibit the board from dealing exclusively with Friendly; indeed, it seems to prohibit the board from considering anything other than the highest offering price on the table. However, *Cole* might not be as absolute as it sounds.

In *Cole*, the court found that the directors of the takeover target agreed to accept the lower bid of a white knight and refused to consider a higher bid from a hostile bidder out of self-interest rather than

out of a concern for the best interests of the corporation. Bondholders had threatened to sue the board members if they sold off corporate assets and thereby jeopardized repayment of corporate bonds. The white knight offered to take steps to guarantee payment of the bonds, the hostile bidder refused to take such steps, and the board accepted the white knight's bid and refused to entertain a higher bid from the hostile bidder. Thus, the directors protected themselves from threatened lawsuits by selling to the white knight.

The facts here are just the opposite—because both the hostile takeover bidder (Metro) and certain shareholders (*e.g.*, CRIF) have threatened to sue the board if they decide to accept a bid from the white knight, the board's self-interest would best be served by dealing with Metro, not Friendly. Thus, because the court's main concern in *Cole* appears to be self-dealing, and self-dealing does not seem to be involved in our case, *Cole* probably does not apply. Therefore, the TVTV board is free to decide that the best interests of the corporation, the shareholders, and indeed most other interested persons would be better served by a share exchange with Friendly even if the sale price equivalent is lower than the price offered by Metro, because most of the parties involved are more interested in continuing family friendly programming than in obtaining the highest sale price for their shares.

Finally, note that in either case, a majority of the shares have to approve the merger or sale. [Franklin Corporations Code §251] It seems that the majority would approve an offer from Friendly and would reject an offer from Metro. Thus, dealing with Metro probably would be fruitless.

Multistate Performance Test

State v. White

National Conference of Bar Examiners

Preface

This Multistate Performance Test is a reprint of one of the three MPTs which were administered in July 2001.

The instructions for the test appear on the next page. On the actual MPT, they will appear on the back cover of the test.

INSTRUCTIONS

1. You will have 90 minutes to complete this session of the examination. This performance test is designed to evaluate your ability to handle a select number of legal authorities in the context of a factual problem involving a client.

2. The problem is set in the fictitious state of Franklin, in the fictitious Fifteenth Circuit of the United States. Columbia and Olympia are also fictitious states in the Fifteenth Circuit. In Franklin, the trial court of general jurisdiction is the District Court, the intermediate appellate court is the Court of Appeal, and the highest court is the Supreme Court.

3. You will have two kinds of materials with which to work: a File and a Library. The first document in the File is a memorandum containing the instructions for the task you are to complete. The other documents in the File contain factual information about your case and may include some facts that are not relevant.

4. The Library contains the legal authorities needed to complete the task and may also include some authorities that are not relevant. Any cases may be real, modified, or written solely for the purpose of this examination. If the cases appear familiar to you, do not assume that they are precisely the same as you have read before. Read them thoroughly, as if they all were new to you. You should assume that cases were decided in the jurisdictions and on the dates shown. In citing cases from the Library, you may use abbreviations and omit page references.

5. Your response must be written in the answer book provided. If you are taking this examination on a laptop computer, your jurisdiction will provide you with specific instructions. In answering this performance test, you should concentrate on the materials provided in the File and Library. What you have learned in law school and elsewhere provides the general background for analyzing the problem; the File and Library provide the specific materials with which you must work.

6. Although there are no restrictions on how you apportion your time, you should be sure to allocate ample time (about 45 minutes) to reading and digesting the materials and to organizing your answer before you begin writing it. You may make notes anywhere in the test materials; blank pages are provided at the end of the booklet. You may not tear pages from the question booklet.

7. This performance test will be graded on your responsiveness to the instructions regarding the task you are to complete, which are given to you in the first memorandum in the File, and on the content, thoroughness, and organization of your response.

State v. White

FILE

LIBRARY

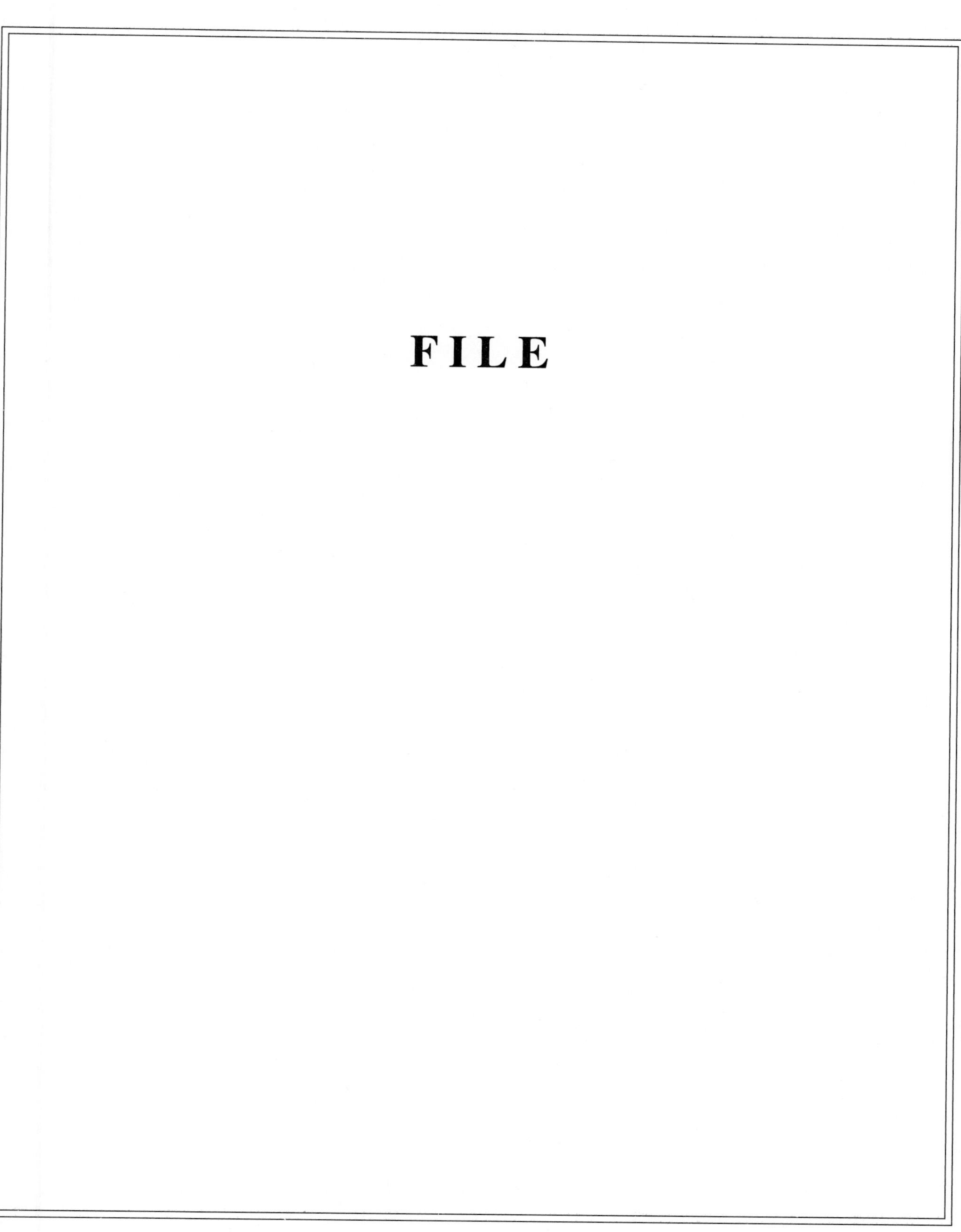

FILE

Office of the Public Defender
Felony Trial Division

TO: Applicant
FROM: Carlos Espinoza, Assistant Public Defender
DATE: July 24, 2001
RE: *State v. James White*

Our client, James White, has been arrested for the knife-murder of his brother Stephen White, and his indictment is pending before the Grand Jury. Last year we represented this client on a charge of aggravated assault, also involving a knife and Stephen. During the course of that representation, we referred him to Grace Peterson, one of the social workers on our staff. She interviewed him, wrote a report for me, and ultimately was instrumental in getting him released from jail and admitted to a hospital for psychiatric treatment. Even though I did not reveal the report or its contents to the court, I was able to persuade the court to release him to the hospital for treatment.

The aggravated assault case is still unresolved because both the prosecutor and the judge agreed to several three-month continuances while the client was in treatment. I had hoped to convince White's brother to help me reach an agreement with the prosecutor to drop those charges. Now, of course, everything is changed, and the prosecutor will, no doubt, try to use whatever he can from the assault case to help prove the murder case.

There was never a trial in the assault case and the only witness to the alleged assault (other than James) is now dead. The prosecutor wants to present, as evidence in the murder case, statements made by James concerning the alleged assault. Accordingly, as part of its case before the Grand Jury, the State has subpoenaed the records of conversations that Peterson had with our client and the report she prepared for me in the assault case. Ms. Peterson has left our office and moved to Italy.

We will file a Motion to Quash the Subpoena with the judge presiding over the Grand Jury. I have drafted the Motion so that it refers only obliquely to what is contained in Peterson's report. I need you to draft a persuasive brief in support of the Motion to Quash to be submitted to the judge *in camera*, along with the social worker's report, to persuade her that the contents of that report are privileged and may not be seen or used by the prosecutor in this case. As you know, in an *in camera* submission, the judge reviews the claimed privileged material outside the presence of the lawyer for the party seeking disclosure of the material. Neither the brief nor the report attached to the brief will be served on opposing counsel. You should bring the specific confidential information in the report to the judge's attention so that the judge will focus on the specific points you have directed her to. Prepare the brief in accordance with the guidelines set forth in the attached office memorandum.

Office of the Public Defender
Felony Trial Division

MEMORANDUM September 8, 1995

TO: Attorneys

FROM: Maurice Abelard

RE: Persuasive Briefs

All persuasive briefs, including Briefs in Support of Motions (also called Memoranda of Points and Authorities), shall conform to the following guidelines.

All briefs shall include a Statement of Facts. The aim of the Statement of Facts is to persuade the tribunal that the facts support our client's position. The facts must be stated accurately; however, emphasis should be placed on the material facts that best support our client's position. The Statement of Facts need not be exhaustive but it must contain key facts sufficient to inform the court of the essence of the dispute and the relief sought.

Our office follows the practice of breaking the argument into its major components and writing carefully crafted subject headings that illustrate the arguments they cover. Avoid writing briefs that contain only a single broad argument heading. The argument heading must succinctly summarize the reasons the tribunal should take the position you are advocating. A heading should be a specific application of a rule of law to the facts of the case and not a bare legal or factual conclusion or a statement of an abstract principle. For example, improper: THE POLICE DID NOT HAVE PROBABLE CAUSE TO ARREST DEFENDANT. Proper: THE FACT THAT DEFENDANT WAS WALKING ALONE IN A HIGH-CRIME AREA AT NIGHT WITHOUT PHOTO IDENTIFICATION WAS INSUFFICIENT TO ESTABLISH PROBABLE CAUSE FOR HIS ARREST.

The body of each argument should identify and analyze applicable legal authority and persuasively argue how the facts and law support our client's position. It is important to use the facts in the argument. Authority supportive of our client's position should be emphasized, but contrary authority also should generally be cited, addressed in the argument, and explained or distinguished. Do not reserve arguments for reply or supplemental briefs.

The lawyer need not prepare a table of contents, a table of cases, a summary of argument, or the index. These will be prepared, where required, after the draft is approved.

IN THE SUPERIOR COURT FOR MONTGOMERY COUNTY
STATE OF FRANKLIN

SUBPOENA DUCES TECUM

State of Franklin

Criminal Case Number 01-7703

vs.

James White, Defendant

TO:
Custodian of Records
Rehabilitation Services Division
Office of the Public Defender
22 Twin Peaks Blvd.
Galewood, Franklin 33988

YOU ARE COMMANDED TO APPEAR before the Grand Jury duly empaneled in the above captioned case at the Montgomery County Courthouse, Room 346, on July 27, 2001 at 10:00 a.m.

YOU ARE COMMANDED TO PRODUCE all reports, notes and any documents regarding the defendant, James White, prepared during the period from September 27, 2000 to date by Grace Peterson, MSW.

Subpoena requested by the Montgomery County State's Attorney's Office.

DATE ISSUED: July 23, 2001

Katherine Klare

Katherine Klare, Clerk

NOTICE: You are liable to Body Attachment and Fine for Failure to Obey This Subpoena.

IN THE SUPERIOR COURT FOR MONTGOMERY COUNTY
STATE OF FRANKLIN

State of Franklin | Criminal Case Number 01-7703

vs. | MOTION TO QUASH SUBPOENA

James White, Defendant

Defendant James White moves this Court to quash the subpoena duces tecum issued by the Montgomery County State's Attorney's Office to Custodian of Records, Rehabilitation Services Division, for notes and records of conversations and interviews pertaining to him and prepared by Grace Peterson, MSW. In support of this motion Defendant states:

1. at the time of Defendant's conversations with her, Grace Peterson
    a. was a social worker duly licensed to practice in the State of Franklin;
    b. was employed by the Office of the Public Defender in its Rehabilitation Services Division; and
    c. was assisting his attorney, Carlos Espinoza, in preparing to defend him in a pending criminal case.
2. all communications between Defendant and Grace Peterson were believed by Defendant to be privileged and confidential.
3. all communications between Defendant and Grace Peterson were privileged under both §§835 and 952 of the Franklin Evidence Code and, therefore, cannot be divulged.
4. Defendant has at no time waived any privilege applicable to the communications.

WHEREFORE, Defendant requests that this Court grant this motion to quash. This motion is supported by an accompanying brief and records filed concurrently under seal for *in camera* review.

Respectfully Submitted,
Office of the Public Defender

By Carlos Espinoza
Carlos Espinoza
Counsel for the Defendant

July 24, 2001

Office of the Public Defender

Felony Trial Division

MEMORANDUM

TO: File of James White

FROM: Carlos Espinoza, Assistant Public Defender

DATE: September 27, 2000

RE: Notes from Interview with James White at Montgomery Jail

Client charged with aggravated assault of his older brother, Stephen, and arraigned this morning. I was appointed as his Public Defender and met with him several hours later. Client has been in jail since arrest last night. Bail set at $25,000.

Client says charge arose from a fight he had with his brother in the house they share. Says he doesn't remember the incident. The police told him that Stephen was cut with a knife and had to be rushed to the hospital for "more than 100 stitches." The noise from the fight was loud enough to alarm some neighbor (he doesn't know which neighbor), who then called the police. It is not the first time the police have come to the house because of fighting between the brothers nor is it the first time client has been arrested. Client says he doesn't remember any of the fights.

Client says he loves his brother and doesn't know why he would fight with him. Says brother is his best friend.

Client is 39-year-old Army veteran who receives disability compensation from the Veteran's Administration (VA) for "a nervous condition." Says he never recovered mentally from his combat experience in the Gulf War and that the VA rates him as 25% disabled. He says he doesn't get enough to live on but that he can't work. Brother Stephen is trustee for a small inheritance left by their parents to support client. Sometimes there is conflict between the brothers over Stephen's decisions about "my money." Client's share of the household expenses in Stephen's house comes from the inheritance. Client says it is unfair that his parents left Stephen in charge of his life but that he also appreciates the many things "my brother does for me." Client admits to heavy drinking when he is depressed. Says he often blacks out. Sometimes he has "episodes" and only learns about them later from others.

Asked client about Stephen's statement to police that says client started argument over Stephen's refusal to provide money for booze and that as the argument got louder client began throwing things at him and then lunged at him with the knife. Client says he doesn't remember but that he wouldn't do something like that to his brother. Explained lawyer-client confidentiality to client. Client revealed he owns large knife he brought home from Gulf War. He keeps the knife hidden under the floor boards in his bedroom, but he insists he never used knife to harm his brother.

Client agrees to meet with Grace Peterson, our social worker, who will help us prepare for a bail reduction motion to get him released on own recognizance. Complicated because brother won't let him return home. Might be willing to accept psychological treatment if it will help him get out of jail.

Called Peterson and she will see him tomorrow morning.

Office of the Public Defender
Rehabilitation Services Division
22 Twin Peaks Blvd.
Galewood, Franklin 33988

TO: Carlos Espinoza

FROM: Grace Peterson, MSW

DATE: September 29, 2000

RE: Report on James White

Client was interviewed for two hours on September 28, 2000 and for one hour on September 29, 2000 after being referred by Assistant Public Defender Carlos Espinoza for evaluation for purposes of preparing a bail reduction motion and possibly for disposition.

Mr. White, 39 years old, has a history of psychiatric disorder. The precise prior diagnosis was not ascertainable, and the client either did not know it or would not reveal it. All of his prior treatment was done at the local VA hospital. Client's history includes military service in a combat situation, so a possible diagnosis is Post Traumatic Stress Disorder, but the interview situation and the amount of time available did not permit a full assessment. Client says he left psychotherapy several years ago "because those VA shrinks are a bunch of quacks and they don't make me feel any happier." He stopped taking medication because "I don't feel like myself when I am taking those head pills." Client was advised of my recommendation that he needed to get back into treatment since he had now apparently injured his brother.

Mr. White's response to being confronted with the allegations against him evolved over the course of the three hours we spent together. He was in deep denial at first, claiming to have no memory of any fight with his brother. As I continued to ask him about his relationship with his brother he said he was sure he didn't do what his brother said he did.

Later, when I told him that his brother would no longer permit him to live in the same house with him, he became enraged. He yelled, "He is lucky I didn't kill him. He makes me so mad! Why does he get to control my life and my money? I wanted to teach him a lesson, to convince him to let me live as I want to, to make my own decisions." I then asked him what made him lose his temper. His

answer, full of profanities and shouting, was to claim that his brother was responsible for everything that was wrong, to deny that his temper was an issue, and to say, "I hope these things I've done to him have taught him his lesson!"

I asked him whether he had ever done anything else to teach his brother a lesson. He said that he had once tried to poison his brother by putting rat poison in some mashed potatoes. He said that his effort failed because Stephen spit out the potatoes after one taste and assumed that the food was spoiled. It is not clear whether this story was truthful and could possibly have been said for the shock value. It is clear that he has fixated on his brother as a perceived persecutor. Without further tests I am unable to express a reliable opinion on whether there is paranoia present, but I would not be surprised to learn that the client is in the early stages of schizophrenia.

My recommendation at this stage is that we try to get him out of jail as soon as possible and into an in-patient facility at the Veterans Administration Hospital. It is clear that he cannot be returned to the living situation that led him to wound his brother, at least until he is properly diagnosed and commits himself to staying on the medication that could control his rage. He said he is willing to voluntarily commit himself to such a facility if it would mean he could get out of jail. I will go to work immediately to secure him a bed in the Anger Management Treatment Program at that facility.

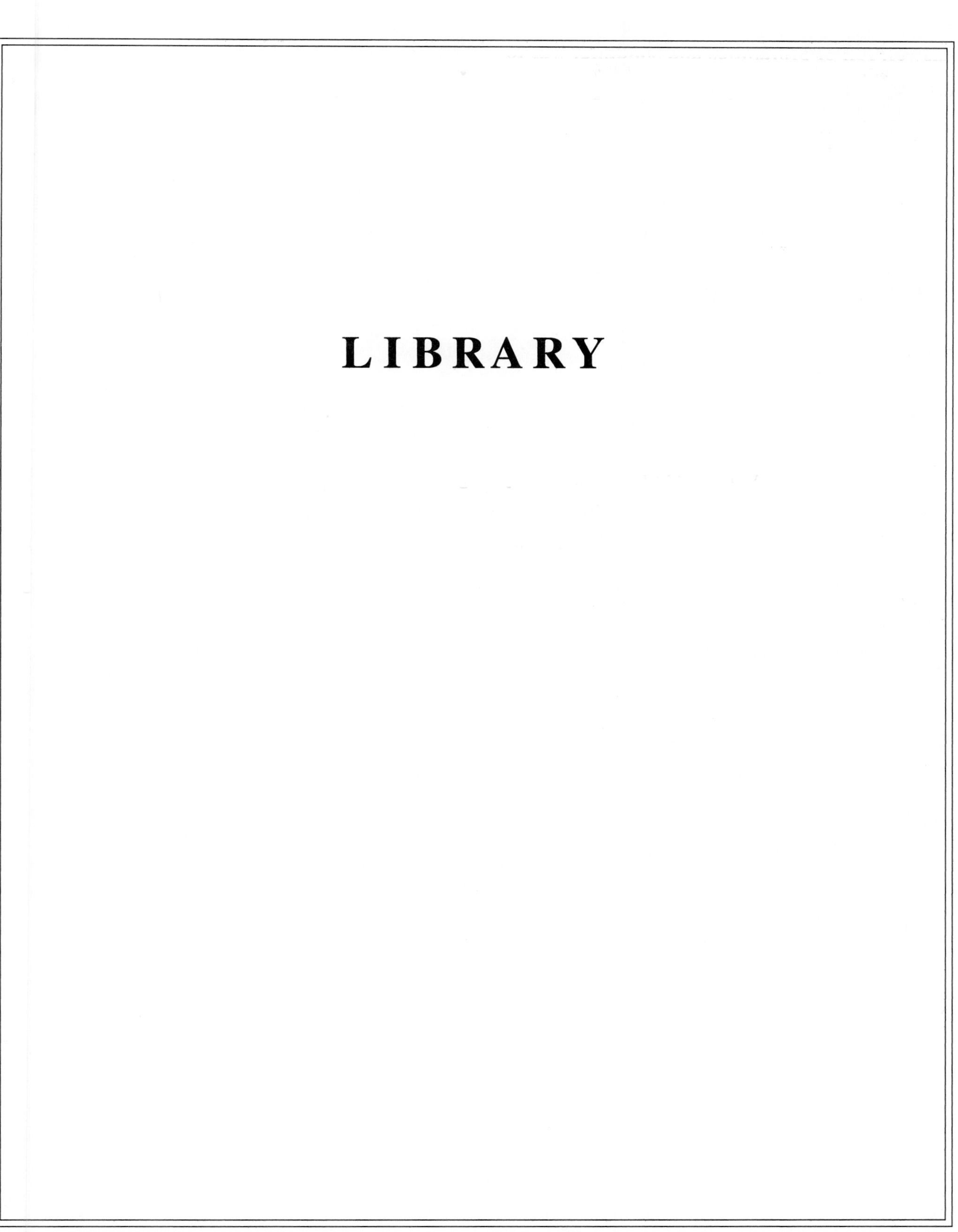

LIBRARY

Franklin Evidence Code

§835. Confidentiality of communications with social workers; Exceptions
No licensed social worker may disclose any information acquired from persons consulting the social worker in a professional capacity except:

(a) with the written consent of the person or, in the case of death or disability, of the person's own personal representative, other person authorized to sue, or the beneficiary of an insurance policy on the person's life, health, or physical condition;

(b) that a social worker shall not be required to treat as confidential a communication that reveals the contemplation or commission of a crime or a harmful act;

(c) that communications and records may be disclosed when a social worker determines that there is a substantial risk of imminent physical injury by the person to the person or others, and the person refuses explicitly to voluntarily accept further appropriate treatment;

(d) when the person waives the privilege by bringing charges against the social worker; or

(e) in any child custody case in which, upon a hearing in chambers, the judge, in the exercise of the judge's discretion, determines that the social worker has evidence bearing significantly on the person's ability to provide suitable custody and that it is more important to the welfare of the child that the information be disclosed than that the relationship between the person and social worker be protected.

* * * *

§952. Confidential communication between client and lawyer
As used in this article, "confidential communication between client and lawyer" means information transmitted between a client and the client's lawyer in the course of that relationship and in confidence by a means which, so far as the client is aware, discloses the information to no third persons other than those who are present to further the interest of the client in the consultation or those to whom disclosure is reasonably necessary for the transmission of the information or the

accomplishment of the purpose for which the lawyer is consulted. "Confidential communication between client and lawyer" also includes a legal opinion formed and the advice given by the lawyer in the course of that relationship.

§953. Lawyer-client privilege

The client, whether or not a party, has a privilege to refuse to disclose, and to prevent another from disclosing, a confidential communication between client and lawyer. A lawyer cannot, without the consent of the client, be examined as to any communication made by the client to the lawyer, or the lawyer's advice given in the course of professional employment; nor can a lawyer's secretary, stenographer, or clerk be examined, without the consent of the lawyer, concerning any fact the knowledge of which has been acquired in such capacity.

§954. When lawyer required to claim privilege

The lawyer who received or made a communication subject to the privilege under this article shall claim the privilege whenever the communication is sought to be disclosed.

§955. Crime or fraud

There is no privilege under this article if the services of the lawyer were sought or obtained to enable or aid anyone to commit or plan to commit a crime or a fraud.

§956. Disclosure necessary to prevent criminal act likely to result in death or bodily harm

There is no privilege under this article if the lawyer reasonably believes that disclosure of any confidential communication relating to representation of a client is necessary to prevent the client from committing a criminal act that the lawyer believes is likely to result in death or substantial bodily harm.

State v. Guthrie

Franklin Supreme Court (1988)

The defendant is charged with murder in the second degree. At a pretrial hearing, the State moved to compel a licensed social worker to disclose communications made to her in her professional capacity by the defendant and other persons. The social worker asserted a social worker's privilege pursuant to Franklin Evidence Code §835. The judge ordered the social worker to disclose "all of the alleged communications" to the judge and to the prosecutor at a pretrial *in camera* hearing. The order also provided that, following this disclosure, the prosecutor was to "inform the judge as to the necessity for the disclosure of any or all of the communications in the case to be tried; that thereafter the judge shall rule as to which of the communications he shall order the social worker to disclose at the trial." The judge subsequently amended his order to permit the defense attorney to be present at the *in camera* hearing. We granted the social worker's application for direct appellate review.

The social worker's brief additionally raises the issue of whether the *in camera* hearing violated Evidence Code §835.

Betsy Diznoff, the social worker involved in this case, is employed by a hospital. The victim, a seven-month-old child, was brought to the hospital on July 9, 1981. She died one week later from her injuries. Shortly after the child was admitted to the hospital, Diznoff was assigned to treat the victim's family. She interviewed the victim's mother as well as the defendant, who was the mother's boyfriend. At the pretrial hearing, the State moved that Diznoff be required to disclose various communications the defendant made to her in which he admitted hitting the child. The State also seeks certain statements made by the defendant allegedly denying any wrongdoing.

Evidence Code §835 prohibits disclosure by a licensed social worker of information acquired from persons consulting the social worker in a professional capacity. This case is concerned with the exception embodied in subsection (b), which states that "a social worker shall not be required to treat as confidential a communication that reveals the contemplation or commission of a crime or a harmful act."

1. *Statutory purpose.* The privilege established by §835 is a legislative recognition that the confidentiality of a person's communications to a social worker is a necessity for successful social work intervention. Whether the protected relationship involves physicians, psychologists or certified social workers, all share the common purpose of encouraging patients or clients fully

to disclose the nature and details of their illnesses or their emotions without fear of later revelation by one in whom they placed their trust and confidence. The purpose of enacting a social worker-client privilege is to prevent the chilling effect that routine disclosures may have in preventing those in need of help from seeking that help. The Legislature has determined that, while the preservation of the confidential relationship is an important objective, under certain circumstances this goal must give way in favor of other societal interests. Therefore, the Legislature has carved out exceptions to the statutory privilege.

2. *Scope of exception.* The pertinent language of the exception embodied in subsection (b) provides that a social worker shall not be required to treat as confidential a communication that reveals the contemplation or commission of a crime or a harmful act.

The social worker has testified before the grand jury concerning statements made by the defendant that fall into this category and is prepared to do so at trial. The social worker testified that, during her interview with the defendant, he admitted that he hit the victim on the night she went to the hospital and also had hit her in the past. It is clear that these statements reveal the commission of a crime or harmful act and are not privileged. The State contends that exception (b) not only encompasses admissions of guilt but also extends to communications that are evidence of consciousness of guilt, such as denials or false statements, and in addition any information that has any bearing upon criminal activity. Diznoff contends that the exception must be construed much more narrowly and that the State's interpretation of the exception would effectively nullify the statute.

The intended scope of the phrase "communication that reveals the contemplation or commission of a crime or a harmful act" is not readily ascertainable from the language used. While it is clear that admissions of a crime or harmful act are intended to be covered by this phrase, it is not clear whether the additional communications that the State seeks are intended to fall within the statutory exception.

The State's reading of subsection (b) is too broad. It would require social workers to disclose all of the information they receive in a professional capacity whenever a crime is involved. It would negate the privilege under this circumstance. We think that the Legislature evidenced two aims by the enactment of the statute and exception (b). The first objective is to encourage individuals in need of help from a social worker to seek that help by ensuring the confidentiality of their communications. The second objective, embodied in subsection (b), is to serve the interests of society in prosecuting those who are guilty of criminal conduct. In enacting subsection (b), the Legislature attempted to balance these two objectives. Exception (b) should be narrowly construed to require disclosure by a social worker of subpoenaed communications that relate directly to the fact or immediate circumstances of a crime. The exception does not extend to all information that might be relevant in the prosecution of a person for a crime. The exception is not intended to allow the State a "fishing expedition" or a convenient discovery device.

In the case before us, the court may compel the social worker to reveal the defendant's admissions of criminal activity. However, the defendant's alleged denials of wrongdoing and false statements to the social worker do not reveal the commission of a crime. While such denials may show a "consciousness of guilt," they do not "reveal" the commission of a crime.

3. *In camera hearing.* The statute does not set forth any procedure by which the trial judge can determine whether communications fall within exception (b). The *in camera* hearing is the proper procedure to allow the judge to determine whether or not the privilege applies to communications made to the social worker.

The State argues that the parties should exchange briefs and that the prosecutor and defense counsel should be present at the *in camera* hearing because the judge may require their assistance in determining the relevance of the communications. The defendant argues that the prosecutor should not receive the defendant's brief in support of his motion nor be present because the disclosure in the presence of the prosecutor is a violation of the client's confidentiality. He argues also that even if the judge rules that certain testimony may not be used at trial, the prosecutor may indirectly use such evidence against the defendant.

We agree that disclosure of the confidential information to the prosecutor or the defense attorney in the *in camera* hearing would frustrate the purpose of the statute unless it falls within one of the statutory exceptions. In most cases, the judge will be able to make the decision whether or not the information is privileged without the parties' assistance. However, if questions arise, the judge may require the assistance of the parties, but must do so without revealing the content of the confidential communications.

Remanded for further proceedings.

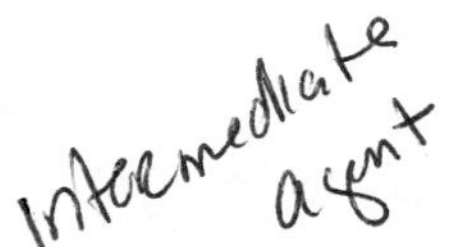

Shea Cargo Company v. Wilson

Franklin Court of Appeal (1951)

James Wilson brought an action for personal injuries against Shea Cargo Company. He alleged that he suffered a brain concussion and nervous shock. At the request of Wilson's attorneys, a physician specializing in nervous and mental diseases, Dr. Joseph Chavkin, twice gave Wilson a neurological and psychiatric examination. In his deposition, Dr. Chavkin testified that there was no physician-patient relationship between him and Wilson; that he did not advise or treat Wilson; that the sole purpose of the examination was to aid Wilson's attorneys in the preparation of a lawsuit for Wilson; and that he was the agent of the attorneys. He refused to answer questions regarding Wilson's condition on the ground that the information sought was privileged under Franklin Evidence Code §952, et seq., Lawyer-Client Privilege. Wilson's counsel also claimed that the information was privileged.

The Superior Court granted Wilson's motion for a protective order and now Defendant filed this interlocutory appeal.

The Physician-Patient Privilege

Dr. Chavkin testified that "there was no physician-patient relationship in the sense that I was examining him for the purpose of giving him advice or treatment . . . nor did I at any time give him any such advice or treatment; so that there wasn't that usual physician-patient relationship." He also filed an affidavit in which he averred that he "has not at any time prescribed for or treated the said James Wilson as a patient or otherwise." Under such circumstances there is no physician-patient privilege under Evidence Code §920.[1] That privilege cannot be invoked when no treatment is contemplated or given. The confidence that is protected is only that which is given to a professional physician during a consultation with a view to curative treatment; for it is that relation only which the law desires to facilitate.

Even if there had been a physician-patient relationship, the privilege would be waived under §920 by Wilson's bringing the action for personal injuries.

The purpose of the privilege is to preclude the humiliation of the patient that might follow disclosure of his ailments. When the patient himself discloses those ailments by bringing an action in which they are in issue, there is no longer any reason for the privilege.

---

[1] §920 says, "*Physician and patient.* A licensed physician cannot, without the consent of his patient, be examined in a civil action, as to any information acquired in attending the patient, which was necessary to enable him to prescribe or act for the patient; . . . provided further, that where any person brings an action to recover damages for personal injuries, such action shall be deemed to constitute a consent by the person bringing such action that any physician who has prescribed for or treated said person and whose testimony is material in said action shall testify . . . ."

The Lawyer-Client Privilege

Although Dr. Chavkin can invoke no privilege of his own and there was no physician-patient privilege in this case, we have concluded that Dr. Chavkin was an intermediate agent for communication between Wilson and his lawyers and that Wilson may therefore invoke the lawyer-client privilege under §953 of the Evidence Code.[2] This privilege is strictly construed, since it suppresses relevant facts that may be necessary for a just decision. It cannot be invoked unless the client intended the communication to be confidential, and only communications made to a lawyer in the course of professional employment are privileged.

The privilege is given on grounds of public policy in the belief that the benefits derived therefrom justify the risk that unjust decisions may sometimes result from the suppression of relevant evidence. Adequate legal representation in the ascertaininent and enforcement of rights or the prosecution or defense of litigation compels a full disclosure of the facts by the client to his lawyer. Unless the client makes known to the lawyer all the facts, the advice that follows will be useless, if not misleading, and much useless litigation may result. Given the privilege, a client can disclose unfavorable facts without fear that the lawyer may be forced to reveal the information confided to the lawyer. The absence of the privilege would convert the lawyer into a mere informer for the benefit of the opponent.

Petitioner contends that under the express terms of §953 only the lawyer and the lawyer's secretary, stenographer, or clerk cannot be examined and that, since Dr. Chavkin was not engaged in any of these capacities, he cannot withhold the information requested.

The statute specifically extends the client's privilege to preclude examination of the lawyer's secretary, stenographer, or clerk regarding communications between lawyer and client to rule out the possibility of their coming within the general rule that the privilege does not preclude the examination of a third person who overhears communications between a client and the client's lawyer. It does not follow, however, that intermediate agents of the lawyer and client may be freely examined. Had Wilson himself described his condition to his lawyers there could be no doubt that the communication would be privileged. It is no less the client's communication to the lawyer when it is given by the client to an agent for transmission to the lawyer. A communication, then, by any form

[2] §953 reads, *Lawyer-client privilege* ". . . A lawyer cannot, without the consent of the client, be examined as to any communication made by the client to the lawyer or the lawyer's advice given in the course of professional employment; nor can a lawyer's secretary, stenographer, or clerk be examined, without the consent of the lawyer, concerning any fact the knowledge of which has been acquired in such capacity."

of agency employed or set in motion either by the client or the lawyer is within the privilege.

This of course includes communications through an interpreter, through a messenger or any other agent of transmission, as well as communications originating with the client's agent and made to the lawyer. It follows, too, that the communications of the lawyer's agent to the lawyer are within the privilege because the lawyer's agent is also the client's sub-agent and is acting as such for the client. Thus, when communication by a client to the client's lawyer regarding the client's physical or mental condition requires the assistance of a physician to interpret the client's condition to the lawyer, the client may submit to an examination by the physician without fear that the latter will be compelled to reveal the information disclosed.

Affirmed.

State v. White

Sample Answer

BRIEF IN SUPPORT OF MOTION TO QUASH SUBPOENA

I. STATEMENT OF FACTS

The defendant, James White, is charged with the knife-murder of his brother Stephen White. The Public Defender's Office is representing him in this matter. Ten months ago, the defendant was charged with the aggravated assault of his brother; the defendant allegedly fought with his brother over money and then stabbed him with a knife. The Public Defender's Office also represented the defendant in the assault case.

The prosecution has now subpoenaed the reports, notes, and other documents concerning the defendant prepared by Grace Peterson, a licensed social worker who was employed by the Public Defender's Office and who interviewed the defendant in the assault case. At that time, Ms. Peterson interviewed the defendant at the request of the defense counsel. The defendant was in police custody after his arrest for aggravated assault, and the defense counsel requested the defendant to meet with Ms. Peterson to help the defense counsel prepare for a bail reduction motion to get the defendant released on his own recognizance, and for possible disposition of the charges.

The defendant agreed to meet with Ms. Peterson after the defense counsel explained lawyer-client confidentiality. The defendant believed all statements made by him to Ms. Peterson were privileged and confidential. The defendant discussed his military and psychiatric history with Ms. Peterson. He also told her that he had no memory of any fight with his brother, and that he was sure he did not stab his brother. However, later in the interview, when Ms. Peterson told him that his brother would not let him back in the house they shared, the defendant became enraged and yelled that "he [the brother] was lucky I didn't kill him," and that he "wanted to teach him [the brother] a lesson," and that he "hopes these things I've done to him have taught him a lesson." Ms. Peterson then asked the defendant if he had ever done anything else to teach his brother a lesson, and the defendant responded that he once tried to poison his brother. Ms. Peterson was not sure that the defendant was telling the truth about the poison story and believed that the defendant may be schizophrenic.

After the interview, Ms. Peterson prepared a report for the defense counsel that included the defendant's military and psychiatric history as well as the statements discussed above. Although the defense counsel did not reveal the contents of the report to the court, he used the information in the report to get the defendant released to a treatment facility. The assault case, however, is still pending because there was no final disposition of the charges. The defendant agreed to voluntarily commit himself for treatment if it would keep him out of jail.

Because Ms. Peterson now lives in Italy, she is unable to testify to statements made by the defendant during the interview. Therefore, the prosecution wants to admit the defendant's statements in her report to prove that the defendant murdered his brother. The defense has filed a motion to quash the state's subpoena because the statements in the report are privileged communications. This brief is in support of the motion to quash. A copy of Ms. Peterson's report is attached and submitted under seal for the court's *in camera* review.

II. ARGUMENT

A. The Defendant's Statements in Ms. Peterson's Report Are Inadmissible Under the Social Worker-Client Privilege Because the Statements Were Made to Ms. Peterson Acting in Her Capacity as a Social Worker and No Exception Applies.

Under Franklin Evidence Code section 835, a licensed social worker may not disclose information acquired from a person who has consulted her in a professional capacity. Clearly, the defendant consulted Ms. Peterson, a licensed social worker, in her professional capacity. Thus, the privilege applies. However, this privilege is not absolute. A social worker may disclose information communicated by a person to the social worker when (i) the information reveals the contemplation or commission of a crime or harmful act; or (ii) the social worker believes that there is a substantial risk of imminent physical injury to the person or another and the person refuses to voluntarily accept appropriate treatment. [Franklin Evidence Code §835(b), (c)]

In *State v. Guthrie*, the Franklin Supreme Court examined the social worker-client privilege and the exception for communications that reveal the contemplation or commission of a crime or harmful act. In *Guthrie*, the defendant was charged with the murder of his girlfriend's baby. After the baby's death, a hospital social worker interviewed the baby's mother and the defendant. The defendant admitted to the social worker that he hit the girlfriend's baby but also denied that he committed any wrongdoing. The state sought to have the social worker disclose these statements under the exception for statements revealing the contemplation or commission of a crime or harmful act, arguing that the exception extended to communications that show consciousness of guilt, such as denials or false statements, and any other communications that have any bearing on criminal conduct.

The *Guthrie* court discussed the rationales behind the social worker-client privilege and the exception: The privilege is necessary to encourage people to get the help they need; thus it is important to ensure confidentiality under the privilege. However, the exception is necessary to promote the societal interest in prosecuting criminal conduct. The court then decided that the state's argument in extending the exception to cover communications concerning consciousness of guilt or any other communications bearing on criminal conduct is too broad; the exception does not extend to all information that might be relevant in prosecuting a person for the crime charged. The exception must be construed narrowly to require disclosure by a social worker only of communications that ***relate directly to the fact or immediate circumstance of a crime***. Thus, the *Guthrie* court held that the social worker was required to reveal only those statements by the defendant that were admissions to criminal conduct, and not denials of wrongdoing or false statements.

In this case, the state has subpoenaed the records of all conversations the defendant had with Ms. Peterson and the report she prepared for the defense counsel. As discussed above, this information is privileged under the Franklin Evidence Code as communications made to a social worker who is acting in her professional capacity. The privilege extends to the report because Ms. Peterson is unavailable to testify. Because the exceptions to the privilege do not apply, the report should not be disclosed to the state under subpoena.

Specifically, the information in the report concerning the defendant's military and psychiatric history is privileged and there is no exception that would allow for its admission. However, the state can argue that although the defendant's military and psychiatric history is inadmissible, certain statements made by the defendant are admissible under the exception for statements revealing the contemplation or commission of a crime or harmful act. The state can argue that the defendant's statements denying any assault on his brother are admissible under the exception because the exception extends to statements that show consciousness of guilt. However, as indicated above, the court in *Guthrie* limited the exception to statements directly related to the fact or immediate circumstance of the crime; denials or false statements are inadmissible. Thus, the defendant's denial would not be admissible.

The state also can argue that the defendant's statement regarding his attempt to poison his brother is admissible under the exception. However, this statement is of doubtful credibility and thus is inadmissible as a false statement. The *Guthrie* court held that false statements are not admissible under the exception. Here, Ms. Peterson could not judge whether the poison story was true; rather, she indicated that the defendant may have said it for "shock value," and she suggested that the story may be a product of schizophrenia. Also, if the story was not true, it could not relate directly to the commission of a crime or harmful act and so it is inadmissible.

The state can also argue that the statements the defendant made that his brother was lucky that he did not kill him, that he wanted to teach his brother a lesson, and that he hopes his actions taught his brother a lesson are admissible under the exception for statements revealing the commission of a crime. The state can argue that these statements relate to the defendant's assault/stabbing of his brother. However, these statements do not directly relate to the commission of a crime. The defendant never admitted to stabbing his brother nor made any reference to the assault or stabbing. Also, the statements were made in anger after finding out that his brother would not let him move back into the house, and thus may be false. Therefore, these statements are inadmissible.

It also should be noted that the exception to the social worker-client privilege that allows the social worker to disclose information when there is a substantial risk of imminent injury to the client or another is not applicable here. This exception does not apply because there is no risk of harm to the defendant's brother because he is dead, and although there may be a generalized fear that the defendant's temper could lead him to harm someone else, there is nothing to indicate that such harm is imminent. Also, the statute requires that the person refuse treatment. Here, the defendant has voluntarily agreed to treatment.

B. The Defendant's Statements in Ms. Peterson's Report Also Are Inadmissible Under the Attorney-Client Privilege Because the Defendant Met with Ms. Peterson and Made Statements to Her at the Request of Defense Counsel to Assist Defense Counsel in Representing the Defendant.

Section 953 of the Franklin Evidence Code provides that a client has a privilege to refuse to disclose and to prevent others from disclosing confidential communications made between the lawyer and client. Section 952 defines "confidential communications" as communications made between the lawyer and client in the course of that relationship which are made in confidence, *i.e.*, by a means that discloses the communications to no third persons except those who are present to further the interests of the client in the consultation or who are reasonably necessary for the transmission of information or accomplishment of the purpose for which the lawyer is consulted. Section 953 also states that a lawyer's secretary, stenographer, or clerk cannot be examined concerning any fact of which has been acquired in such capacity.

In *Shea Cargo Company v. Wilson*, the Franklin Court of Appeals examined whether respondent's statements made to a doctor were inadmissible under the attorney-client privilege. The respondent in *Shea* had brought an action against the petitioner for personal injuries suffered. The petitioner sought to have a doctor who examined the respondent at the request of respondent's attorney testify to the respondent's condition. The petitioner contended that under section 953, only the lawyer and the lawyer's secretary, stenographer, or clerk are prevented from being examined regarding a client's confidential communications, and that the doctor was not engaged in any of those capacities; thus he can be required to disclose the respondent's condition.

The *Shea* court noted that the attorney-client privilege is strictly construed, and that it cannot be invoked unless the client intended a communication to be privileged. The court also noted that the privilege specifically prevents the examination of a lawyer's secretary, stenographer, or clerk regarding

attorney-client communications to rule out the possibility of their coming within the general rule that the privilege does not apply to third persons who overhear attorney-client communications. However, the court stated that it does not follow that intermediate agents of the lawyer and client may be freely examined; the court commented that it is no less the client's communication to the lawyer when given by the client to an agent for transmission to the lawyer. Thus, the *Shea* court held that a communication by any form of agency set in motion by either the client or the lawyer is privileged, and that when the assistance of a physician is necessary to explain the client's physical or mental condition to the lawyer, the client may submit to an examination by the physician without fear that the physician will be compelled to reveal the information disclosed. Therefore, the court held that the doctor could invoke the attorney-client privilege and prevent the disclosure of information relating to the respondent's condition.

In this case, the defense counsel explained attorney-client confidentiality to the defendant and then specifically requested the defendant to meet with Ms. Peterson. Thus, the defendant intended his communications with Ms. Peterson to be privileged. Furthermore, the defense counsel requested the meeting between the defendant and Ms. Peterson to assist the defense counsel in preparing for a bail reduction hearing and to get the defendant released on his own recognizance. The defense counsel also thought that he might be able to dispose of the case based on Ms. Peterson's evaluation of the defendant. Thus, Ms. Peterson is an intermediate agent of the lawyer, and the defendant's interview with her that was summarized in her report was necessary to explain the defendant's mental state to the lawyer and is not subject to disclosure under the attorney-client privilege.

Under Evidence Code section 956, the attorney can disclose confidential communication if necessary to prevent the client from committing a crime the attorney believes is likely to result in death or substantial bodily harm. This exception to the attorney-client privilege does not apply here. At this point, there is no reason to believe that the defendant is likely to harm anyone, as the object of his anger (his brother) is dead.

III. CONCLUSION

The motion to quash the state's subpoena of Grace Peterson's report should be granted because the statements contained in the report are privileged under both the social worker-client privilege and the attorney-client privilege.

Multistate

Performance Test

Whitford v. Newberry
Middle School District

National Conference of Bar Examiners

Preface

This Multistate Performance Test is a reprint of one of the three MPTs which were administered in February 2002.

The instructions for the test appear on the next page. On the actual MPT, they will appear on the back cover of the test.

INSTRUCTIONS

1. You will have 90 minutes to complete this session of the examination. This performance test is designed to evaluate your ability to handle a select number of legal authorities in the context of a factual problem involving a client.

2. The problem is set in the fictitious state of Franklin, in the fictitious Fifteenth Circuit of the United States. Columbia and Olympia are also fictitious states in the Fifteenth Circuit. In Franklin, the trial court of general jurisdiction is the District Court, the intermediate appellate court is the Court of Appeal, and the highest court is the Supreme Court.

3. You will have two kinds of materials with which to work: a File and a Library. The first document in the File is a memorandum containing the instructions for the task you are to complete. The other documents in the File contain factual information about your case and may include some facts that are not relevant.

4. The Library contains the legal authorities needed to complete the task and may also include some authorities that are not relevant. Any cases may be real, modified, or written solely for the purpose of this examination. If the cases appear familiar to you, do not assume that they are precisely the same as you have read before. Read them thoroughly, as if they all were new to you. You should assume that cases were decided in the jurisdictions and on the dates shown. In citing cases from the Library, you may use abbreviations and omit page references.

5. Your response must be written in the answer book provided. If you are taking this examination on a laptop computer, your jurisdiction will provide you with specific instructions. In answering this performance test, you should concentrate on the materials provided in the File and Library. What you have learned in law school and elsewhere provides the general background for analyzing the problem; the File and Library provide the specific materials with which you must work.

6. Although there are no restrictions on how you apportion your time, you should be sure to allocate ample time (about 45 minutes) to reading and digesting the materials and to organizing your answer before you begin writing it. You may make notes anywhere in the test materials; blank pages are provided at the end of the booklet. You may not tear pages from the question booklet.

7. This performance test will be graded on your responsiveness to the instructions regarding the task you are to complete, which are given to you in the first memorandum in the File, and on the content, thoroughness, and organization of your response.

Whitford v. Newberry Middle School District

FILE

LIBRARY

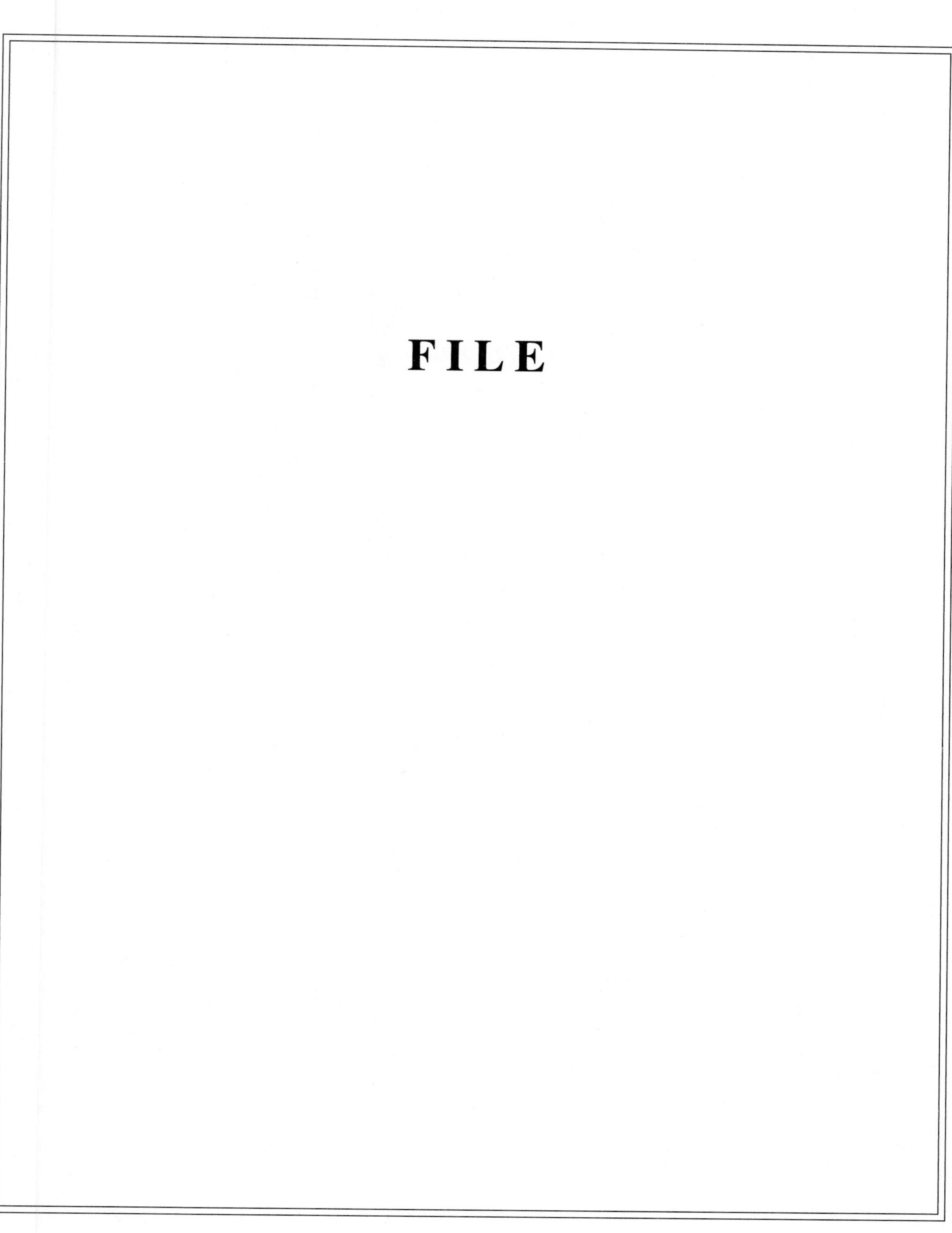

FILE

The Gogh Law Offices
647 Aiden Place
Newberry, Franklin 33616

MEMORANDUM

TO: Applicant
FROM: Sandy Gogh
RE: *Whitford v. Newberry Middle School District*
DATE: February 28, 2002

I was very pleased with the way you handled the evidentiary phase of the motion for preliminary injunction in *Annie Whitford v. Newberry Middle School District.* You will be making the closing argument tomorrow afternoon. Before then, I'd like you to write out your closing argument to prepare for your presentation in court and let me review it.

The court has instructed you to focus your argument on the likelihood of Annie's success on the merits, which you know is a prerequisite for issuance of a preliminary injunction. The judge has already found irreparable injury, so there is no need for you to argue that point.

The closing argument should revolve around the facts that you brought out at the hearing. The School District refused to allow Annie to try out for her school's boys-only volleyball team. Since the District receives federal financial assistance, this refusal violated Annie's rights under Title IX of the Education Amendments of 1972. The refusal deprived her of an equal opportunity, based on gender, to participate in interscholastic athletics.

In the argument, you should tell a persuasive story about why Annie should prevail, highlight the salient facts of that story, and show how the evidence supports the factors that are enumerated in the statute, regulations, and caselaw. It is also important that you preempt the District's position by showing how the District's evidence fails to support its case and, in fact, supports yours. The structure of the argument—*i.e.*, an introduction, main argument, and conclusion—is important. It should be persuasive, organized, well-reasoned, and compelling. You should end it with a clear statement of the relief you are seeking.

UNITED STATES DISTRICT COURT
CENTRAL DISTRICT OF FRANKLIN

Annie Whitford, a minor, by
her best friends and natural
guardians Pearl Whitford and George
Whitford,
Plaintiff
v.
Newberry Middle School District,
Defendant

Case Number 02-CV-1068

TRANSCRIPT OF HEARING ON PLAINTIFF'S
MOTION FOR PRELIMINARY INJUNCTION
February 27, 2002

THE COURT: Okay counsel, let's begin. You may proceed.
APPLICANT: In this case, plaintiff Annie Whitford is a 12-year-old student in the seventh grade at Newberry Middle School. She seeks an order requiring Newberry Middle School District to let her try out for the interscholastic volleyball team at Newberry Middle School. Newberry Middle School is covered by Title IX of the Education Amendments of 1972, which prohibits gender discrimination in school athletic programs. Annie wanted to try out for her school's all-male volleyball team and was informed by the coach that she could not because a District rule prohibits females from playing with or against male students in contact sports.
THE COURT: Is that policy in writing?
APPLICANT: It's attached to my motion, Your Honor. Let me read it into the record: "Boys and girls shall not be permitted to participate in interschool athletic games as mixed teams, nor shall boys' teams and girls' teams participate against each other in interscholastic athletic contests when the sports involved are contact sports or sports in which the purpose or major activity involves physical contact, including football, baseball, basketball, volleyball, wrestling, and ice hockey."
THE COURT: Mr. Perdue, is this a fair summary of the problem?
PERDUE (Counsel for School District): Yes, Your Honor.
THE COURT: Call your first witness, counsel.

THE PLAINTIFF, Annie Whitford, WAS SWORN AND IDENTIFIED.
APPLICANT: Good morning, Annie. I am going to ask you a few questions, okay?
WHITFORD: Okay.
Q: When did you start playing volleyball?
A: When I was about seven years old, in the second grade.
Q: Have you been playing ever since?
A: Yes, constantly. I've played on teams through the YMCA, the Parks and Recreation Department, and the U.S. Volleyball League Juniors Club. I've gone to volleyball camps for the last five summers.
Q: Were there boys on these teams?
A: Yes, they were all co-ed.
Q: I notice you're wearing a T-shirt today that has something to do with volleyball.
A: Yeah, it's my lucky T-shirt. It's the one I got as a special award when my team won the silver medal at the National Junior Olympics this year in New Orleans. I play the position of middle blocker, so the T-shirt says, "Annie Whitford, Middle Blocker, Attacker of the Unwary, She Yields to No One."
Q: Have you received other awards?
A: Yes, I've gotten awards when my teams have won tournaments, and also as the team's Most Valuable Player.
Q: Do you know the win-loss statistics of your teams?
A: Counting it all up, the teams I've played on have won 97 matches and lost only seven. We've taken at least 20 titles.
Q: Annie, what does volleyball mean to you?
A: Volleyball is my life. I play it every day. If I'm not practicing or playing on teams, I'm working on my serves, passes, and spikes against the wall of the gym or behind the school. My goal is to get a scholarship to a college with a great women's volleyball team, like the University of Franklin or Stanford. My parents sure couldn't afford those schools otherwise. Maybe I'll even play in the Olympics one day. In fact, even before that, I've got a real good chance of getting a volleyball scholarship to Prescott next year. It's, like, the top prep school in the state and has got a great volleyball program.
Q: When did you first attend Newberry Middle School?

A: Just this year when my family moved here from out of state.

Q: Why do you want to play on the boys' volleyball team?

A: For one, seventh grade is the first chance you get to play interscholastic volleyball. Also, it's not like there is even a girls' team for me to try out for. Even if there were, I've played with boys on all of my past teams and I've watched the Newberry Middle School volleyball team play. I think that playing with the boys will give me the competition I need to develop my skills.

Q: Annie, suppose the judge decided you should be able to try out, but she waited six months before she made that decision. Would that be okay?

A: Well, I don't want to be impolite, but, like, what would be the point? The season starts in two weeks and only lasts three months. I mean, Prescott scouts and even some colleges wouldn't be able to see me play.

APPLICANT: I have nothing further for this witness.

THE COURT: Cross-examination?

PERDUE: Yes. Thank you, Your Honor.

Q: Annie, have you ever been hurt playing volleyball?

A: Well, just twice. In a tournament game last year, I was hit in the face by a ball. I got a bruised eye and a bloody nose.

Q: Was that ball hit by a boy?

A: Yeah.

Q: Any other injuries?

A: At last summer's volleyball camp, a boy on the other team bumped me at the net and caused me to come down off balance. I came down on my right ankle and sprained it.

Q: So, your injury was caused by coming into physical contact with a boy, isn't that right?

A: Yeah, but he did it intentionally and he got called for a foul because you're not supposed to do that. But you really try hard not to do stuff like that because your team could get penalized.

Q: And, lots of times, when you're scrambling to get the ball, you and your teammates collide, isn't that true?

A: Not lots of times, but sometimes.

Q: Thank you, Annie. Nothing further, Your Honor.

THE COURT: Next?
APPLICANT: The plaintiff calls Karin Wallenstein.
THE WITNESS, Karin Wallenstein, WAS SWORN AND IDENTIFIED.
APPLICANT: Ms. Wallenstein, in what positions are you employed at Newberry Middle School?
WALLENSTEIN: I am the Director of Physical Education and the volleyball coach.
Q: Were you previously employed in school athletics?
A: Yes, after graduating from college, I taught physical education courses for seventh and eighth graders for about six years. After that, I was at different times an assistant coach for the women's volleyball teams at Franklin Community College and Franklin State.
Q: Do you also play volleyball?
A: I play on the "Bruisers" adult co-ed team through the U.S. Volleyball League. I've played since high school.
Q: How many interscholastic sports teams are there at Newberry Middle School?
A: There are 10.
Q: What are they?
A: There are six boys' teams—football, basketball, baseball, ice hockey, volleyball, and wrestling. There are four girls' teams—cross-country, basketball, swimming, and tennis.
Q: Are there any co-ed interscholastic teams?
A: No.
Q: Is there a budget for interscholastic athletics at Newberry?
A: Yes, it pays for things like coaches' salaries, facilities upkeep, equipment and uniform purchases, athlete transportation, and publicity.
Q: What percentage of the athletic budget is spent on the boys' teams?
A: I'd say approximately 70%.
Q: Did you allow Annie Whitford to try out for the school volleyball team?
A: Ultimately, no.
Q: Why?
A: This is a little embarrassing. Being new to Newberry, I didn't even know that the District had a rule barring girls from the volleyball team. I had seen Annie play during P.E. class and she is by far the best player we have in the school—boy or girl. I told her I hoped she would try out.

Q: Did any other female students ask to try out?
A: No, but not for lack of interest.
Q: What do you mean?
A: Unlike me, they knew the rule. Before tryouts I asked some of the girls who played well in class if they were going to try out. They told me it was no use, that, although some of them love to play volleyball, they had given up a long time ago trying to get the school to start a girls' team, or to allow a co-ed team. Once I found out about the rule barring girls, I had to tell Annie she couldn't try out for the team.
Q: How much, if any, physical contact takes place between players during a game of volleyball?
A: We follow U.S. Volleyball League rules, which say volleyball is a non-contact sport. The main activity of the game is hitting the ball back and forth over the net and trying to land the ball in the opponent's court without its being returned successfully. Intentional or threatened physical contact between players can cause the player who acts intentionally or threatens another—and her team—to be penalized, including expulsion from the match.
Q: Thank you, Coach Wallenstein.
THE COURT: Cross-examination?
PERDUE: Thank you, Your Honor. Ms. Wallenstein, isn't it true that volleyball players wear protective padding when they play?
WALLENSTEIN: Most players wear kneepads, and I have seen a few players wear elbow pads.
Q: In a game of volleyball, the six members of one team play on one side of the net and the six members of the opposing team play on the other side, correct?
A: Yes, that's correct.
Q: And, in the course of running for the ball, team members collide with each other, don't they?
A: Not normally, if each player covers her area, but it can happen occasionally.
Q: And sometimes a player in the front line collides at the net with a player from the other team, right?
A: Sometimes.
Q: For example, when trying to spike a ball over the net, a player jumps up to hit the ball, right?
A: Yes.
Q: And that player raises her arm over her head and attempts to slap the ball hard over the net.
A: Yes.

Q: And in trying to make that play, she may physically strike a player on the other team who may be trying to block or pass the ball, right?

A: In my experience, rarely.

Q: Well, isn't it considered a very good play when a player spikes a ball hard over the net?

A: Yes.

Q: And a hard, fast hit over the net that the other team can't respond to is even called a "kill," right?

A: Yes, but certainly not with the aim of "killing" anyone.

Q: In the course of your impressive career as a college coach, how many injuries to players have you observed as a result of physical contact between players?

A: Some.

Q: Because a good player is going to use all her power, speed, and strength to get that volleyball over the net, right?

A: Come on, Mr. Perdue, we are talking about 12-year-old boys and girls.

Q: Ms. Wallenstein, please answer my question.

A: I guess so.

PERDUE: I have no further questions of this witness.

THE COURT: Redirect?

APPLICANT: Briefly, Your Honor. Ms. Wallenstein, do volleyball rules require players to wear knee or elbow pads?

WALLENSTEIN: No.

Q: How about mouth protectors or shin guards?

A: Neither.

Q: Do the rules prohibit players from wearing jewelry?

A: The rules don't but good sense does.

APPLICANT: Nothing further, Your Honor, and the plaintiff rests.

THE COURT: Mr. Perdue?

PERDUE: Your Honor, the District calls its only witness, Grace Huang.

THE WITNESS, Grace Huang, WAS SWORN AND IDENTIFIED.

PERDUE: Ms. Huang, you have been the Superintendent of the Newberry Middle School District for 10 years.

HUANG: Correct.
Q: What, if any, responsibility do you have over the interscholastic athletic programs at the schools in your District?
A: I decide the budget allocations, approve the types and number of interscholastic teams and, with help of counsel, monitor compliance with the law.
Q: Were you responsible for the issuance of the rule at issue in this case?
A: Yes.
Q: What are the reasons for this rule?
A: I read Title IX to prohibit co-ed interscholastic teams in contact sports and the District has concluded that volleyball is a contact sport.
Q: Your Honor, I have nothing further for this witness.
THE COURT: Cross-examination?
APPLICANT: Thank you, Your Honor. Ms. Huang, you have no firsthand experience in school athletics, do you?
HUANG: No, not really.
Q: You have never taught seventh grade students, have you?
A: My previous teaching experience was with high school students.
Q: Am I correct that only seventh and eighth grade students may participate in interscholastic athletic activities in the Newberry Middle School District?
A: Yes, that is correct.
Q: How many students are there in the seventh and eighth grades at Newberry Middle School?
A: Approximately 1,000.
Q: How many of the 1,000 students are female?
A: About 600.
Q: That would make about 400 of the students male?
A: Yes.
Q: Of the 600 female students, approximately how many participate in interscholastic athletics?
A: About 100 among the four girls' teams.
Q: And, of the 400 male students, how many play on interscholastic sports teams?
A: About 200.
Q: In the past, female students at Newberry Middle School have requested the formation

of a girls' interscholastic volleyball team, am I right?
A: I vaguely recall some parents sending me a letter to that effect.
Q: And their request was denied?
A: That's true.
Q: There are talented volleyball players among the female students at Newberry Middle School, aren't there?
A: I don't really know.
Q: I assume you have thought through the reasons why you denied the request for an interscholastic girls' volleyball team?
A: Yes, I have.
Q: Well, some of those reasons are that you have limited facilities, and it would be hard to schedule practice and game times if you had both girls' and boys' teams.
A: Yes.
Q: You might have to hire another coach, and even if you didn't, you'd have to pay Ms. Wallenstein more to take on the extra work.
A: Yes.
Q: You would have to increase your lockers and other facilities to accommodate visiting teams. Is that right?
A: Yes.
Q: This all would cost a great deal of money, wouldn't it?
A: We only have so much money to spend on the athletic programs at each school.
Q: I have nothing further for this witness.
THE COURT: Mr. Perdue, any redirect?
PERDUE: No, the District rests.
THE COURT: Thank you, counsel. I see it's getting late, so let's reconvene tomorrow afternoon for argument. We will get you a transcript with our new simultaneous transcription equipment. Before we adjourn, however, let me say I think it's pretty clear Annie has established that waiting for a trial doesn't do her any good. If her legal theory is right, she will suffer irreparable harm. You have adequately briefed the issue whether the Title IX regulations comport with constitutional equal protection standards so do not argue that point again. I want you to focus your arguments on the likelihood of plaintiff's success on the merits.

[illegible] a girls' [illegible] volleyball team, and [illegible]

A. I vaguely recall some parents [illegible] to that effect.

Q. [illegible]

A. That's true.

Q. There are [illegible] female students at Newberry Middle School, aren't there?

A. I don't really know.

Q. [illegible]

A. Yes, I have.

Q. [illegible]

Q. [illegible]

A. [illegible]

Q. [illegible] is that right?

A. [illegible]

Q. [illegible]

A. We only have [illegible]

Q. [illegible]

[illegible]

[illegible]

[illegible]

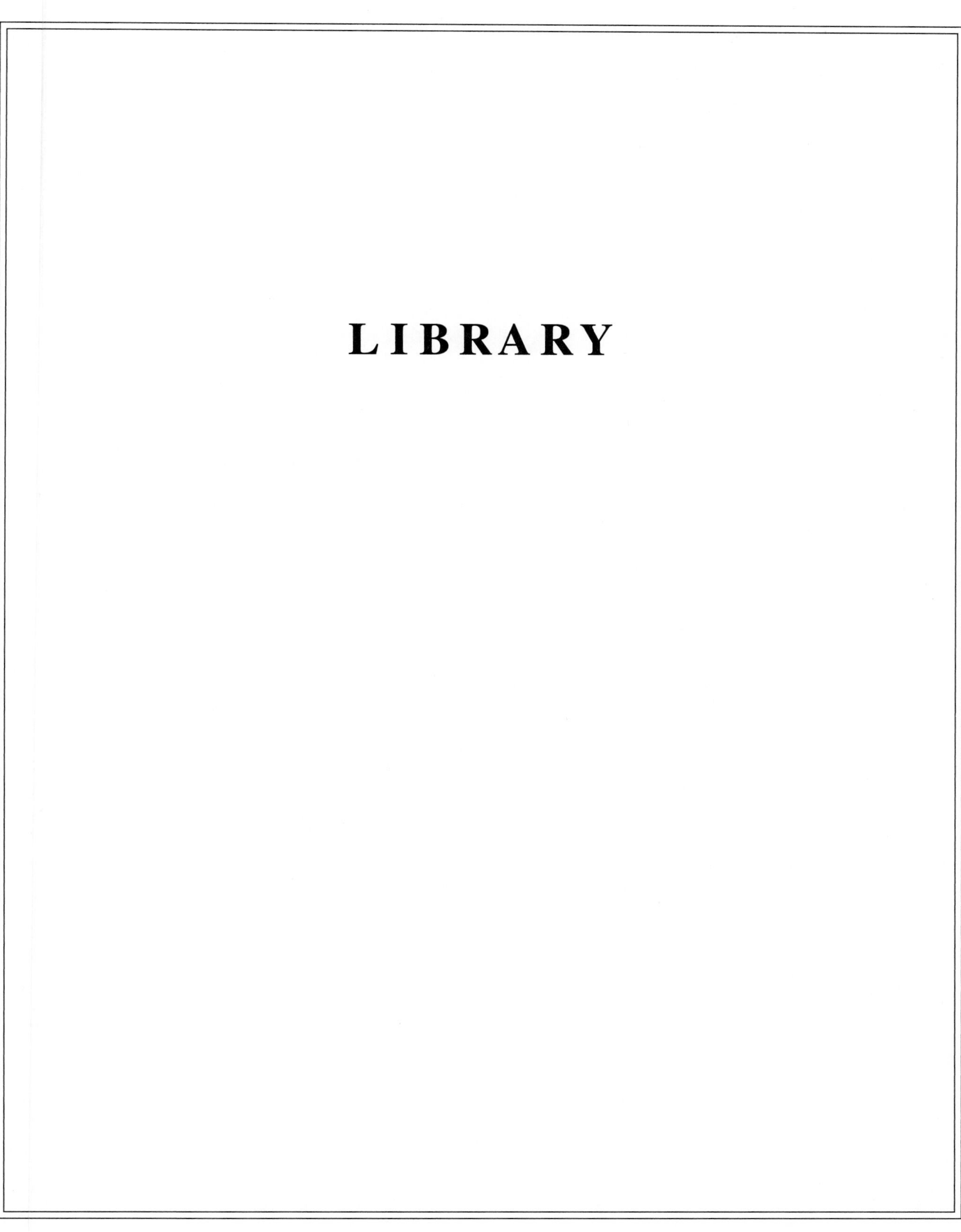

LIBRARY

Title IX of the Education Amendments of 1972
20 United States Code §1681

(a) No person in the United States shall, on the basis of gender, be excluded from participation in, be denied the benefits of, or be subjected to discrimination under any education program or activity receiving Federal financial assistance.

34 Code of Federal Regulations §106.41. Athletics.

(a) General. No person shall, on the basis of gender, be excluded from participation in, be denied the benefits of, be treated differently from another person, or otherwise be discriminated against in any interscholastic athletics offered by a recipient, and no recipient shall provide any such athletics separately on such basis.

(b) Separate teams. Notwithstanding the requirements of paragraph (a) of this section, a recipient may operate or sponsor separate teams in a particular sport for members of each gender where selection for such teams is based upon competitive skill or the activity involved is a contact sport. However, where a recipient operates or sponsors a team in a particular sport for members of one gender but operates or sponsors no such team for members of the other gender, and athletic opportunities for members of that gender have previously been limited, members of the excluded gender must be allowed to try out for the team offered unless the sport involved is a contact sport. For the purposes of this paragraph, contact sports include boxing, wrestling, rugby, ice hockey, football, basketball, and other sports the purpose or major activity of which involves bodily contact.

(c) Equal opportunity. A recipient that operates or sponsors interscholastic, intercollegiate, club or intramural athletics shall provide equal athletic opportunity for members of both genders. In determining whether equal opportunities are available, the following factors will be considered:

(1) Whether the selection of sports and levels of competition effectively accommodate the interests and abilities of members of both genders;

(2) Provision of equipment and supplies;

(3) Scheduling of games and practice time;

(4) Travel and per diem allowance;

(5) Opportunity to receive coaching and academic tutoring;

(6) Assignment and compensation of coaches and tutors;

(7) Provision of locker rooms, practice and competitive facilities;

(8) Provision of medical and training facilities and services;

(9) Provision of housing and dining facilities and services; and

(10) Publicity.

Unequal aggregate expenditures for members of each gender or unequal expenditures for male and female teams if a recipient operates or sponsors separate teams may be considered in assessing equality of athletic opportunity for members of each gender.

Metcalf v. Homer School District

United States Court of Appeal for the Fifteenth Circuit (1998)

Ryan Metcalf, a male student at Homer High School in Homer, Franklin, alleges that he is unlawfully precluded on the basis of his gender from playing interscholastic field hockey because he is not allowed to compete for a place on the only field hockey team at his school, which is the girls' team. The district court ruled in favor of Ryan, under Title IX of the Education Amendments of 1972.

The District argues that its policy prohibiting boys from being members of the girls' field hockey team falls within both of the exceptions set forth in 34 C.F.R. §106.41 (b) concerning the obligations placed upon a recipient when it sponsors a team for members of only one gender and not the other gender. When the sport is a contact sport, the recipient can provide a team for only one gender. When the sport is a non-contact sport, the recipient must provide an opportunity for the excluded gender to try out for the team only when "athletic opportunities for members of that gender have previously been limited." (*Id.*)

The contact sport exception is the broadest exception under Title IX. Whether field hockey is a contact sport depends on whether it is a sport "the purpose or major activity of which involves bodily contact." (*Id.*) An expert testifying on plaintiff's behalf stated that "field hockey is technically, and according to the international rules that govern the game, a non-contact sport. Almost all bodily contact or threatened bodily contact between players is a violation or foul. Any physical contact is incidental."

The District offered its own expert, who explained that the major activities of the sport of field hockey involve running up and down the field attempting to score a goal or prevent the other team from doing so. She stated that these activities "inevitably produce and involve bodily contact." She concluded that field hockey is a contact sport because bodily contact regularly occurs throughout the course of any competitive field hockey game.

Both parties agreed that the "purpose" of field hockey, unlike wrestling, boxing or football, does not involve bodily contact. The district court held that "no major activity of field hockey involves bodily contact and it is, therefore, not a contact sport." We disagree.

The district court's inquiry as to the major activity suggests that bodily contact can be deemed a "major activity" of a sport only if it is sanctioned activity. While the fact that the rules penalize bodily contact is an important factor in determining whether the *purpose* of field hockey involves bodily contact, the regulation does not allow the inquiry to end

there. It requires a further inquiry into whether the *major activity* of field hockey involves bodily contact.

In making this determination, we consider it significant that the rules require mouth protectors and shin guards, prohibit spiked shoes, and prohibit the wearing of jewelry. Such a level of protective rules suggests that bodily contact does in fact occur frequently. Further, even if bodily contact is incidental to the game, it may be an inevitable and frequent occurrence in the game. In sum, both the level of protective rules as well as the inevitability and frequency of bodily contact in the actual game must be analyzed to determine whether the major activities of a sport involve bodily contact.

Applying these factors, we find that field hockey is a contact sport under 34 C.F.R. §106.41(b), and reverse. Because Ryan's Title IX claim is disposed of by our finding that field hockey is a contact sport, it is not necessary to inquire into whether the athletic opportunities of males at Homer High have previously been limited.

Milley v. Arlington School District

United States Court of Appeal for the Fifteenth Circuit (2000)

Tommi-Jo Milley is an extraordinarily gifted female baseball pitcher. Since "T.J." was seven years old, she has pitched in organized baseball teams in programs run by the Arlington Park District and the Arlington Little League. She has also participated in the U.S. Baseball Association Batter-Up and Elks Club competitions. During this period the teams T.J. played on have won 95% of their games. She has received numerous awards recognizing her abilities. In all of these programs, T.J. played with boys.

In the fall of 1999, T.J., now 11, enrolled in sixth grade at Arlington Junior High School in Des Plaines, Franklin. She was then presented with her first opportunity to play interscholastic baseball. There is only one baseball team at Arlington and that is a boys' baseball team. Defendant in this case, the Arlington School District, denied T.J. permission to try out for the boys' baseball team. T.J. and her parents filed this action, seeking injunctive relief requiring defendants to permit her to try out for the boys' team. The district court's grant of summary judgment for the plaintiff is now before us on appeal.

Plaintiff challenges her exclusion from the tryouts under Title IX of the Education Amendments of 1972 and the regulations thereunder. 34 C.F.R. §106.41 subsection (b) requires a recipient of federal funds who sponsors a team in a particular sport only for members of one gender to allow members of the excluded gender to try out for the team if the sport is a non-contact sport and athletic opportunities for members of the excluded gender have previously been limited. The parties stipulate that baseball is not a contact sport. They agree that the sole question on appeal is whether "athletic opportunities . . . have previously been limited" for girls at Arlington.

In interpreting this language, the district court considered the absence of a girls' or a co-ed baseball team at Arlington and held that the District was in violation of Title IX because opportunities for girls in baseball have previously been limited. The court interpreted the regulation's inquiry as sports-specific. We disagree.

The phrase "have previously been limited" must be understood in the context of the entire athletic program. If the district court's construction were adopted, there could never be a situation in a non-contact sport in which a team was limited to a single gender without a corresponding team for the other gender because, by definition, the opportunities in that particular sport would be limited for the excluded gender. It would mean that girls would always be able to argue that they had previously limited athletic

opportunities just because certain sports have traditionally been considered boys' sports, such as baseball.

Our view is consistent with subsection (c) of the regulation, which enumerates ten factors that will be considered in determining whether interscholastic programs provide equal athletic opportunity. That subsection further provides, "Unequal aggregate expenditures for members of each gender or unequal expenditures for male and female teams if a recipient operates or sponsors separate teams may be considered in assessing equality of athletic opportunity for members of each gender." Thus, it is clear that the obligation of an educational institution in complying with the requirements of Title IX cannot be measured only by comparing types of teams available to each gender, but instead must turn on whether disparities of a substantial and unjustified nature exist in the benefits, treatment, services, or opportunities afforded male and female athletes in the institution's sports program as a whole.

The district court's grant of summary judgment for the plaintiff is reversed.

Whitford v. Newberry Middle School District

Sample Answer

Whitford v. Newberry Middle School District

Closing Argument

I represent Annie Whitford on her motion for an order requiring Newberry Middle School District to let her try out for the school's interscholastic volleyball team.

Annie is a twelve-year-old girl who began playing volleyball when she was just seven years old, and in her own words, she has been playing "constantly" ever since. She has played on various co-ed teams and has attended volleyball camps for the last five summers. Through her talented participation on these teams, she has won various awards including Most Valuable Player. She hopes to receive a college scholarship for volleyball, and perhaps one day to play in the Olympics. Clearly, volleyball is a very important part of Annie's life.

Annie began attending Newberry Middle School this year when her family moved to Newberry from out of state. When the school's volleyball coach, Karen Wallenstein, observed Annie playing volleyball, she encouraged her to try out for the volleyball team. But before the tryouts were held, both Ms. Wallenstein and Annie were dismayed to find that Annie would not be permitted to try out because the Newberry School District has a rule barring girls from the boys-only team, and there is no girls team. The district rule is based on the district's determination that volleyball is a contact sport.

Since this court has already determined that irreparable harm will result if an injunction is not granted, the only matter to consider is Annie's likelihood of success at trial. The evidence presented thus far clearly indicates that Annie would prevail at trial. Title IX of the Education Amendments of 1972 prohibits gender discrimination under any education program receiving federal assistance. Under Title IX, a school may sponsor separate athletic teams for girls and boys when the sport involved is a contact sport. However, when a school that receives federal funds sponsors a team for members of one gender but not the other, and athletic opportunities for members of the excluded gender have previously been limited, members of the excluded gender must be allowed to try out for the team offered unless the sport is a contact sport. Two facts are undisputed. Newberry Middle School is a recipient of federal financial assistance, and the school sponsors a volleyball team for boys, but not for girls. The matters in dispute therefore are whether volleyball is a contact sport, and if so, whether athletic opportunities for girls have previously been limited by Newberry School. In this case, the evidence unambiguously shows that the School District erred in classifying volleyball as a contact sport, and that athletic opportunities for girls have previously been limited by the school.

Let us first discuss the evidence showing that the School District has improperly characterized volleyball as a contact sport. The Regulations under Title IX [34 C.F.R. §160.41] list several sports that are considered to be contact sports. The enumerated sports are those in which physical contact is an integral part of the game, such as it is in football and wrestling. The Regulations further define a contact sport as one in which the purpose or major activity involves bodily contact. Volleyball clearly does not meet this definition. Ms. Wallenstein, who is the school's Director of Physical Education and coach of the volleyball team, testified that the school follows the U.S. Volleyball League Rules. Interestingly, the U.S. Volleyball League states that volleyball is not a contact sport. Ms. Wallenstein explained that under the League rules, intentional or threatened physical contact between players can result in penalties and expulsion from the game. Ms. Wallenstein testified that while occasional contact is possible, if each player covers her area, contact normally does not occur. The School District has presented no evidence to rebut the testimony of Ms. Wallenstein. The School District superintendent,

Grace Huang, testified that she simply read Title IX and arrived at the conclusion that volleyball was a contact sport. She gave no justification or reasoning for her conclusion whatsoever. Most likely Ms. Huang was unable to provide a reasoned explanation because, unlike Ms. Wallenstein, she has no experience in school athletics at all. Ms. Wallenstein has many years experience as a Director of Physical Education, physical education teacher, and volleyball coach, and she herself is an experienced volleyball player. Clearly, her testimony regarding the rules and purposes of the game of volleyball is entitled to great weight, especially in the absence of contradictory evidence.

In *Metcalf v. Homer School District,* the court of appeals for this circuit explained that the fact that a sport's rules penalize bodily contact is an important factor in determining whether the purpose of the sport is physical contact. As Ms. Wallenstein indicated, bodily contact is penalized under the rules of the U.S. Volleyball League. This then tends to show that bodily contact is not the purpose of volleyball.

Further inquiry must be made into whether the ***major activity*** of the sport involves bodily contact. Ms. Wallenstein testified that according to the U.S. Volleyball League Rules, the main activity of the game is hitting the ball back and forth over the net and trying to land the ball in the opponent's court. Again, the School District presented no evidence to rebut this testimony. In *Metcalf* the court also considered the level of protection players were required to wear to participate in the sport. For example, field hockey players are required to wear mouth protectors and shin guards, and are prohibited from wearing spiked shoes and jewelry. The court explained that such a level of protective rules indicated that bodily contact is an inevitable and frequent occurrence in the game. The rules of volleyball do not require players to wear any particular protection. Ms. Wallenstein testified that some players wear knee or elbow pads, but these are not required. Neither are mouth protectors or shin guards, and there is no rule prohibiting jewelry. The lack of rules requiring protective equipment indicates that contact is not a major activity of the game of volleyball.

The School District will argue that contact does occur as evidenced by the fact that Annie has been injured while playing volleyball. But in all the time she has been playing, she has only been injured two times. Considering the frequency with which Annie plays volleyball, two injuries in five years is an extremely small number and tends to support her contention that contact is not a normal part of the game. Furthermore, one of those injuries was caused by contact with the ball, not bodily contact with another player. Annie testified that the one time she was injured from bodily contact, the other player was penalized because the contact was intentional.

Considering all of the evidence, volleyball cannot be considered a contact sport. Since volleyball is not a contact sport, Annie must be allowed to try out for her school's team if the court finds that the school has limited athletic opportunities for girls in the past. The evidence clearly demonstrates that they have.

The Regulations list ten factors to be considered in determining whether equal athletic opportunities are available to male and female students. [34 C.F.R. §106.41(c)] Six of those factors are relevant here. Those factors are: whether the selection of sports and levels of competition effectively accommodate the interests and abilities of members of both genders; provision of equipment and supplies; travel and per diem allowance; opportunity to receive coaching and academic tutoring; assignment and compensation of coaches and tutors; and publicity. Inequality under the first factor is demonstrated by the substantial disparity in the number of sports teams available at Newberry for the girls despite the fact that they represent the majority of the student body. Inequality under the other factors is demonstrated by the disparity in the percentage of the athletic budget spent on girls' versus boys' athletic teams.

In *Milley v. Arlington School District*, this circuit's court of appeals explained that a school's athletic program as a whole must be examined to determine if there are disparities of a substantial and unjustified nature in terms of benefits, treatment, services, or opportunities afforded male and female athletes. Substantial disparity is easily demonstrated in this case. Of the 1000 students at Newberry, 600 are girls and 400 are boys. Although girls make up the majority of the student body, the school sponsors only four girls' athletic teams and six teams for boys. Ms. Huang testified that of the 400 male students, approximately half participate in interscholastic sports teams. Of the 600 female students, only about 100 or one-sixth participate. This is not due to lack of interest on the part of the female student body. In the past, female students and their parents have submitted written requests to the superintendent for the formation of a girls' volleyball team. These requests were denied and the reasons Ms. Huang gave for her denial are significant. Ms. Huang testified that she denied the requests in part due to the school's limited facilities, which would make it difficult to schedule practices and games. She further indicated that part of the reason was financial—either another coach would have to be hired, or the current coach paid more, and lockers and other facilities would have to be increased. There is not enough money in the athletic budget for these expenses.

The school's athletics budget pays for the coaches' salaries, upkeep of the facilities, equipment and uniform purchases, athlete transportation, and publicity. Ms. Wallenstein testified that approximately 70% of the athletic budget is spent on the boys' teams. No evidence was presented to rebut this estimate. The disproportionate financial support of the boys' teams, and the disproportionate number of sports offered for girls, despite their majority and despite their requests for more options, indicates that athletic opportunities for female students have been limited at Newberry School.

Annie Whitford is a talented volleyball player. She has shown her ability to excel in this sport on co-ed teams in the past. The Newberry School District erred first in its baseless classification of volleyball as a contact sport. It is not among the sports listed in the Regulations under Title IX, and neither the purpose nor the major activity of the sport includes bodily contact.

Newberry School does not offer an interscholastic volleyball team for girls. In fact, athletic opportunities for female students are quite limited, despite the fact that the majority of the students are female. Annie would clearly be successful on the merits in this case. For these reasons, the court should enter an order allowing Annie Whitford to try out for her school's interscholastic volleyball team. To do otherwise would frustrate the purposes of Title IX.

Multistate Performance Test

State v. Tweedy

National Conference of Bar Examiners

Preface

This Multistate Performance Test is a reprint of one of the three MPTs which were administered in July 2002.

The instructions for the test appear on the next page. On the actual MPT, they will appear on the back cover of the test.

INSTRUCTIONS

1. You will have 90 minutes to complete this session of the examination. This performance test is designed to evaluate your ability to handle a select number of legal authorities in the context of a factual problem involving a client.

2. The problem is set in the fictitious state of Franklin, in the fictitious Fifteenth Circuit of the United States. Columbia and Olympia are also fictitious states in the Fifteenth Circuit. In Franklin, the trial court of general jurisdiction is the District Court, the intermediate appellate court is the Court of Appeal, and the highest court is the Supreme Court.

3. You will have two kinds of materials with which to work: a File and a Library. The first document in the File is a memorandum containing the instructions for the task you are to complete. The other documents in the File contain factual information about your case and may include some facts that are not relevant.

4. The Library contains the legal authorities needed to complete the task and may also include some authorities that are not relevant. Any cases may be real, modified, or written solely for the purpose of this examination. If the cases appear familiar to you, do not assume that they are precisely the same as you have read before. Read them thoroughly, as if they all were new to you. You should assume that cases were decided in the jurisdictions and on the dates shown. In citing cases from the Library, you may use abbreviations and omit page references.

5. Your response must be written in the answer book provided. If you are taking this examination on a laptop computer, your jurisdiction will provide you with specific instructions. In answering this performance test, you should concentrate on the materials provided in the File and Library. What you have learned in law school and elsewhere provides the general background for analyzing the problem; the File and Library provide the specific materials with which you must work.

6. Although there are no restrictions on how you apportion your time, you should be sure to allocate ample time (about 45 minutes) to reading and digesting the materials and to organizing your answer before you begin writing it. You may make notes anywhere in the test materials; blank pages are provided at the end of the booklet. You may not tear pages from the question booklet.

7. This performance test will be graded on your responsiveness to the instructions regarding the task you are to complete, which are given to you in the first memorandum in the File, and on the content, thoroughness, and organization of your response.

State v. Tweedy

FILE

LIBRARY

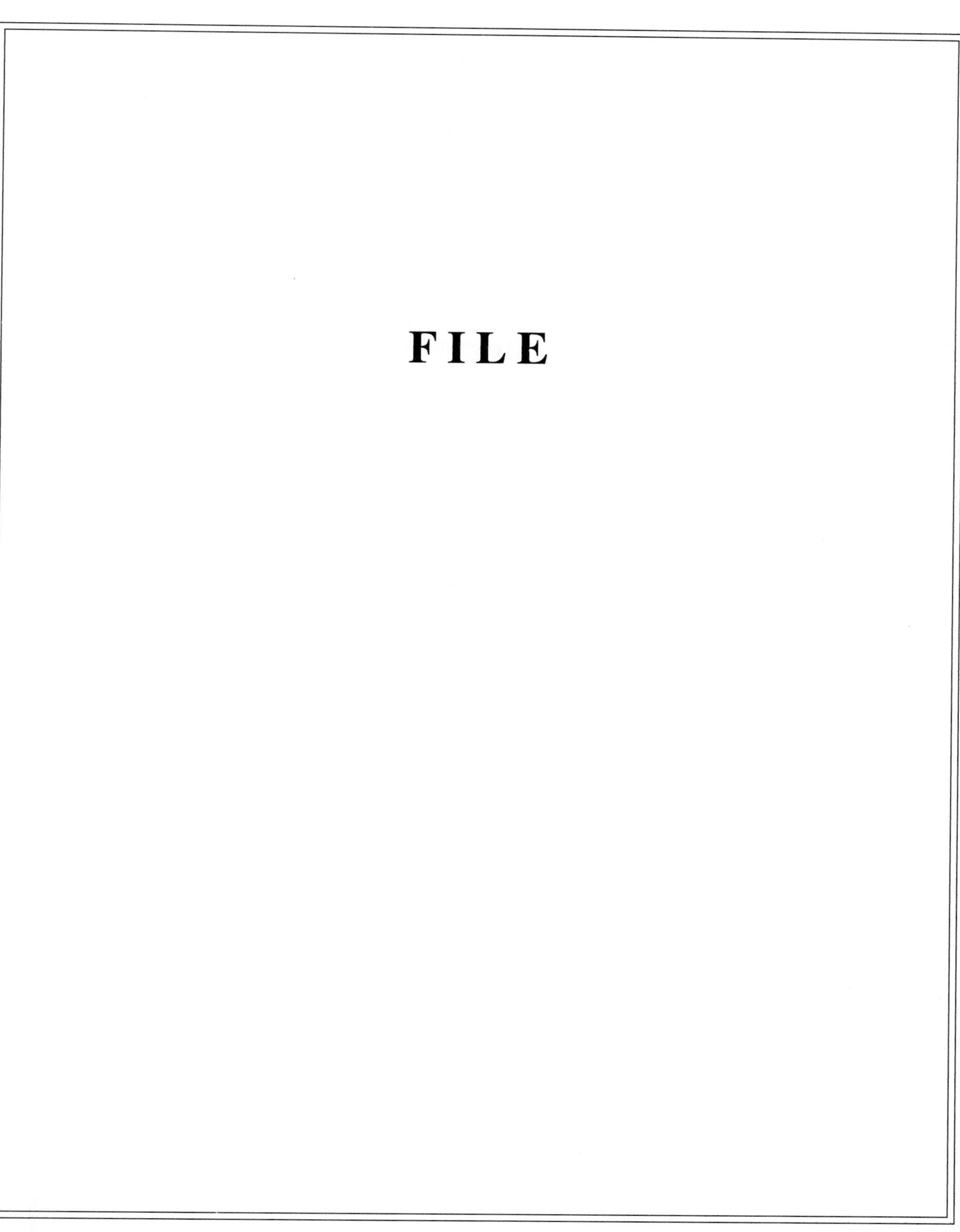

FILE

Office of the District Attorney

DeSoto County
83645 Washington Street
DeSoto, Franklin 33123
(901) 555-1294

TO: Applicant

FROM: Shirley Clay Scott, Assistant District Attorney

RE: Tweedy, James A.

DATE: July 30, 2002

I have been asked to recommend whether we should prosecute Mr. James A. Tweedy. The District Attorney has stated his belief that the case will be difficult to try and that it is unlikely that a conviction can be obtained. I, however, believe that this case is worth pursuing and want to seek a felony indictment against Mr. Tweedy for two counts of endangering the welfare of a child under Penal Code §4304.

Please prepare for my signature a two-part memorandum to the District Attorney. The first part should persuade the District Attorney that we have sufficient admissible evidence to prove all the elements necessary to obtain a conviction. You may assume that we can avoid any hearsay problems that might arise. I know that additional facts may facilitate prosecution, but in this first part you should address only the question of whether we have enough evidence to proceed based on what we *already* know.

In the second part of the memorandum, which should be brief, identify any conflicting or incomplete facts in the File that we will need to further investigate or clarify to facilitate prosecution. Recommend the investigative steps this office should take to develop these additional facts.

INCIDENT NO. 02-3105	DeSoto Police Department Incident Report			Date of Statement 7/17/02
NAME (LAST, FIRST, MIDDLE) OF PERSON GIVING STATEMENT Tweedy, James A.		DOB/AGE 8/3/76	RESIDENCE PHONE None	BUSINESS PHONE None
STREET ADDRESS 1376 Archer Ave, Apt. 27		CITY DeSoto	STATE Franklin	ZIP CODE 33123
STATEMENT TAKEN BY (NAME/BADGE) Mary Lou Higgerson #1361		IN PRESENCE OF		

On the evening of July 16, 2002, and the early morning hours of July 17, officer called to the scene of a fire to investigate possible criminal neglect. Two minor children (the older child three (3) years of age and the younger twenty (20) months) were left in their apartment unattended while father, James A. Tweedy, participated in a social evening with friends.

Before leaving, Tweedy put the children in the bedroom. According to his statement, he secured the bedroom door by inserting two table knives between the door and the jamb. In addition, he locked the main door to the apartment. Tweedy claims he spoke to neighbor, Mrs. England, who had consented to watch out for the children in his absence.

According to another neighbor, Glen Poshard, at approximately 12:05 a.m. a fire started in the building, possibly originating as a result of a defective television set in Tweedy's apartment. Tweedy returned to premises at 3:00 a.m. at which point investigating officer briefly interviewed Tweedy before Tweedy left for the hospital to see if he could find the children.

Firefighter Albert Malone informed officer that unknown visitor to the building, learning from a neighbor that the youngsters were trapped in the bedroom, attempted to remove them but was prevented from doing so by the manner in which the bedroom door had been fastened. Firemen, upon entry, found the children apparently dead in the bedroom of the apartment.

Signature *Mary Lou Higgerson*

INCIDENT NO. 02-3105	DeSoto Police Department Incident Report Addendum		Date of Statement 7/18/02
NAME (LAST, FIRST, MIDDLE) OF PERSON GIVING STATEMENT Wirthin, Harry P.	DOB/AGE 9/2/46	RESIDENCE PHONE 555-5678	BUSINESS PHONE same
LOCATION OF INCIDENT 1376 Archer Ave, Apt. 27	CITY DeSoto	STATE Franklin	ZIP CODE 33123
STATEMENT TAKEN BY (NAME/BADGE) Mary Lou Higgerson #1361	IN PRESENCE OF		

Addendum to Incident Report dated July 17, 2002.

I spoke with Harry P. Wirthin, owner and superintendent of the building occupied by James Tweedy and family. He stated that Tweedy was typical tenant. Only problem was that 4 years ago a small electrical fire occurred in Tweedy's apartment. Apparently, Tweedy's wife, who is now deceased, left a curling iron on in the bathroom and it overheated causing a short that started a fire. No one was in the apartment at the time.

Mr. Wirthin did indicate that on at least two prior occasions he knew the children were left alone in the apartment. He also indicated that the neighbor two floors up, a Mrs. England, occasionally watched the children. I spoke with Mrs. England who indicated that on one or two occasions she had watched the children. She indicated that she had been asked to watch them on the night in question, but that she declined.

A check of DeSoto Licensing & Inspection records indicates that Mr. Wirthin has been cited on 5 occasions within the last 5 years for code violations related to wiring problems in the building. All citations resulted from complaints from tenants about faulty wiring.

Signature Mary Lou Higgerson

INCIDENT NO.	DeSoto Fire Marshal Report	DATE OF INVESTIGATION
02-3105	DeSoto, Franklin	7/17/02

An investigation was conducted on the above-referenced date into the fire at 1376 Archer Ave, Apt. 27.

Cause of fire was electrical problem located in defective television set. This conclusion was easily reached with examination of set and surrounding area. There existed little actual fire damage. Damage was limited to television set and curtains located near the set. Internal part of television set received extensive damage.

Smoke and water damage in contrast was extensive. Level of smoke commensurate with high use of synthetic materials in apartment.

NAME (LAST, FIRST, MIDDLE) OF PERSON MAKING REPORT	TITLE		BUSINESS PHONE
Gatton, Phil	Deputy Fire Marshal		555-8463
STREET ADDRESS OF INVESTIGATION	CITY	STATE	ZIP CODE
1376 Archer Ave, Apt. 27	DeSoto	Franklin	33123
Signature Phil Gatton			

OFFICE OF THE DESOTO COUNTY MEDICAL EXAMINER
Marsha Ryan, J.D., M.D.
Chief Medical Examiner
9765 Garwin Street
DeSoto, Franklin 33123

July 22, 2002

TO: Shirley Clay Scott, Assistant District Attorney

FROM: Marsha Ryan, Chief Medical Examiner

RE: Alma & Fred Tweedy

I got your voice mail concerning the autopsies on the Tweedy children. The autopsies are complete, and I'll send you a copy of the report. The important details, however, are pretty straightforward.

Fred: White male, approximately three years old. General health was good. No evidence of any disease process. Cause of death was smoke inhalation resulting from fire.

Alma: White female, approximately twenty months old. General health was poor. Evidence of congenital heart malformation, which if remained undetected would be life threatening. Cause of death was smoke inhalation resulting from fire.

Let me know if you need anything else.

Transcript of Interview of James Tweedy

by Officer Higgerson

July 22, 2002

Officer: Thank you for coming down, Mr. Tweedy. The night of the fire was horrible and I understand your difficulty in answering all my questions then.

Tweedy: Well, of course, I wanted to get to the hospital as soon as possible, but it was too late.

Officer: Yes, I know. I'm sorry. Now, Mr. Tweedy, I want to state on the record that you do not have to talk with me. Anything you say can and will be used against you. You have the right to be represented by a lawyer. If you cannot afford to hire a lawyer, one will be appointed to represent you.

Tweedy: I know my rights.

Officer: And you are willing to talk to me?

Tweedy: Yes.

Officer: Why did you leave the children alone?

Tweedy: I didn't.

Officer: What do you mean?

Tweedy: I asked Mrs. England to watch them. She said she would be happy to.

Officer: But she didn't come down to the apartment, did she?

Tweedy: Not right when I asked, but she said she'd be down there in a few minutes, after she finished her dishes.

Officer: Then why did you jam the bedroom door the way you did?

Tweedy: This is not a safe neighborhood. The landlord doesn't keep the place in the best shape and I could not trust the locks on the door to the apartment. Look, I did what I could. I even left the TV on to make people think I was home.

Officer: But, it was the bedroom doorjamb that you stuck the knives into.

Tweedy: Well, I couldn't very well do that on the outside door.

Officer: Was it your habit to leave the children unattended?

Tweedy: No.

Officer: Had you ever done it before?

Tweedy: Like I said, I didn't do it this time. I'd asked Mrs. England to watch them.

Officer: Mrs. England denies being asked.

Tweedy: Well, she's lying. Obviously she's afraid that she's going to be blamed. In fact, rather than sitting here and accusing me, you should be asking her why she didn't do what she said she would.

Officer: Mr. Tweedy, were you drinking the night of the fire?

Tweedy: I went to a club that night. Yes, I had a couple beers. I was not drunk. I'm sorry, I think I should talk to an attorney.

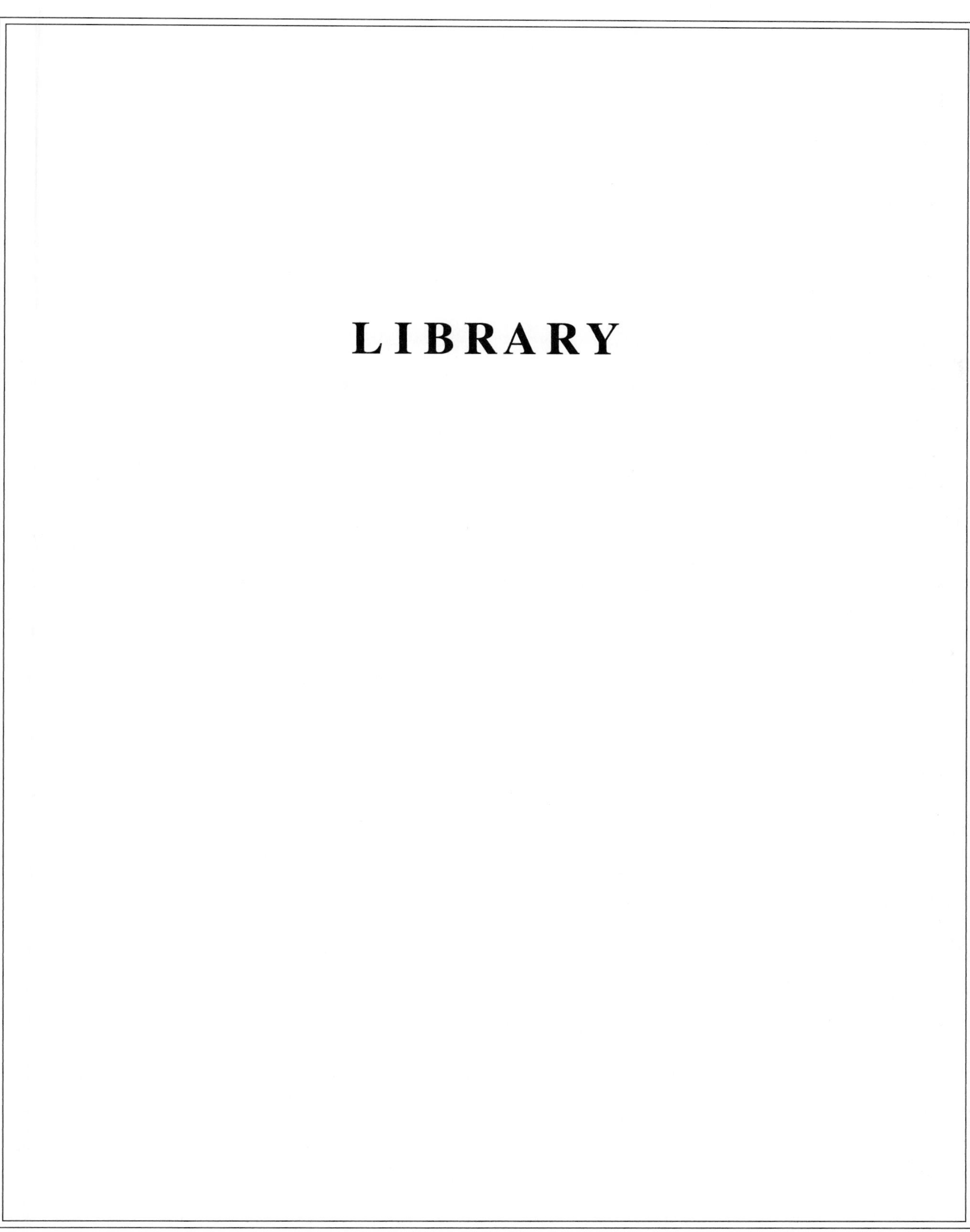

LIBRARY

Franklin Penal Code

§4304. Endangering Welfare of a Child

(a) Offense defined. A parent, guardian, or other person supervising the welfare of a child under 18 years of age commits an offense if he knowingly endangers the welfare of the child by violating a duty of care, protection or support.

(b) Grading. An offense under this section constitutes a felony of the third degree.

Franklin Rules of Evidence

Rule 401. Definition of "Relevant Evidence"

"Relevant evidence" means evidence having any tendency to make the existence of any fact that is of consequence to the determination of the action more probable or less probable than it would be without the evidence.

Rule 402. Relevant Evidence Generally Admissible; Irrelevant Evidence Inadmissible

All relevant evidence is admissible, except as otherwise provided by the Constitution of the State of Franklin, by Act of the Franklin Legislature, by these rules, or by other rules prescribed by the Franklin Supreme Court pursuant to statutory authority. Evidence which is not relevant is not admissible.

Rule 403. Exclusion of Relevant Evidence on Grounds of Prejudice, Confusion, or Waste of Time

Although relevant, evidence may be excluded if its probative value is substantially outweighed by the danger of unfair prejudice, confusion of the issues, or misleading the jury, or by considerations of undue delay, waste of time, or needless presentation of cumulative evidence.

Rule 404. Character Evidence Not Admissible To Prove Conduct; Exceptions; Other Crimes

(a) Character evidence generally. Evidence of a person's character or a trait of character is not admissible for the purpose of proving action in conformity therewith on a particular occasion, except:

(1) Character of accused. Evidence of a pertinent trait of character offered by an accused, or by the prosecution to rebut the same;

(2) Character of victim. Evidence of a pertinent trait of character of the victim of the crime offered by an accused, or by the prosecution to rebut the same, or evidence of a character trait of peacefulness of the victim offered by the prosecution in a homicide case to rebut evidence that the victim was the first aggressor;

* * * *

(b) Other crimes, wrongs, or acts. Evidence of other crimes, wrongs, or acts is not admissible to prove the character of a person in order to show action in conformity therewith. It may, however, be admissible for other purposes, such as proof of motive, opportunity, intent, preparation, plan, knowledge, identity, or absence of mistake or accident, provided that upon request by the accused, the prosecution in a criminal case shall provide reasonable notice in advance of trial, or during trial if the court excuses pretrial notice on good cause shown, of the general nature of any such evidence it intends to introduce at trial.

State v. Miller

Franklin Supreme Court (1992)

Appellant, Rachel Miller, was convicted under Franklin Penal Code §4304, endangering the welfare of a child, following a non-jury trial. Miller was thereafter sentenced to two years' probation. This appeal ensued.

The relevant facts are straightforward and thoroughly tragic. On the evening of November 18, 1989, Miller, with her 22-month-old son, Clarence, visited Antonio Green, the father of the child. Green and Miller are not husband and wife. Green resided in a three-story rooming house. A restaurant was located on the first floor of the premises. Eugenia Orr lived on the second level and Green occupied the top floor.

Father, mother, and child met at a neighborhood tavern and then returned to the rooming house. Earlier in the day, Green had accompanied Orr on a shopping trip; father, mother, and child went directly to Orr's apartment to examine that day's purchases. Miller was not well acquainted with Orr. After some time, Miller went upstairs to Green's room, leaving the child in Orr's apartment in the care of Green because the child was playing with his father's new shoes. When the child tired of this activity, Green took him upstairs to Miller and then returned to the Orr apartment.

Miller washed and changed the child and prepared him for bed. Green's room contained a double bed. Nearby was an electric space heater, which turned out to be in a damaged condition but was then operating. Miller put the child in the bed and then lay down with the child until he fell asleep. Once her son was asleep, Miller decided to go down to the first-floor restaurant to buy some juice for the child. She left Green's apartment with the child asleep in the bed, the space heater operating, and the door to the hallway stairs open. She also left her sweater in the apartment.

When Miller stopped on the second floor en route to the restaurant, Green asked Miller if she would "go clubbing" (visiting bars or nightclubs) with him. She declined, explaining that she had to watch the child and that she was tired and not dressed for the occasion anyway. While she was on the first floor, Green yelled down to her through the common hallway, repeating his request and saying that Orr had agreed to watch the child. Miller agreed to accompany him. She asked Green to bring down her sweater and did not return upstairs. Green brought her the sweater. He had, in fact, not spoken to Orr about watching the child and Orr did not do so.

Green and Miller left the rooming house at approximately 1:00 a.m. and visited two clubs. During this time, they were joined by friends. One of these friends was called as a witness and testified that Miller continually fretted about the child. Returning to the rooming house

after 3:00 a.m., Green and Miller discovered police and fire trucks in the street outside and the building ablaze. The only death resulting from the conflagration was Miller's infant son, who died of smoke inhalation and burns. The space heater was determined to be the cause of the fire. Green was convicted of various criminal charges in connection with the child's death. Miller was convicted of endangering the welfare of her child.

We must consider whether the evidence was sufficient to uphold the verdict of the trial court. We must accept all the evidence and all reasonable inferences that may be drawn from that evidence upon which the factfinder could have based its verdict. If the evidence, viewed in the light most favorable to the state, is not sufficient to establish guilt beyond a reasonable doubt of the crime charged, then the conviction should be overturned.

Miller claims that the evidence presented at trial was insufficient to prove the intent element of the crime with which she was charged. Under Penal Code §4304, a parent or other person supervising the welfare of a child commits a felony if he or she *knowingly* endangers the child. Section 302(b) of the Penal Code defines knowingly:

> (2) A person acts knowingly with respect to a material element of an offense when:
>
> (i) if the element involves the nature of his conduct or the attendant circumstances, he is aware that his conduct is of that nature or that such circumstances exist; and
>
> (ii) if the element involves the result of his conduct, he is aware that it is practically certain that his conduct will cause such a result.

It is clear that §4304 contemplates endangerment either by act or by omission to act. In *State v. Cardwell* (1986), this court established a three-pronged standard for testing the sufficiency of evidence of the intent element under §4304:

> We hold that evidence is sufficient to prove the intent element of the offense of endangering the welfare of a child when the accused is aware of his or her duty to protect the child; is aware that the child is in circumstances that are reasonably likely to result in harm to the child; and has either failed to act or has taken actions so lame or meager that such actions cannot reasonably be expected to be effective to protect the child from physical or psychological harm.

If proof fails on any one of these prongs, the evidence must be found insufficient.

Employing this test, the *Cardwell* court found sufficient evidence of intent where a mother was aware that her child was being subjected to sexual abuse by the stepfather and took wholly ineffectual remedial actions. Specifically, she wrote letters to the stepfather expressing outrage and warning that she would not tolerate such conduct and she made an aborted attempt to move the child to a relative's house.

On the other hand, in *State v. Louie* (1990), this court found insufficient evidence to convict a husband and wife where they knew that their 13-year-old daughter was engaging in sexual activity with an adult and became pregnant against the express warnings of a physician. Louie differed from *Cardwell* in that the parents did not allow the child to remain in a potentially dangerous situation; they simply failed to stop the child from surreptitiously seeking out sexual activity. The court was unwilling to extend culpability, noting that parents could not know everything about their child's activities nor was §4304 intended to punish parents merely because their child becomes pregnant.

Here, the trial court, sitting as factfinder, determined that when Miller left with Green to go clubbing, she was aware that her infant son was in the third-floor room with the space heater on. The court found that by failing to question Green's statement that Orr would watch the child, Miller has evidenced the requisite intent for purposes of §4304. We have difficulty in finding that the evidence is sufficient to satisfy the *Cardwell* tripartite test. It is undisputed that appellant was aware of her duty to protect her child. However, merely leaving the child alone is insufficient to establish the requisite intent. We cannot find as a matter of law that she was aware that she had placed her child in circumstances that were likely to result in harm to the child or that her failure to check on the alleged babysitting arrangements was unreasonable under *Cardwell.*

The trial court specifically credited Miller's testimony that she believed Green when he told her that Orr was watching her child. The logical inference based on this finding is that Miller was not aware that she had left her child unattended. There was no evidence presented at trial that Green was an inherently dishonest person or that Miller had cause to disbelieve him. The trial court has based Miller's culpability under §4304 not on the fact that Miller knowingly left her child alone, but rather that she should not have been so gullible as to believe Green. Undeniably, Miller may have exercised poor judgment on the night in question, and perhaps she is guilty of reckless or negligent conduct in connection with her son's death. However, this is not sufficient for a finding of guilt under §4304. If Miller in fact believed that her son was in the care of another, she did not knowingly place him in circumstances that were reasonably likely to result in harm, and her conduct cannot be adjudged criminal.

Judgment reversed. Appellant discharged.

State v. Shoup

Franklin Supreme Court (1993)

Joseph C. Shoup was tried by jury and was found guilty of homicide by vehicle while driving under the influence of alcohol. Shoup asserts that the trial court committed reversible error by refusing to give the instruction requested by the defense on the issue of causation.

On January 3, 1990, at about 8:00 p.m., appellant was operating an automobile on Oak Street, a narrow alleyway located in the town of Vienna. The passengers in appellant's vehicle were Michelle Shoup, his wife, who was seated in the front passenger seat, and Jean Moll and John Rush, who were in the back seat. Appellant was observed failing to stop for three consecutive stop signs, and the speed of his vehicle was estimated to be approximately 50 to 55 miles per hour.

Appellant drove through the intersection of Oak and Williams Streets without stopping at the stop sign. His vehicle collided with a large dump truck parked in the alleyway near a loading dock at a garment factory. The site of the accident was about 30 to 35 feet from the intersection.

Upon being summoned to the scene of the accident, Charles Harris, the Police Chief for the town of Vienna, observed that appellant smelled strongly of alcohol and that there were several beer cans on the floor of the vehicle. All of the vehicle's occupants were transported for medical treatment. Appellant's wife suffered massive internal injuries and died shortly after being taken by helicopter to Cardinal Medical Center. Appellant was taken to Ashland State Hospital, where, at 9:30 p.m., blood samples were drawn at the request of Chief Harris for the purpose of determining appellant's blood alcohol level. Two blood tests measured appellant's blood alcohol content at 0.176% and 0.175%.

At trial, the defense contended that the legal cause of Michelle Shoup's death had been the illegal parking of the dump truck with which appellant's vehicle collided. Police Chief Harris testified that there had been a no parking sign posted at the loading dock where the dump truck was parked. However, according to Chief Harris, this sign had been placed there by the garment factory and not by the town. Therefore, he was without legal authority to issue tickets for illegal parking at that location. Other testimony established that, despite poor lighting conditions, the dump truck could be seen from the intersection at Oak and Williams Streets. Additionally, both Jean Moll and John Rush described appellant's driving prior to the accident as erratic.

Causation is an essential element of a criminal charge, which the State must prove beyond a reasonable doubt. The tort concept of proximate cause plays no role in a prosecution for criminal homicide. Rather, the State must prove a more direct causal relationship between the defendant's conduct and the victim's death. However, it has never been the law of this State that criminal responsibility must be confined to a sole or immediate cause of death. Criminal responsibility is properly assessed against one whose conduct was a direct and substantial factor in producing the result even though other factors combined with that conduct to achieve the result. Thus, a defendant cannot escape the natural consequences of his act merely because of foreseeable complications.

In this case, a jury could find that appellant's conduct was a direct and substantial factor in bringing about the death of Michelle Shoup. The evidence disclosed that, while intoxicated, appellant drove his vehicle down a narrow, dimly lit alleyway, erratically and at a high rate of speed, failing to stop at three consecutive intersections where stop signs had been posted. Moreover, the evidence suggested that had appellant obeyed the stop sign at the intersection of Oak and Williams Streets, he would have been able to observe the dump truck parked in the alleyway. The fact that the dump truck was parked in the alleyway undoubtedly contributed to the accident. Appellant's conduct started an unbroken chain of causation that directly and substantially led to his wife's death. Because the fact that another vehicle may have been parked in a hazardous manner was a foreseeable circumstance, appellant is not relieved from the natural consequences of his conduct.

Affirmed.

State v. Tweedy

Sample Answer

MEMORANDUM

To: District Attorney
From: Shirley Clay Scott, Assistant District Attorney
Re: Tweedy, James A.
Date: July 30, 2002

I. Prosecution of James A. Tweedy under Franklin Penal Code §4304.

James A. Tweedy's two young children died from smoke inhalation in an electrical fire that started in their apartment while they were there without adult supervision. A careful review of the evidence in this matter indicates that there is sufficient admissible evidence to prosecute James Tweedy under Franklin Penal Code §4304, Endangering the Welfare of a Child.

Section 4304 states that a parent, guardian, or other person supervising the welfare of a child under 18 years of age commits an offense if he knowingly endangers the welfare of the child by violating a duty of care, protection, or support. As discussed below, each element of the offense can be satisfied in this case.

A. The Evidence Shows Tweedy Is the Parent of a Child under Age 18.

James Tweedy is the father and custodial parent of Alma and Fred Tweedy. The children's mother is deceased. The Medical Examiner's report indicates that Alma was 20 months old at the time of her death, and Fred was three years old. Both children were under the age of 18. As the children's father, Tweedy had a duty of care, protection, and support toward them.

B. The Evidence Shows that Tweedy Knowingly Endangered his Children.

Section 4304 contains an element of intent: The endangerment must be committed "knowingly." Penal Code section 302(b) defines "knowingly," and the Franklin Supreme Court interpreted section 302(b) by establishing a three-pronged test for the sufficiency of evidence of the requisite intent. [State v. Miller (1992); State v. Cardwell (1986)] Evidence is sufficient to prove intent when the accused: (1) is aware of his duty to protect the child; (2) is aware that the child is in circumstances that are reasonably likely to result in harm to the child; and (3) has either failed to act or has taken actions so lame or meager that such actions cannot reasonably be expected to be effective to protect the child from physical or psychological harm. In the present case, there is admissible evidence sufficient to satisfy each part of the three-pronged test.

1. Tweedy was aware of his duty to protect his children.

The first prong of the test is that the accused must be aware of his duty to protect the child. In his statement to police, Tweedy indicated that he had asked his neighbor, Mrs. England, if she would watch the children for him. This fact alone shows that Tweedy knew that he was responsible for the children, that they should not be left alone, and that he needed to provide supervision for them. Tweedy stated that he had asked Mrs. England to watch the children in the past, indicating that he recognized his responsibility to provide adult supervision for his children when he could not be with them. These statements are all admissible as relevant evidence under Evidence Rule 401.

Tweedy's other statements to police further indicate his awareness of his duty to protect the children. Tweedy told police that before he left the apartment, he put the children in the bedroom and jammed the bedroom door from the outside by placing knives in the door jamb. He stated that

he did this because the neighborhood was not safe, and that because the landlord did not keep up the building well, he could not trust the locks on the apartment door. He also left the television on to make people think that he was at home. These actions further indicate Tweedy's recognition of his duty to protect the children. Thus it is clear that Tweedy was aware of his duty to protect his children from harm.

2. Tweedy was aware that the children were in circumstances reasonably likely to result in harm.

Under the second prong of the test, the accused must be aware that the child is in circumstances that are reasonably likely to result in harm to the child. While the evidence indicates that Tweedy clearly understood his duty to protect his children from harm ***in general,*** the Franklin Supreme Court has required something more than recognition of a general duty. In both *State v. Cardwell* (1986) and *State v. Louie* (1990), the court indicates that the accused must have been aware that the child was in a potentially dangerous situation due to a specific danger—in this case, the fire. The evidence shows that Tweedy was aware of the danger of electrical fires, as he had experienced a fire in that very apartment four years ago. Tweedy's wife had left a curling iron on in the apartment when no one was home, and a fire resulted when the appliance shorted. It is likely that defense counsel will object to admission of this evidence because evidence of other wrongs, crimes, or acts is inadmissible. However, evidence of the prior fire is admissible under Evidence Rule 404(b), which allows admission of evidence to show knowledge. The fire was not Tweedy's prior act, it was his wife's. In addition, the evidence is not offered to show that either fire was Tweedy's fault, but simply to demonstrate that he was aware of the prior fire. Thus we can show Tweedy had knowledge of the danger of a fire starting from an electrical appliance, such as a television, that is operating in an apartment when no one is there. By leaving the television on, Tweedy knowingly exposed his children to the risk of an electrical fire. The evidence is sufficient to meet the second prong of the test, but it should be noted that further investigation may result in additional evidence of Tweedy's awareness of the risk of fire. (*See* part II, *infra.*)

3. Tweedy's actions to carry out his duty were nonexistent or ineffectual.

Finally, it must be shown that the parent failed to act, or took actions so lame or meager that such actions cannot reasonably be expected to be effective to protect the child. Tweedy claims that he asked Mrs. England to watch the children before he left, and that she said she would do so after she finished washing her dishes. The statement Mrs. England made to police contradicts Tweedy's statement. Mrs. England told the police that she refused to watch the children that night. In any case, the fact remains that Tweedy left the children in the apartment ***knowing*** that they could be there alone for a while either until Mrs. England washed her dishes, or until Tweedy returned.

In *State v. Miller*, a mother left her infant child alone in an apartment. The child died of smoke inhalation when a space heater caused a fire in the apartment. The mother was found not guilty of endangerment because the trial court found her testimony that she was not aware that she left her child unattended was credible. The evidence in that case could reasonably be interpreted to corroborate the mother's testimony that she left the premises believing that someone was with the child. The facts in *Miller* are very different from the facts of this case. Here, Tweedy left the apartment ***knowing full well*** that his children were alone, and could be for some time.

Additionally, unlike the mother in *Miller*, Tweedy's statements that he believed Mrs. England would be coming soon do not appear to be credible. The police report indicates that Mrs. England told

Officer Higgerson that she had refused to watch the children that night. However, while interviewing Tweedy, Officer Higgerson told Tweedy that Mrs. England denied even being asked to watch the children. This inconsistency may have simply been the result of a police interviewing tactic. Clearly it must be cleared up by further investigation, but whichever version is true, both statements contradict Tweedy's statement that Mrs. England was going to watch the children. Further contradictory testimony can be presented by the owner of the building, Mr. Wirthin, who told police that he was aware of at least two prior occasions in which the children were left alone in the apartment. This statement casts doubt on Tweedy's claim that Mrs. England was coming to babysit, and could corroborate Mrs. England's statement either that she refused to watch the children that night or she was never asked.

Even if Tweedy's statements could be found credible, his leaving the apartment knowing that the children were alone and knowing that an electrical fire was possible is sufficient to establish that the actions Tweedy took to protect his children were ineffectual. Tweedy's act of leaving the television on and jamming the bedroom door shut not only failed to protect the children, but also exposed the children to additional potential harm that they could not get out in an emergency than simply being left alone in the apartment.

Thus each part of the *Miller* three-pronged test can be satisfied by admissible evidence and section 4304's intent element can be adequately demonstrated in this case. The final consideration is causation.

C. Tweedy's Conduct Was a Substantial Factor in the Children's Deaths.

Causation is an essential element of any criminal charge, which the State must prove beyond a reasonable doubt. [*See* State v. Shoup (1993)] Criminal responsibility is properly assessed against one whose conduct was a direct and substantial factor in producing the result even though other factors combined with that conduct to achieve the result. [*Id.*] In *State v. Shoup*, the defendant, while driving under the influence of alcohol, ran a stop sign and struck a dump truck that was illegally parked. Shoup's passenger, his wife, was killed in the accident. At trial, Shoup argued that the legal cause of his wife's death was the illegally parked truck. The Franklin Supreme Court upheld Shoup's vehicular homicide conviction stating that his conduct started an unbroken chain of causation that directly and substantially led to his wife's death. Similarly, in this case, Tweedy's conduct started an unbroken chain of causation that directly and substantially led to the death of his children. Tweedy locked the children in the bedroom and left the television on. According to the Fire Marshall's report, the television started the fire that resulted in the smoke that killed the children. Had Tweedy not left the television on, the fire would not have started. Had he not jammed the bedroom door, the children may have been able to escape or be rescued. The television causing an electrical fire and the smoke resulting from the synthetic materials in the apartment were foreseeable possibilities, just as in *Shoup,* an illegally parked vehicle was a foreseeable possibility. It was also foreseeable that in the event of a fire, the children would not be able to escape. In securing the door, ostensibly to prevent a break-in, Tweedy must have foreseen that no one would be able to get in to the children in the event of an emergency. Therefore, just as in the *Shoup* case, Tweedy cannot escape liability for the natural consequences of his conduct merely because of foreseeable complications.

The defense will likely argue that with respect to Alma, there was an intervening factor that resulted in her death. While it is true that the medical examiner found that Alma had a congenital heart malformation, she indicated ***that if this condition was left untreated***, it would be life threatening. She did not indicate that the heart problem was currently life threatening, or that it in any way contributed

to the child's death. Furthermore, Fred, who was older and in good health, also succumbed to smoke inhalation. In light of this, no logical argument can be made that Alma might have survived but for the heart condition.

D. Conclusion.

There is sufficient admissible evidence to prove each element necessary to convict James A. Tweedy of felony child endangerment under section 4304 of the Franklin Penal Code. All of the evidence discussed in the brief is admissible under Rules 401 and 402 of the Franklin Rules of Evidence as relevant evidence.

II. Recommendations for Further Investigation.

There are several other matters that require further investigation, and could possibly lead to more compelling evidence of Tweedy's culpability. First, Mr. Harry Wirthin told police that he knows that the children were left alone in the apartment on at least two prior occasions. An investigator should contact Mr. Wirthin again to find out the circumstances of those occurrences. Also, Mr. Wirthin should be questioned about the circumstances of the previous fire in Tweedy's apartment and whether Tweedy was aware of those circumstances.

Mrs. England should also be interviewed again to determine whether Tweedy asked her to babysit that night. She should be asked about the previous occasions on which she has babysat the children. For example, how often did she babysit? Did he ever secure the door with knives before? If not, this would indicate he was not expecting Mrs. England to come that night. Also, the outside door of the apartment was locked when firefighters tried to enter, so we need to know if Mrs. England had a key to Tweedy's apartment. If not, this would also show that Tweedy was not expecting Mrs. England that night. We should also ask Mrs. England if she has ever refused to babysit before, and if so, does she know what Tweedy did? Did he ever go out anyway?

We should interview Glen Poshard about what he knows, if anything, about Tweedy's leaving the children alone on other occasions.

The police report indicates that a check of city licensing and inspection records revealed that Mr. Wirthin was cited on five occasions in the last five years for code violations relating to wiring problems in the building. All of the citations resulted from complaints from tenants. We need to find out if Tweedy himself ever filed a complaint. We could check with Mr. Wirthin or the city licensing and inspection department about who filed the complaints. It should also be determined whether any notice of these code violations was sent to the residents of the building. If so, this would show that Tweedy was aware of electrical wiring problems in the building, thus making a stronger case that he was aware of a danger of fire in his building. Again, we could check with Mr. Wirthin or the city.

Finally, we may also want to investigate how difficult it is to open the door when knives are in the door jamb, and we should attempt to find out from firefighter Albert Malone who the "unknown visitor" referred to in the incident report is, and, if we find the "visitor," what he or she knows about the incident.

Multistate Performance Test

Vargas v. Monte

National Conference of Bar Examiners

Preface

This Multistate Performance Test is a reprint of one of the three MPTs which were administered in July 2003.

The instructions for the test appear on the next page. On the actual MPT, they will appear on the back cover of the test.

INSTRUCTIONS

1. You will have 90 minutes to complete this session of the examination. This performance test is designed to evaluate your ability to handle a select number of legal authorities in the context of a factual problem involving a client.

2. The problem is set in the fictitious state of Franklin, in the fictitious Fifteenth Circuit of the United States. Columbia and Olympia are also fictitious states in the Fifteenth Circuit. In Franklin, the trial court of general jurisdiction is the District Court, the intermediate appellate court is the Court of Appeal, and the highest court is the Supreme Court.

3. You will have two kinds of materials with which to work: a File and a Library. The first document in the File is a memorandum containing the instructions for the task you are to complete. The other documents in the File contain factual information about your case and may include some facts that are not relevant.

4. The Library contains the legal authorities needed to complete the task and may also include some authorities that are not relevant. Any cases may be real, modified, or written solely for the purpose of this examination. If the cases appear familiar to you, do not assume that they are precisely the same as you have read before. Read them thoroughly, as if they all were new to you. You should assume that cases were decided in the jurisdictions and on the dates shown. In citing cases from the Library, you may use abbreviations and omit page references.

5. Your response must be written in the answer book provided. If you are taking this examination on a laptop computer, your jurisdiction will provide you with specific instructions. In answering this performance test, you should concentrate on the materials provided in the File and Library. What you have learned in law school and elsewhere provides the general background for analyzing the problem; the File and Library provide the specific materials with which you must work.

6. Although there are no restrictions on how you apportion your time, you should be sure to allocate ample time (about 45 minutes) to reading and digesting the materials and to organizing your answer before you begin writing it. You may make notes anywhere in the test materials; blank pages are provided at the end of the booklet. You may not tear pages from the question booklet.

7. This performance test will be graded on your responsiveness to the instructions regarding the task you are to complete, which are given to you in the first memorandum in the File, and on the content, thoroughness, and organization of your response.

INSTRUCTIONS

1. ou will have 90 minutes to complete this session of the examination. This performance test is igned to evaluate your ability to handle a select number of legal authorities in the context of a ual problem involving a client.

2. e problem is set in the fictional state of Franklin, in the fictional Fifteenth Circuit of the United ates. Columbia and Olympia are also fictional states in the Fifteenth Circuit. In Franklin, the trial urt of general jurisdiction is the District Court, the intermediate appellate court is the Court of peal, and the highest court is the Supreme Court.

3. ou will have two kinds of materials with which to work: a File and a Library. The first document the File is a memorandum containing the instructions for the task you are to complete. The other cuments in the File contain factual information about your case and may include some facts that not relevant.

4. e Library contains the legal authorities needed to complete the task and may also include some thorities that are not relevant. Any cases may be real, modified, or written solely for the purpose this examination. If the cases appear familiar to you, do not assume that they are precisely the me as you have read before. Read them thoroughly, as if they all were new to you. You should sume that cases were decided in the jurisdictions and on the dates shown. In citing cases from the brary, you may use abbreviations and omit page references.

5. ur response must be written in the answer book provided. If you are taking the examination on a aptop computer, your jurisdiction will provide you with specific instructions. In answering this rformance test, you should concentrate on the materials provided in the File and Library. What you have learned in law school and elsewhere provides the general background for analyzing the oblem; the File and Library provide the specific materials with which you must work.

6. though there are no restrictions on how you apportion your time, you should be sure to allocate ample time (about 45 minutes) to reading and digesting the materials and to organizing your answer fore you begin writing it. You may make notes anywhere in the test materials; blank pages are ovided at the end of the booklet. You may not tear pages from the question booklet.

7. is performance test will be graded on your responsiveness to the instructions regarding the task u are to complete, which are given to you in the first memorandum in the File, and on the content, oroughness, and organization of your response.

Vargas v. Monte

FILE

LIBRARY

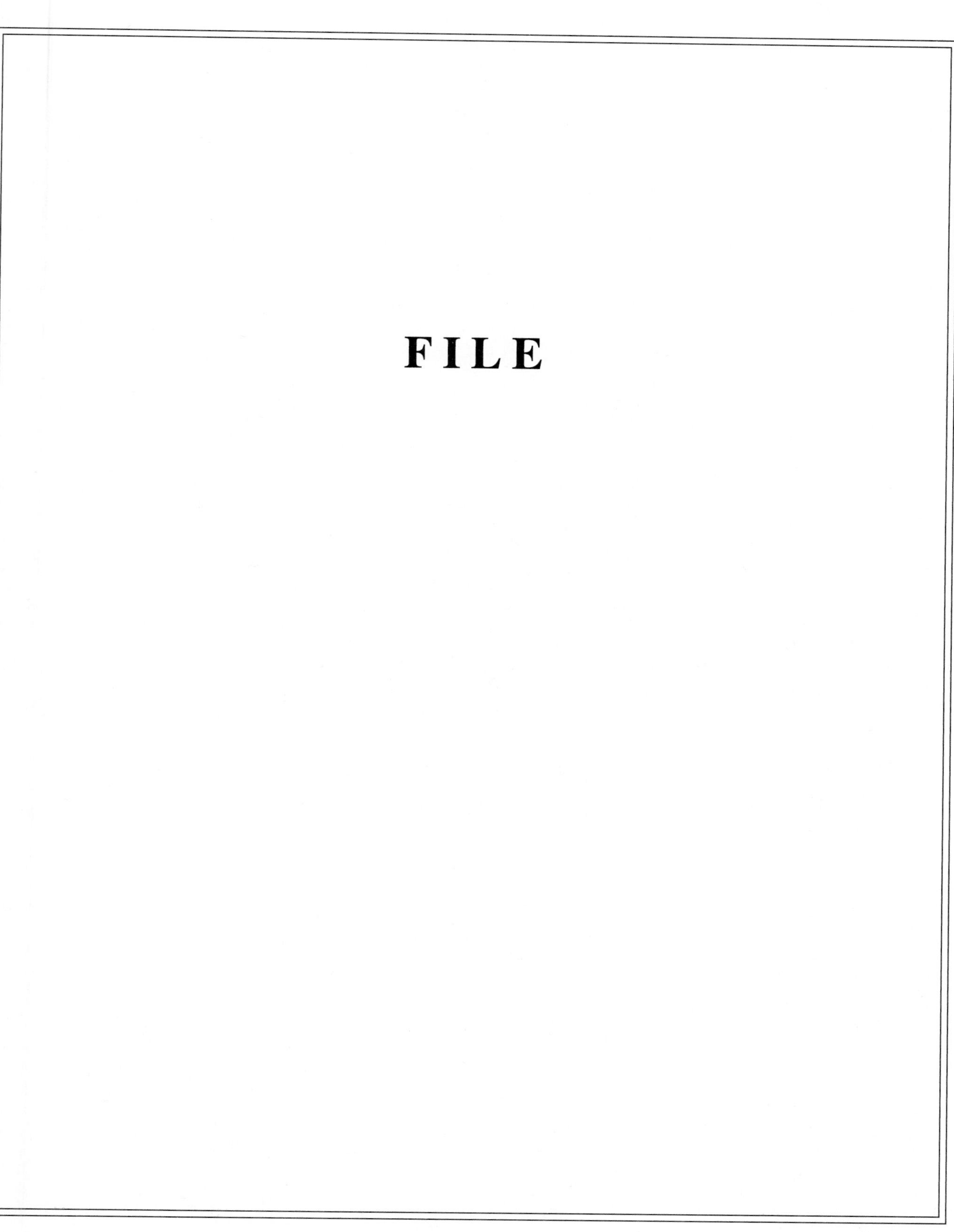

FILE

Norman & Longfellow
Attorneys at Law
405 East Gray, Suite 100
Lakeview, Franklin 33071

MEMORANDUM

To: Applicant
From: Jane Norman
Date: July 29, 2003
Subject: *Vargas v. Monte*

We have nearly completed the bench trial of the *Vargas v. Monte* timber trespass case. Our client, Les Vargas, brought this action against adjoining landowner Carla Monte for wrongfully cutting and removing trees from his property. He is seeking an award of statutory treble damages. The parties have presented their evidence at trial, and the judge has now requested briefs on the issues of whether, based on the evidence adduced at trial, (1) defendant Monte is liable for timber trespass and, if so, (2) whether single, double, or treble damages, or some combination thereof, should be assessed against her.

Please draft a persuasive brief to the court addressing the liability and damages issues outlined above. Our goals are to persuade the judge to hold Monte liable for timber trespass and award Vargas the maximum damages allowable by law based on the evidence, explaining why any lower measure of damages is inappropriate.

Prepare the brief in accordance with the guidelines set forth in the attached office memorandum. We have a statement of stipulated facts in this case so, as pointed out in the brief writing guidelines, you should write only a short introductory statement that reminds the court of the nature of the dispute and our goals. In drafting your arguments, however, you must use all relevant facts that support your arguments.

Norman & Longfellow
Attorneys at Law
405 East Gray, Suite 100
Lakeview, Franklin 33071

MEMORANDUM

September 8, 1995

To: All Lawyers
From: Litigation Supervisor
Subject: Persuasive Briefs

All persuasive briefs shall conform to the following guidelines:

All briefs shall include a Statement of Facts. The aim of the Statement of Facts is to persuade the tribunal that the facts support our client's position. The facts must be stated accurately, although emphasis is not improper. Select carefully the facts that are pertinent to the legal arguments. However, in a brief to a trial court, when there is a statement of stipulated facts, the Statement of Facts section of the brief may be abbreviated. In such cases, the lawyer need only write a short introductory statement and direct the court's attention to the statement of stipulated facts.

The firm follows the practice of breaking the argument into its major components and writing carefully crafted subject headings that illustrate the arguments they cover. Avoid writing briefs that contain only a single broad argument heading. The argument heading should succinctly summarize the reasons the tribunal should take the position you are advocating. A heading should be a specific application of a rule of law to the facts of the case and not a bare legal or factual conclusion or a statement of an abstract principle. For example, improper: THE UNDERLYING FACTS ESTABLISH PLAINTIFF'S CLAIM OF RIGHT. Proper: BY PLACING A CHAIN ACROSS THE DRIVEWAY AND BY REFUSING ACCESS TO OTHERS, PLAINTIFF HAS ESTABLISHED A CLAIM OF RIGHT.

The body of each argument should analyze applicable legal authority and persuasively argue how the facts and law support our client's position. Authority supportive of our client's position should be emphasized, but contrary authority should also generally be cited, addressed in the argument, and explained or distinguished. Do not reserve arguments for reply or supplemental briefing.

The lawyer need not prepare a table of contents, a table of cases, a summary of argument, or an index. These will be prepared, when required, after the draft is approved.

STATEMENT OF STIPULATED FACTS

1. Plaintiff Les Vargas owns property covering several hundred acres of land in Cleveland County, Franklin.

2. Adjoining the Vargas property is a several-hundred-acre parcel of land owned by defendant Carla Monte.

3. Prior to 1880, the two parcels were part of a larger tract of land owned by the United States Government.

4. In 1879, the original survey of this area was conducted by licensed surveyors for the U.S. General Land Office ("USGLO"). The original survey was undertaken for the purpose of subdividing the area into smaller parcels, which were then sold.

5. In 1880, the USGLO transferred to Vargas's and Monte's ancestors their respective parcels. The Vargas family bought the west half and the Monte family bought the east half.

6. As part of the 1879 survey, the one-quarter-mile-long common boundary running north and south between the Vargas and Monte parcels was established and marked.

7. The 1879 survey established section corners that were monumented using wooden posts set in mounds of stone. The lines between these corners were marked by blazing trees along the common boundary. A blaze is a chest-high, smooth surface cut on a tree.

8. Between 2000 and 2002, the boundary line between the parties' properties was resurveyed by the U.S. Department of the Interior, Bureau of Land Management ("BLM"), as part of a larger resurvey of portions of the county. The BLM resurvey is the only licensed survey conducted of these parcels since the original USGLO survey.

9. From March 2000 to January 2002, Carla Monte cut and removed approximately 700 trees from a strip of land along the parties' shared boundary.

EXCERPTS FROM TRIAL TESTIMONY OF PLAINTIFF LES VARGAS

DIRECT EXAMINATION BY JANE NORMAN, Counsel for Plaintiff:

* * * *

Q: How long have you and Carla Monte shared a common property boundary?

A: Well, we each inherited our parcels from our families, who had owned them for generations. So I guess that makes us lifelong neighbors in a sense.

Q: Was the boundary line between your and Ms. Monte's properties clearly delineated before the BLM resurvey?

A: Not at all. There were conflicting blaze marks at various points along the property line, and even some trees sprayed with paint and tagged with construction tape. Members of both families had tried to figure out where the true boundary was, but they eventually gave up.

Q: So, how did you and Ms. Monte deal with the uncertainty surrounding the property line?

A: Well, both of our parcels are big enough that we never really got around to sorting it out. When I heard about the BLM resurvey, I figured that we'd finally know once and for all where the true boundary line was.

* * * *

Q: How would you describe your relationship with Carla Monte?

A: Well, I thought it was pretty neighborly until I found out she was cutting down my trees.

Q: When did you discover this?

A: Sometime during the fall of 2001, when I got a call from a BLM surveyor by the name of Stan Linhart.

Q: Did you do anything as a result of Mr. Linhart's call?

A: Yes. I went out to the boundary between the two properties and saw that dozens of my trees had been chopped down. Everywhere I looked, I saw stumps where there used to be beautiful, mature ponderosa pines.

Q: What, if anything, did you do after you discovered that your trees had been destroyed?

A: I tried to reach Carla, but she never returned my calls. I left messages on her machine asking her to stop destroying my trees. I also posted some signs that said "No Trespassing."

Q: Did your efforts have any effect?

A: When I went back about a month later to check on things, I discovered that even more of my trees had been cut down and hauled off. I couldn't believe that Carla had continued to log in this area and that she'd cut down more of my trees even after I posted the "No Trespassing" signs. That was when I decided to take legal action.

Q: Did Carla Monte have your permission to cut down any of your trees?

A: Absolutely not. In fact, she knew that I'd turned down some lucrative logging contracts with logging companies that wanted to harvest trees on my property.

Q: How did she know this?

A: Well, over the years I told her about a few of the offers I'd received from logging companies. She told me I was silly to turn down these big money offers. She said that if I ever changed my mind, I should let her know because, since she was in the logging business, she wanted the logging rights to my land.

* * * *

CROSS-EXAMINATION BY WILLIAM WARREN, Counsel for Defendant:

* * * *

Q: Mr. Vargas, isn't it true that your family and the family of Ms. Monte had a longstanding agreement about the boundary of the two properties?

A: No, she and I never agreed on the exact boundary. As the landscape changed over the years, it was more and more difficult to determine the exact location of the dividing line. But we knew within a few feet or so where our property line was, especially in the area where she chopped down my trees.

Q: Showing you what has been marked as Defendant's Exhibit A for identification, can you identify it?

A: Well, it looks like a letter with a hand-drawn map from my grandfather, Amos Vargas, to someone by the name of Ben Monte.

Q: You recognize the handwriting of your grandfather, Amos Vargas, don't you?

A: Yes, it seems to be his writing. It looks like his letters that we have in the family collection.

Q: And your grandfather wrote this letter in 1906, didn't he?

A: Well, all I know is the letter says it was written on April 18, 1906.

* * * *

EXCERPTS FROM TRIAL TESTIMONY OF STAN LINHART

DIRECT EXAMINATION BY JANE NORMAN, Counsel for Plaintiff:

* * * * *

Q: As a licensed surveyor for the United States Department of the Interior, Bureau of Land Management, were you involved in the BLM resurvey of Cleveland County?

A: Yes, I was the lead surveyor and the point of contact for local landowners.

Q: Are you familiar with the parcels owned by plaintiff Les Vargas and defendant Carla Monte?

A: I am. The Vargas and Monte parcels were surveyed as part of the BLM resurvey.

* * * * *

Q: Did you have contact with Ms. Monte during the fall of 2001?

A: Yes. We were surveying a stretch of the boundary between the Monte and Vargas parcels when I spotted Ms. Monte and her crew cutting down trees west of the property line, in fact more than 100 feet onto the Vargas parcel. I noticed that she had already cut about 300 trees. When I pointed out to Ms. Monte that she was logging trees on the Vargas parcel, she told me that the trees were on her property.

Q: What specifically did she say to you?

A: She said her grandfather and Vargas's grandfather had agreed on the boundary. Then she pointed to some old blaze marks and paint stains about 20 feet farther west inside the Vargas property and said that the parties had relied on these markings for years. When I pointed out that the true boundary line was more than 100 feet east of the point where she was logging, she said it wasn't fair for BLM to come in and try to change the boundary lines after all these years.

Q: Did the conversation end there?

A: No. I warned her that the boundary markers she was relying on weren't accurate, and I cautioned her against continuing to log there until BLM could complete its resurvey.

Q: Do you know whether Ms. Monte continued logging in that area after you told her this?

A: The very next day I saw her in the same area cutting down more trees on the Vargas property. When I returned to the area a few weeks later to double check some of our survey work, I saw additional evidence of logging by Ms. Monte farther along the shared boundary line, including more stumps on the Vargas side of the property line. By that time, I had already notified Mr. Vargas, and I figured this was something that the two property owners would have to work out.

Q: Can you describe the condition of the boundary line between the Monte and Vargas properties prior to the BLM resurvey?

A: Well, before the resurvey, the boundary line was a real mess and nobody knew exactly where it was located.

Q: Why is that?

A: Because the section lines blazed on trees during the original survey back in the 1800s had deteriorated. Previous attempts had been made to locate and perpetuate the original survey monuments. Over time, these attempts created errors and conflicting blaze marks and other evidence concerning the property boundaries. This problem wasn't limited to the boundary line between the Vargas and Monte properties. It was a widespread and well-known problem throughout the county, which is why we were called in to do the resurvey.

* * * * *

CROSS-EXAMINATION BY WILLIAM WARREN, Counsel for Defendant:

* * * * *

Q: As the surveyor of the boundary between the Vargas and Monte properties, you are aware of the natural features in the area, aren't you?

A: Of course.

Q: So you know where Bella Creek is, correct?

A: Yes.

Q: And that creek bed shifts, doesn't it, Mr. Linhart, depending on whether it's the wet or dry season?

A: Yes, that makes sense.

Q: And over time, creek beds can shift several hundred feet, depending on changing natural conditions, right?

A: Well, several hundred feet may be a stretch but, yes, creek beds have been known to move.

Q: Well, 50 or 100 feet over 100 years wouldn't be a stretch, would it, Mr. Linhart?

A: No, that could happen.

Q: OK. Are you aware of a large outcropping near the north end of the Vargas-Monte properties, known by most local folks as "the big rock"?

A: Yes.

Q: And "the big rock" is north of Bella Creek, right?

A: Right.

Q: And the distance between the bend in Bella Creek and "the big rock" is well over 1,000 feet, isn't it?

A: At least 1,000 feet.

Q: And the area where you saw Ms. Monte logging trees along the Vargas-Monte boundary is between the bend in Bella Creek and "the big rock," correct?

A: That's correct.

EXCERPTS FROM TRIAL TESTIMONY OF DEFENDANT CARLA MONTE

DIRECT EXAMINATION BY WILLIAM WARREN, Counsel for Defendant:

* * * *

Q: Ms. Monte, whose trees did you believe you were cutting down?

A: I thought I was on my side of the boundary line and that the trees belonged to me.

Q: Why did you believe the trees belonged to you?

A: Because I followed the existing blaze marks made by our families over the years and the marks conform to the 1906 agreement between my grandfather, Ben Monte, and Amos Vargas. The Vargas parcel is west of mine, and I made sure I stayed east of the existing blaze marks, which are based on the line between the bend in Bella Creek and "the big rock."

Q: Showing you Defendant's Exhibit A, can you identify this?

A: Yes. It's a copy of a letter to my grandfather from Amos Vargas. There's a hand-drawn map on the letter showing the boundary between the two properties. It's among the family papers passed along to me by my dad before he passed on.

Q: Did you and Mr. Vargas ever discuss the boundary between your properties?

A: We had a few discussions over the years about the poor condition of the boundary line. I thought that he would not object to my logging along the common border, as long as I stayed east of the existing blaze marks.

* * * *

CROSS-EXAMINATION BY JANE NORMAN, Counsel for Plaintiff:

* * * *

Q: Ms. Monte, isn't it true that you knew before you began logging along the Monte-Vargas boundary line that BLM was in the process of resurveying property lines in this area?

A: Yes, I did receive a notification letter from BLM before I began my logging operations.

Q: And you own literally hundreds of acres of land in Cleveland County, don't you?

A: Yes.

Q: And there was nothing to prevent you from logging another section of your land away from the boundary line, was there?

A: Well, the trees that we cut were ready for thinning, and the logging trucks had easy access. But, in any event, I only cut down trees that belonged to me.

Q: But you didn't know for a fact that the trees you harvested were on your property, did you?

A: Based on everything I knew at the time those were my trees.

Defendant's Exhibit A ~~for Identication~~

April 18, 1906

Benjamin Monte
Route 2, Box 4
Belleville, Franklin

Dear Ben,

I know it's been a while since you and I last talked about the north-south boundary line between our parcels in Cleveland County, but I just want to put in writing what I think is the understanding you and I have about that matter.

When you and I were walking the property last summer we looked for the old markers, but we couldn't figure out where they were or where the line ran. The rock piles weren't there, and we could see some scars on some of the older trees but who's to say if they were blaze marks or what.

I know we talked about you and me just arbitrarily setting the boundary and agreeing that that would be it. The line we more or less decided on was a line from the southern boundary, proceeding north along Bella Creek, which is dry most of the year but changes course a bit during the winter months, to where it bends to the west, along the deer path, continuing north to the big rock on the northern boundary. I've drawn a map at the bottom of this letter.

So, as far as I'm concerned, let's agree on that. Okay? If I don't hear back from you, I'll assume it's okay with you.

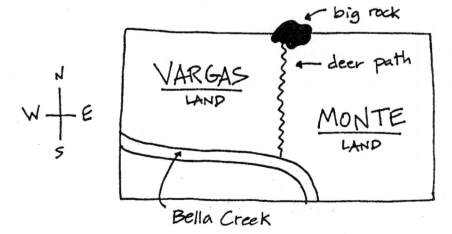

Your friend,

Amos Vargas

Amos Vargas

big rock
deer path
N
W
E
S
VARGAS LAND
MONTE LAND
Bella Creek

United States Department of the Interior
Bureau of Land Management
Franklin State Office
1000 Government Way
Belle Garden, Franklin 33021

May 27, 2000

Carla Monte
14562 Cedar Ridge Drive
Belleville, Franklin 33025

Dear Landowner:

The Bureau of Land Management is conducting a land survey within Cleveland County to determine the boundaries. Records indicate that you are a landowner in the area of our survey and we wish to make you aware of our presence.

Should it become necessary to enter your lands during the course of this survey, Stan Linhart of our Maddock Field Station will attempt to contact you personally for prior permission.

Please notify Mr. Linhart of any locked gates you may have, or if you have questions regarding this survey. He may be contacted at the following address:

Maddock Field Station
332 Clarksburg Drive
Diamond Springs, Franklin 33022

Sincerely,

Cecilia S. Chen

Cecilia S. Chen
Chief, Survey Branch

United States Department of the Interior

Bureau of Land Management

Franklin State Office

1050 Government Way

Belle Fourche, Franklin 55021

May 27, 2009

[illegible]

Dear [illegible]:

The Bureau of Land Management is conducting a land survey in the Cleveland County to determine the [illegible] lines. Records indicate that you are a landowner in the area of our survey and we want to make you aware of our presence.

[illegible]

[illegible]

[illegible]

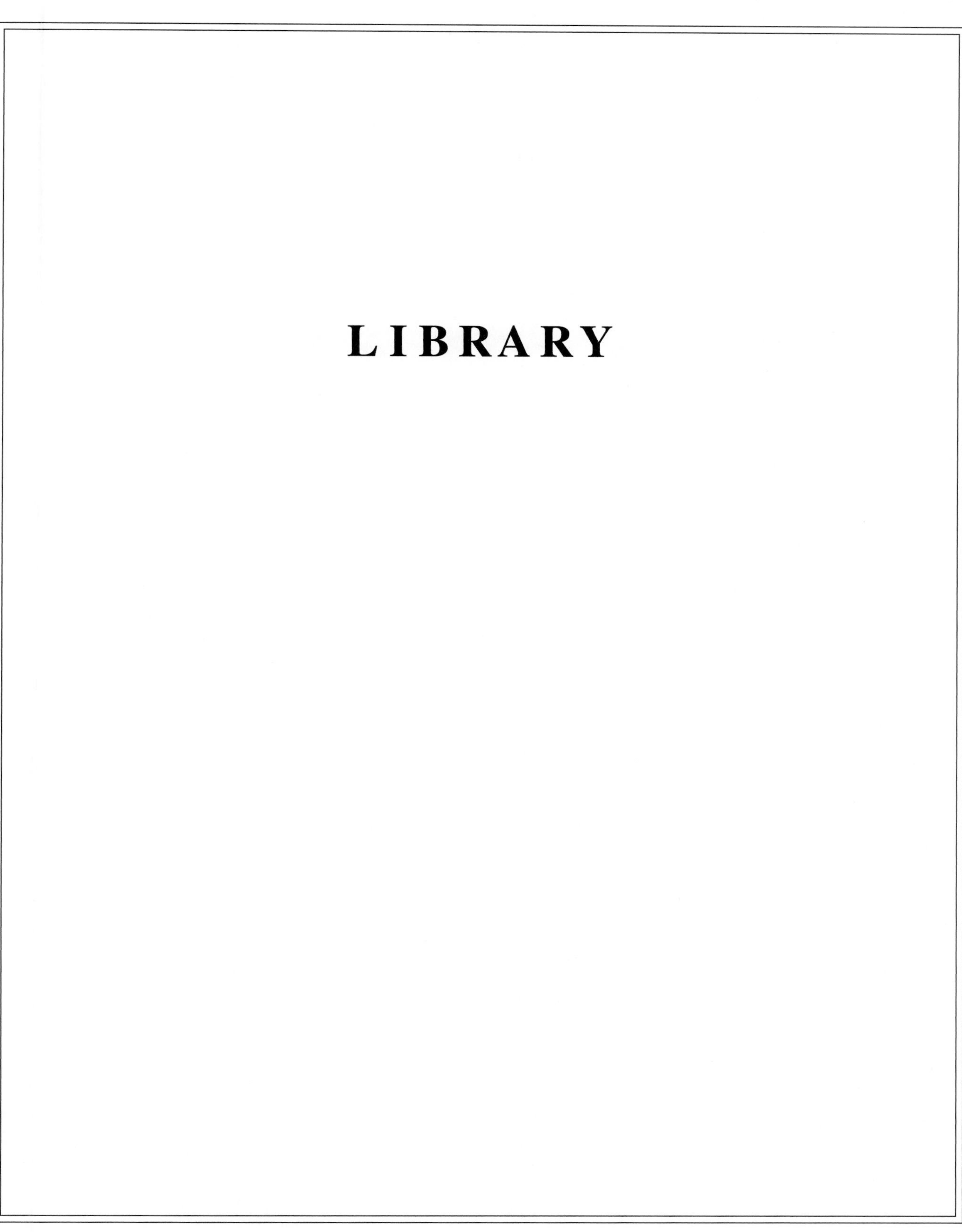

LIBRARY

Franklin Civil Code

§3346. Injuries to timber, trees, or underwood; treble damages; double damages; actual detriment

(a) For wrongful injuries to timber, trees, or underwood upon the land of another, or removal thereof, the measure of damages is three times such sum as would compensate for the actual detriment, except that where the trespass was casual or involuntary, or where the defendant had probable cause to believe that the land on which the trespass was committed was his own or the land of the person in whose service or by whose direction the act was done, the measure of damages shall be twice the sum as would compensate for the actual detriment.

(b) The measure of damages to be assessed against a defendant for any trespass committed while acting in reliance upon a survey of boundary lines which improperly fixes the location of a boundary line, shall be the actual detriment incurred if the trespass was committed by a defendant who relied upon a survey made by a licensed surveyor.

(c) Any action for the damages specified by subdivisions (a) and (b) of this section must be commenced within five years from the date of the trespass.

Anderson v. Flush

Franklin Court of Appeal (1953)

Maggie Anderson brought this action to recover statutory treble damages for injuries to 39 trees in her orchard. She alleges the injuries were caused by the deliberate action of Todd Flush while moving a house along Levin Avenue, a public street, in the course of his house-moving business. The trial judge awarded double, not treble, damages. Anderson appeals the trial court's denial of treble damages. Flush also appeals, claiming that, although he damaged Anderson's trees, double damages are not mandatory and should not have been awarded.

Levin Avenue is bordered on one side by Anderson's orchard and on the other by that of John Koh. The trees in Koh's orchard bordering the avenue are interspersed with telephone poles while those of Anderson's orchard are not. Between the orchards, the paved portion of Levin Avenue is only about 15 feet wide. The damaged trees are on Anderson's property, but their branches extended over the street.

Flush observed that it would be necessary to touch the bordering trees on at least one side of Levin Avenue. He chose to strike those of Anderson because of the telephone poles on Koh's property. He thought that the house would brush by the limbs without causing any extensive damage to the trees. He sawed off some limbs to prevent them from breaking farther back near the trunks and from causing permanent damage to the trees.

The purpose of Civil Code §3346 is to protect trees and timber. The trial court held that Flush's actions were wrongful and the double damages provision of §3346 was mandatory. We agree.

There are three measures of damages depending on the nature of the trespass: (1) for willful and malicious trespass, the court may impose treble damages but must impose double damages; (2) for casual and involuntary trespass, the court must impose double damages; and (3) for trespass in reliance on a survey, actual damages.

Under §3346 the trial court has discretion to determine the circumstances under which to award treble damages. Because treble damages are punitive, the defendant must have acted willfully and maliciously.

While §3346 leaves the imposition of treble damages to the discretion of the court, it places a floor upon that discretion. Double damages must be awarded whether the trespass be willful and malicious or casual and involuntary. The trial court was required to impose no less than double damages.

We must determine whether the trial court abused its discretion in refusing to award treble damages. It is undisputed that the branches of Anderson's trees extended over the street. Since the street is dedicated to public use to its full width irrespective of the paved portion, the trial court was justified in deciding that Flush did not act with malice or a reckless disregard of Anderson's rights. Flush, faced with the dilemma of inflicting what he believed would be slight damage to Anderson's orchard, damage to telephone poles, or blocking a public street for a substantial period of time, acted reasonably to minimize the damage. The trial court did not abuse its discretion in refusing to impose treble damages. Affirmed.

Hardway Lumber v. Thompson

Franklin Court of Appeal (1971)

Hardway Lumber appeals from a judgment awarding it double damages based on the value of timber wrongfully removed from its land, contending the trial court erred in not awarding treble damages pursuant to §3346 of the Franklin Civil Code.

Hardway entered into a 10-year contract with defendant Henry Thompson for the sale of timber on Hardway's land. Five years into the contract, Hardway properly rescinded the agreement by filing a notice with the Recorder of Deeds. While the recording provided constructive notice, it is undisputed that Thompson was never given actual notice of the rescission. Shortly after the rescission, Hardway discovered that Thompson was logging timber on its property. Hardway sued, seeking treble damages.

The trial court concluded (i) Thompson was not aware that Hardway had rescinded the logging contract; (ii) at the time Thompson removed the timber, he believed he had a right to do so; and (iii) Thompson was not acting with malice or ill will toward Hardway.

Although §3346 does not expressly so provide, Franklin courts have held that to award treble damages, the plaintiff must prove that the wrongful act was willful and malicious. Since a defendant rarely admits to such a state of mind, it must frequently be established from the circumstances. Malice may be found when a defendant performs an act with reckless disregard of or indifference to the rights of others.

For example, in *Guernsey v. Wheeler* (Franklin Court of Appeal 1966), the defendant had a contract permitting him to log on a parcel of land known as Sherman's Trust. Prior to removing trees, he was told repeatedly there were conflicting descriptions as to the precise location of Sherman's Trust, but he nonetheless logged a large number of trees. The trial court rejected his claim that he had probable cause to believe he was logging the land covered by his contract. We held that because the trespass was neither casual nor involuntary but was instead committed with a reckless disregard of and indifference to the rights of the owner, treble damages were appropriate.

In the present case, the trial court found that Thompson's acts were not in bad faith; that his motives were not to vex, harass, annoy, or injure Hardway; and that the trespass was committed while attempting to harvest what he thought was his own timber. The trial court did not abuse its discretion. Affirmed.

Blackjack Lumber Company v. Pearlman

Franklin Court of Appeal (1986)

Blackjack Lumber Company brought this action against Frank Pearlman to recover statutory damages for timber trespass under Franklin Civil Code §3346. Pearlman invoked the doctrine of agreed boundary as a defense. The trial court found that predecessors of the parties had agreed upon a boundary between their respective parcels, and decided in Pearlman's favor.

At issue is the boundary line between the northern and southern halves of Section 35. In 1961, Tom Majors purchased the north half from the Union Lumber Company. Majors was uncertain as to the boundary line between the two parcels. In 1962, non-licensed Union Lumber personnel undertook an informal survey of the boundary line and blazed trees (i.e., notched them with an axe) as they went across the boundary line. Majors observed the informal survey as it progressed and agreed with the line that was drawn.

In 1970, Pearlman bought the south half of Section 35 from Union Lumber and agreed with Majors that the line blazed by Union Lumber in 1962 was the boundary line. In 1973, Majors sold the north half to Blackjack Lumber. By this time, Pearlman had flagged the blazed line and the flags were clearly visible on the ground. In 1980, Pearlman conducted logging operations on his property and logged up to the blazed line. On one occasion, Pearlman asked and received Blackjack's permission to install a landing north of the blazed line for convenience in conducting his operations.

In 1982, Blackjack hired a licensed surveyor to survey the boundary line between the two halves of Section 35. This survey showed the boundary to be several hundred feet to the south of the line blazed in 1962.

In cases of uncertainty, courts look with favor upon private agreements fixing and marking boundary lines. This judicially created rule is known as the doctrine of agreed boundary. It is intended to secure repose and prevent litigation. The essential elements of the doctrine are (1) uncertainty about the true boundary line; (2) an agreement between adjoining landowners as to the boundary; (3) an agreed-upon boundary that is identifiable on the ground; and (4) acceptance and acquiescence to the agreed-upon boundary for a period at least equal to the statute of limitations.

The doctrine of agreed boundary applies even where the parties intend to set the boundary along the true property line but fail to do so, due to a mistake. Moreover, there is no requirement that the true location be unascertainable. Here, it is clear neither Majors nor Union Lumber knew the true location of the boundary line.

The trial court found that, after the line was established by Union Lumber, both Union and Majors accepted the marked line, and their successors likewise accepted it for 20 years as the correct location of the boundary line between the two parcels. Acceptance of the line by both Majors and Union Lumber and their successors is sufficient evidence to show an agreement between Majors and Union Lumber that the blazed line was in fact the agreed-upon boundary line between their respective properties. Therefore, we find that the elements for the doctrine of agreed boundary have been satisfied, and the trial court's judgment is affirmed.

Vargas v. Monte

Sample Answer

TRIAL BRIEF

STATEMENT OF FACTS

The parties' Statement of Stipulated Facts is attached to this brief as Exhibit 1.

Defendant Monte has cut approximately 700 trees on Plaintiff Vargas's property despite being notified by Plaintiff and the Bureau of Land Management ("BLM") that the trees were on Plaintiff's land and despite being asked by Plaintiff to stop logging. Defendant claims that she thought she was cutting trees on her own property.

Testimony at trial shows that the original boundary markings had deteriorated to such an extent that the boundary line had become uncertain, and that additional markings on the land over the years further confused the true boundary. Defendant claims that an "agreement" in a 1906 letter from Plaintiff's grandfather to her grandfather established the boundary. The letter, which was offered by Defendant, states that because the parties' grandfathers could not figure out the boundary line, they "more or less decided" to "arbitrarily" set the boundary line by reference to a creek bed that changed from season to season and a deer path that could shift over time. However, although Plaintiff identified the handwriting in the letter as his grandfather's, he apparently had never seen the letter before it was shown to him at trial. He further testified that he and Defendant "had never really got around to sorting . . . [the boundary line] out."

Defendant, who is in the logging business, admitted at trial that she first began to cut trees along the boundary line after being notified by letter of the BLM's intent to resurvey the properties. After she had cut about 300 trees, the BLM surveyor warned her that she was cutting trees more than 100 feet onto Plaintiff's land. The surveyor also notified Plaintiff, who attempted to stop the destruction of his trees by leaving messages on Defendant's answering machine asking her to stop and by posting "No Trespassing" signs on his property. Despite being told by the surveyor that the markers she was relying on were inaccurate, and ignoring Plaintiff's messages and signs, Defendant continued cutting Plaintiff's trees. Furthermore, she knew from prior conversations with Plaintiff that he wanted no logging on his property and that he had turned down lucrative offers from several logging companies. Nevertheless, she continued cutting.

ARGUMENT

I. DEFENDANT'S ACTIONS CONSTITUTE TIMBER TRESPASS FOR WHICH THE DEFENSE OF AGREED BOUNDARY DOES NOT APPLY BECAUSE THERE WAS NEITHER A BOUNDARY AGREEMENT BETWEEN THE PARTIES NOR WAS THE BOUNDARY LINE IDENTIFIABLE.

A. The Agreed Boundary Defense Fails Because Only One of the Required Elements Is Present.

Private agreements between parties to fix boundary lines are recognized by Franklin courts and, if established, are a complete defense to timber trespass. [Blackjack Lumber Co. v. Pearlman (1986)] The court in *Blackjack* stated that in order for the agreed boundary doctrine to be a defense, there must be (i) an uncertain boundary; (ii) an agreement between adjoining landowners as to the boundary; (iii) an agreed-upon boundary that is identifiable on the ground; and (iv) acceptance and acquiescence to

the agreed-upon boundary for a period at least equal to the statute of limitations. The facts in this case do not support the defense of agreed boundary.

Neither party disputes the uncertainty of the 1879 boundary line between Defendant's and Plaintiff's properties. Both Plaintiff and the BLM surveyor, Mr. Linhart, acknowledged that the original markings were uncertain and confusing and that, over the years, additional attempts to mark the boundary made it virtually impossible to ascertain the location of the original line. Even Defendant stated that the boundary markings were in "poor condition." Thus, the first element of the defense is met.

The second element requires that the adjoining landowners have agreed on a boundary line. Defendant claims that she and Plaintiff are bound by a supposed 1906 agreement evidenced by a letter from Plaintiff's grandfather to Defendant's grandfather. The letter proposes an "arbitrary" boundary line based on a shifting creek bed. Even assuming, *arguendo,* that a shifting natural boundary could be a basis for an agreed-upon boundary, there is not a scintilla of evidence that the parties ever agreed to such a boundary. On the contrary, Plaintiff testified that he and Defendant never sorted out the boundary matter. Additionally, although Plaintiff recognized his grandfather's handwriting on the 1906 letter shown to him at trial, he did not recognize the letter itself, which had been in the Defendant's family papers in her possession. Defendant has not put forward any evidence supporting any agreement between her and Plaintiff regarding a boundary but relies solely on the 1906 letter for her agreed boundary defense. However, it is not even clear from the letter that Defendant's grandfather ever agreed to the proposal. The letter concludes with "[I]f I don't hear back from you, I'll assume it's okay with you." Defendant has introduced no evidence that the 1906 proposal was ever agreed to by her grandfather. Defendant's lack of evidence showing the existence of an agreement, either between Plaintiff and herself or between their ancestors, fails to satisfy the second element of the agreed boundary defense—an agreement between adjoining landowners.

Even if the court could find that there had been agreement on a boundary line, the conflicting and confusing boundary marks fail to satisfy the third element of the agreed boundary doctrine—that the boundary be identifiable on the ground. Plaintiff's testimony indicates that the boundary area was marked with "conflicting blaze marks," and "some trees were sprayed with paint and tagged with construction tape." He also noted that members of both families gave up trying to ascertain the true boundary. The BLM surveyor testified that the boundary line was "a real mess" and nobody knew its location anymore. Even Defendant admitted that the boundary line was in "poor condition." It also appears that the original markings were not identifiable back in 1906 when Amos Vargas wrote that "[w]hen you and I were walking the property last summer we looked for the old markers, but we couldn't figure out where they were or where the line ran." Moreover, even the proposed boundary in the 1906 letter was based on a shifting creek bed. Thus, the evidence reveals that there was no identifiable boundary upon which the parties could have agreed, and therefore Defendant failed to meet the third element of the agreed boundary doctrine.

As for the fourth element, because Defendant has failed to satisfy the second and third elements of this defense, it follows that the fourth element, acquiescence or agreement for a certain length of time, also fails. Therefore, Plaintiff has no defense to her actions.

B. Because the Agreed Boundary Doctrine Is Inapplicable, Defendant Is Liable for Timber Trespass Because She Cut and Removed Trees From Plaintiff's Property Without His Permission.

Franklin Civil Code section 3346 makes timber trespass a strict liability tort. Liability is imposed even if a defendant relies on a survey done improperly or circumstances exist that lead a defendant to believe that she is cutting timber on her own land. In the present case, Defendant cut trees on Plaintiff's property without his permission. In fact, she knew that Plaintiff did not want any logging on his land. Defendant is therefore liable to Plaintiff for timber trespass.

II. PLAINTIFF IS ENTITLED TO TREBLE DAMAGES BECAUSE DEFENDANT'S TRESPASS WAS NEITHER CASUAL OR INVOLUNTARY NOR WAS SHE RELYING ON A SURVEY; RATHER, DEFENDANT'S CONDUCT WAS WILLFUL AND MALICIOUS SINCE SHE LOGGED TREES ALONG THE UNIDENTIFIABLE BOUNDARY LINE WITH KNOWLEDGE OF THE PROPOSED SURVEY AND CONTINUED TO DO SO AFTER REPEATED WARNINGS THAT SHE WAS CUTTING TREES ON PLAINTIFF'S PROPERTY.

Franklin Civil Code section 3346 establishes three measures of damages for timber trespass: (i) actual damages are incurred when a defendant trespasses while relying on an improper boundary line fixed by a survey by a licensed surveyor; (ii) double damages are assessed for a casual or involuntary trespass, or where the defendant had probable cause to believe the land was her own, and (iii) treble damages may be imposed for willful and malicious trespass. At least double damages must be imposed when the trespass is not in reliance on a licensed survey. [Anderson v. Flush (1953)]

A. Actual Damages Are Inappropriate Because Defendant Did Not Rely on a Licensed Survey.

Under section 3346, damages for a plaintiff's actual detriment are appropriate only when a defendant trespasses in reliance on a survey made by a licensed surveyor that improperly fixes the boundary line. There is no evidence in the present case that Defendant relied on any survey at all. It is clear from the facts that she did not rely on the 1879 survey because those marks were no longer identifiable by anyone. Accordingly, actual damages are not appropriate here.

B. Defendant's Rush to Log Trees Before an Unidentifiable Boundary Was to Be Surveyed, and Her Continued Logging After Being Warned that She Was Trespassing, Show Willful and Malicious Conduct Entitling Plaintiff to Treble, Not Double, Damages.

Section 3346 requires imposition of double damages for casual and involuntary trespass and for wrongful injuries. However, a court, in its discretion, may impose treble damages upon a finding that a defendant's wrongful conduct was willful and malicious. [Hardway Lumber v. Thompson (1971); Anderson v. Flush] Malice is usually established from the circumstances of a case and is found to exist when a defendant acts with reckless disregard or indifference to the rights of others. [Hardway Lumber v. Thompson]

The damages issue here is whether Plaintiff is entitled to treble damages based on Defendant's willful and malicious conduct or to double damages for casual and involuntary trespass. The relevant cases are *Anderson v. Flush* and *Hardway Lumber v. Thompson*, both of which upheld imposition of double damages for trespass. *Anderson* involved a defendant who damaged overhanging branches of trees while moving a house down a public street, one side of which was lined with telephone poles while the other side was lined with orchard trees. The Franklin Court of Appeals ruled that the trial court did not abuse its discretion by imposing double, instead of treble, damages because the defendant did not act with malice or reckless disregard of the orchard owner's rights since he attempted to prevent permanent damage to the trees.

In *Hardway Lumber*, the court held that treble damages were inappropriate because the defendant cut trees in reliance on a logging contract that had been rescinded but he had no actual notice of the rescission. The court held that double damages were appropriate because the defendant had no intent to injure and he believed he was harvesting trees that were his to harvest.

The facts in the present case are distinguishable from those in the *Anderson* and *Hardway Lumber* cases. Here, Defendant was not using public property nor was she presented with a choice of the lesser evil, as was the defendant in *Anderson*. On the contrary, Defendant could have cut timber elsewhere on her property until after the resurvey was completed. Moreover, Defendant had no logging contract to rely upon, as did the defendant in *Hardway Lumber*; and she knew that Plaintiff wanted no logging of trees from his property. Furthermore, Defendant made no effort to lessen damage to Plaintiff's property, as did the *Anderson* defendant. She instead exhibited a total disregard for Plaintiff's expressed intent not to permit the cutting of his trees. She was in the logging business and yet she did not begin to log trees along the unclear boundary line until ***after*** she had received notice that the boundary was to be resurveyed. Then, after rushing to cut trees in the area, she ignored several warnings from the surveyor that she was trespassing and continued to cut trees on Plaintiff's land. Defendant also ignored Plaintiff's telephone messages and "No Trespassing" signs and continued her logging activities even though she knew she was trespassing. She could have reasonably chosen to wait until after the resurvey to log along the boundary in order to be certain that she would not cut any of Plaintiff's trees. These facts suggest that Defendant acted with such reckless disregard or indifference to Plaintiff's rights as to support a finding of willful and malicious conduct.

The present case is similar to the situation presented in *Guernsey v. Wheeler* (1966), cited in *Hardway Lumber*. The defendant in *Guernsey* ignored repeated warnings that there were conflicting descriptions as to the location of the parcel he had rights to log. The *Guernsey* court, in awarding treble damages, rejected the defendant's claim that he had probable cause to believe he was logging the correct parcel of land, holding that his acts were not casual or involuntary but were instead committed with reckless disregard and indifference to the owner's rights. In the present case, Defendant also ignored repeated warnings and, knowing the impreciseness of the boundary, rushed to log before a resurvey could establish a definite boundary. Even after Defendant knew she was trespassing, she continued to log trees on Plaintiff's property. These facts support a finding that Defendant acted willfully, maliciously, and with reckless disregard of Plaintiff's rights. Accordingly, an award of treble damages for wrongful trespass is supported by the record and would not be an abuse of this honorable court's discretion.

[**EDITOR'S NOTE:** A well written answer arguing that double damages were appropriate for the trees removed ***before*** the surveyor's notice to Defendant that she was logging on Plaintiff's property, and for triple damages for the trees cut thereafter, would probably also have received full credit. However, given that Defendant did not begin to log until after receiving notice of the resurvey and knew Plaintiff's strong opposition to logging, there is enough evidence to argue that she acted willfully and with malice even for the first trees and that therefore triple damages are appropriate.]

Multistate

Performance Test

In re Marian Bonner

National Conference of Bar Examiners

Preface

This Multistate Performance Test is a reprint of one of the three MPTs which were administered in July 2004.

The instructions for the test appear on the next page. On the actual MPT, they will appear on the back cover of the test.

INSTRUCTIONS

1. You will have 90 minutes to complete this session of the examination. This performance test is designed to evaluate your ability to handle a select number of legal authorities in the context of a factual problem involving a client.

2. The problem is set in the fictitious state of Franklin, in the fictitious Fifteenth Circuit of the United States. Columbia and Olympia are also fictitious states in the Fifteenth Circuit. In Franklin, the trial court of general jurisdiction is the District Court, the intermediate appellate court is the Court of Appeal, and the highest court is the Supreme Court.

3. You will have two kinds of materials with which to work: a File and a Library. The first document in the File is a memorandum containing the instructions for the task you are to complete. The other documents in the File contain factual information about your case and may include some facts that are not relevant.

4. The Library contains the legal authorities needed to complete the task and may also include some authorities that are not relevant. Any cases may be real, modified, or written solely for the purpose of this examination. If the cases appear familiar to you, do not assume that they are precisely the same as you have read before. Read them thoroughly, as if they all were new to you. You should assume that cases were decided in the jurisdictions and on the dates shown. In citing cases from the Library, you may use abbreviations and omit page references.

5. Your response must be written in the answer book provided. If you are taking this examination on a laptop computer, your jurisdiction will provide you with specific instructions. In answering this performance test, you should concentrate on the materials provided in the File and Library. What you have learned in law school and elsewhere provides the general background for analyzing the problem; the File and Library provide the specific materials with which you must work.

6. Although there are no restrictions on how you apportion your time, you should be sure to allocate ample time (about 45 minutes) to reading and digesting the materials and to organizing your answer before you begin writing it. You may make notes anywhere in the test materials; blank pages are provided at the end of the booklet. You may not tear pages from the question booklet.

7. This performance test will be graded on your responsiveness to the instructions regarding the task you are to complete, which are given to you in the first memorandum in the File, and on the content, thoroughness, and organization of your response.

In re Marian Bonner

FILE

LIBRARY

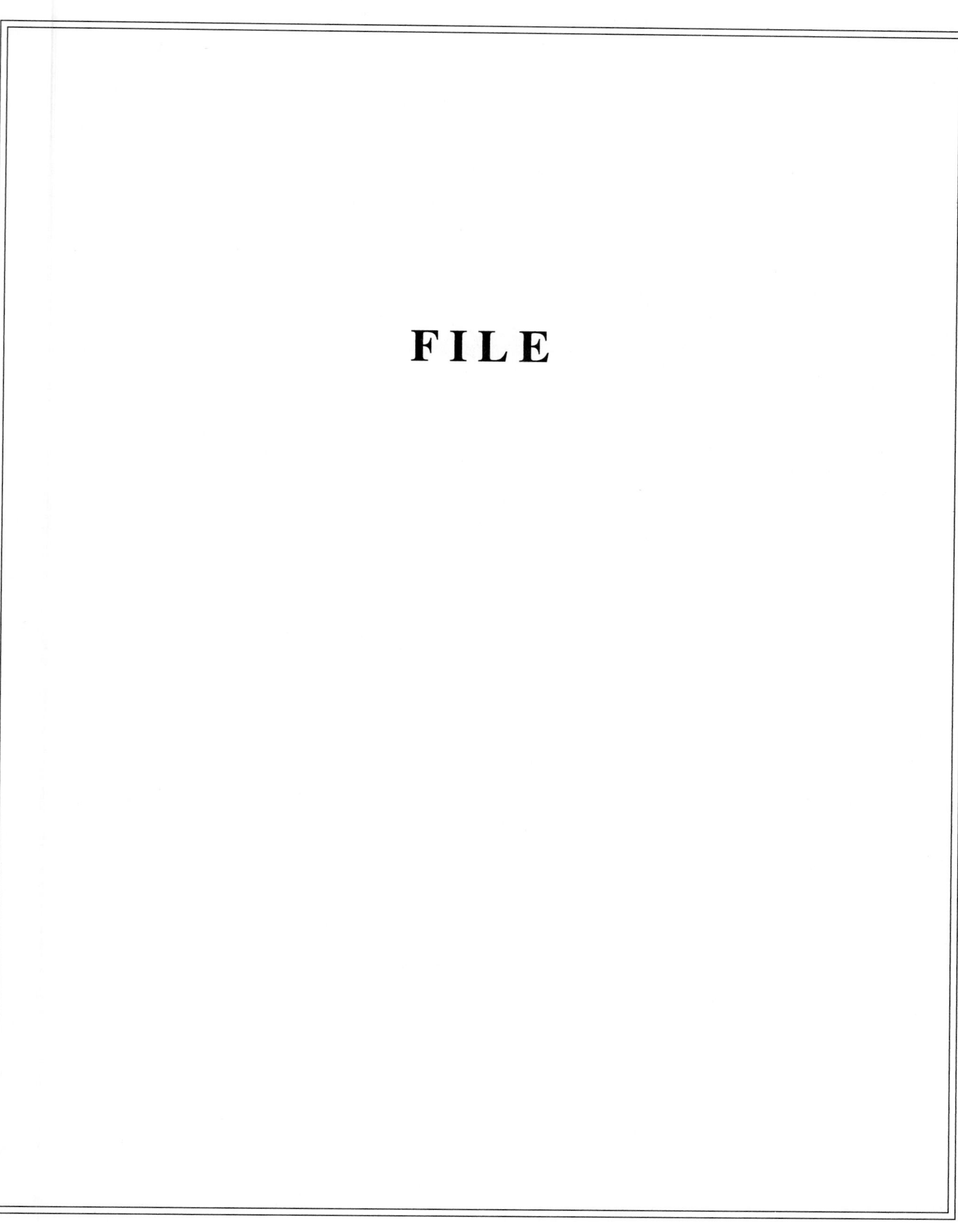
FILE

Andrews, Ewing & Oakman
1656 Barrington Boulevard
Cascade, Franklin 33339

MEMORANDUM

To: Applicant
From: Denise Samuels
Re: Marian Bonner matter

July 27, 2004

Dr. Nicole Hall is the daughter of Dr. Marian Bonner, one of the most prominent educational reformers in this country. Dr. Hall wants to stop the Success for Every Child Association (SECA), a for-profit educational corporation, from the unauthorized use of her deceased mother's writings and name.

We do not yet know if SECA got physical possession of the writings lawfully. Nevertheless, we have enough information to proceed with an action based on Dr. Hall's copyright in the materials and her right to assert a violation of her mother's right of publicity. However, Dr. Hall would prefer to resolve this matter informally. I told her I would write a demand letter to SECA's attorney for her to review.

I need your help in drafting the demand letter to William Drake, the attorney for SECA. We want to convince him that if SECA uses Dr. Bonner's writings and her name, it will infringe on Dr. Hall's copyright and will violate the right of publicity. In fact, SECA might have already violated the right of publicity by announcing its intended plans.

Your letter should contain

- a description of the dispute;
- a brief statement of the salient facts; and
- arguments that support our position concerning copyright infringement and the right of publicity.

Your arguments should incorporate the facts and the authorities.

You should address only Dr. Hall's claims of copyright infringement and violation of the right of publicity. Do not concern yourself with Dr. Hall's potential claims for injunctive relief, damages, or return of the papers themselves. I will address these issues and later amend your letter to include them.

Transcript of Interview with Nicole Hall
July 26, 2004

Attorney: Good to see you, Nicole. The Library Association letter you dropped off is astounding.

Client: So much to take in. But I need to make some decisions quickly to preserve my mother's legacy. You need to help me figure out how to stop this sleazy, so-called educational group from desecrating my mother's name and using it for purposes she would have abhorred. She remained deeply committed to public education, even with its shortcomings. Making a profit from public education was anathema to her. I also don't want them misusing her writings to promote their own agenda.

Attorney: Tell me more of the background. What do you know about your mother's writing?

Client: Not much. She talked about writing another book that would help people understand why she tried all her projects, including those that had gone wrong. But she was constantly on to the next project. I never saw any writing on her desk or in her study. She was very conflicted about her academic impulses to analyze the world and her activist impulses to change it. And, at the end of her life, she became depressed, as well as disheartened. Only the kids in her classes kept her going.

Attorney: Were you involved with your mother during her last years?

Client: Sure. I visited her about twice a month in Stone Park. We got along fine.

Attorney: Tell me why you didn't end up with her papers.

Client: I didn't clean out her house. My niece, Celina Miller, lived close to my mother, and they saw each other often. Celina called me when my mother had her stroke. My mother was able to communicate only a little so there was no chance to discuss anything. In her will, she had given me everything, so I didn't think there was much about property or arrangements to talk about anyway.

Attorney: What happened after she died?

Client: After the small, private memorial service in Stone Park—my mother was very clear that this sort of event was all she wanted—Celina wanted to go through my mother's house and pack things up. I offered to be there, but she wanted to be alone. I thought she sent everything to me. There were no papers. There were photographs and other personal stuff, but no writings.

Attorney: Have you discovered anything since you got the Library Association letter?

Client: I called Celina. She remembered two packing boxes labeled "papers" in a closet with numerous projects done by my mother's students—pottery, mobiles, posters, dioramas. Celina thought the boxes contained student papers. Celina put the boxes in her van, covered them with bags filled with the student projects, and took them to Husein Aboud—a neighbor who had been very kind to my mother—for storage in his garage. Celina meant to return them to the students, but forgot.

Attorney: Do you know how the papers got from the garage to SECA?

Client: Some people Celina thought were from the school contacted her about six months after my mother's death about papers my mother had. Celina thought they meant the student papers so she told them where they were. I called Husein, and he remembered checking with Celina and letting the people take everything. He, too, thought they were from Stone Park schools, but he doesn't know if they actually said that.

Attorney: Anything else?

Client: Nothing now. What do we do?

Attorney: A few preliminaries. Your mother did bequeath everything to you. When we probated your mother's will, all her personal property went to you, including all her personal papers and her copyright in those papers. There is an oddity of copyright law that makes ownership complex. Ownership of the physical papers and ownership of the copyright are independent of each other. When your mother died, both the physical papers and her copyright became yours. Because of this distinction, we have two routes to pursue. We need to get back the physical papers as fast as possible. I will immediately dispatch our best investigator to find out more about how SECA acquired the papers, so we can figure out if SECA obtained them lawfully. We can then decide what to do to get the papers back.

Client: I'm not sure I understand the distinction between ownership of the copyright and the papers themselves.

Attorney: Yes, it is sort of counterintuitive. Let me give you an example. Suppose you write a personal letter and send it to someone. You own the copyright in the letter and you also own the right of publication and distribution, even though the recipient owns the letter.

Client: Okay, now I think I understand. I'd like to move as fast as possible. Who knows what they're doing with my mother's papers.

Attorney: Second, we can move quickly to stop SECA from taking any actions involving the copyrighted material in the papers. We can send a letter demanding that they take no action regarding the papers. We can also include a demand in the letter that SECA stop from violating what is called your mother's right of publicity. They may have already misused her name and renown for

their own purposes. We may need to get SECA to reverse action they've already taken. If this doesn't work, we can file a lawsuit seeking an injunction and damages. Once we learn whether SECA has done anything unlawful in obtaining the papers, we may add a claim for return of the papers themselves.

Client: I'm relieved that there are actions that we can take—quickly.

Attorney: I know and respect SECA's lawyer, Bill Drake, and I believe a letter fully stating our position might resolve everything. SECA could avoid a lot of bad publicity and maybe damages for wrongful actions if they agree not to go ahead with any of their plans or to take any other actions involving use of your mother's name or private writings without your permission. If this letter works, it would be the quickest and cleanest way to resolve the problem. If it doesn't work, we can go ahead with the other plan. We might lose a few days, but this will give SECA's lawyer time to do the right thing.

Client: My mother would have liked this all resolved quietly.

Attorney: I'll prepare a draft of a letter to the lawyer and call you by noon tomorrow.

* * * *

The Franklin Library Association
452 Ocean Boulevard
Franklin City, Franklin 33100

Elizabeth Philips, *Associate Director for Acquisitions*

July 23, 2004

Dr. Nicole Hall
491 Fayette Street
Cascade, Franklin 33337

Dear Dr. Hall:

I write concerning developments of great urgency and significance to the preservation and dissemination of the work of your distinguished mother, Dr. Marian Bonner. The Franklin Library Association just learned that the Success for Every Child Association (SECA) has recently obtained a cache of your mother's personal materials, including letters and journals covering the period from 1952 to 2003, and handwritten drafts of speeches.

Yesterday, SECA, a for-profit educational corporation, announced in a press release and news conference that it had acquired previously unknown materials of great historical and social value written by your mother and is planning to change its name to the Marian Bonner Educational Group. I immediately contacted Louise Boyle, the CEO of SECA, to inquire about the material and SECA's plans for its use. Ms. Boyle referred me to William Drake, counsel for SECA. Mr. Drake said that he could not disclose how SECA had acquired the materials, but he did say that there were more than 300 letters, 50 handwritten speeches, and 10 volumes of journals, spanning the entire length of Dr. Bonner's career and all apparently written in her handwriting. Mr. Drake indicated that, in conjunction with a celebration marking its name change, SECA plans to publish and distribute to all state legislators REDISCOVERING MARIAN BONNER'S LEGACY, a small volume of excerpts from your mother's newly discovered writings that stress the need for attention to the individual needs of each child, the signature focus of SECA. Following the publication, SECA intends to sell your mother's materials to collectors. Furthermore, SECA has already been awarded contracts by state legislators to run pilot programs in three Franklin cities to take over "under-performing" schools. SECA is positioning itself to be the major for-profit educational provider in Franklin and beyond. Identification with your mother's work will advance SECA's commercial goals.

I am sure that you understand the enormous historical significance of your mother's work. There are

large gaps in our understanding of her. Scholars have her groundbreaking book, DISCRIMINATION, PUBLIC EDUCATION, AND DEMOCRACY, and the records from her work as a citizen member on the Franklin Education Commission are in our archives, but there is little personal material that provides insight into developments in her thought and in her evaluation of her own efforts. These materials are more than of utmost importance to scholars, however. They are a legacy for the public, especially for all who care about education, racial equality, and the creation of a better world. It is highly unlikely that research libraries can afford to go head-to-head with wealthy bidders when these materials are sold. In addition, Mr. Drake indicated that SECA intends to sell the materials in separate units, which will mean that they will be dispersed in various sites around the country and may be totally inaccessible or accessible only on a restricted basis.

I write because I fear that you may not be aware of these developments. I have also rather presumptuously assumed that you are concerned about academic and public access to your mother's work. From your own work as a physician in the leadership of public health efforts in Franklin, I know that you have worked tirelessly on behalf of expanding both public understanding and academic research. I am also aware from accounts of the latter years of your mother's life that she was reclusive. Therefore, I have made inferences that may not be correct. I am hopeful that you may wish to initiate action to forestall or halt these developments. The Library Association can do little directly. We are available, however, to assist you. The Library Association may also be able to help if you are interested in pursuing publication of an annotated edition of your mother's papers.

Sincerely yours,

Elizabeth Philips

Elizabeth Philips, Ph.D.
Associate Director for Acquisitions

Dictionary of Historical Biography for The State of Franklin

Marian Bonner (1922-2003) - A noted scholar, dynamic social reformer, and tireless citizen advocate, Marian Bonner played a major role in designing and implementing an innovative strategy for dismantling the system of *de facto* racial segregation in the public school system in Franklin. In 1952, Bonner received a dual Ph.D. from the University of Franklin in American History and Sociology. Her dissertation analyzing the interaction of the complex historical and sociological factors that contributed to actual, although not legally mandated, racial segregation in public schooling in Franklin was published by Franklin University Press in 1954, the year of the United States Supreme Court's decision in *Brown v. Topeka Board of Education* that outlawed *de jure* segregation in public education. Bonner's work provided the first major academic analysis of how eradicating legally imposed segregation of public schools would not by itself produce racially integrated schools. DISCRIMINATION, PUBLIC EDUCATION, AND DEMOCRACY was awarded the prestigious *Hanson Prize in History* in 1955.

While a faculty member in the Sociology Department at the University of Franklin for twelve years, Bonner developed her ideas about how to achieve racially integrated schools. She worked on proposals in the areas of housing and employment. Believing that changes in residential segregation would come slowly, she developed prototypes of public educational systems with flexibly drawn school boundaries based on factors other than geographical location. Throughout her career, Bonner argued that a publicly funded, operated, and controlled school system was essential to racial justice and democratic participation.

Known as "The Great Educator," with a national reputation as a pre-eminent educational reformer, Bonner was chosen in a yearly poll conducted by the *Franklin Daily Times* as Educator of the Year fifteen times. More public schools in Franklin are named after her than any other individual. The Franklin Education Association awarded her its prestigious *Champion of Education Award*, which it has presented only four times in its fifty-year history. In 1986, the Douglas Foundation recognized Bonner with its yearly lifetime achievement award to the citizen of Franklin who most powerfully shaped national policy debate. From 1976 to 1988, Bonner served on the Committee of Trustees for the University of Franklin.

In 1988, despite her considerable power, prestige, and influence, Bonner announced publicly that she was discouraged by the continuing barriers to educational equity, even in Franklin, where many had made sustained efforts to accomplish change. Little is known about the professional and personal sources of Bonner's discontent. Bonner moved to Stone Park, a small town in northern Franklin with a high percentage of African-American residents, where she had grown up and attended public school. She taught first grade at Stone Park Elementary School, where she worked until she died of a stroke in 2003.

See also NOTABLE AMERICAN WOMEN, PROMINENT AMERICAN EDUCATORS, AFRICAN-AMERICANS IN PUBLIC LIFE.

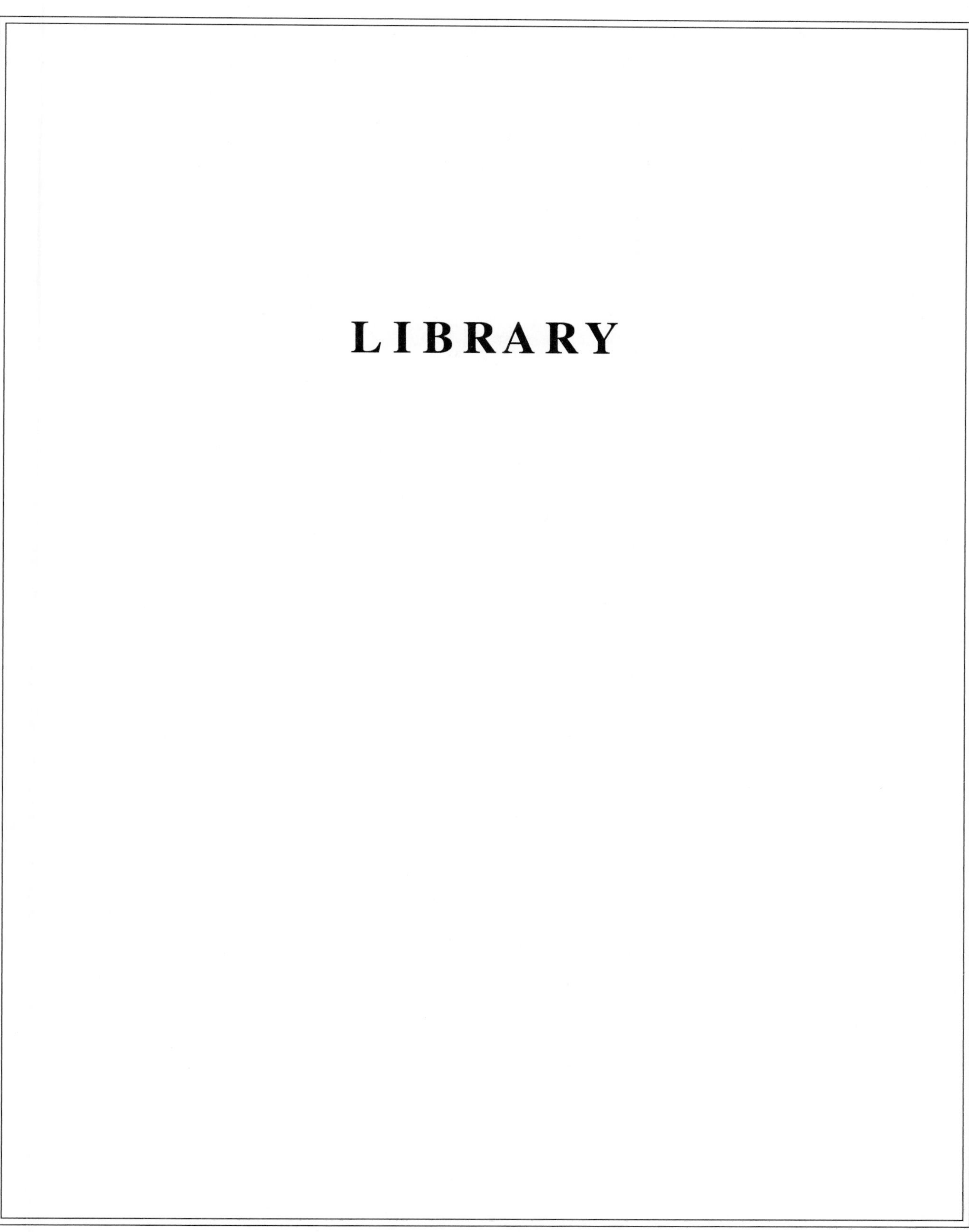
LIBRARY

UNITED STATES CODE

Title 17. Copyright

* * * *

§ 102. Subject matter of copyright: In general

(a) Copyright protection subsists, in accordance with this title, in original works of authorship fixed in any tangible medium of expression, ... Works of authorship include the following categories:

(1) literary works;

* * * *

(4) musical works;

* * * *

§ 106. Exclusive rights in copyrighted works

Subject to section 107 . . . , the owner of a copyright under this title has the exclusive rights to do and to authorize any of the following:

(1) to reproduce the copyrighted work in copies . . .;

* * * *

(3) to distribute copies . . . of the copyrighted work to the public by sale or other transfer of ownership, or by rental, lease, or lending;

* * * *

(5) in the case of literary . . . works, . . . to display the copyrighted work publicly;

* * * *

§ 107. Limitations on exclusive rights: Fair use

Notwithstanding the provisions of section 106 . . . , the fair use of a copyrighted work, including such use by reproduction in copies . . . or by any other means specified by that section, for purposes such as criticism, comment, news reporting, teaching (including multiple copies for classroom use), scholarship, or research, is not an infringement of copyright. In determining whether the use made of a work in any particular case is a fair use the factors to be considered shall include—

(1) the purpose and character of the use, including whether such use is of a commercial nature or is for nonprofit educational purposes;

(2) the nature of the copyrighted work;

(3) the amount and substantiality of the portion used in relation to the copyrighted work as a whole; and

(4) the effect of the use upon the potential market for or value of the copyrighted work.

The fact that a work is unpublished shall not itself bar a finding of fair use if such finding is made upon consideration of all the above factors.

* * * *

§ 201. Ownership of copyright

(a) Initial ownership. Copyright in a work protected under this title vests initially in the author or authors of the work. . . .

* * * *

(d) Transfer of ownership.

(1) The ownership of a copyright may be transferred in whole or in part by any means of conveyance or by operation of law, and may be bequeathed by will or pass as personal property by the applicable laws of intestate succession.

* * * *

§ 501. Infringement of copyright

(a) Anyone who violates any of the exclusive rights of the copyright owner . . . is an infringer of the copyright . . . .

* * * *

Campbell v. Acuff-Rose Music, Inc.

United States Supreme Court (1994)

We are called upon to decide whether 2 Live Crew's commercial parody of Roy Orbison's song, "Oh, Pretty Woman," may be a fair use within the meaning of the Copyright Act of 1976, 17 U.S.C. § 107. The Court of Appeals held that commercial use by 2 Live Crew made it presumptively unfair.

In 1964, Roy Orbison and William Dees wrote a rock ballad called "Oh, Pretty Woman" and assigned their rights in it to respondent Acuff-Rose Music, Inc.

Petitioners Luther R. Campbell, Christopher Wongwon, Mark Ross, and David Hobbs are collectively known as 2 Live Crew, a popular rap music group. In 1989, Campbell wrote a song entitled "Pretty Woman," which he later described as intended, "through comical lyrics, to satirize the original work." Acuff-Rose sued 2 Live Crew and its record company for copyright infringement.

It is uncontested here that 2 Live Crew's song would be an infringement of Acuff-Rose's rights in "Oh, Pretty Woman," under the Copyright Act of 1976, 17 U.S.C. § 106, but for a finding of fair use. The fair use doctrine permits and requires courts to avoid rigid application of the copyright statute when, on occasion, it would stifle the very creativity which that law is designed to foster.

Section 107 of the Copyright Act sets forth four factors to be considered together, in light of the purposes of copyright.

A. The first factor is the purpose and character of the use. § 107(1). The central purpose of this investigation is to see, in Justice Story's words, whether the new work merely "supersede[s] the objects" of the original creation or instead adds something new, with a further purpose or different character, altering the first with new expression, meaning, or message; it asks, in other words, whether and to what extent the new work is "transformative." Although such transformative use is not absolutely necessary for a finding of fair use, the goal of copyright, to promote science and the arts, is generally furthered by the creation of transformative works. Such works thus lie at the heart of the fair use doctrine's guarantee of breathing space within the confines of copyright, and the more transformative the new work, the less will be the significance of other factors, like commercialism, that may weigh against a finding of fair use.

Parody has an obvious claim to transformative value. Like less ostensibly humorous forms of criticism, it can provide social benefit, by shedding light on an earlier work, and, in the process, creating a new one. Parody, like other comment or criticism, may claim fair use under §107.

The "fact that a publication was commercial as opposed to nonprofit is a separate factor that tends to weigh against a finding of fair use." *Harper & Row v. Nation Enterprises* (U.S. Supreme Court, 1985). That tendency will vary with the context. The use, for example, of a copyrighted work to advertise a product, even in a parody, will be entitled to less indulgence under the first

factor of the fair use enquiry than the sale of a parody for its own sake.

B. The second statutory factor, "the nature of the copyrighted work," § 107(2), calls for recognition that some works are closer to the core of intended copyright protection than others, with the consequence that fair use is more difficult to establish when the former works are copied. For example, if a work is unpublished, that is "a key, although not a determinative factor," weighing heavily against a finding of fairness. *See Harper & Row, supra*. Also, courts accord greater copyright protection to creative works, as opposed to those that are factual in nature.

The Orbison original's creative expression for public dissemination falls within the core of the copyright's protective purposes. This fact, however, is not much help since parodies almost invariably copy publicly known, expressive works.

C. The third factor asks whether "the amount and substantiality of the portion used in relation to the copyrighted work as a whole," § 107(3), are reasonable in relation to the purpose of the copying. The enquiry will harken back to the first of the statutory factors, for we recognize that the extent of permissible copying varies with the purpose and character of the use. *See Harper & Row, supra.* "Even substantial quotations might qualify as fair use in a review of a published work or a news account of a speech" but not in a scoop of a soon-to-be-published memoir.

In *Harper & Row*, for example, the *Nation Weekly* had taken only some 300 words out of President Ford's memoirs, but we signaled the significance of the quotations in finding them to amount to the heart of the book, the part most likely to be newsworthy and important in licensing serialization. Whether a substantial portion of the infringing work was copied verbatim from the copyrighted work is a relevant question for it may reveal a dearth of transformative character or purpose under the first factor, or a greater likelihood of market harm under the fourth; a work composed primarily of an original, particularly its heart, with little added or changed, is more likely to be a merely superseding use, fulfilling demand for the original.

D. The fourth fair use factor is "the effect of the use upon the potential market for or value of the copyrighted work." §107(4). Since fair use is an affirmative defense, its proponent would have difficulty carrying the burden of demonstrating fair use without favorable evidence about relevant markets.

When a commercial use amounts to mere duplication of the entirety of an original, it serves as a market replacement for it, making it likely that cognizable market harm to the original will occur. But when, on the contrary, the second use is transformative, market substitution is at least less certain, and market harm may not be so readily inferred. The parody and the original usually serve different market functions.

It was error for the Court of Appeals to conclude that the commercial nature of 2 Live Crew's parody of "Oh, Pretty Woman" rendered it presumptively unfair. The court also erred in holding that 2 Live Crew had necessarily copied excessively from the Orbison original, considering the parodic purpose of the use. We therefore reverse the judgment of the Court of Appeals and remand the case for further proceedings consistent with this opinion.

Martin Luther King, Jr., Center for Social Change, Inc. v. Bolen Products, Inc.

Franklin Supreme Court (1982)

Three certified questions come from the United States Court of Appeals for the Fifteenth Circuit.

The plaintiff is the Martin Luther King, Jr., Center for Social Change (the Center), a non-profit corporation that seeks to promote the ideals of Dr. King. Defendant Bolen Products, Inc., which manufactures and sells plastic products as funeral accessories, developed the concept of marketing a plastic bust of Dr. King.

Bolen sought the endorsement and participation of the Center, but the Center refused. Bolen, nevertheless, hired an artist to prepare a mold and an agent to handle the promotion of the product. Bolen's advertisements offered the bust as "an exclusive memorial" and "an opportunity to support the Martin Luther King, Jr., Center for Social Change." The advertisement stated that "a contribution from your order goes to the King Center for Social Change" and promised a Certificate of Appreciation. Out of the $29.95 purchase price, Bolen set aside 3% ($.90) as a contribution to the Center. The magazine advertisements contained photographs of Dr. King and excerpts from his copyrighted speeches.

On December 19, 1980, plaintiff demanded that defendant cease and desist from further advertisements and sales of the bust, and, on December 31, 1980, moved for a preliminary injunction in United States District Court, which sought (1) an end to the use of the Center's name in advertising and marketing the busts, (2) restraint of any further copyright infringement, and (3) an end to the manufacture and sale of the plastic busts. The court, based on the defendant's agreement to discontinue the use of the Center's name in further promotion, granted this part of the injunction. The court, having found that the defendant had infringed the copyrights, enjoined all further use of the copyrighted material. In ruling on the third request, the court confronted the plaintiff's claim that the manufacture and sale of the busts violated Dr. King's right of publicity, which had passed to his heirs upon Dr. King's death. The district court concluded that it was not necessary to determine whether the right of publicity was devisable in Franklin because Dr. King had not commercially exploited this right during his lifetime.

1. Does Franklin recognize a right of publicity?

This right may be defined as a celebrity's right to the exclusive use of his or her name and likeness, most often asserted by or on behalf of professional athletes and entertainers. This case involves none of those occupations. Dr. King, a Baptist minister, was the foremost leader of the civil rights movement in the United States. He was awarded the Nobel Prize for Peace in 1964. Although not a public official, Dr. King was a public figure.

Franklin has long recognized the right of publicity as developing out of the right of privacy. In *Pavesich v. New England Life Ins. Co.* (Franklin Supreme Court, 1905), the court found that the publication of a person's picture, without his consent, as a part of an advertisement, for the

purpose of exploiting the publisher's business, is a violation of the right of privacy. Although the question was not involved in the case, the court noted that, while the right of privacy is personal, and may die with the person, the relatives of the deceased may, in a proper case, protect the memory of their kinsman, not only from defamation, but also from an unconsented-to invasion. Finding that Pavesich, although an artist, was not recognized as a public figure, the court also left open the question facing us involving the likeness of a public figure.

The right of publicity was first recognized in *Palmer v. Schonhorn Enterprises, Inc.* (Franklin Supreme Court, 1967). In *Palmer,* Arnold Palmer obtained summary judgment against the manufacturer of a golf game that used his name and biography without his consent. The Franklin Supreme Court held that although the publication of biographical data of a well-known figure does not per se violate the right of publicity, the use of that same data for the purpose of capitalizing upon the name by using it in connection with a commercial project other than the dissemination of news or articles or biographies does. "One should not be permitted to commercialize or exploit or capitalize upon another's name, reputation, or accomplishments merely because the accomplishments have been highly publicized." As in *Palmer*, we deal here with the unauthorized use of a person's name and likeness for the commercial benefit of the user, not with a city's use of a celebrity's name to denominate a street or school.

The right of publicity is not absolute. In *Hicks v. Casablanca Records* (1978), the Franklin Supreme Court held that a fictional novel and movie concerning an unexplained eleven-day disappearance by Agatha Christie, author of numerous mystery novels, were permissible under the First Amendment.

The Franklin courts have recognized the rights of private citizens, as well as entertainers, not to have their names and photographs used for the financial gain of the user without their consent, where such use is not authorized as an exercise of the First Amendment. A public figure prominent in religion and civil rights should be entitled to no less protection. We hold that the appropriation of another's name and likeness without consent and for financial gain is a tort in Franklin, whether the person whose name and likeness is used is a private citizen, entertainer, or a public figure. The measure of damages to a public figure for violation of his or her right of publicity is the value of the appropriation to the user.

2. Does the right of publicity survive the death of its owner?

Whether the right of publicity is inheritable is a question of first impression in Franklin. Courts are divided. In *Johnson v. Marvin Studios* (S.D.N.Y. 1975), the court held that since the right of publicity was assignable, it survived the deaths of Stanley Laurel and Oliver Hardy. The court reasoned that, if the right is descendible, the individual is able to transfer the benefits of his labor to his immediate successors and is assured that control over the exercise of the right can be vested in a suitable beneficiary. Furthermore, the court found that advertisers should not receive a windfall in the form of freedom to use with impunity the name or likeness of deceased celebrities who may have worked their entire lives to attain their status. The financial benefits of that labor should go to the celebrities' heirs.

Conversely, in *Lugosi v. Universal Pictures* (California Supreme Court, 1979), the California Supreme Court declared that the right of publicity expires upon the death of the celebrity. Bela Lugosi appeared as Count Dracula in Universal Pictures' movie by that name. Universal entered into a contract with Bella Lugosi that gave Universal the right to exploit *in connection with* the movie all aspects of Lugosi's performance. Lugosi, however, retained the right to exploit his name and likeness in association with the Dracula character for all other purposes. Such a right, protectable during Lugosi's lifetime, did not survive his death. The court held that Lugosi's heirs could not prevent Universal's continued exploitation of Lugosi's portrayal of Count Dracula for purposes not connected to the movie. The California court reasoned that the very decision to exploit name and likeness is a personal one. Because the ancestor did not exploit the flood of publicity received in his lifetime for commercial purposes, the opportunity to have done so should not descend to his heirs. Now that Bela Lugosi is dead, the heirs seek to be the only ones who can exploit their ancestor's personality. The court asked, "Should similar rights automatically transfer to succeeding heirs? May remote descendants obtain damages for the unauthorized commercial use of the name or likeness of their distinguished ancestors? If not, where is the line to be drawn, and who should draw it?" Assuming that some durational limitation would be appropriate, the court thought that setting the limit went beyond the scope of judicial authority.

Recognizing important policy concerns on both sides of this judicial uncertainty, we hold that in Franklin the right of publicity may, in certain circumstances, survive the death of its owner and is inheritable. We are particularly concerned with exploitation for commercial purposes of the publicity right of a celebrity when the fame arises from noncommercial endeavors. Furthermore, we see no public purpose that would be served by the exploitation of a public figure's name and likeness. Therefore, we hold that, in Franklin, the right of publicity of a public figure survives his or her death if the unauthorized exploitation of that public figure for commercial purposes would not serve to reward or encourage effort and creativity that serve some significant public purpose.

3. Must the owner of the right of publicity have commercially exploited that right before it can survive?

A well-known minister may avoid exploiting his prominence during life because to do otherwise would impair his ministry. Should his election not to take commercial advantage of his position during life result in permitting others to exploit his name and likeness after his death? In our view, a person who avoids exploitation during life is entitled to have his or her image protected against exploitation after death just as much if not more than a person who exploited his image during life.

Dr. King could have exploited his name and likeness during his lifetime. That this opportunity was not appealing to him does not mean that others have the right to use his name and likeness in ways he himself chose not to do. Nor does it strip his family and estate of the right to control, preserve, and extend his status and memory, and to prevent unauthorized exploitation by others.

In re Marian Bonner

Sample Answer

Dear Mr. Drake:

I am writing to inform you about the dispute that has arisen between my client, Dr. Nicole Hall, the daughter of Dr. Marian Bonner and the sole beneficiary under her will, and your client, the Success for Every Child Association (SECA). Dr. Hall has recently been informed that SECA possesses boxes containing Dr. Bonner's writings which it intends to use, in conjunction with Dr. Bonner's name, to further SECA's commercial interests. I'm sending this letter with the goal of reaching an amicable agreement with SECA to refrain from its proposed infringement of Dr. Hall's copyright and unauthorized use of Dr. Bonner's writings and name, and to return the papers to their rightful owner, Dr. Hall. Such a resolution would preclude litigation with a possibility of extensive damages and the accompanying adverse publicity to SECA.

The salient facts are as follows: Dr. Hall inherited all of her mother's property, including all of her writings. Since Dr. Bonner, up to her death, had not transferred ownership of either her papers or the copyrights therein to anyone, ownership of the papers and copyrights therefore passed to Dr. Hall. Dr. Bonner's lifework was the development of a plan that would achieve racial integration in Franklin public schools. SECA is surely aware that Dr. Bonner was adamant in her belief that a publicly funded, operated, and controlled school system is essential to racial justice and democratic participation. The idea of making a profit from public education was abhorrent to her. Dr. Bonner's work and influence in shaping our national policy debate on public education was widely recognized and respected, both here in Franklin and nationwide.

The Franklin Library Association recently sent Dr. Hall a letter informing her that SECA, a private, for-profit corporation in the business of running certain public schools pursuant to a contract with the State of Franklin, has acquired possession of approximately 300 letters, 50 speeches, and 10 volumes of journals, all of which are in Dr. Bonner's handwriting. Moreover, SECA has announced its plans to change its name to the "Marian Bonner Educational Group." Dr. Hall was also informed that SECA plans to publish a volume entitled "Rediscovering Marian Bonner's Legacy," consisting of excerpts from Dr. Bonner's writings, which SECA plans to distribute to state legislators to announce SECA's name change. The chosen excerpts will emphasize Dr. Bonner's fervent belief that attention must be given to the needs of each child, a phrase that just happens to mimic SECA's corporate "signature focus." SECA then plans to sell the Bonner writings, separately, to the highest bidders.

If SECA takes these proposed actions, it will infringe Dr. Hall's copyright in the materials and violate the right of publicity that Dr. Hall inherited from her mother.

Dr. Hall's Protectible Copyright

Dr. Hall inherited the copyright to her mother's writings. These writings are subject to copyright protection under 17 U.S.C. sections 102 *et seq.* They qualify under section 102 because they are original works of authorship that are fixed in a tangible medium of expression, *i.e.*, on paper in Dr. Bonner's handwriting. They can most likely be classified as "literary works." Although ownership of the papers themselves and ownership of the copyrights are two separate rights, the original owner of the papers and copyrights, Dr. Bonner, by her will transferred ***both*** papers and copyrights to Dr. Hall. This type of transfer is allowed under section 201. Therefore, even if SECA's possession of the papers is legal, the copyrights legally belong to Dr. Hall, thus giving her the exclusive right to reproduce the writings, to publicly distribute copies by sale or by other means of transferring ownership, and to publicly display the writings. [17 U.S.C. §106]

We anticipate that SECA will claim fair use of the papers. As you know, fair use permits certain uses of copyrighted work that do not constitute infringement. Fair use is an affirmative defense which SECA

would have to prove to be absolved of copyright infringement. [*See* Campbell v. Acuff-Rose Music, Inc.] Under the facts here, SECA clearly cannot establish fair use upon consideration of the determinative four factors of section 107 which are further explained in *Campbell*.

1. **Purpose and Character of Use:** The first factor to consider is the purpose and character of the use, including whether it is of a commercial nature or is for nonprofit educational purposes. [17 U.S.C. §107(1)] This factor involves a two-prong analysis: (i) whether the work is transformative, and (ii) whether the intended use is for commercial gain. [Campbell]

The commercial use of a copyright can be a fair use if it is "transformative," which is a use that "adds something new, with a further purpose or different character, altering the [original] with new expression, meaning, or message." [Campbell] If Dr. Hall's information is accurate, SECA's plans to publish and distribute a volume of Dr. Bonner's writings is not transformative because it intends merely to select various excerpts from the writings, print them, and distribute them presumably without comment, critique, or other editing that would give a new meaning to, or message from, Dr. Bonner's writings. Thus, this use is clearly not transformative.

SECA also plans to announce its name change by publishing and distributing to state legislators excerpts of Dr. Bonner's writings that stress the necessity of taking care of each child's needs. This would not be considered a use for nonprofit educational purposes. We know that SECA has operated a pilot program for the state in a few schools and is now seeking contracts with the state to run under-performing Franklin schools. Its publication and distribution of the volume to Franklin legislators is an obvious attempt to enhance its reputation and improve its standing with the very same legislators who have the power to award contracts for operation of state schools. The distribution of the volume is clearly for a commercial purpose as is SECA's plan to sell Dr. Bonner's papers to the highest bidders. Although commercial use, standing alone, is not necessarily determinative, "it is a separate factor that tends to weigh against a finding of fair use." [Campbell—citing Harper v. Row] Therefore, SECA's purely commercial motive along with the lack of any transformative use strongly precludes a finding of fair use.

2. **Nature of Copyrighted Work:** The second factor considered in determining fair use is the nature of the copyrighted work. [17 U.S.C. §107(2)] The court in *Campbell* stated that the fact that a work is unpublished weighs heavily against a finding of fair use, and that "some works are closer to the core of intended copyright protection than others." [Campbell—citing Harper and Row] Courts also grant greater copyright protection to creative works, as opposed to works factual in nature. [Campbell]

Dr. Bonner's papers were both unpublished and creative, containing her own ideas and theories and not just facts. Dr. Hall believes that her mother intended to write another book, presumably based on the ideas and theories recorded in her papers. The Library Association's letter states that the papers possessed by SECA are the only source of information that illuminate the development of Dr. Bonner's ideas and her evaluation of her efforts to reform schools. If Dr. Bonner had planned to write another book about why she tried all her projects, her papers containing her thoughts and plans would be at the "core of intended copyright protection" as source materials for her book. To allow SECA to use them would nullify that protection, thus requiring a finding against fair use.

3. **Amount and Substantiality of Portion Used in Relation to Work as a Whole:** The third factor is the amount and substantiality of the portion used in relation to the copyrighted work as a whole; that is, whether those portions of the writings intended for use by SECA are reasonable in relation to the copyrighted work as a whole, both in terms of substance and amount. [Campbell] This question overlaps

the question as to whether the parts used are verbatim reproductions or transformative. The volume of excerpts that SECA plans to publish for legislators will highlight Dr. Bonner's belief in the necessity of giving each child's needs individual attention. This is the basic tenet underlying Dr. Bonner's educational theories. It is apparent that SECA intends to copy excerpts, word for word, in order to create an illusion that its corporate focus is to implement Dr. Bonner's goals. Even if the excerpts are but a small portion of Dr. Bonner's writings, they represent the central theme of her educational research and aspirations. The Library Association notes that these excerpts, relating to Dr. Bonner's basic theories, are the ones of greatest importance to scholars and the public. There is no doubt that the excerpts containing Dr. Bonner's core ideas are substantive parts of the entire writings. Even when small portions are used, fair use can be denied by courts, especially when the excerpts used are verbatim and have no transformative character [Campbell], as is the case here.

Furthermore, SECA plans to sell ***all*** of Dr. Bonner's papers, piecemeal, to the highest bidders, an act that would be an infringement of Dr. Hall's ***exclusive*** right, under 17 U.S.C. section 106(3) to distribute the writings. Because of the substantive nature of the excerpts, which go to the heart of Dr. Bonner's research and thought processes, the third factor also negates a finding of fair use.

4. Effect on Potential Market for or Value of Work: The fourth factor regarding fair use is the effect of the use on the potential market for, or value of, the copyrighted work. [17 U.S.C. §107(4)] The court in *Campbell* held that when a commercial use is merely a duplication of an original, it replaces the market for the original, thus harming the market. [Campbell] Here the excerpts volume is a mere duplication of some of Dr. Bonner's work and the sale of all of her original work clearly harms the market.

There are actually two markets here: (i) state legislators who have authority to award contracts, and (ii) collectors who will pay money for Dr. Bonner's work. Both markets clearly belong to Dr. Hall, successor to her mother's writings. Dr. Hall is a leader in public health efforts and as such she seeks to expand public understanding and academic research. Similarly, she is interested in expanding her mother's educational ideas and goals. Any plan she may have for putting into practice her mother's lifelong work, as expressed in the papers, could only be accomplished through the legislators and the legislative process. Dr. Hall's hope of implementing her mother's plans would be futile if SECA had already preempted the legislative market by distributing the volume of excerpts. Moreover, SECA's intention to break the papers into lots to sell separately to collectors would completely preempt that market as well. There would be no market remaining for the sale of papers by Dr. Hall, should she wish to do so.

In addition, the piecemeal sale of the papers to private collectors by SECA would destroy the academic and research market. According to the Library Association, Dr. Bonner's papers are of the "utmost importance to scholars" in that they would provide "insight into her thought and in her evaluation of her own efforts." The papers held in collector's hands would likely be scattered around the world, effectively denying access to not only the academic world, but also would prevent public access to papers important to those interested in public education, racial equality, and other subjects covered in Dr. Bonner's papers. It is overwhelmingly obvious that SECA's proposed actions, amounting to a mere duplication of part or all of the writings, would effectively destroy all relevant markets for the original writings.

Consideration of the four factors clearly demonstrates that SECA's proposed uses of Dr. Bonner's writings do not constitute fair use and will infringe on Dr. Hall's copyright. Accordingly, Dr. Hall demands that SECA abandon any and all plans to use the writings of Dr. Bonner that would infringe Dr. Hall's rights.

Dr. Hall's Right of Publicity

The right of publicity is also at stake here. This right consists of "a celebrity's right to the exclusive use of his or her name and likeness." [Martin Luther King, Jr., Center for Social Change, Inc. v. Bolen

Products, Inc.] This right is recognized in Franklin and applies to private and public figures. According to *Bolen Products*, the right is violated "...by using [the name] in connection with a commercial project other than dissemination of news or articles or biographies. . . ." That case also held that the right of publicity survives the death of a public figure if the unauthorized use is for commercial purposes and does not serve "to reward or encourage effort and creativity" that serves some significant public purpose.

Dr. Bonner clearly was a public figure. She was known as "The Great Educator," preeminent in her field, and had received numerous public awards and honors, both nationally and in Franklin. She was chosen Educator of the Year for 15 years by the *Franklin Daily Times*, was a Trustee for the University of Franklin, and had more Franklin public schools named after her than any other person. [*See* Dictionary of Historical Biography for the State of Franklin]

As a public figure, Dr. Bonner had a right of publicity that descended to Dr. Hall by will. Franklin law protects Dr. Hall's right against SECA's unauthorized commercial use for a multitude of reasons: Dr. Bonner's fame arose from her lifelong efforts for racial integration in, and improvement of, public schools—purely noncommercial efforts, while SECA's planned uses are for commercial purposes. SECA's planned uses would not reward Dr. Hall nor enhance her mother's reputation. In fact, Dr. Bonner would find such profiteering from public education repugnant, and SECA's planned uses would deprive Dr. Hall of valuable rights. Those uses also would not "reward or encourage effort or creativity that serves some significant public purpose." Rather they would do nothing more than further SECA's own commercial interests.

It is irrelevant that Dr. Bonner never sought to exploit her name in a commercial manner. As the court in *Bolen Products* held, " . . . a person who avoids exploitation during life is entitled to have his or her image protected against exploitation after death just as much if not more than a person who exploited his image during life."

Note that by announcing in a press release and news conference that it intended to change its name to the Marian Bonner Educational Group, SECA has already violated Dr. Hall's right of publicity, and must immediately halt any further actions to use the Bonner name.

In view of the copyright infringement and violation of the right of publicity described above, it is imperative that SECA refrain from using Dr. Bonner's name and writings. Compliance with this demand will not only save SECA the expense of litigation and subsequent damages, but will also preclude the negative publicity attendant to its misuse of Dr. Bonner's name and writings. Because of the need for immediate action to prevent harm to Dr. Hall's rights and Dr. Bonner's reputation, it is necessary that I receive your response to this demand within seven days in order to avoid further action by Dr. Hall.

Very truly yours,

Denise Samuels

Multistate Performance Test

Graham Realty, Inc. v. Brenda Chapin

National Conference of Bar Examiners

Preface

This Multistate Performance Test is a reprint of one of the three MPTs which were administered in July 2004.

The instructions for the test appear on the next page. On the actual MPT, they will appear on the back cover of the test.

INSTRUCTIONS

1. You will have 90 minutes to complete this session of the examination. This performance test is designed to evaluate your ability to handle a select number of legal authorities in the context of a factual problem involving a client.

2. The problem is set in the fictitious state of Franklin, in the fictitious Fifteenth Circuit of the United States. Columbia and Olympia are also fictitious states in the Fifteenth Circuit. In Franklin, the trial court of general jurisdiction is the District Court, the intermediate appellate court is the Court of Appeal, and the highest court is the Supreme Court.

3. You will have two kinds of materials with which to work: a File and a Library. The first document in the File is a memorandum containing the instructions for the task you are to complete. The other documents in the File contain factual information about your case and may include some facts that are not relevant.

4. The Library contains the legal authorities needed to complete the task and may also include some authorities that are not relevant. Any cases may be real, modified, or written solely for the purpose of this examination. If the cases appear familiar to you, do not assume that they are precisely the same as you have read before. Read them thoroughly, as if they all were new to you. You should assume that cases were decided in the jurisdictions and on the dates shown. In citing cases from the Library, you may use abbreviations and omit page references.

5. Your response must be written in the answer book provided. If you are taking this examination on a laptop computer, your jurisdiction will provide you with specific instructions. In answering this performance test, you should concentrate on the materials provided in the File and Library. What you have learned in law school and elsewhere provides the general background for analyzing the problem; the File and Library provide the specific materials with which you must work.

6. Although there are no restrictions on how you apportion your time, you should be sure to allocate ample time (about 45 minutes) to reading and digesting the materials and to organizing your answer before you begin writing it. You may make notes anywhere in the test materials; blank pages are provided at the end of the booklet. You may not tear pages from the question booklet.

7. This performance test will be graded on your responsiveness to the instructions regarding the task you are to complete, which are given to you in the first memorandum in the File, and on the content, thoroughness, and organization of your response.

INSTRUCTIONS

1. You will have 90 minutes to complete this session of the examination. This performance test is designed to evaluate your ability to handle a select number of legal authorities in the context of a factual problem involving a client.

2. The problem is set in the fictitious state of Franklin, in the fictitious Fifteenth Circuit of the United States. Columbia and Olympia are also fictitious states in the Fifteenth Circuit. In Franklin, the trial court of general jurisdiction is the District Court, the intermediate appellate court is the Court of Appeal, and the highest court is the Supreme Court.

3. You will have two kinds of materials with which to work: a File and a Library. The first document in the File is a memorandum containing the instructions for the task you are to complete. The other documents in the File contain factual information about your case and may include some facts that are not relevant.

4. The Library contains the legal authorities needed to complete the task and may also include some authorities that are not relevant. Any cases may be real, modified, or written solely for the purpose of this examination. If the cases appear familiar to you, do not assume that they are precisely the same as you have read before. Read them thoroughly, as if they all were new to you. You should assume that cases were decided in the jurisdictions and on the dates shown. In citing cases from the Library, you may use abbreviations and omit page references.

5. Your response must be written in the answer book provided. If you are taking the examination on a laptop computer, your jurisdiction will provide you with specific instructions. In answering this performance test, you should concentrate on the materials provided in the File and Library. What you have learned in law school and elsewhere provides the general background for analyzing the problem; the File and Library provide the specific materials with which you must work.

6. Although there are no restrictions on how you apportion your time, you should be sure to allocate ample time (about 45 minutes) to reading and digesting the materials and to organizing your answer before you begin writing it. You may make notes anywhere in the test materials; blank pages are provided at the end of the booklet. You may not tear pages from the question booklet.

7. This performance test will be graded on your responsiveness to the instructions regarding the task you are to complete, which are given to you in the first memorandum in the File, and on the content, thoroughness, and organization of your response.

Graham Realty, Inc. v. Brenda Chapin

FILE

LIBRARY

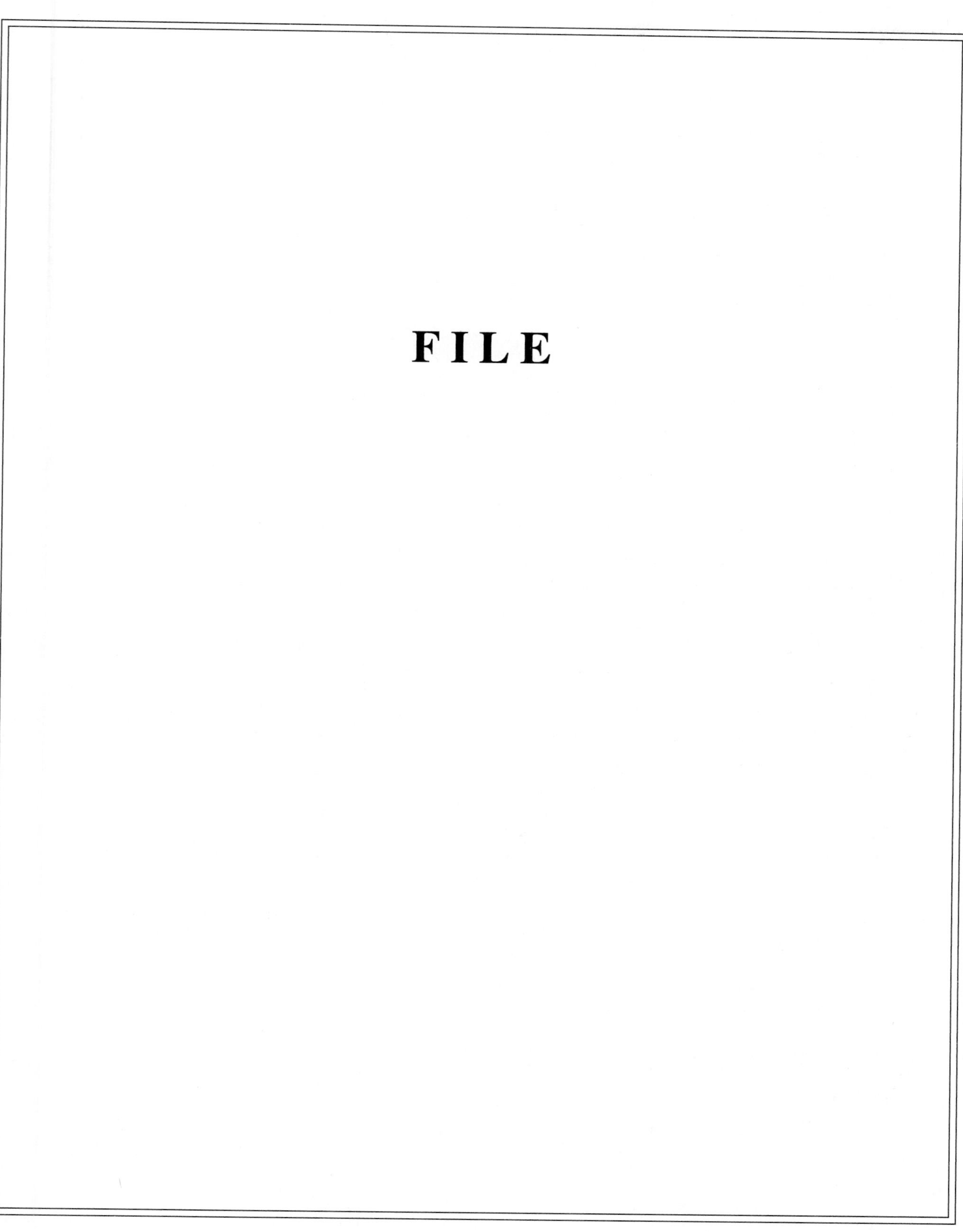

FILE

The Legal Aid Society
Briggs Neighborhood Office
Civil Division
Avon, Franklin 33210

To: Applicant
From: Joseph Murray, Supervising Attorney
Date: July 27, 2004
Re: *Graham Realty, Inc. v. Brenda Chapin*

Our client, Brenda Chapin, is a tenant living in an apartment owned by Graham Realty, Inc. (GRI). She has withheld her monthly rent of $1,000 for seven months because of the poor condition of her apartment. GRI is suing her for eviction and recovery of back rent. We have tried to settle the matter, but negotiations have broken off because of GRI's refusal to make any concessions regarding much-needed repairs in our client's apartment and the common areas of the building. The matter is set to be heard next week before the Housing Division Court.

To successfully defend against GRI's suit for eviction and recovery of back rent, we will have to prove that GRI breached the implied warranty of habitability. Assuming that we can prove such a breach, we also intend to seek damages available to Ms. Chapin as a result of GRI's breach.

Please draft a case planning memo for the summary eviction proceeding before the Housing Division Court. Citing the relevant legal authority, your memo should identify:

1) the elements we must establish to prove that GRI breached the implied warranty of habitability and the evidence available to establish these elements; and

2) the remedies available to Ms. Chapin, the elements of those remedies, and the evidence available to us to establish those elements. (You need not concern yourself with admissibility issues.)

You should also discuss whether there is any relief that Ms. Chapin might be entitled to pursue that *cannot* be obtained in this summary proceeding. If there is, state what it is and explain why.

Follow our office's "Case Planning Memorandum Guidelines" in drafting your memo. These guidelines include an excerpt of a case planning memorandum used in an unrelated case. As the guidelines instruct, do not include a separate statement of facts because here at the Legal Aid Society, these memos are strictly internal documents used to prepare for court.

The Legal Aid Society ***March 4, 2004***

Case Planning Memorandum Guidelines

Our office follows the practice of using a case planning memorandum (CPM) to prepare for court. A CPM is an internal document that identifies and evaluates, as applicable, the client's claims, counterclaims, defenses, and/or remedies. For each of these, cite the **Legal Authority,** including statutory and case law as applicable; the **Elements** that must be proven in order to establish the client's right to prevail; and the **Supporting Evidence** available to establish each element, including testimonial evidence, documentary evidence, and physical evidence.

A CPM should not include a separate statement of facts, as it is intended as a reference tool for attorneys already familiar with the case. Attached as an example is an excerpt from a CPM drafted for *Jimenez v. Brown Apartments,* a case we litigated in January 2002.

Excerpt from *Jimenez* Case Planning Memorandum

Claim: Breach of Franklin Fair Housing Law/Unlawful Housing Discrimination

Legal Authority: Section 530 of the Franklin Fair Housing Law prohibits a landlord from rejecting a prospective tenant's rental application solely because the application does not meet a particular income-to-rent ratio. A landlord's rejection of an application, notwithstanding the tenant's proof of actual ability to pay, is prima facie evidence of a violation of this section. *(Mooney v. Lutz Management Co.)*

Element #1: The landlord refused to lease residential premises to a prospective tenant because the tenant did not meet the minimum income-to-rent ratio.

Evidence available to show Brown Apartments refused to rent to David Jimenez based on his income level:

- Testimony of Jimenez that he completed Brown's standard rental application form, including providing information about his income.
- Copy of the application Jimenez submitted to Brown.
- Copy of Brown's standard rental application form, stating (in very fine print) that all tenants must have monthly income equal to four times monthly rent.
- Letter from Brown rejecting Jimenez's rental application.

Element #2: The prospective tenant established actual ability to pay rental amount.

Evidence available to show Jimenez's actual ability to pay rent charged by Brown:

- Jimenez's bank statement showing $5,000 in savings account.
- Written financial reference from previous landlord.

Remedy: Punitive Damages

Legal Authority: A court will award punitive damages to a tenant for a violation of §530 when such conduct is a pervasive practice by a landlord. *(Chong v. Riverside Apartments, LLC*—punitive damages upheld where landlord exhibited repeated disregard for the rights accorded tenants under §530)

Element: The landlord's pervasive practice is to reject applicants based on income level without considering actual ability to pay rent.

Evidence available to prove that Brown's pervasive practice violates §530:

- Copy of Brown's standard rental application form.
- Testimony of Brown's rental agent that the standard rental application form is used for *all* prospective tenants in Brown's five high-rise complexes in Avon.
- Copy of Brown's rental agent manual, which states that "rental agents must screen each prospective tenant for compliance with minimum income requirements using payroll statements only. . . ."

The Legal Aid Society
Briggs Neighborhood Office
Civil Division
Avon, Franklin 33210

To: File
From: Virginia Eilson, Intake Officer
Date: July 26, 2004
Re: Intake Notes: *Graham Realty, Inc. v. Brenda Chapin*

I interviewed Brenda Chapin, who has retained us to represent her in the summary eviction proceeding that is pending against her, *Graham Realty, Inc. v. Brenda Chapin.*

Client resides at Graham Towers, on the seventh floor in apartment 7B. Graham Towers is owned by Graham Realty, Inc. (GRI). When client moved into the apartment a year ago, some repairs were needed. She doesn't want to move if the apartment is repaired. "The housing market is so tight that I don't think I can find anything that would be better than this place at the price, but I want it to be fixed up." Client says her block is becoming "fancier." Herb London, GRI's building manager, told Ms. Albert, the owner of the grocery store at the corner and a friend of Ms. Chapin, that GRI wants to cash in on these apartments.

Client has about two years left on a 3-year lease at $1,000 per month. Utilities are not included in the rent. Graham Towers is a large and very old apartment building in the Briggs section of Avon. The apartment consists of two bedrooms, a living room, bathroom, and kitchen.

Client lives in the apartment with her two daughters, Harriett, age 3, and Mary, age 14. Her husband passed away two years ago. She was initially shown the apartment by Herb London. At that time, she noticed some of the repairs that were needed. Mr. London assured her that the repairs would be made, and she signed the lease. She paid rent for five months, but repairs weren't made and things got worse. Beginning in January 2004, client stopped paying her rent to try and force the owner to make the needed repairs.

Now GRI is suing to evict her and to collect the $7,000 in back rent.

Client complains that the bathroom ceiling leaks. A few chunks of plaster have fallen, injuring her daughter Mary (see copy of letter in file). Client wants to be reimbursed for daughter's medical bills as well as her (client's) lost wages. The ceiling looks like it is about to fall. One wall in the bathroom is discolored by a smelly, slimy green fungus that is spreading. She says the smell is overpowering.

Herb London promised to repair numerous cracks and holes in walls in the apartment and to paint. Nothing has been done to date. More plaster is falling from ceilings and walls. The entire apartment needs painting and plastering. "Why should I have to keep my promise to pay rent if he didn't keep his promise to fix the place?"

Heat and hot water sometimes don't work. Client has had to use her electric stove to heat apartment sometimes and has had to buy and use electric space heater. She has had to heat water on the stove to use for washing dishes and bathing. The space heater cost $79. Her electric bills have skyrocketed because of her additional use of the heater and the stove.

Client is very angry about rats. There are rat holes in the bedrooms and kitchen. She regularly sets traps and has killed four rats. GRI's building superintendent (Victor) came up and killed a rat once. She has had to throw away food in boxes (cereal, rice, etc.) after rats got into them. Rat droppings are everywhere, but there is no extermination service. Her daughters complain that they are afraid that the rats will come out as soon as the lights are turned off at night. She wants GRI punished for ignoring her situation.

In addition, the elevator has been unreliable, sometimes out of service for three to four days at a time. All of neighbors get angry when elevator is broken.

Client says she has constantly complained. Speaks to Victor often and has called London many times. She doesn't usually get through but leaves messages on London's answering machine and with secretary. Sent a letter to Herb London listing complaints; see copy of letter in file. She has taken pictures of some of the conditions (will bring them in if we need them) and reported her problems to the Avon Department of Buildings. Inspector came several times and gave her a copy of report. See copy of report in file. At the time of the inspections, the hot water was working.

Client believes that the repairs should be made immediately. She is willing to pay some of rent but "not much" from time she moved in until the repairs are completed. "Why should I pay good money for an apartment that is in bad condition and not worth nearly what GRI is charging? Some of my neighbors have moved out. Mr. London isn't renting those vacant units. Victor told me he's holding on to them, waiting for the rest of us to give up and leave in disgust. I really don't want to be forced out, but I refuse to pay $1,000 a month to live in a dump."

804 7th Avenue, Apt. 7B,
Avon, Franklin 33210
May 21, 2004

Mr. Herb London
Graham Realty, Inc.
222 French St.
Avon, Franklin 33210

Re: Problems in Graham Towers Apt. 7B

Dear Mr. London,

Over the past months, I have repeatedly called your office in an effort to get you to make repairs in my apartment. Usually when I call and give your secretary my name, I am told that you are not in. Other times I have left a message on your answering machine. On the few occasions when you have actually taken my calls, I have explained that there are a number of problems in the apartment. In all, my notes indicate that I have called eight times to complain.

In addition to my phone calls to you, I have spoken with Victor, the building superintendent, on many occasions about the problems in my apartment. I have even shown him the conditions that need to be fixed. Each time we talk, he tells me that he needs your permission before he can do anything. In spite of all my attempts, no repairs have been made in my apartment.

I am now upset about three particularly disturbing developments. First, two weeks ago, while my 14-year-old daughter, Mary, was using the bathroom, a large chunk of plaster fell from the ceiling, knocking her to the floor and causing a gash in her scalp, which required 10 stitches to close. This was very painful and we are both quite upset. My daughter missed a day of school and I missed a day of work. We also had to pay the hospital, and when I asked you to reimburse me, you refused. All of this could have been prevented if you had fixed the leaks in the ceiling that I have been complaining about for months.

Second, as you well know, we frequently do not have any heat in the building. When this happens, we are forced to make do by operating our electric stove, as well as the space heater we were forced to buy. It still isn't warm enough in the bedrooms. Furthermore, it is not safe to run the stove all night long. While we do not want to do anything that creates a fire hazard, we also do not want to freeze on cold nights.

Finally, late last night, Mary woke me up screaming because she was awakened by a rat that ran across her bed. We have complained about the rats before, but the problem is getting worse. My daughters are afraid to go to sleep for fear that a rat will bite them.

This situation is intolerable. You must do something to repair our apartment immediately, pay my daughter's medical bills, and compensate us for the pain you have caused. Thank you.

Very truly,

Brenda Chapin

Brenda Chapin

City of Avon Department of Buildings, Office of the Building Inspector

Violation Report

Address: **804 7th Avenue, Apt. 7B**, Avon, Franklin 33210
Date: July 6, 2004

HPD#	Range	Block	Lot	CD	Census Tract	Stories	A Units	B Units	Owner
3394	801-807	90210	2141	10	21800	8	100	0	Graham Realty Inc.

There are 5 violations listed below for Apartment 7B. Arranged by category-
A class: 0 B class: 2 C class: 3

Class Definitions

A: "Non-hazardous," such as minor leaks, chipping or peeling paint when no children under the age of six live in the home, or lack of signs designating floor numbers. An owner has 90 days to correct an A violation before fines will be assessed.

B: "Hazardous," such as public doors not self-closing, inadequate lighting in public areas or lack of posted Certificate of Occupancy. An owner has 30 days to correct a B violation before fines will be assessed.

C: "Immediately hazardous," such as inadequate fire exits, the presence of rodents or lead-based paint, or lack of heat, hot water, electricity, or gas. An owner has 24 hours to correct a C violation before fines will be assessed.

Apt.	Date Reported	Hazard Class	Violation ID #	Description
7B	February 2004	B	270421	repair broken or defective plastered surfaces and paint walls and ceilings in the entire apartment.
7B	February 2004	C	270422	abate the nuisance consisting of rodents in entire apartment.
7B	March 2004	B	321123	abate the nuisance consisting of evidence of a water leak on the bathroom ceiling.
7B	March 2004	C	321124	abate the nuisance consisting of mold-like substance existing along the south wall of the bathroom from ceiling to floor.
All	April 2004	C	398927	restore elevator service.

Avon Gazette

Section C: Real Estate July 20, 2004

Uptown Boomtown

By Emily Saylor

Marianne Conrad moved to Graham Towers fourteen years ago, when more than half the apartments were vacant and neighborhood drug dealers preyed on residents. Now the courtyard mailboxes carry the names of lawyers and doctors alongside those of pensioners, and rumors of co-op conversion swirl.

"A year ago, I could have bought a house in the Briggs section of Avon, but not now," Ms. Conrad says. "I can't afford it. And I'm basically middle-class. Unless you're upper management and making close to $300,000, I don't think anyone else can afford it, either. Today, a shell of a building in this area goes for $250,000. And I'm talking about no roof, no windows."

She's determined, however, not to let this boom pass her by completely. "I'm a social character, and I know lots of folks in Briggs, so I hear about things," Ms. Conrad says. "I'm always looking for my little niche, so I went three months ago and got a real estate license. Now if I hear about a house, I need to sell it."

Reaction to these changes is mixed at Graham Towers. Most tenants are pleased to see recent renovations to the building's exterior. However, longtime residents are apprehensive about the gentrification of the towers. According to Ms. Conrad, they are also concerned that "management is trying to force existing tenants out by ignoring necessary repairs so they can bring in well-heeled tenants and charge substantially higher rents."

In 1994, movie producer Dan Jackson used Graham Towers as the all-too-believable setting for a crack factory in "Broken Dreams." Ten years later, a company Jackson co-founded with his sister, Nicki, is just as keenly capturing the moment: Urban Box Office Network is the first major media outlet to move its headquarters to Briggs. Given the trend at Graham Towers and in the neighborhood, it won't be the last.

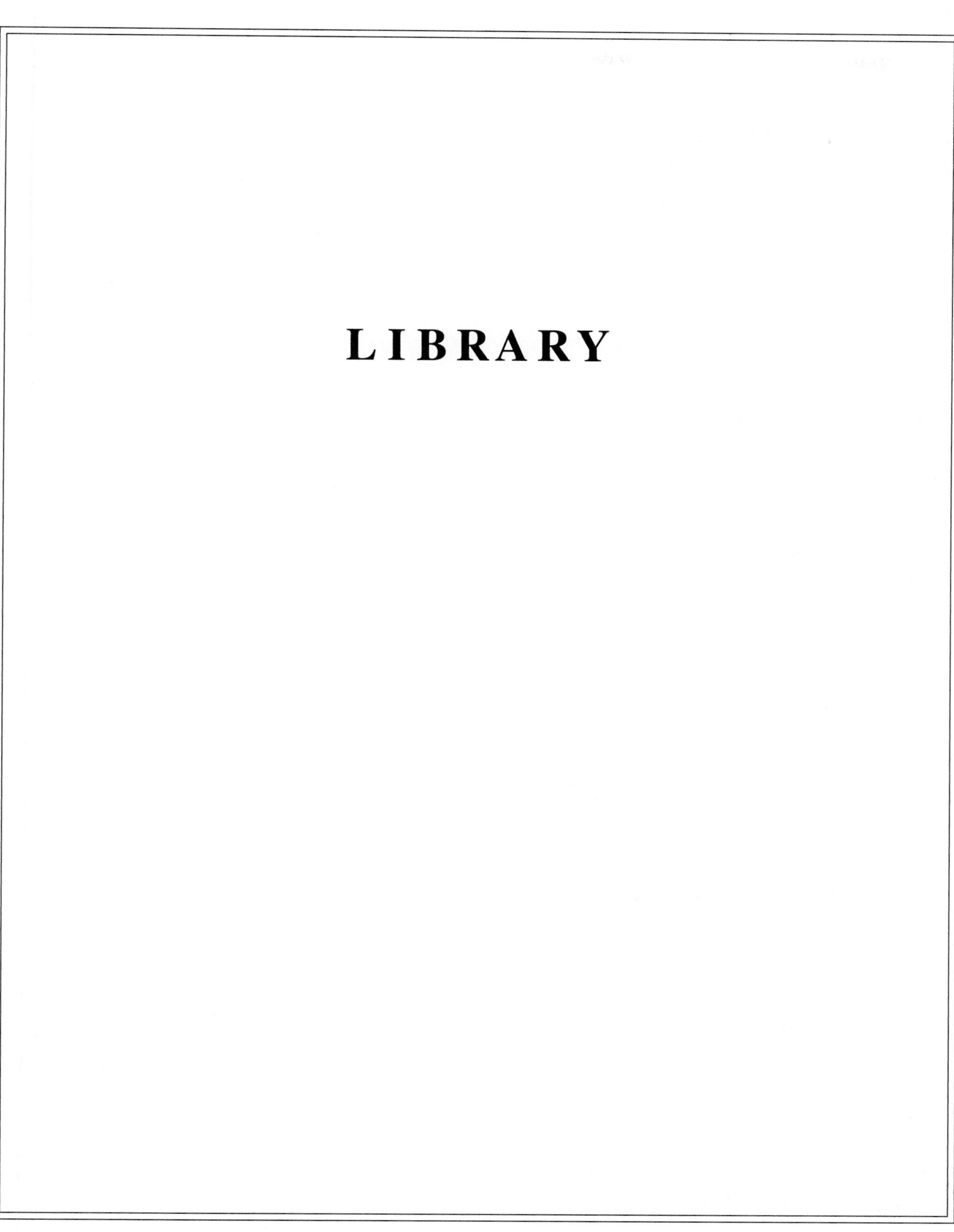

LIBRARY

Franklin Real Property Law

§500. Warranty of habitability

1. In every written or oral lease or rental agreement for residential premises, the landlord shall be deemed to warrant that

   (a) the premises so leased or rented and all areas used in connection therewith in common with other tenants or residents are fit for human habitation and for the uses reasonably intended by the parties; and

   (b) the occupants of such premises shall not be subjected to any conditions that would be dangerous, hazardous, or detrimental to their life, health, or safety.

2. Any agreement by a lessee or tenant of a dwelling waiving or modifying the rights as set forth in this section shall be void as contrary to public policy.

3. In determining the amount of damages sustained by a tenant, the court shall not require expert testimony.

Franklin District Court Act

§240. Housing Division of the Franklin District Court

A division of the court shall be devoted to actions and proceedings involving the enforcement of state and local laws for the establishment and maintenance of housing standards.

All summary proceedings to recover possession of residential premises or to remove tenants therefrom and to render judgment for rent due, including those cases in which a tenant alleges a defense relating to a stay of eviction proceedings or any action for rent abatement upon failure to make repairs, shall be brought in the Housing Division of the Franklin District Court.

Regardless of the relief originally sought by a party, the court may employ any remedy, program, procedure, or sanction authorized by law for the enforcement of housing standards that are effective to accomplish compliance or to protect and promote the public interest. This shall include, but not be limited to, the reduction of rent through abatement as well as the imposition of remedial and punitive damages.

Virgil v. Landy

Franklin Court of Appeal (1997)

Defendant appeals from a judgment rendered by the Housing Division of the Franklin District Court. The court ordered defendant landlord to pay plaintiff damages in the amount of $4,945 as reimbursement of all rent paid and additional compensatory damages. The award covered a 14-month period during which plaintiff rented a residential apartment in defendant's apartment building. On appeal, defendant raises two issues: first, whether the court correctly calculated the amount of damages; and second, whether the court's award to plaintiff of the entire amount of rent paid to defendant was proper since plaintiff remained in possession of the apartment for the entire 14-month period.

In October 1995, plaintiff began occupying an apartment in defendant's apartment building. Plaintiff has paid all rent due under her tenancy. Upon moving into the apartment, plaintiff discovered a broken kitchen window. Defendant promised to repair it, but, after waiting a week and fearing that her two-year-old grandchild might cut himself on the shards of glass, plaintiff repaired the window at her own expense. After moving in, plaintiff discovered that the toilet would flush only by dumping pails of water into it. The toilet remained mechanically inoperable throughout the period of plaintiff's tenancy. In addition, the bathroom light and wall outlet were inoperable. Plaintiff also discovered that the water pipes leaked down the walls of her back bedroom. As a result of this leakage, a large section of plaster fell from the back bedroom ceiling onto her bed and her grandson's crib. These conditions were brought to the attention of the defendant, but he never corrected them. Plaintiff moved her and her grandson's bedroom furniture into the living room and ceased using the back bedroom.

The court held that the state of disrepair of plaintiff's apartment, which was known to the defendant, substantially reduced the value of the leasehold from the agreed rental value and constituted a breach of the implied warranty of habitability. The district court based its award of damages on the breach of this warranty and on breach of an express contract. Defendant argues that, because plaintiff never abandoned the demised premises, it was error to award her the full amount of rent paid.

A lease is a contract between the landlord and the tenant wherein the landlord promises to deliver and maintain the demised premises in habitable condition and the tenant promises to pay rent for such habitable premises.

In the rental of any residential dwelling unit an implied warranty exists in the lease, whether oral or written, that the landlord will deliver over and maintain, throughout the period of the tenancy, premises that are safe, clean, and fit for human habitation. *See* Franklin Real Property Law § 500. The implied warranty of habitability covers all defects in the essential facilities of the residence. This implied warranty of habitability cannot be waived.

A substantial violation of an applicable housing code shall constitute prima facie evidence that there has been a breach of the warranty of habitability. One or two minor violations standing alone that do not affect the health or safety of the tenant shall be considered *de minimis* and not a breach of the warranty.

Regardless of whether there are Housing Code violations, in determining whether there has been a breach of the implied warranty of habitability, courts should inquire whether the claimed defect has an impact on the safety or health of the tenant.

In order to bring a cause of action for breach of the implied warranty of habitability, the tenant must first show that he or she notified the landlord of the deficiency or defect not known to the landlord and allowed a reasonable time for its correction.[1]

The statute, Franklin Real Property Law §500, and its companion provision, §240 of Franklin District Court Act, give the court wide latitude in assessing damages. The measure of rent abatement damages shall be the difference between the value of the dwelling as warranted and the value of the dwelling as it exists in its defective condition. In determining the fair rental value of the dwelling as warranted, the court may look to the agreed-upon rent as something the two parties have agreed to as proper for the premises as impliedly warranted. Then the court should consider testimony and other evidence to determine the percentage reduction of habitability or usability by the tenant attributable to the defects.

In determining the percentage reduction of habitability, the trial court should consider the area affected, the amount of time the tenant is exposed to the defect, the degree of discomfort and annoyance the defect imposes, the quality of the defect as health-threatening or just intermittently annoying, and the extent to which such a defect causes the tenant to find the premises uninhabitable. For example, damages are recoverable when the tenant cannot bathe comfortably because there is inadequate hot water, or must worry about insect infestation spreading disease, or must avoid certain rooms if there is inadequate weather protection.

The tenant's damages are calculated by reducing the agreed rent by this percentage reduction of habitability, and multiplying the difference by the number of months of occupancy. The tenant will be liable only for the reasonable rental value, if any, of the property in its imperfect condition during the tenant's period of occupancy.

Damages for discomfort and annoyance are not susceptible to precise calculation. For that reason, the damages awarded for rent abatement, including discomfort and annoyance, may not exceed the total rent otherwise due. Accordingly, because we hold that a 100% rent abatement is the maximum that may be awarded to a tenant in an ordinary breach of implied warranty case, we reverse the trial court's decision awarding $1,500 in additional compensatory damages.

[1] As we held in *Rosenbaum v. Chavkin* (1990), a tenant may, where there has been a breach of the implied warranty of habitability, withhold the payment of rent. That permits the tenant to shift the burden and expense of bringing suit to the landlord, who can better afford to bring the action, and to then raise the breach of the implied warranty of habitability as a counterclaim.

Separate damages, however, are available for remedial measures taken by the tenant when the landlord is notified of the defect but fails to remedy it within a reasonable time, and the tenant has incurred out-of-pocket expenses to remedy the defect. In this case, the tenant paid for the repair of a window. Accordingly, the trial court's award of $225 for remedial measures was proper.

Punitive damages may also be awarded in the proper circumstances to punish conduct that is morally culpable. Such an award serves to deter a wrongdoer from repetitions of the same or similar actions. And it tends to encourage prosecution of a claim by a victim who might not otherwise incur the expense or inconvenience of private action.

As we have repeatedly held, when a landlord, after receiving notice of a defect, persistently fails to make repairs that are essential to the health and safety of the tenant, the landlord is morally culpable and an award of punitive damages is proper. *See Main v. Stocker Realty* (Franklin Court of Appeal, 1996). When such behavior points to the bad spirit and wrong intention of the defendant, and would support a finding of willful and wanton or fraudulent conduct, punitive damages may be increased.

The trial court denied an award to plaintiff of punitive damages without explaining why. The record evinces a pattern of intentional conduct on the part of defendant for which the term "slumlord" surely was coined. Defendant's conduct was culpable and demeaning to plaintiff and clearly expressive of a wanton disregard of plaintiff's rights.

The trial court found that defendant was aware of defects in the essential facilities of plaintiff's apartment and promised plaintiff that repairs would be made, but never fulfilled those promises. These findings point to the bad spirit and wrong intention of the defendant, and would support a finding of willful and wanton or fraudulent conduct. We remand to give the trial court the opportunity to reconsider or explain its refusal to award punitive damages.

Affirmed in part, reversed in part, and remanded.

Bashford v. Schwartz

Franklin Court of Appeal (2001)

This appeal is from an order of the Housing Division of the District Court, which denied a motion by petitioner landlord to sever respondent tenant's counterclaims. The issue presented is whether the aggrieved tenant may raise in this summary eviction proceeding a counterclaim seeking damages for the loss of property that allegedly occurred as a result of the landlord's failure to provide adequate security.

The tenant stated that for a number of months she had complained to the landlord that the front door to her apartment was insecure and required replacement. This was never done. She stated that following her complaints an intruder forced open her front door and burglarized her apartment. Respondent asserts that she is entitled to damages for loss of property based on the landlord's failure to replace the front door.

While tenants may, in this nonpayment proceeding, counterclaim for damages sustained by reason of landlord's breach of the implied warranty of habitability as embodied in §500 of the Franklin Real Property Law, the proper measure of those contract damages is the difference between the fair market value of the premises if they had been as warranted, as measured by the rent reserved under the lease, and the value of the premises during the period of the breach. *See Virgil v. Landy* (Franklin Court of Appeal, 1997).

Where questions of negligence, proximate cause, and damages are contested and require discovery and proof that would delay the summary proceedings, those claims are more appropriately tried outside the limited sphere of the landlord-tenant proceeding. While §240 contains language giving the Housing Division Court authority to "employ any remedy," the point is that these are *summary* proceedings intended to allow quick and effective resolution of traditional landlord-tenant disputes and enforcement of the Housing Code. The Housing Division of the District Court, according to the legislation that created it, is "devoted to actions and proceedings involving the enforcement of state and local laws for the establishment and maintenance of housing standards. . . ." (Franklin District Court Act §240).

Reversed.

Graham Realty, Inc. v. Brenda Chapin

Sample Answer

To: Joseph Murray
From: Applicant
Re: *Graham Realty, Inc. v. Brenda Chapin–Case Planning Memorandum*

Claim: Defense to Eviction Action

I. BREACH OF IMPLIED WARRANTY OF HABITABILITY

Legal Authority: Franklin Real Property Law section 500 implies in every residential lease a warranty that the premises are fit for human habitation and the uses reasonably intended, and that the occupants will not be subjected to dangerous or hazardous conditions or those that are detrimental to their life, health, or safety. Also, notice of the defect must be given to the landlord, Graham Realty, Inc. ("GRI"), and the landlord must be allowed a reasonable time for repairs. [Virgil v. Landy] Under *Virgil v. Landy*, "[a] substantial violation of an applicable housing code shall constitute prima facie evidence that there has been a breach of the warranty of habitability."

Element #1: Ms. Chapin is the lessee and tenant of apartment 7B in Graham Towers.

Evidence:

- Copy of the written lease signed by Ms. Chapin (presumably she can produce it).
- Testimony of Ms. Chapin that she and her daughters have occupied apartment 7B for one year.

Element #2: The premises are not fit for human habitation or the uses reasonably intended by the parties.

Evidence:

- Testimony of Ms. Chapin as to the defects in the apartment. From the inception of their residency, she and her family have been subjected to water leaks and a spreading "smelly, slimy green fungus" in the bathroom, falling plaster, cracks and holes in the walls, rat infestation, and erratic hot water, heat, and elevator service.
- Testimony of Ms. Chapin's 14-year-old daughter, Mary, as to those same defects.
- Copy of the Avon Department of Buildings Violation Report ("Violation Report"), showing notice of five violations—two "hazardous" violations and three "immediately hazardous" violations.

Element #3: The defects in the apartment subject the occupants to conditions that are dangerous, hazardous, or detrimental to their life, health, and safety.

Evidence:

- Copy of the Violation Report listing three "immediately hazardous" violations (the rat infestation, faulty elevator, and mold on the bathroom wall) and two "hazardous" violations (the defective plaster and paint and the water leak in the bathroom ceiling).
- Testimony of Ms. Chapin as to these conditions and also as to the lack of hot water, which affects their health (*e.g.*, by not being able to clean dishes and other areas of the apartment with hot water and being unable to maintain regular personal hygiene), and the lack of heat, requiring them to leave their stove and electric space heater on all night, which presents a fire hazard.
- Testimony of Mary as to those same conditions.

Element #4: The tenant gave notice to the landlord.

Evidence:

- Testimony of Ms. Chapin that when she was first shown the apartment by Herb London, GRI's building manager, she asked him about certain defects and he agreed to fix them. Also, testimony that she called him at least eight times to request repairs and has also left phone messages and can produce notes she made of the calls and messages to Mr. London.

- Testimony of Mr. London about his conversations with Ms. Chapin both when he showed her the apartment and when he spoke with her on the phone, and about any phone messages he received from her. (His secretary might be able to testify to the phone messages.)

- Copy of the letter Ms. Chapin wrote to Mr. London, on May 21, 2004, listing some of the defects and requesting their repair.

- Copy of the Violation Report, which would have been given to GRI.

- Testimony of Ms. Chapin that on many occasions, she reported the rats and other defects to Victor, GRI's building superintendent, who killed a rat in her apartment.

II. RENT ABATEMENT

Legal Authority: Franklin District Court Act section 240 provides for rent abatement as a remedy for breach of the warranty of habitability. The measure of rent abatement is stated in *Virgil v. Landy* as "the difference between the value of the dwelling as warranted and the value of the dwelling as it exists in its defective condition." The court determines the amount of rent abatement by considering the following factors:

(i) The area affected;
(ii) The amount of time the occupant was exposed to the defects;
(iii) The degree of discomfort and annoyance the defect imposes;
(iv) The quality of the defects as health-threatening as opposed to just intermittently annoying; and
(v) The extent to which the defects cause the tenant to find the premises uninhabitable.
[Virgil v. Landy]

The tenant is liable for only "the reasonable rent value, if any, of the property in its imperfect condition during the tenant's period of occupancy." [Virgil v. Landy] A 100% rent abatement is the maximum that may be awarded. [Virgil v. Landy] Franklin District Court Act section 240 gives the court wide latitude in assessing damages. Franklin Real Property Law section 500 provides that expert testimony is not required to determine a tenant's damages.

Element #1: The fair rental value of the apartment in its warranted condition.

Evidence:

- Copy of the lease between Ms. Chapin and GRI which establishes a monthly rent of $1,000. In *Virgil,* the court stated that the agreed-upon rent is a proper measure of the fair rental value of the dwelling as warranted.

Element #2: The factors considered by the court in estimating the percentage of rent abatement are:

Evidence:
(i) Regarding the area affected:

- Testimony of Ms. Chapin as to the apartment's layout: two bedrooms, a living room, bathroom, and kitchen.
- Testimony of Ms. Chapin as to the apartment's defects: bathroom ceiling leak and a spreading mold-like substance on a wall, falling plaster and cracks and holes in walls throughout the apartment, the entire apartment needs painting and plastering, the presence of rats and rat holes in the kitchen and bedrooms, and the sporadic availability of heat and hot water.
- Testimony of Mary as to those defects.
- Testimony of Ms. Chapin that she has caught four rats and that Victor came up and killed a rat once and that rat droppings are everywhere. She can also relate having to throw away food after rats got into the packages.
- Testimony of Victor about the rats.
- Copies of photos taken by Ms. Chapin of the visible defects and the Violation Report.
- Testimony of Ms. Chapin's neighbors as to the erratic elevator service, heat, and hot water.
- Copies of her electric bills and a receipt for the space heater to show lack of heat and hot water.

(ii) Regarding the amount of time the Chapin family has been exposed to the defective conditions.

- Testimony of Ms. Chapin that they have been exposed to some of these conditions from the first day they moved into the apartment (even before that, when Herb London first showed her the apartment and he promised to make repairs).
- Testimony of Mary as to those conditions.
- Copy of the Violation Report to show how long the violations listed therein have persisted on official records.
- Testimony of the building inspector about the conditions he recorded in the Violation Report (although the report itself may be sufficient).
- Testimony of Ms. Chapin as to the frequency, duration, and total time the elevator was inoperable and the unavailability of consistent heat and hot water, and presumably how long there has been a rat infestation.
- Testimony of Ms. Chapin's neighbors as to those conditions.

- Copies of Ms. Chapin's electric bills, which will corroborate the periods of time during which she has been without heat and hot water and show the increased use of electricity for her stove and space heater.

(iii) Regarding the degree of discomfort and annoyance imposed by the defects:

- Testimony of Ms. Chapin regarding fear of rats and resulting inability to sleep, difficulty in maintaining personal hygiene and washing dishes without hot water, repeated calls to landlord, worry over the safety of using stove and space heater to provide heat, falling plaster, fungus in the bathroom, etc.

- Testimony of Mary about those conditions, especially about the rats and about being injured by the falling plaster.

- Copy of the hospital report to substantiate Mary's injury.

- A statement from Mary's school about her absence due to her injury by the chunk of plaster.

- A copy of the letter to Mr. London which corroborates the discomfort: "It . . . isn't warm enough in the bedrooms," "Mary woke me up screaming because she was awakened by a rat . . .," ". . . a large chunk of plaster fell from the ceiling, knocking [Mary] to the floor and causing a gash in her scalp, which required 10 stitches. . . ."

- Testimony of Ms. Chapin that when the elevator was not functioning, it caused extreme discomfort as her apartment is on the seventh floor.

- Testimony of Ms. Chapin's neighbors which perhaps can corroborate some of the discomfort-causing defects regarding lack of heat and hot water, erratic elevator service, and rat infestation.

- Receipt for the space heater.

- Sample of rat droppings found in the apartment and food packages chewed by the rats, and plaster that has fallen from ceiling.

(iv) Regarding the quality of the defects as health-threatening as opposed to just intermittently annoying:

- Testimony of Ms. Chapin as to the deleterious effects on her family arising from the lack of heat and hot water (*e.g.*, inability to wash dishes, safety concerns from using the stove for heating purposes, threat of harm from falling plaster, health hazards caused by rats and their droppings, and the spreading green fungus).

- Testimony of Mary about those conditions and her injury from the falling plaster.

- Copy of the hospital bill substantiating Mary's injury.

- Copy of the Violation Report listing three "immediately hazardous" violations and two "hazardous" violations.

(v) Regarding the extent to which the defects caused the Chapins to find the premises uninhabitable:

- Testimony of Ms. Chapin (and perhaps Mary) that the defects required her to: heat water on the stove to bathe and do dishes; run the stove and/or space heater in order to heat the apartment and that, even with the space heater, "[i]t still isn't warm enough in the bedrooms. . . ."; worry about the fire hazards attendant to operating a stove and/or space heater for heating purposes; and the inability of her children to sleep because of fears of rats.

- Copy of the letter to Mr. London stating that "[t]his situation is intolerable."

III. REMEDIAL (OUT-OF-POCKET) DAMAGES TO REMEDY DEFECTS

Legal Authority: Franklin District Court Act section 240 provides that a court has great leeway in fashioning remedies, including imposition of remedial (and punitive) damages. The court in *Virgil v. Landy* interpreted section 240 to provide for out-of-pocket damages when a landlord has been notified of a defect and fails to remedy it within a reasonable time. The items for which Ms. Chapin can request out-of-pocket damages are the space heater and the amount of her electric bills attributable to the lack of heat and hot water and perhaps replacement costs of food that she had to discard because of rat infestation and the traps used to trap rats. [*Note*: The court in *Bashford v. Schwartz* denied recovery of damages for loss of property in a summary proceeding in Housing Court. Thus, a claim for damages arising from plaster hitting Mary should not be raised here.]

Element #1: The landlord was notified of the defects by Ms. Chapin:

Evidence:

- Testimony of Ms. Chapin about her repeated phone calls to Mr. London, speaking to him a few times and leaving messages for him the other times regarding repair of the defects.

- Testimony of Ms. Chapin that she spoke with Victor, showing him the defects and requesting repairs, and she can produce her letter to Mr. London for corroboration of her requests to Victor.

- Copy of the letter to Mr. London stating that she had to buy a space heater because of a lack of heat.

- Testimony of Victor about the lack of hot water (and other defects). (He may not be a good witness but we may want to call him.)

Element #2: The landlord failed to repair the defects within a reasonable time.

Evidence:

- Testimony of Ms. Chapin that none of the defects has been repaired despite her numerous requests.

- Copy of the Violation Report which demonstrates that no repairs have been done.

Element #3: Ms. Chapin incurred out-of-pocket expenses in an effort to alleviate reported defects.

Evidence:

- Testimony of Ms. Chapin that she was "forced" to buy a space heater when her apartment had no heat (and presumably she can produce a receipt); that when there was no heat, she had to run the electric oven for warmth; and that when there was no heat, she had to heat water on the electric stove for purposes of washing dishes and for bathing.

- Copies of her electric bills to demonstrate the above-average charges she incurred due to a lack of hot water and heat.

- Receipt for space heater.

- Testimony of Ms. Chapin regarding the cost of the food she had to discard because of rat infestation and the cost of the rat traps and maybe she has some receipts. Maybe Victor, who killed a rat in the apartment, can also testify to the loss of food resulting from the rats.

IV. PUNITIVE DAMAGES

Legal Authority: Franklin District Court Act section 240 authorizes the imposition of punitive damages in this type of proceeding. Furthermore, "when a landlord, after receiving notice of a defect, persistently fails to make repairs that are essential to the health and safety of the tenant, the landlord is morally culpable and an award of punitive damages is proper. [Virgil v. Landy—citing Main v. Stocker Realty] *Virgil* also holds that when a landlord's behavior indicates his "bad spirit and wrong intention" and can "support a finding of willful and wanton or fraudulent conduct, punitive damages may be increased."

Element #1: The landlord had notice of defects that were detrimental to the Chapins's essential needs for their health and safety.

Evidence:

- Evidence already discussed in support of I., Element #3; II., Element #2(iv); and III., Element #1 is relevant here.

- Testimony of Ms. Chapin that she reported the rats (and presumably all of the defects) during her "many" complaints to Victor and Mr. London.

- Copies of the letter to Mr. London showing notice of lack of heat and the rat infestation.

- Copy of the Violation Report showing that GRI had notice, among other defects, of rodents in the apartment, mold on a bathroom wall, and elevator service in need of repair—all listed as "immediately hazardous" defects, and the defective paint and plaster and water leaking into the bathroom ceiling, defects that are "hazardous" to the tenant. The Violation Report would have been given to GRI.

- Testimony of the other tenants in the building about the elevator service and presumably about the lack of hot water and heat and rat infestation.

- Copies of Ms. Chapin's photos of the defects in her apartment, which would include the leaking ceiling, mold, and falling plaster and peeling paint.

Element #2: The landlord persistently failed to make repairs essential to the tenants' health and safety.

Evidence:

- Testimony of Ms. Chapin that, after repeated requests to Mr. London and Victor for necessary repairs, not a single defect was repaired.

- Copy of the Violation Report that required GRI to repair the elevator, abate the mold problem, and rid the apartment of rats within 24 hours of the notice. Repairs that should have been completed by now have not been made. [*Note:* The Violation Report gave GRI 30 days to repair the paint and plaster and fix the bathroom water leak. Since only 21 days have elapsed since the Report, GRI still has nine days to remedy these defects pursuant to the city code. However, Ms. Chapin can testify that she gave notice of all of the defects, including lack of heat and hot water (also hazardous to her family's health and safety) more than 30 days ago in her letter and calls to Mr. London and also in her complaints to Victor. Ms. Chapin can produce the notes she made of her calls to Mr. London, which she presumably dated.]

Element #3: The landlord's conduct indicates "bad spirit and wrong intention" so as to support a finding of willful and wanton or fraudulent conduct.

Evidence:

- Testimony of Ms. Chapin, her letter to Mr. London, and the Violation Report regarding notice of hazardous defects in the apartment which were persistently ignored by GRI, indicating the bad spirit and wrong intention of its conduct.

- Copy of the *Avon Gazette* article, from which one would deduce that the intention of GRI is to allow conditions in the apartment building to deteriorate so much that tenants will move out, allowing GRI to "cash in" on the gentrification of the neighborhood.

- Testimony of Ms. Chapin that Victor told her that Mr. London is not renting vacated apartments because he is "waiting for the rest of us to give and leave in disgust." Perhaps Victor's testimony can be obtained.

- Testimony of Ms. Chapin as to Mr. London's assurances when he first showed the apartment to her that repairs would be made to defects she pointed out to him, and that she signed her lease in reliance on these assurances, unaware that GRI did not intend to make any repairs. This would indicate fraud.

V. REMEDIES NOT OBTAINABLE IN THIS SUMMARY PROCEEDING

Legal Authority: The court in *Bashford v. Schwartz* held that when issues of negligence, proximate cause, and damages are contested, thus requiring discovery and proof which would delay a summary proceeding, such claims are not appropriate in Housing Division Court. Instead, according to *Bashford*, they "are more appropriately tried outside the limited sphere of the landlord-tenant proceeding." Franklin District Court Act section 240 permits only remedial and punitive damages.

- Ms. Chapin wants reimbursement for medical costs incurred to treat Mary's head wound sustained when plaster fell on her head. She also wants reimbursement for one day's lost wages arising from Mary's injury. These damages are not remedial (out-of-pocket), as authorized in section 240 because they were not used to remedy a defect but rather involve personal injury to Mary.

- Ms. Chapin's letter to Mr. London demands "reimbursement for the pain you have caused us." If this is a request for pain and suffering caused by GRI's refusal to make repairs, it too is outside the parameters of remedial damages, and should be tried in a proceeding separate from the present summary proceeding.

Multistate Performance Test

In re Clarke Corporation

National Conference of Bar Examiners

Preface

This Multistate Performance Test is a reprint of one of the three MPTs which were administered in July 2005.

The instructions for the test appear on the next page. On the actual MPT, they will appear on the back cover of the test.

INSTRUCTIONS

1. You will have 90 minutes to complete this session of the examination. This performance test is designed to evaluate your ability to handle a select number of legal authorities in the context of a factual problem involving a client.

2. The problem is set in the fictitious state of Franklin, in the fictitious Fifteenth Circuit of the United States. Columbia and Olympia are also fictitious states in the Fifteenth Circuit. In Franklin, the trial court of general jurisdiction is the District Court, the intermediate appellate court is the Court of Appeal, and the highest court is the Supreme Court.

3. You will have two kinds of materials with which to work: a File and a Library. The first document in the File is a memorandum containing the instructions for the task you are to complete. The other documents in the File contain factual information about your case and may include some facts that are not relevant.

4. The Library contains the legal authorities needed to complete the task and may also include some authorities that are not relevant. Any cases may be real, modified, or written solely for the purpose of this examination. If the cases appear familiar to you, do not assume that they are precisely the same as you have read before. Read them thoroughly, as if they all were new to you. You should assume that cases were decided in the jurisdictions and on the dates shown. In citing cases from the Library, you may use abbreviations and omit page references.

5. Your response must be written in the answer book provided. If you are taking this examination on a laptop computer, your jurisdiction will provide you with specific instructions. In answering this performance test, you should concentrate on the materials provided in the File and Library. What you have learned in law school and elsewhere provides the general background for analyzing the problem; the File and Library provide the specific materials with which you must work.

6. Although there are no restrictions on how you apportion your time, you should be sure to allocate ample time (about 45 minutes) to reading and digesting the materials and to organizing your answer before you begin writing it. You may make notes anywhere in the test materials; blank pages are provided at the end of the booklet. You may not tear pages from the question booklet.

7. This performance test will be graded on your responsiveness to the instructions regarding the task you are to complete, which are given to you in the first memorandum in the File, and on the content, thoroughness, and organization of your response.

In re Clarke Corporation

FILE

LIBRARY

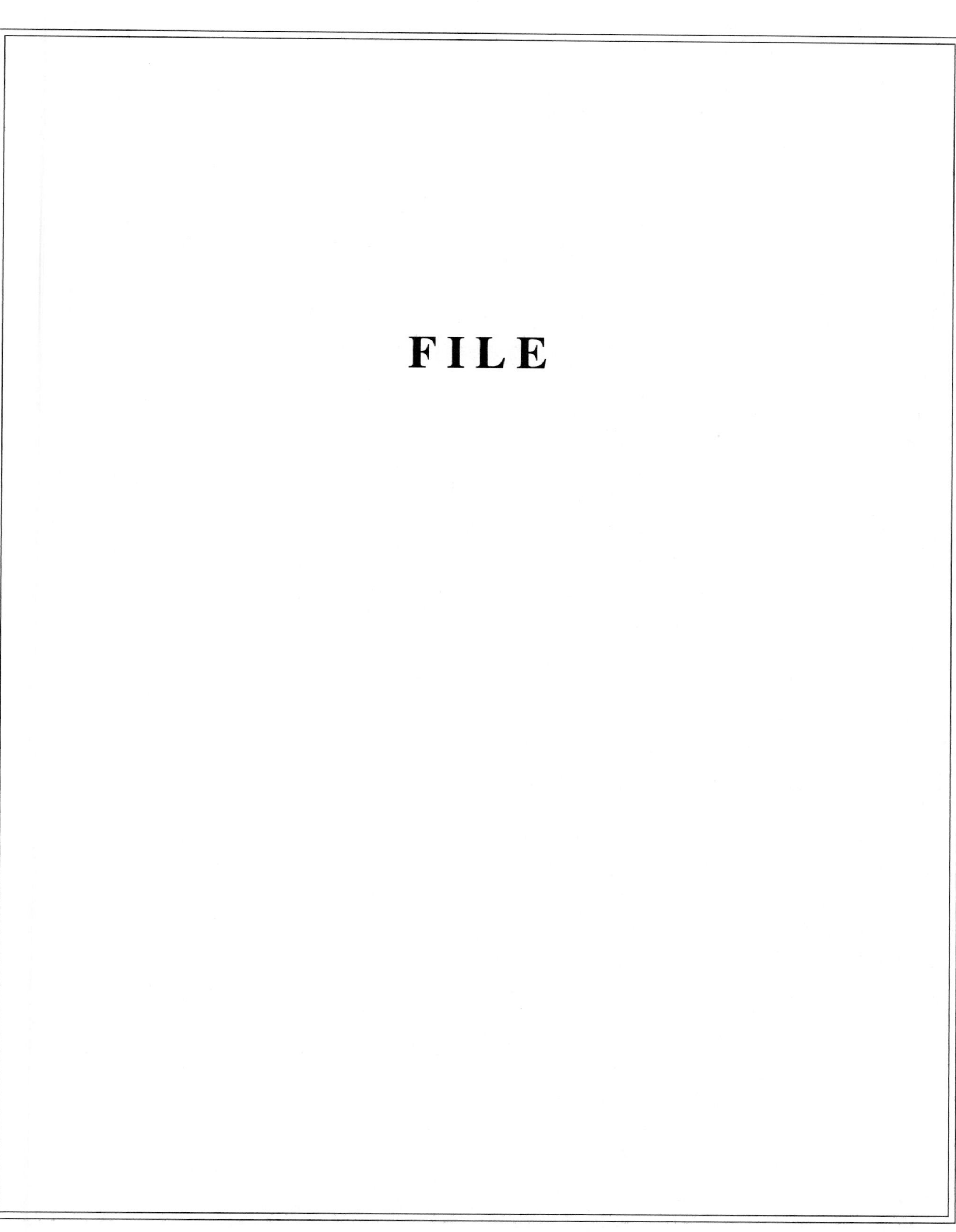
FILE

MacKenzie, Asp & Norman LLP
Attorneys at Law
550 Enterprise Blvd., Suite 2500
Cypress, Franklin 33337

INTEROFFICE MEMORANDUM

TO: Applicant
FROM: Margaret MacKenzie
DATE: July 26, 2005
SUBJECT: *In re Clarke Corporation*

Our client, Clarke Corporation (Clarke), has been threatened with a products liability action. The specific allegations against Clarke concern an X-ray enhancing contrast dye substance known as "PureView" originally manufactured by Santoy Enterprises and then, briefly, by Clarke following Clarke's acquisition as an asset purchaser of Santoy's Drug Manufacturing Division. Mary Regan alleges her husband's death was caused by doses of PureView administered to him more than two decades ago.

As a general rule, there is no corporate successor liability in this situation. There are, however, four traditional exceptions to the general rule. I have determined that none of them applies here, so do not address them. A fifth, more recently created exception, called the product line successor rule, does give me some concern.

Please draft for my signature an opinion letter to Jasmine Clarke, Clarke's president, explaining whether the product line successor rule can be invoked to impose liability on Clarke Corporation for Mr. Regan's death. You need not be concerned with whether PureView was in fact defective because those facts have not yet been developed.

I'm attaching a memorandum regarding our firm's practice in writing opinion letters. Please follow these guidelines in preparing your letter.

MacKenzie, Asp & Norman LLP
Attorneys at Law
550 Enterprise Blvd., Suite 2500
Cypress, Franklin 33337

INTEROFFICE MEMORANDUM

TO: Associates

SUBJECT: Opinion Letters

DATE: September 8, 1995

The firm follows these guidelines in preparing opinion letters to clients:

- Begin the letter with a brief introductory statement of the question.
- Provide a concise one-sentence answer to the question.
- Write a brief statement of the facts relevant to the question.
- Identify and analyze all issues raised by the question. Be sure to discuss the relevant facts and authorities that support your conclusion. Because this is an opinion letter, analyze each theory or issue and all elements or factors of each issue.

Remember to write in a way that clearly addresses the legal issues but also allows the client to follow your reasoning and the logic of your conclusions.

MacKenzie, Asp & Norman LLP
Attorneys at Law
550 Enterprise Blvd., Suite 2500
Cypress, Franklin 33337

INTEROFFICE MEMORANDUM

TO: File
FROM: Margaret MacKenzie
SUBJECT: Interview of Jasmine Clarke, President of Clarke Corporation
DATE: July 25, 2005

- Clarke Corporation (Clarke) is a family-owned pharmaceutical company founded by Ms. Clarke's father, Benjamin Clarke, approximately 30 years ago. Ms. Clarke has been president of the company since her father's retirement in 2002.
- For the first 10 or so years of operation, Clarke specialized in the development and manufacture of blood-thinning medications. In approximately 1985, the company began exploring options for expanding its operations to include other product lines. To that end, it entered into discussions with several unrelated entities, including Santoy Enterprises, concerning a possible merger or acquisition. Ultimately, Clarke decided to acquire Santoy's Drug Manufacturing Division (DMD).
- Prior to the negotiations concerning DMD, Clarke and Santoy had never done any business together or, for that matter, been business competitors, since they manufactured different types of medical and pharmaceutical products.
- DMD comprised approximately 80% of Santoy's manufacturing operations. The other 20% consisted of a fledgling Industrial Chemicals Division that manufactured certain chemical solvents.
- "PureView," a contrast dye material used for enhancing medical X-rays, was one of five pharmaceutical products manufactured by DMD. PureView was DMD's least profitable product, accounting for less than 5% of DMD's total sales.
- Clarke's acquisition of DMD was accomplished through an Asset Purchase Agreement dated September 1, 1990 (copy attached), whereby Clarke purchased certain assets from and assumed certain liabilities of Santoy in exchange for cash consideration of $2.5 million. No stock of either corporation was transferred in connection with the transaction. None of Santoy's officers, directors or shareholders became affiliated with Clarke, although Clarke hired most of DMD's existing employees.

- The $2.5 million purchase price was the subject of intense arm's-length negotiations and constituted adequate consideration for the assets purchased. In retrospect, Ms. Clarke believes that Clarke paid more than it should have for DMD, since the DMD products have never been as profitable as initially projected.
- Following the sale of DMD, pursuant to the terms of the Asset Purchase Agreement, Santoy changed its corporate name to "Sentinel Enterprises."
- Sentinel invested the proceeds from the sale of DMD into its fledgling Industrial Chemical Division, which never took off. Having sold its other assets to Clarke, Sentinel was forced to shut down its operations. In 1992, two years after the DMD transaction, Sentinel filed for bankruptcy and its assets were liquidated.
- After acquiring DMD, Clarke initially continued to manufacture the five former Santoy products using identical manufacturing processes and the same product names that had been used by Santoy. Although Clarke solicited former Santoy customers for business, Clarke informed all existing and prospective customers that it, not Santoy, was now the manufacturer of those products.
- In March 1991, just six months after the DMD acquisition, Clarke discontinued production of PureView. The market just wasn't there for the product, and sales had declined precipitously due to the introduction of new X-ray technology that eventually rendered contrast dye products such as PureView virtually obsolete.
- Since then, Clarke has not manufactured or sold PureView or any similar product. Clarke does, however, continue to manufacture the four other unrelated pharmaceutical products that it purchased from Santoy, which collectively account for about 15% of Clarke's total business.
- Three months ago, a report surfaced in the *Journal of American Medicine* linking PureView exposure to certain forms of cancer. The report was based on a study that tracked 100 individuals who received doses of PureView more than two decades ago. The study found that within the past few years several of those individuals had developed rare, life-threatening cancerous tumors caused by their exposure to PureView.
- This is the first time that PureView has been linked to any serious medical illness. Before the study, only occasional minor complications (such as mild swelling and soreness) had been known to result from its use.
- Last week Ms. Clarke received a letter from a law firm representing the widow of a man who received doses of PureView more than two decades ago and who recently died from a malignant tumor. (*See* attached demand letter.)

- Ms. Clarke is very concerned about her company's potential liability for injuries that may have been caused by Santoy-manufactured PureView over the nearly 20 years that Santoy produced the substance. She wants our legal advice on whether Clarke could be held liable for these claims by virtue of its acquisition of DMD.

ASSET PURCHASE AGREEMENT
BETWEEN
SANTOY ENTERPRISES, INC. ("Seller")
AND CLARKE CORPORATION ("Purchaser")

* * * *

ARTICLE II
THE ASSET PURCHASE

2.1 Upon the terms and subject to the conditions of this Agreement, Seller sells, assigns, and transfers to Purchaser, free and clear of all encumbrances, Seller's Drug Manufacturing Division (the "Business") and all assets, licenses, permits, contracts, operations and rights owned by Seller and constituting the Business (the "Purchased Assets"), including:

(i) All manufacturing facilities, machinery, and equipment;

(ii) All items of inventory;

(iii) All laboratory supplies and related research materials;

* * * *

(vi) All customer lists and mailing lists used in the Business;

* * * *

(viii) All trade secrets, royalty rights, work notes, market studies, consultants' reports, and similar property used in the Business;

(ix) All goodwill associated with the Business;

(x) All rights, title and interest in the names "Santoy," "Santoy Drugs," . . . and "PureView," and any variants thereof, and any related logos, trademarks, trade names or service marks incorporating such names;

* * * *

2.3 Purchase Price. In consideration of the transfer to Purchaser of the Purchased Assets, Purchaser agrees to deliver to Seller the sum of $2,500,000.

* * * *

2.5 Assumption of Liabilities.

(a) General Limitation on Liabilities. Seller shall transfer the Purchased Assets to Purchaser free and clear of all encumbrances, and Purchaser shall not, by virtue of its purchase of the Purchased Assets, assume or become responsible for any liabilities or obligations of Seller except liability for leases, contracts, and other agreements entered into by Seller in the ordinary course of business prior to this Agreement.

(b) Offer of Employment. Purchaser shall offer employment as of the date hereof to all of Seller's active employees in the Business ("Transferred Employees"). Purchaser shall keep on its payroll all Transferred Employees who accept Purchaser's offer of employment except for those who may resign or be terminated for cause, for at least 90 days after the date of this Agreement.

* * * *

ARTICLE V

* * * *

5.5 Change of Name. Seller will amend its Articles of Incorporation within ten (10) business days after the date of this Agreement to change its corporate name to a name dissimilar to the name by which Seller is presently known.

* * * *

5.9 Noncompetition Agreement of Seller. For a period of five (5) years, Seller shall not, directly or indirectly, (i) engage in the manufacture, sale or distribution of products similar in type or performing the same general purpose as those manufactured in the Business, or (ii) own, manage, operate or control, or participate in the ownership, management, operation or control of, any business which directly or indirectly competes with the Business.

* * * *

IN WITNESS WHEREOF, the Parties have executed this Agreement as of September 1, 1990.

SANTOY ENTERPRISES, INC.

By: Daniel Santoy

Name: Daniel Santoy
Title: President

CLARKE CORPORATION

By: Benjamin Clarke

Name: Benjamin Clarke
Title: President

BENTLEY, PABLO & SUMMER LLP
ATTORNEYS AT LAW

July 21, 2005

Ms. Jasmine Clarke, President
Clarke Corporation
800 Robinson Blvd.
Cypress, Franklin 33337

Dear Ms. Clarke:

We are writing on behalf of our client, Mary Regan, concerning the death of her husband, Thomas Regan, resulting from a malignant tumor caused by his exposure to PureView, a contrast dye material used for X-ray purposes.

As you know, PureView was manufactured by Clarke Corporation's predecessor, Santoy Enterprises, from 1970 to 1990. In 1983, Mr. Regan received several doses of PureView in connection with the treatment of an injury. He developed a fatal malignant tumor as a result of his exposure to PureView and died on November 29, 2004.

In 1990, Clarke Corporation purchased Santoy Enterprises. Clarke, as the successor to the original manufacturer of PureView, is liable for all damages resulting from Mr. Regan's exposure to PureView. *Gray v. Ballard* (Franklin Supreme Court 1987).

We expect Clarke Corporation, as a respectable family-run business, to take responsibility for its liability and fully compensate Mrs. Regan for her husband's untimely demise.

Should you wish to resolve this matter without resort to litigation and thereby avoid the substantial time and expense as well as negative publicity entailed by a lengthy court action, please contact me immediately.

Please be advised that we will pursue any and all legal recourse available on behalf of our client, including the filing of a civil action for products liability against Clarke Corporation, if we do not hear from you within 10 days of the date of this letter.

Sincerely,

William H. Bentley

William H. Bentley, Esq.
Managing Partner

405 TIMBERDELL DRIVE • PURCELL, FRANKLIN • 33331
PHONE: (832) 555-7220 • FAX: (832) 555-7225

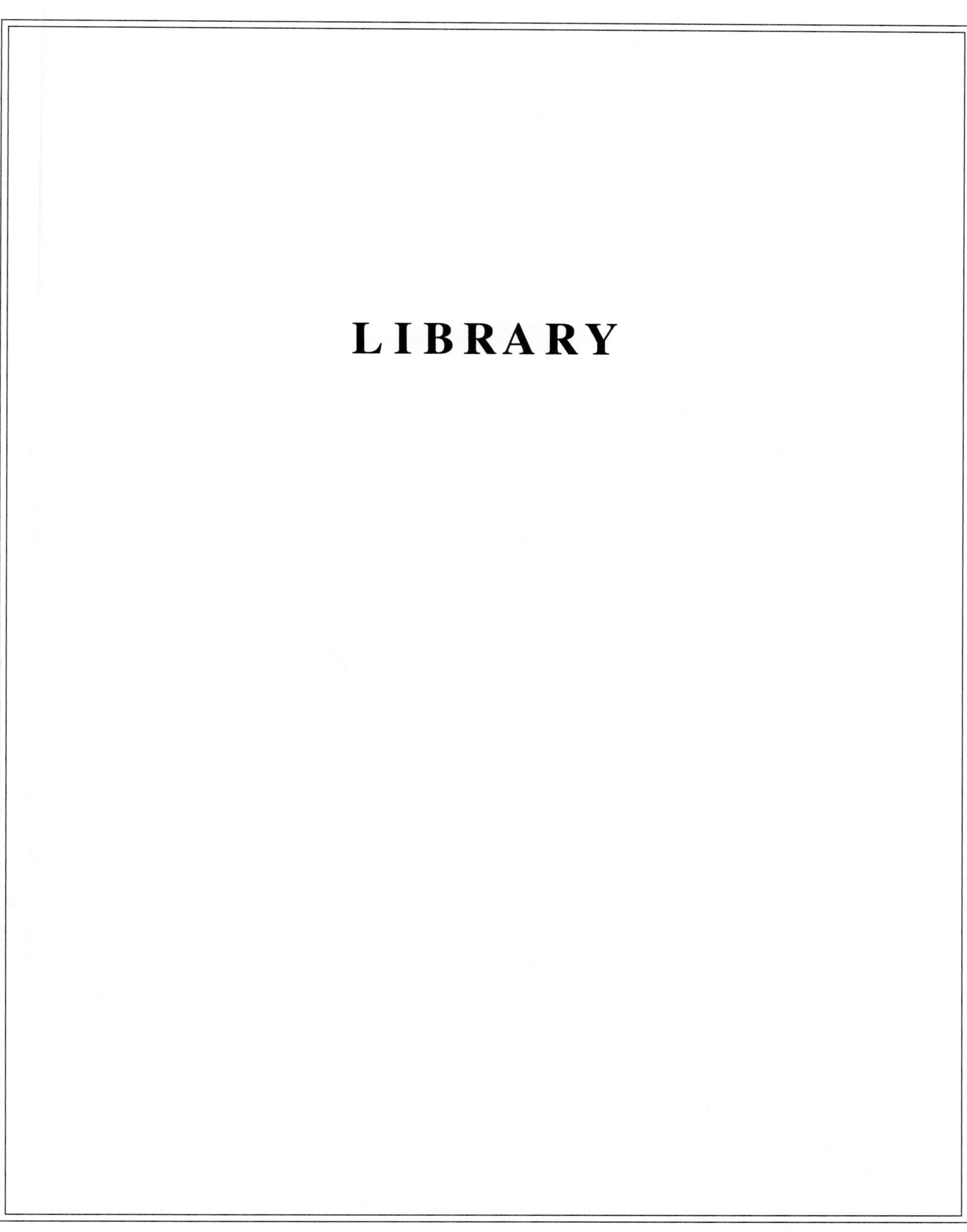

LIBRARY

Gray v. Ballard Corporation

Franklin Supreme Court (1987)

Claiming damages for injury from a defective ladder, Michael Gray brought a products liability claim against defendant Ballard Corporation (Ballard II). Ballard II neither manufactured nor sold the ladder. However, prior to Gray's injury, Ballard II succeeded to the business of the ladder's manufacturer, the now dissolved "Ballard Corporation" (Ballard I), through a purchase of Ballard I's assets for adequate cash consideration. The trial court entered summary judgment for Ballard II and Gray appeals.

Gray alleged in his complaint that on March 24, 1979, he fell from a defective ladder while working on a construction project. It is undisputed that the ladder involved in the accident was an "old" model manufactured by Ballard I, and that Ballard II was not the manufacturer. Hence, the principal issue addressed by the parties' submissions on the motion for summary judgment was the presence or absence of any factual basis for imposing any of Ballard I's liability as manufacturer of the ladder upon Ballard II as successor to Ballard I's manufacturing business.

On July 1, 1978, Ballard I sold to Ballard II, then known as Thunderbird Corporation (Thunderbird), its "stock in trade, fixtures, equipment, trade name, inventory and goodwill," as well as its interest in the real property used for its manufacturing activities. Ballard II paid Ballard I and its principal stockholders total cash consideration of $350,000 for the assets and goodwill of Ballard I. As part of the sale transaction, Ballard I agreed "to dissolve its corporate existence as soon as practical." The possibility of Ballard II being liable for defects in products manufactured or sold by Ballard I was not specifically discussed nor was any provision expressly made therefor. Two months after the sale, Ballard I dissolved.

The tangible assets acquired by Ballard II included Ballard I's manufacturing plant, machinery, offices, office fixtures and equipment, and inventory. Ballard II used these assets to continue manufacturing operations without interruption. The factory personnel remained the same, the former general manager of Ballard I remained with the business as a paid consultant for about six months after the takeover, and identical manufacturing processes were used for producing the ladders. The "Ballard" name continued to be used for all ladders produced after the change of ownership. Ballard II also acquired Ballard I's lists of customers, whom it solicited, and it continued to employ the salespersons and representatives who had sold ladders for Ballard I. Aside from a redesign of the logo on company letterhead, there was no indication on any printed materials that a new company was manufacturing Ballard ladders,

and Ballard II's representatives were instructed not to notify customers of the change in ownership.

Our discussion of the law starts with the rule ordinarily applied to determine successor liability in the context of an asset purchase transaction. The general rule is that a corporation that purchases the principal assets of another corporation in an arm's-length transaction is not liable for the debts and liabilities of the selling corporation. However, the courts have traditionally recognized four exceptions to this rule: (1) the purchaser has expressly agreed to assume liability; (2) the transaction amounts to a de facto merger of the two corporations; (3) the purchaser is a mere continuation of the seller; or (4) the transfer of assets to the purchaser is for the fraudulent purpose of escaping liability for the seller's debts.

If this approach were determinative of Ballard II's liability to Gray, we would be required to affirm the summary judgment. None of the four traditional exceptions for imposing liability on the purchasing corporation is present here. However, we have concluded that Gray's products liability claim could be pursued under a new exception to the general rule against corporate successor liability and that summary judgment must therefore be reversed.

The traditional rule against successor liability and the exceptions thereto are designed to protect commercial creditors and shareholders. They do not take into account the public policies underlying strict tort liability for defective products. The purpose of strict tort liability is to ensure that the costs of injuries resulting from defective products are not borne by the injured persons who are powerless to protect themselves. Rather, the costs should be borne by the manufacturers that put such products on the market and are able to spread throughout their customer base the cost of compensating those injured.

Under the circumstances here, imposing liability upon a successor to the original manufacturer is justified where the plaintiff can meet each of the following three conditions: (1) the virtual destruction of plaintiff's remedies against the original manufacturer caused by the successor's acquisition of the business, (2) the successor's ability to assume the original manufacturer's risk-spreading role, and (3) the fairness of requiring the successor to assume responsibility for defective products as a consequence of the successor enjoying the original manufacturer's goodwill in its continued operation of the business. We turn to an analysis of each of these conditions in the context of the present case.

Condition 1. We assume that Gray was injured as a result of defects in a ladder manufactured by Ballard I and therefore could assert liability against Ballard I. However, the practical value of this right of recovery against the original manufacturer was vitiated by the purchase of

Ballard I's tangible assets, trade name, and goodwill, and the dissolution of Ballard I in accordance with the purchase agreement. The injury giving rise to Gray's claim against Ballard I did not occur until more than six months after Ballard I dissolved. Thus, even if Gray could obtain a judgment on his claim against the dissolved and assetless Ballard I, he would face formidable and probably insuperable obstacles in attempting to obtain satisfaction of the judgment from former stockholders or directors. These barriers to Gray obtaining redress from the dissolved Ballard I set him (and similarly situated victims of defective products) apart from persons entitled to recovery against a dissolved corporation for claims that were capable of being known at the time of its dissolution.

Condition 2. While depriving Gray of redress against the ladder's manufacturer, Ballard I, the transaction by which Ballard II acquired Ballard I's name and operating assets had the further effect of transferring to Ballard II the resources that had previously been available to Ballard I for meeting its responsibilities to those injured by its defective ladders. These resources included not only the physical plant, manufacturing equipment, and inventories, but also the know-how available through the records of manufacturing designs, the continued employment of the factory personnel, and the consulting services of Ballard I's general manager. With these facilities and sources of information, Ballard II had virtually the same capacity as Ballard I to estimate the risks of claims for injuries from defects in previously manufactured ladders for purposes of obtaining insurance coverage or planning self-insurance. Moreover, the acquisition of the Ballard enterprise gave Ballard II the opportunity formerly enjoyed by Ballard I of passing on to purchasers of new "Ballard" products the costs of meeting these risks. Immediately after the acquisition, it was Ballard II, not Ballard I, that was in a position to promote the paramount policy of the strict products liability rule by spreading throughout its customer base the cost of compensating otherwise defenseless victims of manufacturing defects.

Condition 3. Imposing liability on Ballard II for injuries caused by Ballard I's defective products is fair vis-à-vis Ballard II in view of its acquisition of Ballard I's trade name, goodwill, and customer lists, its continuing production of the same line of ladders, and its holding itself out to potential and existing customers as the same enterprise. This deliberate albeit legitimate exploitation of Ballard I's established reputation as a going concern manufacturing a specific product line gave Ballard II a substantial benefit that its predecessor could not have enjoyed without the burden of potential liability for injuries from previously manufactured units.

Imposing liability upon successor manufacturers in the position of Ballard II has two consequences. First, it causes the successor taking the benefit of the original manufacturer's goodwill

to also bear the burden of defective products. Second, it prevents the predecessor from reaping a windfall by selling its assets at an inflated price that does not reflect successor liability and then liquidating, thereby avoiding responsibility for subsequent injuries from its defective products. Here, by taking over and continuing the established business of producing and distributing Ballard ladders, Ballard II became an integral part of the overall manufacturing enterprise that should bear the cost of injuries resulting from defective products.

In sum, we recognize a new exception, the product line successor rule, to the traditional rule governing successor liability. Where all three of the conditions discussed above have been satisfied, a party that acquires a business and continues to manufacture the acquired product line assumes liability for defects in units of the same product line that had previously been manufactured by the entity from which the business was acquired.

Reversed.

Shatner v. Burger Company

Franklin Court of Appeal (1999)

Dennis Shatner appeals from the trial court's entry of summary judgment in favor of Burger Company, the successor to asbestos distributor Oliver Corp, in this products liability action for asbestos-related injuries.

In 1998, Shatner filed a complaint against Burger alleging that he developed mesothelioma, a latent asbestos-related disease that can manifest itself 30 to 40 years after asbestos exposure, as a result of exposure to asbestos products during his employment as a pipefitter from 1948 through 1979. Burger moved for summary judgment on the grounds that it had no liability as a "product line successor" to Oliver Corp, the corporation alleged to have distributed the asbestos to which Shatner was exposed during his career as a pipefitter.

In 1960, Burger purchased the asbestos distribution assets of Oliver Corp. As consideration for the sale, Burger agreed to pay $3.7 million in cash at closing. As part of the agreement, Oliver Corp agreed to change its name so that Burger could use the "Oliver Corp" name in connection with the asbestos distribution business. Accordingly, Oliver Corp changed its name to Laurel Products. In 1962, 15 months after the asset purchase, Laurel Products dissolved. Burger played no part in the decision to dissolve Laurel Products, nor could it have, as it had no board members in common with Laurel Products, owned no stock in the corporation, and exercised no control over the entity. Furthermore, there was no provision in the original asset purchase agreement between Burger and Oliver Corp requiring the dissolution of the selling corporation. Three years after acquiring Oliver Corp, Burger left the asbestos business when it sold the goodwill and assets of its asbestos distribution business to an unrelated and now defunct entity.

Shatner asserts that Burger is liable under the three-condition "product line successor" test first enunciated in *Gray v. Ballard* (Franklin Supreme Court, 1987).

The first condition to be considered in deciding whether to impose product line successor liability is whether the successor's acquisition of the original manufacturer's business caused the virtual destruction of the plaintiff's remedies against that manufacturer. In *Gray*, the manufacturer/predecessor was dissolved within two months after the successor's purchase of the assets, trade name, and goodwill, in accordance with the purchase agreement. Thus, by virtue of the very terms of the agreement, that the predecessor would dissolve "as soon as practical," the predecessor ceased to exist as a business entity and the plaintiff's remedies against it were destroyed. The successor corporation, in a very real sense, caused the destruction of

the remedy by its acquisition of everything the predecessor possessed, which made it an ongoing business concern answerable for its predecessor's liabilities.

Following *Gray*, the court in *Kramer v. Macintosh Inc.* (Franklin Court of Appeal 1995) held that the first condition was satisfied where the successor corporation, by purchasing nearly all of the assets of the financially strapped predecessor and obtaining financial and managerial control over the predecessor, substantially contributed to the predecessor's demise.

The same cannot be said of Burger's purchase of Oliver Corp. The corporate entity that had been Oliver Corp continued to exist as Laurel Products for 15 months, when it was dissolved and liquidated by its sole shareholder, LP International, a corporation with absolutely no affiliation to Burger. The undisputed evidence showed that Oliver Corp obtained $3.7 million in cash as adequate consideration for its asbestos business assets, that it continued as an ongoing corporate entity for 15 months after the sale, and that Burger played no role in its decision to dissolve, as the two entities had no corporate overlap. The legitimate considerations of fairness that were implicated by the circumstances in *Gray* and *Kramer* are not present here. To conclude that the first condition has been satisfied under the facts of this case would essentially eviscerate the general rule of successor *nonliability* by potentially exposing successors to liability in every case where the predecessor eventually and unilaterally dissolved after selling off its assets.

The second condition addressed by the court in *Gray* was whether the successor corporation had acquired from the predecessor those resources essential to its ability to meet its responsibility to people injured by product defects. In *Gray*, the successor corporation not only acquired its predecessor's physical plant, manufacturing equipment, and inventories, but also the know-how available through the records of manufacturing designs, the continued employment of the factory personnel, and the consulting services of the predecessor's general manager. With these resources the court concluded that the successor had essentially the same capacity as its predecessor to estimate the risks of claims against it for injuries caused by product defects and to make appropriate arrangements for insurance.

The court in *Rollins v. Hardy Systems* (Franklin Court of Appeal 1997) similarly imposed liability on the successor to a manufacturer of custom-made kelp dryers. It held that the successor, which had purchased the predecessor's ongoing business, including its name, goodwill, tools, machinery, and equipment, was in a position to protect itself from loss by expressly providing for that risk when negotiating the sale terms with the predecessor and by spreading the costs of injuries among its current customers. The court determined that, because the successor had continued in the same general business, it was liable, regardless of whether it continued to make the specific injurious product.

The Burger/Oliver Corp transaction certainly has many of the same characteristics as *Gray* and *Rollins*. Burger purchased the Oliver Corp name, physical plant facilities, and machinery, and Oliver Corp's employees became Burger's employees. The differences, however, are crucial. First, in *Gray* and *Rollins*, the defendant successor corporation was still a going concern engaged in the same business as its predecessor at the time the action against it was initiated. In this case, Burger sold Oliver Corp to an unrelated entity 31 years before Shatner brought his action to recover for his injuries. Second, the record before us indicates that Burger entered and then left the asbestos business well before the government began to regulate asbestos and long before the health risks of asbestos were well known. Thus, unlike the defendants in *Gray* and *Rollins,* who could reasonably anticipate injuries to those using their products, Burger had no way to calculate the health risks posed by asbestos and incorporate those risks into its pricing and insurance decisions.

Finally, the third condition's benefit/burden balance leads us to conclude that it would be unfair to impose product line successor liability on Burger. The passage of 35 years since Burger was engaged in the asbestos business, the short (39 months) time period it spent in the business, the impossibility at the time of envisioning the need to spread such an enormous but then unknown risk, the payment of adequate consideration for the business, and the fact that Oliver Corp continued as a corporate entity with substantial assets until dissolving without Burger's involvement, support our conclusion.

We appreciate that the product line successor rule is intended to protect the victims of manufacturing defects and to spread the cost of compensating those victims. Still, where a policy rests upon fairness, as does product line successor liability, the question of fairness must itself be applied with an even hand. The undisputed evidence presented here weighs against imposition of product line successor liability on Burger.

Affirmed.

In re Clarke Corporation

Sample Answer

Jasmine Clarke, President
Clarke Corporation
800 Robinson Blvd.
Cypress, Franklin 33337

Dear Ms. Clarke:

As you know, Mary Regan has threatened to file a products liability suit against Clarke Corporation, as the corporate successor to the manufacturer of PureView dye. Ms. Regan believes that her husband's exposure to the dye caused a malignant tumor, which resulted in his death. The purpose of this letter is to explore this question: Is Clarke Corporation liable, under the product line successor rule established by the Franklin Supreme Court in *Gray v. Ballard Corporation*, for any injury allegedly caused by the PureView dye?

The answer to that question is no. The rule does not apply to our situation because at least two of the three conditions have not been met, specifically that the purchase of Santoy Enterprises did not result in destruction of remedies and that it would not be fair to hold Clarke Corporation liable.

STATEMENT OF FACTS

After arms-length negotiations, on September 1, 1990, Clarke Corporation ("Clarke") purchased Santoy Enterprise's Drug Manufacturing Division ("DMD"), leaving Santoy with 20% of its assets (a chemical solvent manufacturing division). The purchase agreement stated that Clarke acquired from DMD all manufacturing facilities, machinery, inventory, all lab supplies and related research materials, customer lists, trade names and secrets, goodwill, and other assets. Clarke hired most of DMD's employees, although none of Santoy's officers, directors, or shareholders became affiliated with Clarke. Clarke paid $2.5 million for the acquisition—there was no exchange of shares.

The agreement also contained a general limitations on liabilities clause, a five-year noncompetition clause, and a clause requiring Santoy to change its name within 10 days of the agreement. Santoy changed its name to Sentinel Enterprises. Two years later, Sentinel filed for bankruptcy and was dissolved.

PureView, an X-ray contrast dye product, was one the five products included in the sale and had accounted for less than 5% of DMD's sales. Clarke continued to manufacture the five products, utilizing identical procedures and product names as those used by Santoy but using Clarke's manufacturing facilities. Clarke informed customers that it, and not Santoy, was now the manufacturer. Six months after the purchase (March 1991), Clarke ceased manufacture of PureView because the dye had become technologically obsolete. Clarke continued manufacturing the remaining four unrelated products which constitute approximately 15% of Clarke's business.

Three months ago, the *Journal of American Medicine* reported a link between the use, more than 20 years ago, of PureView and a rare and potentially fatal type of cancer. PureView has never before been linked to any serious medical condition. Ms. Regan now demands that Clarke, as Santoy's successor, assume liability for Mr. Regan's death.

ANALYSIS

In *Gray v. Ballard Corporation,* the Franklin Supreme Court set forth a new rule of corporate successor liability. *Gray* concerned a successor ladder manufacturer that continued manufacturing the same product that caused the injury. The court held that public policy—*i.e.,* protection of innocent victims and the spreading of the risk throughout the customer base—called for the creation of this new rule: A

corporate successor can be held liable for the original manufacturer's product defects when: (i) the purchase virtually destroys all remedies against the original manufacturer; (ii) the successor is able to assume the original manufacturer's risk-spreading function; ***and*** (iii) it is fair for the successor to assume liability since it has assumed the original manufacturer's goodwill.

There are many facts in our case that are similar to those in *Gray*. As in *Gray*, Clarke purchased the manufacturing facilities, machinery, inventory, trade names and secrets, customer and mailing lists, goodwill, and other assets of DMD. Factory personnel remained nearly the same because Clarke hired most of DMD's employees. Clarke continued to manufacture in an identical manner the same DMD products, using DMD's product names, and solicited DMD's customers. Also as in *Gray*, DMD dissolved after the sale, thus depriving potential plaintiffs of a remedy for injuries from product defects.

However, there are crucial facts in our case that distinguish it from *Gray*. In fact, our case is much closer to *Shatner v. Burger Company*, in which the appellate court held that the product line successor rule was inapplicable to a successor to an asbestos distributor. *Shatner* discusses each of the three conditions set forth in *Gray* separately. We will now look at each in light of our case.

A. Purchase Virtually Destroys All Remedies Against Original Manufacturer

Clarke's purchase of DMD did not destroy all remedies against Santoy. The agreement in *Gray* required the original manufacturer to dissolve after the sale. There was no such requirement in our purchase agreement, only that Santoy change its name and not compete for five years. Neither of these requirements caused Santoy to go out of business; in fact, Santoy continued its business for two more years under the name of Sentinel.

The agreement in *Gray* did not specifically discuss liability for defective products. Our purchase agreement also does not specifically mention liability for defective products, but it does state that Clarke will not be liable for Santoy's obligations ***except for*** leases, contracts, and other pre-sale agreements made in the ordinary course of business before the purchase agreement. While it may not be persuasive, we can at least argue that our agreement limited Clarke's liability to leases, contracts, etc., and excludes liability for defective products.

Kramer v. Macintosh Inc., another appellate court case, held that this first requirement was met when the successor corporation purchased nearly all of the predecessor's assets and obtained financial and managerial control. Although Clarke purchased 80% of Santoy's assets, Santoy used those funds to operate its chemical solvent manufacturing business for two more years as Sentinel. Also, Clarke had no control over Sentinel's operations. As in *Shatner*, there was no corporate overlap between Clarke and Sentinel, and thus Clarke had no control, financial or managerial, over Sentinel's actions. Clarke played no role in Sentinel's decision to dissolve.

Thus, the first condition has not been met. To find otherwise ". . .would essentially eviscerate the general rule of successor *nonliability* by potentially exposing successors to liability in every case where the predecessor eventually and unilaterally dissolved after selling off its assets." [Shatner v. Burger Company]

B. Purchaser's Ability to Spread Risks

Although Clarke discontinued manufacture of PureView six months after the purchase, this may not persuade a court that Clarke was relieved of the ability to spread risks among its remaining DMD products. Clarke still manufactures the other four DMD products included in the purchase, the sale of which constitutes 15% of its business. The appellate court in *Rollins v. Hardy Systems* held that a successor that had purchased its predecessor's machinery, tools, goodwill, and name had the ability to cover its risk by including it as a factor in the purchase price and by the price charged to customers. This risk-spreading ability continues even after the defective product is no longer manufactured. Thus, it is likely that a court will find that Clarke can still spread its risk based on its pricing of the remaining four DMD products.

We can argue that our case is closer to *Shatner* than *Rollins*. As in *Shatner*, Clarke discontinued manufacture of the product many years before the claim arose and it had left the business of making the dye long before any health risks were known. We can argue that Clarke could not calculate the risk and incorporate those risks into its pricing or insurance. However, Clarke acquired Santoy's trade secrets, supplies, research materials, equipment, etc., and so it arguably is in the same position as Santoy was to assess the risks. This fact combined with the fact that Clarke continues to manufacture four of the DMD products will likely render this argument unpersuasive.

Therefore, although the second *Gray* condition probably has been met, Clarke will not be liable unless all three requirements of the product line successor rule have been fulfilled.

C. Fairness of Assumption of Liability

The third condition requires a balancing of the benefits and burdens—that is, whether it is fair to impose liability on Clarke for a defective product manufactured by Santoy because Clarke purchased Santoy's goodwill as well as the product. It appears that our case is more like *Shatner* than *Gray*, and that the burdens likely outweigh the benefits flowing from the goodwill.

One of the reasons underlying the *Gray* decision was to prevent corporations from selling at an inflated price and then dissolving, thereby avoiding liability for defective product injuries. In *Gray*, the predecessor dissolved its corporation two months after the sale, as required by the purchase agreement. Thus, the successor had a role in the dissolution and could fairly be held responsible for products liability. Clarke had no role in Sentinel's decision to dissolve, the sale was for fair compensation, and Sentinel remained in business for two years.

Also, the injury in *Gray* occurred approximately nine months after the purchase, and the successor clearly relied on its predecessor's goodwill by holding itself out to customers as the same manufacturer, never notifying them of the change of ownership. The goodwill Clarke acquired in relation to PureView was short-lived (six months before the product became obsolete), and the injury occurred many years before the purchase. Furthermore, customers did not rely on Santoy's reputation since Clarke notified them that Clarke was now the manufacturer. Thus, Clarke received little goodwill attributable to PureView.

Looking at *Shatner*, the successor there continued manufacture of the product for 39 months after the purchase. The court found that because of the short manufacturing period and the very long period between the successor's ownership of the business and assertion of the injury, it would be unfair to impose product liability 35 years later, especially when it was not previously possible to spread an unknown risk among the asbestos products. Similarly, Clarke manufactured PureView for only six months, and Mr. Regan was injected with PureView more than 20 years ago, seven years before Clarke's purchase. Moreover, it was nearly 15 years after Clarke ceased manufacture that a possible risk attributable to the product was discovered. Like the successor in *Shatner*, Clarke has had no opportunity to "spread the risk," either by factoring it into the Santoy assets purchase price or by the prices charged to customers of the remaining four DMD products since the defect has just now been discovered.

In light of the above, it would be unfair to impose liability on Clarke.

CONCLUSION

The product line successor rule is inapplicable to Clarke because at least two of the three *Gray* requirements have not been met. Clarke's acquisition from Santoy was not the cause of the predecessor's dissolution and therefore Clarke was not responsible for destruction of remedies for product defects. Moreover, a balancing of the benefits and burdens indicates that it is unfair to impose product liability on Clarke.

Sincerely yours,
Margaret MacKenzie

Multistate Performance Test

In re Mistover Acres LLC

National Conference of Bar Examiners

Preface

This Multistate Performance Test is a reprint of one of the two MPTs which were administered in July 2007.

The instructions for the test appear on the next page. On the actual MPT, they will appear on the back cover of the test.

INSTRUCTIONS

1. You will have 90 minutes to complete this session of the examination. This performance test is designed to evaluate your ability to handle a select number of legal authorities in the context of a factual problem involving a client.

2. The problem is set in the fictitious state of Franklin, in the fictitious Fifteenth Circuit of the United States. Columbia and Olympia are also fictitious states in the Fifteenth Circuit. In Franklin, the trial court of general jurisdiction is the District Court, the intermediate appellate court is the Court of Appeal, and the highest court is the Supreme Court.

3. You will have two kinds of materials with which to work: a File and a Library. The first document in the File is a memorandum containing the instructions for the task you are to complete. The other documents in the File contain factual information about your case and may include some facts that are not relevant.

4. The Library contains the legal authorities needed to complete the task and may also include some authorities that are not relevant. Any cases may be real, modified, or written solely for the purpose of this examination. If the cases appear familiar to you, do not assume that they are precisely the same as you have read before. Read them thoroughly, as if they all were new to you. You should assume that cases were decided in the jurisdictions and on the dates shown. In citing cases from the Library, you may use abbreviations and omit page references.

5. Your response must be written in the answer book provided. If you are taking this examination on a laptop computer, your jurisdiction will provide you with specific instructions. In answering this performance test, you should concentrate on the materials provided in the File and Library. What you have learned in law school and elsewhere provides the general background for analyzing the problem; the File and Library provide the specific materials with which you must work.

6. Although there are no restrictions on how you apportion your time, you should be sure to allocate ample time (about 45 minutes) to reading and digesting the materials and to organizing your answer before you begin writing it. You may make notes anywhere in the test materials; blank pages are provided at the end of the booklet. You may not tear pages from the question booklet.

7. This performance test will be graded on your responsiveness to the instructions regarding the task you are to complete, which are given to you in the first memorandum in the File, and on the content, thoroughness, and organization of your response.

In re Mistover Acres LLC

FILE

LIBRARY

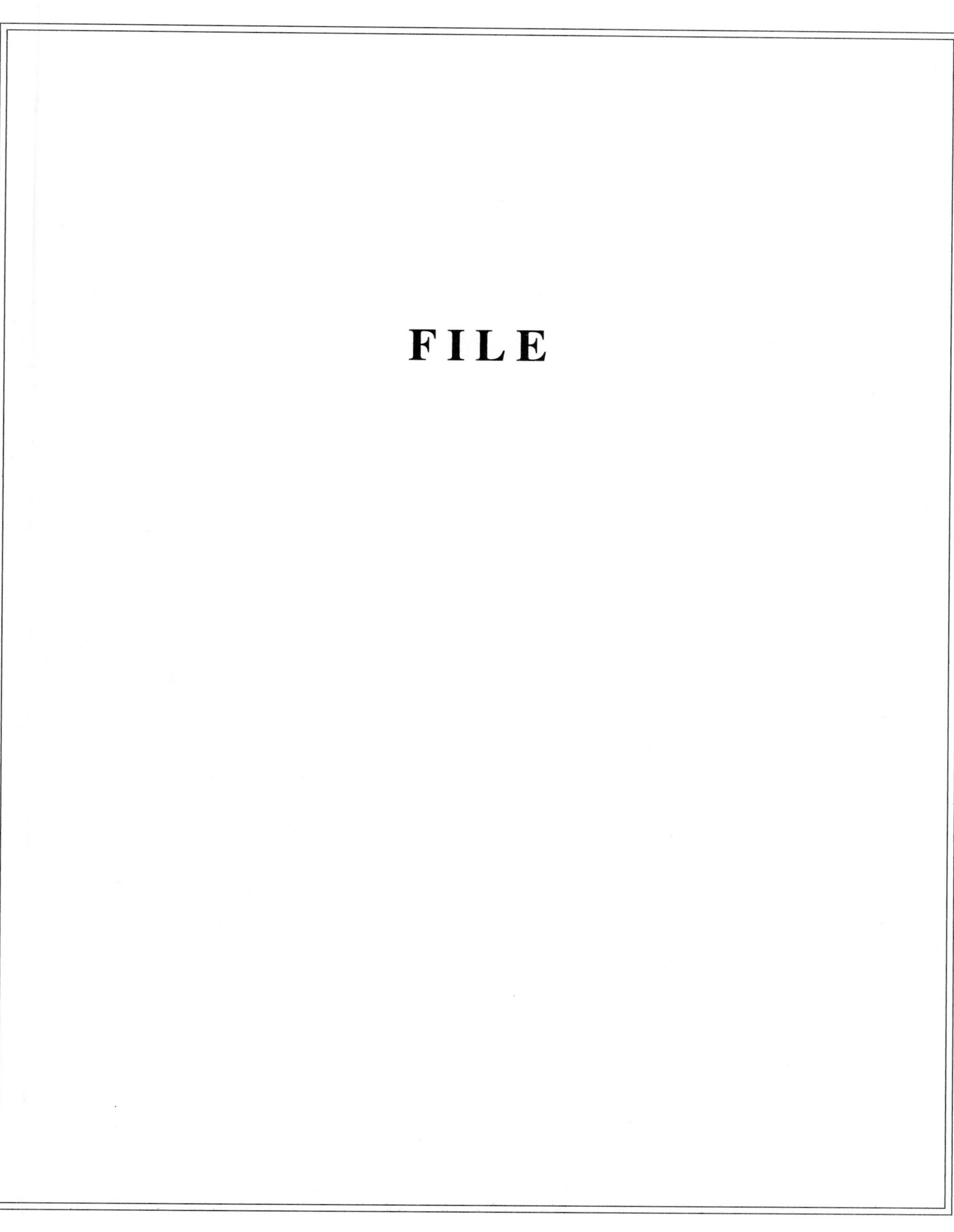

FILE

PALKOVICH, VAN EVERY & DOOLEY
ATTORNEYS AT LAW
3034 Sutton Avenue
Banford, Franklin 33518

TO: Applicant
FROM: Lyle Palkovich
RE: Mistover Acres LLC
DATE: July 24, 2007

We have been retained by Petra Flynn, one of three members of Mistover Acres LLC ("Mistover"), a Franklin limited liability company, to review a claim made against Mistover by Genesee Trout, Inc., for damage to its trout farm caused by the aerial crop dusting of a pesticide, MU-83, on Mistover's fields. Mistover is a well-respected grower and seller of apples, salad greens, and herbs.

We are representing Petra Flynn in her individual capacity. Mistover has its own legal counsel. Ms. Flynn has come to us because she is concerned about her potential personal liability for the harm claimed by the trout farm. She believes that Mistover's organization completely shields her from personal liability for Mistover's business-related activities, but she is understandably troubled by the demand letter from Genesee Trout's counsel. Another concern I have is whether the aerial crop dusting of MU-83 constituted an ultrahazardous activity, thereby raising the possibility of strict liability. The next meeting with Ms. Flynn on this matter is scheduled for July 31, 2007.

Please prepare an objective memorandum analyzing the following questions under Franklin law:

1) Can Ms. Flynn be held personally liable for the damage done by the aerial crop dusting?
2) Did the aerial crop dusting of MU-83 constitute an ultrahazardous activity?

You need not prepare a separate statement of facts, but in each part of the memorandum you should incorporate the relevant facts, analyze the applicable legal authorities, and explain how the facts and law affect your analysis. A carefully crafted subject heading should precede each discussion section. For the purpose of your analysis, assume that the aerial crop dusting caused the damage to the trout farm.

Client Interview Notes: Petra Flynn

July 17, 2007

Petra Flynn is one of three members of Mistover Acres LLC. The other two members are Petra's brother, Gilbert Flynn, and their cousin, Chip Kendall. They formed Mistover after Petra and Gil inherited two adjoining parcels of land in Sutton Township. Mistover grows apples, herbs, and unusual varieties of lettuce that have become very popular in gourmet restaurants. Under the terms of the Mistover Acres LLC Operating Agreement, Petra and Gil lease their land, about 60 acres, to the business. Petra and Gil do some work for Mistover, but as Chip has the expertise in agriculture, most of the decisions regarding planting are left to him. Petra supervises the marketing and sale of Mistover's produce.

Petra has come to the firm for advice regarding her potential personal liability for claims made by Genesee Trout, Inc., in a demand letter its attorneys sent to Mistover's office. She is concerned about Mistover being liable for such a large claim, as it has yet to turn a profit and Chip invested all the money he had in Mistover when they organized it five years ago. According to Petra, Chip "is essentially judgment proof," and Gil's financial situation has always been precarious. She fears that, because she has substantial assets of her own, any lawsuit by Genesee Trout will try to target her as a "deep-pocket" defendant.

Sutton Township is an area of rolling hills that has long been agricultural. In the 1990s, farmers experienced economic difficulties, but in recent years, small-scale, specialized producers like Mistover have been reviving the local economy. A number of these producers are devoted to organic agricultural practices. For example, across the road from Mistover is Haakon Farms, where the owner sells goat cheese made with the milk from her own herd. And, as noted in the demand letter, Genesee Trout's trout farm lies just east of Mistover.

According to Petra, the three members began Mistover to put into practice their belief that consumers deserved another option besides the bland fruits and vegetables grown by factory farms that dominate the selections in most supermarkets. Nonetheless, neither she nor Gil was particularly thrilled when Chip suggested growing new lettuce varieties. Mistover's heirloom apple varieties were selling well and the lettuce varieties could not be successfully raised in amounts needed for sale without the use of some chemical fertilizers and pesticides, which they generally try to avoid. Chip, however, persuaded them that these rare lettuces would soon be "must have" salad greens in the best restaurants, and that the price

Mistover could charge would soon generate enough income to allow it to expand into other vegetable crops. Chip also argued that, as one of the only operations offering a unique and locally grown lettuce variety, Mistover would earn a reputation for being an innovator in the gourmet produce market.

Mistover first grew lettuce two years ago and the crop did well. Last year, however, Chip discovered leaf slugs on the plants. If nothing had been done about the leaf slugs, they could have destroyed one-third of the crop. Chip proposed using a pesticide, but Petra expressed concerns about the marketing consequences, as they had always emphasized that Mistover's produce was locally grown with minimal chemicals. They researched pesticides together and ultimately selected MU-83, a new pesticide. Petra then ordered it last year through an agricultural supplier; MU-83 is not available to the general public. Chip walked through the fields with some of Mistover's seasonal help and sprayed the lettuce crop with MU-83. It was effective, but the labor costs of the pesticide application were high.

When Chip found the leaf slugs again this season, he determined that the slugs were more numerous than last year and that hand spraying would involve even higher labor costs. Before joining Mistover, when he lived in Columbia, Chip had worked one growing season using his small airplane to dust large corn and wheat fields with pesticides and herbicides. He and Petra decided to use aerial crop dusting, and Petra ordered more MU-83. The Franklin Environmental Code requires posting for aerial crop dusting, and Petra ensured that the proper notice was posted on the Sutton Township website, at the Town Hall, and at three other public places.

Chip sprayed the fields with MU-83 on March 28, 2007. Petra was at Mistover that afternoon and watched Chip take off in his airplane, circle the farm buildings, and then fly over the plants at a height of about 20 feet to apply the MU-83. She did not observe the yellow cloud described in the letter from Genesee Trout's attorneys, but does recall that there was a light breeze blowing from the west, which possibly could have carried MU-83 in the direction of the trout ponds. Two days later she and Chip walked through the fields and verified that the MU-83 had killed any visible leaf slugs.

The lettuce, Mistover's best crop yet, was picked and sold at a prime price. Until the letter from Genesee Trout's attorneys arrived, none of the LLC members had heard any complaints about the MU-83 aerial crop dusting or their farming activities in general. Petra will come in next week to discuss the situation.

FRENCH & ISENBERG, LLP
ATTORNEYS AT LAW
222 SHEFFIELD AVE
CENTRALIA, FRANKLIN 33530

July 17, 2007

Ms. Petra Flynn
Mistover Acres LLC
P.O. Box 572
Derby, Franklin 38440

Re: Genesee Trout, Inc.

Dear Ms. Flynn:

We represent Genesee Trout, Inc., the owner of the trout farm that abuts Mistover Acres on its eastern edge. On March 28, 2007, our client's employees observed a crop-dusting airplane flying over the fields of Mistover Acres, spraying a yellow-colored substance. They then observed a yellow cloud drifting over Genesee Trout's fish ponds. In the months since that date, a higher-than-expected percentage of our client's trout stock has died, and the number of successful egg hatchings has substantially declined. The water in the fish ponds has been tested and has been found to contain significant levels of the pesticide MU-83. The cost to clean the ponds and restock the trout will exceed $1 million. Genesee Trout is also concerned that MU-83 will leech into the local water supply.

The presence of MU-83 in the Genesee Trout fish ponds, the resulting decline in the trout stock and egg hatchings, and the potential damage to the water supply were caused by Mistover Acres LLC's aerial crop dusting on March 28, 2007.

Genesee Trout, Inc., is willing to settle its claims against Mistover Acres LLC. However, if a settlement cannot be reached, our client has instructed us to pursue legal action against Mistover Acres LLC and its members. If you are willing to discuss settlement, please respond to this letter within two weeks of its receipt.

Sincerely,

Walter French

Walter French

OPERATING AGREEMENT OF MISTOVER ACRES LLC

This OPERATING AGREEMENT is entered into by Petra Flynn, Gilbert Flynn, and Chip Kendall for the purpose of organizing a limited liability company pursuant to the Franklin Limited Liability Company Act, §601 *et seq.*

1. **Name and Purpose:** The limited liability company shall be known as MISTOVER ACRES LLC (hereinafter "the LLC"). Its purpose is to grow and market apples and other produce for sale at farmers' markets and to restaurants and other commercial establishments.

2. **Members:** The members of the LLC are Petra Flynn, Gilbert Flynn, and Chip Kendall.

3. **Capital Contributions:** The capital contributions of the respective members shall be as follows:

   a. Chip Kendall: $50,000 (fifty thousand dollars).
   b. Petra Flynn: $10,000 (ten thousand dollars).
   c. Gilbert Flynn: $10,000 (ten thousand dollars).

4. **Lease of Agricultural Land:** On or before the date of filing of the Articles of Organization, leases will be entered into between the LLC and Petra Flynn, and the LLC and Gilbert Flynn, for the two adjoining 30-acre parcels on Schmidt Road, Derby, Franklin, identified as Tracts 37 and 38 of Sutton Township Certified Survey 2713. The LLC shall have the exclusive right to lease these parcels for as long as the LLC continues in existence or until such time as the members agree to terminate the leases.

5. **Management:** With respect to acquisition of capital assets by the LLC, or the addition of new members or employees of the LLC, the undersigned members shall in all cases act as a group, with a majority vote or consent of the members required to take action. Day-to-day decisions regarding planting and harvesting are delegated to Chip Kendall until the members agree otherwise. The marketing and sale of the LLC's produce shall be supervised by Petra Flynn.

6. **Sharing in Distributions and Profits:** For the first five (5) years of the LLC's existence, the profits, if any, will be reinvested into the LLC's operations. If any profit is realized in subsequent years, 50 percent (50%) will be reinvested into the LLC, and the remainder will be distributed in equal shares to the members.

7. **Accounting:** Members shall receive annual financial reports containing the LLC's balance sheet and a statement showing the net capital appreciation or depreciation.

8. **Applicable Law:** All questions concerning the construction, validity and interpretation of this agreement and the performance of the obligations imposed by this agreement shall be governed by the laws of the State of Franklin.

Dated: February 15, 2002

Petra Flynn
Petra Flynn

Gilbert Flynn
Gilbert Flynn

Chip Kendall
Chip Kendall

USER'S GUIDE FOR MU-83 APPLICATION

Thank you for selecting an AgriShield, Inc., product to protect your crops! MU-83 is an effective pesticide for use on all crops, including those intended for human consumption. Studies by the University of Franklin Agricultural College have demonstrated that it is 98% successful in completely eradicating pests such as rootworm, boll weevils, and leaf slugs, when applied according to directions. It is suitable for application by hand, tractor-pulled spraying rig, or aerial dusting by airplane. Aerial dusting should occur at a distance no higher than 30 feet from the intended target area.

* * * *

As with all pesticides, persons applying MU-83 should use caution and be aware that pesticide "drift" (the movement of pesticide droplets or particles in the air from the targeted field to non-target areas) is always a risk of pesticide application. Drift and runoff may be toxic to aquatic organisms in neighboring areas. Drift will occur with every application. The amount of drift is subject to various controllable and uncontrollable factors, such as time of application, concentration, wind gusts, weather changes, and the physical characteristics of pesticide droplets or aerosols. Apply this product only in accordance with application instructions found on the label.

WARNING: IMPROPER USE OR APPLICATION OF MU-83 MAY CAUSE SERIOUS INJURY OR DEATH.

SUTTON TOWNSHIP

PUBLIC NOTICE

In accordance with the Franklin Environmental Code, §22(1), Mistover Acres LLC hereby gives public notice that it will conduct aerial crop dusting of the following pesticide on the date indicated:

Pesticide: MU-83

The pesticide application will occur on March 28, 2007 on the following described property in Sutton Township:

> The two adjoining 30-acre parcels identified as Tracts 37 and 38 of Sutton Township Certified Survey 2713, according to the records of the Clerk and Recorder of Washington County, Franklin, and also known as Mistover Acres LLC, 200 W. Schmidt Rd.

For further information, contact:

Petra Flynn
200 W. Schmidt Road
Derby, Franklin 33510
(920) 555-1085

Dated this 25th day of March, 2007

Mistover Acres LLC

by Petra Flynn

Petra Flynn, its authorized representative

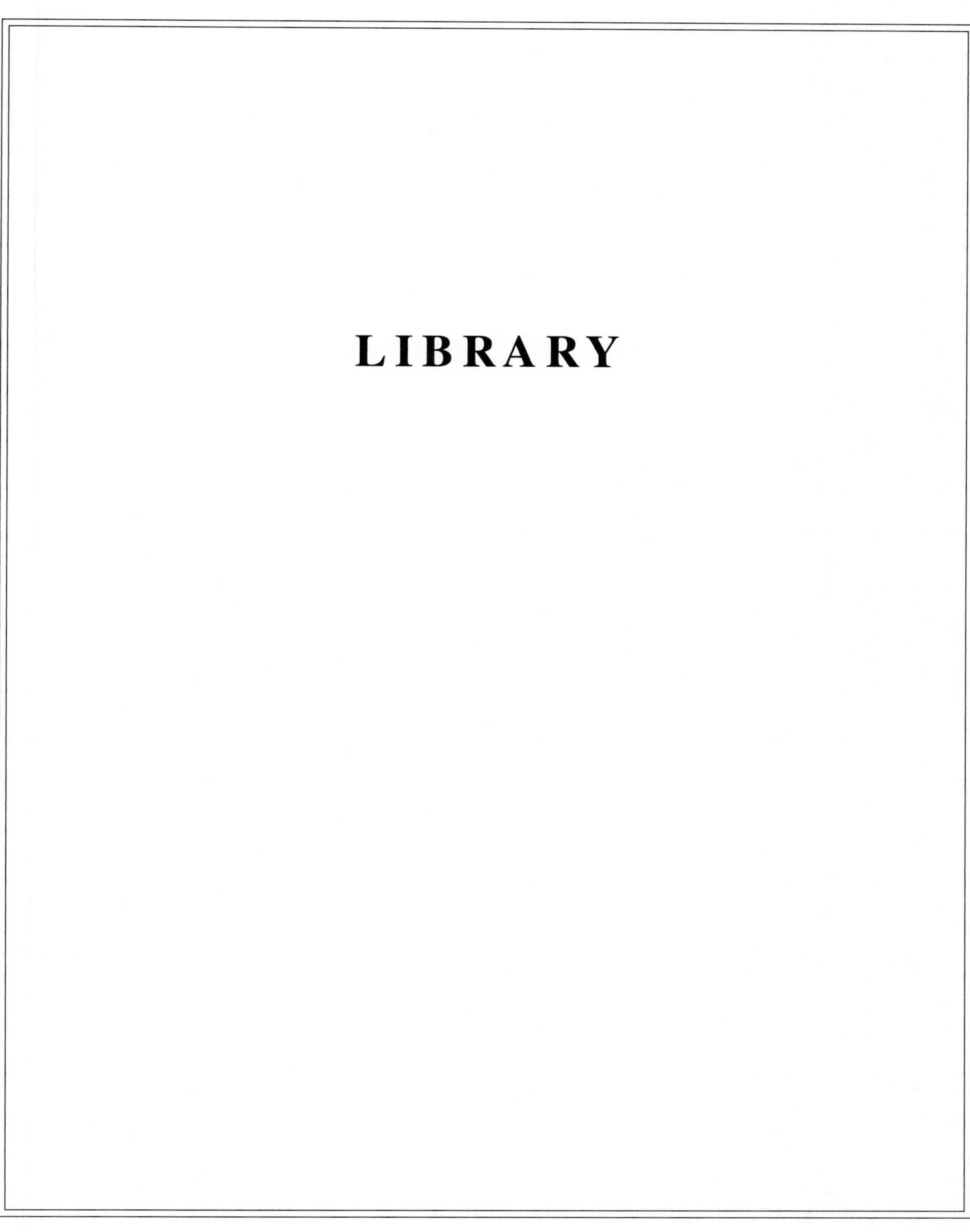

LIBRARY

Franklin Limited Liability Company Act

§601 General Purposes.

(1) A limited liability company may be organized under this Act for any lawful purpose . . . .

(2) Unless otherwise provided in an operating agreement, a limited liability company organized and existing under this Act has the same powers as an individual to do all things necessary and convenient to carry out its business, including but not limited to all of the following:

(a) Sue and be sued, complain and defend in its own name.

(b) Purchase, take, receive, lease, or otherwise acquire and own, hold, improve, use, and otherwise deal in or with real or personal property or any legal or equitable interest in real or personal property, wherever situated.

(c) Sell, convey, mortgage, lease, and otherwise dispose of all or any part of its property . . . .

(d) Make contracts and guarantees; incur liabilities. . . .

* * * *

(g) Elect or appoint managers, agents, and employees of the limited liability company, define their duties, and fix their compensation.

* * * *

§605 Liability of members.

(1) The debts, obligations, and liabilities of a limited liability company, whether arising in contract, tort, or otherwise, shall be solely the debts, obligations, and liabilities of the limited liability company.

(2) Except as otherwise provided in this Act or by written agreement of a member, a member of a limited liability company is not personally liable solely by reason of being a member of the limited liability company for any debt, obligation, or liability of the limited liability company, whether that liability or obligation arises in contract, tort, or otherwise, or for the acts or omissions of any other member, agent, or employee of the limited liability company.

(3) Nothing in this section shall be construed to affect the liability of a member of a limited liability company to third parties for the member's participation in tortious conduct.

(4) A member of a limited liability company is not a proper party to a proceeding by or against a limited liability company solely by reason of being a member of the limited liability company, except where the object of the proceeding is to enforce a member's right against or liability to the limited liability company or as otherwise provided in an operating agreement.

Hodas v. Ice LLC

Franklin Court of Appeal (2004)

This is an action to recover damages for injuries sustained in a motor vehicle accident. The complaint alleged that on March 18, 2000, between 12:00 a.m. and 1:45 a.m., Tony Veit and Todd Hodas were patrons of the Firefly Bar in Groton, Franklin. The Firefly Bar is owned by Ice LLC. Defendants Duncan O'Malley, Joe Kaufman, and Victor Casellano are the only members of Ice LLC.

While at the Firefly Bar, Veit consumed large quantities of alcohol. Despite his being obviously intoxicated, the defendants and/or their employees continued to serve him. Veit and Hodas, both grossly intoxicated, left the Firefly in Veit's car. While speeding, Veit lost control of the vehicle and hit a tree. Veit died at the scene and Hodas was seriously injured.

Hodas claims that the defendants were negligent and reckless in their conduct by selling any alcohol to an obviously intoxicated person. O'Malley, Kaufman, and Casellano argue that they were entitled to summary judgment because liability cannot attach solely by virtue of the fact that they were members of Ice LLC, the entity that owned the bar. The trial court denied the summary judgment motion. We granted O'Malley, Kaufman, and Casellano leave to bring this interlocutory appeal.

DISCUSSION

It is undisputed that Ice LLC is a Franklin limited liability company organized under the Franklin Limited Liability Company Act (FLLCA), §601 *et seq*. The original property lease agreement identifies Ice LLC as Lessee, acting through its members O'Malley and Kaufman. A liquor license application for the bar states that Casellano invested $80,000 in Ice LLC to be used for the purpose of renovating the building in Groton that houses the Firefly Bar. The Ice LLC operating agreement names the three as the sole members of the LLC.

A limited liability company, or "LLC," is a business entity that combines the attributes of a partnership for federal income tax purposes with the limited liability protections that a corporation provides to shareholders. Like a partnership, an LLC allows the owners, called members, to participate in the management of the business. LLCs are typically governed by operating agreements. The provisions pertaining to the liability of LLC members are found in §605 of the FLLCA.

The FLLCA generally provides that a member of an LLC is not personally liable for acts or debts of the company solely by reason of being a member. Nevertheless, a member may be personally liable if the person participates in tortious conduct.

O'Malley and Kaufman contend that tort liability of an LLC member is limited to conduct committed *outside* the member role. We reject this approach as contravening the corporate and agency principles upon which the liability of LLC members is based. Nor does the language of the FLLCA support such a restriction. We recognize, however, that the "participation in tortious conduct" standard does not impose tort liability on a member for performing what is merely a general administrative duty. *See Lee v. Bayrd* (Franklin Ct. App. 1985) (no tort liability where corporate officer not shown to have authorized, directed, or participated in tortious act). There must be some participation; liability of individuals is derived from individual activities. This standard thus comports with the principle that members are not liable based only on their status.

O'Malley, Kaufman, and Casellano argue that this view of limited liability defeats the language of §605(2) that bars tort liability predicated solely by reason of an individual's status as a member of the LLC. We disagree. The phrase "solely by reason of" refers to liability based upon membership or management *status*. It does not immunize a member's *conduct*. It is not inconsistent to protect a member from vicarious liability (*e.g.*, for the tortious acts of another LLC member or employee), while imposing liability when the member participates in a tort. In short, liability of LLC members is limited, but not to the extent claimed by O'Malley, Kaufman, and Casellano.

O'Malley and Kaufman

The complaint alleges that O'Malley and Kaufman failed to properly supervise and train their personnel and failed to monitor their patrons to ensure safety.

O'Malley and Kaufman both admitted at their depositions that they were at the bar on March 17, 2000, into the morning hours of the 18th, and that the place was very busy. Kaufman stated that he usually deals with the customers and personnel. O'Malley testified that on that night, he was "all over the place, making sure everyone was doing what they were supposed to, greeting customers and doing other 'PR' work." Neither defendant could affirm or deny whether he had personally served alcohol to Veit.

O'Malley and Kaufman would not be liable solely because of their status as members of Ice LLC. But the FLLCA does not affect the liability of an LLC member who participates in tortious conduct, whether or not that conduct is on behalf of the LLC. *See* §605(3). Given the participation of O'Malley and Kaufman in the operations of the business, there are material issues of fact which precluded the granting of summary judgment. *See Goff v. PureMilk LLC* (Franklin Ct. App. 1997) (summary judgment inappropriate where agreement required LLC's member/manager to provide human resources and consulting services to LLC and extent of member's/manager's participation in tortious conduct was unknown). A trial is necessary to develop the facts relating to allegations of O'Malley and Kaufman's participation in the

alleged torts. For this reason, the court affirms the denial of summary judgment as to O'Malley and Kaufman.

Casellano

There was no evidence before the trial court that Casellano was at the Firefly Bar on March 17, 2000, or that he participated in the business operations at any point in time relevant to the allegations in the complaint. To support his claim for Casellano's liability, Hodas referred to the liquor license application that was signed and filed by Casellano, a trade name certificate recorded in the Groton Land Records listing Casellano as one of the persons involved in the business known as the Firefly Bar, and the operating agreement designating Casellano as a member of the LLC.

These documents clearly demonstrate that Casellano was a member of Ice LLC in March 2000. Nothing else has been presented as a basis for Casellano's liability. Hodas could not overcome the fact that his claim for liability is based solely upon Casellano's status as a member of the LLC. Section 605(2) of the FLLCA precludes liability based on membership status alone. Further, a member is not liable for the acts or omissions of any other member of the limited liability company. For this reason, the court reverses the denial of summary judgment as to Casellano.

Affirmed in part, reversed in part, and remanded for further proceedings.

Thurman v. Ellis

Franklin Court of Appeal (2003)

Defendant Gwen Ellis appeals from a judgment entered on a jury verdict awarding damages to plaintiff Adele Thurman in the amount of $50,000. The issue before us is whether the trial court erred in instructing the jury that breeders of pit bull dogs are strictly liable for any harm caused by their animals on the basis that raising pit bulls is an ultrahazardous activity.

Ellis has bred pit bulls for several years. Thurman was injured when, on a visit to Ellis's home, the mother of the current litter attacked her while she was holding a puppy. Thurman suffered deep wounds to her arm and hand before Ellis could restrain the dog. Although Thurman alleged three other counts in her complaint, only the claim for strict liability based on an ultrahazardous activity is before us on appeal.

Those who engage in ultrahazardous activities are, as a general rule, subject to strict liability for the harm caused to the innocent as a result of the activity. When determining whether an activity is ultrahazardous, we apply §520 of the Restatement (Second) of Torts, which requires analysis of six factors: (1) existence of a high degree of risk of some harm to the person, land, or chattels of others; (2) likelihood that the resulting harm will be great; (3) inability to eliminate the risk by the exercise of reasonable care; (4) extent to which the activity is not a matter of common usage; (5) inappropriateness of the activity to the place where it is carried on; and (6) extent to which the activity's value to the community is outweighed by its dangerous attributes. *Sisson v. City of Bremerton* (Franklin Sup. Ct. 1975). This is a totality of the circumstances test. No one factor is determinative.

In Franklin, assessment of the §520 factors has resulted in the imposition of strict liability for firework displays; rock blasting where injury occurred to property on an adjacent lot; emissions from chemical separation as part of weapons-grade plutonium production; and a common carrier's transportation of large quantities of gasoline. Under the same analysis of the factors in §520, Franklin courts have held that the following activities are *not* ultrahazardous: household use of water, electricity, or gas; operation of oil and gas wells in rural areas; and ground damage caused by the crash landing of aircraft.

Sisson provides a detailed example of the court's reasoning when applying the §520 factors. There, it was alleged that the city's demolition project, which caused the collapse of the retaining walls that protected the plaintiffs' homes, constituted an ultrahazardous activity rendering the city strictly liable for the damage. The court emphasized that the inability to

eliminate the risk by the exercise of reasonable care would generally carry more weight than the other factors, but that this factor alone was not dispositive of whether an activity is ultrahazardous. Moreover, while the availability and relative costs, economic and otherwise, of alternative methods for conducting the activity are basic to the inquiry, the court stressed that an activity that was ultrahazardous in one context is not necessarily ultrahazardous for all occasions. Ultimately, the court held that the record was inadequate to determine whether the demolition project was ultrahazardous.

Fredricks v. Centralia Fire Dept. (Franklin Ct. App. 1999) explained that the value of an activity to the community will at times negate factors that would otherwise favor imposing strict liability. In *Fredricks*, it was claimed that the fire department had conducted an ultrahazardous activity in putting out a fire and that water used to put out the fire had spread toxic waste to adjoining properties, requiring costly cleanup. The court reasoned that, while firefighting presented a high degree of risk, the value to the community far outweighed the inherent dangers of the activity. In addition, referring to the fifth factor, the court noted that there was no reasonable basis for the plaintiff's claim, as it "defied logic to argue that it is inappropriate to carry out firefighting at the site of a fire." *Id.*

Here, Ellis disputes the evidence of a high degree of risk of harm. She testified that, until the attack on Thurman, none of her dogs had behaved violently. Her expert, a nationally known breeder, opined that pit bulls are good-tempered, loyal animals, unless specifically trained to be aggressive. Thurman, however, presented the opinions of a veterinarian and an authority on pit bulls to show that years of breeding had created an aggressive breed that was easily provoked, especially if an animal thought its young were in danger.

While the precise degree of risk posed by pit bulls is uncertain, it is undisputed that because of the pit bull's powerful jaw structure, it is extremely difficult to open the dog's mouth once it bites someone or something. This practically ensures that anyone bitten by a pit bull will sustain a severe injury. In addition, the fact that Ellis was breeding pit bulls in her home in a residential neighborhood, in close proximity to young children, as opposed to a less populated area or at least a location with sufficient space for an outdoor dog kennel, leads us to conclude that the activity was being conducted in an inappropriate place. Ellis correctly points out that no city ordinance banned breeding dogs such as pit bulls within city limits. However, the fact that an activity is legal is not a defense to a claim that the activity is ultrahazardous. The first, second, and fifth factors support holding Ellis strictly liable for the harm caused by her dogs.

Turning to the fourth factor, we recognize that dog breeding in general is a common activity.

While not as numerous as many breeds, pit bulls are not so rare that raising them should be considered uncommon. Nevertheless, we conclude that, with this breed, exercise of reasonable care is unlikely to eliminate the risk of severe injury, as pit bulls that have never bitten might, without warning, attack an individual perceived to be a threat and inflict grave injury. There was testimony from both parties' experts that preventive measures were possible, such as keeping muzzles on the adult dogs. But dogs cannot be muzzled all the time, and we are not persuaded that the availability of such measures overcomes the other factors favoring the conclusion that raising pit bulls in the circumstances identified here is an ultrahazardous activity. Finally, unlike the situation in *Fredricks*, the public benefit of the activity does not justify insulating the defendant from strict liability.

It is undisputed that the attack by Ellis's pit bull resulted in Thurman's injuries and therefore causation is not in doubt. Accordingly, we conclude that there is sufficient evidence to establish that by raising pit bulls in a residential neighborhood, Ellis engaged in an ultrahazardous activity. The trial court did not err in giving the ultrahazardous instruction.

Affirmed.

In re Mistover Acres LLC

Sample Answer

To: Lyle Palkovich
From: Applicant
Re: Mistover Acres LLC
Date: July 24, 2007

MEMORANDUM

This memorandum addresses the potential personal liability of our client, Petra Flynn, a member of Mistover Acres LLC ("Mistover"), for damage incurred by Genesee Trout, Inc.'s trout farm on March 28, 2007, as well as the likelihood that the aerial crop dusting carried out by Mistover constituted an ultrahazardous activity. Although both questions are close calls, the balance of all relevant factors indicates that Ms. Flynn can be held personally liable for the damage, and that the aerial crop dusting constituted an ultrahazardous activity.

I. Personal Liability of Petra Flynn for Damage Allegedly Caused by Aerial Crop Dusting on March 28, 2007.

Under Franklin law, a member of an LLC is not personally liable solely by reason of being a member of the company for any obligation or liability of the company, whether arising in contract, tort, or otherwise unless the member so provides by written agreement. [Franklin Limited Liability Company Act ("FLLCA") §605] However, the statute does not insulate the member from liability for her own participation in tortious conduct. [FLLCA §605(3)]

The case of *Hodas v. Ice LLC* sets forth the parameters of personal liability of members of an LLC. After reviewing FLLCA section 605, the court stated that a member of an LLC is not personally liable for acts solely by reason of being a member, nor will tort liability lie for a member's performance of a general administrative duty [*see* Lee v. Bayrd, cited in *Hodas* for the proposition that there is no tort liability if a corporate officer was not shown to have authorized, directed, or participated in the tortious act]. However, if an LLC member participates in the tortious conduct, she may be held personally liable, and that personal liability is not limited to torts committed outside her role as a member of the LLC.

Ms. Flynn is one of three members of Mistover, a Franklin limited liability company ("LLC"). There is no indication that she entered into a written agreement that subjected her to personal liability. Thus, any theory of tort liability must be based on Ms. Flynn's personal participation in the allegedly tortious conduct. Hence, it is necessary to examine Ms. Flynn's actions relative to the facts.

Pursuant to the Mistover LLC Operating Agreement, Ms. Flynn agreed to supervise the marketing and sale of Mistover's produce. Day-to-day decisions regarding planting and harvesting are delegated to Chip Kendall. Mr. Kendall persuaded the other members to grow the new type of lettuce which required chemical pesticides. When leaf slugs were discovered on Mistover's lettuce plants, Ms. Flynn and Mr. Kendall researched pesticides together and selected MU-83. Ms. Flynn ordered this pesticide through an agricultural supplier, and Mr. Kendall applied the pesticide by hand. Although the application was effective, labor costs were high.

When the slugs returned, Mr. Kendall decided that the slugs were more numerous and that hand spraying would be even costlier. Thus, he and Ms. Flynn decided to employ aerial crop dusting. Ms.

Flynn ordered more MU-83. Pursuant to requirements of the Franklin Environmental Code, she posted public notices of the aerial crop dusting. When Mr. Kendall sprayed the fields on March 28, 2007, Ms. Flynn was present. She observed Mr. Kendall take off in his plane and fly over the plants at an approximate height of 20 feet to apply the MU-83. Two days later, she walked through the fields with Mr. Kendall and verified that the MU-83 had killed any visible leaf slugs.

It is important to view Ms. Flynn's actions in light of the principle that she is not subject to tort liability for performance of a general administrative duty. An argument could be made that Mr. Kendall, as the member in charge of planting and harvesting, was responsible for any tortious conduct because he selected the crop, discovered the need for pesticides, and administered the pesticide by plane, presumably deciding the time and details of the dusting. Ms. Flynn's involvement fell solely under her administrative duties: Ordering the pesticide and posting the notices mandated by the Franklin Environmental Code clearly fall within the scope of her general administrative duties as a member of the LLC, and her marketing duties would not make her personally liable for any damage to Genesee Trout. Also, the inspection of the fields occurred two days after the aerial spraying; thus, it occurred after the allegedly tortious conduct took place. Therefore, the inspection would not have involved Ms. Flynn in personal tortious conduct.

Nevertheless, we cannot overlook Ms. Flynn's actions that go beyond administrative duties. She researched pesticides and decided, together with Mr. Kendall, to use MU-83. Also, she participated in the decision to repeat the application of the pesticide by means of aerial crop dusting, and she was present as Mr. Kendall applied the pesticide. Although it is a close call, these actions may well constitute a sufficient level of personal participation so as to justify the imposition of personal tort liability on Ms. Flynn. The facts do suggest that these particular actions may have gone beyond the parameters of "general administrative duties." Therefore, we must inform Ms. Flynn that, while she will not be held liable solely by virtue of her membership in the LLC, it is possible that she will be found to have engaged in a level of personal participation in the allegedly tortious conduct that she may subject her to personal liability.

II. Aerial Crop Dusting of MU-83 as an Ultrahazardous Activity.

The question of whether the aerial crop dusting of MU-83 constituted an ultrahazardous activity calls for an analysis of six factors that are referred to in section 520 of the Restatement (Second) of Torts. On balance, it appears that the factors tilt slightly in favor of finding that this activity was an ultrahazardous activity.

When determining whether an activity is ultrahazardous, the state of Franklin applies section 520 of the Restatement (Second) of Torts. [Thurman v. Ellis] Section 520 lists six factors to consider: (i) the existence of a high degree of risk of some harm to the person, land, or chattels of others; (ii) the likelihood that the resulting harm will be great; (iii) the inability to eliminate the risk by reasonable care; (iv) the extent to which the activity is not a matter of common usage; (v) the inappropriateness of the activity to the place where it is carried on; and (vi) the extent to which the activity's value to the community is outweighed by its dangerous attributes. No single factor is solely determinative; the court must examine the totality of all circumstances. Following is an analysis of each factor:

Factor (i)–high degree of risk: The User's Guide for MU-83 Application ("the guide") states that users of the product should use caution and be aware that "drift" (*i.e.,* movement of droplets or particles in the air from the targeted area to non-target areas) is always a risk. In fact, the guide states that "[d]rift will occur with every application." It also states that "drift and runoff may be toxic to

aquatic organisms in neighboring areas," such as what may have happened to Genesee's trout. Finally, the guide states in bold print that improper use or application of the product may cause serious injury or death.

These statements from the guide indicate that when Mistover conducted the aerial spraying, there would almost certainly be some drift with potential toxicity. Thus, the conclusion is that Factor (i) would be decided in favor of a finding that the aerial crop dusting was ultrahazardous.

Factor (ii)–likelihood of great harm: The language of the guide (*i.e.*, drift ***"may"*** be toxic; improper use ***"may"*** cause serious injury or death) does not shed much light on the issue of the likelihood that harm will be great. In fact, arguably the guide suggests that if used properly, the harm will not be serious, and Mr. Kendall applied the pesticide in accordance with the guide. Although we are to assume that the aerial crop dusting caused the damage to the trout farm, it is not clear that serious harm was likely at the time of spraying. This is to be contrasted with the situation in *Thurman,* where the court stated that being bitten by a pit bull would almost assuredly result in a severe injury. Thus, because it is uncertain that the aerial crop dusting here at issue was likely to result in great harm, Factor (ii) would probably be decided in favor of a finding that the crop dusting was not ultrahazardous.

Factor (iii)–inability to eliminate risk: As previously noted, no single factor is solely determinative of the issue of whether an activity is ultrahazardous. However, as the *Thurman* court noted, the court in *Sisson v. City of Bremerton* emphasized that the inability to eliminate risk by the exercise of reasonable care generally carries more weight than the other factors. Thus, this factor is very important.

According to the guide, drift will always occur. The amount of drift will vary according to several factors, some of which are controllable (*e.g.*, time of day, concentration, and means of application), while others are uncontrollable (*e.g.*, wind gusts, weather changes, and the physical characteristics of pesticide droplets or aerosols). As stated above, the warning that improper use or application may cause serious injury or death may be taken as an indication that proper use might eliminate or lessen the probability of serious harm. However, such a contention appears quite weak and pales in comparison to the uncontrollable factors presented by wind, weather, and physical characteristics of the droplets. Thus, it appears that reasonable care at best could limit, but not eliminate, the risk posed by the aerial crop dusting. Consequently, Factor (iii) would be decided in favor of a finding that the crop dusting was ultrahazardous.

Factor (iv)–matter of common usage: It does not appear that the use of pesticides is uncommon in the area. Last year, Mistover applied pesticide (albeit by hand). Also, we are told that "a number" of the agricultural producers in the area use organic practices; this implies that some producers do not follow such practices, and thus it is likely that they use pesticides.

An argument can be made that it is uncommon to employ ***aerial*** application of the pesticide, but this argument holds little merit. The guide refers to aerial dusting as a suitable method of application. Also, since the Franklin Environmental Code requires posting notice prior to aerial dusting, it can be inferred that such an activity is not necessarily uncommon. Thus, Factor (iv) would be decided in favor of a finding that the crop dusting was not ultrahazardous.

Factor (v)–inappropriateness of activity in area: The court will consider the activity in light of the area in which it occurred. In *Thurman v. Ellis,* the court concluded that breeding of pit bulls in a residential neighborhood was inappropriate to the place where such activity was conducted, even though it was a legal activity. In contrast, the court in *Fredricks v. Centralia Fire Department* (cited in *Thurman*), stated that despite the hazards involved in firefighting, such an activity is appropriate to the community.

Mistover is located in an area that has long been agricultural. Clearly, pesticide spraying in an agricultural area would normally be considered appropriate. However, over the years, a number of small scale, specialized producers devoted to organic practices have begun operating in the area. Given Mistover's rather close proximity to such operations, it is likely that the aerial spraying, with its concomitant risk of drift, would not be appropriate to the place where it occurred. Thus, the aerial spraying is more like the pit bull breeding at issue in *Thurman* than it is to the firefighting at issue in *Fredricks*.

It could be argued that the spraying was appropriate because the Franklin Environmental Code notice requirements impliedly approve such activity. Such an argument has no merit because the fact that an activity is legal is not a defense to a claim that it is ultrahazardous. [Thurman v. Ellis] Therefore, Factor (v) would be decided in favor of a finding that the crop dusting was ultrahazardous.

Factor (vi)–value to community vs. dangerous attributes: The *Thurman* court cited *Fredericks v. Centralia Fire Department* for the proposition that the value of an activity to a community might negate factors that would otherwise favor the imposition of strict liability. Specifically, the court in *Fredericks* found that the value of firefighting outweighed the inherent dangers of such an activity.

At first glance, it may seem that the availability of a new type of lettuce is not of such great value to the community that it is worth risking damage to aquatic life and to another's business. However, an argument can be made that pesticide use is important, not only for Mistover's crop, but for others' crops if the leaf slug population was not kept under control. How strong this argument is depends on the other crops in the area and the extent of organic farming, but it is likely that the value of aerial spraying to the community is not outweighed by the dangerous attributes of such activity. Factor (vi) would probably be decided in favor of a finding that the crop dusting was not ultrahazardous.

The above analysis shows that the balance of factors for determining whether the aerial spraying was ultrahazardous is extremely close. Note, however, that the factor pertaining to inability to eliminate risk by reasonable care carries more weight than the other factors. The inability to eliminate the risk, in conjunction with the virtual certainty of some pesticide drift to nearby properties, tips the balance in favor of a finding that the aerial crop dusting was ultrahazardous. Because of the potentially serious consequences, Mistover should have continued to use hand application, despite the additional expense involved with that method.

[**EDITOR'S NOTE:** Because the issue of whether the aerial spraying was ultrahazardous under these facts is a close call, a well written answer that decided that the activity was ***not*** ultrahazardous could also have received full credit provided that it supported that result through a reasonable analysis of the law and facts.]

Multistate

Performance Test

Williams v. A-1 Automotive Center

National Conference of Bar Examiners

Preface

This Multistate Performance Test is a reprint of one of the two MPTs which were administered in July 2008.

The instructions for the test appear on the next page. On the actual MPT, they will appear on the back cover of the test.

INSTRUCTIONS

1. You will have 90 minutes to complete this session of the examination. This performance test is designed to evaluate your ability to handle a select number of legal authorities in the context of a factual problem involving a client.

2. The problem is set in the fictitious state of Franklin, in the fictitious Fifteenth Circuit of the United States. Columbia and Olympia are also fictitious states in the Fifteenth Circuit. In Franklin, the trial court of general jurisdiction is the District Court, the intermediate appellate court is the Court of Appeal, and the highest court is the Supreme Court.

3. You will have two kinds of materials with which to work: a File and a Library. The first document in the File is a memorandum containing the instructions for the task you are to complete. The other documents in the File contain factual information about your case and may include some facts that are not relevant.

4. The Library contains the legal authorities needed to complete the task and may also include some authorities that are not relevant. Any cases may be real, modified, or written solely for the purpose of this examination. If the cases appear familiar to you, do not assume that they are precisely the same as you have read before. Read them thoroughly, as if they all were new to you. You should assume that cases were decided in the jurisdictions and on the dates shown. In citing cases from the Library, you may use abbreviations and omit page references.

5. Your response must be written in the answer book provided. If you are taking this examination on a laptop computer, your jurisdiction will provide you with specific instructions. In answering this performance test, you should concentrate on the materials provided in the File and Library. What you have learned in law school and elsewhere provides the general background for analyzing the problem; the File and Library provide the specific materials with which you must work.

6. Although there are no restrictions on how you apportion your time, you should be sure to allocate ample time (about 45 minutes) to reading and digesting the materials and to organizing your answer before you begin writing it. You may make notes anywhere in the test materials; blank pages are provided at the end of the booklet. You may not tear pages from the question booklet.

7. This performance test will be graded on your responsiveness to the instructions regarding the task you are to complete, which are given to you in the first memorandum in the File, and on the content, thoroughness, and organization of your response.

Williams v. A-1 Automotive Center

FILE

LIBRARY

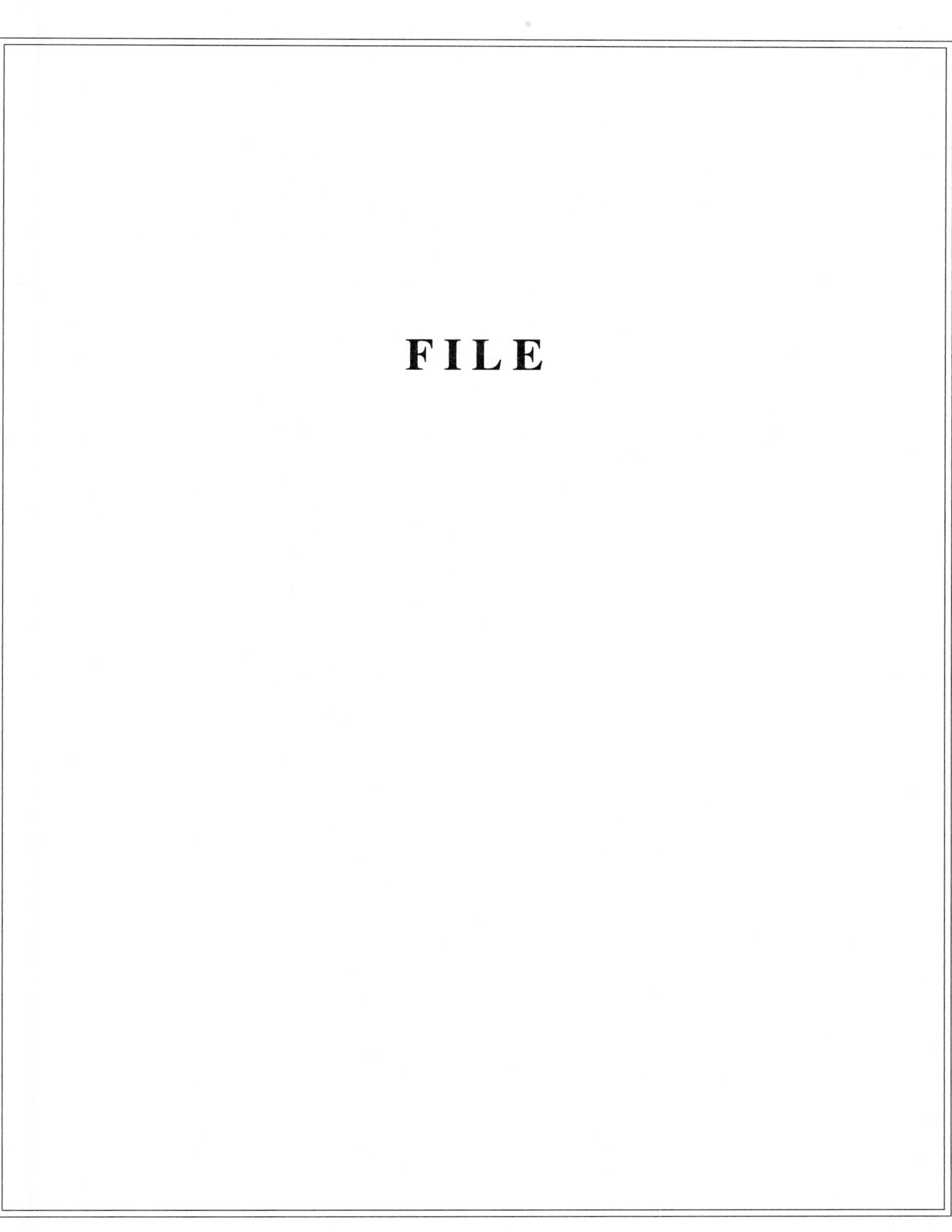

FILE

MILLER & KILLEBREW LLP
ATTORNEYS AT LAW
450 FLAMINGO DRIVE, SUITE 1000
CLEAR BAY, FRANKLIN 33002

MEMORANDUM

To: Applicant
From: Tania Miller
Re: Williams v. Biggs d/b/a A-1 Automotive Center
Date: July 29, 2008

We represent Robert Williams in a dispute with A-1 Automotive Center (A-1), concerning repairs that A-1 made to his minivan. He wants us to file a lawsuit on his behalf.

I believe Mr. Williams may be able to sue A-1 for fraud. I'm attaching notes of my interview with Mr. Williams and my memorandum to the file identifying four potentially actionable statements.

Please complete the following tasks:

1. Write a memo analyzing which of the four statements are actionable and which are not, and explaining the reasons for each of your conclusions.

2. For each statement that you determine to be actionable, draft a separate cause of action for fraud. Be sure to follow our firm's drafting guidelines for causes of action.

MILLER & KILLEBREW LLP

OFFICE MEMORANDUM

To: Attorneys
From: Tania Miller
Re: Drafting Causes of Action
Date: September 5, 2004

In pleading a cause of action, firm practice requires attorneys to draft the minimum allegations necessary to plead the required legal elements of the claim, presented in separately numbered paragraphs. The practice of pleading the required legal elements minimizes the risk of the court dismissing an action for failure to state a claim.

For example, a complaint for negligence must usually allege four elements: that the defendant had a duty, that the defendant breached that duty, that the defendant's breach was the proximate cause of injury to the plaintiff, and that this injury caused the plaintiff to suffer compensable damages. The following complaint for negligence provides an example of a negligence pleading consistent with the firm's pleadings practice:

1. When driving his car on the streets of Franklin City, Joe McMann owed other persons using the streets the duty to drive his car as a reasonable and prudent person would.
2. On December 5, 2002, Joe McMann breached his duty by driving his car at a speed in excess of the posted speed limit and through a red light at the corner of First Avenue and K Street in Franklin City.
3. When Joe McMann breached his duty, his car struck Sally Young, who was a pedestrian lawfully walking in a crosswalk at the intersection of First Avenue and K Street.
4. As a result of Joe McMann's breaching his duty, Sally Young suffered serious bodily injury and other damages.

Client interview notes: Robert Williams
July 24, 2008

Met with new client Robert Williams this morning concerning his dispute with A-1 Automotive Center (A-1). A-1 is a small auto-repair shop located in Navasota, Franklin, which is owned and operated by Aaron Biggs.

Last month, Williams and his family were planning to leave for a one-week vacation in Ocean City, Columbia. He intended to drive to Ocean City in his 2003 Dodge minivan. At that time, the minivan had approximately 75,000 miles on the odometer and was in perfect working condition.

Williams saw an advertisement in a local newspaper in which A-1 offered an oil change and fluid check for $29.95, and decided to take advantage of it. On Thursday, June 5, 2008, he called A-1 and spoke with Biggs, who told him to bring in the minivan and said that A-1 would do the work right away.

When Williams arrived, he was informed by Biggs that his minivan would have to be test-driven. Williams told Biggs that he would like to go along. After waiting around for half an hour, however, he saw his minivan being driven around the corner by one of the shop's mechanics. When the mechanic returned from the test-drive, Williams saw him talking and joking about something with Biggs. A few minutes later, Biggs walked over and told Williams that although the minivan was shifting fine, there might be a little slippage in the transmission, and that A-1 would have to find what was causing the problem. Because Biggs could not estimate how long that would take, Williams took a bus home.

Williams was home no more than 15 minutes when he received a call from Biggs telling him that there were problems with the minivan's transmission. Biggs told Williams that he had "checked and found a notification from Dodge about a defect causing the gears to grind down." Williams expressed surprise that there could be any problem with the transmission when the vehicle had been running perfectly, and he told Biggs not to take the transmission out of the minivan until he arrived.

When Williams arrived at the shop about 45 minutes later, the transmission had already been removed from his minivan and disassembled. Biggs told Williams, "Your transmission is going to fail, and soon!" Biggs gave him the option of having his old transmission repaired for about $1,400 or purchasing a rebuilt transmission from A-1's stock at a cost of around $1,700.

Although Williams originally had had no intention of putting a rebuilt transmission into his minivan, at that point he felt he had no choice. He had no expertise in automotive repair, he was planning to leave for his vacation the next day, and Biggs told him that it would take three days to repair his own transmission but that a rebuilt transmission could be installed by that evening. Williams told Biggs to install the rebuilt transmission. Biggs then said, "It would also help if we installed an extra cooler to keep it from running hot." Williams told Biggs that if the minivan had needed an extra cooler, the manufacturer would have installed one. With that, Biggs dropped the subject.

Williams picked up the minivan that evening and paid the bill. As Williams left the shop, Biggs told him, "I guarantee the job."

Williams took the minivan home and parked it in his garage. Later that evening, he noticed transmission oil all over the garage floor. He decided to delay his vacation and take the minivan back to A-1. When Williams looked at his receipt, however, he discovered that it was stamped "NO GUARANTEE." The next morning, when he called A-1 to inquire why this was the case, Biggs told him that because he had elected not to have the extra cooler installed, A-1 could not guarantee the transmission. That same day, Williams took the minivan to Mission Dodge, a local dealership, and told them about his experience with A-1. Mission discovered that the minivan's transmission was in fact his original transmission and not a rebuilt one. (Domestic car manufacturers mark engine transmission casings with the vehicle's serial number.) Mission also told Williams that Dodge had not circulated any notification about any problems with the transmissions in its 2003 minivans. Mission charged Williams $128 to repair the transmission leak, which had been caused by A-1's improper reinstallation of the transmission.

On June 17, 2008, after he returned from vacation, Williams called A-1 and attempted to get his money back. Biggs told Williams that he would look into it. Williams called back several times to follow up with Biggs. Each time, Biggs told him that he was still looking into the matter. Williams came to us to bring suit.

MILLER & KILLEBREW LLP
ATTORNEYS AT LAW
450 FLAMINGO DRIVE, SUITE 1000
CLEAR BAY, FRANKLIN 33002

MEMORANDUM

To: File
From: Tania Miller
Re: Williams Matter
Date: July 25, 2008

Note to file—Further research needed to determine whether any of the following statements by Biggs might support a cause of action for fraud:

1. Biggs had "found a notification from Dodge about a defect causing the gears to grind down."
2. "Your transmission is going to fail, and soon!"
3. "It would also help if we installed an extra cooler to keep it from running hot."
4. "I guarantee the job."

RECEIPT

A-1 Automotive Center
4834 West Avenue
Navasota, Franklin 33017
(222) 555-2115
FIRST CLASS SERVICE

Invoice #: I0023059
Date: June 5, 2008
Page: 1

Customer: Robert Williams Address: 17159 Springfield Ct. City: Diamond Springs, FR 33015 Home Phone: (222) 555-3591 Work Phone: (222) 555-6705	Vehicle: 2003 Dodge Grand Caravan Minivan License: E47-S19 V.I.N.: JH5SV9257RS928599 Engine: V6/150hp/3.8L Mileage: 75,249
Parts	Labor
REBUILT TRANSMISSION, INCLUDING HOUSING, GEARS, SEALS, PLANETARY ASSEMBLY, SPRAGS, TORQUE CONVERTER, PAN GASKET, FILTER, BANDS, SOLENOID, AND FRONT PUMP; DRAIN AND REPLACE TRANSMISSION FLUID $1400.00	CUSTOMER REQUESTED WE REPLACE ORIGINAL TRANSMISSION WITH REBUILT TRANSMISSION INSTEAD OF REPAIRING ORIGINAL 6.25 hrs @ $60.00/hr $375.00
	Labor: $375.00 Parts: $1400.00 Other Fees: $0.00 Supplies: $0.00 Subtotal: $1775.00 Sales Tax: $112.00 Total: $1887.00 Paid: $1887.00 Balance Due: $0.00

NO GUARANTEE

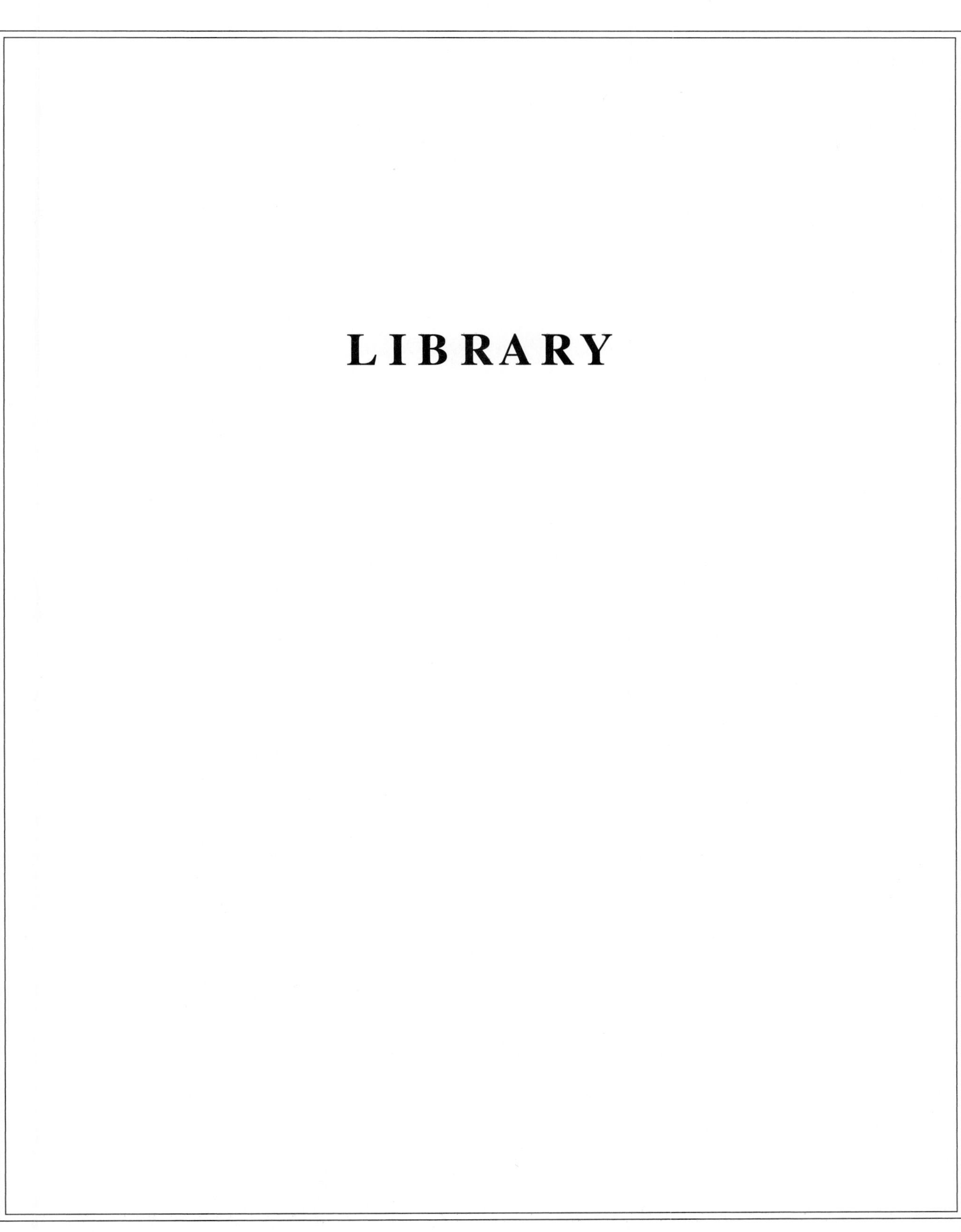

LIBRARY

Foster v. Panera

Franklin Court of Appeal (2003)

This action was brought to recover damages for fraud. Plaintiff Danielle Foster appeals from the trial court's dismissal of the action for failure to state a claim against defendants Ted Panera and Abbey Furniture Company (collectively "defendants").

PLAINTIFF'S ALLEGATIONS

The pertinent allegations in the complaint are as follows:

On or about May 7, 2001, Foster told Panera, the store manager at Abbey Furniture Company, that she wished to purchase a certain set of bedroom furniture, which included a solid wood headboard. All of the items were present in the store except for the headboard. Panera told Foster that the headboard was at the store's warehouse and would be delivered to her with the other items.

Unknown to Foster, Panera made this representation knowing that it was false and intending to induce Foster's purchase of the furniture. Relying on this representation, Foster ordered and paid for the bedroom set, specifically including the solid wood headboard. She would not have ordered or purchased the bedroom set, nor any of its individual components, had she known that it would not include the matching headboard. When the furniture was delivered to Foster with a brass headboard, instead of the solid wood headboard, Foster telephoned Panera, who apologized and said that the correct headboard would be delivered to her soon. However, during the ensuing weeks and months, Panera told Foster that the headboard was on order, under manufacture, in storage, or in delivery, providing various delivery dates. The solid wood headboard was never delivered.

Panera knew that these later representations were false and, in making them, intended that Foster would be induced to keep the furniture and refrain from canceling the order. Relying on Panera's statements, Foster kept the furniture and waited for delivery of the wood headboard. Had she known that the statements were false, she would have canceled the order, returned the furniture, and demanded a refund. But because she was the customer in this transaction and because Panera, as the store manager, presumably had familiarity with the whereabouts of store inventory, Foster relied on his representations as being true.

Foster has stored but has not used the furniture. Defendants have not removed it from Foster's home, nor have they refunded the purchase price. As a direct and proximate result of Panera's initial misrepresentation, Foster was induced to purchase the bedroom set and was damaged thereby.

As a direct and proximate result of Panera's later misrepresentations, Foster was induced to store unwanted furniture, and to refrain from canceling the contract and obtaining a refund, all to her damage in the amount of $3,500.

DEFENDANTS' MOTION TO DISMISS

Defendants filed a motion to dismiss the complaint on the ground that "the complaint fails to state a claim upon which relief may be granted against defendants." The motion was granted, and this appeal ensued.

ANALYSIS

In reviewing a trial court's grant of a motion to dismiss, we accept the plaintiff's allegations as true and give her the benefit of all fair implications therefrom. A complaint for fraud must allege the following elements: (1) a material misrepresentation of fact by the defendant, (2) made with knowledge of its falsity, (3) made with intent to deceive or induce reliance, (4) reasonable reliance by the plaintiff upon the misrepresentation, and (5) loss by the plaintiff as a proximate result of the misrepresentation.

Every element of the cause of action for fraud must be specifically pleaded and the facts constituting the fraud must be alleged with sufficient particularity to allow a defendant to understand fully the nature of the charge made. It is not sufficient to allege fraud in general terms, or in terms which amount to mere conclusions.

Defendants contend that the representations were not material and therefore cannot support an action for fraud. We disagree.

A representation is material if a reasonable person would consider it important in deciding to enter into the transaction. Here, the complaint indicates that Foster asked for a solid wood headboard, and that Panera repeatedly confirmed its eventual availability. A reasonable person seeking a solid wood headboard would have considered these assertions to be an important factor in the sale. The allegations thus clearly demonstrate that the representations were material.

CONCLUSION

Foster has properly stated a fraud claim. The judgment of the trial court dismissing the complaint is reversed, and the case remanded for proceedings consistent with this opinion.

Madison v. Brooks

Franklin Court of Appeal (1979)

This action was brought by plaintiff Jean Madison to rescind, on the ground of fraud, a written contract for the sale of certain plant nursery stock. The district court granted defendant Walter Brooks's motion to dismiss for failure to state a claim upon which relief could be granted. The sole question on appeal is whether a statement that is an expression of opinion may be actionable as fraud.

The complaint alleges that prior to executing the contract, Brooks told Madison that he had grafted 52,000 dormant buds in the trees comprising the nursery stock and that Madison "would surely see 60 to 70 percent of the dormant buds growing and producing trees." The parties stipulate that in fact only 30 percent of the dormant buds grew and produced trees.

Brooks contends that the so-called misrepresentation was the mere expression of an opinion and not a statement of a fact, and therefore could not constitute actionable fraud. He insists that a vendor has the right to freely express an opinion as to what will or will not happen in the future in relation to the sale of the property under consideration, and that such statements do not constitute actionable fraud.

As a general rule, fraud cannot be predicated upon the mere expression of an opinion which is understood to be only an estimate or a judgment. The person to whom such a statement is made has no right to rely upon the statement, and does so at his peril. For example, an auto dealer's representations that the vehicle "was a good car" and that it was "about the best one they had" were not actionable as fraud. *Bender v. Fiat Corp.* (Fr. Ct. App. 1986). Nor was the statement that certain seeds were "top quality tomato seeds" definitive enough as to how the product would perform but instead was merely the grower's opinion that the seeds were top quality. *Novotny v. Ford Farms* (Fr. Sup. Ct. 1999).

However, there is an exception to this rule where the opinion relates to a subject as to which the parties do not have equal knowledge or means of ascertaining the truth. Where the party making the misrepresentation has special knowledge of the facts underlying the opinion, or "is possessed of superior knowledge respecting such matters, with a design to deceive and mislead," the positive assertion of a matter, which stated in another form might be a mere opinion, may be actionable if the statement was false. *Novotny*. In *Novotny*, the grower also described the tomato seeds as "ones that would produce drought-resistant plants that would bear firm, uniform fruit that would not bruise during shipment." The court held that *this* statement could be the basis for a fraud action. *Id. See also Wong v. Hall Lumber, Ltd.* (Fr. Ct. App. 2004) (statement made by salesman that windows were

coated in a preservative that would "protect against rot and decay for at least 10 years" constituted an actionable statement).

The complaint's allegations fall within the exception. In addition to alleging that Brooks told Madison that she "would surely see 60 to 70 percent of the dormant buds growing and producing trees," the complaint alleges that Brooks knew that the dormant buds were poorly handled and would almost certainly not grow properly. The complaint also alleges that Madison relied upon Brooks's skill in the business and that Madison, who was not an expert in the field of horticulture, did not possess reasonable means of ascertaining the truth of Brooks's statement.

When we review the granting of a motion to dismiss for failure to state a claim, we take the well-pleaded allegations of fact as true. Taking these allegations as true, the statement that Madison "would surely see 60 to 70 percent of the dormant buds growing and producing trees" would be equivalent to a misrepresentation of fact, satisfying that essential element of common law fraud.

Accordingly, the trial court should not have dismissed the complaint. We reverse and remand.

Rogers v. Statewide Insurance Co.

Franklin Court of Appeal (1995)

Plaintiff Michelle Rogers appeals from a judgment entered after the trial court granted defendant Statewide Insurance Company's motion to dismiss her complaint for failure to state a claim upon which relief may be granted. The sole issue on appeal concerns the circumstances under which an unfulfilled promise to perform is actionable as fraud at common law. We conclude that when the promise is made with no intent to perform, it constitutes a misrepresentation of fact. If the other elements of fraud are present, a cause of action for fraud exists.

Rogers alleges as follows: She was involved in an auto accident with Andy Bosch, an insured of defendant. Bosch's liability was reasonably clear. Rogers obtained an estimate of $3,200 to repair her vehicle. Statewide represented to her that she was authorized to have her vehicle repaired at Capitol Ford, that Statewide's obligation to indemnify her for her damages was reasonably clear, and that Statewide would pay her for all such repairs immediately upon their completion. Rogers relied on the representations and brought her vehicle to be repaired. However, Statewide refused to pay for the repairs or to indemnify her. Because Rogers lacked the funds to complete the repairs or to obtain the release of her vehicle, she was left without its use for an extended period of several weeks until Statewide eventually settled her claim.

The gist of Rogers's fraud claim is that Statewide said it *would* pay for her repairs *immediately upon their completion*, and that it failed to do so, that Rogers could not afford to have the repairs completed or redeem her vehicle, and that she lost the use of the car for several weeks. The critical alleged misrepresentation as to immediate payment upon completion did not involve a past or existing material fact. Rather, it involved a promise to perform at some future time.

A promise is a statement of intention to perform some action in the future. If the maker of a promise honestly intends to follow through on that intention at the time of the promise, the statement cannot give rise to an action for fraud. However, if at the time of making the promise the promisor has no plans to perform, he has misrepresented his present intention, which would be a misrepresentation of fact. It is that misrepresentation that can support an action for fraud. To state such a claim, one must specifically allege, among other things, that the promisor did not intend to perform at the time the promise was made. Rogers's complaint does not contain such an allegation. Therefore, the motion to dismiss was proper.

Affirmed.

Williams v. A-1 Automotive Center

Sample Answer

MEMORANDUM

To: Tania Miller
From: Applicant
Re: Williams v. Biggs d/b/a/ A-1 Automotive Center

In Franklin, a complaint for fraud must allege the following elements: "(1) a material misrepresentation of fact by the defendant; (2) made with the knowledge of its falsity; (3) made with intent to deceive or induce reliance; (4) reasonable reliance by the plaintiff upon the misrepresentation; and (5) loss by the plaintiff as a proximate result of the misrepresentation." [Foster v. Panera (Fr. Ct. App. 2003)]

Analyses of the four statements made by Biggs to our client, Robert Williams, indicates that two of the statements may be actionable.

Statement 1: Biggs had "found a notification from Dodge about a defect causing the gears to grind down."

Biggs told Mr. Williams that there were problems with the minivan's transmission and then made the above statement. This is a misrepresentation because there was no such notification from Dodge, according to Mission Dodge, a Dodge dealer who repaired the minivan after A-1 allegedly rebuilt the transmission. Biggs said he "checked and found a notification from Dodge . . . ." This statement shows that he knew that his statement was false when he made it to Mr. Williams and did not just make an error in thinking that there was such a notification. He intended that Mr. Williams rely on the alleged notification in order to charge him for work on the transmission. A misrepresentation is material if it would induce a reasonable person to consider it important in deciding to enter the transaction. [Foster v. Panera] A reasonable person would consider a notification from the manufacturer important in deciding whether to repair or replace the transmission, and thus it was reasonable for Mr. Williams, who had no expertise regarding automotive repairs, to rely on the statement of an owner and operator of a car repair business that there was a notification and to authorize the work. As a result of the material misrepresentation, Mr. Williams suffered damages in the amount of $1887 paid to Biggs and $128 paid to Mission Dodge to repair the transmission leak caused by Biggs improperly reinstalling the transmission.

Statement 2: Biggs also told Williams, "Your transmission is going to fail, and soon!"

This statement could appear to be an expression of an opinion rather than a statement of fact. In *Madison v. Brooks* (Fr. Ct. App. 2005), the court held that "fraud cannot be predicated upon the mere expression of an opinion which is understood to be only an estimate or a judgment. The person to whom such a statement is made has no right to rely upon the statement." However, the *Madison* court found an exception to this rule when the parties involved have unequal knowledge. If the person making the statement "is possessed of superior knowledge respecting such matters, with a design to deceive or mislead," the statement may be actionable if false. [Madison v. Brooks—*quoting* Novotny v. Ford Farms (Fr. Sup. Ct. 1999)]

Here, Mr. Williams had no expertise regarding automotive repairs when he took the minivan to Biggs for an oil change. Biggs, who owned and operated an automotive repair business, held himself out as

having such expertise. Thus, Biggs had superior knowledge respecting the state of the transmission. At the time he made the statement, Biggs knew it to be false and intended to deceive Mr. Williams about the need for repair work. The minivan had no apparent transmission problems when Mr. Williams brought in the minivan, and the fact that Biggs lied about the notification from Dodge as the reason to do the repair work shows that he could not point to any reason to believe that the transmission would fail soon. Furthermore, he did not replace the transmission with a rebuilt one as charged for on the receipt, but merely replaced the original transmission (as shown by the minivan's serial number on the allegedly repaired transmission). Thus, Biggs used his superior knowledge to lie to Mr. Williams with the intent to deceive him. The statement is material because a reasonable person would consider a statement by a knowledgeable mechanic about the transmission important. It was reasonable for Mr. Williams to rely upon Biggs's expertise as a mechanic when Biggs said the transmission would soon fail and to allow repairs to the transmission. Mr. Williams suffered damages of $1887 paid to Biggs and $128 paid to Mission Dodge when he relied on Biggs's statement.

Note that Franklin case law supports our case. Mr. Williams's reliance is similar to that of the buyer in *Madison v. Brooks* who had no experience in grafting and growing trees and relied on the experienced seller's statements about the growth of buds. In *Novotny*, a statement by the grower that tomato seeds would produce drought-resistant plants that would bear fruit that would not bruise during shipment was actionable because of the superior knowledge of the grower. In *Wong v. Hall Lumber, Ltd.* (Fr. Ct. App. 2004), a salesman's statement that windows were coated with a preservative that would "protect against rot and decay for at least 10 years" was also actionable under the *Madison* exception. Thus, these cases buttress our argument that Mr. Williams has a cause of action.

Statement 3: "It would also help if we installed an extra cooler to keep it from running hot."

Although this statement is false and meant to deceive Mr. Williams because Biggs knew that there was nothing wrong with the transmission in the minivan, it is not actionable because Mr. Williams did not rely on the misrepresentation. He elected not to have an extra cooler installed. Also, he had already agreed to have the rebuilt transmission installed before Biggs even mentioned the cooler. Thus, this statement did not enter into his decision to allow Biggs to do repair work. Furthermore, because no cooler was installed, Mr. Williams suffered no damages as a result of the statement. For these reasons, the statement is not actionable.

Statement 4: "I guarantee the job."

This statement could be considered a promise and thus not actionable. In *Rogers v. Statewide Insurance Co.* (Fr. App. Ct. 1995), the court held that "if the maker of a promise honestly intends to follow through on that intention at the time of the promise, the statement cannot give rise to an action for fraud." However, the court further held that "if at the time of making the promise the promisor has no plans to perform, he has misrepresented his present intention . . ." and that misrepresentation can support an action for fraud. In our case, when Biggs made his promise to guarantee the work, he did not intend to perform. As Mr. Williams was leaving the shop, Biggs said, "I guarantee the job." But that was ***after*** he had already given Mr. Williams a receipt that was stamped "NO GUARANTEE." Clearly he did not intend to follow through on his promise when he made it. Also, when Mr. Williams later asked Biggs why there was no guarantee, Biggs told him that the work could not be guaranteed because Mr. Williams elected not to have the extra cooler installed. However, Biggs made his promise to guarantee the work ***after*** Williams had refused the extra cooler. This also shows that Biggs did not intend to guarantee the job at the time he made the promise. Therefore, the statement could be actionable if the other elements of fraud are found.

Here the element of reasonable reliance is lacking. When Mr. Williams decided to authorize the repair work, the statement of guarantee had not even been made. Biggs did not offer his guarantee until after the work was finished and Mr. Williams had paid the bill. Clearly Mr. Williams did not rely on the statement.

COMPLAINTS:

Williams v. Aaron Biggs d/b/a/ A-1 Automotive Center

1. On June 5, 2008, Plaintiff Robert Williams took his 2003 Dodge Minivan to A-1 Automotive Center ("A-1"), owned and operated by Defendant Aaron Biggs, to have the oil changed. After an A-1 mechanic drove the minivan, Defendant Biggs told Robert Williams that there might be slippage in the transmission and that it would take more time to discover the cause. Upon arriving home, Robert Williams received a phone call from Defendant Biggs who made the material misrepresentation that he had "checked and found a notification from Dodge about a defect causing the gears to grind down."

2. Defendant Biggs knew at the time he made this statement that it was false because there had been no notifications sent by Dodge regarding transmissions in 2003 minivans.

3. Defendant Biggs made the statement to Robert Williams with the intent to deceive him and to induce him to authorize A-1 to make unnecessary repairs and to pay for those repairs.

4. Robert Williams, who had no expertise regarding automotive repairs, reasonably relied on the statement by Biggs, who as an owner/operator of an automotive repair business held himself out as having superior knowledge regarding automotive repairs. Robert Williams would not have authorized or paid for the repairs had he known the statement was false.

5. As a direct and proximate result of his reasonable reliance on Defendant Biggs's false statement, Robert Williams paid for unnecessary repairs, which actually were never performed, and was damaged in the amount of $1887 paid to A-1, plus $128 paid to Mission Dodge to repair the transmission leak caused by A-1 when it replaced the original transmission.

Williams v. Aaron Biggs d/b/a/ A-1 Automotive Center

1. On June 5, 2008, Plaintiff Robert Williams took his 2003 Dodge minivan to A-l Automotive Center ("A-1"), owned and operated by Defendant Aaron Biggs, to have it the oil changed. After an A-1 mechanic drove the minivan, Defendant Biggs told Robert Williams that there might be slippage in the transmission and that it would take more time to discover the cause. Upon arriving home, Robert Williams received a phone call from Defendant Biggs who said that he had "checked and found a notification from Dodge about a defect causing the gears to grind down." Defendant Biggs knew his statement was false because Dodge had not issued such a notification. Robert Williams returned to A-1 to find that A-1 had removed the transmission from the minivan and disassembled it, contrary to his instructions not to remove the transmission until he arrived. Defendant Biggs then made the material misrepresentation to Robert Williams that, "Your transmission is going to fail, and soon!"

2. Defendant Biggs knew this statement to be false at the time that he made it: He knew there was no notification from Dodge about transmission problems and that Robert Williams reported no problems

with the transmission. He also knew that the transmission was not going to fail soon because he did not install a rebuilt transmission as Robert Williams instructed but merely put the old one back into the minivan. This is evidenced by the fact that the transmission allegedly rebuilt had the vehicle's serial number on its casing, establishing that it was the minivan's original transmission.

3. Defendant Biggs made this statement to Robert Williams with the intent to deceive him and to induce him to authorize A-1 to make unnecessary repairs and to pay for those repairs.

4. Robert Williams, who had no expertise in automotive repairs, reasonably relied on Defendant Biggs's statements, who as an owner/operator of an automotive repair business held himself out as having superior knowledge regarding automotive repairs. Robert Williams would not have authorized or paid for the repairs had he known the statement was false.

5. As a direct and proximate result of his reasonable reliance on Defendant Biggs's false statement, Robert Williams paid for unnecessary repairs, which actually were never performed, and was damaged in the amount of $1887 paid to A-1, plus $128 paid to Mission Dodge to repair the transmission leak caused by A-1 when it improperly replaced the original transmission.